TERRORISM

Documents of International and Local Control

VOLUME 90

TERRORISM

Documents of International and Local Control

VOLUME 90

PRESIDENTIAL POWERS AND THE GLOBAL WAR AGAINST TERRORISTS

Douglas C. Lovelace Jr., Esquire
Senior National Security Strategist

Oceana®
NEW YORK

OXFORD
UNIVERSITY PRESS

Oxford University Press, Inc., publishes works that further Oxford University's objective of excellence in research, scholarship, and education.

Published by Oxford University Press, Inc.
198 Madison Avenue, New York, New York 10016

Cataloging-in-Publication information is available from the Library of Congress.

ISSN 1062-4007
Terrorism: Documents of International and Local Control

ISBN: 978-0-19-538102-3 (v. 90)

Note to Readers:
This publication is designed to provide accurate and authoritative information in regard to the subject matter covered. It is based upon sources believed to be accurate and reliable and is intended to be current as of the time it was written. It is sold with the understanding that the publisher is not engaged in rendering legal, accounting, or other professional services. If legal advice or other expert assistance is required, the services of a competent professional person should be sought. Also, to confirm that the information has not been affected or changed by recent developments, traditional legal research techniques should be used, including checking primary sources where appropriate.

(Based on the Declaration of Principles jointly adopted by a Committee of the American Bar Association and a Committee of Publishers and Associations.)

TABLE OF CONTENTS

VOLUME 90

PRESIDENTIAL POWERS AND THE GLOBAL WAR AGAINST TERRORISTS

DOCUMENTS

PREFACE

PRESIDENTIAL POWERS AND THE GLOBAL WAR AGAINST TERRORISTS

The theme of this volume is the separation and distribution of war-making powers among the branches of the federal government, with a particular emphasis on presidential powers. The balance has changed significantly over the last half-century. The provisions of the U.S. Constitution are no longer as clearly understood as they were during the world wars. Since World War II, the United states has been in an era of wars of limited liability; that is, wars that are not fought to ensure national survival, but to improve America's security posture. Consequently, those wars, or conflicts, do not mobilize the entire nation and take on the nature expressed by the Prussian military theorist, Carl von Clausewitz, as the continuation of politics by other means.

Since the politics underlying war fall mostly within the foreign policy arena, the area in which the President is the principal actor, within our constitutional separation of powers scheme, it comes as no surprise that there has been a steady drift of war-making powers away from the Legislative Branch to the Executive. This, mostly incremental, migration has been tolerable, even manageable, largely because wars of limited liability are episodic. Consequently, differences between the branches of government exposed by applications of military power in various contingencies can be sorted out during the inter-conflict periods, or at least *modi vivendi* can be established.

Also, while not claiming that wars of limited liability have not been costly to the nation, they have not caused the American public and political elite to remain as deeply engaged in the politics of war-making, as they might have been in the early 1940s. Thus, ambiguity as to which branch of government has responsibility and authority for which war-making powers has been allowed to grow within our national understanding of the separation of powers. To address the uncertainty, or even confusion, over appropriate roles for the Legislative and Executive Branches, the first half of this volume offers documents that bring separation of war-making powers issues, as they are viewed today, into clear view.

Another dimension to the debate over war-making powers has developed. Now, a new type of war, even more perplexing than wars of limited liability, has arrived on the scene: the Global War Against Terrorists, or the Long War, as some call it, to account for its presumed multi-generational duration. This new type of war, for those who think it is actually a war, adds additional confounding aspects to modern warfare, by applying pressure on fundamental concepts of liberal democracy, such as individual rights and civil liberties. While transient compromises of rights and liberties during times of national crisis are not absent from American history, today even the smallest deviations from constitutional principles create angst, given the indeterminate nature and duration of this new type of war. Unfortunately, the attacks on individual rights and civil liberties occasioned by this new form of war have not been small, but widespread and crucial. The President, as Commander-In-Chief, is the most likely governmental entity to abridge freedoms, as he strives to ensure a safe America.

While many aspects of the Global War Against Terrorists have insidious but pernicious effects on American democracy, the second half of this volume perforce is limited to a discussion of only two: Executive Branch invasion of individual privacy through the Federal Bureau of Investigation's use of National Security Letters and the resort to often "warrantless" wiretapping, eavesdropping, or data-mining, for the purpose of gathering information and intelligence useful for combating elusive, loosely linked terrorists. The Executive Branch does not sacrifice even the smallest degree of civil liberties lightly. It is faced with defeating an amorphous and enigmatic enemy that has the potential to cause enormous harm to the nation and Americans abroad. The tension between national security and civil liberties is quite pronounced today and is easily illustrated by a review of these two topic areas. The volume provides primary source documents to enable readers to assess the extent to which our nation is achieving the correct balance.

A. LEGAL BASES FOR EMPLOYING U.S. MILITARY POWER

LEGAL BASES FOR EMPLOYING UNITED STATES MILITARY POWER IN THE WAR AGAINST TERRORISM

Commentary

What are the legal bases for using U.S. military power internationally? Does the separation of powers intended by the framers of the U.S. Constitution remain operative? Does appropriate balance in war-making powers exist between the Legislative and Executive Branches? Is the war against terrorists actually a war, as contemplated by Article II of the U.S. Constitution? Has the United States entered an era of wars of limited liability and, if so, are extant laws sufficient for assigning proper roles to the U.S. Congress and the president? These are perplexing questions that require answers arrived at through careful thought.

Although there have been eleven formal congressional declarations of war, the last occurred over a half-century ago. Typically, the declarations were in response to attacks on the United States, its citizens, or its other interests and were directed at nation states. Today, many argue that the concept of a formal declaration of war is obsolete. Instead, we see U.S. presidents seeking congressional authorizations for the use of force, while in some cases, presidents place U.S. forces in harm's way without express congressional approval. How the country goes about wielding its military instrument of national power has both domestic and international consequences. Moreover, the ambiguity and complexity of the Global War Against Terrorists make the proper division of responsibility for war-making much more difficult to discern and understand.

The first section of this volume provides historical background on the enactment of declarations of war and authorizations for the use of force and analyzes their legal effects, under international and domestic law. The documents provided include discussions of statutes that give the president and the Executive Branch significant standby authority. Additionally, this first section presents a comprehensive collection of the statutes that are triggered by a declaration of war, a declaration of national emergency, and/or the existence of a state of war. This section also provides a summary of the congressional procedures applicable to the enactment of a declaration of war or authorization for the use of force, including measures under the War Powers Resolution.

The documents provided in this first section then move to a thorough analysis of the War Powers Resolution (P.L. 93-148), passed in 1973 over the veto of President Nixon. We recall that at that time America was anguishing over its experience in Vietnam and blamed entry into the war on inadequately checked presidential authority, notwithstanding the Gulf of Tonkin Resolution passed by Congress in 1964. That measure authorized the president to take all necessary steps, including the use of armed force, to assist any member or protocol state of the Southeast Asia Collective Defense Treaty that requested assistance in defense of its freedom. Subsequent analyses of the basis for the Resolution, as well as its sufficiency for taking the nation to war, led not only to repeal of the Resolution, but eventually to passage of the the War Powers Resolution (WPR). But, has the WPR served its intended purpose? If not, should it?

The War Powers Resolution (WPR) was to define legislative and executive interaction in decisions to send American military forces into harm's way. In the event that the president contemplates introducing U.S. forces into hostile situations in exercise of his constitutional authority as Commander-in-Chief, the WPR requires him, in every possible instance, to consult first with Congress, to report and consult with Congress regularly thereafter, and withdraw any committed forces within sixty days, unless Congress acts to authorize the action. In passing the WPR, Congress interpreted the U.S. Constitution to mean that as Commander-in-Chief, the president may introduce U.S. Armed Forces into hostilities, or imminent hostilities only pursuant to a congressional declaration of war or other specific statutory authorization, or during a national emergency resulting from an attack upon U.S. territory or citizens. The difficulty of applying the WPR in this era of wars of limited liability is readily apparent, especially when one combines the president's Commander-in-Chief powers with his foreign policy powers and applies them to the Global War Against Terrorists.

In practice, presidents have complied with the requirements of the WPR to varying degrees; however, presidential compliance has typically been accompanied by the caveat that the president's actions should not be construed as acknowledging the constitutionality of the WPR. Various separation of power scholars have argued that if the framers of the U.S. Constitution had intended to give Congress the power to commence war, they would have written it into the Constitution. They argue that the president, as Commander-in-Chief, therefore, has the power to commence war. They argue further, that the Commander-in-Chief also is empowered to conduct war and end war, powers limited only by the war resources made available by Congress. Therefore, they hold, the WPR, if fully executed, would upset the balance of war-making powers provided by Articles I and II of the U.S. Constitution. Several proposals have been made to modify or repeal the WPR, but none have been acted upon. The Congressional Research Service

(CRS) War Powers Resolution report correctly notes that three general schools of thought exist, regarding whether the WPR requires revision. The first holds that no revision is necessary, because the WPR has achieved its purpose to a satisfactory degree; that is, it has caused better communications between the Executive and Legislative Branches during times of crisis and has effectively served as a restraint on presidential adventurism. This view is made more acceptable by the seeming lack of interest in any branch of government to put the constitutionality of the WPR to a definitive test.

Another view is that the WPR should be repealed because it unconstitutionally inhibits the president's effectiveness in formulating and implementing U.S. foreign policy because of the time limits it imposes. Some argue further that the WPR provides for inappropriate congressional influence over the deployment and employment of U.S. military forces, powers assigned to the Commander-in-Chief by the U.S. Constitution. Nonetheless, successive presidents have not found the WPR overly constraining or burdensome to at least partially comply with the provisions of the WPR, albeit with the frequent constitutional disclaimer. Not only has such compliance been generally satisfactory to Congress, it also has provided political footing for presidents to seek authorizations for the use of force.

Third, some believe that the WPR has not provided Congress sufficient influence on decisions to deploy and commit U.S. forces and should be strengthened. Those of this view argue that in too many instances, presidents have unilaterally introduced military forces into hostilities and committed the nation to a course of war without adequate congressional consultation, much less authorization. This position includes the claim that if Congress did have more definitive powers, it would act to restrain the president when appropriate. Evidence to support that imbedded argument is quite limited, however.

In most cases in which presidents have introduced U.S. forces into hostilities, Congress had passed a resolution of some sort authorizing the action. The war powers tension between the Legislative and Executive Branches most often arises after forces are committed to what turns out to be a politically unpopular conflict. In that situation, Congress would very much like to influence decisions such as what the war objectives should be, when are they achieved, how many military members should be permitted to participate in the action, what level of violence they should be permitted to employ, and when the war should be brought to an end. But, to the frustration of many members of Congress, the U.S. Constitution implies that those types of decisions are the president's, as Commander-in-Chief.

The rather strange situation in which the WPR exists is that neither Congress, the president, nor the Supreme Court is anxious to press the issue of whether the resolution is constitutional. The Legislative and

Executive Branches each fear losing constitutional ground to the other. The Judicial Branch has signaled that it might elect not to decide the issue, seeing it as a political issue to be resolved by the other branches through political debate, interaction, and compromise.

People often observe that Congress can easily control presidential adventurism with respect to committing the nation to armed conflict since it decides whether to authorize and appropriate funds for such actions. The argument goes that if the president takes military action that Congress does not approve of, Congress can force the withdrawal of the forces by withholding funding. Although that argument seems to have a certain academic logic, it has not proven viable.

The sacrifices made by the young women and men who comprise the U.S. armed forces are recognized and respected by the larger society. The U.S. military, as an institution, is consistently ranked highest among the most trusted professions in the nation. In short, Americans support their men and women in uniform and do not suffer lightly elected officials who do not. Members of Congress, therefore, are very reluctant to use the power of the purse to force the president to withdraw forces from ongoing operations for fear of being viewed as insensitive to the equipment, supplies, material, and moral support needed by those who serve. Congress's self-imposed restraint in this regard leaves it with little choice but to rely on the only partially functioning WPR in its attempts to reign in the president.

For these reasons and others that become apparent when one reads the documents contained in this first section, a contemporary study of the distribution of war-making powers between the Legislative and Executive branches would be incomplete without consideration of the events leading up to passage of the WPR, how it has been viewed by successive Congresses and presidents, the role it plays today, and its prospects for future efficacy. The documents in this section shed considerable light on the resolution and help the reader understand the increased salience of the WPR, during this era of long-term, persistent conflict, in which the United States must involve itself in limited conflicts. The war powers section concludes with a case study of sorts that helps illuminate and add texture to the policies and other information provided in the preceding documents. The fact that the war in Iraq, Operation Iraqi Freedom, proceeded from a congressional resolution for the "Authorization for Use of Military Force Against Iraq," which was signed by President Bush on October 16, 2002, has not prevented the war from becoming very unpopular in the U.S. Congress, as well as within the American polity. Many members of Congress now search for ways to force the president to withdraw U.S. forces from Iraq. For the reasons explained above, few legislators are willing to state publicly that all funding for the war should be terminated.

Instead they call for a reduction of funding that would force the president to adopt a war strategy that would permit the withdrawal of forces over time, although there is considerable variation in opinion on what should be the appropriate timeframe. This approach by members of Congress takes the separation of war-making powers to a new level of analysis; i.e., should Congress, through its power of the purse, be able to shape the manner in which the president, as Commander-in-Chief, conducts the war? Stated differently, is it constitutional for Congress to set parameters for the strategy the president may develop and employ, by setting funding limits that constrain the Commander-in-Chief's strategic options?

The final document in this section discusses the constitutional allocation of war powers between Congress and the president, and includes a review of what the Judicial Branch has had to say on the topic. It acknowledges Congress's power to rescind prior military authorization but pragmatically admits the limited effect such an act would have, absent a corresponding reduction of war funding. The report takes on the issue of the extent to which, if any, Congress may shape the war effort through funding, drawing upon court cases and previous congressional action. The report purports to analyze the principal arguments that could be made to support increased congressional control of the war effort, but does so with a discernable legislative bias. Consequently, it concludes, for example, that limiting the number or troops that may serve in a war is within Congress' authority to allocate resources for military operations. The analysis provided, however, does not consider the issue of congressional reluctance to limit funding for troops deployed in harm's way. To some extent, that self-restraint makes a legal conclusion that Congress has the constitutional power to do so less germane.

The president has taken the position that Congress may not act in ways that determine or even limit the strategic, operational, and tactical courses of action that the president may pursue—that the constitutional power to conduct war rests with the Commander-in-Chief. The president's constitutional interpretation would countenance the complete cutoff of funding by Congress, but not reductions tailored to shape or eliminate strategic options the president might choose to develop and execute. The Iraq war, although claimed to be integral to the Global War Against Terrorists, may become so traumatizing to the American public as to create an environment similar to that witnessed near the end of the Vietnam War. If the American public turns decidedly anti-Iraq War and begins to question the process that allowed America to become so deeply involved in, and entrapped by, an overwhelmingly unpopular war, the issue of the proper allocation of war powers between the Legislative and Executive Branches may ripen anew, with even greater urgency than at the end of the Vietnam War. A new look at the WPR may be in the offing.

DOCUMENT NO. 1

DECLARATIONS OF WAR AND AUTHORIZATIONS FOR THE USE OF MILITARY FORCE: HISTORICAL BACKGROUND AND LEGAL IMPLICATIONS

CRS Report
RL31133

March 8, 2007

Jennifer K. Elsea
Legislative Attorney
American Law Division
&
Richard F. Grimmett
Specialist in National Defense
Foreign Affairs, Defense, and Trade Division

Summary

From the Washington Administration to the present, Congress and the President have enacted 11 separate formal declarations of war against foreign nations in five different wars. Each declaration has been preceded by a presidential request either in writing or in person before a joint session of Congress. The reasons cited in justification for the requests have included armed attacks on United States territory or its citizens and threats to United States rights or interests as a sovereign nation.

Congress and the President have also on a number of occasions enacted authorizations for the use of force instead of declarations of war. Most commonly, such measures have authorized the use of force against either a named country or unnamed hostile nations in a given region. In most cases, the President has requested the authority, but Congress has sometimes given the President less than what he asked for. In contrast to the declarations of war, not all authorizations for the use of force have resulted in actual combat. Both declarations and authorizations require the signature of the President in order to become law.

In contrast to an authorization, a declaration of war in itself creates a state of war under international law and legitimates the killing of enemy combatants, the seizure of its property, and the apprehension of enemy aliens. At one time, a declaration was deemed a necessary legal prerequisite to a war and was also thought to terminate diplomatic and commercial relations and most treaties between the combatants. In the modern era, the international legal consequences of declarations have become less determinate; in fact, declarations have rarely been issued since World War II. Perhaps most important, neither a declaration nor an authorization is necessary to trigger application of the laws of war, such as the Hague and Geneva Conventions; for that, the fact of armed conflict is the controlling circumstance.

With respect to domestic law, a declaration of war automatically triggers many standby statutory authorities conferring special powers on the President with respect to the military, foreign trade, transportation, communications, manufacturing, alien enemies, etc. In contrast, no standby authorities appear to be triggered automatically by an authorization for the use of force. Most standby authorities do not require a declaration of war to be actualized but can be triggered by a declaration of national emergency or simply by the existence of a state of war. Declarations of war and authorizations for the use of force waive the time limitations otherwise applicable to the use of force imposed by the War Powers Resolution.

This report provides historical background on the enactment of declarations of war and authorizations for the use of force and analyzes their legal effects under international and domestic law. It also sets forth their texts in two appendices. Because the statutes that confer standby authority on the President and the executive branch potentially play such a large role in an armed conflict to which the United States is a party, the report includes an extensive listing and summary of the statutes that are triggered by a declaration of war, a declaration of national emergency, and/or the existence of a state of war. The report concludes with a summary of the congressional procedures applicable to the enactment of a declaration of war or authorization for the use of force and to measures under the War Powers Resolution. The report will be updated as circumstances warrant.

Introduction

Article I, § 8, of the Constitution vests in Congress the power "to declare War." Pursuant to that power, Congress has enacted eleven declarations of war during the course of American history relating to five different wars, the most recent being those that were adopted during World War II. In addition, Congress has adopted a number of authorizations for the use of military force, the most recent being the joint resolution enacted on

October 16, 2002, authorizing the use of military force against Iraq. To buttress the nation's ability to prosecute a war or armed conflict, Congress has also enacted numerous statutes which confer standby authority on the President or the executive branch and are activated by the enactment of a declaration of war, the existence of a state of war, or the promulgation of a declaration of national emergency.

This report examines a number of topics related to declarations of war and authorizations for the use of military force by the United States.[1] It (1) provides historical background on each of the declarations of war and on several major authorizations for the use of force that have been enacted; (2) analyzes the implications of declarations of war and authorizations for the use of force under both international law and domestic law; (3) lists and summarizes the more than 250 standby statutory authorities that can come into effect pursuant to a declaration of war, the existence of a state of war, and/or a declaration of national emergency; (4) describes the procedures in Congress governing the consideration of declarations of war and authorizations for the use of force, including the procedures under the War Powers Resolution; and (5) sets forth in two appendices the texts of all of the declarations of war and the major authorizations for the use of force that have been enacted. The report does not address the issue of the constitutionality of Presidential uses of military force absent a declaration of war or authorization for the use of force. The report will be updated as circumstances warrant.

Previous Declarations of War

From the Washington Administration to the present, there have been eleven separate formal declarations of war against foreign nations enacted by Congress and the President, encompassing five different wars—the War of 1812 with Great Britain, the War with Mexico in 1846, the War with Spain in 1898, the First World War, and the Second World War.[2] In each case the enactment of a formal declaration of war has been preceded by a presidential request to Congress for such an action, either in writing or in person before a joint session of Congress. In each such message requesting a war declaration, the President has cited what he deemed compelling reasons for doing so. These reasons have included armed attacks on United States territory or its citizens, and attacks on or direct threats to United States rights or interests as a sovereign nation. In the nineteenth century all declarations of war were passed by the Congress in the form of a bill. In the

[1] CRS analysts and attorneys in addition to the listed authors have contributed to various parts of this report: David Ackerman, Elizabeth Bazan, Richard Beth, and Charles Doyle.

[2] See Figure 1 for presidential and congressional actions taken regarding all formal declarations of war by the United States. See Appendix I for the texts of these declarations.

twentieth century all declarations of war were passed by the Congress in the form of a joint resolution. In every instance the measures were adopted by majority vote in both the House and the Senate and were signed into law by the President.[3] The last formal declaration of war was enacted on June 5, 1942, against Rumania during World War II.[4]

The circumstances of President McKinley's request for a declaration of war against Spain in 1898 stand in singular contrast to all the others. McKinley's request for a declaration of war on April 25, 1898, was approved by a voice vote of both Houses of Congress on that date. His request was made after Spain had rejected a U.S. ultimatum that Spain relinquish its sovereignty over Cuba and permit Cuba to become an independent state. This ultimatum was supported by a joint resolution of Congress, signed into law on April 20, 1898, that among other things, declared Cuba to be independent, demanded that Spain withdraw its military forces from the island, and directed and authorized the President to use the U.S. Army, Navy and militia of the various states to achieve these ends. The war with Spain in 1898, in short, was not principally based on attacks on the United States but on a U.S. effort to end the Cuban insurrection against Spain, bring about Cuban independence, and restore a stable government and order on the island—outcomes that were believed by the United States to advance its interests.[5]

In the twentieth century, without exception, presidential requests for formal declarations of war by Congress were based on findings by the President that U.S. territory or sovereign rights had been attacked or threatened by a foreign nation. Although President Wilson had tried to maintain U.S. neutrality after the outbreak of the First World War, he regarded the German decision on February 1, 1917, to engage in unrestricted submarine warfare against all naval vessels in the war zone, including those of neutral states, to be an unacceptable assault on U.S. sovereign rights which the German Government had previously pledged to respect. Wilson's request

---

[3] It is beyond the scope of this report to detail the often complex circumstances underlying the nature, motivations, and timing of presidential requests for war declarations. Those matters have been the subject of important debates among scholars. The texts of specific presidential messages requesting a declaration of war are found in Richardson, James D. (ed.) *A Compilation of the Messages and Papers of the Presidents* (20 vol., Washington, 1897–1917.) as follows: Madison: Vol. II, pp. 484–490.; Polk: Vol. V, pp. 2287–2293.; McKinley: Vol. XIII, pp. 6296–6297; Wilson: Vol. XVI, pp. 8226–8233 (for Germany) and Vol. XVI, pp. 8399–8406 (for Austria-Hungary); Rosenman, Samuel I. (comp.) The Public Papers and Addresses of Franklin D. Roosevelt, 1941. New York, Harper & Brothers, 1950), pp. 514–515 (for Japan) and pp. 532 (for Germany and Italy); Rosenman, Samuel I. (comp.) The Public Papers and Addresses of Franklin D. Roosevelt, 1942. New York, Harper & Brothers, 1950), pp. 257 (declarations for Bulgaria, Hungary and Rumania).

[4] Act of Jun. 5, 1942, ch. 325, 56 Stat. 307.

[5] Richardson, Messages and Papers of the Presidents, Vol XIII, pp. 6296–6297. Act of Apr. 25, 1898, ch. 189, 30 Stat. 364. Joint Resolution of April 20, 1898, [Res. 24] 30 Stat. 738. An earlier message by McKinley requesting authorization to use U.S. military force to resolve the Cuban-Spanish conflict was submitted to Congress on April 11, 1898. Richardson, Messages and Papers of the Presidents, Vol. XIII, pp. 6281–6292.

to Congress for a declaration of war against Germany on April 2, 1917, stated that war had been "thrust upon the United States" by Germany's actions. Congress passed a joint resolution declaring war which the President signed on April 6, 1917. Wilson delayed requesting a war declaration against Austria-Hungary until December 4, 1917. He did so then because that state, a German ally in the war, had become an active instrument of Germany against the United States. Congress quickly passed a joint resolution declaring war which the President signed on December 7, 1917.[6]

President Franklin D. Roosevelt requested a declaration of war against Japan on December 8, 1941, because of direct military attacks by that nation against U.S. territory, military personnel and citizens in Hawaii and other outposts in the Pacific area. The House and the Senate passed the requested declaration and the President signed it into law that same day. After Germany and Italy each declared war on the United States on December 11, 1941, President Roosevelt asked Congress to respond in kind by recognizing that a state of war existed between the United States and those two nations. Congress passed separate joint resolutions declaring war on both nations which the President signed on December 11, 1941.[7] On June 2, 1942, President Roosevelt asked that Congress declare war on Bulgaria, Hungary and Rumania, nations that were under the domination of Germany, were engaged in active military actions against the United States, and had themselves declared war on the United States. Congress passed separate joint resolutions declaring war on each of these nations. The President signed these resolutions on June 5, 1942.[8]

There is a striking similarity of language in the eight declarations of war passed by the Congress in the twentieth century. They all declare that a "state of war" exists between the United States and the other nation. With the one exception of the declaration of war against Austria-Hungary on December 7, 1917, the other seven declarations characterize the state of war as having been "thrust upon the United States" by the other nation. All eight of these twentieth century declarations of war state in identical language that the President is—

> authorized and directed to employ the entire naval and military forces of the United States and the resources of the Government to carry on war against [the 'Government' of the particular nation]; and to bring the

[6] Richardson, Messages and Papers of the Presidents, Vol. XVI, pp. 8226–8233. Act of Apr. 6, 1917, ch.1, 40 Stat.1. [Germany]. Richardson, Messages and Papers of the Presidents, Vol. XVI, pp. 8399–8406. Act of Dec. 7, 1917, ch. 1, 40 Stat. 429. [Austria-Hungary].

[7] Rosenman, *Public Papers of President Roosevelt, 1941,* pp. 514–515. Act of Dec. 8, 1941, ch. 561,55 Stat. 795. [Japan]; Rosenman,*Public Papers of President Roosevelt 1941,*p. 532. Act of Dec. 11, 1941, ch. 564, 55 Stat. 796. [Germany]. Act of Dec. 11, 1941, ch. 565, 55 Stat. 797.[Italy].

[8] Rosenman, *Public Papers of President Roosevelt, 1942,* p. 257. Act of Jun. 5, 1942, ch. 323, 56 Stat. 307. [Bulgaria]. Act of Jun. 5, 1942, ch. 324, 56 Stat. 307. [Hungary]. Act of Jun. 5, 1942, ch. 325, 56 Stat. 307. [Rumania].

conflict to a successful termination all of the resources of the country are hereby pledged by the Congress of the United States.

The complete texts of the eleven declarations of war are set forth in Appendix I.

Key Dates And Actions Related To Formal U.S. Declarations Of War

1812—Great Britain	Madison asked June 1, 1812. House passed on June 4, 1812 (79-49). Senate passed on June 17, 1812 (19-13). President signed on **June 18, 1812**. Act of Jun. 18, 1812, ch. 102, 2 Stat. 755. Terminated by Treaty of Ghent, which entered into force on Feb. 17, 1815. 8 Stat. 218, Treaty Series 109.
1846—Mexico	Polk asked May 11, 1846. House passed on May 11, 1846 (174-14). Senate passed on May 12, 1846 (40-2). President signed on May 13, 1846. Act of **May 13, 1846**, ch.16, 9 Stat. 9. Terminated by Treaty of Guadalupe Hidalgo, which entered into force on May 30, 1848. 9 Stat. 922, Treaty Series 207.
1898—Spain	McKinley asked April 25, 1898. Senate and House passed on **April 25, 1898**, by voice votes. McKinley signed on April 25, 1898. Act of Apr. 25, 1898, ch. 189, 30 Stat. 364. The bill made the war date retroactive to April 21, 1898. Terminated by Treaty of Paris, which entered into force on April 11, 1899. 30 Stat. 1754, Treaty Series 343.
1917—World War I (Germany)	Wilson asked April 2, 1917. Senate passed on April 4, 1917 (82-6). House passed on April 6, 1917 (373-50). President signed on **April 6, 1917**. Act of Apr. 6, 1917, ch.1, 40 Stat. 1. Terminated by Act of July 2, 1921, ch. 40, 42 Stat. 105, which declared the state of war between the U.S. and Germany to be at an end. Formally recognized by the Treaty on Establishment of Friendly Relations, which entered into force Nov. 11, 1921. 42 Stat. 1939, Treaty Series 658.
1917—World War I (Austria-Hungary)	Wilson asked December 4, 1917. House passed on December 7, 1917 (365-1). Senate passed on December 7, 1917(74-0). President signed on **December 7, 1917**. Act of Dec. 7, 1917, ch.1, 40 Stat. 429. Terminated by Act of July 2, 1921, ch. 40, 42 Stat. 105, which declared the state of war between the U.S. and the two successor states and governments to the Austro-Hungarian monarchy—Austria and Hungary—to be at an end. Formally recognized by the Treaty on Establishment of Friendly Relations with Austria, which entered into force Nov. 8, 1921 (42 Stat. 1939, Treaty Series 658) and the Treaty on Establishing Friendly Relations with Hungary, which entered into force Dec. 17, 1921. 42 Stat. 1951, Treaty Series 660.
1941—World War II (Japan)	Roosevelt asked December 8, 1941. Senate passed on December 8, 1941 (82-0). House passed on December 8, 1941 (388-1). President signed on **December 8, 1941**. Act of Dec. 8, 1941, ch. 561, 55 Stat. 795. Terminated by Treaty of Peace with Japan, which entered into force Apr. 28, 1952. 3 UST 3169, TIAS 2490.

1941—World War II (Germany)	Roosevelt asked **December 11, 1941**. Senate passed on December 11, 1941 (88-0). House passed on December 11, 1941 (393-0). President signed on December 11, 1941. Act of Dec. 11, 1941, ch. 564, 55 Stat. 796. Terminated by Act of October 19, 1951, ch. 519, 65 Stat. 541.
1941— World War II (Italy)	Roosevelt asked December 11, 1941. Senate passed on December 11, 1941 (90-0). House passed on December 11, 1941 (399-0). President signed on **December 11, 1941**. Act of Dec. 11, 1941, ch. 565, 55 Stat. 796. Terminated by Treaty of Peace with Italy, which entered into force Sept. 15, 1947. 4 UST 311, 61 Stat. 1245.
1942—World War II (Bulgaria)	Roosevelt asked June 2, 1942. House passed on June 3, 1942 (357-0). Senate passed on June 4, 1942 (73-0). President signed on **June 5, 1942**. Act of Jun. 5, 1942, ch. 323, 56 Stat. 307. Terminated by Treaty of Peace with Bulgaria, which entered into force Sept. 15, 1947. 4 UST 429, 61 Stat. 1915.
1942—World War II (Hungary)	Roosevelt asked June 2, 1942. House passed on June 3, 1942 (360-0). Senate passed on June 4, 1942 (73-0). President signed on **June 5, 1942**. Act of Jun. 5, 1942, ch. 324, 56 Stat. 307. Terminated by Treaty of Peace with Hungary, which entered into force Sept. 15, 1947. 4 UST 453, 61 Stat. 2065.
1942—World War II (Rumania)	Roosevelt asked June 2, 1942. House passed on June 3, 1942 (361-0). Senate passed on June 4, 1942 (73-0). President signed on **June 5, 1942**. Act of Jun. 5, 1942, ch. 325, 56 Stat. 307. Terminated by Treaty of Peace with Rumania, which entered into force Sept. 15, 1947. 4 UST 403, 61 Stat. 1757.

Key Statutory Authorizations for the Use of Military Force

From the Administration of President John Adams to the present, there have been various instances when legislation has been enacted authorizing the use of military force by the President instead of formally declaring war. In most cases such legislation has been preceded by a specific request by the President for such authority. During the Presidencies of John Adams and Thomas Jefferson, these Chief Executives noted in messages to Congress that Congressional authorizations for use of force would be appropriate to enable the United States to protect its interests from predatory actions by foreign powers, in particular attacks on U.S. commercial vessels and persons on the high seas by France and by Tripoli. Congress responded with specific authorizations for the use of force under the President's direction in 1798 against France and in 1802 against Tripoli. In 1815 President James Madison formally requested that Congress declare war against the Regency of Algiers in response to its attacks on U.S. citizens and commerce in the Mediterranean. Congress responded with an Act authorizing the President to utilize U.S. armed vessels to be used against Algerian naval attacks but did not declare war.

In the period following World War II, Presidential requests for authority to use military force, when made, have usually been for broad authority to use U.S. military force in a specific region of the world in order to defend U.S. interests or friendly states as the President deems appropriate. More recently, due to an expansive interpretation of the President's constitutional authority as Commander-in-Chief of the Armed Forces and of his inherent powers to use force without Congressional authorization, the President has welcomed *support* from the Congress in the form of legislation authorizing him to utilize U.S. military forces in a foreign conflict or engagement in support of U.S. interests, but has not taken the view that he is *required* to obtain such authorization.

What follows is a brief overview of key legislative authorizations of the use of military force by the President from the Administration of John Adams to the present.[9] Appendix 2 provides the complete text of these specific authorizations.

France 1798

The United States during the 1790s had remained neutral in the conflict in Europe between France and Great Britain and had only begun to develop a Navy. During the Administration of President John Adams, relations with France deteriorated as American commercial ships were frequently seized by French naval vessels. In response, in his message to Congress on May 16, 1797, President Adams argued that it would be prudent for the Congress to enact legislation that would address the actions of the French by authorizing, among other things, the use of U.S. naval vessels to defend against attacks on American shipping and citizens engaged in lawful commerce abroad. President Adams reiterated, in a message of March 19, 1798, his view of the necessity for Congressional action on his recommendations for the adoption of measures to protect American seafaring citizens and commerce.[10]

Congress subsequently responded to the President's recommendations by passing legislation "more effectually to protect the Commerce and Coasts of the United States" authorizing the President to instruct commanders of

---

[9] There have been numbers of scholarly works written that address, in depth, the circumstances surrounding most of the measures discussed herein. It is beyond the scope of this report to itemize fully the complex diplomatic, political and military motivations that led to their enactment. For general background see Bemis, Samuel Flagg, A Diplomatic History of the United States, New York, Holt, Rinehart and Winston, 5th ed. 1965; DeConde, Alexander, A History of American Foreign Policy, New York, Charles Scribner's Sons, 3rd ed., 2 vol. 1978; Bailey, Thomas A., A Diplomatic History of the American People, Englewood Cliffs, Prentice Hall, Inc., 10th ed. 1980.

[10] The text of President John Adams messages to Congress are found in Richardson, James D. (ed.) A *Compilation of the Messages and Papers of the Presidents* (20 vol., Washington, 1897–1917), Vol. I, pp. 223–229, 254–255; Also in Annals of the Congress of the United States, 5th. Congress, 1st session, pp.54–59, 1271–1272.

U.S. armed vessels to act against any "armed vessel" found to have committed or attempting to commit "depredations on the vessels" belonging to United States citizens, and to retake any ship or vessel of United States citizens that may have been captured by non-U.S. armed vessels.[11] The legislation was signed into law on May 28, 1798, Congress passed additional legislation, signed into law on July 9, 1798, that authorized the President to instruct commanders of U.S. Navy warships to "subdue, seize and take any armed French vessel which shall be found within the jurisdictional limits of the United States, or elsewhere, on the high seas. . . ." The President was further granted the authority to grant special commissions to "owners of private armed ships and vessels of the United States," to permit them to lawfully subdue, seize, and capture "any armed French vessel," and to recapture U.S. vessels, goods and effects of U.S. citizens with the same authority as U.S. Navy vessels, subject to instructions given by the President.[12]

Tripoli 1802

President Thomas Jefferson, in response to attacks on U.S. commercial shipping in the Mediterranean Sea by vessels under the control of the Bey of Tripoli, noted in his message to Congress of December 8, 1801, that it would be prudent for Congress to authorize the use of U.S. Navy forces to protect U.S. shipping against Tripoli, including permitting them to take offensive action against Tripolitan vessels.[13] Congress responded by passing legislation, enacted on February 6, 1802, that authorized the President to "equip, officer, man, and employ such of the armed vessels of the United States as may be judged requisite by the President of the United States, for protecting effectually the commerce and seamen thereof on the Atlantic ocean, the Mediterranean and adjoining seas." The President was also authorized to utilize the U.S. Navy "to subdue, seize and make prize of all vessels, goods and effects belonging to the Bey of Tripoli, or his subjects . . . and to cause to be done all such other acts of precaution or hostility as the state of war will justify, and may, in his opinion, require." The President was further granted the authority to grant special commissions to "owners of private armed vessels of the United States," to permit them to lawfully subdue and seize "any Tripolitan vessel, goods or effects" with the same authority as U.S. Navy vessels, subject to instructions given by the President.[14]

---

[11] Act of May 28, 1798, ch. 48, 2 Stat. 561.

[12] Act of July 9, 1798, ch. 68, 2 Stat. 578.

[13] The text of President Thomas Jefferson's message to Congress is found in Richardson, James D. (ed.) *A Compilation of the Messages and Papers of the Presidents* (20 vol., Washington, 1897–1917), Vol. I, pp. 314–320; Also in Annals of the Congress of the United States, 7th Congress, 1st session, pp. 12–16.

[14] Act of February 6, 1802, ch. 4, 1 Stat. 129.

Algeria 1815

President James Madison, after the conclusion of a peace treaty with Great Britain ending the War of 1812, sought authority to use the U.S. Navy to take action against vessels of the ruler and Regency of Algeria that had been seizing U.S. commercial vessels in the Mediterranean area. Due to acts of "overt and direct warfare against the citizens of the United States," President Madison, on February 23, 1815, recommended that Congress declare the "existence of a state of war between the United States and the Dey and Regency of Algiers."[15] Congress did not declare war but did pass legislation, enacted on March 3, 1815, that authorized the President to use the U.S. Navy, "as judged requisite by the President" to protect the "commerce and seamen" of the United States on the "Atlantic Ocean, the Mediterranean and adjoining seas." The President was also authorized to utilize the U.S. Navy to seize "all vessels, goods and effects belonging to the Dey of Algiers, or to his subjects . . . and to cause to be done all such other acts of precaution or hostility as the state of war will justify, and may, in his opinion, require." The President was further granted the discretionary authority to grant special commissions to "owners of private armed vessels of the United States," to permit them to lawfully subdue, seize, and capture "any Algerine vessel, goods or effects" with the same authority as U.S. Navy vessels, subject to instructions given by the President.[16]

Suppression of Piracy 1819–1823

During the years after the War of 1812, there was a notable increase in the number of attacks on U.S. commercial shipping vessels in and around the Caribbean and Latin American coastal waters. Some of this was stimulated by the chaotic conditions attendant to the struggles for independence by South American colonies of Spain. Pirates attacked not only Spanish vessels in the region, but vessels of other nations generally. In response to calls for action against these predatory attacks on their vessels, American shippers petitioned Congress for action to protect them from pirates. In response, on March 3, 1819, legislation was enacted "to protect the commerce of the United States, and punish the crime of piracy." This legislation authorized the President to employ "the public armed vessels" of the United States as he deemed necessary to protect "the merchant vessels of the United States and their crews from piratical aggressions and depredations." This legislation further authorized the President to instruct the commanders of the "public armed vessels of the United States" to take various actions to combat piracy, including attacking and seizing pirates and their vessels. The legislation also authorized U.S. vessels attacked by pirates to take actions against their

[15] The text of President James Madison's message to Congress is found in Richardson, James D. (ed.) *A Compilation of the Messages and Papers of the Presidents* (20 vol., Washington, 1897–1917), Vol. II, p. 539; Also in Annals of the Congress of the United States, 13th Congress, 3rd session, p. 269.

[16] Act of March 3, 1815, Chap. 90, 3 Stat. 230.

aggressors and seize their ships. The legislation further established penalties for those that engaged in piracy. This 1819 statute was subsequently made permanent law on January 30, 1823. It has been amended, but the current text, found in Title 33 of the United States Code, contains substantially the same language as was enacted in March of 1819.[17]

Formosa 1955

In a message to Congress on January 24, 1955, President Dwight Eisenhower, detailed a series of "provocative political and military actions" by the Chinese Communist government that he believed established a "pattern of aggressive purpose." That purpose was the "conquest of Formosa." This situation, said Eisenhower, posed a "serious danger to the security of our country and of the entire Pacific area and indeed to the peace of the world." The President believed that the U.S. should not wait for the United Nations to take steps to deal with the situation but should be prepared to use its own armed forces "to assure the security of Formosa and the Pescadores." President Eisenhower stated that authority for "some of the actions which might be required would be inherent in the authority of the Commander-in-Chief." He noted that, pending Congressional action, he "would not hesitate, so far as my Constitutional powers extend, to take whatever emergency action might be forced upon us to protect the rights and security of the United States." However, he stated that a "suitable Congressional resolution would clearly and publicly establish the authority of the President as Commander-in-Chief to employ" the U.S. armed forces "promptly and effectively" as he deemed necessary to deal with the circumstances. Such a resolution would "make clear the unified and serious intentions of our Government, our Congress and our people."[18]

In response to the President's request, Congress passed legislation on January 29, 1955, that authorized the President to "employ the Armed Forces of the United States as he deems necessary for the specific purpose of securing and protecting Formosa, and the Pescadores against armed attack. . . ." The President was also authorized to take "such other measures as he judges to be required or appropriate in assuring the defense of Formosa and the Pescadores." The resolution stated that it would expire when the President determined and reported to Congress that the "peace and security of the area is reasonably assured. . . .[19] The resolution was subsequently repealed in 1974.[20]

[17] For a detailed treatment of the problem of piracy in the West Indies during the U.S. early national period see Francis B.C. Bradlee. Piracy in the West Indies and Its Suppression. Salem: The Essex Institute, 1923 [reprinted 1970 by MacDonald and Janes, London]. Also see chapter 12 in Craig L. Symonds. Navalists and Antinavalists. Newark: University of Delaware Press, 1980.

[18] Public Papers of the Presidents of the United States. Dwight D. Eisenhower. 1955, Washington. U.S. Government Printing Office, 1959, pp. 207–211.

[19] P.L. 84-4, 69 Stat. 7, January 29, 1955. The House passed H.J.Res. 159 by a vote of 410–3 on January 25, 1955; the Senate passed the joint resolution by a vote of 85–3 on January 28, 1955.

[20] P.L. 93-475, § 3, 88 Stat. 1439, October 26, 1974.

Middle East 1957

In a special message to Congress on January 5, 1957, President Dwight D. Eisenhower requested Congressional support for a program of military and economic cooperation with nations in the general area of the Middle East to "deal with the possibility of Communist aggression, direct or indirect" against nations in that region. As one component of this military and economic assistance program, President Eisenhower sought authority to employ the "armed forces of the United States to secure and protect the territorial integrity and political independence of such nations, requesting such aid, against overt armed aggression from any nation controlled by International Communism." The President emphasized that such authority would not be utilized by him "except at the desire of the nation attacked."[21]

In response, the Congress passed legislation, enacted on March 9, 1957, that, among other things, authorized the President "to undertake, in the general area of the Middle East, military assistance programs with any nation or group of nations of that area desiring such assistance." The joint resolution further provided that "if the President determines the necessity thereof, the United States is prepared to use armed forces to assist any such nation or group of such nations requesting assistance against armed aggression from any country controlled by international communism: *Provided*, that such employment shall be consonant with the treaty obligations of the United States and with the Constitution of the United States." The President was also to report to Congress on his action under the joint resolution between January and July of each year. The joint resolution further provided that it would expire when the President determined that the "peace and security of the nations in the general area of the Middle East" was "reasonably assured" or should Congress terminate it earlier by passage of a concurrent resolution.[22] The resolution has not been formally repealed.[23]

---

[21] Public Papers of the Presidents of the United States. Dwight D. Eisenhower. 1957, Washington. U.S. Government Printing Office, 1958, pp. 6, 11–15.

[22] P.L. 85-7, 71 Stat. 5 March 9, 1957 [H.J. Res. 117]. The Senate Committees on Foreign Relations and Armed Services, in a joint report, noted that in considering the legislation various strongly held views had been "vigorously expressed" regarding the constitutional powers of the President and of the Congress, as well as the proper constitutional procedure to be followed in the situation contemplated by the legislation. The final legislative language adopted reflected this debate. This language had, the Senate committees said, "the virtue of remaining silent on the question of the relationship between the Congress and the President with respect to the use of the Armed Forces for the objectives stated in the resolution." The Senate committees also argued that although there was sharp division as to the "proper constitutional processes" to follow in support of the President's request, there was none regarding the substantive policy involved. They stated that "the clear statement of policy in section 2 of the resolution as reported is preferable to a blanket authorization to the President to use the Armed Forces in this area." U.S. Congress. Senate. Committees on Foreign Relations and Armed Services, 85th Congress, 1st session, Senate Report 70, February 14, 1957, [to accompany S.J. Res. 19], pp. 1, 8–9. The text of the Senate bill was adopted by the Congress in lieu of that of the House bill. The Senate passed the joint resolution, H.J. Res. 117, as amended, by a vote of 72–19 on March 5, 1957; the House passed H.J. Res. 117 with the Senate amendments by a vote of 350–60 on March 7, 1957. The joint resolution was signed on March 9, 1957.

[23] The resolution is codified at 22 U.S.C.A. §§ 1961–65.

Southeast Asia 1964

In the early 1960s the United States had been providing military assistance and support to the government of South Vietnam. Over time tensions, associated with the U.S. military presence in Southeast Asia and support for the South Vietnamese government, grew between the U.S. and the communist government of North Vietnam. On August 2, 1964, a U.S. destroyer, the U.S.S. Maddox, while in international waters off the coast of North Vietnam (the Gulf of Tonkin) was attacked by North Vietnamese torpedo boats. The attack was repulsed. The State Department protested to the North Vietnamese government and noted that grave consequences would follow additional offensive actions against U.S. forces. Subsequently, on August 4, further attacks by North Vietnamese vessels against U.S. destroyers were reported to Washington. President Lyndon Johnson responded on August 4 by sending U.S. military aircraft to bomb "gunboats and certain supporting facilities" in North Vietnam that had allegedly been used in the actions against U.S. naval vessels. After meeting with Congressional leaders, President Johnson on August 5, 1964, formally requested a resolution of Congress that would "express the support of the Congress for all necessary action to protect our armed forces and to assist nations covered by the SEATO Treaty."[24]

Congress responded to President Johnson's request by passing a joint resolution to "promote the maintenance of international peace and security in southeast Asia." This legislation has come to be popularly known as the "Gulf of Tonkin resolution." This joint resolution, enacted on August 10, 1964, stated that "the Congress approves and supports the determination of the President, as Commander-in-Chief, to take all necessary measures to repel any armed attack against the forces of the United States and to prevent further aggression." The joint resolution further stated that "[c]onsonant with the Constitution of the United States and the Charter of the United Nations and in accordance with its obligations under the Southeast Asia Collective Defense Treaty, the United States is, therefore, prepared, as the President determines, to take all necessary steps, including the use of armed force, to assist any member or protocol state of the Southeast Asia Collective Defense Treaty requesting assistance in defense of its freedom." The joint resolution stated that it would expire whenever the President determined that the "peace and security of the area is reasonably assured" or if Congress chose to terminate it earlier by concurrent resolution.[25] Congress repealed the resolution in 1971.[26]

[24] Public Papers of the Presidents of the United States. Lyndon B. Johnson. 1963–64, Washington. U.S. Government Printing Office, 1965, pp. 927, 930–932.

[25] P.L. 88-408, 78 Stat. 384, August 10, 1964. The House passed H.J. Res. 1145 on August 7, 1964 by a vote of 414–0; the Senate passed it on August 7, 1964 by a vote of 88–2. This joint resolution was later repealed in 1971 by P.L. 91-672, § 12, 84 Stat. 2053 (1971).

[26] P.L. 91-672, § 12, 84 Stat. 2055, January 12, 1971.

Lebanon 1983

On July 6, 1982, President Ronald Reagan announced he would send a small contingent of U.S. troops to participate in a multinational force for temporary peacekeeping in Lebanon. When the forces began to land on August 25, President Reagan reported this action to Congress but did not cite section 4(a)(1) of the War Powers Resolution,[27] and said the agreement with Lebanon ruled out any combat responsibilities. After overseeing the departure of the Palestine Liberation Organization force, the U.S. Marines in the first Multinational Force left Lebanon on September 10, 1982. The second dispatch of Marines to Lebanon began on September 20, 1982. President Reagan announced that the United States, France, and Italy had agreed to form a new multinational force to return to Lebanon for a limited period of time to help maintain order until the lawful authorities in Lebanon could discharge those duties. The action followed three events that took place after the withdrawal of the first group of U.S. Marines: the assassination of Lebanon President-elect Bashir Gemayel, the entry of Israeli forces into West Beirut, and the massacre of Palestinian civilians by Lebanese Christian militiamen.

On September 29, 1982, President Reagan submitted a report to Congress that 1,200 Marines had begun to arrive in Beirut, but again he did not cite section 4(a)(1), of the War Powers Resolution, stating that the American force would not engage in combat. As a result of incidents in which U.S. Marines were killed or wounded, there was controversy in Congress on whether the President's report should have been filed under section 4(a)(1). In mid-1983 Congress passed the Lebanon Emergency Assistance Act of 1983 requiring statutory authorization for any substantial expansion in the number or role of U.S. Armed Forces in Lebanon. It also included a section that stated:

> Nothing in this section is intended to modify, limit, or suspend any of the standards and procedures prescribed by the War Powers Resolution of 1973.[28]

President Reagan reported on the Lebanon situation again on August 30, 1983, still not citing section 4(a)(1), after fighting broke out between various factions in Lebanon and two Marines were killed. The level of fighting heightened; and as the Marine casualties increased and the action enlarged, there were more calls in Congress for invocation of the War Powers Resolution. Several Members of Congress said the situation had changed since the President's first report and introduced legislation that took various approaches. Senator Charles Mathias introduced S.J. Res. 159 stating that the time limit specified in the War Powers Resolution had begun on

[27] For an explanation of the requirements of the War Powers Resolution, *see infra* at 27–28.
[28] P.L. 98-43, 97 Stat. 214, June 27, 1983 [S. 639].

August 31, 1983, and authorizing the forces to remain in Lebanon for a period of 120 days after the expiration of the 60-day period. Representative Thomas Downey introduced H.J. Res. 348 directing the President to report under section 4(a)(1) of the War Powers Resolution. Senator Robert Byrd introduced S.J. Res. 163 finding that section 4(a)(1) of the War Powers Resolution applied to the present circumstances in Lebanon. The House Appropriations Committee approved an amendment to the continuing resolution for FY1984 (H.J. Res. 367), sponsored by Representative Clarence Long, providing that after 60 days, funds could not be "obligated or expended for peacekeeping activities in Lebanon by United States Armed Forces," unless the President had submitted a report under section 4(a)(1) of the War Powers Resolution. A similar amendment was later rejected by the full body, but it reminded the Administration of possible congressional actions.

On September 20, 1983, congressional leaders and President Reagan agreed on a compromise resolution invoking section 4(a)(1) of the War Powers Resolution and authorizing the Marines to remain for 18 months. The Multinational Force in Lebanon Resolution became the first legislation to be handled under the expedited procedures of the War Powers Resolution. On September 28 the House passed H.J. Res. 364 by a vote of 270 to 161. On September 29 the Senate passed S.J. Res. 159 by a vote of 54 to 46. The House accepted the Senate bill by a vote of 253 to 156 later the same day. The President signed the joint resolution into law on October 12, 1983. As passed, the joint resolution contained four occurrences that would terminate the authorization before eighteen months: (1) the withdrawal of all foreign forces from Lebanon, unless the President certified continued U.S. participation was required to accomplish specified purposes; (2) the assumption by the United Nations or the Government of Lebanon of the responsibilities of the Multinational Force; (3) the implementation of other effective security arrangements; or (4) the withdrawal of all other countries from participation in the Multinational Force. Congress also determined in the joint resolution that the requirements of section 4(a)(1) of the War Powers Resolution became operative on August 29, 1983.[29]

In a statement made on signing S.J. Res. 159 on October 12, 1983, President Reagan expressed appreciation for the support for the U.S. presence and policies in Lebanon he believed were embodied in the legislation. He sharply differed, however, with various "findings, determinations, and assertions" by the Congress on certain matters. He stated his concerns about the practical problems associated with section 4(a)(1) of the War Powers Resolution, and the wisdom and constitutionality of section 5(b). President Reagan noted that in signing the Lebanon resolution it was important for him to state

[29] P.L. 98-119, 97 Stat. 805, October 12, 1983 [S.J. Res. 159].

> that I do not and cannot cede any of the authority vested in me under the Constitution as President and as Commander in Chief of United States Armed Forces. Nor should my signing be viewed as any acknowledgment that the President's constitutional authority can be impermissibly infringed by statute, that congressional authorization would be required if and when the period specified in section 5(b) of the War Powers Resolution might be deemed to have been triggered and the period had expired, or that section 6 of the Multinational Force in Lebanon Resolution may be interpreted to revise the constitutional authority to deploy United States Armed Forces.[30]

Iraq 1991

On August 2, 1990, Iraqi troops under the direction of President Saddam Hussein invaded Kuwait, seized its oil fields, installed a new government in Kuwait City, and moved toward the border with Saudi Arabia. A week after the invasion, on August 9, President George H.W. Bush reported to Congress "consistent with the War Powers Resolution" that he had deployed U.S. armed forces to the region prepared to take action with others to deter further Iraqi aggression. He noted that he did not believe involvement in hostilities was imminent. Throughout the rest of 1990, President Bush continued to work to establish an international coalition opposed to Iraq's aggression, while continuing to deploy additional U.S. military reinforcements into Saudi Arabia and the Persian Gulf region. By the end of the year approximately 350,000 U.S. forces had been deployed to the area.[31]

As the prospect of a war without congressional authorization increased, on November 20, 1990, Representative Ron Dellums and 44 other Democratic Members of Congress sought a judicial order enjoining the President from offensive military operations in connection with Operation Desert Shield unless he consulted with and obtained an authorization from Congress. On December 13, Judge Harold Greene of the federal district court in Washington denied the injunction, holding that the controversy was not ripe for judicial resolution because a majority of Congress had not sought relief and the executive branch had not shown sufficient commitment to a definitive course of action.[32]

By January, 1991, President Bush had secured the support of the United Nations and an international coalition to use force, if necessary, to free Kuwait

---

[30] Public Papers of the Presidents of the United States. Ronald Reagan. 1983, Washington. U.S. Government Printing Office, 1985, pp.1444–1445. Shortly afterward, on October 23, 1983, 241 U.S. Marines in Lebanon were killed by a suicide truck bombing, raising fresh questions in Congress and U.S. public opinion about U.S. participation in the Lebanon peacekeeping endeavor. On February 7, 1984, President Reagan announced the Marines would be redeployed and on March 30, 1984, reported to Congress that U.S. participation in the Multinational Force in Lebanon had ended.

[31] For an overview of Congressional actions during the fall and winter of 1990 as well as the President's actions in response to the events in the Persian Gulf, *see* CRS, *The War Powers Resolution: After Twenty-Eight Years* (RL31185), by Richard F. Grimmett, pp. 24–28.

[32] Dellums v. Bush, 752 F. Supp. 1141 (D.D.C. 1990).

from Iraqi occupation. U.N. Resolution 678 of November 29, 1990, authorized all U.N. member states "to use all necessary means" to implement various U.N. resolutions seeking to end Iraqi occupation of Kuwait. It set a January 15, 1991 deadline for Iraq to implement fully all relevant U.N. resolutions relating to its invasion of Kuwait. On January 8, 1991, President George H.W. Bush, in a letter to the congressional leaders, requested a congressional resolution supporting the use of all necessary means to implement U.N. Security Council Resolution 678. He stated that he was "determined to do whatever is necessary to protect America's security" and that he could "think of no better way than for Congress to express its support for the President at this critical time." It is noteworthy that the President's request for a resolution was a request for congressional "support" for his undertaking in the Persian Gulf, not for "authority" to engage in the military operation. In a press conference on January 9, 1991, President Bush reinforced this distinction in response to questions about the use of force resolution being debated in Congress. He was asked whether he thought he needed the resolution, and if he lost on it would he feel bound by that decision. President Bush in response stated: "I don't think I need it. . . . I feel that I have the authority to fully implement the United Nations resolutions." He added that he felt that he had "the constitutional authority—many attorneys having so advised me."[33]

On January 12, 1991, both houses passed the "Authorization for Use of Military Force Against Iraq Resolution." Section 2(a) of that joint resolution authorized the President to use U.S. Armed Forces pursuant to U.N. Security Council Resolution 678 to achieve implementation of the earlier Security Council resolutions. Section 2(b) required as a precondition that the President would first have to report to Congress that the United States had used all appropriate diplomatic and other peaceful means to obtain compliance by Iraq with the Security Council resolution and that those efforts had not been successful. Section 2(c) stated that it constituted specific statutory authorization within the meaning of Section 5(b) of the War Powers Resolution. Section 3 required the President to report every 60 days on efforts to obtain compliance of Iraq with the U.N. Security Council resolution.[34]

In his statement made when signing H.J.Res. 77 into law, President Bush said the following:

> As I made clear to congressional leaders at the outset, my request for congressional support did not, and my signing this resolution does not, constitute

[33] Public Papers of the Presidents of the United States. George Bush 1991. Washington, U.S. Government Printing Office, 1992, pp. 13–14, 19–20.

[34] The House passed H.J. Res. 77 by a vote of 250 to 183. The Senate passed S.J. Res. 2 and then accepted the language in H.J. Res. 77. The Senate vote was 52 to 47. P.L. 102-1, 105 Stat. 3, January 14, 1991. On January 12, to emphasize the congressional power to declare war, the House also adopted by a vote of 302 to 131 H.Con. Res. 32 expressing the sense that Congress must approve any offensive military actions against Iraq; the Senate did not act on the measure.

> any change in the long-standing positions of the executive branch on either the President's constitutional authority to use the Armed Forces to defend vital U.S. interests or the constitutionality of the War Powers Resolution.

He added that he was pleased that "differences on these issues between the President and many in the Congress have not prevented us from uniting in a common objective."[35] On January16, 1991, President Bush made the determination required by P.L. 102-1 that diplomatic means had not and would not compel Iraq to withdraw from Kuwait. On January 18, he reported to Congress "consistent with the War Powers Resolution" that he had directed U.S. forces to commence combat operations on January 16.[36]

Terrorist Attacks against the United States (World Trade Center and the Pentagon) 2001

On September 11, 2001, terrorists hijacked four U.S. commercial airliners, crashing two into the twin towers of the World Trade Center in New York City, and another into the Pentagon building in Arlington, Virginia. The fourth plane crashed in Shanksville, Pennsylvania near Pittsburgh, after passengers struggled with the highjackers for control of the aircraft. The death toll from these incidents was nearly 3000. President George W. Bush characterized these attacks as more than acts of terror. "They were acts of war," he said. He added that "freedom and democracy are under attack," and he asserted that the United States would use "all of our resources to conquer this enemy."[37]

In the days immediately after the September 11 attacks, the President consulted with the leaders of Congress on appropriate steps to take to deal with the situation confronting the United States. One of the things that emerged from discussions was the concept of a joint resolution of the Congress authorizing the President to take military steps to deal with the parties responsible for the attacks on the United States. Between September 13 and 14, draft language of such a resolution was discussed and negotiated by the President's representatives and the House and Senate leadership of both parties. Other members of both Houses suggested language for consideration. On Friday, September 14, 2001, the text of a joint resolution

---

35 Public Papers of the Presidents of the United States. George Bush 1991. Washington, U.S. Government Printing Office, 1992, p. 40. Subsequently, on June 20,1992, President Bush reiterated his view of his constitutional authority during remarks to the Texas State Republican Convention in Dallas, Texas. On that occasion President Bush said: "Some people say, why can't you bring the same kind of purpose and success to the domestic scene as you did in Desert Shield and Desert Storm? And the answer is: I didn't have to get permission from some old goat in the United States Congress to kick Saddam Hussein out of Kuwait. That's the reason." Public Papers of the Presidents of the United States. George Bush 1992–93. Washington, U.S. Government Printing Office, 1993, p. 995.

36 Public Papers of the Presidents of the United States. George Bush 1991. Washington, U.S. Government Printing Office, 1992, p. 42, 52. Emphasis added.

37 Presidential statement of September 12, 2001. Office of the White House Press Secretary. See White House website at [http: //whitehouse.gov/news/releases].

was introduced. It was first considered and passed by the Senate in the morning of September 14, as Senate Joint Resolution 23, by a vote of 98-0. The House of Representatives passed it later that evening, by a vote of 420-1, after tabling an identical resolution, H.J.Res. 64, and rejecting a motion to recommit by Representative John Tierney that would have had the effect, if passed and enacted, of requiring a report from the President on his actions under the resolution every 60 days.[38]

President Bush signed the measure into law on September 18, 2001.[39] The joint resolution authorizes the President

> to use all necessary and appropriate force against those nations, organizations, or persons he determines planned, authorized, committed, or aided the terrorist attacks that occurred on September 11, 2001, or harbored such organizations or persons, in order to prevent any future acts of international terrorism against the United States by such nations, organizations or persons.

The joint resolution further states that Congress declares that this resolution is intended to "constitute specific statutory authorization within the meaning of section 5(b) of the War Powers Resolution." Finally, the joint resolution also states that "[n]othing in this resolution supercedes any requirement of the War Powers Resolution."

A notable feature of P.L. 107-40 is that, unlike all other major legislation authorizing the use of military force by the President, this joint resolution authorizes military force against not only nations but also organizations and persons linked to the September 11, 2001, attacks on the United States. This authorization of military action against organizations and persons is unprecedented in American history, with the scope of its reach yet to be determined. The authorization of use of force against unnamed nations is more consistent with some previous instances where authority was given to act against unnamed states as appropriate when they became aggressors or took military action against the United States or its citizens.

President George W. Bush in signing S.J. Res. 23 on September 18, 2001, stated that the Congress had acted "wisely, decisively, and in the finest traditions of our country." He thanked the "leadership of both Houses for their role in expeditiously passing this historic joint resolution." He noted that he had had the "benefit of meaningful consultations with members of the Congress" since the September 11 attacks and that he would "continue

[38] For background on discussions regarding the resolution see *Washington Post*, September 13, 2001, p.A3; *CQ Daily Monitor*, September 13, 2001, p.2, 6; *CQ Daily Monitor*, September 14, 2001, p.2; Washington Post, September 14, 2001, p. A30; The New York Times, September 14, 2001, p.A19; *Roll Call*, September 20, 2001, p.17; and Abramowitz, David, "The President, the Congress, and Use of Force: Legal and Political Considerations in Authorizing Use of Force Against International Terrorism," 43 *Harvard International Law Journal* 71 (2002). The debate on S. J. Res. 23 is found in 107 CONG. REC. S9416–S9421 and H5638–H5683 (daily edition September 14, 2001).

[39] P.L. 107-40 (September 18, 2001); 115 Stat. 224.

to consult closely with them as our Nation responds to this threat to our peace and security." President Bush also asserted that S.J. Jes. 23 "recognized the authority of the President under the Constitution to take action to deter and prevent acts of terrorism against the United States." He also stated that "in signing this resolution, I maintain the longstanding position of the executive branch regarding the President's constitutional authority to use force, including the Armed Forces of the United States, and regarding the constitutionality of the War Powers Resolution."[40]

The Bush Administration has interpreted P.L. 107-40 broadly, to confirm the President's authority as Commander-in-Chief to conduct antiterrorism operations anywhere in the world, including within the United States.[41] In 2004, the Supreme Court affirmed the President's powers to detain "enemy combatants" captured in Afghanistan as part of the necessary force authorized by Congress, but found that detainees could challenge their detention in federal court.[42] In light of the Supreme Court decisions, the Administration interprets the joint resolution to authorize any measures that can be characterized as fundamental incidents of the conduct of war, even where such measures are otherwise prohibited by statute (at least so long as the statute in question contemplates a statutory exception). Thus, the Administration has cited the joint resolution to support the President's power to detain persons he has deemed to be "enemy combatants" (whether citizens or aliens and without regard to the location or circumstances of their capture)[43] and to conduct electronic surveillance of communications within the United States without following the procedures prescribed in FISA.[44] The Supreme Court in 2006 held that P.L. 107-40 does not override the UCMJ as it pertains to the trial of captured combatants for violations of the law of war.[45]

---

40 Statement of the President on September 18, 2001. President Signs Authorization for Use of Military Force bill. Office of the White House Press Secretary. September 18, 2001. See White House website at [http://whitehouse.gov/news/releases].

41 For a detailed legislative history of the joint resolution addressing its intended scope, see CRS Report RS22357, *Authorization For Use Of Military Force in Response to the 9/11 Attacks (P.L. 107-40): Legislative History*, by Richard F. Grimmett.

42 For an overview of the 2004 Supreme Court decisions regarding the authorization to use military force, see CRS Report RS21884, *The Supreme Court and Detainees in the War on Terrorism: Summary and Analysis*.

43 *See* CRS Report RL31724, Detention of American Citizens as Enemy Combatants, by Jennifer K. Elsea.

44 U.S. Department of Justice White Paper on NSA Legal Authorities ("Legal Authorities Supporting the Activities of the National Security Agency Described by the President") (PDF) (Jan. 19,2006) [http://news.findlaw.com/hdocs/docs/nsa/dojnsa11906wp.pdf]. For an analysis of the Administration position as presented prior to the DOJ White Paper, see *CRSMemorandum, Presidential Authority to Conduct Warrantless Electronic Surveillance to Gather Foreign Intelligence Information*, by Elizabeth Bazan and Jennifer K. Elsea, Jan. 5, 2006.

45 Hamdan v. Rumsfeld, 548 U.S. __ (2006), *rev'g 415* F.3d 33 (D.C. Cir. 2005). For a summary and analysis, see CRS Report RS22466, *Hamdan v. Rumsfeld: Military Commissions in the 'Global War on Terrorism,'* by Jennifer K. Elsea.

Authorization for Use of Force Against Iraq 2002

In the summer of 2002, the Bush Administration made public its views regarding what it deemed a significant threat to U.S. interests and security posed by the prospect that Iraq had or was acquiring weapons of mass destruction. Senior members of the Bush Administration cited a number of violations of U.N. Security Council resolutions by Iraq regarding the obligation imposed at the end of the Gulf War in 1991 to end its chemical, biological and nuclear weapons programs. On September 4, 2002, President Bush met with leaders from both Houses and parties at the White House. At that meeting the President stated that he would seek Congressional support, in the near future, for action deemed necessary to deal with the theat posed to the United States by the regime of Saddam Hussein of Iraq. The President also indicated that he would speak to the United Nations shortly and set out his concerns about Iraq.

On September 12, 2002, President Bush addressed the U.N. General Assembly and set out the history of Iraqi misdeeds over the last two decades and the numerous times that Iraq had not fulfilled its commitments to comply with various U.N. Security Council resolutions, including disarmament, since the Gulf War of 1991. He stated that the United States would work with the U.N. Security Council to deal with Iraq's challenge. However, he emphasized that if Iraq refused to fulfill its obligations to comply with U.N. Security Council resolutions, the United States would see that those resolutions were enforced.[46]

Subsequently, on September 19, 2002, the White House sent a "draft" joint resolution to House Speaker Dennis Hastert, House Minority Leader Richard Gephardt, Senate Majority Leader Thomas Daschle and Senate Minority Leader Trent Lott. This draft would have authorized the President to use military force not only against Iraq but "to restore international peace and security in the region." Subsequently introduced as S.J. Res. 45 on September 26, it served as the basis for an extensive debate over the desirability, necessity, and scope of a new Congressional authorization for the use of force. The Senate used this bill as the focus for a debate which began, after cloture was invoked, on October 3. The Senate debate continued from October 4 until October 11, 2002, and involved consideration of numerous amendments to the measure. In the end the Senate adopted H.J. Res. 114 in lieu of S.J. Res. 45.

The draft measure was not formally introduced in the House. Instead, the vehicle for House consideration of the issue was H.J. Res. 114. Cosponsored by Speaker Hastert and Minority Leader Gephardt and introduced on

---

[46] See the White House website for comments by the President to the Congressional leaders and to the U.N. under news (Sept.) at [http://www.whitehouse.gov/news/releases/2002/09/].

October 2, 2002, H.J. Res. 114 embodied modifications to the White House draft that were agreeable to the White House, most House and Senate Republicans, and the House Democratic leadership. The House International Relations Committee reported out a slightly amended version of the joint resolution on October 7, 2002 (H. Report 107-721). The House adopted the rule governing debate on the joint resolution (H. Res. 474) on October 8, 2002; and debated the measure until October 10, when it passed H.J. Res. 114 by a vote of 296-133. Subsequently, the Senate passed the House version of H.J. Res 114 on October 11 by a vote of 77-23, and President Bush signed the Authorization for Use of Military Force against Iraq Resolution of 2002 into law on October 16, 2002.[47]

In signing H.J. Res. 114 into law, President Bush noted that by passing this legislation the Congress had demonstrated that "the United States speaks with one voice on the threat to international peace and security posed by Iraq." He added that the legislation carried an important message that "Iraq will either comply with all U.N. resolutions, rid itself of weapons of mass destruction, and . . . its support for terrorists, or will be compelled to do so." While the President noted he had sought a "resolution of support" from Congress to use force against Iraq, and appreciated receiving that support, he also stated that

> . . . my request for it did not, and my signing this resolution does not, constitute any change in the long-standing positions of the executive branch on either the President's constitutional authority to use force to deter, prevent, or respond to aggression or other threats to U.S. interests or on the constitutionality of the War Powers Resolution.

The President went on to state that on the "important question of the threat posed by Iraq", his views and goals and those of the Congress were the same. He further observed that he had extensive consultations with the Congress in the past months, and that he looked forward to "continuing close consultation in the months ahead." He stated his intent to submit written reports to Congress every 60 days on matters "relevant to this resolution."[48]

The central element of P.L. 107-243 is the authorization for the President to use the armed forces of the United States

> as he determines to be necessary and appropriate in order to—(1) defend the national security of the United States against the continuing threat posed by Iraq; and (2) enforce all relevant United Nations Security Council resolutions regarding Iraq.

---

[47] P.L. 107-243; 116 Stat. 1498. For a detailed side-by-side comparison of the House and Senate versions of the authorization of force against Iraq legislation and proposed amendments *see* CRS, *Authorization of Use of U.S. Armed Forces Against Iraq: Side-by-Side Comparison of Selected Legislative Proposals* (RL31596), by Dianne Rennack.

[48] For text of President Bush's signing statement for H.J. Res. 114 see the State Department's Washington File entry at [http://usinfo.state.gov/topical/pol/usandun/02101606.htm].

As predicates for the use of force, the statute requires the President to communicate to Congress his determination that the use of diplomatic and other peaceful means will not "adequately protect the United States . . . or . . . lead to enforcement of all relevant United Nations Security Council resolutions" and that the use of force is "consistent" with the battle against terrorism. Like P.L. 102-1 and P.L. 107-40, the statute declares that it is "intended to constitute specific statutory authorization within the meaning of section 5(b) of the War Powers Resolution." It also requires the President to make periodic reports to Congress "on matters relevant to this joint resolution." Finally, the statute expresses Congress' "support" for the efforts of the President to obtain "prompt and decisive action by the Security Council" to enforce Iraq's compliance with all relevant Security Council resolutions.

Public Law 107-243 clearly confers broad authority on the President to use force. In contrast to P.L. 102-1, the authority granted is not limited to the implementation of previously adopted Security Council resolutions concerning Iraq but includes "all relevant . . . resolutions." Thus, it appears to incorporate future resolutions concerning Iraq that may be adopted by the Security Council as well as those adopted prior to the enactment of P.L. 107-243. The authority also appears to extend beyond compelling Iraq's disarmament to implementing the full range of concerns expressed in those resolutions. Unlike P.L. 107-40, the President's exercise of the authority granted is **not** dependent upon a finding that Iraq was associated in some direct way with the September 11, 2001, attacks on the U.S. Moreover, the authority conferred can be used for the broad purpose of defending "the national security of the United States against the continuing threat posed by Iraq." Nevertheless, P. L. 107-243 is narrower than P.L. 107-40 in that it limits the authorization for the use of force to Iraq. It also requires as a predicate for the use of force that the President determine that peaceful means cannot suffice and that the use of force against Iraq is consistent with the battle against terrorism.[49] P. L. 107-243 further limits the force used to that which the President determines is "necessary and appropriate." Finally, as with P.L. 107-40, the statutory authorization for use of force granted to the President in P.L. 107-243 is not dependent for its exercise upon prior authorization by the U.N. Security Council.

P.L. 107-243 does not contain explicit time requirements or call for the withdrawal of U.S. troops by any specific date or set of criteria. Presumably, continued force is authorized so long as Iraq poses a continuing threat to

[49] In March 2003, President George W. Bush reported to Congress the determination that was required by P.L. 107-243 regarding his exercise of authority for military operations against Iraq. House Document 108–50. March 19, 2003. A report in connection with Presidential Determination under Public Law 107–243. Communication from the President of the United States transmitting a report consistent with Section 3(b) of the Authorization for Use of Military Force Against Iraq Resolution of 2002.

the United States and the U.S. military presence is not inconsistent with relevant U.N. resolutions. While it may be argued that the specific threats posed by Iraq during Saddam Hussein's regime that were emphasized in the preamble to PL 107-243 no longer exist, it seems reasonable to conclude that the authorization to use force includes authority to use the military to occupy Iraq, consistent with the international law of armed conflict, until a new government is able to maintain control over the territory.[50] This conclusion is bolstered by U.N. Security Council resolutions adopted in the aftermath of the invasion. Despite the initial lack of consensus regarding the legality of the invasion, the Security Council adopted subsequent resolutions recognizing the occupation of Iraq and generally supporting the coalition's plans for bringing about a democratic government in Iraq. Resolution 1511 (Oct. 16, 2003), in paragraph 13

> authorizes a multinational force under unified command to take all necessary measures to contribute to the maintenance of security and stability in Iraq, including for the purpose of ensuring necessary conditions for the implementation of the timetable and programme as well as to contribute to the security of the United Nations Assistance Mission for Iraq, the Governing Council of Iraq and other institutions of the Iraqi interim administration, and key humanitarian and economic infrastructure.

Resolution 1546 reaffirmed the authorization for the multinational force (MNF) in Resolution 1511, "noting" that "the presence of the multinational force in Iraq is at the request of the incoming Interim Government of Iraq." The terms of the mandate for the MNF are expressed in paragraph 12, in which the Security Council

> [d]ecides further that the mandate for the multinational force shall be reviewed at the request of the Government of Iraq or twelve months from the date of this resolution, and that this mandate shall expire upon the completion of the political process set out in paragraph four [of Resolution 1546], and declares that it will terminate this mandate earlier if requested by the Government of Iraq.

The termination of the UN mandate for the MNF is tied directly to the completion of the political process rather than to any specific date set for that event. In Resolution 1637 (Nov. 11, 2005), the Security Council reiterated its finding that "the situation in Iraq continues to constitute a threat to international peace and security," and extended the MNF mandate until 31 December 2006, to be reviewed at the request of the Iraqi government or no later than 15 June 2006. On June 9, 2006, the Iraqi foreign minister requested the continued presence of the MNF,[51] making it likely that the mandate will be extended at least until December 2007. As long as the U.N.

---

[50] For an overview of the process, see *Iraq: Transition to Sovereignty*, CRS Report RS21820.

[51] Letter from Hoshyar Zebari, Minister for Foreign Affairs of the Republic of Iraq, to the United Nations, U.N. Doc. SC/2006/377 (June 9, 2006).

mandate remains in force and the situation in Iraq continues to pose a threat, no new authorization will be required. What would happen in the event the Security Council reaches an impasse on extending the mandate is less clear. Congress is free to alter, through legislation, the nature of U.S. participation at any time.

Implications Under International Law

Traditionally, peace and war have been deemed under international law to be distinctive forms of relations between states. Thus, peace has been defined as

> a condition in which States maintain order and justice, solve their problems by cooperation, and eliminate violence. It is a condition in which States respect each other's sovereignty and equality, refrain from intervention and the threat or use of force and cooperate with one another in accordance with the treaties which they have concluded.[52]

War, in contrast, has been described as "a condition of armed hostility between States,"[53] "a contention, through the use of armed force, between states, undertaken for the purpose of overpowering another."[54] War has been said to terminate or suspend the laws and customs that prevail in peacetime and to substitute for them the laws of war. Under the traditional laws of war enemy combatants can be killed, prisoners of war taken, the enemy's property seized or destroyed, enemy aliens interned, and other measures necessary to subdue the enemy and impose the will of the warring state taken.[55] Moreover, the existence of a state of war traditionally has been deemed to terminate diplomatic and commercial relations and most of the treaty obligations existing between the warring States.[56] A state of

---

[52] Skubiszewski, Krzysztof, "Peace and War," *Encyclopedia of Public International Law*, Vol 4 (1982), at 74–75.

[53] Hyde, Charles Cheney, *International Law Chiefly as Interpreted and Applied by the United States*, Vol. 3 (1945), at 1686.

[54] von Glahn, Gerhard, *Law Among Nations* (6th ed.) (1992), at 669.

[55] In his treatise *Law of Nations* (1858), at 346, Emmerich de Vattel stated the general principles governing the conduct of war as follows:

> As soon, therefore, as we have declared war, we have a right to do against the enemy whatever we find necessary for the attainment of that end—for the purpose of bringing him to reason, and obtaining justice and security from him.
>
> The lawfulness of the end does not give us a real right to anything further than barely the means necessary for the attainment of that end. Whatever we do beyond that, is reprobated by the law of nature, is faulty, and condemnable at the tribunal of conscience. Hence it is that the right to such or such acts of hostility varies according to circumstances. What is just and perfectly innocent in war, in one particular situation, is not always so on other occasions. Right goes hand in hand with necessity and the exigency of the case, but never exceeds them.

[56] Cushman K. Davis, *A Treatise on International Law* (1901), at 141 stated:

> War abrogates all treaties between the belligerents; its suspends all commercial intercourse and relations between their respective subjects, and makes them unlawful; it dissolves all partnerships between subjects of the belligerents; it suspends the operation of all executory contracts

war also has brought into play the law of neutrality with respect to relations between the belligerent and non-belligerent States.

In this traditional understanding a declaration of war has been deemed, in and of itself, to have the effect of creating a state of war and changing the relationship between the states involved from one of peace to one of war. That has been the case even if no hostilities actually occur. Some question exists as to whether international law traditionally deemed a declaration of war to be a necessary prerequisite to the existence of a state of war;[57] but it is clear that under international law a declaration of war has been viewed as "creating the legal status of war . . . [and giving] evidence that peace has been transmuted into war, and that the law of war has replaced the law of peace."[58]

Authorizations for the use of force, in contrast, have not been seen as automatically creating a state of war under international law. The U.S. Court of Claims, in construing the statutes authorizing the limited use of force against France in 1798, described how their effects differed from those that followed in the wake of a war:

> [Our naval vessels] might seize armed vessels only, and only those armed vessels which had already committed depredations, or those which were on our coast for the purpose of committing depredations, and they might retake an American vessel captured by such an armed vessel. This statute is a fair

---

during the war. . . . It open a great gulf of non-intercourse between the two nations, and imposes disability upon the subjects of each to do any kind of civil business with those of the other. . . .

57 Commentators differ on this issue. Grotius claimed that a declaration was a necessary precondition to the existence of a war. *See* Ingrid *Detter, The Law of* War (2000), at 10. Vattel said a declaration communicated to the enemy was demanded by "humanity" prior to the inception of a war, served as an inducement to the enemy to "terminate the difference without the effusion of blood," and was "the constant practice among the powers of Europe." Vattel, *supra* note 55, at 315. But he also stated that "there seems to be no absolute necessity for a formal declaration of war to render it legal." *Id.* at 316. *Kent's Commentary on International Law* (1878), at169–171, stated:

> . . . [I]t has become settled by the practice of Europe that war may lawfully exist by a declaration which is unilateral only, or without a declaration on either side. It may begin with mutual hostilities. Since the Peace of Versailles in 1763, formal declarations of war of any kind seem to have been discontinued, and all the necessary and legitimate consequences of war flow at once from a state of public hostilities, duly recognized, and explicitly announced, by a domestic manifesto or State paper."

A legal requirement of a formal declaration of war was included in the Hague Convention (III) Relative to the Opening of Hostilities, negotiated in 1907 and ratified by 42 countries (including the U.S.), which stated as follows:

> The Contracting Powers recognize that hostilities between themselves must not commence without previous and explicit warning, in the form either of a reasoned declaration of war or of an ultimatum with conditional declaration of war.

Although this treaty remains in effect for its Parties, its requirement regarding a declaration of war has generally fallen into desuetude; and a declaration generally is no longer regarded as a legal prerequisite to the use of force. Von Glahn, *supra* note 54, at 600, states: ". . . [G]eneral opinion has sanctioned a commencement of hostilities without issuing a declaration of war or other formal notice of intent to resort to the use of force."

58 Eagleton, Clyde, "The Form and Function of the Declaration of War," 38 *American Journal of International Law* 19, 21 (1938).

> illustration of the class of laws enacted at this time; they directed suspension of commercial relations until the end of the next session of Congress, not indefinitely . . . ; they gave power to the President to apprehend the subjects of hostile nations whenever he should make "public proclamation" of war . . . , and no such proclamation was made; they gave him authority to instruct our armed vessels to seize French "armed," not merchant, vessels . . . , together with contingent authority to augment the army in case war should break out or in case of imminent danger of invasion. . . .
>
> If war existed, why authorize our armed vessels to seize French armed vessels? War itself gave that right, as well as the right to seize merchantmen which the statutes did not permit. If war existed why empower the President to apprehend foreign enemies? War itself placed that duty upon him as a necessary and inherent incident of military command. Why, if there was war, should a suspension of commercial intercourse be authorized, for what more complete suspension of that intercourse could there be than the very fact of war?
>
> There was no declaration of war; the tribunals of each country were open to the other—an impossibility were war in progress; diplomatic and commercial intercourse were admittedly suspended; but during many years there was no intercourse between England and Mexico, which were not at war; there was retaliation and reprisal, but such retaliations and reprisals have often occurred between nations at peace; there was a near approach to war, but at no time was one of the nations turned into an enemy of the other in such manner that every citizen of the one became the enemy of every citizen of the other; finally, there was not that kind of war which abrogated treaties and wiped out, at least temporarily, all pending rights and contracts, individual and national.[59]

Whether this traditional understanding of war and of the effect of a declaration of war continues to be viable is a matter of considerable dispute among scholars. The right of a state to initiate war, many contend, has been outlawed by such international agreements as the Kellogg-Briand Peace Pact and the Charter of the United Nations. In the Kellogg-Briand Peace Pact,[60] for instance, the Parties stated that they "condemn recourse to war for the solution of international controversies, and renounce it as an instrument of national policy in their relations with one another."[61] After World War II the Nuremberg Tribunal gave teeth to this commitment by ruling that the Pact rendered aggressive war illegal under international law and makes those who plan and wage such a war guilty of a crime.[62] The Charter

---

[59] Gray v. United States, 21 Ct.Cl. 340, 373 (1886).

[60] Treaty Providing for the Renunciation of War As an Instrument of National Policy, 46 Stat. 2343 (1929); TS 796; 2 Bevans 732.

[61] *Id.*, Art. I.

[62] The Tribunal stated:

> In the opinion of the Tribunal, the solemn renunciation of war as an instrument of national policy necessarily involves the proposition that such a war is illegal in international law; and

of the United Nations, in turn, states one of its purposes to be "to save succeeding generations from the scourge of war," and it requires its Members "to refrain from the threat or use of force against the territorial integrity or political independence of any State, or in any other manner inconsistent with the Purposes of the United Nations."[63] Moreover, it provides for a system of collective security through the Security Council as the primary means of maintaining or restoring international peace and security.[64] Both instruments, it is contended, recognize that the concept of war as a legal right of states, except in self-defense,[65] has been superseded. (The United States, of course, is a Party not only to the Charter but also to the Pact, and it still regards the latter as continuing to be in force.[66]) Whether the traditional concept of war remains valid has been further complicated by the increasing participation in armed conflict of non-State actors such as insurgents, freedom fighters, and terrorists.

Moreover, the clarity of the consequences of a state of war in traditional international law has become muddied in the modern era. Most States since 1945, even when engaged in armed conflict, have resisted describing the conflict as a war.[67] States so engaged have not always automatically terminated diplomatic and commercial relationships,[68] and the discontinuance of treaty obligations has increasingly been deemed to require a treaty-by-treaty examination.[69] Moreover, conventions that attempt to regulate the means used to wage war, such as the Hague Conventions and other more recent agreements,[70] and those that attempt to ameliorate the consequences of

---

that those who plan and wage such a war, with its inevitable and terrible consequences, are committing a crime in so doing.

See "International Military Tribunal (Nuremberg): Judgment and Sentences," 41 *American Journal of International Law* 172, 218 (1947).

63 UN Charter, 59 Stat. 1031, Preamble and Article 2(4).

64 *Id.* Ch. VII.

65 The right of self-defense is explicitly recognized in Article 51 of the Charter, which states that "Nothing in the present Charter shall impair the inherent right of individual or collective self-defence if an armed attack occurs against a Member of the United Nations. . . ."

66 Department of State, *Treaties in Force: A List of Treaties and other International Agreements of the United States in Force on January 1, 2002* (Aug. 2002), at 454.

67 Dieter Fleck, ed., *The Handbook of Humanitarian Law in Armed Conflicts* (1995), at 39.

68 The modern codification of the law of diplomatic relations—the Vienna Convention on Diplomatic Relations, 23 UST 3227 (1972)—does not specifically address the effect of a declaration of war or of an authorization for the use of force but does address what is required in cases of "armed conflict." Whenever diplomatic relations are broken, the Convention requires that diplomatic privileges and immunities not cease until the diplomat leaves the country and that the receiving state assist diplomats and their families in leaving "at the earliest possible moment, . . . even in case of armed conflict" (Articles 38 and 44). The Convention also requires that a state respect and protect the premises of a diplomatic mission and its property and archives during any time in which diplomatic relations have been broken, including "in the case of armed conflict" (Article 45(a)).

69 The modern tendency appears to be to deem treaties as remaining in effect to the greatest extent possible. *See generally*, von Glahn, Gerhard, *Law Among Nations* (1992), at 715–716.

70 *See* The Hague Convention Respecting the Laws and Customs of War on Land, 32 Stat. 1803 (1902); the Hague Convention (III) Relative to the Opening of Hostilities, 36 Stat. 2259 (1910); the Hague Convention (IV) Respecting the Laws and Customs of War on Land, 36 Stat. 2277 (1910); the Hague Convention (V) Respecting the Rights and Duties of Neutral Powers and Persons in Case of War on

war for certain categories of persons, such as the Geneva Conventions,[71] are deemed to apply to armed conflicts regardless of what label the Parties attach to them. A state of war still gives rise to "a mutual right to kill in battle,"[72] triggers application of the various conventions regulating the means of waging war as well as of the general principles of necessity and proportionality, and brings into play the Geneva Conventions. But its other legal consequences seemingly have become less determinate.

Perhaps as a consequence of these developments, declarations of war have fallen into disuse and are virtually never issued in modern conflicts. One commentator asserts that since 1945 "[t]here are no cases of a formal declaration of war having been delivered by one state to another through diplomatic channels. . . ."[73] As noted above, the United States last declared war in 1942 against Rumania and has since adopted only authorizations for the use of force.

Thus, declarations of war may have become anachronistic in contemporary international law. The legal right of States to engage in war has seemingly become constrained (for other than defensive purposes), and the most salient international laws regarding the means of waging war and the protection of certain categories of persons apply to the circumstance of armed conflict regardless of whether war has been declared. That circumstance can arise in the wake of an authorization to use force as well. States likely still retain a right to issue declarations of war, at least in exercising the right of self-defense; and such a declaration seemingly would still automatically create a state of war. But it is not clear that the legal consequences under international law that would flow from a declaration differ dramatically from those that occur if an armed conflict comes into being pursuant to an authorization for the use of force.

Land, 36 Stat. 2310 (1910); the Hague Convention (VII) Relative to the Laying of Automatic Submarine Contact Mines, 36 Stat. 2332 (1910); the Hague Convention (IX) Concerning Bombardment by Naval Forces in Time of War, 36 Stat. 2351 (1910); the Hague Convention (XI) Relative to Certain Restrictions With Regard to the Exercise of the Right of Capture in Naval War, 36 Stat. 2396 (1910); the Hague Convention (XIII) Concerning the Rights and Duties of Neutral Powers in Naval War, 36 Stat. 2415 (1910); The Protocol for the Prohibition of the Use in War of Asphyxiating, Poisonous or other Gases, and of Bacteriological Methods of Warfare, 26 UST 571(1975) and The Convention on the Prohibition of Military or Any Other Hostile Use of Environmental Modification Techniques, 31 UST 333 (1980). The United States, it might be noted, is a Party to all of these conventions.

[71] The four Geneva Conventions apply to the treatment of those in the armed forces who are wounded and sick in the field, those who are shipwrecked, prisoners of war, and civilian populations. *See* Convention (I) for the Amelioration of the Condition of the Wounded and Sick in Armed Forces in the Field, 6 UST 3114 (1956); Convention (II) for the Amelioration of the Condition of the Wounded, Sick, and Shipwrecked Members of Armed Forces at Sea, 6 UST 3217 (1956); Convention (III) Relative to the Treatment of Prisoners of War, 6 UST 3316 (1956); and Convention (IV) Relative to the Protection of Civilian Persons in Time of War, 6 UST 3516 (1956).

[72] Alexander Hamilton, "The Examination No. 1," (Dec. 17, 1801), reprinted in 25 *The Papers of Alexander Hamilton* 455 (Syrett, ed., 1977), quoted in J. Gregory Sidak, "To Declare War," 41 *Duke Law Journal* 27 (1991), at 62. The full quote reads: "War, of itself, gives to the parties a mutual right to kill in battle. . . . This is a rule of natural law; a necessary and inevitable consequence of the state of war."

[73] *Id.* at 203.

Implications Under Domestic Law

Early American jurisprudence drew a distinction between general, or perfect, war and limited, or imperfect, war, and understood a declaration of war under Article I, § 8, of the Constitution to commit the nation to a general war. Justice Washington, *in Bas v. Tinghy*,[74] described the distinction as follows:

> It may, I believe, be safely laid down, that every contention by force between two nations, in external matters, under the authority of their respective governments, is not only war, but public war. If it be declared in form, it is called *solemn*, and is of the perfect kind; because one whole nation is at war with another whole nation; and *all* the members of the nation declaring war are authorised to commit hostilities against all the members of the other, in every place, and under every circumstance. In such a war all the members act under a general authority, and all the rights and consequences of war attach to their condition.
>
> . . . [H]ostilities may subsist between two nations more confined in its nature and extent; being limited as to places, persons, and things; and this is more properly termed *imperfect war;* because not solemn, and because those who are authorised to commit hostilities, act under special authority, and can go no farther than to the extent of their commission. Still, however, it is *public war*, because it is an external contention, by force, between some of the members of the two nations, authorised by the legitimate powers.[75]

Justice Chase, more simply, stated: "Congress is empowered to declare a general war, or congress may wage a limited war; limited in place, in objects, and in time."[76]

Thus, at least in the 18th and 19th centuries, authorizations for the use of force were understood to be included within Congress' power to declare war and to have narrower legal consequences than declarations of war. Declarations were reserved for general war against particular countries and empowered the President "to use the whole land and naval force of the United States" (United Kingdom in 1812), "to employ the militia, naval, and military forces of the United States" (Mexico in 1846), or "to use the entire land and naval forces of the United States" (Spain in 1898) to prosecute the war. Authorizations, in contrast, allowed the President to use the American navy against the vessels of France, the Bey of Tripoli, and the Dey of Algiers, or against piracy generally.

[74] U.S. (4 Dall.) 37, 40 (1800).
[75] *Id.*
[76] *Id.* at 43.

In the modern era authorizations have sometimes been quite broad[77]; and some have, arguably, been equivalent in scope to a declaration of war. But the domestic legal consequences that flow from such authorizations still are substantially more limited than those that would flow from a declaration of war.

Both declarations of war and authorizations for the use of force have the effect of eliminating the time limits otherwise imposed on the President's use of the armed forces under the War Powers Resolution; and both may legitimate the killing of foreign officials that might otherwise be prohibited by the executive order on assassinations. The capture of enemy combatants on the battlefield and their detention until hostilities have subsided is implied in an authorization to use ground forces, just as it would be included in a formal declaration of war.

But a declaration of war automatically brings into effect a number of statutes that confer special powers on the President and the Executive Branch, especially concerning measures that have domestic effect. A declaration, for instance, activates statutes that empower the President to interdict all trade with the enemy, order manufacturing plants to produce armaments and seize them if they refuse, control transportation systems in order to give the military priority use, and command communications systems to give priority to the military. A declaration triggers the Alien Enemy Act, which gives the President substantial discretionary authority over nationals of an enemy state who are in the United States. It activates special authorities to use electronic surveillance for purposes of gathering foreign intelligence information without a court order under the Foreign Intelligence Surveillance Act. It automatically extends enlistments in the armed forces until the end of the war, can make the Coast Guard part of the Navy, gives the President substantial discretion over the appointment and reappointment of commanders, and allows the military priority use of the natural resources on the public lands and the continental shelf.

An authorization for the use of force does not automatically trigger any of these standby statutory authorities. Some of them can come into effect if a state of war in fact comes into being after an authorization for the use of force is enacted; and the great majority of them, including many of the most sweeping ones, can be activated if the President chooses to issue a proclamation of a national emergency. But an authorization for the use of

[77] *See,* e.g., P.L. 107-40(Sept. 18,2001) (authorizing the President to use "all necessary and appropriate force against those nations, organizations, or persons he determines planned, authorized, committed, or aided the terrorist attacks that occurred on September 11, 2001. . . .") and P.L. 107-243 (Oct. 16, 2002) (authorizing the President to the use the armed forces "as he determines to be necessary and appropriate in order to—(1) defend the national security of the United States against the continuing threat posed by Iraq; and (2) enforce all relevant United Nations Security Council resolutions regarding Iraq."

force, in itself and in contrast to a declaration of war, does not trigger any of these standby authorities.

The following subsections give an overview of some of the more salient domestic legal consequences of a declaration of war or authorization for the use of force. They are followed by a section setting forth a detailed list of the standby statutory authorities that can be triggered by a declaration of war, a state or war, and/or a proclamation of national emergency.

The War Powers Resolution

Both a declaration of war and an authorization for the use of force have significant implications with respect to the War Powers Resolution (WPR).[78] The WPR was enacted over President Nixon's veto in 1973 purportedly to restore a Congressional role in authorizing the use of force that was thought by many to have been lost in the Cold War and the Vietnam War. To that end the WPR mandates that the President consult with the Congress "in every possible instance" prior to introducing U.S. armed forces into hostilities and regularly afterwards. Section 4(a) of the WPR further requires the President, "in the absence of a declaration of war," to report to Congress within 48 hours in any case in which United States Armed Forces are introduced —

(1) into hostilities or into situations where imminent involvement in hostilities is clearly indicated by the circumstances;

(2) into the territory, airspace or waters of a foreign nation, while equipped for combat, except for deployments which relate solely to supply, replacement, repair, or training of such forces; or

(3) in numbers which substantially enlarge United States Armed Forces equipped for combat already located in a foreign nation.

Section 5(b) of the Resolution, in turn, requires that if a report has been submitted or was required to be submitted under § 4(a)(1) above, the President shall terminate the involvement of U.S. forces unless Congress

(1) has declared war or has enacted a specific authorization for such use of United States Armed Forces;

(2) has extended by law such sixty-day period, or

(3) is physically unable to meet as a result of an armed attack upon the United States.[79]

Thus, congressional enactment of either a declaration of war or an authorization for the use of force pursuant to § 5(b) has the effect of tolling the 60–90 day withdrawal mandate of the WPR.

---

[78] 50 U.S.C.A. § 1541 *et seq.*

[79] *Id.*, § 1544(b).

Each of the last three authorizations for the use of force enacted—the 1991 Gulf War authorization, the September 18, 2001, authorization with respect to terrorist attacks, and the October 16, 2002, authorization with respect to Iraq—have explicitly stated that they constitute the authorization required by § 5(b) of the WPR. Each, in other words, has tolled the 60–90 day limitation that the WPR otherwise would impose on the use of military force by the President. All three authorizations have further specified that "[n]othing in this resolution supercedes any requirement of the War Powers Resolution." That appears to mean that the consultation and reporting requirements of the WPR still apply.

Trading with the Enemy Act and the International Emergency Economic Powers Act

Two related statutes, the Trading With the Enemy Act[80] (TWEA) and the International Emergency Economic Powers Act[81] (IEEPA), grant the President extraordinary powers to control foreign-owned property and foreign trade transactions with designated countries under certain exceptional circumstances. TWEA comes into effect upon a declaration of war or the existence of a state of war, while IEEPA is triggered solely by a presidential declaration of national emergency. Neither statute is triggered by an authorization for the use of force (unless, in the case of TWEA, the authorization eventually leads to the existence of a state of war). IEEPA is the authority most commonly invoked to freeze or block the assets of foreign states, companies, or individuals located within the jurisdiction of the United States.

Until 1977 the broad range of economic authorities granted by TWEA could be exercised both in times of war and in times of national emergency. However, in 1977 Congress limited the prospective application of TWEA to times of declared or undeclared war only and enacted IEEPA to apply during times of a national emergency declared by the President. Under TWEA the President may

(A) investigate, regulate, or prohibit, any transactions in foreign exchange, transfers of credit or payments or payments between, by, through, or to any banking institution, and the importing, exporting, hoarding, melting, or earmarking of gold or silver coin or bullion, currency or securities, and

(B) investigate, regulate, direct and compel, nullify, void, prevent or prohibit, any acquisition, holding, withholding, use, transfer, withdrawal, transportation, importation or exportation of, or dealing in, or exercising any right, power, privilege with respect to, or transactions

[80] 50 U.S.C. App. §§ 1 *et seq.*
[81] 50 U.S.C. §§ 1701 *et seq.*

> involving, any property in which any foreign country or a national thereof has any interest, by any person, or with respect to any property, subject to the jurisdiction of the United States; and any property or interest of any foreign country or national thereof shall vest, when, as, and upon the terms, directed by the President, in such agency or person as may be designated from time to time by the President, and upon such terms and conditions as the President may prescribe such interest or property shall be held, used, administered, liquidated, sold, or otherwise dealt with in the interest of and for the benefit of the United States. . . .[82]

IEEPA replicates many of TWEA's powers to regulate international transactions,[83] but it does not include TWEA authorities relative to purely domestic transactions, the regulation of bullion, and seizure of records.[84] It also does not contain TWEA's general authority to take title to foreign assets. But Congress did amend IEEPA in the "USA Patriot Act" in 2001 to authorize the President to confiscate and take title to

> any property, subject to the jurisdiction ofthe United States, of any foreign person, foreign organization, or foreign country that he determines has planned, authorized, aided or engaged in . . . hostilities or attacks against the United States. . . .[85]

Congress further amended both IEEPA and TWEA in the recently enacted "Terrorism Risk Insurance Act of 2002" to provide that the assets of foreign terrorist states that have been frozen in the U.S. pursuant to either statute may be used to satisfy civil judgments against them.[86]

As noted, IEEPA is triggered solely by a declaration of national emergency, while TWEA applies in time of war. Thus, TWEA is not dependent upon a declaration of war, but it can be triggered by such a declaration. Neither appears to be triggered by an authorization for the use of force, unless and until, in the case of TWEA, a state of war actually develops.

Other Economic Authorities

As noted, a declaration of war gives the President full authority over trade relations with the enemy. Other statutes triggered by a declaration give the President the authority to order plants to convert to the production of armaments and to seize those that refuse to do so,[87] to take control of the Tennessee Valley Authority in order to manufacture explosives or for other

---

[82] 50 U.S.C.A. Appx. § 5(b).
[83] 50 U.S.C.A. § 1702, as amended by P.L. 107-56, Title I, § 106 (Oct. 26, 2001).
[84] Staff of the House Ways and Means Committee, 105th Cong., *Overview and Compilation of U.S. Trade Statutes*, ch. 5 (WMCP 105–4, 1997).
[85] P.L. 107-56, Title I, § 106 (Oct. 26, 2001).
[86] P.L. 107-297, Title II, § 201 (Nov. 26, 2002).
[87] 10 U.S.C.A. § 2538.

military purposes,[88] to assume control of transportation systems for military purposes,[89] to condemn land for military uses,[90] to have the right of first refusal over natural resources,[91] and to take control of communications facilities.[92] It also gives the President full power over agricultural exports.[93] An authorization for the use of force, in itself, does not trigger any of these authorities.

Alien Enemy Act

First enacted in 1798, the Alien Enemy Act[94] broadly authorizes the President to deport, detain, or otherwise condition the stay of alien enemies in the U.S. in cases of "declared war" or "any invasion or predatory incursion . . . perpetrated, attempted, or threatened against the territory of the United States by any foreign nation or government. . . ." The Act implements the internationally recognized right of every nation to protect itself during times of war from individuals whose primary allegiance lies with a hostile foreign power. Given this premise, the Supreme Court has observed that "[e]xecutive power over enemy aliens, undelayed and unhampered by litigation, has been deemed, throughout our history, essential to wartime security."[95]

The President must publicly proclaim the event that gives rise to activation of the Act and make regulations regarding the treatment of those aliens. But once he does so, his power to "apprehend, restrain, secure, and remove" enemy aliens extends to all "natives, citizens, denizens, or subjects of the hostile nation or government, being of the age of fourteen years and upward, who shall be in the United States and not actually naturalized."[96] The President may intern or remove enemy aliens or set lesser restraints on them, and may adopt any "regulations which are found necessary in the premises and for the public safety."[97] Thus, President Woodrow Wilson, for example, barred alien enemies during World War I from possessing firearms and explosives, coming within a half a mile of a military facility or munitions factory, residing in certain areas, possessing certain communications equipment, and publishing certain types of materials. President Roosevelt authorized similar restrictions during World War II and, additionally, set up

88 16 U.S.C.A. § 831s.
89 10 U.S.C.A. § 2644.
90 10 U.S.C.A. §§ 2663(b) and 2664(d).
91 43 U.S.C.A. § 1314(b).
92 47 U.S.C.A. § 606(a).
93 7 U.S.C.A. § 5712(c).
94 50 U.S.C. §§ 21 *et seq.*
95 *Johnson v. Eisentrager*, 339 U.S. 763, 774 (1950).
96 50 U.S.C. § 21.
97 *Id.*

over 100 community hearing boards to make internment recommendations to the Attorney General.[98]

The procedural rights of aliens who are subject to the Alien Enemy Act are drastically restricted compared with those that aliens otherwise enjoy, including hearing rights under the removal provisions of the Immigration and Nationality Act.[99] The scope of judicial review is equally circumscribed.[100] Among the few rights recognized under the Act, alien enemies subjected to removal may, if not chargeable with "actual hostility" or other crime against public safety, be entitled to the time allowed by applicable treaty or order to wind up his or her affairs here.[101] A very limited right to judicial review under a petition for a writ of habeas corpus also is recognized. Generally, however, the power of the President to control alien enemies under the Act is extraordinary.

As noted, the Act does not appear to be triggered solely by an authorization for the use of force.

Criminal Law

There are a number of civilian federal criminal law provisions that apply explicitly to specified conduct in time of war. They do not appear to distinguish between circumstances involving a declaration of war and other situations in which a state of war may exist absent a declaration of war. Thus, these statutes may be triggered by a declaration of war, but they also may apply in circumstances where a state of war is deemed to exist. Consequently, they do not appear to be triggered by an authorization for the use of force, unless and until a state of war develops. These statutes include, for example:[102]

(a) 18 U.S.C.A. § 443 (willful secreting, mutilating, obliterating or destroying records of a war contractor, that is, a holder of a prime or subcontract connected with or related to the prosecution of a war);

(b) 18 U.S.C.A. § 757 (procuring the escape of a prisoner of war held by the United States or any of its allies or the escape of an apprehended or interned enemy alien held by the United States or its allies; aiding or assisting such escape or assisting the prisoner of war or enemy alien after his escape; or attempting or conspiring to do any of the above);

---

98 *See* J. Gregory Sindak, War, Liberty, and Enemy Aliens, 67 N. Y. *U.L. Rev.* 1402, 1412–1419 (1992). President Roosevelt also, of course, ordered thousands of Japanese-American citizens interned; but he did not rely explicitly on the Alien Enemy Act to do so.

99 8 U.S.C. §§ 1101 *etseq. See, e.g.*, 8 U.S.C. § 240.

100 *See Ludecke v. Watkins*, 335 U.S. 160 (1948) ("The very nature of the President's power to order the removal of all enemy aliens rejects the notion that courts may pass judgment upon the exercise of his discretion.").

101 50 U.S.C.A. § 22.

102 This list is intended to provide examples, rather than to be exhaustive.

(c) 18 U.S.C.A. § 792 (harboring or concealing persons known or believed to have committed or to be about to commit an offense under 18 U.S.C. §§ 793 or 794);

(d) 18 U.S.C.A. § 793 (gathering, transmitting or losing information related to the national defense with the intent or reason to believe that it is to be used to the injury of the United States or to the benefit of a foreign nation. Includes, among other things, such actions with respect to information on any place in which any vessel, aircraft, arms, munitions, or other materials or instruments for use in time of war are being prepared, repaired, stored, or are the subject of research or development; or with respect to any prohibited place so designated by the President by proclamation in time or war or in case of national emergency in which anything for the use of the Army, Navy, or Air Force is being prepared, constructed, or stored);

(e) 18 U.S.C.A. § 794 (gathering or delivering information relating to the national defense with the intent or reason to believe that it is to be used to the injury of the United States or to the advantage of a foreign nation. Subsection (b) deals with recording, publishing, or communicating or attempting to elicit information regarding movements, numbers, condition or disposition of Armed Forces, ships, aircraft or war materials, with the intent that the information be communicated to the enemy in time of war. It also covers communicating to the enemy in time of war information on plans or conduct of naval or military operations or defense measures.)[103]

(f) 18 U.S.C.A. § 1091 (genocide in time of peace or in time of war);

(g) 18 U.S.C.A. § 1653 (aliens who are found and taken on the sea making war against the United States or engaging in piracy against U.S. vessels or property);

(h) 18 U.S.C.A. § 2153 (when the United States is at war or when a national emergency has been declared, willful destruction of war material, war premises, or war utilities, with intent or reason to believe that such actions may injure, interfere with, or obstruct the United States or associate nations in their war or defense activities; and conspiracy to do so);

(i) 18 U.S.C.A. § 2154 (in times of war or national emergency, willfully producing defective war material, war premises, or war utilities

[103] It should be noted that other espionage provisions in 18 U.S.C.A. §§ 793–799 do not explicitly require a state or time of war to apply, but would presumably apply in wartime as well as peacetime. Unlawful communication of, receipt of, tampering with, or disclosure of restricted data with respect to special nuclear material is addressed in 42 U.S.C.A. §§ 2274–77. Here again, wartime is not distinguished from other times in the application of these provisions.

with intent to injure, interfere with, or obstruct the war or defense activities of the United States or associate nations);

(j) 18 U.S.C.A. § 2381 and U.S. Constitution, Art. 3, Sec. 3, Cl. 1 (while owing allegiance to the United States, levying war against the United States or adhering to its enemies, giving them aid and comfort. Constitution requires confession in open court or testimony of two witnesses to the same overt act to convict for treason);

(k) 18 U.S.C.A. § 2382 (misprision of treason);

(l) 18 U.S.C.A. § 2384 (seditious conspiracy to overthrow or destroy by force the Government of the United States or to levy war against the United States);

(m) 18 U.S.C.A. § 2388 (willfully engaging in certain activities in time of war with intent to adversely affect armed forces of the United States or to obstruct enlistment or recruitment; conspiracy to do so; harboring a person knowing or having reason to believe that the person has engaged in such conduct);

(n) 18 U.S.C.A. § 2389 (recruiting soldiers or sailors within U.S. jurisdiction to engage in armed hostilities against the United States); and

(o) 18 U.S.C.A. § 2441 (war crimes).

It should also be noted that other federal and state criminal law provisions,[104] which do not draw distinctions between conduct in time of war and at other times, also apply during wartime.[105] For example, 18 U.S.C.A. § 175 prohibits knowing development, stockpiling, acquisition, possession or retention of any biological agent, toxin, or delivery system for use as a weapon, or knowing assistance to a foreign state to do so. 18 U.S.C.A. § 229, with certain exceptions, prohibits similar conduct with respect to chemical weapons. 18 U.S.C.A. § 831 prohibits specific transactions or actions involving nuclear materials, while 42 U.S.C.A. § 2284 deals with sabotage of nuclear facilities or fuel. 18 U.S.C.A. § 2332a prohibits certain uses of weapons of mass destruction. Other explosives offenses are covered in 18 U.S.C.A. § 844. Hostage-taking is addressed in

---

[104] The provisions noted in this paragraph are intended as examples, rather than as an exhaustive list.

[105] There are also a number of provisions in 18 U.S.C.A. §§ 958–67 that may be triggered by conduct during wars involving other nations with whom the United States is at peace or during wars in which the United States is neutral. These deal, for example, with: enlisting in the service of a foreign government to serve in war against a nation with whom the United States is at peace; taking part in or facilitating a military or naval expedition against a friendly nation; strengthening the armed vessel of a foreign nation which is at war with a nation with whom the United States is at peace; arming a vessel to be used against a friendly nation; authorizing the taking out or attempting to take out of a U.S. port a detained vessel of a belligerent nation; delivering an armed vessel to a belligerent nation in a conflict in which the United States is neutral; or authorizing the taking out or attempting to take out of a U.S. port a vessel the departure of which has been prohibited in aid of neutrality.

18 U.S.C. § 1203, while kidnaping is covered by 18 U.S.C.A. § 1201. 18 U.S.C.A. § 1116 deals with murder or manslaughter of foreign officials, official guests, or internationally protected persons. 18 U.S.C.A. § 1114 addresses the murder or attempted murder of federal officers and employees, including members of the uniformed services, while they are engaged in or on account of the performance of official duties. It also covers murder or attempted murder of any person assisting an officer or employee of the United States in the performance of those duties or on account of that assistance.[106]

There are also criminal law provisions applicable to the military in the Uniform Code of Military Justice, 10 U.S.C.A. §§ 841 *et seq*. Some of these provisions apply specifically in times of war. These will be treated separately in the subsequent section of this report on "Military Personnel."[107]

Foreign Intelligence Surveillance

The Foreign Intelligence Surveillance Act (FISA), as amended, in pertinent part, authorizes electronic surveillance, physical searches, and the use of pen registers and trap and trace devices to gather foreign intelligence information and sets out the procedures and circumstances under which each of these investigative tools may be used.[108] In the event of a declaration of war, FISA authorizes the use of each of these investigative tools to gather foreign intelligence for up to 15 days without a court order. For electronic surveillance subsequent to a declaration of war, FISA provides, at 50 U.S.C.A. § 1811, that:

> Notwithstanding any other law, the President, through the Attorney General, may authorize electronic surveillance without a court order under this subchapter to acquire foreign intelligence information for a period not to exceed fifteen calendar days following a declaration of war by the Congress.

[106] Some of these statutes are among a number of federal statutes which implicitly or explicitly have extraterritorial application. This raises a question as to whether or to what extent the existence of a state of open hostilities or a declaration of war would affect the availability of extraterritorial application of such provisions. Time constraints do not permit an exploration of this issue in this report. For a general discussion of extraterritorial application of federal criminal law, including appendices addressing federal criminal laws which enjoy express extraterritorial application and federal crimes subject to federal prosecution when committed overseas, see, CRS, *Extraterritorial Application of American Criminal Law,* (Report 94–166S), by Charles Doyle.

[107] Moreover, by operation of the Military Extraterritorial Jurisdiction Act of 2000, 18 U.S.C.A. §§ 3261–3267, contractors and other civilians who accompany American armed forces overseas are subject to federal prosecution for the commission of various common law crimes such as murder (18 U.S.C.A. § 1111), rape (18 U.S.C.A. § 2241), assault (18 U.S.C.A. § 113), kidnaping (18 U.S.C.A. § 1201), and the like.

[108] Electronic surveillance under FISA is addressed at 50 U.S.C.A. §§ 1801 *et seq.;* foreign intelligence physical searches are addressed at 50 U.S.C. §§ 1821 *et seq.;* and pen registers and trap and trace devices under FISA are dealt with at 50 U.S.C. §§ 1841 *et seq.*

In the context of physical searches, 50U.S.C.A. § 1829 includes language similar to that in § 1811:

> Notwithstanding any other provision of law, the President, through the Attorney General, may authorize physical searches without a court order under this subchapter to acquire foreign intelligence information for a period not to exceed 15 calendar days following a declaration of war by the Congress.

For pen registers and trap and trace devices, 50 U.S.C.A. § 1844 provides that

> Notwithstanding any other provision of law, the President, through the Attorney General, may authorize the use of a pen register or trap and trace device without a court order under this subchapter to acquire foreign intelligence information for a period not to exceed 15 calendar days following a declaration of war by Congress.

None of these provisions appears to be triggered by an authorization for the use of force.

In addition to the foregoing provisions, FISA has been amended to authorize the use of these investigative tools without a court order for foreign intelligence purposes in "emergency" circumstances as determined by the Attorney General. To do so the Attorney General must (1) find that an emergency exists, (2) determine that the factual basis for the issuance of an order to approve such surveillance, physical search, or pen register or trap and trace device also exists, (3) advise a judge of the U.S. Foreign Intelligence Surveillance Court (FISC) that a decision to use the emergency authority has been made, and (4) apply to the FISC judge so notified for a court order as soon as practicable (but no later than within 72 hours in the case of an electronic surveillance or physical search or 48 hours in the case of a pen register or trap and trace device).[109] These provisions do not expressly address the question of whether such emergency procedures might be triggered either by an authorization for the use of force or by a Congressional declaration of war. However, depending upon the circumstances involved, these emergency powers, or other provisions within FISA,[110] might be utilized.

---

[109] For pertinent criteria and procedures applicable to such emergency situations, see 50 U.S.C. §§ 1805(f) (electronic surveillance), 1824(e) (physical search), or 1843 (pen register or trap and trace device. This authority is applicable only to gathering foreign intelligence information not concerning a United States person or information to protect against international terrorism or clandestine intelligence activities, provided that such an investigation of a U.S. person may not be conducted solely on the basis of First Amendment protected activities).

[110] *See, e.g.*, 50 U.S.C. § 1802 (electronic surveillance directed solely at acquisition of communications, not involving U.S. persons, of a foreign government or governments or components thereof, factions of a foreign nation or nations not substantially composed of U.S. persons, or entities openly acknowledged to be directed and controlled by a foreign government or governments, without a court order for periods up to one year in specific circumstances; this provision also covers electronic surveillance directed solely at acquisition of technical intelligence, other than spoken communications

Assassination

As noted in the foregoing discussion of criminal law, 18 U.S.C.A. § 1116 makes it a crime to kill or attempt to kill a "foreign official, official guest, or internationally protected person." The term "foreign official" includes, among others, a Chief of State or the political equivalent thereof while he or she is in the United States. "Internationally protected person" covers, among others, a Chief of State or the political equivalent thereof, whenever such person is in a country other than his or her own. This criminal provision does not apply to the killing or attempted killing of an internationally protected person in his or her own country. The United States courts may exercise jurisdiction over the killing or attempted killing of internationally protected persons in violation of 18 U.S.C. § 1116 committed outside the United States where the victim is a representative, officer, employee or agent of the United States; where a perpetrator is a U.S. national; or where an offender is later found in the United States.

In addition, Part 2.11 of Executive Order 12333 forbids any person employed by or acting on behalf of the United States Government from engaging in, or conspiring to engage in, assassination. Part 2.12 of that executive order further prohibits any agency of the Intelligence Community from participating in or requesting any person to undertake activities forbidden by the order. The executive order does not define "assassination," nor does either the criminal statute or the executive order specifically address the applicability of the prohibition to an armed conflict in which the U.S. is engaged. However, in times of war, the targeting of an enemy's command and control structures may be regarded as strategically important, is lawful under international law, likely is not intended to be barred by E.O. 12333, and does not appear to be covered by 18 U.S.C. § 1116. Hence, a declaration of war, because it creates a state of war regardless of whether actual hostilities have occurred, arguably creates a situation where such an act is not prohibited by domestic law. Less clear is the effect of an authorization for the use of force. Once a state of war comes into existence following such an authorization, then the legal situation appears to be the same as with a declaration. But prior to that development, the legal effect of an authorization for the use of force on the assassination ban appears somewhat ambiguous.

An executive order may be revoked by the President through another executive order. To the extent that an executive order is issued pursuant to authority granted by statute, Congress may repeal it or terminate the underlying statutory authority upon which it rests. The assassination ban is part of an executive order issued by President Reagan in 1981 under both

---

of individuals, from property or premises of such foreign governments, factions, or entities). For a more detailed discussion of FISA, see CRS, *The Foreign Intelligence Surveillance Act: An Overview of the Statutory Framework and Recent Judicial Decisions* (RL30465), by Elizabeth B. Bazan.

statutory and constitutional authority. The order does not indicate the nature of the authority underlying the assassination ban in particular. If one were to argue that a statutory basis for the ban exists, then one might contend that an authorization for a use of force would, by implication, modify the ban or repeal it with respect to the context in which the use of force was authorized.

The Defense Production Act of 1950

Conversely, declarations of war or authorizations for the use of force do not appear to have any particular consequences for the broad authorities conferred by the Defense Production Act of 1950 (DPA), as amended.[111] The DPA was first enacted in 1950 to mobilize the nation's productive capacity after the outbreak of the Korean War. It currently plays a key role in enabling the United States to maintain a national defense/military readiness capability that will support a rapid and effective response to any threat to U.S. national security, including "an attack on the United States." The DPA has been reauthorized and amended a number of times, most recently in 2003. The original 1950 act contained seven titles, four of which were rescinded in 1953.[112] Currently, three titles of the DPA are in effect, and they are due to expire on September 30, 2008, unless renewed.[113] The authorities contained in the act are not triggered by any particular event but are continuously available "to ensure the national defense preparedness, which is essential to national security. . . ."[114]

Title I (Priorities and Allocations)

This title[115] provides the President with the authority to require the priority performance of defense contracts and to allocate scarce critical and strategic materials essential to the national defense. This authority may also be extended to support the military requirements of allied nations when such extension is in the U.S. national defense interest. Priority contract performance, especially as implemented with respect to industrial resources, is intended to ensure sources of supply and timely delivery of required items for defense purposes.[116]

---

[111] 50 U.S.C.A. App. §§ 2061 *et seq.*

[112] Titles II, IV, V, and VI pertained to Korean War-era economic stabilization measures (controlling prices, wages, credit, etc.).

[113] P.L. 108-195, § 2 (Dec. 19, 2003) extended the sunset date for these provisions from September 30, 2003 to.

[114] 50 U.S.C.A. App. § 2062.

[115] *Id.* §§ 2071–2078.

[116] Similar authority to require the priority performance of defense contracts, including those for the Nuclear Regulatory Commission, if the President determines that "it is in the interest of national security" to do so, is conferred by 50 U.S.C.A. App. § 468. That statute also authorizes the President to take immediate possession of any plant, mine, or other facility that fails to honor such a priority

The post-Cold War use of this authority includes the 1990–1991 operations in the Persian Gulf (Desert Shield/Storm). During this operation, such items as computer and communications equipment, Global Positioning System receivers, chemical warfare protective clothing, and medical supplies were urgently required by both U.S. and Allied nation forces. More recently, DPA authority has been used to ensure timely delivery of critically needed items to support the deployment of U.S. and NATO troops in Bosnia and nearby areas and the availability of natural gas in California's energy crisis in December, 2000, and January, 2001.

Title I contains a section that prohibits the President from exercising his priorities and allocations authority unless he makes certain findings supporting the need for such action. Additional sections provide the President with authority relating to the hoarding of designated materials, penalties for the violation of any provision of Title I, small business preferences, etc.

Title III (Expansion of Productive Capacity and Supply)

This title[117] is used only in cases where domestic sources are required and domestic firms cannot, or will not, act on their own to meet a national defense production need. Because private firms may be reluctant to invest in production capabilities for a new material unless a near-term demand for the material is relatively certain, Title III authorizes the use of financial incentives to expand defense-related productive capacity of critical components, critical technology items, and industrial resources "essential to the national defense." These financial incentives include loan guarantees, direct federal loans, purchases, purchase guarantees, and installation of equipment in contractor facilities. The authorities conferred in this title become broader in times of a national emergency declared by the President or Congress.

Title VII (General Provisions)

This title[118] includes various provisions with relevance to defense industrial preparedness. Examples include (a) Section 708, which authorizes the President to provide antitrust defenses to private firms participating in voluntary agreements aimed at solving production and distribution problems involving national defense preparedness; (b) Section 710, which establishes a National Defense Executive Reserve (NDER) composed of recognized experts from various segments of the private sector and government (except full-time federal) employees for training for possible employment in the

---

requirement, including steel production facilities that fail to honor priority directives regarding the apportionment of steel to entities producing steel products or materials for the armed forces.

117 *Id.* §§ 2077 and 2091–2099

118 *Id*, §§ 2151–2170.

federal government in the event of an emergency; and (c) Section 721, a provision popularly known as the "Exon-Florio Amendment," which authorizes the President to suspend or prohibit the acquisition, merger, or takeover of a domestic firm by a foreign firm if such action would threaten to impair national security.[119]

Insurance Contracts

Another domestic legal issue implicated by declarations of war and authorizations for the use of force is their effect, if any, on insurance contracts, particularly with respect to clauses that exclude coverage for "acts of war." The overwhelming characterization of the events of September 11, 2001, as an "act of war" by public officials, sovereigns, international organizations, and the media, for instance, caused concern that insurance companies and the courts would interpret so called "war risk" exclusion clauses in the pertinent insurance contracts to deny claims related to the attacks. However, even a declaration of war by Congress does not appear to have an authoritative effect upon the construction of material terms contained in private contracts. The intent of the parties, not the description of Congress, is what is most relevant to understanding whether the events of September 11 or any future terrorist attacks constitute "acts of war" within the meaning of private contracts,[120] and it is not uncommon for such exclusion clauses in insurance contracts to be given narrow constructions in order to allow recovery to the insured.[121]

In the leading case in this area, *Pan American World Airways, Incorporated v. Aetna Casualty and Surety Company*,[122] a j et was hijacked and destroyed by political dissidents in the Middle East. "Notwithstanding the obvious political overtones of the event," the court ruled that "the hijacking was too contained to come under the war or insurrection exclusion."[123] A rule of causation and a rule of identity informed this conclusion. According to the *Pan Am* decision, when a court interprets an insurance policy excluding from coverage any injuries "caused by" a certain class of conditions, "the causation inquiry stops at the efficient physical cause of the loss; it does not

119 For a more extensive discussion of the Act, *see* CRS, *Defense Production Act: Purpose and Scope* (RS20587), by David E. Lockwood.

120 Under New York law, insurance policies are to be interpreted in accordance with their terms. *See* Continental Insurance Company v. Arkwright Mutual Insurance Company, 102 F.3d 30 (2d Cir. 1996). *See also* Shneiderman v. Metropolitan Casualty, 14 A.D.2d 284 (N.Y. 1961) (holding that "an insurance policy is generally a contract with the average man who presumably is unfamiliar with the existence of a state of war from the strictly political, military and/or legal standpoint.")

121 *See, e.g.*, Hammond v. National Life and Accident Insurance Co., 243 So.2d 902 (La. App.), *cert. den.*, 258 La. 347, 246 So.2d 196 (La. 1971) (war exclusion clauses in two accidental death policies held not to preclude payment of double indemnity benefits for the death of a U.S. sailor on board an aircraft carrier in the Tonkin Gulf caused by crew error rather than hostile action on the grounds the phrase "in time of war" in the policies was ambiguous and, therefore, should be construed against the insurer).

122 505 F.2d 989 (2nd Cir. 1974).

123 *Id.* at 1009. Jefferey W. Stempel, Law of Insurance Contract Disputes § 1.02[a] (2001).

trace events back to their metaphysical beginnings."[124] In the *Pan Am* case, the court examined contract language excluding from coverage losses caused by a "military or usurped power" and stated that an act causing such a loss "must be at least that of a de facto government."[125] On the facts of the case, the court then found that the terrorist organization that high-jacked the Pan Am airplane "was not a de facto government in the sky over London when the 747 was taken"[126] and held that the exclusion clause, therefore, did not apply.

This issue will not likely arise with respect to any future acts of terrorism on U.S. territory. In the aftermath of September 11, 2001, Congress enacted the Terrorism Risk Insurance Act to ensure the availability of commercial insurance coverage for losses due to acts of terrorism.[127]

Military Personnel

A number of provisions of the U.S. Code concern crimes under the Uniform Code of Military Justice, the activation of the reserves, the role of the Coast Guard, tax benefits for military personnel, and disability and death as the result of combat duty. None appear necessarily to require a declaration of war to be applicable, but a declaration can trigger their application.

Crimes under the UCMJ

Various crimes defined under the Uniform Code of Military Justice (i.e., the UCMJ, set out at 10 U.S.C.A. §§ 801 *et seq.)* occur either primarily or exclusively in the context of states of hostilities (e.g., "misbehavior before the enemy" under section 899; "subordinate compelling surrender" under section 900; "improper use of countersign" under section 901; "forcing a safeguard" under section 902; "aiding the enemy" under section 904; "misconduct as prisoner" under section 905; and rules concerning "spies" under section 906). Several of these crimes either only occur or occur in aggravated form "in time of war." The Manual for Courts Martial sets out Rules for Court Martial. Rule 103(19) defines the expression "time of war," as follows:

> For purpose *[sic]* of . . . implementing the applicable paragraphs of Parts IV and V of this Manual only, "time of war" means a period of war declared by Congress or the factual determination by the President that the existence of hostilities warrants a finding that a "time of war" exists for purposes of . . . Parts IV and V of this manual.

---

124 *Pan Am,* 505 F.2dat 1006. See also *Kimmins Indus. Service Corp. v. Reliance Ins. Co.,* 19 F.3d 78, 81 (2nd Cir. 1994), *Album Realty Co. v. American Home Assurance Co.,* 176 A.D.2d at 514, *quoting Home Insurance Co. v. American Insurance Co.,* 147 A.D.2d 353, 354(1989).

125 *Pan Am,* 505 F.2d at 1006.

126 *Id.*

127 For an overview, see CRS Report RS21979, *Terrorism Risk Insurance: An Overview,* by Baird Webel.

Thus, a congressional declaration is not indispensable to prosecutions of these crimes but can trigger their application. They do not appear to be triggered by an authorization for the use of force unless a state of war develops.

The jurisdiction of the military expands during time of war. The UCMJ permits trial by court-martial of "persons serving with or accompanying an armed force in the field" in time of war (see 10 U.S.C.A. § 802(a)(10)). In this context, the phrase "in time of war" has been interpreted to mean only during wars declared by Congress (see Robb v. United States, 456 F.2d 768 (Ct. Cl. 1972)). In time of war or conditions of martial law, military commissions may provide a special venue for trying persons not otherwise subject to the UCMJ.[128] Military jurisdiction expands during war to cover civilians accused of violating sections 904 or 906 (aiding the enemy and spying), as well as other "offenders or offenses that by . . . the law of war may be tried by military commissions, provost courts, or other military tribunals" (§ 821), at least insofar as the Constitution permits.[129]

Activation of Reserves

Chapter 1209 of title 10 of the United States Code (10 U.S.C.A. §§ 12301 *et seq*.) relates generally to activation of reserve forces. The Ready Reserve forces include members of the Army National Guard and the Air National Guard (see 10 U.S.C.A. § 10145(b)). The authority conferred under sections 12302 through 12304 can be exercised without a congressional declaration of war or national emergency; but those sections only allow reserve forces to be called to active duty for fixed statutory periods (i.e., up to 24 months under sections 12302 and 12303 and up to 270 days under section 12304). By contrast, the authority conferred under section 12301 can be exercised "[i]n time of war or of national emergency declared by Congress" and allows reserve forces to be called to active duty "for the duration of the war or national emergency and for six months thereafter." The Standby Reserve (as distinguished from the Ready Reserve and Selected Reserve forces) can only be called to active service under the authority conferred by section 12301 (see section 12306). While the Retired Reserve can be called to active service for up to 12 months under 10 U.S.C.A. § 688, it can be called to service "for the duration" under the authority conferred by section 12301 (see section 12307). So-called "stop loss" authority is conferred under section 12305. This authority allows the President to "suspend any provision of law relating to promotion, retirement, or separation" with respect to persons called to active service under sections 12301, 12302, and 12304.

---

128 *See* CRS, *Terrorism and the Law of War: Trying Terrorists as War Criminals before Military Commissions* (RL31191), by Jennifer Elsea (providing a general background of U.S. history of military commissions).
129 *See Exparte* Milligan, 71 U.S. (4 Wall.) 2 (1866).

This means that, when persons have been called to active service "for the duration" under the authority conferred by section 12301, otherwise applicable rules concerning promotions, retirements, and separations may not apply. Thus, for all of these sections, a declaration of war is not a necessary predicate, but it can trigger the application of section 12301 and related provisions. Reemployment rights for reservists called to active duty available under the Uniformed Services Employment and Reemployment Rights Act (USERRA, 38 U.S.C.A. §§ 4301 *et seq.)* and benefits available through the Service members Civil Relief Act (50 U.S.C.A. App. §§ 501—596) do not require a declaration of war, but depend generally on the authority under which the call to active duty was made, and may vary according to whether service was rendered during a period of war.

Coast Guard

Section 3 of title 14 of the United States Code specifies that "[u]pon the declaration of war if Congress so directs in the declaration or when the President directs, the Coast Guard shall operate as a service in the Navy. . . ."[130] Thus, a congressional declaration of war is not indispensable to bring the Coast Guard under the control of the Navy, but it would have that effect.

Tax Provisions

There are several provisions of the Internal Revenue Code which apply to taxpayers involved directly or indirectly with war. A congressional declaration of war is not needed to render any of these provisions applicable.

Perhaps the most significant relevant provision of the Internal Revenue Code is section 112 under which some or all of the pay received by members of the uniformed services for active service in a combat zone is excluded from gross income (i.e., is received tax-free). The term "combat zone" is specially defined for purposes of this rule and means an area so designated by the President of the United States in an Executive Order, and such an Executive Order must be issued to make the tax exemption apply. No reference is made in this provision to any declaration by Congress of the existence of a state of war and, by its express terms, it applied to service in the Korean and Vietnam conflicts.

The pay of POWs and those listed as "missing in action" is also exempt (see (IRC § 112(d)).

In addition, pay received tax-free because of IRC § 112 is exempt from federal income-tax withholding under IRC § 3401(a)(1). Due dates for filing returns and for paying taxes, according to IRC § 7508, are deferred for members of

[130] The language "if Congress so directs in the declaration" was added by P.L. 109-241 (2006).

the uniformed services serving in a combat zone designated by the President for purposes of IRC § 112. Telephone calls originating from combat zones designated under IRC § 112 are exempt from the federal excise tax that would otherwise apply (see IRC § 4253(d)). The so-called "additional estate tax" does not apply in the case of the estate of a member of the Armed Forces who is killed in action in a combat zone designated under IRC § 112 or who dies as a result of wounds, disease, or injury suffered in such a combat zone (see IRC § 2201).

An exemption from federal income tax for the current taxable year and the preceding taxable year is allowed under IRC § 692 for a member of the Armed Forces who dies in a combat zone designated under IRC § 112 or who dies as a result of wounds, disease, or injury suffered in such a combat zone, and such an exemption is also allowed in the case of a civilian federal employee killed in any military action involving the United States (see IRC § 692).

Special rules for spouses of persons who become missing in action also appear in the Code (see IRC §§ 2(a)(3) and 6013).

Disability and Death

Subchapter II of chapter 11 of title 38 of the United States Code (38 U.S. C. §§ 1110 *et seq.*) relates to "wartime disability compensation." Relevant disability must result from personal injury suffered or disease contracted in the line of duty in active military, naval, or air service "during a period of war."[131] Thus, there is no explicit requirement of a congressional declaration of war. On the other hand, such a declaration would obviously assure that the particular period of hostilities in question is indeed a period of war. Some other veterans' benefits depend on whether the person seeking benefits served during a period of war.

Chapter 13 of title 38 of the United States Code (38 U.S.C.A. §§ 1301 *et seq.)* relates to service-connected deaths. Compensation in connection with such deaths is accorded without regard to whether or not they occurred during or as a result of a war declared by Congress.

Rules under 38 U.S.C.A. § 2402 relating to the eligibility of members of the Armed Forces who die while on active duty to be buried in national cemeteries (including Arlington National Cemetery) and other rules concerning burial benefits are not contingent on a congressional declaration of war.

[131] For a list of "periods of war," see CRS Report RS21405, *Periods of War,* by Barbara Salazar Torreon. For information about requirements to qualify for veterans' benefits, see CRS Report RL33113, *Veterans Affairs: Basic Eligibility for Disability Benefit Programs,* by Douglas Reid Weimer.

Itemization of Standby Statutory Authorities

Under ordinary circumstances the President exercises the powers conferred on him by the Constitution and by statutes enacted by Congress. As noted in the preceding section, in extraordinary circumstances a number of additional statutory powers may become available; and his Constitutional powers are likely to be given a generous interpretation by the courts. The standby statutory authorities potentially available to the President and the executive branch number in the hundreds. Some are triggered by a declaration of war, some by the existence of a state of war (and, thus, also by a declaration of war), and some pursuant to a declaration or the existence of national emergency. Most can be triggered by one or more of the foregoing circumstances. None of these special authorities appears to be triggered by an authorization for the use of force (unless and until it leads to a state of war). With respect to those statutes that are triggered by the existence of a national emergency or of a state or time of war, the determination of whether such a condition exists would be made in the first instance by the executive branch.

Those authorities that require a declaration of national emergency as a predicate for coming into effect are not automatically activated by such a declaration. National emergency powers can be exercised only pursuant to the strictures of the National Emergencies Act.[132] In addition to requiring that the President publicly declare a national emergency, that Act requires that he specify the emergency statutory authorities that he intends to use prior to their use and that he publish that information in the *Federal Register* and report it to Congress.[133] (On September 14, 2001, President Bush, for example, took this step by issuing a "Declaration of National Emergency by Reason of Certain Terrorist Attacks" and specifying ten statutory authorities that he intended to use.[134]) Moreover, the Act provides that Congress can terminate a declared emergency at any time by joint resolution and that, in any event, the emergency declaration and any statutory powers activated pursuant to it expire after one year unless the President specifically renews the declaration.[135]

The following subsections identify the standby authorities that become available to the President and the executive branch upon (1) a declaration of war, (2) the existence of a state of war, and (3) pursuant to a declaration

---

132 50 U.S.C.A. § 1601 *et seq.*

133 *Id.* §§ 1621 and 1631.

134 Proclamation 7463 (Sept. 14, 2001); 66 Fed. Reg. 48199 (Sept. 18, 2001). For further background on the enactment of the National Emergencies Act and to track the emergency authorities invoked by President Bush, *see* CRS Report RS21017, *Terrorist Attacks and National Emergency Declarations,* by Harold C. Relyea.

135 *Id.* § 1622.

of national emergency.[136] It is important to emphasize that a declaration of war activates not only the statutes listed in the first subsection but also—because a declaration of war automatically creates a state of war—those listed in the second section. The latter statutes are listed separately because they can come into effect even if a declaration of war is never adopted.

Within each subsection, the statutes are listed in the order in which they appear in the U.S. Code. The lists exclude the statutes detailed above concerning criminal law and taxes as well as the disaster relief authorities contained in the "Robert T. Stafford Disaster Relief and Emergency Assistance Act."[137]

(1) Statutory Authorities Triggered by a Declaration of War

Many of following provisions can be triggered by circumstances other than a declaration of war. But all would come into effect upon enactment of a declaration of war:

Congressional Budget Act

2 U.S.C.A. § 198(b)—provides that the rule mandating that Congress adjourn sine die by July 31 of each year unless each House adopts a concurrent resolution, "shall not be applicable in any year if on July 31 of such year a state of war exists pursuant to a declaration of war by the Congress."

2 U.S.C.A. § 641—provides that the requirement that amendments to a reconciliation bill not increase budget outlays or decrease budget outlay reductions, revenues, or revenue increases unless they include offsetting budget outlay reductions or revenue increases does not apply "if a declaration of war by the Congress is in effect."

2 U.S.C.A. § 642(a) (West Supp. 2001)—provides that the requirement making bills, amendments, motions, and conference reports which provide new budget authority that would exceed what Congress has set forth in the concurrent resolution on the budget for that fiscal year or that would reduce revenues below what has been set forth in that concurrent resolution out of order in the House does not apply "when a declaration of war by the Congress is in effect."

---

[136] These lists are based on several LEXIS searches using the search terms "national w/2 emergency," "state or time w/2 war," and "declaration w/2 war," and are current through August 1, 2006. The results of an earlier version of these searches were also compared to, and supplemented by, a study done under contract for the Office of Mobilization Preparedness in the Federal Emergency Management Agency in 1992 by the System Planning Corporation—*Emergency Executive Authorities* (Contract EMW-91-C-3644).

[137] 42 U.S.C.A. §§ 5121 *et seq.*

2 U.S.C.A. § 643(b)(2) (West Supp. 2001)—provides that the requirement making any bill, amendment, motion, or conference report that exceeds the discretionary spending limits set forth in 2 U.S.C.A. App. 901(c) out of order in the Senate does not apply "if a declaration of war by the Congress is in effect or a joint resolution pursuant to sections 907a and 908 of this title has been enacted."

2 U.S.C.A. § 907a(b)—states that sequestration reports and orders and certain other requirements of the Budget Act are precluded or suspended "upon the enactment of a declaration of war" but that the sequestration procedures are restored "effective with the first fiscal year that begins in the session after the state of war is concluded by Senate ratification of the necessary treaties. . . ."

Agricultural Exports

7 U.S.C.A. § 5712(c)—allows the President to prohibit or curtail the export of any agricultural commodity "during a period for which the President has declared a national emergency or for which the Congress has declared war."

Armed Forces

10 U.S.C.A. § 123b—provides that the President may waive the statutory ceiling placed on the number of members of the armed forces who may be stationed abroad in any fiscal year "if the President declares an emergency" and that the ceiling "does not apply in the event of a declaration of war or an armed attack on any member nation of the North Atlantic Treaty Organization, Japan, the Republic of Korea, or any other ally of the United States."

10 U.S.C.A. § 2350j(e)(3)(A)—allows the Secretary of Defense to carry out a military construction project financed by contributions from designated countries or regional organizations without prior explanation and justification to Congress if the project is necessary to support the armed forces "by reason of a declaration of war, or a declaration by the President of a national emergency pursuant to the National Emergencies Act that is in force at the time of the commencement of the project."

10 U.S.C.A. § 2662(g)—provides that the congressional notice and wait provisions governing certain real property transactions by the Secretary of a military department and by the GSA for the Department of Defense do not apply, *inter alia,* if the transaction results from "a declaration of war . . . or a declaration of a national emergency by the President pursuant to the National Emergencies Act."

10 U.S.C.A. § 2808(a)—provides that the Secretary of Defense and the Secretaries of the military departments, with his authorization, may "without regard to any other provision of law" undertake military construction

projects "not otherwise authorized by law" if necessary to support the use of the armed forces "in the event of a declaration of war or the declaration by the President of a national emergency under the National Emergencies Act that requires use of the armed forces."

Coast Guard

14 U.S.C.A. § 3, as amended by P.L. 109-241 (2006)—provides that the Coast Guard shall operate as a service in the Navy "upon the declaration of war if Congress so directs in the declaration or when the President directs. . . ."

14 U.S.C.A. § 661, as amended by P.L. 107-295, § 105 (Nov. 25, 2002)—provides that the President may, if there is in effect a declaration of war or national emergency at the end of any fiscal year, suspend any end-strength limitation prescribed by law for any military or civilian component of the Coast Guard for a period not to exceed 6 months after the end of the war or national emergency.

14 U.S.C.A. § 724, as amended by P.L. 107-295, § 105 (Nov. 25, 2002)—provides that the President may, if there is in effect a declaration of war or national emergency at the end of any fiscal year, suspend any end-strength limitation prescribed by law for the number of officers in the Coast Guard Reserve for a period not to exceed 6 months after the end of the war or national emergency.

Small Business Administration

15 U.S.C.A. § 636(n)—provides for the deferral of the repayment of interest and principal on direct loans by the SBA to a member of a reserve component who is ordered to active duty during a "period of military conflict," defined to mean "a period of war declared by Congress [or] a period of national emergency declared by the Congress or the President. . . ."

Unilateral Trade Sanctions

22 U.S.C.A. § 7203 —provides that the prohibition in the "Trade Sanctions Reform and Export Enhancement Act of 2000" barring the President from imposing new unilateral agricultural or medical sanctions without the approval of Congress does not apply with respect to the imposition of such a sanction against a foreign country or entity "(A) pursuant to a declaration of war against the country or entity; (B) pursuant to specific statutory authorization for the use of the Armed Forces of the United States against the country or entity; (C) against which the Armed Forces of the United States are involved in hostilities; or (D) where imminent involvement by the Armed Forces of the United States in hostilities against the country or entity is clearly indicated by the circumstances. . . ."

Armed Forces Retirement Home

24 U.S.C.A. § 412—provides that "persons who . . . served in a war theater during a time of war declared by Congress" are eligible to become residents of an Armed Forces Retirement Home.

Statutes of Limitation

28 U.S.C.A. § 2416(d)—provides that, for the purpose of computing the time limitation periods for commencing court actions brought by the United States, "there shall be excluded all periods during which . . . the United States is in a state of war declared pursuant to Article I, Section 8, of the Constitution of the United States."

Deferral of Civil Works Projects

33 U.S.C.A. § 2293—authorizes the Secretary of the Army, "in the event of a declaration of war or a declaration by the President of a national emergency in accordance with the National Emergencies Act that requires or may require use of the Armed Forces," to terminate or defer Army civil works projects that he determines are not essential to the national defense and to apply the resources to projects that are essential.

Nuclear Regulatory Commission

42 U.S.C.A. § 2138—authorizes the Nuclear Regulatory Commission to suspend any licenses it has granted relating to the production or use of special nuclear material, to order the recapture of any such material, and to order the operation of any such facility, "if the Commission finds it necessary to the common defense and security . . . whenever the Congress declares that a state of war or national emergency exists."

Enemy Alien Act

50 U.S.C.A. § 21—authorizes the President to "apprehend, restrain, secure, and remove" alien enemies . . . whenever there is a declared war between the United States and any foreign nation or government, or any invasion or predatory incursion is perpetrated, attempted, or threatened against the territory of the United States by any foreign nation or government, and the President makes public proclamation of the event."

National Defense Stockpile

50 U.S.C.A. § 98f(a)(2)—authorizes any person designated by the President, "(1) at any time the President determines the release of such materials is required for purposes of the national defense or (2) in time of war declared by the Congress or during a national emergency," to use, sell, or otherwise

dispose of materials in the National Defense Stockpile that the designee determines are "required for purposes of the national defense."[138]

Chemical and Biological Warfare Agents

50 U.S.C.A. § 1515—authorizes the President to suspend the provisions of law governing the production, transportation, location, testing, and disposal of lethal chemical and biological warfare agents "during the period of any war declared by Congress and during the period of any national emergency declared by Congress or by the President."

50 U.S.C.A. § 1521—authorizes the Secretary of Defense to defer the destruction of up to 10 percent of the stockpile of lethal chemical agents and munitions beyond December 31, 2004, "in the event of a declaration of war by the Congress or of a national emergency by the President or the Congress or if the Secretary of Defense determines that there has been a significant delay in the acquisition of an adequate number of binary chemical weapons to meet the requirements of the Armed Forces."

National Emergencies Act

50 U.S.C.A. § 1641—requires the President, "when the President declares a national emergency, or Congress declares war," to maintain a file and index of all significant orders issued during such emergency or war, to transmit such orders to the Congress, and to report to Congress each six months on the total expenditures during that period that are attributable to the exercise of emergency authorities conferred by such declaration.

Foreign Intelligence Surveillance Act (FISA)

50 U.S.C.A. § 1811—provides that notwithstanding any other law, the President may authorize electronic surveillance without a court order under FISA "to acquire foreign intelligence information for a period not to exceed fifteen calendar days following a declaration of war by the Congress."

50 U.S.C.A. § 1829—provides that notwithstanding any other law, the President may authorize physical searches without a court order under FISA "to acquire foreign intelligence information for a period not to exceed 15 calendar days following a declaration of war by the Congress."

50 U.S.C.A. § 1844—provides that notwithstanding any other provision of law, the President may authorize the use of a pen register or trap and trace device without a court order under FISA "to acquire foreign intelligence information for a period not to exceed 15 calendar days following a declaration of war by Congress."

---

[138] For purposes of this authority, "national emergency" is defined to mean "a general declaration of emergency with respect to the national defense made by the President or by the Congress. 50 U.S.C.A. § 58h-3.

Selective Service Act

50 U.S.C.A. App. § 454(a)—provides that the President can vary the specified standards for physical and mental fitness of inductees into the armed forces "except in time of war or national emergency declared by the Congress"; that those who voluntarily enlist cannot have their enlistment extended without their consent "until after a declaration of war or national emergency by the Congress"; and that various exceptions from requirements of service in the reserves or from orders to active duty without consent do not apply "in time of war or national emergency declared by Congress."

50 U.S.C.A. App. § 456—provides that various exceptions to liability for induction into the armed forces for veterans of World War II and members of the Reserves and the National Guard do not apply "after a declaration of war or national emergency made by the Congress" and that the exception for those who have had a close relative killed in the line of duty does not apply "during the period of a war or a national emergency declared by Congress."

(2) Statutory Authorities Triggered by the Existence of a State of War (and Thus Also by a Declaration of War)

In addition to the statutes that are explicitly triggered by a declaration of war, a number come into the effect if a state of war, or period of war, or simply "war" exists. Because a declaration of war automatically creates a state of war, these authorities also are triggered by the enactment of a declaration of war. But they can come into effect even if no declaration of war is adopted. As is the case with respect to many of the statutes in the foregoing subsection, many of these statutes can also be triggered pursuant to a declaration of national emergency. The statutes are set forth in the order in which they appear in the U.S. Code:

Administrative Procedure

5 U.S.C.A. § 551(1)—excludes "military authority exercised in the field in time of war or in occupied territory" from the definition of "agency" for purposes of general administrative procedure.

5 U.S.C.A. § 701(b)—excludes "military authority exercised in the field in time of war or in occupied territory" from the definition of "agency" for purposes of judicial review of administrative procedure.

Federal Employees

5 U.S.C.A. § 5335(b)—requires that step increases mandated for federal civil service employees be preserved for those employees whose civilian service is interrupted by "service with the armed forces or by service in

essential non-Government civilian employment during a period of war or national emergency."

5 U.S.C.A. § 5343(e)(3)—requires that step increases mandated for federal prevailing rate employees be preserved for those employees whose civilian service is interrupted by "service with the armed forces or by service in essential non-Government civilian employment during a period of war or national emergency."

5 U.S.C.A. § 6323(d)(1)—allows up to 44 days of leave for a military reserve technician who is on active duty except "during a war or national emergency declared by the President or Congress."

5 U.S.C.A. § 8114(e)(3)—prohibits accounting for "bonus or pay for particularly hazardous service in time of war" when computing pay to compensate government employees for work injuries.

5 U.S.C.A. § 8332(g)—provides that a civil service employee who leaves his civilian position to serve in the military "during the period of a war, or of a national emergency as proclaimed by the President or declared by Congress" is deemed not to be separated from his civil service position for purposes of determining his or her creditable service for retirement purposes, unless the military service extends beyond 5 years.

Aliens

8 U.S.C.A. § 1182(a)(8)—provides that any person "who has departed from or who has remained outside the United States to avoid or evade training or service in the armed forces in time of war or a period declared by the President to be a national emergency" is ineligible to receive a visa and inadmissible into the United States, and is thus ineligible for citizenship.

8 U.S.C.A. § 1231(b)(2)—provides that when the Attorney General decides that it is "impracticable, inadvisable, inconvenient, or impossible" to remove an alien to the country where the alien is a citizen or subject because the "United States is at war," the alien may be removed to the "country that is host to a government in exile of the country of which the alien is a citizen or subject" or to "a country . . . that is very near to the country that is host to a government in exile of the country of which the alien is a citizen or subject" or to "a country . . . that is very near to the country of which the alien is a citizen or subject."

8 U.S.C.A. § 1425—makes any person who deserted or shall desert the armed forces or left the United States with the intent to avoid the draft at "any time during which the United States has been or shall be at war" ineligible to become a naturalized citizen of the United States.

8 U.S.C.A. § 1438—authorizes the Attorney General to naturalize former United States citizens who lost citizenship by serving "in the military, air,

or naval forces of any country at war with a country with which the United States was at war after December 7, 1941, and before September 2, 1945."

8 U.S.C.A. § 1442(a)—authorizes the Attorney General to naturalize an alien from a country with which the United States is at war after the alien's loyalty to the United States is established if the alien's application for naturalization was "pending at the beginning of the state of war and the applicant is otherwise entitled to admission to citizenship."

8 U.S.C.A. § 1455(d)—prohibits the Attorney General from charging or collecting a naturalization fee "during the time when the United States is at war" from an alien in the military, air, or naval service of the United States for filing an application for naturalization or issuing a certificate of naturalization upon admission to citizenship.

8 U.S.C.A. § 1481(a)(3)and(6)—provides that a person who is a national of the United States whether by birth or naturalization shall lose his nationality by serving in the armed forces of a foreign state "if such armed forces are engaged in hostilities against the United States" and by voluntarily making "a formal written renunciation of nationality . . . whenever the United States shall be in a state of war" and the Attorney General approves such renunciation as "not contrary to the interests of national defense."

Armed Forces

10 U.S.C.A. § 123—authorizes the President to "suspend the operation of any provision of law relating to the promotion, involuntary retirement, or separation of commissioned officers of the Army, Navy, Air Force, Marine Corps, or Coast Guard Reserve . . . in time of war, or of a national emergency declared by Congress or the President" until one year after the war or national emergency terminates.

10 U.S.C.A. § 123a—authorizes the President to defer any end-strength limitation prescribed by law for any military or civilian component of the armed forces if "there is in effect a war or national emergency" until six months after the war or national emergency terminates.

10 U.S.C.A. § 152(a)—provides that "in time of war there is no limit on the number of reappointments" the President may make of the same person to the two-year position of Chairman of the Joint Chiefs of Staff.

10 U.S.C.A. § 154(a)—provides that "in time of war there is no limit on the number of reappointments" the President may make of the same person to the two-year position of Vice Chairman of the Joint Chiefs of Staff.

10 U.S.C.A. § 155 (f)(4)—lifts the four-year limitation on the tours of duty of officers assigned or detailed to duty on the Joint Staff of the Joint Chiefs of Staff "in time of war; or during a national emergency declared by the President or Congress."

10 U.S.C.A. § 194(e)—lifts the caps on the number of armed forces and civilian employees that can be assigned or detailed to permanent duty in management headquarters activities or otherwise in the Defense Agencies and DOD Field Activities "in time of war; or during a national emergency declared by the President or Congress."

10 U.S.C.A. § 351—authorizes the President to "arm, have armed, or allow to be armed" any watercraft or aircraft used as a means of transportation "on, over, or under water" during a "war and at any other time when the President determines that the security of the United States is threatened by the application, or the imminent danger of application, of physical force by any foreign government or agency against the United States, its citizens, the property of its citizens, or their commercial interests."

10 U.S.C.A. § 519—provides that "in time of war or of national emergency declared by Congress" enlistments in the armed forces shall be for the duration of the war or emergency plus six months.

10 U.S.C.A. § 527—allows the President to suspend the limitations placed on the number of general officers in the Army, Air Force, and Marines and of flag officers in the Navy, and the number of such officers who may be designated in various ranks, "in time of war, or of national emergency declared by Congress or the President" until up to one year after the war or national emergency terminates.

10 U.S.C.A. § 603(a)—allows the President to appoint "any qualified person" to any officer grade in the Army, Navy, Air Force, and Marines up to major general or rear admiral "in time of war, or of national emergency declared by the Congress or the President" for up to 2 years or 6 months after the war or national emergency has terminated, whichever occurs first.

10 U.S.C.A. § 620(d)—allows the Secretary of a military department to exclude a reserve officer ordered to active duty "during a war or national emergency" from the active duty roster of officers.

10 U.S.C.A. § 671—provides that "in time of war or a national emergency declared by Congress or the President" basic training may not be less than 12 weeks (except for certain health care professionals).

10 U.S.C.A. § 688(f)—waives the 12-month limitation on the period for which retired members of the armed forces can be recalled to active duty and the prohibition on recalling certain categories of retired officers to active duty "in time of war or of national emergency declared by Congress or the President."

10 U.S.C.A. § 690(c)—waives the limitation on the number of retired general officers and flag officers who may be on active duty at any one time "in time of war or of national emergency declared by Congress or the President."

10 U.S.C.A. § 708(d)—allows the Secretary of a military department to cancel a leave of absence granted for educational purposes "in time of war, or of national emergency declared by Congress or the President."

10 U.S.C.A. § 712—allows the President to detail members of the armed forces to any foreign country he deems advisable to assist in military matters "during a war or a declared national emergency."

10 U.S.C.A. § 721—waives the limitation on the percentage of officers who can be assigned for up to six months to positions external to their armed force "during any period of war or of national emergency declared by Congress or the President."

10 U.S.C.A. § 772(e)—authorizes a person not on active duty who served honorably "in time of war" in the Army, Navy, Air Force, or Marine Corps to bear the title, and, "when authorized by regulations prescribed by the President," wear the uniform, of the "highest grade held by him during that war."

10 U.S.C.A. § 802(a)—subjects "persons serving with or accompanying an armed force in the field . . . in time of war" to the Uniform Code of Military Justice.[139]

10 U.S.C.A. § 843—provides that a person charged with "absence without leave or missing movement in time of war," or with any offense punishable by death, may be tried and punished at any time without limitation and that a person charged with an "offense the trial of which in time of war is certified to the President by the Secretary concerned to be detrimental to the prosecution of the war or inimical to the national security" may be tried and punished up to "six months after the termination of hostilities as proclaimed by the President or by a joint resolution of Congress."

10 U.S.C.A. § 871(b)—allows the Secretary of a military department to commute a court-martial sentence of dismissal to a reduction in grade "in time of war or national emergency."

10 U.S.C.A. § 885(c)—provides that any person found guilty of desertion or attempt to desert the armed forces shall be punished, "if the offense is committed in time of war," by death or "such other punishment as a court-martial may direct."

10 U.S.C.A. § 890—provides that any member of the armed forces who "willfully disobeys a lawful command of his superior commissioned officer" shall be punished, "if the offense is committed in time of war," by death or "such other punishment as a court-martial may direct."

---

[139] Although the statute does not require a formal declaration of war, military courts have interpreted section 802(a), to the extent it would subject civilians to military jurisdiction, to apply only during a declared war. *See* United States v. Averette, 17 USCMA 363 (1968), *followed by* Robb v. United States, 456 F.2d 768 (Ct. Cl. 1972).

10 U.S.C.A. § 901—provides that any person subject to the UCMJ who "in time of war discloses the parole or countersign to any person not entitled to receive it" or who gives to another who is entitled to receive and use the parole or countersign a "different parole or countersign from that which, to his knowledge, he was authorized and required to give," shall be punished by death or such other punishment as a court-martial may direct.

10 U.S.C.A. § 905—provides that any person subject to the UCMJ who, "while in the hands of the enemy in time of war," acts to the detriment of other prisoners to receive favorable treatment or maltreats his fellow prisoners without justifiable cause shall be punished as a court-martial may direct.

10 U.S.C.A. § 906—provides that "any person who in time of war is found lurking as a spy or acting as a spy" with respect to the armed forces or defense entities shall be tried by a court-martial and, if convicted, be punished by death.

10 U.S.C.A. § 913—provides that any sentinel or look-out who is found drunk or sleeping at his post, or who leaves it before he is relieved, shall be punished by death if the offense is committed "in time of war" and by such other punishment as a court-martial may direct at other times.

10 U.S.C.A. § 978(e)—allows the President to suspend the requirement that persons seeking to enlist in the armed forces be tested for drug and alcohol use and dependency "in time of war, or time of emergency declared by Congress or the President."

10 U.S.C.A. § 1104(d)—provides that members of the armed forces on active duty "during and immediately following a period of war, or during and immediately following a national emergency involving the use of the armed forces in armed conflict" may receive health-care services from the Department of Veterans Affairs.

10 U.S.C.A. § 1161(a)—provides that no commissioned officer may be dismissed from any armed force except by sentence of a general court-martial, in commutation of a sentence of a general court-martial, or "in time of war, by order of the President."

10 U.S.C.A. §§ 1201(b) and 1203(b)—provides that the Secretary of a military department may allow a member of his armed force to retire on disability even though the disability is less than 30 percent under the standard schedule of rating disabilities used by the Department of Veterans Affairs if the member has at least 20 years of service and the disability was incurred "in line of duty in time of war or national emergency."

10 U.S.C.A. § 1491(e)—allows the Secretary of Defense to waive the requirement that a funeral honors detail be provided for the funeral of any veteran if "necessary . . . to meet the requirements of war, national emergency, or a contingency operation or other military requirements."

10 U.S.C.A. § 1580—allows the Secretary of Defense or of the military department concerned to designate any employee of DOD as an emergency essential employee if they provide immediate support to combat operations in a combat zone "in connection with a war, a national emergency declared by Congress or the President, or the commencement of combat operations of the armed forces in the zone."

10 U.S.C.A. § 2208—allows the Secretary of Defense to waive the requirement that Congress be given written notification of the advance billing of a customer of a working-capital fund "during a period of war or national emergency."

10 U.S.C.A. § 2366(c)—authorizes the President to suspend the operation of any provision related to the survivability testing and lethality testing required before full-scale production of any major systems and munitions programs "in time of war or mobilization."

10 U.S.C.A. § 2457(b)—states as policy the dispersal of manufacturing facilities and standardization of equipment among North Atlantic Treaty Organization members to "minimize potential economic hardship to parties to the agreements and increase the survivability, in time of war."

10 U.S.C.A. § 2461(h)—provides that the conditions and prerequisites to the privatization of a DOD commercial or industrial type function do "not apply during war or during a period of national emergency declared by the President or Congress."

10 U.S.C.A. § 2538—authorizes the President, through the head of any department, to seize any plant that is "equipped to manufacture, or that in the opinion of the head of that department is capable of being readily transformed into a plant for manufacturing, arms or ammunition, parts thereof, or necessary supplies for the armed forces" and to manufacture products at such plant "in time of war or when war is imminent," if the head of the plant refuses to cooperate with an order for arms or supplies.

10 U.S.C.A. § 2539—provides that the Secretary of Defense may maintain a list of privately owned plants in the United States that have a capacity "sufficient to warrant conversion into ammunition plants in time of war or when war is imminent," and may obtain complete information as to the equipment of each of those plants.

10 U.S.C.A. § 2552—provides that the Secretary of a military department may lend equipment under the jurisdiction of that department that is on hand, and that can be temporarily spared, to "any organization formed by the American National Red Cross that needs it for instruction and practice for the purpose of aiding the Army, Navy, or Air Force in time of war."

10 U.S.C.A. § 2632—allows the Secretary of a military department to provide transportation for employees working in a private plant that is manufacturing

material for that department "during a war or a national emergency declared by Congress or the President."

10 U.S.C.A. § 2644—authorizes the Secretary of Defense in "time of war" to take possession and assume control of all or part of any system of transportation to transport troops, war material, and equipment, or "for other purposes related to the emergency."

10 U.S.C.A. § 2663(b)—provides that, "in time of war or when war is imminent," the United States may, immediately upon the filing of a petition for condemnation, acquire any interest in land, including temporary use, needed for the site, construction, or operation of fortifications, coast defenses, or military training camps, the construction and operation of plants for the production of nitrate and other compounds and the manufacture of explosives or other munitions of war, or the development and transmission of power for the operation of these production plants.

10 U.S.C.A. § 2664(d)—provides that, in "time of war or when war is imminent," the Secretary of a military department or the Secretary of Transportation may, immediately upon the filing of a petition for condemnation, take and use property related to logging that is needed for production of aircraft, vessels, dry docks, or equipment for them, the procurement of supplies for aircraft, vessels, and dry docks, or housing for persons employed by the Army, Navy, Air Force, or Marine Corps.

10 U.S.C.A. § 2733(b)—extends the time that a claim brought against the United States for damage to or loss of real property, damage to or loss of personal property, or personal injury or death caused by an officer, employee, or a member of the Army, Navy, Air Force, Marine Corps, or Coast Guard that arose in "time of war or armed conflict, or if such a war or conflict intervened," from two years after it accrues to two years after the war or armed conflict is terminated.

10 U.S.C.A. § 3014(f)(4)—provides that the ceilings on the number of members of the armed forces, civilians, officers, and general officers that may be assigned or detailed for duty in the Office of the Secretary of the Army and on the Army Staff "do not apply in time of war or during a national emergency declared by the President or Congress."

10 U.S.C.A. § 3033(a)(1)—allows the President to reappoint a Chief of Staff of the Army for an additional term of four years "in time of war or during a national emergency declared by Congress."

10 U.S.C.A. § 3063(b)—allows the Secretary of the Army to discontinue or consolidate the basic branches of the Army designated by statute "for the duration of any war, or of any national emergency declared by Congress."

10 U.S.C.A. § 3691—provides that officers of the Army who have aeronautical ratings as observers may be rated as flying officers in "time of war."

10 U.S.C.A. § 4780(a)—authorizes the Secretary of the Army to acquire by lease any building, or part of a building, in the District of Columbia that may be needed for military purposes in "time of war or when war is imminent."

10 U.S.C.A. § 5014(f)(4)—provides that the ceilings on the number of members of the armed forces, civilians, officers, and general and flag officers that may be assigned or detailed for duty in the Office of the Secretary of the Navy, the Office of the Chief of Naval Operations, and the Headquarters Marine Corps "do not apply in time of war or during a national emergency declared by the President or Congress."

10 U.S.C.A. § 5033—allows the President to reappoint a Chief of Naval Operations for an additional term of four years "in time of war or during a national emergency declared by Congress."

10 U.S.C.A. § 5043—allows the President to reappoint a Commandant of the Marine Corps for an additional term of four years "in time of war or national emergency declared by Congress."

10 U.S.C.A. § 5133(c)—provides that "except in time of war, any officer of a staff corps who has served as a chief of bureau for a full term is exempt from sea duty."

10 U.S.C.A. § 5450—provides that the limitation to ten on the number of retired flag officers who may be on active duty at any one time in the Regular Navy does not apply "in time of war or national emergency."

10 U.S.C.A. § 5540(b)—provides that, "except in time of war," each member of the Navy and Marine Corps who is serving on a naval vessel, whose term of enlistment has expired, and who desires to return to the United States but is retained by a senior officer "as essential to the public interest," is entitled to an increase in basic pay of 25 percent.

10 U.S.C.A. § 6485—provides that members of the Fleet Reserve and Fleet Marine Corps Reserve may be ordered to active duty "in time of war or national emergency declared by Congress, for the duration of the war or national emergency and for six months thereafter, (and) in time of national emergency declared by the President. . . ."

10 U.S.C.A. § 6486—provides that the Secretary of the Navy may not release a member of the Fleet Reserve or the Fleet Marine Corps Reserve from active duty "in time of war or national emergency declared by Congress or by the President" unless certain conditions are met.

10 U.S.C.A. § 6911(b)—provides that "except in time of war or emergency declared by Congress," 20 percent of the aviation cadets procured in each fiscal year shall be procured from qualified enlisted members of the Regular Navy and the Regular Marine Corps.

10 U.S.C.A. § 6972—provides that the crypt and window spaces of the Naval Academy Chapel may be used only for memorials to officers of the Navy who have successfully commanded a fleet or squadron in battle or who have "received the thanks of Congress for conspicuously distinguished services in time of war."

10 U.S.C.A. § 7224—authorizes the Secretary of the Navy to designate persons who can be transported and subsisted on naval vessels at government expense "in time of war or during a national emergency declared by the President."

10 U.S.C.A. § 7226—provides that the Secretary of the Navy shall prescribe a suitable pennant to be known as the Naval Reserve yacht pennant to be flown by a yacht or similar vessel if "the vessel has been designated by the Secretary, under such regulations as he prescribes, as suitable for service as a naval auxiliary in time of war."

10 U.S.C.A. § 7722—provides that "whenever in time of war" the Secretary of the Navy certifies to a court, or to a judge of a court, that the prosecution of a suit would tend to endanger the security of naval operations in the war, or would tend to interfere with those operations, all further proceedings in the suit shall be stayed.

10 U.S.C.A. § 7724—provides that, "if in time of war, with respect to any claim against the United States on which a suit would lie," the Secretary of the Navy certifies to the court in which proceedings are pending for the taking of certain depositions, that the proceedings would tend to endanger or interfere with the security of the United States, "then the proceedings may not be started or, if they have been started, they shall, when the certificate is filed, be stayed."

10 U.S.C.A. § 8014(f)(4)—provides that the ceilings on the number of members of the armed forces, civilians, officers, and general officers that can be assigned or detailed for duty in the Office of the Secretary of the Air Force do not apply "in time of war or during a national emergency declared by the President or Congress."

10 U.S.C.A. § 8033(a)(1)—allows the President to reappoint the Chief of Staff of the Air Force for an additional term of four years "in time of war or during a national emergency declared by Congress."

10 U.S.C.A. § 8257(d)—provides that, "except in time of war or of emergency declared by Congress," at least 20 percent of the aviation cadets designated in each fiscal year shall be selected from members of the Regular Air Force or the Regular Army who are eligible and qualified.

10 U.S.C.A. § 8691—provides that officers of the Air Force who have aeronautical ratings as observers may be rated as flying officers in "time of war."

10 U.S.C.A. § 9773(c)—provides that in selecting sites for air bases and depots and in determining the alteration or enlargement of existing air bases or depots, the Secretary of the Air Force shall consider the need "to permit, in time of peace, training and effective planning in each strategic area for the use and expansion of commercial, municipal, and private flying installations in time of war."

10 U.S.C.A. § 9780(a)—authorizes the Secretary of the Army to acquire by lease any building, or part of a building, in the District of Columbia that may be needed for military purposes in "time of war or when war is imminent."

Reserves

10 U.S.C.A. § 10102—states the purpose of the reserves to be "to provide trained units and qualified persons available for active duty in the armed forces, in time of war or national emergency, and at such other times as the national security may require."

10 U.S.C.A. § 12006—allows the President, "in time of war, or of national emergency," to suspend the statutory ceilings placed on the number of reserve commissioned officers, reserve general officers, and rear admirals in the Army, Navy, Air Force, and Marine Corps reserves for up to one year beyond the end of the war or national emergency, notwithstanding the earlier termination date prescribed by the National Emergencies Act.

10 U.S.C.A. § 12103—extends enlistments in the reserves that are in effect "at the beginning of a war or of a national emergency declared by Congress," or that are entered into during such a war or emergency, and that would otherwise expire, until six months after the war or emergency has ended, unless earlier terminated by the Secretary concerned.

10 U.S.C.A. § 12243—allows the President to suspend any law relating to the promotion or mandatory retirement or separation of permanent reserve warrant officers "in time of war, or of emergency declared after May 29, 1954, by Congress or the President."

10 U.S.C.A. § 12301—allows the Secretary of a military department, "in time of war or of national emergency declared by Congress, or when otherwise authorized by law," to order any reserve unit or member to active duty without their consent for the duration of the war or emergency and up to six months thereafter, and allows reserves on inactive or retired status to be called up if those on active status or in the inactive National Guard are insufficient.

10 U.S.C.A. § 12311—provides that if an agreement between the Secretary and a member of the reserves specifying a set term of active duty expires "during a war or during a national emergency declared by Congress or the President," the Reserve may be kept on active duty without his consent.

10 U.S.C.A. § 12313—limits the discretion of the Secretary concerned to release a Reserve from active duty "in time of war or of national emergency declared by Congress or the President. . . ."

10 U.S.C.A. § 12316—provides that a Reserve who is called up "for a period of more than 30 days in time of war or national emergency" and who is otherwise entitled to a pension, retired or retainer pay, or disability compensation shall receive either that compensation, if it is greater, or the pay and allowances prescribed for the duty he is performing.

10 U.S.C.A. § 14317, as amended by P.L. 108-136, § 512(a) (Nov. 24, 2003)—provides that reserve officers not on the active-duty list when ordered to active duty "in time of war or national emergency" may be considered for promotion by a mandatory or special selection board; or in the case of an officer who "is serving on active duty in support of a contingency operation, by a vacancy promotion board."

10 U.S.C.A. § 16163, as added by P.L. 108-375, § 527(a) (Oct. 28, 2004)—provides educational assistance to reservists who "served on active duty in support of a contingency operation for 90 consecutive days or more" after September 11, 2001, and to members of the National Guard who "performed full time National Guard duty under section 502 (f) of title 32 for 90 consecutive days or more when authorized by the President or Secretary of Defense for the purpose of responding to a national emergency declared by the President and supported by Federal funds."

10 U.S.C.A. § 16201, as amended by P.L. 107-107, § 539 (Dec. 28, 2001)—provides that the Secretary of each military department may provide financial assistance to persons in training for degrees in medicine or dentistry or other health professions specialties "critically needed in war time" in exchange for a commitment to subsequent service in the Ready Reserve, including the possibility of being ordered to active duty "in time of war or national emergency."

10 U.S.C.A. § 18235—bars the Secretary of Defense from disposing or allowing the use of facilities for the reserves in any manner that would interfere with their use "in time of war or national emergency, by other units of the armed forces or by the United States for any other purpose."

10 U.S.C.A. § 18236—bars a state from disposing or allowing the use of facilities constructed for the reserves with the help of a federal grant in any manner that would interfere with their use "in time of war or national emergency, by other units of the armed forces or by the United States for any other purpose."

Trading with the Enemy Act

12 U.S.C.A. § 95a—authorizes the President, "during the time of war . . . through any agency that he may designate," to investigate, regulate, or

prohibit, any transactions in foreign exchange, or transactions "involving any property in which any foreign country or a national thereof has any interest."

Coast Guard

14 U.S.C.A. § 2—provides that the Coast Guard "shall maintain a state of readiness to function as a specialized service in the Navy in time of war, including the fulfilment of Maritime Defense Zone responsibilities."

14 U.S.C.A. § 275—allows the President, "in time of war, or of national emergency declared by the President or Congress," to suspend any section of this chapter with respect to the selection, promotion, or involuntary separation of Coast Guard officers and to promote to the next higher grade any officer serving on active duty in the grade of ensign or above and any warrant officer serving on active duty in a grade below chief warrant officer, until up to six months after the end of the war or national emergency.

14 U.S.C.A. § 331—allows the Secretary to order any regular officer of the Coast Guard on the retired list to active duty "in time of war or national emergency."

14 U.S.C.A. § 359—allows the Commandant to order any enlisted member of the Coast Guard on the retired list to active duty "in times of war or national emergency."

14 U.S.C.A. § 367—allows an enlisted member of the Coast Guard to be detained beyond the term of his enlistment "during a period of war or national emergency as proclaimed by the President, and, in the interest of national defense," for up to six months after the end of the war or emergency.

14 U.S.C.A. § 371—requires that at least 20 percent of the aviation cadets procured in each fiscal year be qualified enlisted members of the Coast Guard, "except in time of war or national emergency."

14 U.S.C.A. § 508—provides that any "person who is convicted by court martial for desertion from the Coast Guard in time of war" and is consequently dismissed or dishonorably discharged, shall afterwards not be enlisted, appointed or commissioned in any military or naval service under the United States "unless he is restored to duty in time of war."

14 U.S.C.A. § 636—allows commissioned and warrant officers of the Coast Guard to perform all of the functions of a notary public "in time of war or national emergency."

14 U.S.C.A. § 652—provides that legal changes lifting restrictions on the Navy "for the duration of a war or national emergency proclaimed by the President," including those regarding procurement and personnel, shall automatically apply to the Coast Guard.

14 U.S.C.A. § 660(a)—allows the Secretary to provide transportation to and from work for persons employed by a private plant manufacturing material for the Coast Guard "during a war or during a national emergency declared by Congress or the President."

14 U.S.C.A. § 722—allows the President to suspend any part of the subchapter concerning commissioned officers in the Coast Guard Reserve "in time of war or national emergency declared by Congress."

Federal Energy Regulatory Commission

16 U.S.C.A. § 824a(c)—allows the Federal Energy Regulatory Commission to order the temporary connection of electric energy facilities and such generation, delivery, interchange, or transmission of electric energy as in its judgment will best meet the emergency and serve the public interest "during the continuance of any war in which the United States is engaged, or whenever the Commission determines that an emergency exists by reason of a sudden increase in the demand for electric energy, or a shortage of electric energy, or of fuel or water for generating facilities, or other causes."

Tennessee Valley Authority

16 U.S.C.A. § 831d(g)—directs the Tennessee Valley Authority to maintain a plant "for the production of explosives in the event of war or a national emergency" unless Congress releases it from the obligation.

16 U.S.C.A. § 831s—reserves to the government the right, "in case of war or national emergency," to take control of the TVA "for the purpose of manufacturing explosives or for other war purposes."

Imports

19 U.S.C.A. § 1318—allows the Secretary of the Treasury, "whenever the President shall by proclamation declare an emergency to exist by reason of a state of war, or otherwise," to have additional time to perform any act prescribed by the Tariff Act of 1930, as amended, and to permit the import of food, clothing, and medical supplies for use in emergency relief work free of duty.

Neutrality

22 U.S.C.A. § 441—provides that when the President finds that there exists "a state of war between foreign states," the President shall issue a proclamation naming the states involved and shall revoke such proclamation when the "state of war . . . shall have ceased."

Miscellaneous

22 U.S.C.A. § 1623—provides that a commission authorized to settle international claims "shall have jurisdiction to receive, examine, adjudicate,

and render a final decision" with respect to claims between the United States government and a foreign government "exclusive of governments against which the United States declared the existence of a state of war during World War II."

22 U.S.C.A. § 4056(f)—deems that a member of the Foreign Service who has left the Service to enter military service "during a period of war, or national emergency proclaimed by the President or declared by the Congress" has not, for retirement benefit purposes, left the Service unless more than 5 years expire.

Accounting and Contracts

31 U.S.C.A. § 3522(b)(3)—extends the time for the armed forces to submit accounts to the Comptroller General from the usual 60 days to 90 days "during a war or national emergency and for 18 months after the war or emergency ends."

Contracts

31 U.S.C.A. § 3727—allows a contract with DOD, the General Services Administration, and the Department of Energy to provide, or to be changed without consideration to provide, that a future payment under a contract to an assignee is not subject to reduction or setoff "during a war or national emergency proclaimed by the President or declared by law and ended by proclamation or law."

National Guard

32 U.S.C.A. § 104—authorizes the President, in time of peace, to detail a commissioned officer of the Regular Army to perform the duties of chief of staff for each fully organized division of the Army National Guard in order "to insure prompt mobilization of the National Guard in time of war or other emergency."

32 U.S.C.A. § 111—permits the President to suspend various statutory provisions relating to federal recognition of promotions in the Army and Air National Guard "in time of war, or of emergency declared by Congress."

Armed Forces

32 U.S.C.A. § 703(b)—provides that "in time of actual or threatened war, the United States may requisition for military use" supplies and military publications bought by a state or territory "for cash, at cost plus transportation" from the Army or Air Force.

32 U.S.C.A. § 715(b)—provides that "in time of war or armed conflict or if such a war or armed conflict intervenes within two years after it accrues,

and if good cause is shown," the time within which a claim against the United States for property loss, personal injury or death caused by the National Guard must be filed is extended from two years from the time the claim accrued to "two years after the war or armed conflict is terminated."

National Oceanic and Atmospheric Administration

33 U.S.C.A. § 3030—allows the President, "in time of emergency declared by the President or by the Congress, and in time of war," to suspend all or any part of the laws pertaining to the promotion of commissioned officers in the National Oceanic and Atmospheric Administration (NOAA).

33 U.S.C.A. § 854a-1—provides that the laws that pertain to the temporary appointment or advancement of commissioned officers "in time of war or national emergency" in the Navy shall also apply to personnel in NOAA, subject to a few limitations.

33 U.S.C.A. § 3063—provides that the Secretaries of Defense and Commerce shall prescribe regulations governing the duties to be performed by NOAA "in time of war" and providing for the cooperation of NOAA with the military departments "in time of peace in preparation for its duties in time of war."

Ocean Dumping

33 U.S.C.A. § 1902—states that provisions applying pollution control standards derived from the MARPOL Protocol to warships, naval auxiliaries, and vessels owned by the United States, other than submersibles, shall not apply "during time of war or a declared national emergency."

33 U.S.C.A. § 2503—lifts the prohibition on the ocean dumping of potentially infectious medical waste by public vessels "during time of war or a declared national emergency."

Patents

35 U.S.C.A. § 181—provides that an order by the Commissioner of Patents that a patent or patent application be kept secret for national security reasons, which otherwise must be renewed each year, shall remain in effect "during a time when the United States is at war" and for one year following the cessation of hostilities and "during a national emergency declared by the President" and for six months thereafter.

Armed Forces

37 U.S.C.A. § 202—entitles an officer in the Coast Guard who holds a permanent appointment as rear admiral (lower half) on the retired list, and who "in time of war or national emergency has served satisfactorily on

active duty for two years in that grade or in a higher grade," to the pay of a rear admiral when on active duty.

37 U.S.C.A. § 301(d)—provides that "in time of war, the President may suspend the payment of incentive pay" to members of a uniformed service for certain hazardous duties.

37 U.S.C.A. § 301a(c)—provides that "in time of war, the President may suspend the payment of aviation career incentive pay" to members of a uniformed service.

37 U.S.C.A. § 304(e)—provides that "in time of war, the President may suspend the payment of diving duty pay" to members of a uniformed service.

37 U.S.C.A. § 407(d)—provides that the exceptions to the prohibition on members of the uniformed services receiving more than one dislocation allowance a year "does not apply in time of national emergency or in time of war."

37 U.S.C.A. § 901—provides that "in time of war, an officer of an armed force who is serving with troops operating against an enemy and who exercises, under assignment in orders issued by competent authority, a command above that pertaining to his grade," is entitled to the pay and allowances "appropriate to the command so exercised."

37 U.S.C.A. § 909, as added by P.L. 107-107, § 623 (Dec. 28, 2001)—authorizes the continuation of special pay or incentive pay for members of the armed forces who are involuntarily retained on duty under §§ 123 or 12305 of Title 10 unless "in time of war" the President suspends the authority under which the special pay or incentive pay was given.

Veterans' Care

38 U.S.C.A. § 8111A—authorizes the Secretary of the Department of Veterans' Affairs to provide hospital care, nursing home care, and medical services to members of the Armed Forces on active duty "during and immediately following a period of war, or a period of national emergency declared by the President or the Congress that involves the use of the Armed Forces in armed conflict."

Reemployment Rights

38 U.S.C.A. § 4303(16))—includes within the definition of "uniformed services" for purposes of entitlement to the reemployment and other rights protected by the statute "the Armed Forces, the Army National Guard and the Air National Guard . . ., the commissioned corps of the Public Health Service, and any other category of persons designated by the President in time of war or national emergency."

38 U.S.C.A. § 4312(c))—limits the reemployment rights of those absent from their jobs because of service in the uniformed service to five years unless a longer absence is because the individual, *inter alia,* was "ordered to or retained on active duty (other than for training) under any provision of law because of a war or national emergency declared by the President or Congress, as determined by the Secretary concerned."

Sale of War Supplies to Foreign States

(139) 40 U.S.C.A. § 1310, recodified from § 314 byP.L. 107-217 (Aug. 17, 2002)—authorizes the President to sell war supplies, materials, and equipment, and the buildings, plants, and equipment necessary for their production, "to any foreign State or Government, engaged in war against any Government with which the United States is at war."

Defense Structures in the District of Columbia

40 U.S.C.A. § 8722(b)(2), recodified from § 71d by P.L. 107-217 (Aug. 21, 2002)—excludes from the consultation procedures mandated for federal and D.C. agencies with the National Capital Planning Commission for construction projects in D.C. "structures erected by the Department of Defense during wartime or national emergency within existing military, naval, or Air Force reservations, except that the appropriate defense agency shall consult with the Commission as to any developments which materially affect traffic or require coordinated planning of the surrounding area."

Public Health Service

42 U.S.C.A. § 211 (k)—allows commissioned officers in the Regular Corps of the Public Health Service to be recommended for promotion to any higher grade in their category, including the director grade, whether or not a vacancy exists in such grade, "in time of war or of national emergency proclaimed by the President."

42 U.S.C.A. § 213—provides that commissioned officers of the armed forces and their surviving beneficiaries shall, "with respect to active service performed by such officers . . . in time of war" be entitled to all rights, privileges, immunities, and benefits now or hereafter provided "under any law of the United States in the case of commissioned officers of the Army or their surviving beneficiaries on account of active military service, except retired pay and uniform allowances."

42 U.S.C.A. § 217—authorizes the President to use the Public Health Service, "in time of war, or of emergency proclaimed by the President . . . in such manner as shall in his judgment promote the public interest" and, "in time of war, or of emergency involving the national defense proclaimed by the President," to declare the commissioned corps of the Service to be a

military service constituting a branch of the land and naval forces of the United States subject to the Uniform Code of Military Justice.

Infectious Diseases

42 U.S.C.A. § 266—authorizes the Surgeon General, on recommendation of the National Advisory Health Council, to "provide by regulations for the apprehension and examination, in time of war," of any individual reasonably believed to be infected with a disease that is the "probable source of infection to members of the armed forces of the United States orto individuals engaged in the production or transportation of arms, munitions, ships, food, clothing, or other supplies for the armed forces."

Nuclear Energy

42 U.S.C.A. § 2165—authorizes the commission that controls information on atomic energy development in the United States "during the state of war or period of national disaster due to enemy attack to employ individuals and to permit individuals access to Restricted Data prior to completion of a security investigation report . . ."

Public Lands

43 U.S.C.A. § 155—states that the provisions of the Engle Act governing the use of the public lands of the United States by the Department of Defense for defense purposes shall not apply "in time of war or national emergency hereafter declared by the President or Congress."

Natural Resources

43 U.S.C.A. § 1314 (b)—gives the United States, "in time of war or when necessary for national defense," the right of first refusal to purchase any portion of lands and natural resources which are "specifically recognized, confirmed, established, and vested in and assigned to the respective States and others."

43 U.S.C.A. § 134 1(b)—provides that, "in time of war," the United States shall have the right of first refusal to purchase at the market price all or any portion of "any mineral produced from the outer Continental Shelf."

43 U.S.C.A. § 1341(c)—allows the Secretary of the Interior to suspend leases on the outer Continental Shelf, on the recommendation of the Secretary of Defense, "during a state of war or national emergency declared by the Congress or the President of the United States after August 7, 1953."

43 U.S.C.A. § 1353 (f)—clarifies that "nothing in this section" related to the federal purchase and disposition of oil and gas shall prohibit the right of the United States to purchase any oil or gas produced on the outer Continental Shelf "in time of war."

Destruction of Records

44 U.S.C.A. § 3311—provides that "during a state of war between the United States and another nation, or when hostile action by a foreign power appears imminent," the head of an agency may authorize the destruction of records in his legal custody "situated in a military or naval establishment, ship, or other depository outside the territorial limits of continental United States."

Shipping

46 U.S.C.A. § 133—exempts hospital ships in the ports of the United States "in time of war, from all dues and taxes imposed on vessels by the laws of the United States, and from all pilotage charges."

46 U.S.C.A. § 5116—provides that a person causing or allowing the alteration, concealment, or removal of an official mark placed on a vessel by the government, "except to make a lawful change or to escape enemy capture in time of war," commits a class A misdemeanor.

46 U.S.C.A. § 53107, added P.L. 108-136, sec. 3531 (Nov. 24, 2003)—requires the Secretary of Transportation to include in each operating agreement with merchant security fleet contractors an Emergency Preparedness Agreement providing that, "upon a request by the Secretary of Defense during time of war or national emergency, or whenever determined by the Secretary of Defense to be necessary for national security or contingency operation . . ., a contractor for a vessel covered by an operating agreement under this chapter shall make available commercial transportation resources (including services)."

46 U.S.C.A. § 7113—provides that a licensed master, mate, pilot, or engineer of a vessel propelled by machinery or carrying hazardous liquid cargoes in bulk is not "liable to draft in time of war, except for performing duties authorized by the license."

46 U.S.C.A. App. § 835—prohibits, "when the United States is at war or during any national emergency, the existence of which is declared by proclamation of the President," the transfer of any vessel or shipyard to noncitizens without the approval of the Secretary of Transportation.

46 U.S.C.A. App. § 1132)—provides reemployment rights for certain merchant seamen subject to certification by the Secretary of Transportation, *inter alia,* that the individual was employed on a vessel "that is owned, chartered, or controlled by the United States and used by the United States for a war, armed conflict, national emergency, or maritime mobilization need. . . ."

46 U.S.C.A. App. § 1187b(a)(2)—requires that the owners or operators of U.S. flag vessels included in the Maritime Security Fleet enter into an Emergency Preparedness Agreement that requires them to make available

commercial transportation resources "upon a request by the Secretary of Defense during time of war or national emergency, or whenever determined by the Secretary of Defense to be necessary for national security . . . " and that supersedes any other agreement regarding "vessel availability in time of war or national emergency."

46 U.S.C.A. App. § 2002—authorizes the Secretary of Transportation to award a decoration or medal to an individual for service in the merchant marine "in time of war or national emergency proclaimed by the President or Congress, or during operations by the Armed Forces of the United States outside the continental United States under conditions of danger to life and property."

Communications

47 U.S.C.A. § 308—allows the Federal Communications Commission to waive the requirement of a formal written application for construction permits and station licenses, and modifications and renewals thereof, "during a national emergency proclaimed by the President or declared by Congress and during the continuance of any war in which the United States is engaged and when such action is necessary for the national defense or security or otherwise in furtherance of the war effort."

47 U.S.C.A. § 606(a)—authorizes the President, "during the continuance of a war in which the United States is engaged," to direct that communications carriers give preference or priority to "such communications as in his judgment may be essential to the national defense and security"; to use the armed forces to prevent any obstruction of interstate or foreign communication by radio or wire "during any war in which the United States is engaged"; and to suspend or amend all rules and regulations governing wire communications, to close any facility or station for wire communication, and to authorize the use or control of any such facility by the government "upon proclamation . . . that there exists a state or threat of war involving the United States."

47 U.S.C.A. § 606(c)—authorizes the President, "upon proclamation by the President that there exists war or a threat of war, or a state of public peril or disaster or other national emergency, or in order to preserve the neutrality of the United States," to close any radio station or other device capable of emitting electromagnetic radiations which can be used as a navigational aid beyond five miles.

Railroads

49 U.S.C.A. § 11124(a)—authorizes the President, "during time of war or threatened war," to direct the Transportation Board to "give preference or priority to the movement of certain traffic" and to direct all rail carriers

within the Board's jurisdiction to "adopt every means within their control to facilitate and expedite" military traffic.

Protection of Ships and Harbors

50 U.S.C.A. § 191—authorizes the Secretary of Transportation, "whenever the President by proclamation or Executive order declares a national emergency to exist by reason of actual or threatened war, insurrection, invasion, or disturbance or threatened disturbance of the international relations of the United States," to adopt rules and regulations governing the anchorage and movement of all vessels, foreign and domestic, in the territorial waters of the United States and, if necessary, to take possession of such vessels; and also authorizes the President, "whenever the President finds that the security of the United States is endangered by reason of actual or threatened war, or invasion, or insurrection or subversive activity, or of disturbances or threatened disturbances of the international relations of the United States," to take steps to safeguard all vessels, harbors, ports, and waterfront facilities in the United States against destruction, loss, or injury.

Federal Emergency Management Agency

50 U.S.C.A. § 404(b)—provides that one function of the Director of the Federal Emergency Management Agency is to advise the President about programs for the "effective use in time of war of the Nation's natural and industrial resources for military and civilian needs, for the maintenance and stabilization of the civilian economy in time of war, and for the adjustment of such economy to war needs and conditions, policies for unifying, in time of war, the activities of Federal agencies and departments engaged in or concerned with production, procurement, distribution, or transportation of military or civilian supplies, materials, and products, and the relationship between potential supplies of, and potential requirements for, manpower, resources, and productive facilities in time of war."

CIA Retirement Plan

50 U.S.C.A. § 2083—provides that a participant in the CIA retirement plan who, "during the period of any war or of any national emergency as proclaimed by the President or declared by the Congress," leaves to enter military service shall not be deemed as separated from the agency for purposes of the retirement plan unless the military service extends beyond five years.

Trading with the Enemy Act

50 U.S.C.A. App. § 2—defines "the beginning of the war," for purposes of the "Trading with the Enemy Act of 1917," as "midnight ending the day on which Congress has declared, or shall declare war or the existence of a state of war."

50 U.S.C.A. App. § 5(b)—provides extensive authority to the President, "during time of war . . . through any agency that he may designate," to regulate economic transactions with foreign countries and nationals, including the power to block any enemy property within the jurisdiction of the United States and to vest title to that property in the United States.

50 U.S.C.A. App. § 9—authorizes the President, "in time of war or during any national emergency declared by the President," to sell foreign assets frozen under TWEA notwithstanding the existence of a suit by a person claiming that the property was improperly frozen or that he is otherwise legally entitled to the property if "the interest and welfare of the United States require the sale. . . ."

50 U.S.C.A. App. § 10—provides that any citizen or corporation of the United States or corporation desiring to "manufacture, or cause to be manufactured, a machine, manufacture, composition of matter, or design, or to carry on, or to use any trade-mark, print, label or cause to be carried on, a process under any patent or copyrighted matter owned or controlled by an enemy or ally of enemy at any time during the existence of a state of war" may apply to the President for a license.

50 U.S.C.A. App. § 38—provides that any person in the United States may legally donate and deliver any article intended to be used solely to relieve human suffering to persons in a country with which the United States was at war "at any time after the date of cessation of hostilities."

(3) Statutory Authorities Triggered by Declaration or Existence of National Emergency

As noted, many of the statutes in the previous two subsections can also be triggered not only by a declaration of war or the existence of a state of war but also by a declaration of national emergency. There are, in addition, a number of statutes that can be triggered only upon a declaration of national emergency or the existence of such an emergency. These standby authorities do not automatically come into effect upon the issuance of a declaration of national emergency but only in conformity with the procedures set forth in the National Emergencies Act. The statutes, listed in the order in which they appear in the U.S. Code Annotated, include the following:

Federal Employees

5 U.S.C.A. § 3326—allows retired members of the armed forces to be appointed to civil service positions in the Department of Defense for 180 days after their retirement if "a state of national emergency exists."

5 U.S.C.A. § 5303—allows the President, "because of national emergency or serious economic conditions affecting the general welfare," to alter the annual adjustment in pay schedules that would otherwise be effective.

5 U.S.C.A. § 5304a—allows the President, "because of national emergency or serious economic conditions affecting the general welfare," to alter the locality-based comparability pay increases that would otherwise be effective.

Agriculture

7 U.S.C.A. § 1332(c)—requires the Secretary of Agriculture to increase or terminate a national marketing quota for wheat in case of "a national emergency or . . . a material increase in the demand for wheat." (Note: This authority was suspended from 1996 to 2002. *See* 7 U.S.C.A. § 7301(a).)

7 U.S.C.A. § 1371(b)—requires the Secretary of Agriculture to increase or terminate a national marketing quota or acreage allotment for cotton, rice, peanuts, or tobacco if necessary to meet "a national emergency or . . . a material increase in export demand."

7 U.S.C.A. § 1444(e)(4)—allows the Secretary of Agriculture to require a set-aside of cropland if he determines that the "total supply of agricultural commodities will, in the absence of such a set-aside, be excessive taking into account the need for an adequate carryover to maintain reasonable and stable supplies and prices and to meet a national emergency."

7 U.S.C.A. § 1444(h)(5)(A)(1)—allows the Secretary of Agriculture to limit the acreage planted to extra long staple cotton if he determines that the "total supply of extra long staple cotton, in the absence of such limitation, will be excessive taking into account the need for an adequate carryover to maintain reasonable and stable prices and to meet a national emergency."

7 U.S.C.A. § 1736y(3)—declares it to be the policy of the United States that the export of agricultural commodities and products should not be prohibited or limited except "in time of a national emergency declared by the President under the Export Administration Act (50 App. U.S.C.A. §§ 2401 *et seq.).*

7 U.S.C.A. § 1743(a)(6)—allows the Commodity Credit Corporation to dispose of commodity set-asides "in accordance with the directions of the President . . . to meet any national emergency declared by the President."

7 U.S.C. § 1982, as added P.L. 108-375, § 664 (Oct. 28, 2004)—provides relief from certain agricultural loan obligations for reservists mobilized under any "provision of law during a war or during a national emergency declared by the President or Congress."

7 U.S.C.A. § 4208(b)—provides that the policies stated in the "Farmland Protection Policy Act (7 U.S.C.A. §§ 4201-4208) do not apply "to the acquisition or use of farmland for national defense purposes during a national emergency."

Armed Services

10 U.S.C.A. § 1064—authorizes members of the National Guard called to duty during a federally declared disaster or "a national emergency declared by the President or Congress" to use commissary stores and MWR retail facilities.

10 U.S.C.A. § 2304—allows the Secretaries of the military departments and the Department of Transportation as well as the Administrator of NASA to exclude a particular source from a competitive procurement procedure or to solicit bids only from particular sources when it would be in the interest of national defense in having a facility, producer, manufacturer, or other supplier "available for furnishing the property or service in case of a national emergency or industrial mobilization."

10 U.S.C.A. § 4025—prescribes that "during a national emergency declared by the President" the regular working hours of laborers producing military supplies or munitions for the Army are 8 hours a day and 40 hours a week, but allows these limits to be exceeded under regulations prescribed by the Secretary of the Army.

10 U.S.C.A. §9025—provides that "during a national emergency declared by the President" the working hours of laborers and mechanics employed by the Department of the Air Force are 8 hours a day and 40 hours a week but allows the Secretary of the Air Force to alter these hours by regulation.

10 U.S.C.A. § 12302—allows the Secretary of a military department, "in time of national emergency declared by the President after January 1, 1953, or when otherwise authorized by law," to order any member or unit of the Ready Reserve to active duty without their consent for up to 24 months.

Fort McHenry

(16) 16 U.S.C.A. § 440—allows Fort McHenry to be closed "in case of a national emergency" and to be used for military purposes "during the period of the emergency."

Customs Service

19 U.S.C.A. § 1318(b)—authorizes the Secretary of the Treasury, "when necessary to respond to a national emergency declared under the National Emergencies Act," to temporarily eliminate, consolidate, or relocate any office of the Customs Service, modify its hours of service or services rendered, and "take any other action necessary to respond directly to the national emergency. . . ."

Student Financial Aid

20 U.S.C.A. § 1070 note, added P. L. 108-76 (Aug. 18, 2003), extended to September 30, 2007 by P.L. 109-78—authorizes the Secretary of Education

to waive or modify statutory and regulatory provisions applicable to student financial aid programs "during the national emergency . . . declared by the President on September 14, 2001, or subsequent national emergencies declared by the President by reason of terrorist attacks" to provide relief to persons affected by the terrorist attacks of September 11, 2001.

Barro Colorado Island

20 U.S.C.A. § 79—directs that Barro Colorado Island in Gatun Lake in the Canal Zone be left in its natural state for scientific observation and investigation "except in the event of declared national emergency."

Foreign Relations[140]

22 U.S.C.A. § 2318(a)—authorizes the President, if "an unforeseen emergency exists which requires immediate military assistance to a foreign country or international organization" to provide up to $ 100 million in defense articles and services apart from the authority of the Arms Export Control Act but only upon notice to Congress.

22 U.S.C.A. § 4103(c)—allows the President to suspend any statutory provision relating to labor-management relations in the Foreign Service "if the President determines in writing that the suspension is necessary in the interest of national security because of an emergency."

National Oceanographic and Atmospheric Administration

33 U.S.C.A. § 3061—authorizes the President, "whenever in his judgment a sufficient national emergency exists," to transfer such vessels, equipment, stations, and commissioned officers of NOAA to a military department "as he may deem in the best interests of the country."

Red Cross

36 U.S.C.A. § 300104—bars the election of members of the Board of Governors by proxy except "if the board believes a national emergency makes attendance at the national convention impossible."

Veterans' Affairs

38 U.S.C.A. § 1721—authorizes the Secretary of the Department of Veterans' Affairs to prescribe rules for good conduct by those receiving services in Department facilities "during a period of national emergency (other than a period of war or an emergency described in section 8111 A of this title)."

[140] It might be noted that 21 U.S.C.A. § 1901(a) states as a Congressional finding that "[t]here is a national emergency resulting from the activities of international narcotics traffickers and their organizations that threatens the national security, foreign policy, and economy of the United States"; but it is not clear whether any special authorities are intended to be triggered by this provision.

Davis-Bacon Act

40 U.S.C.A. § 3147, recodified from § 276a-5 by P.L. 107-217 (Aug. 21, 2002)—allows the President to suspend the requirements of the Davis-Bacon Act mandating that laborers and mechanics on federal and D.C. construction and public works projects be paid prevailing wages "in the event of a national emergency."

Real Property and Contracts

40 U.S.C.A. § 545, as recodified from § 484(e)(3) by P.L. 107-217 (Aug. 21, 2002)—allows GSA to negotiate disposal and contracts for disposal of surplus property without first seeking public bids "but subject to obtaining such competition as is feasible under the circumstances, if necessary in the public interest during the period of a national emergency declared by the President or the Congress. . . ."

40 U.S.C.A. § 93, as recodified from § 534 by P.L. 107-217 (Aug. 21, 2002)—allows GSA to waive the procedures otherwise applicable to the disposal or acquisition of real property in urban areas "during any period of national emergency proclaimed by the President."

U.S.C.A. § 253—authorizes executive agencies to use noncompetitive procurement procedures if "it is necessary to award the contract to a particular source or sources in order (A) to maintain a facility, producer, manufacturer, or other supplier available for furnishing property or services in case of a national emergency or to achieve industrial mobilization. . . ."

Public Health Service

42 U.S.C.A. § 204—authorizes the Public Health Service to maintain a Reserve Corps "for the purpose of securing a reserve for duty in the Service in time of national emergency."

Prohibition of Compensation

42 U.S.C.A. § 1712—bars employees of contractors of the U.S. providing services outside of the U.S. who suffer injury or death from a war hazard from receiving compensation if they have been "convicted in a court of competent jurisdiction of any subversive act against the United States or any of its allies, committed after the declaration by the President on May 27, 1941, of the national emergency. . . ."

Relocation

42 U.S.C.A. § 4625(c)(3)—waives the requirement in the Uniform Relocation Assistance Act that a person displaced from their dwelling by a project of a federal agency or one undertaken with federal financial assistance not be

required to move until afforded a reasonable opportunity to relocate to a comparable dwelling in the case of "a national emergency declared by the President."

Resources

42 U.S.C.A. § 6393(a)(2)(A)—waives the requirement that a minimum of 30 days be allowed for comment on proposed rules and regulations to implement the domestic supply availability and standby energy authorities of the Energy Policy and Conservation Act "if the President finds that such waiver is necessary to act expeditiously during an emergency affecting the national security of the United States."

Merchant Marine

46 U.S.C.A. § 8103(h)(1)—allows the President to suspend the citizenship requirements that otherwise apply to the officers and seamen on documented vessels of the U.S. "during a proclaimed national emergency."

46 U.S.C.A. § 8301(d)—allows the Secretary of the Department in which the Coast Guard is operating to suspend the requirements relating to the number of licensed individuals that vessels subject to inspection must have "during a national emergency proclaimed by the President."

46 U.S.C.A. App. § 1202(d)—permits the Secretary of Transportation to terminate any charter of DOT vessels "whenever the President shall proclaim that the security of the national defense makes it advisable, or during any national emergency declared by proclamation of the President."

46 U.S.C.A. App. § 1242—authorizes the Secretary of Transportation to requisition or purchase any vessel or other watercraft owned by citizens of the United States "whenever the President shall proclaim that the security of the national defense makes it advisable or during any national emergency declared by proclamation of the President" and to transfer the possession or control of any such vessel or watercraft to any other department or agency of the government.

Airports

49 U.S.C.A. § 40101 note, as added by P.L. 107-71, § 114(g) (Nov. 19, 2001)—gives the Under Secretary of Transportation responsible for the Transportation Security Administration the authority "during a national emergency" to coordinate all domestic transportation and oversee the transportation-related responsibilities of other non-military federal departments and agencies but states that this authority "shall not supersede" the authority of other federal departments and agencies related to transportation.

49 U.S.C.A. § 40101 note, as added by P.L. 107-71, § 127 (Nov. 19, 2001)—authorizes the Secretary of Transportation "during a national emergency affecting air transportation or intrastate air transportation" to grant complete or partial waivers from restrictions that would otherwise apply regarding the carriage by aircraft of freight, mail, emergency medical supplies, personnel, or patients.

49 U.S.C.A. § 47152(5)—provides that the United States, "during a national emergency declared by the President or Congress," is entitled to use, control, or possess any part of a public airport that is on surplus property donated by the government.

49 U.S.C.A. § 196—provides that at any time vessels can be requisitioned under 46 U.S.C.A. § 1242, *supra,* which can come into effect "whenever the President shall proclaim that the security of the national defense makes it advisable or during any national emergency declared by proclamation of the President," the President may also purchase or requisition merchant vessels not owned by U.S. citizens and lying idle in U.S. waters "which the President finds necessary to the national defense."

Modification of Defense Contracts

50 U.S.C.A. § 1435—provides that the President's authority to modify defense contracts in order to "facilitate the national defense" without regard to other provisions of law regarding the making, performance, amendment, or modification of contracts is effective "only during a national emergency declared by Congress or the President" and for six months after the termination thereof.

10 U.S.C.A. § 4544, added by P.L.108-375, § 353 (Oct. 28, 2004)—Working-capital funded Army industrial facility contracts with non-Army entities must include an indemnification clause to preclude government liability "including [for] any damages or injury arising out of a decision by the Secretary of the Army or the Secretary of Defense to suspend or terminate an activity, or any portion thereof, during a war or national emergency or to require the facility to perform other work or provide other services on a priority basis"

National Emergencies Act

50 U.S.C.A. § 1631—requires the President, whenever he "declares a national emergency," to specify in the declaration or by subsequent executive orders published in the *Federal Register* and transmitted to Congress which emergency statutory authorities he or other officers will exercise, prior to their exercise.

International Economic Emergency Powers Act

50 U.S.C.A. § 1701—authorizes the President to exercise the extensive powers with respect to the property of, and economic transactions with,

a foreign country or entity granted by the International Emergency Economic Powers Act (IEEPA) "to deal with any unusual and extraordinary threat, which has its source in whole or substantial part outside the United States, to the national security, foreign policy, or economy of the United States, if the President declares a national emergency with respect to such threat."

50 U.S.C.A. § 1702—exempts from any economic embargo imposed under IEEPA donations of articles such as food, clothing, and medicine intended to relieve human suffering unless the President determines, *inter alia,* that such donations "would seriously impair his ability to deal with any national emergency declared under section 1701 of this title."

50 U.S.C.A. § 1706—provides that foreign assets frozen pursuant to IEEPA may remain frozen beyond the date of the termination of the national emergency if necessary "on account of claims involving such country or its nationals."

Selective Service Act

50 U.S.C.A. App. § 460(e)—provides that the statutory ceiling on the number of armed forces personnel who may be assigned to the Selective Service System does not apply "during a time of war or a national emergency declared by Congress or the President" and mandates that the System be maintained as an active standby organization capable of immediate operation "in the event of a national emergency."

Defense Production Act

50 U.S.C.A. App. § 2091(a)(3)—provides that certain conditions that are prerequisite to the President's exercise of the authority under Title III to provide guarantees for the financing of contracts or other operations deemed necessary for the "procurement of materials or performance of services for the national defense" do not apply "during periods of national emergency declared by Congress or the President."

50 U.S.C.A.App. §2091(e)(1)(D)—provides that the aggregate ceiling of $50 million on the total amount of financing guarantees that can be outstanding under Title III and certain other conditions may be waived "during periods of national emergency declared by the Congress or the President."

50 U.S.C.A. App. § 2092—provides that certain Presidential determinations that are prerequisite to the making of direct federal loans under Title III for the expansion of productive capacity and supply for the national defense do not apply and that the aggregate ceiling of $50 million on such loans and certain other procedural requirements may be waived "during periods of national emergency declared by the Congress or the President."

50 U.S.C.A. App. § 2093—provides that a number of conditions and prerequisites to the exercise of the authority under Title III to expand the productive capacity and supply of private industry for national defense purposes by means of purchase and resale of an industrial resource, a critical technology item, or a critical and strategic raw material may be waived "during periods of national emergency declared by the Congress or the President."

Congressional Procedures for Declaring War or Authorizing the Use of Force

The following section discusses how Congress would act on a joint resolution or bill to declare war or authorize the use of force if the House and Senate were to consider that measure under the regular procedures of each house. It also describes how a measure declaring war or authorizing the use of force would be considered under the procedures contained in the War Powers Resolution of 1973.[141]

Regular Procedures

The Senate's published precedents do not suggest that a measure proposing to declare war or authorize the use of force, if considered outside the framework of the War Powers Resolution, would be immune from the potentially laborious process to which other bills and joint resolutions are subject (except those that benefit from special expedited procedures under rule-making statutes). For example, a joint resolution declaring war or authorizing the use of force presumably would not be eligible for immediate floor consideration at the time it is introduced, and it presumably would be subject to possible delays resulting from the Senators' exercise of their right to debate at length.

Similarly, the precedents of the House apparently do not grant privilege to a joint resolution declaring war or authorizing the use of force either under the "leave to report" authority that House rules and precedents give to certain House committees or as a question of the privileges of the House. Concerning the latter, former House Parliamentarian Wm. Holmes Brown has observed that "Rule IX [on questions of privilege] is concerned not with the privileges of the Congress as a legislative branch, but only with the privileges of the House itself." Thus, neither the enumeration of legislative powers in Article I, sec. 8 of the Constitution nor the prohibition of that article against any withdrawal from the Treasury except by enactment of

[141] P.L. 93-148. 87 Stat. 555 *et. seq.* 50 U.S.C. §§ 1541 *et. seq.*

an appropriation renders a measure purporting to exercise or limit those powers a question of the privileges of the House.[142]

Because a joint resolution declaring war or authorizing the use of force proposes to exercise a constitutional power of "the Congress as a legislative branch," not of the House alone, it would seem, therefore, not to qualify as a question of privilege. If so, the House would consider the joint resolution according to its established procedures for dealing with other legislative measures,[143] unless the proposed declaration or authorization were to be considered under the terms of the War Powers Resolution.

Congress has adopted eight declarations of war during the 20th century—two at the outset of U.S. involvement in World War I and six in the course of World War II. House and Senate consideration of the initial declarations in each of these wars is illustrative of the process that Congress followed. On both occasions, the House and Senate acted to declare war in response to urgent presidential requests made personally before joint sessions of Congress. In light of the importance that most Members attached to these requests, it is not surprising that, in both cases, the two houses acted on the joint resolutions quickly and without following all their regular legislative procedures.

By way of illustration, the following is a brief summary of how the House and Senate considered the initial joint resolutions to declare war in 1917 and 1941.

World War I

Congress convened on April 2, 1917, and on that evening, President Wilson addressed both houses to request that Congress declare war against Germany. Immediately after the President's address, Senator Martin introduced S.J. Res. 1, to declare war, which was referred to the Committee on Foreign Relations. Also on April 2, Representative Flood introduced a companion resolution, H.J. Res 24, which was referred to the Committee on Foreign Affairs.

The Senate committee reported S.J. Res. 1 with an amendment on the following day. Senator LaFollette objected to a unanimous consent request that the Senate consider the measure immediately. Consequently, the joint resolution had to lie over for a day, pursuant to paragraph 4(a) of Senate Rule XVII. On April 4, the Senate agreed by unanimous consent to consider the joint resolution, agreed to the committee amendment, and, after considerable debate, passed the joint resolution by a roll call vote of 82-6.

---

142 Wm. Holmes Brown, House Practice: A Guide to the Rules, Precedents and Procedures of the House. Washington, U.S. Govt. Print. Off., 1996, p. 692.

143 The House floor discussion on April 4, 1917, concerning procedures for considering H.J. Res. 24, supports this interpretation by implication.

The House committee reported H.J. Res. 24 on April 4, and the House then agreed, by unanimous consent, to consider the measure on the following day "under the general rules of the House." Because the joint resolution, once reported, was placed on the Union Calendar, "the general rules of the House" required that it be considered in Committee of the Whole. Consequently, when the House convened on April 5, Representative Flood moved that the House resolve into Committee of the Whole to consider H.J. Res. 24. Before the House agreed to his motion, however, it also agreed to Representative Flood's unanimous consent request that the House instead consider S.J. Res. 1, which the Senate already had passed. After much debate, and after rejecting two amendments in Committee of the Whole and a motion to recommit with instructions in the House, the House passed S.J. Res. 1 by a roll call vote of 373-50.

World War II

On December 8, 1941, President Roosevelt addressed a joint session of Congress and asked for a declaration of war against Japan. Immediately after the joint session ended, the Senate reconvened and, following a live quorum call, Senator Connolly introduced a joint resolution declaring war. At Senator Connolly's request, and by unanimous consent, the Senate agreed to consider the joint resolution immediately, without committee consideration. Within minutes, and after brief statements by Senators Connolly and Vandenberg, the Senate passed the joint resolution by a roll call vote of 82-0.

Also immediately after the President's address, the House acted by considering and agreeing to Representative McCormack's motion to suspend the rules and pass H.J. Res. 254, which Representative McCormack introduced at that time. December 8 being a Monday, suspension motions were in order on that day. Immediately after the House passed H.J. Res. 254 by a roll call vote of 388-1, the House received a message from the Senate that it already had passed its joint resolution, now numbered S.J. Res. 116. The House then agreed to Representative McCormack's unanimous consent request that the House take the Senate joint resolution from the Speaker's table and agree to it. This action was necessary in order for both houses to pass the same measure, making it eligible to be presented to the President for his signature.

Congressional Procedures Under the War Powers Resolution

Enactment of the War Powers Resolution in November 1973 created special expedited procedures by which the House and Senate can act on joint resolutions or bills to declare war or authorize the use of force, if those measures are considered in accordance with the other, related provisions of that law.[144]

These expedited procedures were enacted into law as part of the War Powers Resolution as an exercise of the constitutional rule-making powers of the House and Senate. Article I of the Constitution empowers each house to set its own rules. When Congress enacts into law provisions that affect only the internal operations of the House or Senate, or both, those provisions are known as rule-making provisions of law that are enacted pursuant to this grant of power under Article I. Such rule-making provisions have exactly the same force and effect as provisions contained in the Standing Rules of the House and Senate.[145] Consequently, the house to which certain rule-making provisions apply may enforce, ignore, waive, suspend, supplement, or amend them by its own unilateral action, as it sees fit. For example, the House could adopt a special rule, or the Senate could agree to a unanimous consent request, that would supersede some or all of the procedures described here.

Section 4(a) of the War Powers Resolution directs the President to submit a report to Congress within 48 hours after U.S. armed forces are introduced "into hostilities or into situations where imminent involvement in hostilities is clearly indicated by the circumstances."[146] Section 5(a) provides for the receipt and for the referral to committee of any such presidential report. Under Section 5(b), the President is required to terminate use of the armed forces within 60 calendar days (90 days in some circumstances) after submitting his report unless Congress takes any one of several actions. One of these actions is to declare war; another is to "enact a specific authorization for such use of United States Armed Forces" as an alternative to declaring war. Under another section of the War Powers Resolution, Congress can also adopt a bill or joint resolution at any time requiring the President to remove the armed forces unless a declaration of war or statutory authorization has been enacted.[147]

Section 6 of the War Powers Resolution contains the expedited, or "fast-track," procedures that were included in the law to enable the House and Senate to

144 These expedited procedures are ambiguous in several respects. The description presented here should not be considered a substitute for consultations with the House or Senate Parliamentarian.

145 Other examples of rule-making provisions of law are the various congressional procedures enacted as part of the Congressional Budget and Impoundment Control Act of 1974 and related laws, and the "fast-track" provisions found in the Trade Act of 1974 and related laws.

146 Presidential reports also are required under two other conditions enumerated in Sec. 4(a).

147 Priorto 1983, the WPR provided that Congress could mandate the removal of U.S. armed forces by adopting a concurrent resolution. Given the virtual certainty that this procedure was unconstitutional following the Supreme Court's decision in June, 1983, in INS v. Chadha, 462 U.S. 919 (1983), Congress added a new provision to the War Powers Resolution later in 1983 providing for expedited procedures for a bill or joint resolution to require the removal of U.S. armed forces. *See* 50 U.S.C.A. § 1546a.

act within the 60 calendar-day period on a bill or joint resolution contemplated by Section 5(b).[148]

If, under Section 6(a), such a measure is introduced at least 30 calendar days before the end of the 60-day period, the measure is referred to the House International Relations Committee or the Senate Foreign Relations Committee, as the case may be. That committee is required to report one such measure, with its recommendations, not later than 24 calendar days before the end of the 60-day period. This provision suggests that the committee can report the measure with the committee's proposed amendments, if any. The subsection also provides that its provisions are to govern "unless such House shall otherwise determine by the yeas and nays." In other words, the House or Senate can, by a rollcall vote decided by a simple majority, release its committee from the obligation to report a measure proposing to declare war or to take some other action enumerated in Section 5(b).

If the House or Senate committee does report, it is not required to report the measure favorably. Instead, it may report it unfavorably or without recommendation. But what if either the Senate or House committee fails to report a covered bill or joint resolution within the time permitted? The Senate Parliamentarian has stated that the Senate Foreign Relations Committee would be automatically discharged if it failed to report as required by this subsection. The House Parliamentarian has stated that, should the House International Relations Committee fail to report in a timely manner, a privileged motion to discharge that committee would be in order on the House floor.

Section 6(b) governs initial House and Senate floor consideration of a joint resolution reported from committee pursuant to Section 6(a). Under Section 6(b), the bill or joint resolution, once reported (or once the committee is discharged), "shall become the pending business" of the House or Senate, as the case may be. By making a covered measure the pending business on the House or Senate floor, the War Powers Resolution evidently makes the measure privileged for floor consideration in the House (without the need for the Rules Committee to report a special rule for that purpose), or obviates the need for a motion (that usually is debatable) to proceed to the measure's consideration in the Senate. Because Section 6(b) contains no provisions to the contrary, the measure presumably would be amendable on the floor of either house to the same extent as any other bill or joint resolution that house considers, or could be tabled.

Section 6(b) goes on to require that the House or Senate vote on final passage of the measure within three calendar days after having become the

[148] A subsequent section of the WPR mandates expedited procedures for House and Senate consideration of a bill or joint resolution requiring the removal of U.S. armed forces. *See* 50 U.S.C.A. § 1546a.

pending business, "unless such House shall otherwise determine by yeas and nays." The effect of this subsection probably is more significant for the Senate than the House, because it is designed to preclude a filibuster on the Senate floor. In addition, the last provision of the subsection evidently gives either house options to adjust the timing and length of floor consideration by adopting any of several conceivable motions by rollcall vote. For example, either house might agree by motion to postpone consideration of the measure to a date certain. Alternatively, either house might dispose of the measure by a rollcall vote in favor of a motion to table or recommit it or to postpone its consideration indefinitely. Under the same authority, the House or Senate also might be able to shorten the debate to less than three calendar days or to extend the time for debate.

Sections 6(c) and 6(d) address the process for the House and Senate to reach agreement when each has passed a measure covered by Section 5(b). In summary, Section 6(c) provides for expedited committee and floor action in one house on a covered measure that the other house already has passed. Finally, Section 6(d) states that if a conference is necessary to reach a compromise between House and Senate versions of a covered measure, the conferees are to be appointed "promptly," the conferees are to report in either agreement or disagreement within specified time periods, and the two houses are to act on the conference report before the end of the 60-day period.

These last two subsections raise the problem that no rules or rule-making statute can compel the House and Senate to reach agreement. All that expedited procedures can do is to require that the conferees report, and that the House and Senate act on their report, by a time certain. The War Powers Resolution cannot ensure that both houses will agree on the same position by the end of the 60-day period. If the two houses were unable to agree by the end of the 60 days, that situation presumably would be reflected in (1) votes by one or both houses to reject a conference report in agreement, or (2) votes by both houses to agree to a conference report in disagreement (in other words, votes in each house to accept the report of the conferees that they were unable to reach agreement within the time allotted them). In either case, there is nothing in the statute that would preclude the two houses from appointing a new conference committee that might present a new conference report in agreement at some later date. However, a conference report filed in the Senate after the expiration of the 60-day period might well be subject to extended debate because, presumably, consideration of the report no longer would be governed by Section 6. Instead, the report would be considered under the Senate's regular procedures.

Appendix 1. Texts of Formal Declarations of War by the United States

War with Great Britain 1812

(Act of Jun. 18, 1812, ch. 102, 2 Stat755)

CHAP. CII.—*An Act declaring War between the United Kingdom of Great Britain and Ireland and the dependencies thereof, and the United States of America and their territories.*

Be it enacted by the Senate and House of Representatives of the United States of America in Congress assembled, That war be and the same is hereby declared to exist between the United Kingdom of Great Britain and Ireland and the dependencies thereof, and the United States of America and their territories; and that the President of the United States is hereby authorized to use the whole land and naval force of the United States to carry the same into effect, and to issue to private armed vessels of the United States commissions or letters of marque and general reprisal, in such form as he shall think proper, and under the seal of the United States, against the vessels, goods, and effects of the government of the said United Kingdom of Great Britain and Ireland, and the subjects thereof.

APPROVED, June 18, 1812.

[Terminated by Treaty of Ghent, entered into force Feb. 17, 1815. 8 Stat. 218, Treaty Series 109.]

War with Mexico 1846

(Act of May 13, 1846, ch. 16, 9 Stat. 9)

CHAP. XVI.—*An Act providing for the Prosecution of the existing War between the United States and the Republic of Mexico.*

Whereas, by the act of the Republic of Mexico, a state of war exists between that Government and the United States:

Be it enacted by the Senate and House of Representatives of the United States of America in Congress assembled, That, for the purpose of enabling the government of the United States to prosecute said war to a speedy and successful termination, the President be, and he is hereby, authorized to employ the militia, naval, and military forces of the United States, and to call for and accept the services of any number of volunteers, not exceeding fifty thousand, who may offer their services, either as cavalry, artillery, infantry, or riflemen, to serve twelve months after they shall have arrived at the place of rendezvous, or to the end of the war, unless sooner discharged, according to the time for which they shall have been mustered into service; and that the sum often millions of dollars, out of any moneys in the treasury, or to come into the treasury, not otherwise appropriated, be, and the same is hereby, appropriated for the purpose of carrying the provisions of this act into effect.

SEC. 2. *And be it further enacted,* That the militia, when called into the service of the United States by virtue of this act, or any other act, may, if in the opinion of the President of the United States the public interest requires it, be compelled to serve for a term not exceeding six months after their arrival at the place of rendezvous, in any one year, unless sooner discharged.

SEC. 3. *And be it further enacted,* That the said volunteers shall furnish their own clothes, and if cavalry, their own horses and horse equipments; and when mustered into service shall be armed at the expense of the United States.

SEC. 4. *And be it further enacted,* That said volunteers shall, when called into actual service, and while remaining therein, be subject to the rules and articles of war, and shall be, in all respects except as to clothing and pay, placed on the same footing with similar corps of the United States army; and in lieu of clothing every noncommissioned officer and private in any company, who may thus offer himself, shall be entitled, when called into actual service, to receive in money a sum equal to the cost of clothing of a non-commissioned officer or private (as the case may be) in the regular troops of the United States.

SEC 5. *And be it further enacted,* That the said volunteers so offering their services shall be accepted by the President in companies, battalions, squadrons, and regiments, whose officers shall be appointed in the manner prescribed by law in the several States and Territories to which such companies, battalions, squadrons, and regiments, shall respectively belong.

SEC. 6. *And be it further enacted,* That the President of the United States be, and he is hereby, authorized to organize companies so tendering their service into battalions or squadrons, battalions and squadrons into regiments, regiments into brigades, and brigades into divisions, as soon as the number of volunteers shall render such organization, in his judgment, expedient; and the President shall, if necessary, apportion the staff, field, and general officers among the respective States and Territories from which the volunteers shall tender their services as he may deem proper.

SEC 7. *And be it further enacted,* That the volunteers who may be received into the service of the United States by virtue of the provisions of this act, and who shall be wounded or otherwise disabled in the service, shall be entitled to all the benefit which may be conferred on persons wounded in the service of the United States.

SEC 8. *And be it further enacted,* That the President of the United States be, and he is hereby, authorized forthwith to complete all the public armed vessels now authorized by law, and to purchase or charter, arm, equip, and man, such merchant vessels and steam boats as, upon examination, may be found fit, or easily converted into armed vessels fit for the public service, and in such number as he may deem necessary for the protection of the seaboard, lake coast, and the general defense of the country.

SEC. 9. *And be it further enacted,* That whenever the militia or volunteers are called and received into the service of the United States, under the provisions of this act, they shall have the organization of the army of the United States, and shall have the same pay and allowances; and all mounted privates, non-commissioned officers, musicians, and artificers, shall be allowed 40 cents per day for the use and risk of their horses, except of horses actually killed in action; and if any mounted volunteer, private, non-commissioned officer, musician, or artificer, shall not keep himself provided with a serviceable horse, the said volunteer shall serve on foot.

APPROVED, May 13, 1846.

[Terminated by Treaty of Guadalupe Hidalgo, entered into force May 30, 1848. 9 Stat. 922, Treaty Series 207.]

War with Spain 1898

(Act of Apr. 25, 1898, ch. 189, 30 Stat. 364)

CHAP. 189—An Act Declaring that war exists between the United States of America and the Kingdom of Spain.

Be it enacted by the Senate and House of Representatives of the United States of America in Congress assembled, First. That war be, and the same is hereby, declared to exist, and that war has existed since the twenty-first day of April, anno Domini eighteen hundred and ninety-eight, including said day, between the United States of America and the Kingdom of Spain.

Second. That the President of the United States be, and he hereby is, directed and empowered to use the entire land and naval forces of the United States, and to call into the actual service of the United States the militia of the several States, to such extent as may be necessary to carry this Act into effect.

APPROVED, April 25, 1898.

[Terminated by Treaty of Paris, entered into force Apr. 11, 1899. 30 Stat. 1754, Treaty Series 343.]

War with Germany 1917

(Act of Apr. 6, 1917, ch. 1, 40 Stat. 1)

CHAP. 1.—Joint Resolution Declaring that a state of war exists between the Imperial German Government and the Government and the people of the United States and making provision to prosecute the same.

Whereas the Imperial German Government has committed repeated acts of war against the Government and the people of the United States of America: Therefore be it

Resolved by the Senate and House of Representatives of the United States of America in Congress assembled, That the state of war between the United States and the Imperial German Government which has thus been thrust upon the United States is hereby formally declared; and that the President be, and he is hereby, authorized and directed to employ the entire naval and military forces of the United States and the resources of the Government to carry on war against the Imperial German Government; and to bring the conflict to a successful termination all of the resources of the country are hereby pledged by the Congress of the United States.

APPROVED, April 6, 1917.

[Terminated by Act of July 2, 1921, [S.J. Res. 16] ch. 40, 42 Stat. 105 which declared the state of war between the U.S. and Germany to be at an end. Recognized by Treaty on Establishment of Friendly Relations, entered into force Nov. 11, 1921. 42 Stat. 1939, Treaty Series 658.]

War with Austria-Hungary 1917

(Act of Dec. 7, 1917, ch. 1, 40 Stat. 429)

CHAP. 1,—*Joint Resolution Declaring that a state of war exists between the Imperial and Royal Austro-Hungarian Government and the Government and the people of the United States, and making provision to prosecute the same.*

Whereas the Imperial and Royal Austro-Hungarian Government has committed repeated acts of war against the Government and the people of the United States of America: Therefore be it

Resolved by the Senate and House of Representatives of the United States of America in Congress assembled, That a state of war is hereby declared to exist between the United States of America and the Imperial and Royal Austro-Hungarian Government; and that the President be, and he is hereby, authorized and directed to employ the entire naval and military forces of the United States and the resources of the Government to carry on war against the Imperial and Royal Austro-Hungarian Government; and to bring the conflict to a successful termination all the resources of the country are hereby pledged by the Congress of the United States.

APPROVED, December 7, 1917.

[Terminated by Act of July 2, 1921, [S.J. Res. 16] ch. 40, 42 Stat. 105 which declared the state of war between the U.S. and Austria, a successor state and government to the Austro-Hungarian monarchy, to be at an end. 42 Stat. 105. This was recognized by a Treaty on Establishment of Friendly Relations, entered into force Nov. 8, 1921. 42 Stat. 1939, Treaty Series 658. The Act of July 2, 1921, also declared the state of war between the U.S. and Hungary, a successor state and government to the Austro-Hungarian monarchy, to be at an end. This was recognized by a Treaty on Establishing Friendly Relations, entered into force Dec. 17, 1921. 42 Stat. 1951, Treaty Series 660.]

War with Japan 1941

(Act of Dec. 8, 1941, ch. 561, 55 Stat. 795)

[Chapter 561]

JOINT RESOLUTION

Declaring that a state of war exists between the Imperial Government of Japan and the Government and the people of the United States and making provisions to prosecute the same.

Whereas the Imperial Government of Japan has committed unprovoked acts of war against the Government and the people of the United States of America: Therefore be it

Resolved by the Senate and House of Representatives of the United States of America in Congress assembled, That the state of war between the United States and the Imperial Government of Japan which has thus been thrust upon the United States is hereby formally declared; and the President is hereby authorized and directed to employ the entire naval and military forces of the United States and the resources of the Government to carry on war against the Imperial Government of Japan; and, to bring the conflict to a successful termination, all of the resources of the country are hereby pledged by the Congress of the United States.

APPROVED, December 8, 1941, 4:10 p.m., E.S.T.

[Terminated by Treaty of Peace with Japan, entered into force Apr. 28, 1952. 3 UST 3169, TIAS 2490.]

War with Germany 1941

(Act of Dec. 11, 1941, ch. 564, 55 Stat. 796)

[CHAPTER 564]

JOINT RESOLUTION

Declaring that a state of war exists between the Government of Germany and the Government and the people of the United States and making provision to prosecute the same.

Whereas the Government of Germany has formally declared war against the Government and the people of the United States of America: Therefore be it

Resolved by the Senate and House of Representatives of the United States of America in Congress assembled, That the state of war between the United States and the Government of Germany which has thus been thrust upon the United States is hereby formally declared; and the President is hereby authorized and directed to employ the entire naval and military forces of the United States and the resources of the Government to carry on war against the Government of Germany; and, to bring the conflict to a successful termination, all of the resources of the country are hereby pledged by the Congress of the United States.

APPROVED, December 11, 1941, 3:05 p.m., E.S.T.

[Terminated by [H.J. Res. 289] Act of October 19, 1951, ch. 519, 65 Stat. 541]

War with Italy 1941

(Act of Dec. 11, 1941, ch. 565, 55 Stat. 797)

[CHAPTER 565]

JOINT RESOLUTION

Declaring that a state of war exists between the Government of Italy and the Government and the people of the United States and making provision to prosecute the same.

Whereas the Government of Italy has formally declared war against the Government and the people of the United States of America: Therefore be it

Resolved by the Senate and House of Representatives of the United States of America in Congress assembled, That the state of war between the United States and the Government of Italy which has thus been thrust upon the United States is hereby formally declared; and the President is hereby authorized and directed to employ the entire naval and military forces of the United States and the resources of the Government to carry on war against the Government of Italy; and, to bring the conflict to a successful termination, all of the resources of the country are hereby pledged by the Congress of the United States.

APPROVED, December 11, 1941, 3:06 p.m., E.S.T.

[Terminated by Treaty of Peace with Italy, entered into force Sept. 15, 1947. 4 UST 311,61 Stat. 1245.]

War With Bulgaria 1942

(Act of Jun. 5, 1942, ch. 323, 56 Stat. 307)

[CHAPTER 323]

JOINT RESOLUTION

Declaring that a state of war exists between the Government of Bulgaria and the Government and the people of the United States and making provisions to prosecute the same.

Whereas the Government of Bulgaria has formally declared war against the Government and the people of the United States of America: Therefore be it

Resolved by the Senate and House of Representatives of the United States of America in Congress assembled, That the state of war between the United States and the Government of Bulgaria which has thus been thrust upon the United States is hereby formally declared; and the President is hereby authorized and directed to employ the entire naval and military forces of the United States and the resources of the Government to carry on war against the Government of Bulgaria; and, to bring the conflict to a successful termination, all of the resources of the country are hereby pledged by the Congress of the United States.

APPROVED, June 5, 1942.

[Terminated by Treaty of Peace with Bulgaria, entered into force Sept. 15, 1947. 4 UST 429, 61 Stat. 1915.]

War with Hungary 1942

(Act of Jun. 5, 1942, ch. 324, 56 Stat. 307)

[CHAPTER 324]

JOINT RESOLUTION

Declaring that a state of war exists between the Government of Hungary and the Government and the people of the United States and making provisions to prosecute the same.

Whereas the Government of Hungary has formally declared war against the Government and the people of the United States of America: Therefore be it

Resolved by the Senate and House of Representatives of the United States of America in Congress assembled, That the state of war between the United States and the Government of Hungary which has thus been thrust upon the United States is hereby formally declared; and the President is hereby authorized and directed to employ the entire naval and military forces of the United States and the resources of the Government to carry on war against the Government of Hungary; and, to bring the conflict to a successful termination all of the resources of the country are hereby pledged by the Congress of the United States.

APPROVED, June 5, 1942.

[Terminated by Treaty of Peace with Hungary, entered into force Sept. 15, 1947. 4UST453, 61 Stat. 2065.]

War with Rumania 1942

(Act of Jun. 5, 1942, ch. 325, 56 Stat. 307)

[CHAPTER 325]

JOINT RESOLUTION

Declaring that a state of war exists between the Government of Rumania and the Government and the people of the United States and making provisions to prosecute the same.

Whereas the Government of Rumania has formally declared war against the Government and the people of the United States of America: Therefore be it

Resolved by the Senate and House of Representatives of the United States of America in Congress assembled, That the state of war between the United States and the Government of Rumania which has thus been thrust upon the United States is hereby formally declared; and the President is hereby authorized and directed to employ the entire naval and military forces of the United States and the resources of the Government to carry on war against the Government of Rumania; and, to bring the conflict to a successful termination, all of the resources of the country are hereby pledged by the Congress of the United States.

APPROVED, June 5, 1942.

[Terminated by Treaty of Peace with Rumania, entered into force Sept. 15, 1947. 4UST403, 61 Stat. 1757.]

Appendix II. Texts of Key Authorizations of Use of Force

Protection of the Commerce and Coasts of the United States

(Act of May 28, 1798, ch. 48, 1 Stat. 561)

CHAP. XLVIII.—*An Act more effectually to protect the Commerce and Coasts of the United States.*

Whereas armed vessels sailing under authority or pretence *[sic]* of authority from the Republic of France, have committed depredations on the commerce of the United States, and have recently captured the vessels and property of citizens thereof, on and near the coasts, in violation of the law of nations, and treaties between the United States and the French nation. Therefore:

Be it enacted by the Senate and House of Representatives of the United States of America in Congress assembled, That it shall be lawful for the President of the United States, and he is hereby authorized to instruct and direct the commanders of the armed vessels belonging to the United States to seize, take and bring into any port of the United States, to be proceeded against according to the laws of nations, any such armed vessel which shall have committed or which shall be found hovering on the coasts of the United States, for the purpose of committing depredations on the vessels belonging to citizens thereof;—and also to retake any ship or vessel, of any citizen or citizens of the United States which may have been captured by any such armed vessel.

APPROVED, May 28, 1798.

Protection of the Commerce of the United States

(Act of July 9, 1798, ch. 68, 1 Stat. 578)

CHAP. LXVIII—*An Act further to protect the Commerce of the United States.*

SECTION 1. *Be it enacted by the Senate and House of Representatives of the United States of America in Congress assembled,* That the President of the United States shall be, and he is hereby authorized to instruct the commanders of the public armed vessels which are, or which shall be employed in the service of the United States, to subdue, seize and take any armed French vessel, which shall be found within the jurisdictional limits of the United States, or elsewhere, on the high seas, and such captured vessel, with her apparel, guns and appurtenances, and the goods or effects which shall be found on board the same, being French property, shall be brought within some port of the United States, and shall be duly proceeded against and condemned as forfeited; and shall accrue and be distributed, as by law is or shall be provided respecting the captures which shall be made by the public armed vessels of the United States.

SEC. 2. *And be it further enacted,* That the President of the United States shall be, and he is hereby authorized to grant to the owners of private armed ships and vessels of the United States, who shall make application thereof, special commissions in the form which he shall direct, and under the seal of the United States; and such private armed vessels, when duly commissioned, as aforesaid, shall have the same license and authority for the subduing, seizing and capturing any armed French vessel, and for the recapture of the vessels, goods and effects of the people of the United States, as the public armed vessels of the United States may by law have; and shall be, in like manner, subject to such instructions as shall be ordered by the President of the United States, for the regulation of their conduct. And the commissions which shall be granted, as aforesaid, shall be revocable at the pleasure of the President of the United States.

SEC. 3. *Provided, and be it further enacted,* That every person intending to set forth and employ an armed vessel, and applying for a commission, as aforesaid, shall produce in writing the name, and a suitable description of the tonnage and force of the vessel, and the name and place of residence of each owner concerned therein, the number of the crew and the name of the commander, and the two officers next in rank appointed for such vessel; which writing shall be signed by the person or persons making such application, and filed with the Secretary of State, or shall be delivered to any other officer or person who shall be employed to deliver out such commissions, to be by him transmitted to the Secretary of State.

SEC. 4. *And provided, and be it further enacted,* That before any commission, as aforesaid, shall be issued, the owner or owners of the ship or vessel for which the same shall be requested, and the commander thereof, for the time being, shall give bond to the United States, with at least two responsible sureties, not interested in such vessel, in the penal sum of seven thousand dollars; or if such vessel be provided with more than one hundred and fifty men, then in the penal sum of fourteen thousand dollars; with condition that the owners, and officers, and crews who shall be employed on board of such commissioned vessel, shall and will observe the treaties and laws of the United States and the instructions which shall be given them for the regulation of their conduct: And will satisfy all damages and injuries which shall be done or committed contrary to the tenor thereof, by such vessel, during her commission, and to deliver up the same when revoked by the President of the United States.

SEC. 5. *And be it further enacted,* That all armed French vessels, together with their apparel, guns and appurtenances, and any goods or effects which shall be found on board the same, being French property, and which shall be captured by any private armed vessel or vessels of the United States, duly commissioned, as aforesaid, shall be forfeited, and shall accrue to the owners thereof, and the officers and crews by whom such captures shall be made; and on due condemnation had, shall be distributed according to any agreement which shall be between them; or in failure of such agreement, then by the discretion of the court before whom such condemnation shall be.

SEC. 6. *And be it further enacted,* That all vessels, goods and effects, the property of any citizen of the United States, or person resident therein, which shall be recaptured, as aforesaid, shall be restored to the lawful owners, upon payment by them, respectively, of a just and reasonable salvage, to be determined by the mutual agreement of the parties concerned, or by the decree of any court of the United States having maritime jurisdiction according to the nature of each case: *Provided,* that such allowance shall not be less than one eighth, or exceeding one half of the full value of such recapture, without any deduction. And such salvage shall be distributed to and among the owners, officers and crews of the private armed vessel or vessels entitled thereto, according to any agreement which shall be between them; or in case of no agreement, then by the decree of the court who shall determine upon such salvage.

SEC. 7. *And be it further enacted,* That before breaking bulk of any vessel which shall be captured, as aforesaid, or other disposal or conversion thereof, or of any articles which shall be found on board the same, such capture shall be brought into some port of the United States, and shall be libelled and proceeded against before the district court of the same district; and if after a due course of proceedings, such capture shall be decreed as forfeited in the district court, or in the circuit court of the same district, in the case of any appeal duly allowed, the same shall be delivered to the owners and captors concerned therein, or shall be publicly sold by the marshal of the same court, as shall be finally decreed and ordered by the court. And the same court, who shall have final jurisdiction of any libel or complaint of any capture, as aforesaid, shall and may decree restitution, in whole or in part, when the capture and restraint shall have been made without just cause, as aforesaid; and if made without probable cause, or otherwise unreasonably, may order and decree damages and costs to the party injured, and for which the owners, officers and crews of the private armed vessel or vessels by which such unjust capture shall have been made, and also such vessel or vessels shall be answerable and liable.

SEC. 8. *And be it further enacted,* That all French persons and others, who shall be found acting on board any French armed vessel, which shall be captured, or on board of any vessel of the United States, which shall be captured, or on board of any vessel of the United States, which shall be recaptured, as aforesaid, shall be reported to the collector of the port in which they shall first arrive, and shall be delivered to the custody of the marshal, or of some civil or military officer of the United States, or of any state in or near such port; who shall take charge for their safe keeping and support, at the expense of the United States.

APPROVED, July 9, 1798.

Protection of the Commerce and Seamen of the United States Against the Tripolitan Cruisers

(Act of February 6, 1802, ch. 4, 2 Stat.129)

CHAP. IV.—*An Act for the protection of the Commerce and Seamen of the United States, against the Tripolitan Cruisers.*

Whereas the regency of Tripoli, on the coast of Barbary, has commenced a predatory warfare against the United States:

Be it enacted by the Senate and House of Representatives of the United States of America in Congress assembled, That it shall be lawful fully to equip, officer, man, and employ such of the armed vessels of the United States as may be judged requisite by the President of the United States, for protecting effectually the commerce and seamen thereof on the Atlantic ocean, the Mediterranean and adjoining seas.

SEC. 2. *And be it further enacted,* That it shall be lawful for the President of the United States to instruct the commanders of the respective public vessels aforesaid, to subdue, seize and make prize of all vessels, goods, and effects, belonging to the Bey of Tripoli, or to his subjects, and to bring or send the same into port, to be proceeded against, and distributed according to the law; and also to cause to be done all such other acts of precaution or hostility as the state of war will justify, and may, in his opinion, require.

SEC. 3. *And be it further enacted,* That on the application of, the owners of private armed vessels of the United States, the President of the United States may grant to them special commissions, in the form which he shall direct, under the seal of the United States; and such private armed vessels, when so commissioned, shall have the like authority for subduing, seizing, taking, and bringing into port, any Tripolitan vessel, goods or effects, as the before-mentioned public armed vessels may by law have; and shall therein be subject to the instruction which may be given by the President of the United States for the regulation of their conduct; and their commissions shall be revocable at his pleasure. *Provided,* that before any commission shall be granted, as aforesaid, the owner or owners of the vessel for which the same may be requested, and the commander thereof, for the time being, shall give bond to the United States, with at least two responsible sureties, not interested in such vessel, in the penal sum of seven thousand dollars; or, if such vessel be provided with more than one hundred and fifty men, in the penal sum of fourteen thousand dollars, with condition for observing the treaties and laws of the United States, and the instructions which may be given, as aforesaid; and also, for satisfying all damages and injuries which shall be done, contrary to the tenor thereof, by such commissioned vessel; and for delivering up the commission, when revoked by the President of the United States.

SEC. 4. *And be if further enacted,* That any Tripolitan vessel, goods or effects, which shall be so captured and brought into port, by any private armed vessel of the United States, duly commissioned, as aforesaid, may be adjudged good prize, and thereupon shall accrue to the owners and officers, and men of the capturing vessel, and shall be distributed according to the agreement which shall have been made between them, or, in failure of such agreement, according to the discretion of the court having cognizance of the capture.

SEC. 5. *And be it further enacted,* That the seamen may be engaged to serve in the navy of the United States for a period not exceeding two years; but the President may discharge the same sooner, if in his judgment, their services may be dispensed with.

APPROVED, February 6, 1802.

[Repealed by P.L. 1028, 84th Congress, 2d Sess (August 10, 1956); 70A Stat. 644, sec. 53(b)]

Protection of the Commerce and Seamen of the United States Against the Algerine Cruisers

(Act of March 3, 1815, ch. 90, 3 Stat. 230)

CHAP. XC.—*An Act for the protection of the commerce of the United States against the Algerine cruisers.*

Whereas the Dey of Algiers, on the coast of Barbary, has commenced a predatory warfare against the United States —

Be it enacted by the Senate and House of Representatives of the United States of America, in Congress assembled, That it shall be lawful fully to equip, officer, man and employ such of the armed vessels of the United States as may be judged requisite by the President of the United States for protecting effectually the commerce and seamen thereof on the Atlantic Ocean, the Mediterranean and adjoining seas.

SEC. 2. *And be it further enacted,* That it shall be lawful for the President of the United States to instruct the commanders of the respective public vessels aforesaid, to subdue, seize, and make prize of all vessels, goods and effects of or belonging to the Dey of Algiers, or to his subjects, and to bring or send the same into port, to be proceeded against and distributed according to law; and, also, to cause to be done all such other acts of precaution or hostility, as the state of war will justify, and may in his opinion require.

SEC. 3. *And be it further enacted,* That on the application of the owners of private armed vessels of the United States, the President of the United States may grant them special commissions in the form which he shall direct under the seal of the United States; and such private armed vessels, when so commissioned, shall have the like authority for subduing, seizing, taking and bringing into port any Algerine vessel, goods or effects, as the before-mentioned public armed vessels may by law have; and shall therein be subject to the instructions which may be given by the President of the United States for the regulation of their conduct; and their commissions shall be revokable at his pleasure. *Provided,* That before any commission shall be granted as aforesaid, the owner or owners of the vessels of which the same may be requested, and the commander thereof for the time being shall give bond to the United States, with at least two responsible sureties, not interested in such vessel, in the penal sum of seven thousand dollars, or if such vessel be provided with more than one hundred and fifty men, in the penal sum of fourteen thousand dollars, with condition for observing the treaties and laws of the United States, and the instructions which may be given as aforesaid, and also for satisfying all damages and injuries which shall be done contrary to the tenor thereof by such commissioned vessel, and for delivering up the commission when revoked by the President of the United States.

SEC. 4. *And be if further enacted,* That any Algerine vessel, goods, or effects which may be so captured and brought into port, by any private armed vessel, of the United States, duly commissioned as aforesaid, may be adjudged good prize, and thereupon shall accrue to the owners, and officers, and men of the capturing vessel, and shall be distributed according to the agreement which shall have been made between them, or, in failure of such agreement, according to the discretion [of] the court having cognisance of the capture.

APPROVED, March 3, 1815.

[Repealed by P.L. 1028, 84th Congress, 2d Sess (August 10, 1956); 70A Stat. 644, sec. 53(b)]

Suppression of Piracy

(33 U.S.C. §§ 381-387. R.S. §§ 4293-4299. R.S. § 4293,4294, and 4295 are derived from the Acts of Mar. 3, 1819, ch. 77, 3 Stat. 510 and 512; Jan. 30, 1823, 3 Stat. 513, ch. 7, 3 Stat. 721. R.S.§ 4296 is derived from the Acts of March 3, 1819, ch. 77, 3 Stat. 513; Jan. 30, 1823, ch. 7, 3 Stat. 721; Aug. 5, 1861, ch. 48, 12 Stat. 314. R.S. §§ 4297, 4298, and 4299 are derived from the Act of Aug. 5, 1861, ch. 48, 12 Stat. 315.)

TITLE 33. CHAPTER 7.

§ 381. Use of public vessels to suppress piracy

The President is authorized to employ so many of the public armed vessels as in his judgement the service may require, with suitable instructions to the commanders thereof, in protecting the merchant vessels of the United States and their crews from piratical aggressions and depredations.

§ 382. Seizure of piratical vessels generally

The President is authorized to instruct the commanders of the public armed vessels of the United States to subdue, seize, take, and send into any port of the United States, any armed vessel or boat, or any vessel or boat, the crew whereof shall be armed, and which shall have attempted or committed any piratical aggression, search, restraint, depredation, or seizure, upon any vessel of the United States, or of the citizens thereof, or upon any other vessel; and also to retake any vessel of the United States, or its citizens, which may have been unlawfully captured upon the high seas.

§ 383. Resistance of pirates by merchant vessels

The commander and crew of any merchant vessel of the United States, owned wholly, or in part, by a citizen thereof, may oppose and defend against any aggression, search, restraint, depredation, or seizure, which shall be attempted upon such vessel, or upon any other vessel so owned, by the commander or crew of any armed vessel whatsoever, not being a public armed vessel of some nation in amity with the United States, and may subdue and capture the same; and may also retake any vessel so owned which may have been captured by the commander or crew of any such armed vessel, and send the same into any port of the United States.

§ 384. Condemnation of piratical vessels

Whenever any vessel, which shall have been built, purchased, fitted out in whole or in part, or held for the purpose of being employed in the commission of any piratical aggression, search, restraint, depredation, or seizure, or in the commission of any other act of piracy as defined by the law of nations, or from which any piratical aggression, search, restraint, depredation, or seizure shall have been first attempted or made, is captured and brought into or captured in any port of the United States, the same shall be adjudged and condemned to their use, and that of the captors after due process and trial in any court having admiralty jurisdiction, and which shall be holden for the district into which such captured vessel shall be brought; and the same court shall thereupon order a sale and distribution thereof accordingly, and at its discretion.

§ 385. Seizure and condemnation of vessels fitted out for piracy

Any vessel built, purchased, fitted out in whole or in part, or held for the purpose of being employed in the commission of any piratical aggression, search, restraint, depredation, or seizure, or in the commission of any other act of piracy, as defined by the law of nations, shall be liable to be captured and brought into any port of the United States if found upon the high seas, or to be seized if found in any port or place within the United States, whether the same shall have actually sailed upon any piratical expedition or not, and whether any act of piracy shall have been committed or attempted upon or from such vessel or not; and any such vessel may be adjudged and condemned, if captured by a vessel authorized as hereinafter mentioned [33 USCS § 386] to the use of the United States, and to that of the captors, and if seized by a collector [the Secretary of the Treasury], surveyor or marshal, then to the use of the United States.

§ 386. Commissioning private vessels for seizure of piratical vessels

The President is authorized to instruct the commanders of the public armed vessels of the United States, and to authorize the commanders of any other armed vessels sailing under the authority of any letters of marque and reprisal granted by Congress, or the commanders of any other suitable vessels, to subdue, seize, take, and, if on the high seas, to send into any port of the United States, any vessel or boat built, purchased, fitted out, or held as mentioned in the preceding section [33 USCS § 385].

§ 387. Duties of officers of customs and marshals as to seizure

The collectors of the several ports of entry [the Secretary of the Treasury] the surveyors of the several ports of delivery [the Secretary of the Treasury] and the marshals of the several judicial districts within the United States, shall seize any vessel or boat built, purchased, fitted out, or held as mentioned in section forty-two hundred and ninety-seven [33 USCS § 385], which may be found within their respective ports or districts, and to cause the same to be proceeded against and disposed of as provided by that section.

Authorization for the President to Employ the Armed Forces of the United States for Protecting the Security of Formosa, the Pescadores, and Related Positions and Territories of That Area

(Act of January 29, 1955, ch.4, 69 Stat. 7. [H.J. Res. 159, P.L. 84-4])

P.L. 4, CHAPTER 4 —. *Joint Resolution authorizing the President to employ the Armed Forces of the United States for protecting the security of Formosa, the Pescadores and related positions and territories of that area.*

Whereas the primary purpose of the United States, in its relations with all other nations, is to develop and sustain a just and enduring peace for all; and

Whereas certain territories in the West Pacific under the jurisdiction of the Republic of China are now under armed attack, and threats and declarations have been and are being made by the Chinese Communists that such armed attack is in aid of and in preparation for armed attack on Formosa and the Pescadores,

Whereas such armed attack if continued would gravely endanger the peace and security of the West Pacific Area and particularly of Formosa and the Pescadores; and

Whereas the secure possession by friendly governments of the Western Pacific Island chain, of which Formosa is a part, is essential to the vital interests of the United States and all friendly nations in or bordering upon the Pacific Ocean; and

Whereas the President of the United States on January 6, 1955, submitted to the Senate for its advice and consent to ratification a Mutual Defense Treaty between the United States of America and the Republic of China, which recognizes that an armed attack in the West Pacific area directed against territories, therein described, in the region of Formosa and the Pescadores, would be dangerous to the peace and safety of the parties to the treaty: Therefore be it

Resolved by the Senate and House of Representatives of the United States of America in Congress assembled, That the President of the United States be and he hereby is authorized to employ the Armed Forces of the United

States as he deems necessary for the specific purpose of securing and protecting Formosa, and the Pescadores against armed attack, this authority to include the securing and protection of such related positions and territories of that area now in friendly hands and the taking of such other measures as he judges to be required or appropriate in assuring the defense of Formosa and the Pescadores.

This resolution shall expire when the President shall determine that the peace and security of the area is reasonably assured by international conditions created by action of the United States or otherwise, and shall so report to the Congress.

APPROVED, January 29, 1955, 8:42 a.m.

[Repealed by P.L. 93-475 [S. 3473] Oct. 26, 1975. 88 Stat. 1439]

Promotion of Peace and Stability in the Middle East

(P.L. 85-7, 71 Stat. 5, March 9, 1957 [H.J. Res. 117])

P.L. 85-7—*Joint Resolution, To promote peace and stability in the Middle East.*

Resolved by the Senate and House of Representatives of the United States of America in Congress assembled, That the President be and hereby is authorized to cooperate with and assist any nation or group of nations in the general area of the Middle East desiring such assistance in the deve lopment of economic strength dedicated to the maintenance of national independence.

SEC. 2. The President is authorized to undertake, in the general area of the Middle East, military assistance programs with any nation or group of nations of that area desiring such assistance. Furthermore, the United States regards as vital to the national interest and world peace the preservation of the independence and integrity of the nations of the Middle East. To this end, if the President determines the necessity thereof, the United States is prepared to use armed forces to assist any such nation or group of such nations requesting assistance against armed aggression from any country controlled by international communism: *Provided,* That such employment shall be consonant with the treaty obligations of the United States and with the Constitution of the United States.

SEC. 3. The President is hereby authorized to use during the balance of fiscal year 1957 for economic and military assistance under this joint resolution not to exceed $200,000,000 from any appropriation now available for carrying out the provisions fo the Mutual Security Act of 1954, as amended, in accord with the provisions of such Act: *Provided,* That, whenever the President determines it to be important to the security of the United States, such use may be under the authority of section 401 (a) of the Mutual Security Act of 1954, as amended (except that the provisions of section 105 (a) thereof shall not be waived), and without regard to the provisions of section 105 of the Mutual Security Appropriation Act, 1957: *Provided further,* That obligations incurred in carrying out the purposes of the first sentence of section 2 of this joint resolution shall be paid only out of appropriations for military assistance, and obligations incurred in carrying out the purposes of the first section of this joint resolution shall be paid only out of appropriations other than those for military assistance. This authorization is in addition to other existing authorizations with respect to the use of such appropriations. None of the additional authorization contained in this section shall be used until fifteen days after the Committee on Foreign Relations of the Senate, the Committee on Foreign Affairs of the House of Representatives, the Committees on Appropriations of the Senate and the House of Representatives and, when military assistance is involved, the Committees on Armed Services of the Senate and the House of Representatives have been furnished a report showing the object of the proposed use, the country for the benefit of which such use is intended, and the particular appropriation or appropriations for carrying out the provisions of the Mutual Security Act of 1954, as amended, from which the funds are proposed to be derived: *Provided,* That funds available under this section during the balance of fiscal year 1957 shall, in the case of any such report submitted during the last fifteen days of the fiscal year, remain available for use under this section for the purposes stated in such report for a period of twenty days following the date of submission of such report. Nothing contained in this joint resolution shall be construed as itself authorizing the appropriation of additional funds for the purpose of carrying out the provisions of the first section or of the first sentence of section 2 of this joint resolution.

SEC. 4. The President should continue to furnish facilities and military assistance, within the provisions of applicable law and established policies, to the United Nations Emergency Force in the Middle East, with a view to maintaining the truce in that region.

SEC. 5. The President shall within the months of January and July of each year report to the Congress his action hereunder.

SEC. 6. This joint resolution shall expire when the President shall determine that the peace and security of the nations in the general area of the Middle East are reasonably assured by international conditions created by action of the United Nations or otherwise except that it may be terminated earlier by a concurrent resolution of the two Houses of Congress.

APPROVED, March 9, 1957.

Maintenance of International Peace and Security in Southeast Asia

(P.L. 88-408, 78 Stat. 384, August 10, 1964 [H.J.Res. 11450])

P.L. 88-408, 78 Stat.—*Joint Resolution, To promote the maintenance of international peace and security in southeast Asia.*

Whereas naval units of the Communist regime in Vietnam, in violation of the principles of the Charter of the United Nations and of international law, have deliberately and repeatedly attacked the United States naval vessels lawfully present in international waters, and have thereby created a serious threat to international peace; and

Whereas these attacks are part of a deliberate and systematic campaign of aggression that the Communist regime in North Vietnam has been waging against its neighbors and the nations joined with them in the collective defense of their freedom; and

Whereas the United States is assisting the peoples of southeast Asia to protect their freedom and has no territorial, military or political ambitions in that area, but desires only that these peoples should be left in peace to work out their won destinies in their own way: Now, therefore, be it

Re solved by the Senate and House of Representatives of the United States of America in Congress assembled, That the Congress approves and supports the determination of the President, as Commander in Chief, to take all necessary measures to repel any armed attack against the forces of the Untied States and to prevent further aggression.

SEC. 2. The United States regards as vital to its national interest and to world peace the maintenance of international peace and security in southeast Asia. Consonant with the Constitution of the United States and the Charter of the United Nations and in accordance with its obligations under the Southeast Asia Collective Defense Treaty, the United States is, therefore, prepared, as the President determines, to take all necessary steps, including the use of armed force, to assist any member or protocol state of the Southeast Asia Collective Defense Treaty requesting assistance in defense of its freedom.

SEC. 3. This resolution shall expire when the President shall determine that the peace and security of the area is reasonably assured by international conditions created by action of the United Nations or otherwise, except that it may be terminated earlier by concurrent resolution of the Congress.

APPROVED, August 10, 1964

[Repealed by P.L. 91-672 [H.R. 15628] January 12, 1971. 84 Stat. 2053]

Multinational Force in Lebanon

(P.L. 98-119, 97 Stat. 805, October 12, 1983 [S.J. Res. 159])

P.L. 98-119, 97 Stat. 805—*Joint Resolution providing statutory authorization under the War Powers Resolution for continued United States participation in the multinational peacekeeping force in Lebanon in order to obtain withdrawal of all foreign forces from Lebanon.*

Resolved by the Senate and House of Representatives of the United States of America in Congress assembled,

SHORT TITLE

SECTION 1. This joint resolution may be cited as the "Multinational Force in Lebanon Resolution".

FINDINGS AND PURPOSE

SEC. 2. (a) The Congress finds that—

(1) the removal of all foreign forces from Lebanon is an essential United States foreign policy objective in the Middle East;

(2) in order to restore full control by the Government of Lebanon over its own territory, the United States is currently participating in the multinational peacekeeping force (hereafter in this resolution referred to as the "Multinational Force in Lebanon") which was established in accordance with the exchange of letters between the Governments of the United States and Lebanon dated September 25, 1982;

(3) the Multinational Force in Lebanon better enables the Government of Lebanon to establish its unity, independence, and territorial integrity;

(4) progress toward national political reconciliation in Lebanon is necessary; and

(5) United States Armed Forces participating in the Multinational Force in Lebanon are now in hostilities requiring authorization of their continued presence under the War Powers Resolution.

(b) The Congress determines that the requirements of section 4(a)(1) of the War Powers Resolution became operative on August 29, 1983. Consistent with section 5(b) of the War Powers Resolution, the purpose of this joint resolution is to authorize the continued participation of the United States Armed forces in the Multinational Force in Lebanon.

(c) The Congress intends this joint resolution to constitute the necessary specific statutory authorization under the War Powers Resolution for continued participation by United States Armed Forces in the Multinational Force in Lebanon.

AUTHORIZATION FOR CONTINUED PARTICIPATION OF UNITED STATES ARMED FORCES IN THE MULTINATIONAL FORCE IN LEBANON

SEC. 3. The President is authorized, for purposes of section 5(b) of the War Powers Resolution, to continue participation by United States Armed Forces in the Multinational Force in Lebanon, subject to the provisions of section 6 of this joint resolution. Such participation shall be limited to performance of the functions, and shall be subject to the limitations, specified in the agreement establishing the Multinational Force in Lebanon as set forth in the exchange of letters between the Governments of the United States and Lebanon dated September 25, 1982, except that this shall not preclude such protective measures as may be necessary to ensure the safety of the Multinational Force in Lebanon.

REPORTS TO THE CONGRESS

SEC. 4. As required by section 4(c) of the War Powers Resolution, the President shall report periodically to the Congress with respect to the situation in Lebanon, but in no event shall he report less often than once every three months. In addition to providing the information required by that section on the status, scope, and duration of hostilities involving the Unites States Armed Forces, such reports shall describe in detail —

(1) the activities being performed by the Multinational Force in Lebanon;

(2) the present composition of the Multinational Force in Lebanon, including a description of the responsibilities and deployment of the armed forces of each participating country;

(3) the results of efforts to reduce and eventually eliminate the Multinational Force in Lebanon;

(4) how continued United States participation in the Multinational Force in Lebanon is advancing United States foreign policy interests in the Middle East; and

(5) what progress has occurred toward national political reconciliation among all Lebanese groups.

STATEMENTS OF POLICY

SEC. 5. (a) The Congress declares that the participation of the armed forces of other countries in the Multinational Force in Lebanon is essential to maintain the international character of the peacekeeping function in Lebanon.

(b) The Congress believes that it should continue to be the policy of the United States to promote continuing discussions with Israel, Syria, and Lebanon with the objective of bringing about the withdrawal of all foreign troops from Lebanon and establishing an environment which will permit the Lebanese Armed Forces to carry out their responsibilities in the Beirut area.

(c) It is the sense of the Congress that, not later than one year after the date of enactment of this joint resolution and at least once a year thereafter, the United States should discuss with the other members of the Security Council of the United Nations the establishment of a United Nations peacekeeping force to assume the responsibilities of the Multinational Force in Lebanon. An analysis of the implications of the response to such discussions for the continuation of the Multinational Force in Lebanon shall be included in the reports required under paragraph (3) of section 4 of this resolution.

DURATION OF AUTHORIZATION FOR UNITED STATES PARTICIPATION IN THE MULTINATIONAL FORCE IN LEBANON

SEC. 6. The participation of United States Armed Forces in the Multinational Force in Lebanon shall be authorized for purposes of the War Powers Resolution until the end of the eighteen-month period beginning on the date of enactment of this resolution unless the Congress extends such authorization, except that such authorization shall terminate sooner upon the occurrence of any one of the following:

(1) the withdrawal of all foreign forces from Lebanon, unless the President determines and certifies to the Congress that continued United States Armed Forces participation in the Multinational Force in Lebanon is required after such withdrawal in order to accomplish the purposes specified in the September 25, 1982, exchange of letters providing for the establishment of the Multinational Force in Lebanon; or

(2) the assumption by the United Nations or the Government of Lebanon of the responsibilities of the Multinational Force in Lebanon; or

(3) the implementation of other effective security arrangements in the area; or

(4) the withdrawal of all other countries from participation in the Multinational Force in Lebanon.

INTERPRETATION OF THIS RESOLUTION

SEC. 7. (a) Nothing in this joint resolution shall preclude the President from withdrawing United States Armed Forces participation in the Multinational Force in Lebanon if circumstances warrant, and nothing in this joint resolution shall preclude the Congress by joint resolution from directing such a withdrawal.

(b) Nothing in this joint resolution modifies, limits or supersedes any provision of the War Powers Resolution or the requirement of section 4(a) of the Lebanon Emergency Assistance Act of 1983, relating to congressional authorization for any substantial expansion in the number or role of United States Armed Forces in Lebanon.

CONGRESSIONAL PRIORITY PROCEDURES FOR AMENDMENTS

SEC. 8. (a) Any joint resolution or bill introduced to amend or repeal this Act shall be referred to the Committee on Foreign Affairs of the House of Representatives or the Committee on Foreign Relations of the Senate, as the case may be. Such joint resolution or bill shall be considered by such committee within fifteen calendar days and may be reported out, together with its recommendations, unless such House shall otherwise determine pursuant to its rules.

(b) Any joint resolution or bill so reported shall become the pending business of the House in question (in the case of the Senate the time for debate shall be equally divided between the proponents and the opponents) and shall be voted on within three calendar days thereafter, unless such House shall otherwise determine by the yeas and nays.

(c) Such a joint resolution or bill passed by one House shall be referred to the committee of the other House named in subsection (a) and shall be reported out by such committee together with its recommendations within fifteen calendar days and shall thereupon become the pending business of such House and shall be voted upon within three calendar days, unless such House shall otherwise determine by the yeas and nays.

(d) In the case of any disagreement between the two Houses of Congress with respect to a joint resolution or bill passed by both Houses, conferees shall be promptly appointed and the committee of conference shall make and file a report with respect to such joint resolution within six calendar days after the legislation is referred to the committee of conference. Notwithstanding any rule in either House concerning the printing of conference reports in the Record or concerning any delay in the consideration of such reports, such report shall be acted on by both Houses not later than six calendar days after the conference report is filed. In the event the conferees are unable to agree within forty-eight hours, they shall report back to the respective Houses in disagreement.

APPROVED, October 12, 1983.

Authorization of the Use of U.S. Armed Forces Pursuant to U.N. Security Council Resolution 678 with Respect to Iraq

(P.L. 102-1, 105 Stat. 3, January 14, 1991 [H.J. Res. 77])

P.L. 102-1, 105 Stat. 3—*To authorize the use of United States Armed Forces pursuant to United Nations Security Council Resolution 678.*

Whereas the Government of Iraq without provocation invaded and occupied the territory of Kuwait on August 2, 1990;

Whereas both the House of Representatives (in H.J. Res. 658 of the 101st Congress) and the Senate (in S.Con. Res. 147of the 101st Congress) have condemned Iraq's invasion of Kuwait and declared their support for international action to reverse Iraq's aggression;

Whereas, Iraq's conventional, chemical, biological, and nuclear weapons and ballistic missile programs and its demonstrated willingness to use weapons of mass destruction pose a grave threat to world peace;

Whereas the international community has demanded that Iraq withdraw unconditionally and immediately from Kuwait and that Kuwait's independence and legitimate government be restored;

Whereas the United Nations Security Council repeatedly affirmed the inherent right of individual or collective self-defense in response to the armed attack by Iraq against Kuwait in accordance with Article 51 of the United Nations Charter;

Whereas, in the absence of full compliance by Iraq with its resolutions, the United Nations Security Council in Resolution 678 has authorized member states of the United Nations to use all necessary means after January 15, 1991, to uphold and implement all relevant Security Council resolutions and to restore international peace and security to the area; and

Whereas Iraq has persisted in its illegal occupation of, and brutal aggression against Kuwait: Now, therefore, be it

Resolved by the Senate and House of Representatives of the United States of America in Congress assembled,

SECTION 1. SHORT TITLE

This joint resolution may be cited as the "Authorization for Use of Military Force Against Iraq Resolution".

SEC. 2. AUTHORIZATION FOR USE OF UNITED STATES ARMED FORCES

(a) AUTHORIZATION.—The President is authorized, subject to subsection (b), to use United States Armed Forces pursuant to United Nations Security Council Resolution 678 (1990) in order to achieve implementation of Security Council Resolutions 660, 661, 662, 664, 665, 666, 667, 669, 670, 674, and 677.

(b) REQUIREMENT FOR DETERMINATION THAT USE OF MILITARY FORCE IS NECESSARY.—Before exercising the authority granted in subsection (a), the President shall make available to the Speaker of the House of Representatives and the President pro tempore of the Senate his determination that —

(1) the United States has used all appropriate diplomatic and other peaceful means to obtain compliance by Iraq with the United Nations Security Council resolution cited in subsection (a); and

(2) that those efforts have not been and would not be successful in obtaining such compliance.

(c) WAR POWERS RESOLUTION REQUIREMENTS. —

(1) SPECIFIC STATUTORY AUTHORIZATION.—Consistent with section 8(a)(1) of the War Powers Resolution, the Congress declares that this section is intended to constitute specific statutory authorization within the meaning of section 5(b) of the War Powers Resolution.

(2) APPLICABILITY OF OTHER REQUIREMENTS. —Nothing in this resolution supersedes any requirement of the War Powers Resolution.

SEC. 3. REPORTS TO CONGRESS.

At least once every 60 days, the President shall submit to the Congress a summary on the status of efforts to obtain compliance by Iraq with the resolutions adopted by the United Nations Security Council in response to Iraq's aggression.

APPROVED, January 14, 1991.

Authorization of the Use of U.S. Armed Forces Against Those Responsible for the Recent Attacks Launched Against the United States

(P.L. 107-40, 115 Stat. 224, September 18, 2001 [S. J. Res. 23])

To authorize the use of United States Armed Forces against those responsiblefor the recent attacks launched against the United States.

Whereas, on September 11, 2001, acts of treacherous violence were committed against the United States and its citizens, and

Whereas, such acts render it both necessary and appropriate that the United States exercise its rights to self-defense and to protect United States citizens both at home and abroad, and

Whereas, in light of the threat to the national security and foreign policy of the United States posed by these grave acts of violence, and

Whereas, such acts continue to pose an unusual and extraordinary threat to the national security and foreign policy of the United States,

Whereas the President has authority under the Constitution to take action to deter and prevent acts of international terrorism against the United States.

Resolved by the Senate and the House of Representatives of the United States of America in Congress assembled.

SECTION 1. SHORT TITLE

This joint resolution may be cited as the "Authorization for Use of Military Force"

SECTION 2. AUTHORIZATION FOR USE OF UNITED STATES ARMED FORCES

(a) That the President is authorized to use all necessary and appropriate force against those nations, organizations, or persons he determines planned, authorized, committed, or aided the terrorist attacks that occurred on September 11, 2001, or harbored such organizations or persons, in order to prevent any future acts of international terrorism against the United States by such nations, organizations or persons.

(b) War Powers Resolution Requirements

(1) SPECIFIC STATUTORY AUTHORIZATION—Consistent with section 8(a)(1) of the War Powers Resolution, the Congress declares that this section is intended to constitute specific statutory authorization within the meaning of section 5(b) of the War Powers Resolution.

(2) APPLICABILITY OF OTHER REQUIREMENTS—Nothing in this resolution supercedes any requirement of the War Powers Resolution.

APPROVED, September 18, 2001.

Authorization of the Use of Force Against Iraq Resolution of 2002

(P.L. 107-243, 116 Stat. 1498, October 16, 2002 [H.J. Res. 114])

To authorize the use of United States Armed Forces against Iraq.

Whereas in 1990 in response to Iraq's war of aggression against and illegal occupation of Kuwait, the United States forged a coalition of nations to liberate Kuwait and its people in order to defend the national security of the United States and enforce United Nations Security Council resolutions relating to Iraq;

Whereas after the liberation of Kuwait in 1991, Iraq entered into a United Nations sponsored cease-fire agreement pursuant to which Iraq unequivocally agreed, among other things, to eliminate its nuclear, biological, and chemical weapons programs and the means to deliver and develop them, and to end its support for international terrorism;

Whereas the efforts of international weapons inspectors, United States intelligence agencies, and Iraqi defectors led to the discovery that Iraq had large stockpiles of chemical weapons and a large scale biological weapons program, and that Iraq had an advanced nuclear weapons development program that was much closer to producing a nuclear weapon than intelligence reporting had previously indicated;

Whereas Iraq, in direct and flagrant violation of the cease-fire, attempted to thwart the efforts of weapons inspectors to identify and destroy Iraq's weapons of mass destruction stockpiles and development capabilities, which finally resulted in the withdrawal of inspectors from Iraq on October 31, 1998;

Whereas in Public Law 105-235 (August 14, 1998), Congress concluded that Iraq's continuing weapons of mass destruction programs threatened vital United States interests and international peace and security, declared Iraq to be in "material and unacceptable breach of its international obligations" and urged the President "to take appropriate action, in accordance with the Constitution and relevant laws of the United States, to bring Iraq into compliance with its international obligations";

Whereas Iraq both poses a continuing threat to the national security of the United States and international peace and security in the Persian Gulf region and remains in material and unacceptable breach of its international obligations by, among other things, continuing to possess and develop a significant chemical and biological weapons capability, actively seeking a nuclear weapons capability, and supporting and harboring terrorist organizations;

Whereas Iraq persists in violating resolution of the United Nations Security Council by continuing to engage in brutal repression of its civilian population thereby threatening international peace and security in the region, by refusing to release, repatriate, or account for non-Iraqi citizens wrongfully detained by Iraq, including an American serviceman, and by failing to return property wrongfully seized by Iraq from Kuwait;

Whereas the current Iraqi regime has demonstrated its capability and willingness to use weapons of mass destruction against other nations and its own people;

Whereas the current Iraqi regime has demonstrated its continuing hostility toward, and willingness to attack, the United States, including by attempting in 1993 to assassinate former President Bush and by firing on many thousands of occasions on United States and Coalition Armed Forces engaged in enforcing the resolutions of the United Nations Security Council;

Whereas members of al Qaida, an organization bearing responsibility for attacks on the United States, its citizens, and interests, including the attacks that occurred on September 11, 2001, are known to be in Iraq; Whereas Iraq continues to aid and harbor other international terrorist organizations, including organizations that threaten the lives and safety of United States citizens;

Whereas the attacks on the United States of September 11, 2001, underscored the gravity of the threat posed by the acquisition of weapons of mass destruction by international terrorist organizations;

Whereas Iraq's demonstrated capability and willingness to use weapons of mass destruction, the risk that the current Iraqi regime will either employ those weapons to launch a surprise attack against the United States or its Armed Forces or provide them to international terrorists who would do so, and the extreme magnitude of harm that would result to the United States and its citizens from such an attack, combine to justify action by the United States to defend itself;

Whereas United Nations Security Council Resolution 678 (1990) authorizes the use of all necessary means to enforce United Nations Security Council Resolution 660 (1990) and subsequent relevant resolutions and to compel Iraq to cease certain activities that threaten international peace and security, including the development of weapons of mass destruction and refusal or obstruction of United Nations weapons inspections in violation of United Nations Security Council Resolution 687 (1991), repression of its civilian population in violation of United Nations Security Council Resolution 688 (1991), and threatening its neighbors or United Nations operations in Iraq in violation of United Nations Security Council Resolution 949 (1994);

Whereas in the Authorization for Use of Military Force Against Iraq Resolution (Public Law 102-1), Congress has authorized the President "to use United States Armed Forces pursuant to United Nations Security Council Resolution 678 (1990) in order to achieve implementation of Security Council Resolution 660, 661, 662, 664, 665, 666, 667, 669, 670, 674, and 677";

Whereas in December 1991, Congress expressed its sense that it "supports the use of all necessary means to achieve the goals of United Nations Security Council Resolution 687 as being consistent with the Authorization of Use of Military Force Against Iraq Resolution (Public Law 102-1)," that Iraq's repression of its civilian population violates United Nations Security Council Resolution 688 and "constitutes a continuing threat to the peace, security, and stability of the Persian Gulf region," and that Congress, "supports the use of all necessary means to achieve the goals of United Nations Security Council Resolution 688";

Whereas the Iraq Liberation Act of 1998 (Public Law 105-338) expressed the sense of Congress that it should be the policy of the United States to support efforts to remove from power the current Iraqi regime and promote the emergence of a democratic government to replace that regime;

Whereas on September 12, 2002, President Bush committed the United States to "work with the United Nations Security Council to meet our common challenge" posed by Iraq and to "work for the necessary resolutions," while also making clear that "the Security Council resolutions will be enforced, and the just demands of peace and security will be met, or action will be unavoidable";

Whereas the United States is determined to prosecute the war on terrorism and Iraq's ongoing support for international terrorist groups combined with its development of weapons of mass destruction in direct violation of its obligations under the 1991 cease-fire and other United Nations Security Council resolutions make clear that it is in the national security interests of the United States and in furtherance of the war on terrorism that all relevant United Nations Security Council resolutions be enforced, including through the use of force if necessary;

Whereas Congress has taken steps to pursue vigorously the war on terrorism through the provision of authorities and funding requested by the President to take the necessary actions against international terrorists and terrorist organizations, including those nations, organizations, or persons who planned, authorized, committed, or aided the terrorist attacks that occurred on September 11, 2001, or harbored such persons or organizations;

Whereas the President and Congress are determined to continue to take all appropriate actions against international terrorists and terrorist organizations, including those nations, organizations, or persons who planned, authorized, committed, or aided the terrorist attacks that occurred on September 11, 2001, or harbored such persons or organizations;

Whereas the President has authority under the Constitution to take action in order to deter and prevent acts of international terrorism against the United States, as Congress recognized in the joint resolution on Authorization for Use of Military Force (Public Law 107-40); and

Whereas it is in the national security interests of the United States to restore international peace and security to the Persian Gulf region: Now, therefore, be it

Resolved by the Senate and House of Representatives of the United States of America in Congress assembled,

SECTION 1. SHORT TITLE

This joint resolution may be cited as the "Authorization for Use of Military Force Against Iraq Resolution of 2002."

SEC. 2. SUPPORT FOR UNITED STATES DIPLOMATIC EFFORTS

The Congress of the United States supports the efforts by the President to—

(1) strictly enforce through the United Nations Security Council all relevant Security Council resolutions regarding Iraq and encourages him in those efforts; and

(2) obtain prompt and decisive action by the Security Council to ensure that Iraq abandons its strategy of delay, evasion and noncompliance and promptly and strictly complies with all relevant Security Council resolutions regarding Iraq.

SEC. 3. AUTHORIZATION FOR USE OF UNITED STATES ARMED FORCES

(a) Authorization.—The President is authorized to use the Armed Forces of the United States as he determines to be necessary and appropriate in order to —

(1) defend the national security of the United States against the continuing threat posed by Iraq; and

(2) enforce all relevant United Nations Security Council resolutions regarding Iraq.

(b) Presidential Determination.—In connection with the exercise of the authority granted in subsection (a) to use force the President shall, prior to such exercise or as soon thereafter as may be feasible, but no later than 48 hours after exercising such authority, make available to the Speaker of the House of Representatives and the President pro tempore of the Senate his determination that —

(1) reliance by the United States on further diplomatic or other peaceful means alone either (A) will not adequately protect the national security of the United States against the continuing threat posed by Iraq or (B) is not likely to lead to enforcement of all relevant United Nations Security Council resolutions regarding Iraq; and

(2) acting pursuant to this joint resolution is consistent with the United States and other countries continuing to take the necessary actions against international terrorist and terrorist organizations, including those nations, organizations, or persons who planned, authorized, committed or aided the terrorist attacks that occurred on September 11, 2001.

(c) War Powers Resolution Requirements. —

(1) Specific statutory authorization.—Consistent with section 8(a)(1) of the War Powers Resolution, the Congress declares that this section

is intended to constitute specific statutory authorization within the meaning of section 5(b) of the War Powers Resolution.

(2) Applicability of other requirements.—Nothing in this joint resolution supersedes any requirement of the War Powers Resolution.

SEC. 4. REPORTS TO CONGRESS.

(a) Reports.—The President shall, at least once every 60 days, submit to the Congress a report on matters relevant to this joint resolution, including actions taken pursuant to the exercise of authority granted in section 3 and the status of planning for efforts that are expected to be required after such actions are completed, including those actions described in section 7 of the Iraq Liberation Act of 1998 (Public Law 105-338).

(b) Single Consolidated Report.—To the extent that the submission of any report described in subsection (a) coincides with the submission of any other report on matters relevant to this joint resolution otherwise required to be submitted to Congress pursuant to the reporting requirements of the War Powers Resolution (Public Law 93-148), all such reports may be submitted as a single consolidated report to the Congress.

(c) Rule of Construction.—To the extent that the information required by section 3 of the Authorization for Use of Military Force Against Iraq Resolution (Public Law 102-1) is included in the report required by this section, such report shall be considered as meeting the requirements of section 3 of such resolution.

APPROVED, October 16, 2002.

DOCUMENT NO. 2

THE WAR POWERS RESOLUTION: AFTER THIRTY-THREE YEARS

CRS Report
RL32267

May 1, 2007

Richard F. Grimmett
Specialist in National Defense
Foreign Affairs, Defense, and Trade Division

Summary

This report discusses and assesses the War Powers Resolution, its application since enactment in 1973, providing detailed background on a variety of cases where it was utilized, or issues of its applicability were raised. It will be revised biannually.

In the post-Cold War world, Presidents have continued to commit U.S. Armed Forces into potential hostilities, sometimes without a specific authorization from Congress. Thus the War Powers Resolution and its purposes continues to be a potential subject of controversy. On June 7, 1995 the House defeated, by a vote of 217-201, an amendment to repeal the central features of the War Powers Resolution that have been deemed unconstitutional by every President since the law's enactment in 1973. In 1999, after the President committed U.S. military forces to action in Yugoslavia without congressional authorization, Representative Tom Campbell used expedited procedures under the Resolution to force a debate and votes on U.S. military action in Yugoslavia, and later sought, unsuccessfully, through a federal court suit to enforce Presidential compliance with the terms of the War Powers Resolution.

The War Powers Resolution (P.L. 93-148) was passed over the veto of President Nixon on November 7, 1973, to provide procedures for Congress and the President to participate in decisions to send U.S. Armed Forces into hostilities. Section 4(a)(1) requires the President to report to Congress any introduction of U.S. forces into hostilities or imminent hostilities. When such a report is submitted, or is required to be submitted, section 5(b) requires that the use of forces must be terminated within 60 to 90 days unless Congress authorizes such use or extends the time period. Section 3 requires that the "President in every possible instance shall consult with Congress before introducing" U.S. Armed Forces into hostilities or imminent hostilities.

From 1975 through 2006, Presidents have submitted 121 reports as the result of the War Powers Resolution, but only one, the 1975 *Mayaguez* seizure, cited section 4(a)(1) which triggers the time limit, and in this case the military action was completed and U.S. armed forces had disengaged from the area of conflict when the report was made. The reports submitted by the President since enactment of the War Powers Resolution cover a range of military activities from embassy evacuations to full scale combat military operations, such as the Persian Gulf conflict, and the 2003 war with Iraq, the intervention in Kosovo and the anti-terrorism actions in Afghanistan. In some instances U.S. Armed Forces have been used in hostile situations without formal reports to Congress under the War Powers Resolution. On one occasion, Congress exercised its authority to determine that the requirements of section 4(a)(1) became operative on August 29, 1983, through passage of the Multinational Force in Lebanon Resolution (P.L. 98-119). In 1991 and 2002, Congress authorized, by law, the use of military force against Iraq. In several instances neither the President, Congress, nor the courts have been willing to trigger the War Powers Resolution mechanism.

Introduction

Under the Constitution, the war powers are divided between Congress and the President. Among other relevant grants, Congress has the power to declare war and raise and support the armed forces (Article I, section 8), while the President is Commander in Chief (Article II, section 2). It is generally agreed that the Commander in Chief role gives the President power to utilize the armed forces to repel attacks against the United States, but there has long been controversy over whether he is constitutionally authorized to send forces into hostile situations abroad without a declaration of war or other congressional authorization.

Congressional concern about Presidential use of armed forces without congressional authorization intensified after the Korean conflict. During the Vietnam war, Congress searched for a way to assert authority to decide when the United States should become involved in a war or the armed forces be utilized in circumstances that might lead to hostilities. On November 7, 1973, it passed the War Powers Resolution (P.L. 93-148) over the veto of President Nixon. The main purpose of the Resolution was to establish procedures for both branches to share in decisions that might get the United States involved in war. The drafters sought to circumscribe the President's authority to use armed forces abroad in hostilities or potential hostilities without a declaration of war or other congressional authorization, yet provide enough flexibility to permit him to respond to attack or other emergencies.

The record of the War Powers Resolution since its enactment has been mixed, and after 30 years it remains controversial. Some Members of Congress believe the Resolution has on some occasions served as a restraint on the use of armed forces by Presidents, provided a mode of communication, and given Congress a vehicle for asserting its war powers. Others have sought to amend the Resolution because they believe it has failed to assure a congressional voice in committing U.S. troops to potential conflicts abroad. Others in Congress, along with executive branch officials, contend that the President needs more flexibility in the conduct of foreign policy and that the time limitation in the War Powers Resolution is unconstitutional and impractical. Some have argued for its repeal.

This report examines the provisions of the War Powers Resolution, actual experience in its use from its enactment in 1973 through October 2001, and proposed amendments to it. Appendix A lists instances which Presidents have reported to Congress under the War Powers Resolution, and Appendix B lists representative instances of the use of U.S. armed forces that were not reported.

Provisions of the War Powers Resolution (P.L. 93-148)

Title

Section 1 establishes the title, "The War Powers Resolution." The law is frequently referred to as the "War Powers Act," the title of the measure passed by the Senate. Although the latter is not technically correct, it does serve to emphasize that the War Powers Resolution, embodied in a joint resolution which complies with constitutional requirements for lawmaking, is a law.

Purpose and Policy

Section 2 states the Resolution's purpose and policy, with Section 2(a) citing as the primary purpose to "insure that the collective judgment of both the Congress and the President will apply to the introduction of United States Armed Forces into hostilities, or into situations where imminent involvement in hostilities is clearly indicated by the circumstances, and to the continued use of such forces in hostilities or in such situations."

Section 2(b) points to the Necessary and Proper Clause of the Constitution as the basis for legislation on the war powers. It provides that "Under Article I, section 8, of the Constitution it is specifically provided that Congress shall have the power to make all laws necessary and proper for carrying into execution, not only its own powers but also all other powers vested by the Constitution in the Government of the United States. . . ."

Section 2(c) states the policy that the powers of the President as Commander in Chief to introduce U.S. armed forces into situations of hostilities or imminent hostilities "are exercised only pursuant to —

(1) a declaration of war,

(2) specific statutory authorization, or

(3) a national emergency created by attack upon the United States, its territories or possessions, or its armed forces."

Consultation Requirement

Section 3 of the War Powers Resolution requires the President "in every possible instance" to consult with Congress before introducing U.S. Armed Forces into situations of hostilities and imminent hostilities, and to continue consultations as long as the armed forces remain in such situations. The House report elaborated:

> A considerable amount of attention was given to the definition of **consultation.** Rejected was the notion that consultation should be synonymous with merely being informed. Rather, consultation in this provision means that a decision is pending on a problem and that Members of Congress are being asked by the President for their advice and opinions and, in appropriate circumstances, their approval of action contemplated. Furthermore, for consultation to be meaningful, the President himself must participate and all information relevant to the situation must be made available.[1]

The House version specifically called for consultation between the President and the leadership and appropriate committees. This was changed to less specific wording in conference, however, in order to provide more flexibility.

Reporting Requirements

Section 4 requires the President to report to Congress whenever he introduces U.S. armed forces abroad in certain situations. Of key importance is section 4(a)(1) because it triggers the time limit in section 5(b). Section 4(a)(1) requires reporting within 48 hours, in the absence of a declaration of war or congressional authorization, the introduction of U.S. armed forces "into hostilities or into situations where imminent involvement in hostilities is clearly indicated by the circumstances."

[1] U.S. Congress. H.Rept. 93-287, p. 6.

Some indication of the meaning of hostilities and imminent hostilities is given in the House report on its War Powers bill:

> The word **hostilities** was substituted for the phrase **armed conflict** during the subcommittee drafting process because it was considered to be somewhat broader in scope. In addition to a situation in which fighting actually has begun, **hostilities** also encompasses a state of confrontation in which no shots have been fired but where there is a clear and present danger of armed conflict. **"Imminent hostilities"** denotes a situation in which there is a clear potential either for such a state of confrontation or for actual armed conflict.[2]

Section 4(a)(2) requires the reporting of the introduction of troops "into the territory, airspace or waters of a foreign nation, while equipped for combat, except for deployments which relate solely to supply, replacement, repair, or training of such forces." According to the House report this was to cover

> the initial commitment of troops in situations in which there is no actual fighting but some risk, however small, of the forces being involved in hostilities. A report would be required any time combat military forces were sent to another nation to alter or preserve the existing political status quo or to make the U.S. presence felt. Thus, for example, the dispatch of Marines to Thailand in 1962 and the quarantine of Cuba in the same year would have required Presidential reports. Reports would not be required for routine port supply calls, emergency aid measures, normal training exercises, and other noncombat military activities.[3]

Section 4(a)(3) requires the reporting of the introduction of troops "in numbers which substantially enlarge United States Armed Forces equipped for combat already located in a foreign nation." The House report elaborated:

> While the word "substantially" designates a flexible criterion, it is possible to arrive at a common-sense understanding of the numbers involved. A 100% increase in numbers of Marine guards at an embassy—say from 5 to 10—clearly would not be an occasion for a report. A thousand additional men sent to Europe under present circumstances does not significantly enlarge the total U.S. troop strength of about 300,000 already there. However, the dispatch of 1,000 men to Guantanamo Bay, Cuba, which now has a complement of 4,000 would mean an increase of 25%, which is substantial. Under this circumstance, President Kennedy would have been required to report to Congress in 1962 when he raised the number of U.S. military advisers in Vietnam from 700 to 16,000.[4]

[2] U.S. Congress. H.Rept. 93-287, p. 7.
[3] U.S. Congress. H.Rept. 93-287, p. 7.
[4] U.S. Congress. H.Rept. 93-287, p. 8.

All of the reports under Section 4(a), which are to be submitted to the Speaker of the House and the President pro tempore of the Senate, are to set forth:

(A) the circumstances necessitating the introduction of United States Armed Forces;

(B) the constitutional and legislative authority under which such introduction took place; and

(C) the estimated scope and duration of the hostilities or involvement.

Section 4(b) requires the President to furnish such other information as Congress may request to fulfill its responsibilities relating to committing the nation to war.

Section 4(c) requires the President to report to Congress periodically, and at least every six months, whenever U.S. forces are introduced into hostilities or any other situation in section 4(a).

The objectives of these provisions, the conference report stated, was to "ensure that the Congress by right and as a matter of law will be provided with all the information it requires to carry out its constitutional responsibilities with respect to committing the Nation to war and to the use of United States Armed Forces abroad."[5]

Congressional Action

Section 5(a) deals with congressional procedures for receipt of a report under section 4(a)(1). It provides that if a report is transmitted during a congressional adjournment, the Speaker of the House and the President pro tempore of the Senate, when they deem it advisable or if petitioned by at least 30% of the Members of their respective Houses, shall jointly request the President to convene Congress in order to consider the report and take appropriate action.

Section 5(b) was intended to provide teeth for the War Powers Resolution. After a report "is submitted or is required to be submitted pursuant to section 4(a)(1), whichever is earlier", section 5(b) requires the President to terminate the use of U.S. Armed Forces after 60 days unless Congress (1) has declared war or authorized the action; (2) has extended the period by law; or (3) is physically unable to meet as a result of an armed attack on the United States. The 60 days can be extended for 30 days by the President if he certifies that "unavoidable military necessity respecting the safety of United States Armed Forces" requires their continued use in the course of bringing about their removal.

[5] U.S. Congress. H.Rept. 93–547, p. 8.

Section 5(c) requires the President to remove the forces at any time if Congress so directs by concurrent resolution; the effectiveness of this subsection is uncertain because of the 1983 Supreme Court decision on the legislative veto. It is discussed in Part II of this report.

Priority Procedures

Section 6 establishes expedited procedures for congressional consideration of a joint resolution or bill introduced to authorize the use of armed forces under section 5 (b). They provide for:

(a) A referral to the House Foreign Affairs [International Relations] or Senate Foreign Relations Committee, the committee to report one measure not later than 24 calendar days before the expiration of the 60 day period, unless the relevant House determines otherwise by a vote;

(b) The reported measure to become the pending business of the relevant House and be voted on within three calendar days, unless that House determines otherwise by vote; in the Senate the debate is to be equally divided between proponents and opponents;

(c) A measure passed by one House to be referred to the relevant committee of the other House and reported out not later than 14 calendar days before the expiration of the 60 day period, the reported bill to become the pending business of that House and be voted on within 3 calendar days unless determined otherwise by a vote;

(d) Conferees to file a report not later than four calendar days before the expiration of the 60 day period. If they cannot agree within 48 hours, the conferees are to report back in disagreement, and such report is to be acted on by both Houses not later than the expiration of the 60 day period.

Section 7 establishes similar priority procedures for a concurrent resolution to withdraw forces under section 5(c). For a recent use of these procedures see the section on the legislative veto, below.

Interpretive Provisions

Section 8 sets forth certain interpretations relating to the Resolution. Section 8(a) states that authority to introduce armed forces is not to be inferred from any provision of law or treaty unless it specifically authorizes the introduction of armed forces into hostilities or potential hostilities and states that it is "intended to constitute specific statutory authorization within the meaning of this joint resolution." This language was derived from a Senate measure and was intended to prevent a security treaty or military appropriations act from being used to authorize the introduction of troops. It was also aimed against using a broad resolution like the Tonkin Gulf Resolution[6] to justify hostilities abroad. This resolution had stated that the United States was prepared to take all necessary steps, including use of armed force, to assist certain nations, and it was cited by Presidents and many Members as congressional authorization for the Vietnam war.

> Section 8(b) states that further specific statutory authorization is not required
>
> to permit members of United States Armed Forces to participate jointly with members of the armed forces of one or more foreign countries in the headquarters operations of high-level military commands which were established prior to the date of enactment of this joint resolution and pursuant to the United Nations Charter or any treaty ratified by the United States prior to such date.

This section was added by the Senate to make clear that the resolution did not prevent U.S. forces from participating in certain joint military exercises with allied or friendly organizations or countries. The conference report stated that the "high-level" military commands meant the North Atlantic Treaty Organization, (NATO), the North American Air Defense Command (NORAD) and the United Nations command in Korea.

Section 8(c) defines the introduction of armed forces to include the assignment of armed forces to accompany regular or irregular military forces of other countries when engaged, or potentially engaged, in hostilities. The conference report on the War Powers Resolution explained that this was language modified from a Senate provision requiring specific statutory authorization for assigning members of the Armed Forces for such purposes. The report of the Senate Foreign Relations Committee on its bill said:

> The purpose of this provision is to prevent secret, unauthorized military support activities and to prevent a repetition of many of the most controversial and regrettable actions in Indochina. The ever deepening ground combat involvement of the United States in South Vietnam began with the assignment of U.S. "advisers" to accompany South Vietnamese units on combat patrols; and in Laos, secretly and without congressional authorization, U.S. "advisers" were deeply engaged in the war in northern Laos.[7]

Section 8(d) states that nothing in the Resolution is intended to alter the constitutional authority of either the Congress or the President. It also specifies that nothing is to be construed as granting any authority to introduce troops that would not exist in the absence of the Resolution. The House report said that this provision was to help insure the constitutionality of

[6] P.L. 88–408, approved August 10, 1964; repealed in 1971 by P.L. 91-672.
[7] U.S. Congress. S.Rept. 93-220, p. 24.

the Resolution by making it clear that nothing in it could be interpreted as changing the powers delegated by the Constitution.

Section 9 is a separability clause, stating that if any provision or its application is found invalid, the remainder of the Resolution is not to be affected.

Constitutional Questions Raised

From its inception, the War Powers Resolution was controversial because it operated on the national war powers, powers divided by the Constitution in no definitive fashion between the President and Congress. Congress adopted the resolution in response to the perception that Presidents had assumed more authority to send forces into hostilities than the framers of the Constitution had intended for the Commander-in-Chief. President Nixon in his veto message challenged the constitutionality of the essence of the War Powers Resolution, and particularly two provisions.[8] He argued that the legislative veto provision, permitting Congress to direct the withdrawal of troops by concurrent resolution, was unconstitutional. He also argued that the provision requiring withdrawal of troops after 60–90 days unless Congress passed legislation authorizing such use was unconstitutional because it checked Presidential powers without affirmative congressional action. Every President since the enactment of the War Powers Resolution has taken the position that it is an unconstitutional infringement on the President's authority as Commander-in-Chief.

War Powers of President and Congress

The heart of the challenge to the constitutionality of the War Powers Resolution rests on differing interpretations by the two branches of the respective war powers of the President and Congress. These differing interpretations, especially the assertions of Presidential authority to send forces into hostile situations without a declaration of war or other authorization by Congress, were the reason for the enactment of the Resolution.

The congressional view was that the framers of the Constitution gave Congress the power to declare war, meaning the ultimate decision whether or not to enter a war. Most Members of Congress agreed that the President as Commander in Chief had power to lead the U.S. forces once the decision to wage war had been made, to defend the nation against an attack, and perhaps in some instances to take other action such as rescuing American citizens. But, in this view, he did not have the power to commit armed forces to war. By the early 1970s, the congressional majority view was that the constitutional balance of war powers had swung too far toward the

[8] United States. President (Nixon). Message vetoing House Joint Resolution 542, A Joint Resolution Concerning the War Powers of Congress and the President. October 24, 1973. H.Doc. 93–171.

President and needed to be corrected. Opponents argued that Congress always held the power to forbid or terminate U.S. military action by statute or refusal of appropriations, and that without the clear will to act the War Powers Resolution would be ineffective.

In his veto message, President Nixon said the Resolution would impose restrictions upon the authority of the President which would be dangerous to the safety of the Nation and "attempt to take away, by a mere legislative act, authorities which the President has properly exercised under the Constitution for almost 200 years."

The War Powers Resolution in section 2(c) recognized the constitutional powers of the President as Commander-in-Chief to introduce forces into hostilities or imminent hostilities as "exercised only pursuant to (1) a declaration of war, (2) specific statutory authorization, or (3) a national emergency created by attack upon the United States, its territories or possessions, or its armed forces." The executive branch has contended that the President has much broader authority to use forces, including for such purposes as to rescue American citizens abroad, rescue foreign nationals where such action facilitates the rescue of U.S. citizens, protect U.S. Embassies and legations, suppress civil insurrection, implement the terms of an armistice or cease-fire involving the United States, and carry out the terms of security commitments contained in treaties.[9]

Legislative Veto

On June 23, 1983, the Supreme Court in *INS* v. *Chadha,* ruled unconstitutional the legislative veto provision in section 244(c)(2) of the Immigration and Nationality Act.[10] Although the case involved the use of a one-House legislative veto, the decision cast doubt on the validity of any legislative veto device that was not presented to the President for signature. The Court held that to accomplish what the House attempted to do in the *Chadha* case "requires action in conformity with the express procedures of the Constitution's prescription for legislative action: passage by a majority of both Houses and presentment to the President." On July 6, 1983, the Supreme Court affirmed a lower court's decision striking down a provision in another law[11] that permitted Congress to disapprove by concurrent (two-House) resolution.[12]

---

[9] U.S. Congress. House. Committee on International Relations. War Powers: A Test of Compliance relative to the Danang Sealift, the Evacuation of Phnom Penh, the Evacuation of Saigon, and the Mayaguez Incident. Hearings, May 7 and June 4, 1975. Washington, U.S. Govt. Printing Off., 1975. p. 69.

[10] 462 U.S. 919(1983).

[11] Federal Trade Commission Improvements Act of 1980.

[12] Process Gas Consumers Group v. Consumer Energy Council, 463 U.S. 1216 (1983).

Since section 5(c) requires forces to be removed by the President if Congress so directs by a concurrent resolution, it is constitutionally suspect under the reasoning applied by the Court.[13] A concurrent resolution is adopted by both chambers, but it does not require presentment to the President for signature or veto. Some legal analysts contend, nevertheless, that the War Powers Resolution is in a unique category which differs from statutes containing a legislative veto over delegated authorities.[14] Perhaps more important, some observers contend, if a majority of both Houses ever voted to withdraw U.S. forces, the President would be unlikely to continue the action for long, and Congress could withhold appropriations to finance further action. Because the War Powers Resolution contains a separability clause in section 9, most analysts take the view that the remainder of the joint resolution would not be affected even if section 5(c) were found unconstitutional.[15]

Congress has taken action to fill the gap left by the possible invalidity of the concurrent resolution mechanism for the withdrawal of troops. On October20, 1983, the Senate voted to amend the War Powers Resolution by substituting a joint resolution, which requires presentment to the President, for the concurrent resolution in section 5(c), and providing that it would be handled under the expedited procedures in section 7. The House and Senate conferees agreed not to amend the War Powers Resolution itself, but to adopt a free standing measure relating to the withdrawal of troops. The measure, which became law, provided that any joint resolution or bill to require the removal of U.S. armed forces engaged in hostilities outside the United States without a declaration of war or specific statutory authorization would be considered in accordance with the expedited procedures of section 601(b) of the International Security and Arms Export Control Act of 1976,[16] except that it would be amendable and debate on a veto limited to 20 hours.[17] The priority procedures embraced by this provision applied in the Senate only. Handling of such a joint resolution by the House was left to that Chamber's discretion.

---

13 Celada, Raymond. J. Effect of the Legislative Veto Decision on the Two-House Disapproval Mechanism to Terminate U.S. Involvement in Hostilities Pursuantto Unilateral Presidential Action. CRS Report, August 24, 1983.

14 Gressman, Prof. Eugene. In U.S. Congress. House. Committee on Foreign Affairs. The U.S. Supreme Court Decision Concerning the Legislative Veto. Hearings, July 19,20, and 21, 1983. 98th Congress, 1st sess. Washington, U.S. GPO, 1983, p. 155–157. Buchanan, G. Sidney. In Defense of the War Powers Resolution: Chadha Does Not Apply. Houston Law Review, Vol. 22, p. 1155; Ely, John Hart. Suppose Congress Wanted a War Powers Act that Worked. Columbia Law Review, Vol. 88, p. 1379 (see p. 1395–1398).

15 U.S. Congress. House. Committee on Foreign Affairs. U.S. Supreme Court Decision Concerning the Legislative Veto, Hearings, p. 52.

16 P.L. 94-329, signed June 30, 1976.

17 Senate amendment to S. 1324. Section 1013, State Department Authorization Act for FY1984, P.L. 98–164, approved November 22, 1983. Codified at 50 U.S.C., sect.1546a (1994).

House Members attempted to use section 5(c) to obtain a withdrawal of forces from Somalia. On October 22, 1993, Representative Benjamin Gilman introduced H.Con.Res. 170, pursuant to section 5(c) of the War Powers Resolution, directing the President to remove U.S. Armed Forces from Somalia by January 31, 1994. Using the expedited procedures called for in section 5(c), the Foreign Affairs Committee amended the date of withdrawal to March 31, 1994, (the date the President had already agreed to withdraw the forces), and the House adopted H.Con. Res. 170. The Foreign Affairs Committee reported:[18]

> Despite such genuine constitutionality questions, the committee acted in accordance with the expedited procedures in section 7. The committee action was premised on a determination that neither individual Members of Congress nor Committees of Congress should make unilateral judgments about the constitutionality of provisions of law.

Despite the use of the phrase "directs the President", the sponsor of the resolution and Speaker of the House Thomas Foley expressed the view that because of the *Chadha* decision, the resolution would be non-binding. The March 31, 1994, withdrawal date was later enacted as section 8151 of P.L. 103–139, signed November 11, 1993.

Automatic Withdrawal Provision

The automatic withdrawal provision has become perhaps the most controversial provision of the War Powers Resolution. Section 5(b) requires the President to withdraw U.S. forces from hostilities within 60-90 days after a report is submitted or required to be submitted under section 4(a)(1). The triggering of the time limit has been a major factor in the reluctance of Presidents to report, or Congress to insist upon a report, under section 4(a)(1).

Drafters of the War Powers Resolution included a time limit to provide some teeth for Congress, in the event a President assumed a power to act from provisions of resolutions, treaties, or the Constitution which did not constitute an explicit authorization. The Senate report called the time limit "the heart and core" of the bill that "represents, in an historic sense, a restoration of the constitutional balance which has been distorted by practice in our history and, climatically, in recent decades."[19] The House report emphasized that the Resolution did not grant the President any new authority or any freedom of action during the time limits that he did not already have.

---

[18] H.Rept. 103–329, November 5, 1993, p. 2. See below for further discussion of the Somalia case.

[19] The Senate bill had a time limit of 30 days. U.S. Congress. Senate. Committee on Foreign Relations. War Powers. Report to accompany S. 440. S.Rept. 93–220, 93d Congress, 1st Session. p. 28.

Administration officials have objected that the provision would require the withdrawal of U.S. forces simply because of congressional inaction during an arbitrary period. Since the resolution recognizes that the President has independent authority to use armed forces in certain circumstances, they state, "on what basis can Congress seek to terminate such independent authority by the mere passage of time?"[20] In addition, they argue, the imposition of a deadline interferes with successful action, signals a divided nation and lack of resolve, gives the enemy a basis for hoping that the President will be forced by domestic opponents to stop an action, and increases risk to U.S. forces in the field. The issue has not been dealt with by the courts.

Major Cases and Issues Prior to the Persian Gulf War

Perceptions of the War Powers Resolution tended to be set during the Cold War. During the 1970s the issues revolved largely around the adequacy of consultation. The 1980s raised more serious issues of Presidential compliance and congressional willingness to use the War Powers Resolution to restrain Presidential action. With regard to Lebanon in 1983, Congress itself invoked the War Powers Resolution, but in the 1987–1988 Persian Gulf tanker war Congress chose not to do so. Following is a summary of major U.S. military actions and the issues they raised relating to the War Powers Resolution from its enactment in 1973 to August 1990.[21]

Vietnam Evacuations and Mayaguez: What Is Consultation?

As the Vietnam war ended, on three occasions, in April 1975, President Ford used U.S. forces to help evacuate American citizens and foreign nationals. In addition, in May 1975 President Ford ordered the retaking of a U.S. merchant vessel, the *SS Mayaguez* which had been seized by Cambodian naval patrol vessels. All four actions were reported to Congress citing the War Powers Resolution. The report on the Mayaguez recapture was the only War Powers report to date to specifically cite section 4(a)(1), but the question of the time limit was moot because the action was over by the time the report was filed.

Among the problems revealed by these first four cases were differences of opinion between the two branches on the meaning of consultation.

[20] Sofaer, Abraham D. Prepared statement in: U.S. Congress. Senate. Committee on Foreign Relations. The War Power After 200 Years: Congress and the President at a Constitutional Impasse. Hearings before the Special Subcommittee on War Powers. July 13-September 29, 1988. S.Hrng. 100–1012. p. 1059.

[21] Appendix A lists in chronological order all reports to Congress related to the War Powers Resolution from the first in 1975 through 2003. Appendix B lists representative instances of the deployment to or use of armed forces in potentially hostile situations which were not reported under the Resolution. Appendix C gives the complete text of the War Powers Resolution.

The Ford Administration held that it had met the consultation requirement because the President had directed that congressional leaders be notified prior to the actual commencement of the introduction of armed forces. The prevailing congressional view was that consultation meant that the President seek congressional opinion, and take it into account, prior to making a decision to commit armed forces.[22]

Iran Hostage Rescue Attempt: Is Consultation Always Necessary and Possible?

After an unsuccessful attempt on April 24, 1980, to rescue American hostages being held in Iran, President Carter submitted a report to Congress to meet the requirements of the War Powers Resolution, but he did not consult in advance. The Administration took the position that consultation was not required because the mission was a rescue attempt, not an act of force or aggression against Iran. In addition, the Administration contended that consultation was not possible or required because the mission depended upon total surprise.

Some Members of Congress complained about the lack of consultation, especially because legislative-executive meetings had been going on since the Iranian crisis had begun the previous year. Just before the rescue attempt, the Senate Foreign Relations Committee had sent a letter to Secretary of State Cyrus Vance requesting formal consultations under the War Powers Resolution. Moreover, shortly before the rescue attempt, the President outlined plans for a rescue attempt to Senate Majority Leader Robert Byrd but did not say it had begun. Senate Foreign Relations Committee Chairman Frank Church stressed as guidelines for the future: (1) consultation required giving Congress an opportunity to participate in the decision making process, not just informing Congress that an operation was underway; and (2) the judgment could not be made unilaterally but should be made by the President and Congress.[23]

El Salvador: When Are Military Advisers in Imminent Hostilities?

One of the first cases to generate substantial controversy because it was never reported under the War Powers Resolution was the dispatch of U.S. military advisers to El Salvador. At the end of February 1981, the Department of State announced the dispatch of 20 additional military advisers to El Salvador to aid its government against guerilla warfare. There were

[22] U.S. Congress. House. Committee on International Relations. War Powers: A Test of Compliance Relative to the Danang Sealift, the Evacuation of Phnom Penh, the Evacuation of Saigon, and the Mayaguez Incident. Hearings, May 7 and June 4, 1975. Washington, U.S. Govt. Print. Off., 1975. P. 3.

[23] U.S. Congress. Senate. Committee on Foreign Relations. The situation in Iran. Hearing, 96th Congress, 2nd session. May 8, 1980. Washington, U.S. Govt. Print. Off., 1980. P. iii.

already 19 military advisers in El Salvador sent by the Carter Administration. The Reagan Administration said the insurgents were organized and armed by Soviet bloc countries, particularly Cuba. By March 14, the Administration had authorized a total of 54 advisers, including experts in combat training.

The President did not report the situation under the War Powers Resolution. A State Department memorandum said a report was not required because the U.S. personnel were not being introduced into hostilities or situations of imminent hostilities. The memorandum asserted that if a change in circumstances occurred that raised the prospect of imminent hostilities, the Resolution would be complied with. A justification for not reporting under section 4(a)(2) was that the military personnel being introduced were not equipped for combat.[24] They would, it was maintained, carry only personal sidearms which they were authorized to use only in their own defense or the defense of other Americans.

The State Department held that section 8(c) of the War Powers Resolution was not intended to require a report when U.S. military personnel might be involved in training foreign military personnel, if there were no imminent involvement of U.S. personnel in hostilities. In the case of El Salvador, the memorandum said, U.S. military personnel "will not act as combat advisors, and will not accompany Salvadoran forces in combat, on operational patrols, or in any other situation where combat is likely."

On May 1, 1981, eleven Members of Congress challenged the President's action by filing suit on grounds that he had violated the Constitution and the War Powers Resolution by sending the advisers to El Salvador. Eventually there were 29 co-plaintiffs, but by June 18, 1981, an equal number of Members (13 Senators and 16 Representatives) filed a motion to intervene in the suit, contending that a number of legislative measures were then pending before Congress and that Congress had ample opportunity to vote to end military assistance to El Salvador if it wished.

On October 4, 1982, U.S. District Court Judge Joyce Hens Green dismissed the suit. She ruled that Congress, not the court, must resolve the question of whether the U.S. forces in El Salvador were involved in a hostile or potentially hostile situation. While there might be situations in which a court could conclude that U.S. forces were involved in hostilities, she ruled, the "subtleties of fact-finding in this situation should be left to the political branches." She noted that Congress had taken no action to show it believed the President's decision was subject to the War Powers Resolution.[25] On November 18, 1983, a Federal circuit court affirmed the dismissal and on

[24] Congressional Record, March 5, 1981, V. 127, p. 3743.
[25] *Crockett v. Reagan*, 558 F. Supp. 893 (D.D.C. 1982).

June 8, 1984, the Supreme Court declined consideration of an appeal of that decision.[26]

As the involvement continued and casualties occurred among the U.S. military advisers, various legislative proposals relating to the War Powers Resolution and El Salvador were introduced. Some proposals required a specific authorization prior to the introduction of U.S. forces into hostilities or combat in El Salvador.[27] Other proposals declared that the commitment of U.S. Armed Forces in El Salvador necessitated compliance with section 4(a) of the War Powers Resolution, requiring the President to submit a report.[28]

Neither approach was adopted in legislation, but the Senate Foreign Relations Committee reported that the President had "a clear obligation under the War Powers Resolution to consult with Congress prior to any future decision to commit combat forces to El Salvador."[29] On July 26, 1983, the House rejected an amendment to the Defense Authorization bill (H.R. 2969) to limit the number of active duty military advisers in El Salvador to 55, unless the President reported any increase above that level under section 4(a)(1) of the War Powers Resolution.[30] Nevertheless, the Administration in practice kept the number of trainers at 55.

Honduras: When Are Military Exercises More than Training?

Military exercises in Honduras in 1983 and sub sequent years raised the question of when military exercises should be reported under the War Powers Resolution. Section 4(a)(2) requires the reporting of introduction of troops equipped for combat, but exempts deployments which relate solely to training.

On July 27, 1983, President Reagan announced "joint training exercises" planned for Central America and the Caribbean. The first contingent of U.S. troops landed in Honduras on August 8, 1983, and the series of ground and ocean exercises continued for several years, involving thousands of ground troops plus warships and fighter planes.

The President did not report the exercises under the War Powers Resolution. He characterized the maneuvers as routine and said the United States had been regularly conducting joint exercises with Latin American countries

---

[26] 720 F. 2d 1355 (D.C. Cir. 1983), cert. denied, 467 U.S. 1251 (1984).

[27] On March 8, 1982, Senator Robert Byrd introduced the War Powers Resolution Amendment of 1982 (S. 2179) specifically providing that U.S. armed forces shall not be introduced into El Salvador for combat unless (1) the Congress has declared war or specifically authorized such use; or (2) such introduction was necessary to meet a clear and present danger of attack on the United States or to provide immediate evacuation of U.S. citizens. Similar bills were introduced in the House, e.g. H.R. 1619 and H.R. 1777 in the 98th Congress.

[28] H.Con. Res. 87, 97th Congress.

[29] Report on S.J. Res. 158, Sec. III, S.Rept. 97–470, June 9, 1982.

[30] *Congressional Record*, House, July 26, 1983, pp. 20924–20925.

since 1965. Some Members of Congress, on the other hand, contended that the exercises were part of a policy to support the rebels or "contras" fighting the Sandinista Government of Nicaragua, threatening that government, and increased the possibility of U.S. military involvement in hostilities in Central America.

Several Members of Congress called for reporting the actions under the War Powers Resolution, but some sought other vehicles for congressional control. In 1982, the Boland amendment to the Defense Appropriations Act had already prohibited use of funds to overthrow the Government of Nicaragua or provoke a military exchange between Nicaragua or Honduras.[31] Variations of this amendment followed in subsequent years. After press reports in 1985 that the option of invading Nicaragua was being discussed, the Defense Authorization Act for Fiscal Year 1986 stated the sense of Congress that U.S. armed forces should not be introduced into or over Nicaragua for combat.[32] In 1986, after U.S. helicopters ferried Honduran troops to the Nicaraguan border area, Congress prohibited U.S. personnel from participating in assistance within land areas of Honduras and Costa Rica within 120 miles of the Nicaraguan border, or from entering Nicaragua to provide military advice or support to paramilitary groups operating in that country.[33] Gradually the issue died with peace agreements in the region and the electoral defeat of the Sandinista regime in Nicaragua in 1990.

Lebanon: How Can Congress Invoke the War Powers Resolution?

The War Powers Resolution faced a major test when Marines sent to participate in a Multinational Force in Lebanon in 1982 became the targets of hostile fire in August 1983. During this period President Reagan filed three reports under the War Powers Resolution, but he did not report under section 4(a)(1) that the forces were being introduced into hostilities or imminent hostilities, thus triggering the 60-90 day time limit.

On September 29, 1983, Congress passed the Multinational Force in Lebanon Resolution determining that the requirements of section 4(a)(1) of the War Powers Resolution became operative on August 29, 1983.[34] In the same resolution, Congress authorized the continued participation of the Marines in the Multinational Force for 18 months. The resolution was a compromise between Congress and the President. Congress obtained the President's

---

[31] The initial statutory restriction was contained in the Continuing Appropriations Resolution for 1983, P.L. 97–377. This was followed by a $24 million ceiling on intelligence agency support in FY1984.

[32] Sec. 1451 of P.L.99–145, approved November 8, 1985. A similar provision was contained in the defense authorization for 1988–1989, sec.1405 of P.L.100–180, approved December 4, 1987.

[33] Continuing Appropriations Resolution, P. L. 99–591, approved October 30, 1986. Continued in P.L. 100–202, approved December 22, 1987.

[34] P.L. 98–119, approved October 12, 1983.

signature on legislation invoking the War Powers Resolution for the first time, but the price for this concession was a congressional authorization for the U.S. troops to remain in Lebanon for 18 months.

The events began on July 6, 1982, when President Reagan announced he would send a small contingent of U.S. troops to a multinational force for temporary peacekeeping in Lebanon. Chairman of the House Foreign Affairs Committee Clement Zablocki wrote President Reagan that if such a force were sent, the United States would be introducing forces into imminent hostilities and a report under section 4(a)(1) would be required. When the forces began to land on August 25, President Reagan reported but did not cite section 4(a)(1) and said the agreement with Lebanon ruled out any combat responsibilities. After overseeing the departure of the Palestine Liberation Organization force, the Marines in the first Multinational Force left Lebanon on September 10, 1982.

The second dispatch of Marines to Lebanon began on September 20, 1982. President Reagan announced that the United States, France, and Italy had agreed to form a new multinational force to return to Lebanon for a limited period of time to help maintain order until the lawful authorities in Lebanon could discharge those duties. The action followed three events that took place after the withdrawal of the first group of Marines: the assassination of Lebanon President-elect Bashir Gemayel, the entry of Israeli forces into West Beirut, and the massacre of Palestinian civilians by Lebanese Christian militiamen.

On September 29, 1982, President Reagan submitted a report that 1,200 Marines had begun to arrive in Beirut, but again he did not cite section 4(a)(1), saying instead that the American force would not engage in combat. As a result of incidents in which Marines were killed or wounded, there was again controversy in Congress on whether the President's report should have been filed under section 4(a)(1). In mid-1983 Congress passed the Lebanon Emergency Assistance Act of 1983 requiring statutory authorization for any substantial expansion in the number or role of U.S. Armed Forces in Lebanon. It also included Section 4(b) that stated:

> Nothing in this section is intended to modify, limit, or suspend any of the standards and procedures prescribed by the War Powers Resolution of 1983.[35]

President Reagan reported on the Lebanon situation for the third time on August 30, 1983, still not citing section 4(a)(1), after fighting broke out between various factions in Lebanon and two Marines were killed.

---

[35] P.L. 98–43, approved June 27, 1983.

The level of fighting heightened, and as the Marine casualties increased and the action enlarged, there were more calls in Congress for invocation of the War Powers Resolution. Several Members of Congress said the situation had changed since the President's first report and introduced legislation that took various approaches. Senator Charles Mathias introduced S. J. Res. 159 stating that the time limit specified in the War Powers Resolution had begun on August 31, 1983, and authorizing the forces to remain in Lebanon for a period of 120 days after the expiration of the 60-day period. Representative Thomas Downey introduced H.J.Res. 348 directing the President to report under section 4(a)(1) of the War Powers Resolution. Senator Robert Byrd introduced S.J. Res. 163 finding that section 4(a)(1) of the war powers resolution applied to the present circumstances in Lebanon. The House Appropriations Committee approved an amendment to the continuing resolution for FY1984 (H.J. Res. 367), sponsored by Representative Clarence Long, providing that after 60 days, funds could not be "obligated or expended for peacekeeping activities in Lebanon by United States Armed Forces," unless the President had submitted a report under section 4(a)(1) of the War Powers Resolution. A similar amendment was later rejected by the full body, but it reminded the Administration of possible congressional actions.

On September 20, congressional leaders and President Reagan agreed on a compromise resolution invoking section 4(a)(1) and authorizing the Marines to remain for 18 months. The resolution became the first legislation to be handled under the expedited procedures of the War Powers Resolution. On September 28, the House passed H.J.Res. 364 by a vote of 270 to 161. After three days of debate, on September 29, the Senate passed S.J.Res. 159 by a vote of 54 to 46. The House accepted the Senate bill by a vote of 253 to 156. As passed, the resolution contained four occurrences that would terminate the authorization before eighteen months: (1) the withdrawal of all foreign forces from Lebanon, unless the President certified continued U.S. participation was required to accomplish specified purposes; (2) the assumption by the United Nations or the Government of Lebanon of the responsibilities of the Multinational Force; (3) the implementation of other effective security arrangements; or (4) the withdrawal of all other countries from participation in the Multinational Force.[36]

Shortly afterward, on October 23, 1983, 241 U.S. Marines in Lebanon were killed by a suicide truck bombing, bringing new questions in Congress and U.S. public opinion about U.S. participation. On February 7, 1984, President Reagan announced the Marines would be redeployed and on, March 30, 1984, reported to Congress that U.S. participation in the Multinational Force in Lebanon had ended.

[36] P.L. 98–119, signed October 12, 1983.

Grenada: Do the Expedited Procedures Work?

On October 25, 1983, President Reagan reported to Congress "consistent with" the War Powers Resolution that he had ordered a landing of approximately 1900 U.S. Army and Marine Corps personnel in Grenada. He said that the action was in response to a request from the Organization of Eastern Caribbean States which had formed a collective security force to restore order in Grenada, where anarchic conditions had developed, and to protect the lives of U.S. citizens.

Many Members of Congress contended that the President should have cited section 4(a)(1) of the War Powers Resolution, which would have triggered the 60–90 day time limitation. On November 1, 1983, the House supported this interpretation when it adopted, by a vote of 403–23, H.J Res. 402 declaring that the requirements of section 4(a)(1) had become operative on October 25. The Senate did not act on this measure and a conference was not held. The Senate had adopted a similar measure on October 28 by a vote of 64 to 20, but on November 17 the provision was deleted in the conference report on the debt limit bill to which it was attached.[37] Thus both Houses had voted to invoke section 4(a)(1), but the legislation was not completed.

On November 17, White House spokesman Larry Speakes said the Administration had indicated that there was no need for action as the combat troops would be out within the 60-90 day time period. Speaker Thomas O'Neill took the position that, whether or not Congress passed specific legislation, the War Powers Resolution had become operative on October 25. By December 15, 1983, all U.S. combat troops had been removed from Grenada.

Eleven Members of Congress filed a suit challenging the constitutionality of President Reagan's invasion of Grenada. A district judge held that courts should not decide such cases unless the entire Congress used the institutional remedies available to it.[38] An appellate court subsequently held that the issue was moot because the invasion had been ended.[39]

Libya: Should Congress Help Decide on Raids to Undertake in Response to International Terrorism?

The use of U.S. forces against Libya in 1986 focused attention on the application of the War Powers Resolution to use of military force against international terrorism.

---

[37] U.S. Congress. H.Rept. 98–566 on H.J.Res. 308; Senate amendment numbered 3. Congressional Record November 17, 1983, p. H10189.

[38] *Conyers v. Reagan*, 578 F. Supp. 323 (D.D.C. 1984).

[39] *Conyers v. Reagan*, 765 F.2d 1124 (D.C. Cir. 1985).

Tensions between the United States and Libya under the leadership of Col. Muammar Qadhafi had been mounting for several years, particularly after terrorist incidents at the Rome and Vienna airports on December 27, 1985. On January 7, 1986, President Reagan said that the Rome and Vienna incidents were the latest in a series of brutal terrorist acts committed with Qadhafi's backing that constituted armed aggression against the United States.

The War Powers issue was first raised on March 24, 1986, when Libyan forces fired missiles at U.S. aircraft operating in the Gulf of Sidra. In response, the United States fired missiles at Libyan vessels and at Sirte, the Libyan missile site involved. The U.S. presence in the Gulf of Sidra, an area claimed by Libya, was justified as an exercise to maintain freedom of the seas, but it was widely considered a response to terrorist activities.

Subsequently, on April 5, 1986, a terrorist bombing of a discotheque in West Berlin occurred and an American soldier was killed. On April 14 President Reagan announced there was irrefutable evidence that Libya had been responsible, and U.S. Air Force planes had conducted bombing strikes on headquarters, terrorist facilities, and military installations in Libya in response.

The President reported both cases to Congress although the report on the bombing did not cite section 4(a)(1) and the Gulf of Sidra report did not mention the War Powers Resolution at all. Since the actions were short lived, there was no issue of force withdrawal, but several Members introduced bills to amend the War Powers Resolution. One bill called for improving consultation by establishing a special consultative group in Congress.[40] Others called for strengthening the President's hand in combating terrorism by authorizing the President, notwithstanding any other provision of law, to use all measures he deems necessary to protect U.S. persons against terrorist threats.[41]

Persian Gulf, 1987: When Are Hostilities Imminent?

The War Powers Resolution became an issue in activities in the Persian Gulf after an Iraqi aircraft fired a missile on the *USS Stark* on May 17, 1987, killing 37 U.S. sailors. The attack broached the question of whether the Iran-Iraq war had made the Persian Gulf an area of hostilities or imminent hostilities for U.S. forces. Shortly afterwards, the U.S. adoption of a policy of reflagging and providing a naval escort of Kuwaiti oil tankers through the Persian Gulf raised full force the question of whether U.S. policy was

[40] S.J.Res. 340, introduced May 8, 1986. The bill was not acted upon, but the proposal was later incorporated in other proposed amendments. See below, section on amendments.

[41] S. 2335 and H.R. 4611, Anti-Terrorism Act of 1986, introduced April 17, 1986. Not acted upon.

risking involvement in war without congressional authorization. During 1987 U.S. Naval forces operating in the Gulf increased to 11 major warships, 6 minesweepers, and over a dozen small patrol boats, and a battleship-led formation was sent to the Northern Arabian Sea and Indian Ocean to augment an aircraft carrier battle group already there.

For several months the President did not report any of the deployments or military incidents under the War Powers Resolution, although on May 20, 1987, after the *Stark* incident, Secretary of State Shultz submitted a report similar to previous ones consistent with War Powers provisions, but not mentioning the Resolution. No reports were submitted after the *USS Bridgeton* struck a mine on July 24, 1987, or the U.S.-chartered *Texaco-Caribbean* struck a mine on August 10 and a U.S. F-14 fighter plane fired two missiles at an Iranian aircraft perceived as threatening.

Later, however, after various military incidents on September 23, 1987, and growing congressional concern, the President began submitting reports "consistent with" the War Powers Resolution and on July 13, 1988, submitted the sixth report relating to the Persian Gulf.[42] None of the reports were submitted under section 4(a)(1) or acknowledged that U.S. forces had been introduced into hostilities or imminent hostilities. The Reagan administration contended that the military incidents in the Persian Gulf, or isolated incidents involving defensive reactions, did not add up to hostilities or imminent hostilities as envisaged in the War Powers Resolution. It held that "imminent danger" pay which was announced for military personnel in the Persian Gulf on August 27, 1987, did not trigger section 4 (a)(1). Standards for danger pay, namely, "subject to the threat of physical harm or danger on the basis of civil insurrection, civil war, terrorism, or wartime conditions," were broader than for hostilities of the War Powers Resolution, and had been drafted to be available in situations to which the War Powers Resolution did not apply.[43]

Some Members of Congress contended that if the President did not report under section 4(a)(1), Congress itself should declare such a report should have been submitted, as it had in the Multinational Force in Lebanon Resolution. Several resolutions to this effect were introduced, some authorizing the forces to remain, but none were passed.[44] The decisive votes on the subject took place in the Senate. On September 18, 1987, the Senate voted 50-41 to table an amendment to the Defense authorization bill (S. 1174) to apply the provisions of the War Powers Resolution. The Senate also sustained points of order against consideration of S.J.Res. 217, which would

[42] For the reports, see list above under section on reporting requirements.
[43] Questions submitted to Department of State and responses thereto, March 30, 1988, in War Powers Resolution, Relevant Documents, Correspondence, Reports, p. 97–99.
[44] Bills to this effect in the House included H.J.Res. 387, introduced October 22, 1987, which also authorized the continued presence of U.S. forces in the Gulf.

have invoked the War Powers Resolution, on December 4, 1987, and a similar bill the following year, S.J.Res. 305, on June 6, 1988.

The Senate opted for a different approach, which was to use legislation to assure a congressional role in the Persian Gulf policy without invoking the War Powers Resolution. Early in the situation, both Chambers passed measures requiring the Secretary of Defense to submit a report to Congress prior to the implementation of any agreement between the United States and Kuwait for U.S. military protection of Kuwaiti shipping, and such a report was submitted June 15, 1987. Later, the Senate passed a measure that called for a comprehensive report by the President within 30 days and provided expedited procedures for a joint resolution on the subject after an additional 30 days.[45] The House did not take action on the bill.

As in the case of El Salvador, some Members took the War Powers issue to court. On August 7, 1987, Representative Lowry and 110 other Members of Congress filed suit in the U.S. District Court for the District of Columbia, asking the court to declare that a report was required under section 4(a)(1). On December 18, 1987, the court dismissed the suit, holding it was a nonjusticiable political question, and that the plaintiffs' dispute was "primarily with fellow legislators."[46]

Compliance with the consultation requirement was also an issue. The Administration developed its plan for reflagging and offered it to Kuwait on March 7, 1987, prior to discussing the plan with Members of Congress. A June 15, 1987, report to Congress by the Secretary of Defense stated on the reflagging policy, "As soon as Kuwait indicated its acceptance of our offer, we began consultations with Congress which are still ongoing."[47] This was too late for congressional views to be weighed in on the initial decision, after which it became more difficult to alter the policy. Subsequently, however, considerable consultation developed and the President met with various congressional leaders prior to some actions such as the retaliatory actions in April 1988 against an Iranian oil platform involved in mine-laying.

With recurring military incidents, some Members of Congress took the position that the War Powers Resolution was not being complied with, unless the President reported under section 4(a)(1) or Congress itself voted to invoke the Resolution. Other Members contended the Resolution was working by serving as a restraint on the President, who was now submitting

[45] Byrd-Warner amendment to S.J.Res. 194, adopted by Senate October 21, 1987.

[46] Lowry v. Reagan, 676 F. Supp. 333 (D.D.C. 1987). See also CRS Report RL30352, *War Powers Litigation Since the Enactment of the War Powers Resolution,* by David M. Ackerman.

[47] Weinberger, Caspar W. Secretary of Defense. A Report to the Congress on Security Arrangements in the Persian Gulf. June 15, 1987, p. 14.

reports and consulting with Congress.[48] Still other Members suggested the Persian Gulf situation was demonstrating the need to amend the War Powers Resolution.

As a result of the Persian Gulf situation, in the summer of 1988 both the House Foreign Affairs Committee and the Senate Foreign Relations Committee, which established a Special Subcommittee on War Powers, undertook extensive assessments of the War Powers Resolution. Interest in the issue waned after a ceasefire between Iran and Iraq began on August 20, 1988, and the United States reduced its forces in the Persian Gulf area.

Invasion of Panama: Why Was the War Powers Issue Not Raised?

On December 20, 1989, President Bush ordered 14,000 U.S. military forces to Panama for combat, in addition to 13,000 already present. On December 21, he reported to Congress under the War Powers Resolution but without citing section 4(a)(1). His stated objectives were to protect the 35,000 American citizens in Panama, restore the democratic process, preserve the integrity of the Panama Canal treaties, and apprehend General Manuel Noriega, who had been accused of massive electoral fraud in the Panamanian elections and indicted on drug trafficking charges by two U.S. Federal courts. The operation proceeded swiftly and General Noriega surrendered to U.S. military authorities on January 3. President Bush said the objectives had been met, and U.S. forces were gradually withdrawn. By February 13, all combat forces deployed for the invasion had been withdrawn, leaving the strength just under the 13,597 forces stationed in Panama prior to the invasion.

The President did not consult with congressional leaders before his decision, although he did notify them a few hours in advance of the invasion. Members of Congress had been discussing the problem of General Noriega for some time. Before Congress adjourned, it had called for the President to intensify unilateral, bilateral, and multilateral measures and consult with other nations on ways to coordinate efforts to remove General Noriega from power.[49] The Senate had adopted an amendment supporting the President's use of appropriate diplomatic, economic, and military options "to restore constitutional government to Panama and to remove General Noriega from his illegal control of the Republic of Panama", but had defeated an amendment authorizing the President to use U.S. military

[48] When asked about abiding by the War Powers Resolution, President Reagan said "we are complying with a part of that act, although we do not call it that. But we have been consulting the Congress, reporting to them and telling them what we're doing, and in advance . . ." Press conference of October 22, 1987. *The New York Times*, October 23, 1987, p. A8.

[49] P.L. 101–162, signed November 21, 1989.

force to secure the removal of General Noriega "notwithstanding any other provision of law."[50]

The Panama action did not raise much discussion in Congress about the War Powers Resolution. This was in part because Congress was out of session. The first session of the 101st Congress had ended on November 22, 1989, and the second session did not begin until January 23, 1990, when the operation was essentially over and it appeared likely the additional combat forces would be out of Panama within 60 days of their deployment. Moreover, the President's action in Panama was very popular in American public opinion and supported by most Members of Congress because of the actions of General Noriega. After it was over, on February 7, 1990, the House Passed H.Con.Res. 262 which stated that the President had acted "decisively and appropriately in ordering United States forces to intervene in Panama."

Major Cases and Issues in the Post-Cold War World: United Nations Actions

After the end of the Cold War in 1990, the United States began to move away from unilateral military actions toward actions authorized or supported by the United Nations. Under the auspices of U.N. Security Council resolutions, U.S. forces were deployed in Kuwait and Iraq, Somalia, former Yugoslavia/Bosnia, and Haiti. This raised the new issue of whether the War Powers Resolution applied to U.S. participation in U.N. military actions. It was not a problem during the Cold War because the agreement among the five permanent members required for Security Council actions seldom existed. An exception, the Korean war, occurred before the War Powers Resolution was enacted.[51]

The more basic issue—under what circumstances congressional authorization is required for U.S. participation in U.N. military operations—is an unfinished debate remaining from 1945. Whether congressional authorization is required depends on the types of U.N. action and is governed by the U.N. Participation Act (P.L. 79-264, as amended), as well as by the War Powers Resolution and war powers under the Constitution. Appropriations action by Congress also may be determinative as a practical matter.

[50] Amendments to National Drug Control Strategy bill, S. 1711, October 5, 1989.

[51] In that case, the Soviet Union had absented itself from the Council temporarily, and the Security Council requested members to supply the Republic of Korea with sufficient military assistance to repel the invasion of North Korea. President Truman ordered U.S. air, naval, and ground forces to Korea to repel the attack without authorization from Congress. Senator Robert Taft complained on January 5, 1951, "The President simply usurped authority in violation of the laws and the Constitution, when he sent troops to Korea to carry out the resolution of the United Nations in an undeclared war."

For armed actions under Articles 42 and 43 of the United Nations Charter, Section 6 of the U.N. Participation Act authorizes the President to negotiate special agreements with the Security Council *"which shall be subject to the approval of the Congress by appropriate Act or joint resolution"*, providing for the numbers and types of armed forces and facilities to be made available to the Security Council. Once the agreements have been concluded, further congressional authorization is not necessary, but no such agreements have been concluded.

Section 7 of the United Nations Participation Act, added in 1949 by P.L. 81-341, authorizes the detail of up to 1,000 personnel to serve in any non-combatant capacity for certain U.N. peaceful settlement activities. The United States has provided personnel to several U.N. peacekeeping missions, such as observers to the U.N. Truce Supervision Organization in Palestine since 1948, that appear to fall within the authorization in Section 7 of the Participation Act. Controversy has arisen when larger numbers of forces have been deployed or when it appears the forces might be serving as combatants.

The War Powers Resolution neither excludes United Nations actions from its provisions nor makes any special procedures for them. Section 8(a)(2) states that authority to introduce U.S. Armed Forces into hostilities shall not be inferred from any treaty unless it is implemented by legislation specifically authorizing the introduction and stating that it is intended to constitute specific statutory authorization within the meaning of the War Powers resolution.[52] One purpose of this provision was to ensure that both Houses of Congress be affirmatively involved in any U.S. decision to engage in hostilities pursuant to a treaty, since only the Senate approved a treaty.[53]

From 1990 through 1999, Congress primarily dealt with the issue on a case by case basis, but Members also enacted some measures seeking more control over U.S. participation in future peacekeeping actions wherever they might occur. The Defense Appropriations Act for FY1994 stated the sense of Congress that funds should not be expended for U.S. Armed Forces serving under U.N. Security Council actions unless the President consults with Congress at least 15 days prior to deployment and not later than 48 hours after such deployment, except for humanitarian operations.[54]

[52] Such a statement was made in the Authorization for Use of Military Force against Iraq Resolution, P.L. 102–1, signed January 14, 1991, and in S.J.Res. 45, authorizing the use of force in Somalia for one year, as passed by the Senate on February 4, 1993, and amended by the House on May 25, 1993; a conference was not held.

[53] U.S. Congress. Senate. Committee on Foreign Relations. War Powers; report to accompany S. 440. June 14, 1973. S.Rept. 93–220.

[54] Sec.8153, Department of Defense Appropriation Act for FY1994, H.R. 3116, P.L. 103–139, signed November 11, 1993.

The Defense Authorization Act for FY1994 required a report to Congress by April 1, 1994, including discussion of the requirement of congressional approval for participation of U.S. Armed Forces in multinational peacekeeping missions, proposals to conclude military agreements with the U.N. Security Council under Article 43 of the U.N. Charter, and the applicability of the War Powers Resolution and the U.N. Participation Act.[55] In 1994 and 1995, Congress attempted to gain a greater role in U.N. and other peacekeeping operations through authorization and appropriation legislation. A major element of the House Republicans' Contract with America, H.R. 7, would have placed notable constraints on Presidential authority to commit U.S. forces to international peacekeeping operations. Senator Dole's, S. 5, The Peace Powers Act, introduced in January 1995, would have also placed greater legislative controls on such operations. General and specific funding restrictions and Presidential reporting requirements were passed for peacekeeping operations underway or in prospect. Some of these legislative enactments led to Presidential vetoes. These representative legislative actions are reviewed below as they apply to given cases.[56]

Persian Gulf War, 1991: How Does the War Powers Resolution Relate to the United Nations and a Real War?

On August 2, 1990, Iraqi troops under the direction of President Saddam Hussein invaded Kuwait, seized its oil fields, installed a new government in Kuwait City, and moved on toward the border with Saudi Arabia. Action to repel the invasion led to the largest war in which the United States has been involved since the passage of the War Powers Resolution. Throughout the effort to repel the Iraqi invasion, President Bush worked in tandem with the United Nations, organizing and obtaining international support and authorization for multilateral military action against Iraq.

A week after the invasion, on August 9, President Bush reported to Congress "consistent with the War Powers Resolution" that he had deployed U.S. armed forces to the region prepared to take action with others to deter Iraqi aggression. He did not cite section 4(a)(1) and specifically stated, "I do not believe involvement in hostilities is imminent."

The President did not consult with congressional leaders prior to the deployment, but both houses of Congress had adopted legislation supporting efforts to end the Iraqi occupation of Kuwait, particularly using economic sanctions and multilateral efforts. On August 2, shortly before its recess, the Senate by a vote of 97-0 adopted S.Res. 318 urging the President "to act immediately, using unilateral and multilateral measures, to seek the

[55] Sec. 1502 (11), Defense Authorization Act for FY1994, P.L. 103–160, signed November 30, 1993.

[56] For background see CRS Report RL33557, *Peacekeeping and Related Stability Operations: Issues of U.S. Military Involvement*, by Nina M. Serafino.

full and unconditional withdrawal of all Iraqi forces from Kuwaiti territory" and to work for collective international sanctions against Iraq including, if economic sanctions prove inadequate, "additional multilateral actions, under Article 42 of the United Nations Charter, involving air, sea, and land forces as may be needed . . ." Senate Foreign Relations Committee Chairman Pell stressed, however, that the measure did not authorize unilateral U.S. military actions. Also on August 2, the House passed H.R. 5431 condemning the Iraqi invasion and calling for an economic embargo against Iraq.

The United Nations imposed economic sanctions against Iraq on August 7, and the United States and United Kingdom organized an international naval interdiction effort.[57] Later, on August 25, the U.N. Security Council authorized "such measures as may be necessary" to halt shipping and verify cargoes that might be going to Iraq.

Both Houses adopted measures supporting the deployment, but neither measure was enacted. On October 1, 1990, the House passed H.J.Res. 658 supporting the action and citing the War Powers Resolution without stating that Section 4(a)(1) had become operative. The resolution quoted the President's statement that involvement in hostilities was not imminent. Representative Fascell stated that H.J.Res. 658 was not to be interpreted as a Gulf of Tonkin resolution that granted the President open-ended authority, and that it made clear that "a congressional decision on the issue of war or peace would have to be made through joint consultation." The Senate did not act on H.J. Res. 658.

On October 2, 1990, the Senate by a vote of 96-3 adopted S.Con.Res. 147, stating that "Congress supports continued action by the President in accordance with the decisions of the United Nations Security Council and in accordance with United States constitutional and statutory processes, including the authorization and appropriation of funds by the Congress, to deter Iraqi aggression and to protect American lives and vital interest in the region." As in the House, Senate leaders emphasized that the resolution was not to be interpreted as an open-ended resolution similar to the Gulf of Tonkin resolution. The resolution made no mention of the War Powers Resolution. The House did not act on S.Con.Res. 147. Congress also supported the action by appropriating funds for the preparatory operation, called Operation Desert Shield, and later for war activities called Operation Desert Storm.

[57] On August 17, 1990, Acting Secretary of State Robert M. Kimmitt sent a formal letter to Congress (not mentioning the War Powers Resolution) stating, "It is not our intention or expectation that the use of force will be required to carry out these operations. However, if other means of enforcement fail, necessary and proportionate force will be employed to deny passage to ships that are in violation of these sanctions."

Some Members introduced legislation to establish a special consultation group, but the Administration objected to a formally established group. On October 23, 1990, Senate Majority Leader Mitchell announced that he and Speaker Foley had designated Members of the joint bipartisan leadership and committees of jurisdiction to make themselves available as a group for consultation on developments in the Persian Gulf. By this time U.S. land, naval, and air forces numbering more than 200,000 had been deployed.

After the 101st Congress had adjourned, President Bush on November 8, 1990, ordered an estimated additional 150,000 troops to the Gulf. He incurred considerable criticism because he had not informed the consultation group of the buildup although he had met with them on October 30. On November 16, President Bush sent a second report to Congress describing the continuing and increasing deployment of forces to the region. He stated that his opinion that hostilities were not imminent had not changed. The President wrote, "The deployment will ensure that the coalition has an adequate offensive military option should that be necessary to achieve our common goals." By the end of the year, approximately 350,000 U.S. forces had been deployed to the area.

As the prospect of a war without congressional authorization increased, on November 20, 1990, Representative Ron Dellums and 44 other Democratic Members of Congress sought a judicial order enjoining the President from offensive military operations in connection with Operation Desert Shield unless he consulted with and obtained an authorization from Congress. On November 26, 11 prominent law professors filed a brief in favor of such a judicial action, arguing that the Constitution clearly vested Congress with the authority to declare war and that Federal judges should not use the political questions doctrine to avoid ruling on the issue. The American Civil Liberties Union also filed a memorandum in favor of the plaintiffs. On December 13, Judge Harold Greene of the Federal district court in Washington denied the injunction, holding that the controversy was not ripe for judicial resolution because a majority of Congress had not sought relief and the executive branch had not shown sufficient commitment to a definitive course of action.[58] However, throughout his opinion Judge Greene rejected the Administration's arguments for full Presidential war powers.

On November 29, 1990, U.N. Security Council Resolution 678 authorized member states to use "all necessary means" to implement the Council's resolutions and restore peace and security in the area, unless Iraq complied with the U.N. resolutions by January 15, 1991. As the deadline for Iraqi

[58] Dellums v. Bush, 752 F. Supp. 1141 (D.D.C. 1990).

withdrawal from Kuwait neared, President Bush indicated that if the Iraqi forces did not withdraw from Kuwait, he was prepared to use force to implement the U.N. Security Council resolutions. Administration officials contended that the President did not need any additional congressional authorization for this purpose.[59]

After the 102nd Congress convened, on January 4, 1991, House and Senate leaders announced they would debate U.S. policy beginning January 10. A week before the January 15 deadline, on January 8, 1991, President Bush, in a letter to the congressional leaders, requested a congressional resolution supporting the use of all necessary means to implement U.N. Security Council Resolution 678. He stated that he was "determined to do whatever is necessary to protect America's security" and that he could "think of no better way than for Congress to express its support for the President at this critical time." It is noteworthy that the President's request for a resolution was a request for congressional "support" for his undertaking in the Persian Gulf, not for "authority" to engage in the military operation. In a press conference on January 9, 1991, President Bush reinforced this distinction in response to questions about the use of force resolution being debated in Congress. He was asked whether he thought he needed the resolution, and if he lost on it would he feel bound by that decision. President Bush in response stated: "I don't think I need it . . . I feel that I have the authority to fully implement the United Nations resolutions." He added that he felt that he had "the constitutional authority—many attorneys having so advised me."[60]

On January 12, 1991, both houses passed the "Authorization for Use of Military Force Against Iraq Resolution" (P.L. 102-1).[61] Section 2(a) authorized the President to use U.S. Armed Forces pursuant to U.N. Security Council Resolution 678 to achieve implementation of the earlier Security Council resolutions. Section 2(b) required that first the President would have to report that the United States had used all appropriate diplomatic and other peaceful means to obtain compliance by Iraq with the Security Council resolution and that those efforts had not been successful. Section 2(c) stated that it was intended to constitute specific statutory authorization within the meaning of Section 5(b) of the War Powers Resolution. Section 3

[59] Statement by Secretary of Defense Richard Cheney. U.S. Congress. Senate. Committee on Armed Services. Crisis in the Persian Gulf Region: U.S. Policy Options and Implications. September 11-December 3, 1990, S.Hrg. 101–1071, pp. 701–2.

[60] Weekly Compilation of Presidential Documents. January 14, 1991. Vol. 27, No. 2, pp.17–18; pp. 24–25.

[61] The House passed H.J. Res. 77 by a vote of 250 to 183. The Senate passed S.J. Res. 2 and then considered H.J.Res. 77 as passed. The Senate vote was 52 to 47. The bill became P.L. 102–1, signed January 14, 1991. On January 12, to emphasize the congressional power to declare war, the House also adopted by a vote of 302 to 131 H.Con.Res. 32 expressing the sense that Congress must approve any offensive military actions against Iraq; the Senate did not act on the measure.

required the President to report every 60 days on efforts to obtain compliance of Iraq with the U.N. Security Council resolution.

In his statement made after signing H.J.Res. 77 into law, President Bush said the following: "As I made clear to congressional leaders at the outset, my request for congressional support did not, and my signing this resolution does not, constitute any change in the long-standing positions of the executive branch on either the President's constitutional authority to use the Armed Forces to defend vital U.S. interests or the constitutionality of the War Powers Resolution." He added that he was pleased that "differences on these issues between the President and many in the Congress have not prevented us from uniting in a common objective."[62]

On January 16, President Bush made the determination required by P.L. 102-1 that diplomatic means had not and would not compel Iraq to withdraw from Kuwait. On January 18, he reported to Congress "consistent with the War Powers Resolution" that he had directed U.S. forces to commence combat operations on January 16.

After the beginning of the war Members of Congress strongly supported the President as Commander-in-Chief in his conduct of the war. On March 19, 1991, President Bush reported to Congress that the military operations had been successful, Kuwait had been liberated, and combat operations had been suspended on February 28, 1991.

Prior to passage of P.L. 102-1, some observers questioned the effectiveness of the War Powers Resolution on grounds that the President had begun the action, deployed hundreds of thousands of troops without consultation of Congress, and was moving the Nation increasingly close to war without congressional authorization. After the passage of P.L. 102-1 and the war had begun, Chairman of the House Committee on Foreign Affairs Fascell took the position that "the War Powers Resolution is alive and well"; the President had submitted reports to Congress, and Congress, in P.L. 102-1, had provided specific statutory authorization for the use of force. In his view, the strength and wisdom of the War Powers Resolution was that it established a process by which Congress could authorize the use of force in specific settings for limited purposes, short of a total state of war.

The question is sometimes raised why Congress did not declare war against Iraq. Speaker Foley told the National Press Club on February 7,1991, that

[62] Weekly Compilation of Presidential Documents. January 21, 1991. Vol. 27, No. 3, pp.48–49. Subsequently, on June 20, 1992, during remarks to the Texas State Republican Convention in Dallas, Texas, President Bush said: "Some people say, why can't you bring the same kind of purpose and success to the domestic scene as you did in Desert Shield and Desert Storm? And the answer is: I didn't have to get permission from some old goat in the United States Congress to kick Saddam Hussein out of Kuwait. That's the reason." Weekly Compilation of Presidential Documents. June 29, 1992. Vol. 28, No. 26, pp.1120–1121.

"The reason we did not declare a formal war was not because there is any difference I think in the action that was taken and in a formal declaration of war with respect to military operations, but because there is some question about whether we wish to excite or enact some of the domestic consequences of a formal declaration of war—seizure of property, censorship, and so forth, which the President neither sought nor desired."

Iraq-Post Gulf War: How Long Does an Authorization Last?

After the end of Operation Desert Storm, U.S. military forces were used to deal with three continuing situations in Iraq. These activities raised the issue of how long a congressional authorization for the use of force lasts.

The first situation resulted from the Iraqi government's repression of Kurdish and Shi'ite groups. U.N. Security Council Resolution 688 of April 5, 1991, condemned the repression of the Iraqi civilian population and appealed for contributions to humanitarian relief efforts. On May 17, 1991, President Bush reported to Congress that the Iraqi repression of the Kurdish people had necessitated a limited introduction of U.S. forces into northern Iraq for emergency relief purposes. On July 16, 1991, he reported that U.S. forces had withdrawn from northern Iraq but that the U.S. remained prepared to take appropriate steps as the situation required and that, to this end, an appropriate level of forces would be maintained in the region for "as long as required."

A second situation stemmed from the cease-fire resolution, Security Council Resolution 687 of April 3, 1991, which called for Iraq to accept the destruction or removal of chemical and biological weapons and international control of its nuclear materials. On September 16, 1991, President Bush reported to Congress that Iraq continued to deny inspection teams access to weapons facilities and that this violated the requirements of Resolution 687, and the United States if necessary would take action to ensure Iraqi compliance with the Council's decisions. He reported similar non-cooperation on January 14, 1992, and May 15, 1992.

On July 16, 1992, President Bush reported particular concern about the refusal of Iraqi authorities to grant U.N. inspectors access to the Agricultural Ministry. The President consulted congressional leaders on July 27, and in early August the United States began a series of military exercises to take 5,000 U.S. troops to Kuwait. On September 16, 1992, the President reported, "We will remain prepared to use all necessary means, in accordance with U.N. Security Council resolutions, to assist the United Nations in removing the threat posed by Iraq's chemical, biological, and nuclear weapons capability."

The third situation was related to both of the earlier ones. On August 26, 1992, the United States, Britain, and France began a "no-fly" zone, banning

Iraqi fixed wing and helicopter flights south of the 32nd parallel and creating a limited security zone in the south, where Shi'ite groups were concentrated. After violations of the no-fly zones and various other actions by Iraq, on January 13, 1993, the Bush Administration announced that aircraft from the United States and coalition partners had attacked missile bases in southern Iraq and that the United States was deploying a battalion task force to Kuwait to underline the U.S. continuing commitment to Kuwait's independence. On January 19, 1993, President Bush reported to Congress that U.S. aircraft had shot down an Iraqi aircraft on December 27, 1992, and had undertaken further military actions on January 13, 17, and 18.

President Clinton said on January 21, 1993, that the United States would adhere to the policy toward Iraq set by the Bush Administration. On January 22 and 23, April 9 and 18, June 19, and August 19, 1993, U.S. aircraft fired at targets in Iraq after pilots sensed Iraqi radar or anti-aircraft fire directed at them. On September 23, 1993, President Clinton reported that since the August 19 action, the Iraqi installation fired upon had not displayed hostile intentions.

In a separate incident, on June 28, 1993, President Clinton reported to Congress "consistent with the War Powers Resolution" that on June 26 U.S. naval forces at his direction had launched a Tomahawk cruise missile strike on the Iraqi Intelligence Service's main command and control complex in Baghdad and that the military action was completed upon the impact of the missiles. He said the Iraqi Intelligence Service had planned the failed attempt to assassinate former President Bush during his visit to Kuwait in April 1993.

The question was raised as to whether the Authorization for the Use of Force in Iraq (P.L. 102-1) authorized military actions after the conclusion of the war. P.L. 102-1 authorized the President to use U.S. armed forces pursuant to U.N. Security Council Resolution 678 to achieve implementation of previous Security Council Resolutions relating to Iraq's invasion of Kuwait. The cease-fire resolution, Security Council Resolution 687, was adopted afterwards and therefore not included in Resolution 678.

Congress endorsed the view that further specific authorization was not required for U.S. military action to maintain the cease-fire agreement. Specifically, section 1095 of P.L. 102-190 stated the sense of Congress that it supported the use of all necessary means to achieve the goals of Security Council Resolution 687 as being consistent with the Authorization for Use of Military Force Against Iraq Resolution. Section 1096 supported the use of all necessary means to protect Iraq's Kurdish minority, consistent with relevant U.N. resolutions and authorities contained in P.L. 102-1. The issue of Congressional authorization was debated again in 1998. On March 31, 1998, the House passed a Supplemental Appropriations bill (H.R. 3579) that would have banned the use of funds appropriated in it for the conduct of offensive operations against Iraq, unless such operations were specifically authorized by law. This provision was dropped in the conference with the Senate.

A more broad-gauged approach to the issue of Congressional authorization of military force was attempted in mid-1998. On June 24, 1998, the House passed H.R. 4103, the Defense Department Appropriations bill for FY1999, with a provision by Representative David Skaggs that banned the use of funds appropriated or otherwise made available by this Act "to initiate or conduct offensive military operations by United States Armed Forces except in accordance with the war powers clause of the Constitution (Article 1, Section 8), which vests in Congress the power to declare and authorize war and to take certain specified, related actions." The Skaggs provision was stricken by the House-Senate conference committee on H.R. 4103.

As events developed, beginning in late 1998, and continuing into the period prior to the U.S. military invasion of Iraq in March 2003, the United States conducted a large number of ad-hoc air attacks against Iraqi ground installations and military targets in response to violations of the Northern and Southern "no-fly zones" by the Iraqi, and threatening actions taken against U.S. and coalition aircraft enforcing these "no-fly" sectors. Congressional authorization to continue these activities was not sought by the President, nor were these many incidents reported under the War Powers Resolution. The "no-fly zones" activities were terminated following the 2003 War with Iraq.

Somalia: When Does Humanitarian Assistance Require Congressional Authorization?

In Somalia, the participation of U.S. military forces in a U.N. operation to protect humanitarian assistance became increasingly controversial as fighting and casualties increased and the objectives of the operation appeared to be expanding.

On December 4, 1992, President Bush ordered thousands of U.S. military forces to Somalia to protect humanitarian relief from armed gangs. Earlier, on November 25, the President had offered U.S. forces, and on December 3, the United Nations Security Council had adopted Resolution 794 welcoming the U.S. offer and authorizing the Secretary-General and members cooperating in the U.S. offer "to use all necessary means to establish as soon as possible a secure environment for humanitarian relief operations in Somalia." The resolution also called on member states to provide military forces and authorized the Secretary-General and the states concerned to arrange for unified command and control.

On December 10, 1992, President Bush reported to Congress "consistent with the War Powers Resolution" that on December 8, U.S. armed forces entered Somalia to secure the air field and port facility of Mogadishu and that other elements of the U.S. armed forces were being introduced into Somalia to achieve the objectives of U.N. Security Council Resolution 794. He said the forces would remain only as long as necessary to establish a secure environment for humanitarian relief operations and would then turn over responsibility for maintaining this environment to a U.N. peacekeeping force. The President said that it was not intended that the U.S. armed forces become involved in hostilities, but that the forces were equipped and ready to take such measures as might be needed to accomplish their humanitarian mission and defend themselves. They would also have the support of any additional U.S. forces necessary. By mid-January, U.S. forces in Somalia numbered 25,000.

Since the President did not cite Section 4(a)(1), the 60-day time limit was not necessarily triggered. By February, however, the U.S. force strength was being reduced, and it was announced the United States expected to turn over responsibility for protecting humanitarian relief shipments in Somalia to a U.N. force that would include U.S. troops. On March 26, 1993, the Security Council adopted Resolution 814 expanding the mandate of the U.N. force and bringing about a transition from a U.S.-led force to a U.N.-led force (UNOSOM II). By the middle of May, when the change to U.N. control took place, the U.S. forces were down to approximately 4,000 troops, primarily logistics and communications support teams, but also a rapid deployment force of U.S. Marines stationed on Navy ships.

Violence within Somalia began to increase again. On June 5, 1993, attacks killed 23 Pakistani peacekeepers, and a Somali regional leader, General Aidid, was believed responsible. The next day the U.N. Security Council adopted Resolution 837 reaffirming the authority of UNOSOM II to take all necessary measures against those responsible for the armed attacks. On June 10, 1993, President Clinton reported "consistent with the War Powers Resolution" that the U.S. Quick Reaction Force had executed military strikes to assist UNOSOM II in quelling violence against it. On July 1, President Clinton submitted another report, not mentioning the War Powers Resolution, describing further air and ground military operations aimed at securing General Aidid's compound and neutralizing military capabilities that had been an obstacle to U.N. efforts to deliver humanitarian relief and promote national reconstruction.

From the beginning, a major issue for Congress was whether to authorize U.S. action in Somalia. On February 4, 1993, the Senate had passed S.J.Res. 45 that would authorize the President to use U.S. armed forces pursuant to U.N. Security Council Resolution 794. S.J. Res. 45 stated it was intended to constitute the specific statutory authorization under Section 5(b) of the War Powers Resolution. On May 25, 1993, the House amended S.J.Res. 45 to authorize U.S. forces to remain for one year. S.J.Res. 45 was then sent to the Senate for its concurrence, but the Senate did not act on the measure.

As sporadic fighting resulted in the deaths of Somali and U.N. forces, including Americans, controversy over the operation intensified, and Congress took action through other legislative channels. In September 1993 the House and Senate adopted amendments to the Defense Authorization Act for FY1994 asking that the President consult with Congress on policy toward Somalia, and report the goals, objectives, and anticipated jurisdiction of the U.S. mission in Somalia by October 15, 1993; the amendments expressed the sense that the President by November 15, 1993, should seek and receive congressional authorization for the continued deployment of U.S. forces to Somalia.[63] On October 7, the President consulted with congressional leaders from both parties for over two hours on Somalia policy. On October 13, President Clinton sent a 33-page report to Congress on his Somalia policy and its objectives.

Meanwhile, on October 7 President Clinton said that most U.S. forces would be withdrawn from Somalia by March 31, 1994. To ensure this, the Defense Department Appropriations Act for FY1994, cut off funds for U.S. military operations in Somalia after March 31, 1994, unless the President obtained further spending authority from Congress.[64] Congress approved the use of U.S. military forces in Somalia only for the protection of American military personnel and bases and for helping maintain the flow of relief aid by giving the U.N. forces security and logistical support; it required that U.S. combat forces in Somalia remain under the command and control of U.S. commanders under the ultimate direction of the President.

Earlier, some Members suggested that the U.S. forces in Somalia were clearly in a situation of hostilities or imminent hostilities, and that if Congress did not authorize the troops to remain, the forces should be withdrawn within 60 to 90 days. After a letter from House Foreign Affairs Committee Ranking Minority Member Benjamin Gilman and Senate Foreign Relations Committee Ranking Minority Member Jesse Helms, Assistant Secretary Wendy Sherman replied on July 21, 1993, that no previous Administrations had considered that intermittent military engagements, whether constituting hostilities, would necessitate the withdrawal of forces pursuant to Section 5(b); and the War Powers Resolution, in their view, was intended to apply to sustained hostilities. The State Department did not believe congressional authorization was necessary, although congressional support would be welcome. On August 4, 1993, Representative Gilman asserted that August 4 might be remembered as the day the War Powers Resolution died because combat broke out in Somalia on June 5

---

63 Section 1512, P.L. 103-160, signed November 30, 1993.
64 Sec. 8151 of P.L. 103-139, signed November 11, 1993.

and the President had not withdrawn U.S. forces and Congress had "decided to look the other way." On October 22, 1993, Representative Gilman introduced H.Con.Res. 170 directing the President pursuant to section 5(c) of the War Powers Resolution to withdraw U.S. forces from Somalia by January 31, 1994. The House adopted an amended version calling for withdrawal by March 31, 1994.[65] The Senate did not act on this non-binding measure.

However, the Defense Appropriations Act for FY1995 (P.L. 103-335, signed September 30, 1994) prohibited the use of funds for the continuous presence of U.S. forces in Somalia, except for the protection of U.S. personnel, after September 30, 1994. Subsequently, on November 4, 1994, the U.N. Security Council decided to end the U.N. mission in Somalia by March 31, 1995. On March 3, 1995, U.S. forces completed their assistance to United Nations forces evacuating Somalia.

Another war powers issue was the adequacy of consultation before the dispatch of forces. On December 4, 1992, President Bush had met with a number of congressional leaders to brief them on the troop deployment. In his December 10 report, President Bush stressed that he had taken into account the views expressed in H.Con.Res. 370, S.Con.Res. 132, and P.L. 102-274 on the urgent need for action in Somalia. However, none of these resolutions explicitly authorized U.S. military action.

Former Yugoslavia/Bosnia/Kosovo: What If No Consensus Exists?

Bosnia

The issue of war powers and U.S. participation in United Nations actions was also raised by efforts to halt fighting in the territory of former Yugoslavia, initially in Bosnia. Because some of the U.S. action has been taken within a NATO framework, action in Bosnia has also raised the issue of whether action under NATO is exempt from the requirements of the War Powers Resolution or its standard for the exercise of war powers under the Constitution. Article 11 of the North Atlantic Treaty states that its provisions are to be carried out by the parties "in accordance with their respective constitutional processes," inferring some role for Congress in the event of war. Section 8(a) of the War Powers Resolution states that authority to introduce U.S. forces into hostilities is not to be inferred from any treaty, ratified before or after 1973, unless implementing legislation specifically authorizes such introduction and says it is intended to constitute an authorization within the meaning of the War Powers Resolution. Section 8(b) states that nothing in the War Powers Resolution should be construed to require further authorization for U.S. participation in the

[65] For additional discussion of H.Con. Res. 170, see section on Legislative Veto, above.

headquarters operations of military commands established before 1973, such as NATO headquarters operations.

On August 13, 1992, the U.N. Security Council adopted Resolution 770 calling on nations to take "all measures necessary" to facilitate the delivery of humanitarian assistance to Sarajevo. Many in Congress had been advocating more assistance to the victims of the conflict. On August 11, 1992, the Senate had passed S.Res. 330 urging the President to work for a U.N. Security Council resolution such as was adopted, but saying that no U.S. military personnel should be introduced into hostilities without clearly defined objectives. On the same day, the House passed H. Res. 554 urging the Security Council to authorize measures, including the use of force, to ensure humanitarian relief.

During 1993 the United States participated in airlifts into Sarajevo, naval monitoring of sanctions, and aerial enforcement of a "no-fly zone." On February 10, 1993, Secretary of State Warren Christopher announced that under President Clinton, the United States would try to convince the Serbs, Muslims, and Croats to pursue a diplomatic solution and that if an agreement was reached, U.S. forces, including ground forces, would help enforce the peace. On February 28, 1993, the United States began an airdrop of relief supplies aimed at civilian populations, mainly Muslims, surrounded by fighting in Bosnia.

On March 31, 1993, the U.N. Security Council authorized member states to take all necessary measures to enforce the ban on military flights over Bosnia, the "no-fly zone". NATO planes, including U.S. planes, began patrolling over Bosnia and Herzegovina on April 12, 1993, to enforce the Security Council ban, and the next day, President Clinton reported the U.S. participation "consistent with Section 4 of the War Powers Resolution."

Conflict continued, but the situation was complicated and opinion in Congress and among U.N. and NATO members was divided. President Clinton consulted with about two dozen congressional leaders on potential further action on April 27 and received a wide range of views. On May 2, the Administration began consultation with allies to build support for additional military action to enforce a cease-fire and Bosnian Serb compliance with a peace agreement, but a consensus on action was not reached.

On June 10, 1993, Secretary of State Christopher announced the United States would send 300 U.S. troops to join 700 Scandinavians in the U.N. peacekeeping force in Macedonia.[66] The mission was established under U.N. Security Council Resolution 795 (1992), which sought to prevent the

[66] The name of this area is in dispute. The provisional name, which is used for its designation as a member of the United Nations, is "The Former Yugoslav Republic of Macedonia." This report uses the term "Macedonia" without prejudice.

war in Bosnia from spilling over to neighboring countries. President Clinton reported this action "consistent with Section4 of the War Powers Resolution" on July 9, 1993. He identified U.S. troops as part of a peacekeeping force, and directed in accordance with Section 7 of the U.N. Participation Act.

Planning for U.N. and NATO action to implement a prospective peace agreement included the possibility that the United States might supply 25,000 out of 50,000 NATO forces to enforce U.N. decisions. This possibility brought proposals to require congressional approval before the dispatch of further forces to Bosnia. On September 23, 1993, Senate Minority Leader Robert Dole said he intended to offer an amendment stating that no additional U.S. forces should be introduced into former Yugoslavia without advance approval from Congress. Assistant Secretary of State Stephen Oxman said on October 5 that the Clinton Administration would consult with Congress and not commit American troops to the implementation operation for a peace agreement without congressional support, and that the Administration would act consistent with the War Powers Resolution. Congress sought to assure this in Section 8146 of P.L. 103-139, the Defense Appropriation Act for FY 1994, stating the sense of Congress that funds should not be available for U.S. forces to participate in new missions or operations to implement the peace settlement in Bosnia unless previously authorized by Congress. This provision was sponsored by the Senate by leaders Mitchell and Dole.

At the NATO summit conference in Brussels on January 11, 1994, leaders, including President Clinton, repeated an August threat to undertake air strikes on Serb positions to save Sarajevo and to consider other steps to end the conflict in Bosnia. On February 17, 1994, President Clinton reported "consistent with" the War Powers Resolution that the United States had expanded its participation in United Nations and NATO efforts to reach a peaceful solution in former Yugoslavia and that 60 U.S. aircraft were available for participation in the authorized NATO missions. On March 1, 1994, he reported that on the previous day U.S. planes patrolling the "no-fly zone" under the North Atlantic Treaty Organization (NATO) shot down 4 Serbian Galeb planes. On April 12, 1994, the President reported that on April 10 and 11, following shelling of Gorazde, one of the "safe areas," and a decision by U.N. and NATO leaders, U.S. planes bombed Bosnian Serbian nationalist positions around Gorazde. On August 22, 1994, President Clinton similarly reported that on August 5, U.S. planes under NATO had strafed a Bosnian Serb gun position in an exclusion zone. On September 22, 1994, two British and one U.S. aircraft bombed a Serbian tank in retaliation for Serb attacks on U.N. peacekeepers near Sarajevo; and on November 21 more than 30 planes from the United States, Britain, France, and the Netherlands bombed the runway of a Serb airfield in Croatia.

As the conflict in Bosnia continued, leaders in Congress called for greater congressional involvement in decisions. Senator Dole introduced S. 2042, calling for the United States to end unilaterally its arms embargo, conducted in accordance with a U.N. Security Council Resolution, against Bosnia and Herzegovina. On May 10, 1994, Senate Majority Leader George Mitchell introduced an amendment to authorize and approve the President's decision to carry out NATO decisions to support and protect UNPROFOR forces around designated safe areas; to use airpower in the Sarajevo region; and to authorize air strikes against Serb weapons around certain safe areas if these areas were attacked. The Mitchell amendment favored lifting the arms embargo but not unilaterally; it also stated no U.S. ground combat troops should be deployed in Bosnia unless previously authorized by Congress. The Senate adopted both the Dole proposal, as an amendment, and the Mitchell amendment on May 12, 1994, by votes of 50–49. The less stringent Mitchell amendment passed on a straight party line vote. Yet thirteen Democrats voted for the Dole amendment, indicating a sentiment in both parties to assist the Bosnians in defending themselves. The Senate then adopted S. 2042 as amended. The House did not act on the measure.

The Defense Authorization Act for FY 1995 (P.L. 103-337, signed October 5, 1994) provided, in Section 1404, the sense of the Congress that if the Bosnian Serbs did not accept the Contact Group proposal by October 15, 1994, the President should introduce a U.N. Security Council resolution to end the arms embargo by December 1, 1994; if the Security Council had not acted by November 15, 1994, no funds could be used to enforce the embargo other than those required of all U.N. members under Security Council Resolution 713. That sequence of events occurred and the United States stopped enforcing the embargo. In addition, Section 8100 of the Defense Appropriations Act, FY 1995 (P.L. 103-335, signed September 30, 1994), stated the sense of the Congress that funds made available by this law should not be available for the purposes of deploying U.S. armed forces to participate in implementation of a peace settlement in Bosnia unless previously authorized by Congress.

On May 24, 1995, President Clinton reported "consistent with the War Powers Resolution" that U.S. combat-equipped fighter aircraft and other aircraft continued to contribute to NATO's enforcement of the no-fly zone in airspace over Bosnia-Herzegovina. U.S. aircraft, he noted, are also available for close air support of U.N. forces in Croatia. Roughly 500 U.S. soldiers were still deployed in the former Yugoslav Republic of Macedonia as part of the U.N. Preventive Deployment Force (UNPREDEP). U.S. forces continue to support U.N. refugee and embargo operations in this region.

On September 1, 1995, President Clinton reported "consistent with the War Powers Resolution," that "U.S. combat and support aircraft" had been used beginning on August 29, 1995, in a series of NATO air strikes against Bosnian Serb Army (BSA) forces in Bosnia-Herzegovina that were threatening the U.N.-declared safe areas of Sarajevo, Tuzla, and Gorazde." He noted that during the first day of operations, "some 300 sorties were flown against 23 targets in the vicinity of Sarajevo, Tuzla, Gorazde, and Mostar."

On September 7, 1995 the House passed an amendment to the FY 1996 Department of Defense Appropriations Bill (H.R. 2126), offered by Representative Mark Neumann (R-WI.) that prohibited the obligation or expenditure of funds provided by the bill for any operations beyond those already undertaken. However, in conference the provision was softened to a sense-of-the-Congress provision that said that President must consult with Congress before deploying U.S. forces to Bosnia. The conference report was rejected by the House over issues unrelated to Bosnia on September 29, 1995 by a vote of 151-267. The substitute conference report on H.R. 2126, which was subsequently passed and signed into law, did not include language on Bosnia, in part due to the President's earlier objections to any provision in the bill that might impinge on his powers as Commander-in-Chief. On September 29, the Senate passed by a vote of 94-2 a sense-of-the-Senate amendment to H.R. 2076, the FY 1996 State, Commerce, Justice Appropriations bill, sponsored by Senator Judd Gregg (R-N.H.) that said no funds in the bill should be used for the deployment of U.S. combat troops to Bosnia-Herzegovina unless Congress approves the deployment in advance or to evacuate endangered U.N. peacekeepers. The conference report on H.R. 2076, agreed to by the House and the Senate, included the "sense of the Senate" language of the Gregg amendment.

In response to mounting criticism of the Administration's approach to Bosnian policy, on October 17–18, 1995, Secretary of State Christopher, Secretary of Defense Perry and Joint Chiefs of Staff Chairman Shalikashvili testified before House and Senate Committees on Bosnia policy and the prospect of President Clinton deploying approximately 20,000 American ground forces as part of a NATO peacekeeping operation. During testimony before the Senate Foreign Relations Committee on October 17, Secretary Christopher stated that the President would not be bound by a resolution of the Congress prohibiting sending of U.S. forces into Bosnia without the express prior approval of Congress. Nevertheless, on October 19, 1995, President Clinton in a letter to Senator Robert C. Byrd stated that "[w]hile maintaining the constitutional authorities of the Presidency, I would welcome, encourage and, at the appropriate time, request an expression of support by the Congress" for the commitment of U.S. troops to a NATO implementation force in Bosnia, after a peace agreement is reached.

Subsequently, on October 30, 1995, the House, by a vote of 315-103, passed H.Res. 247, expressing the sense of the House that "no United States Armed forces should be deployed on the ground in the territory of the Republic of Bosnia and Herzegovina to enforce a peace agreement until the Congress has approved such a deployment." On November 13, President Clinton's 9-page letter to Speaker Gingrich stated he would send a request "for a congressional expression of support for U.S. participation in a NATO-led Implementation Force in Bosnia . . . before American forces are deployed in Bosnia." The President said there would be a "timely opportunity for Congress to consider and act upon" his request for support. He added that despite his desire for congressional support, he "must reserve" his "constitutional prerogatives in this area." On November 17, 1995, the House passed (243-171) H.R. 2606, which would "prohibit the use of funds appropriated or otherwise available" to the Defense Department from "being used for the deployment on the ground of United States Armed Forces in the Republic of Bosnia-Herzegovina as part of any peacekeeping operation or as part of any implementation force, unless funds for such deployment are specifically appropriated" by law.

On December 4, 1995, Secretary of Defense Perry announced the deployment of about 1,400 U.S. military personnel (700 to Bosnia/700 to Croatia) as part of the advance elements of the roughly 60,000 person NATO Implementation Force in Bosnia, scheduled to deploy in force once the Dayton Peace Agreement is signed in Paris on December 14, 1995. Secretary Perry noted that once the NATO I-Force was fully deployed, about 20,000 U.S. military personnel would be in Bosnia, and about 5,000 in Croatia.

On December 6, 1995, President Clinton notified the Congress, "consistent with the War Powers Resolution," that he had "ordered the deployment of approximately 1,500 U.S. military personnel to Bosnia and Herzegovina and Croatia as part of a NATO 'enabling force' to lay the groundwork for the prompt and safe deployment of the NATO-led Implementation Force (IFOR)," which would be used to implement the Bosnian peace agreement after its signing. The President also noted that he had authorized deployment of roughly 3,000 other U.S. military personnel to Hungary, Italy, and Croatia to establish infrastructure for the enabling force and the IFOR.

In response to these developments, Congress addressed the question of U.S. ground troop deployments in Bosnia. Lawmakers sought to take action before the final Bosnian peace agreement was signed in Paris on December 14, 1995, following which the bulk of American military forces would be deployed to Bosnia. On December 13, 1995, the House considered H.R. 2770, sponsored by Representative Dornan, which would have prohibited the use of Federal funds for the deployment "on the ground" of U.S. Armed Forces in Bosnia-Herzegovina "as part of any peacekeeping operation, or as part of any implementation force." H.R. 2770 was defeated in the House by a vote of 210-218. On December 13, the House considered two other measures. It approved H.Res. 302, offered by Representative Buyer, by a vote of 287-141. H.Res. 302, anon-binding measure, reiterated "serious concerns and opposition" to the deployment of U.S. ground troops to Bosnia, while expressing confidence, "pride and admiration" for U.S. soldiers deployed there. It called on the President and Defense Secretary to rely on the judgement of the U.S. ground commander in Bosnia and stated that he should be provided with sufficient resources to ensure the safety and well-being of U.S. troops. H.Res. 302, further stated that the U.S. government should "in all respects" be "impartial and evenhanded" with all parties to the Bosnian conflict "as necessary to ensure the safety and protection" of American forces in the region.

Subsequently, the House defeated H.Res 306, proposed by Representative Hamilton, by a vote of 190-237. H.Res 306 stated that the House "unequivocally supports the men and women of the United States Armed Forces who are carrying out their mission in support of peace in Bosnia and Herzegovina with professional excellence, dedicated patriotism and exemplary bravery."

On December 13, the Senate also considered three measures related to Bosnia and U.S. troop deployments. The Senate defeated H.R. 2606 by a vote of 22-77. This bill would have prohibited funds to be obligated or expended for U.S. participation in peacekeeping in Bosnia unless such funds were specifically appropriated for that purpose. The Senate also defeated S.Con.Res. 35, a non-binding resolution of Senators Hutchison and Inhofe. This resolution stated that "Congress opposes President Clinton's decision to deploy" U.S. troops to Bosnia, but noted that "Congress strongly supports" the U.S. troops sent by the President to Bosnia.

The Senate did pass S.J.Res. 44, sponsored by Senators Dole and McCain, by a vote of 69-30. This resolution stated that Congress "unequivocally supports the men and women of our Armed Forces" who were to be deployed to Bosnia. S.J.Res. 44 stated that "notwithstanding reservations expressed about President Clinton's decision" to deploy U.S. forces, "the President may only fulfill his commitment" to deploy them to Bosnia "for approximately one year" if he made a determination to Congress that the mission of the NATO peace implementation force (IFOR) will be limited to implementing the military annex to the Bosnian peace agreement and to protecting itself. The Presidential determination must also state that the United States will "lead an immediate international effort," separate from IFOR, "to provide equipment, arms, training and related logistics assistance of the highest possible quality" to the Muslim-Croat Federation so that it may provide for its own defense. The President could use "existing military drawdown authorities and requesting such additional authority as may be necessary." S.J.Res. 44 also required President Clinton to submit to Congress a detailed report on the armament effort within 30 days, and required regular Presidential reports to Congress on the implementation of both the military and non-military aspects of the peace accords.

The House and Senate did not appoint and direct conferees to meet to reconcile the conflicting elements of the Bosnia related measures each had passed on December 13, 1995. A number of Members and Senators had wished to express their views on the troop deployment before the Dayton Accords were formally signed in Paris. That action had occurred, and the leadership of both parties apparently believed nothing further would be achieved by a conference on the measures passed. As result, no final consensus on a single specific measure was reached on the issue by the two chambers.

The President meanwhile continued with the Bosnian deployment. On December 21, 1995, President Clinton notified Congress "consistent with the War Powers Resolution," that he had ordered the deployment of approximately 20,000 U.S. military personnel to participate in the NATO-led Implementation Force (IFOR) in the Republic of Bosnia-Herzegovina, and approximately 5,000 U.S. military personnel would be deployed in other former Yugoslav states, primarily in Croatia. In addition, about 7,000 U.S. support forces would be deployed to Hungary, Italy, Croatia, and other regional states in support of IFOR's mission. The President ordered participation of U.S. forces "pursuant to" his "constitutional authority to conduct the foreign relations of the United States and as Commander-in-Chief and Chief Executive."[67] Subsequently, President Clinton in December 1996, agreed to provide up to 8,500 ground troops to participate in a NATO-led follow-on force in Bosnia termed the Stabilization Force (SFOR). On March 18, 1998, the House defeated by a vote of 193-225, H.Con. Res. 227, a resolution of Representative Tom Campbell, directing the President, pursuant to section 5(c) of the War Powers Resolution to remove United States Armed Forces from the Republic of Bosnia and Herzegovina. (H. Rept. 105-442).[68]

Kosovo

The issue of Presidential authority to deploy forces in the absence of congressional authorization, under the War Powers Resolution, or otherwise, became an issue of renewed controversy in late March 1999 when President Clinton ordered U.S. military forces to participate in a NATO-led military operation in Kosovo. This action was the focus of a major policy debate over the purpose and scope of U.S. military involvement in Kosovo. The President's action to commit forces to the NATO Kosovo operation also led to a suit in Federal District Court for the District of Columbia by Members of Congress seeking a judicial finding that the President was violating the War Powers Resolution and the Constitution by using military forces in Yugoslavia in the absence of authorization from the Congress.

[67] For additional background see CRS Report RS22324, *Bosnia: Overview of Current Issues*, by Julie Kim.

[68] For additional background see CRS Report RL32392, *Bosnia and Herzegovina: Issues for U.S. Policy*, by Steven Woehrel, and CRS Report RL32282, *Bosnia and Kosovo: U.S. Military Operations*, by Steve Bowman.

The Kosovo controversy began in earnest when on March 26, 1999, President Clinton notified the Congress "consistent with the War Powers Resolution", that on March 24, 1999, U.S. military forces, at his direction and in coalition with NATO allies, had commenced air strikes against Yugoslavia in response to the Yugoslav government's campaign of violence and repression against the ethnic Albanian population in Kosovo. Prior to the President's action, the Senate, on March 23, 1999, had passed, by a vote of 58-41, S.Con.Res. 21, a non-binding resolution expressing the sense of the Congress that the President was authorized to conduct "military air operations and missile strikes in cooperation with our NATO allies against the Federal Republic of Yugoslavia (Serbia and Montenegro)."

Subsequently, the House voted on a number of measures relating to U.S. participation in the NATO operation in Kosovo. On April 28, 1999, the House of Representatives passed H.R. 1569, by a vote of 249-180. This bill would prohibit the use of funds appropriated to the Defense Department from being used for the deployment of "ground elements" of the U.S. Armed Forces in the Federal Republic of Yugoslavia unless that deployment is specifically authorized by law. On that same day the House defeated H.Con. Res. 82, by a vote of 139-290. This resolution would have directed the President, pursuant to section 5(c) of the War Powers Resolution, to remove U.S. Armed Forces from their positions in connection with the present operations against the Federal Republic of Yugoslavia. On April 28, 1999, the House also defeated H.J. Res. 44, by a vote of 2-427. This joint resolution would have declared a state of war between the United States and the "Government of the Federal Republic of Yugoslavia." The House on that same day also defeated, on a 213-213 tie vote, S.Con.Res. 21, the Senate resolution passed on March 23, 1999, that supported military air operations and missile strikes against Yugoslavia. On April 30, 1999, Representative Tom Campbell and 17 other members of the House filed suit in Federal District Court for the District of Columbia seeking a ruling requiring the President to obtain authorization from Congress before continuing the air war, or taking other military action against Yugoslavia.[69]

The Senate, on May 4, 1999, by a vote of 78-22, tabled S.J. Res. 20, a joint resolution, sponsored by Senator John McCain, that would authorize the President "to use all necessary force and other means, in concert with United States allies, to accomplish United States and North Atlantic Treaty Organization objectives in the Federal Republic of Yugoslavia (Serbia and Montenegro)."[70] The House, meanwhile, on May 6, 1999, by a vote of 117-301,

[69] Campbell v. Clinton. Civil Action No. 99–1072.

[70] The McCain joint resolution (S.J.Res. 20) authorizing Presidential action in Yugoslavia was forced to the Senate floor by the Senator's use of the expedited procedures set out in section 6 of the War Powers Resolution for consideration of such resolutions. See debate and discussion in U.S. Congressional Record, Senate, May 3, 1999, pp. S4514–S4572; and May 4, 1999, pp. S4611–S4616 [daily edition].

defeated an amendment by Representative Ernest Istook to H.R. 1664, the FY 1999 defense supplemental appropriations bill, that would have prohibited the expenditure of funds in the bill to implement any plan to use U.S. ground forces to invade Yugoslavia, except in time of war. Congress, meanwhile, on May 20, 1999 cleared for the President's signature, H.R. 1141, an emergency supplemental appropriations bill for FY1999, that provided billions in funding for the existing U.S. Kosovo operation.

The Senate tabled two other amendments that would have restricted military operations by President Clinton in Kosovo. On May 24, 1999, it tabled, by a vote of 52-48, an amendment offered by Senator Arlen Specter to state that no funds available to the Defense Department may be obligated or expended for the deployment of U.S. ground troops to Yugoslavia unless authorized by a declaration of war or a joint resolution authorizing the use of military force. The Specter amendment did not apply to certain actions, such as rescuing U.S. military personnel or citizens.[71] On May 26, 1999 the Senate tabled an amendment, by a vote of 77-21, offered by Senator Bob Smith to prohibit, effective October 1, 1999, the use of funds for military operations in Yugoslavia unless Congress enacted specific authorization in law for the conduct of these operations.[72]

On May 25, 1999, the 60 day had passed since the President notified Congress of his actions regarding U.S. participation in military operations in Kosovo. Representative Campbell, and those who joined his suit, noted to the Federal Court that this was a clear violation of the language of the War Powers Resolution stipulating a withdrawal of U.S. forces from the area of hostilities after 60 days in the absence of congressional authorization to continue, or a Presidential request to Congress for an extra 30 day period to safely withdraw. The President did not seek such a 30 day extension, noting instead his view that the War Powers Resolution is constitutionally defective.

On June 8, 1999, Federal District Judge Paul L. Friedman dismissed the suit of Representative Campbell and others that sought to have the court rule that President Clinton was in violation of the War Powers Resolution and the Constitution by conducting military activities in Yugoslavia without having received prior authorization from Congress. The judge ruled that Representative Campbell and the other Congressional plaintiffs lacked legal standing to bring the suit.[73] On June 24, 1999, Representative Campbell appealed the ruling to the U.S. Court of Appeals for the District of Columbia. The appeals court subsequently agreed to hear the case on an expedited

---

71 U.S. Congressional Record, Senate, May 24, 1999, pp. S5809–S5840 [daily edition].

72 U.S. Congressional Record, Senate, May 26, 1999, pp. S6034–S6040 [daily edition].

73 Seethe June 8, 1999 decision of Judge Friedman of the U.S. District Court for the District of Columbia at 52 F. Supp. 2d 34 (1999).

basis before Judges Silberman, Randolph, and Tatel. On February 18, 2000, the appeals court affirmed the opinion of the District Court that Representative Campbell and his co-plaintiffs lacked standing to sue the President.[74] On May 18, 2000, Representative Campbell and 30 other Members of Congress appealed this decision to the United States Supreme Court. On October 2, 2000, the United States Supreme Court, without comment, refused to hear the appeal of Representative Campbell, thereby letting stand the holding of the U.S. Court of Appeals.[75]

While Representative Campbell's litigation was continuing, Yugoslavia, on June 10, 1999, agreed to NATO conditions for a cease-fire and withdrawal of Yugoslav military and paramilitary personnel from Kosovo, and the creation of a peacekeeping force (KFOR) which had the sanction of the United Nations. Further, on June 10, 1999, the House of Representatives defeated, by a vote of 328-97, an amendment to H.R. 1401, the National Defense Authorization Act for FY 2000-FY 2001, that would have prohibited the use of any Defense Department funding in FY2000 for "military operations in the Federal Republic of Yugoslavia." On that same day, the House approved, by a vote of 270-155, an amendment that deleted, from the House reported version of H.R. 1401, language that would have prohibited any funding for "combat or peacekeeping operations" in the Federal Republic of Yugoslavia.

On June 12, 1999, President Clinton announced and reported to Congress "consistent with the War Powers Resolution" that he had directed the deployment of about "7,000 U.S. military personnel as the U.S. contribution to the approximately 50,000-member, NATO-led security force (KFOR)" currently being assembled in Kosovo. He also noted that about "1,500 U.S. military personnel, under separate U.S. command and control, will deploy to other countries in the region, as our national support element, in support of KFOR." Thus, by the summer of 1999, the President had been able to proceed with his policy of intervention in the Kosovo crisis under the aegis of NATO, the Congress had not achieved any position of consensus on what actions were appropriate in Yugoslavia, and a U.S. District Court had dismissed a congressional lawsuit (a position subsequently affirmed the following year by the Appeals Court, and the U.S. Supreme Court) attempting to stop Presidential military action in Yugoslavia in the absence of prior congressional authorization under the War Powers Resolution.[76]

[74] Campbell v. Clinton, 203 F.3d 19 (D.C. Cir. 2000).
[75] Campbell v. Clinton, *cert. denied,* 531 U.S.815 October 2, 2000).
[76] For detailed discussion of major issues see CRS Report RL31053, *Kosovo and U.S. Policy: Background and Current Issues,* by Julie Kim and Steven J. Woehrel, and CRS Report RL30352, *War Powers Litigation Since the Enactment of the War Powers Resolution,* by David M. Ackerman.

Haiti: Can the President Order Enforcement of a U.N. Embargo?

On July 3, 1993, Haitian military leader Raoul Cedras and deposed President Jean-Bertrand Aristide signed an agreement providing for the restoration of President Aristide on October 30. The United Nations and Organization of American States took responsibility for verifying compliance. In conjunction with the agreement, President Clinton offered to send 350 troops and military engineers to Haiti to help retrain the Haitian armed forces and work on construction projects. A first group of American and Canadian troops arrived on October 6. When additional U.S. forces arrived on October 11, a group of armed civilians appeared intent upon resisting their landing, and on October 12 defense officials ordered the ship carrying them, the *U.S.S. Harlan County*, to leave Haitian waters.

Because the Haitian authorities were not complying with the agreement, on October 13 the U.N. Security Council voted to restore sanctions against Haiti. On October 20, President Clinton reported "consistent with the War Powers Resolution" that U.S. ships had begun to enforce the U.N. embargo. Some Members of Congress complained that Congress had not been consulted on or authorized the action. On October 18, Senator Dole said he would offer an amendment to the Defense Appropriations bill (H.R. 3116) which would require congressional authorization for all deployments into Haitian waters and airspace unless the President made specified certifications. Congressional leaders and Administration officials negotiated on the terms of the amendment. As enacted, section 8147 of P.L. 103-139 stated the sense of Congress that funds should not be obligated or expended for U.S. military operations in Haiti unless the operations were (1) authorized in advance by Congress, (2) necessary to protect or evacuate U.S. citizens, (3) vital to the national security of the United States and there was not sufficient time to receive congressional authorization, or (4) the President reported in advance that the intended deployment met certain criteria.

Enforcement of the embargo intensified. On April 20, 1994, President Clinton further reported "consistent with the War Powers Resolution" that U.S. naval forces had continued enforcement in the waters around Haiti and that 712 vessels had been boarded. On May 6, 1994, the U.N. Security Council adopted Resolution 917 calling for measures to tighten the embargo. On June 10, 1994, President Clinton announced steps being taken to intensify the pressure on Haiti's military leaders that included assisting the Dominican Republic to seal its border with Haiti, using U.S. naval patrol boats to detain ships suspected of violating the sanctions, a ban on commercial air traffic, and sanctions on financial transactions.

As conditions in Haiti worsened, President Clinton stated he would not rule out the use of force, and gradually this option appeared more certain. Many Members continued to contend congressional authorization was necessary for any invasion of Haiti. On May 24, 1994, the House adopted the Goss amendment to the Defense Authorization bill (H.R. 4301) by a vote of 223-201. The amendment expressed the sense of Congress that the United States should not undertake any military action against the mainland of Haiti unless the President first certified to Congress that clear and present danger to U.S. citizens or interests required such action. Subsequently, on June 9 the House voted on the Goss amendment again. This time the House reversed itself and rejected the amendment by a vote of 195-226. On June 27, a point of order was sustained against an amendment to the State Department appropriations bill that sought to prohibit use of funds for any U.N. peacekeeping operation related to Haiti. On June 29, 1994, the Senate in action on H.R. 4226 repassed a provision identical to Section 8147 of P.L. 103-139 but rejected a measure making advance congressional authorization a binding requirement. On August 5 it tabled (rejected) by a vote of 31 to 63 an amendment to H.R. 4606 by Senator Specter prohibiting the President from using U.S. armed forces to depose the military leadership unless authorized in advance by Congress, necessary to protect U.S. citizens, or vital to U.S. interests.

President Clinton sought and obtained U.N. Security Council authorization for an invasion. On July 31, the U.N. Security Council authorized a multinational force to use "all necessary means to facilitate the departure from Haiti of the military leadership . . . on the understanding that the cost of implementing this temporary operation will be borne by the participating Member States" (Resolution 940, 1994).

On August 3, the Senate adopted an amendment to the Department of Veterans Affairs appropriation, H.R. 4624, by a vote of 100-0 expressing its sense that the Security Council Resolution did not constitute authorization for the deployment of U.S. forces in Haiti under the Constitution or the War Powers Resolution. The amendment, however, was rejected in conference. President Clinton said the same day that he would welcome the support of Congress but did not agree that he was constitutionally mandated to obtain it. Some Members introduced resolutions, such as H.Con.Res. 276, calling for congressional authorization prior to the invasion.

On September 15, 1994, in an address to the Nation, President Clinton said he had called up the military reserve and ordered two aircraft carriers into the region. His message to the military dictators was to leave now or the United States would force them from power. The first phase of military action would remove the dictators from power and restore Haiti's democratically elected government. The second phase would involve a much smaller force joining with forces from other U.N. members which would leave Haiti after 1995 elections were held and a new government installed.

While the Defense Department continued to prepare for an invasion within days, on September 16 President Clinton sent to Haiti a negotiating team of former President Jimmy Carter, former Joint Chiefs of Staff Chairman Colin Powell, and Senate Armed Services Committee Chairman Sam Nunn. Again addressing the Nation on September 18, President Clinton announced that the military leaders had agreed to step down by October 15, and agreed to the immediate introduction of troops, beginning September 19, from the 15,000 member international coalition. He said the agreement was only possible because of the credible and imminent threat of multinational force. He emphasized the mission still had risks and there remained possibilities of violence directed at U.S. troops, but the agreement minimized those risks. He also said that under U.N. Security Council resolution 940, a 25-nation international coalition would soon go to Haiti to begin the task of restoring democratic government. Also on September 18, President Clinton reported to Congress on the objectives in accordance with the sense expressed in Section 8147 (c) of P.L. 103-139, the FY1994 Defense Appropriations Act.

U.S. forces entered Haiti on September 1994. On September 21, President Clinton reported "consistent with the War Powers Resolution" the deployment of 1,500 troops, to be increased by several thousand. (At the peak in September there were about 21,000 U.S. forces in Haiti.) He said the U.S. presence would not be open-ended but would be replaced after a period of months by a U.N. peacekeeping force, although some U.S. forces would participate in and be present for the duration of the U.N. mission. The forces were involved in the first hostilities on September 24 when U.S. Marines killed ten armed Haitian resisters in a fire-fight.

On September 19, the House agreed to H.Con.Res. 290 commending the President and the special delegation to Haiti, and supporting the prompt and orderly withdrawal of U.S. forces from Haiti as soon as possible; on September 19, the Senate agreed to a similar measure, S.Res. 259. On October 3, 1994, the House Foreign Affairs Committee reported H.J.Res. 416 authorizing the forces in Haiti until March 1, 1995, and providing procedures for a joint resolution to withdraw the forces. In House debate on October 6 the House voted against the original contents and for the Dellums substitute. As passed, H.J.Res. 416 stated the sense that the President should have sought congressional approval before deploying U.S. forces to Haiti, supporting a prompt and orderly withdrawal as soon as possible, and requiring a monthly report on Haiti as well as other reports. This same language was also adopted by the Senate on October 6 as S.J. Res. 229, and on October 7 the House passed S.J.Res. 229. President Clinton signed S.J. Res. 229 on October 25, 1994 (P.L. 103-423).

After U.S. forces began to disarm Haitian military and paramilitary forces and President Aristide returned on October 15, 1994, the United States began to withdraw some forces. On March 31, 1995, U.N. peacekeeping forces assumed responsibility for missions previously conducted by U.S. military forces in Haiti. By September 21, 1995, President Clinton reported the United States had 2,400 military personnel in Haiti as participants in the U.N. Mission in Haiti (UNMIH), and 260 U.S. military personnel assigned to the U.S. Support Group Haiti. On February 29, 1996, the U.S. Commander of the UNMIH was replaced and U.S. forces ceased to conduct security operations in Haiti, except for self defense. The majority of the 1,907 U.S. military personnel in Haiti were withdrawn by mid-March 1996, and the remainder, who stayed to arrange the dismantlement and repatriation of equipment, were withdrawn in mid-April 1996. After that, a U.S. support unit of 300 to 500 troops, made up primarily of engineers, remained in Haiti carrying out public works such as building bridges, repairing schools, and digging wells. In December 1997, President Clinton ordered the Dept. of Defense to maintain hundreds of U.S. troops in Haiti indefinitely. In September 1999, however, the 106th Congress passed the FY2000 DOD authorization bill (P.L. 106-65) that prohibited DOD funding to maintain a continuous U.S. military presence in Haiti beyond May 31, 2000. The troops were withdrawn by the end of January 2000. According to the conference report accompanying the FY2000DOD authorization bill (H. Rept. 106-301), the President is not prohibited from engaging in periodic theater engagement activities in Haiti.[77]

Terrorist Attacks against the United States (World Trade Center and the Pentagon) 2001: How Does the War Powers Resolution Apply?

On September 11, 2001, terrorists hijacked four U.S. commercial airliners, crashing two into the twin towers of the World Trade Center in New York City, and another into the Pentagon building in Arlington, Virginia. The fourth plane crashed in Shanksville, Pennsylvania near Pittsburgh, after passengers struggled with the highjackers for control of the aircraft. The death toll from these incidents was more than three thousand, making the attacks the most devastating of their kind in United States history. President George W. Bush characterized these attacks as more than acts of terror. "They were acts of war," he said. He added that "freedom and democracy are under attack," and he asserted that the United States would use "all of our resources to conquer this enemy."[78]

In the days immediately after the September 11 attacks, the President consulted with the leaders of Congress on appropriate steps to take to deal with the situation confronting the United States. One of the things that

[77] For further information on Haiti, see Haiti: Issues for Congress, CRS Report RL32294.

[78] Presidential statement of September 12, 2001. Office of the White House Press Secretary. See White House website at [http://whitehouse.gov/news/releases].

emerged from discussions with the White House and congressional leaders was the concept of a joint resolution of the Congress authorizing the President to take military steps to deal with the parties responsible for the attacks on the United States. Between September 13 and 14, draft language of such a resolution was discussed and negotiated by the President's representatives and the House and Senate leadership of both parties. Other members of both Houses suggested language for consideration. On Friday, September 14, 2001, the text of a joint resolution was introduced. It was first considered and passed by the Senate in the morning of September 14, as Senate Joint Resolution 23, by a vote of 98-0. The House of Representatives passed it later that evening, by a vote of 420-1, after tabling an identical resolution, H.J. Res. 64, and rejecting a motion to recommit by Representative John Tierney that would have had the effect, if passed and enacted, of requiring a report from the President on his actions under the resolution every 60 days.[79]

Senate Joint Resolution 23, titled the "Authorization for Use of Military Force," passed by Congress on September 14, 2001, was signed into law on September 18, 2001.[80] The joint resolution authorizes the President

> to use all necessary and appropriate force against those nations, organizations, or persons he determines planned, authorized, committed, or aided the terrorist attacks that occurred on September 11, 2001, or harbored such organizations or persons, in order to prevent any future acts of international terrorism against the United States by such nations, organizations or persons.

The joint resolution further states that Congress declares that this resolution is intended to "constitute specific statutory authorization within the meaning of section 5(b) of the War Powers Resolution." Finally, the joint resolution also states that "[n]othing in this resolution supercedes any requirement of the War Powers Resolution."

A notable feature of S.J.Res. 23 is that unlike all other major legislation authorizing the use of military force by the President, this joint resolution authorizes military force against "organizations and persons" linked to the September 11, 2001 attacks on the United States. Past authorizations of the use of force have permitted action against unnamed nations in specific regions of the world or against named individual nations. This authorization of military action against "organizations or persons" is unprecedented in American history, with the scope of its reach yet to be determined. The authorization of use of force against unnamed nations is more consistent

[79] For background on discussions regarding the resolution see: Washington Post, September 13, 2001, p.A3; CQ Daily Monitor, September 13, 2001, p.2, 6; CQ Daily Monitor, September 14, 2001, p.2; Washington Post, September 14, 2001, p. A30; The New York Times, September 14, 2001, p.A19; Roll Call, September 20, 2001, p.17. The debate on S. J. Res. 23 is found in U.S. Congress. Congressional Record, 107th Congress, 1st session, pp.S9416–S9421 (Senate); H5638–H5683 [daily edition].

[80] P.L. 107–40 (September 18, 2001); 115 Stat. 224.

with some previous instances where authority was given to act against unnamed states as appropriate when they became aggressors or took military action against the United States or its citizens.[81]

President George W. Bush in signing S.J.Res. on September 18, 2001, noted the Congress had acted "wisely, decisively, and in the finest traditions of our country." He thanked the "leadership of both Houses for their role in expeditiously passing this historic joint resolution." He noted that he had had the "benefit of meaningful consultations with members of the Congress" since the September 11 attacks and that he would "continue to consult closely with them as our Nation responds to this threat to our peace and security." President Bush also asserted that S.J.Res. 23 "recognized the authority of the President under the Constitution to take action to deter and prevent acts of terrorism against the United States." He also stated: "In signing this resolution, I maintain the longstanding position of the executive branch regarding the President's constitutional authority to use force, including the Armed Forces of the United States and regarding the constitutionality of the War Powers Resolution."[82]

Prior to its enactment, there was concern among some in Congress that the President might not adhere to the reporting requirements of the War Powers Resolution when he exercised the authority provided in S.J. Res. 23. There appeared to be general agreement that the President had committed himself to consult with the Congress on matters related to his military actions against terrorists and those associated with the attacks on the United States on September 11. On September 24, 2001, President Bush reported to Congress, "consistent with the War Powers Resolution," and "Senate Joint Resolution 23" that in response to terrorist attacks on the World Trade Center and the Pentagon he had ordered the "deployment of various combat-equipped and combat support forces to a number of foreign nations in the Central and Pacific Command areas of operations." The President noted that as part of efforts to "prevent and deter terrorism" he might find it necessary to order additional forces into these and other areas of the world. . . ." He stated that he could not now predict "the scope and duration of these deployments," nor the "actions necessary to counter the terrorist threat to the United States."

Subsequently, on October 9, 2001, President George W. Bush reported to Congress, "consistent with the War Powers Resolution," and "Senate Joint Resolution 23" that on October 7, 2001, U.S. Armed Forces "began combat

---

81 For detailed legislative history of P.L. 107–40 see CRS Report RS22357, *Authorization For Use of Military Force in Response to the 9/11 Attacks (P.L. 107–40): Legislative History, by Richard F. Grimmett.*

82 Statement of the President on September 18, 2001. President Signs Authorization for Use of Military Force bill. Office of the White House Press Secretary. September 18, 2001. See White House website at [http://whitehouse.gov/news/releases].

action in Afghanistan against Al Qaida terrorists and their Taliban supporters." The President stated that he had directed this military action in response to the September 11, 2001 attacks on U.S. "territory, our citizens, and our way of life, and to the continuing threat of terrorist acts against the United States and our friends and allies." This military action was "part of our campaign against terrorism" and was "designed to disrupt the use of Afghanistan as a terrorist base of operations."

Thus, in light of the September 11, 2001 terrorist attacks against United States territory and citizens, the President and the Congress, after consultations, agreed to a course of legislative action that did not invoke the War Powers Resolution itself, but substituted a specific authorization measure, S.J.Res. 23. Pursuit of such an action is contemplated by the language of the War Powers Resolution itself. As of the end of October 2001, President Bush had chosen to state in his reports to Congress that the military actions he had taken relating to the terrorists attacks were "consistent with" both the War Powers Resolution and Senate Joint Resolution 23. His actions follow the practice of his White House predecessors in not formally citing the language of the War Powers Resolution in section 4(a)(1) that would trigger a military forces withdrawal timetable. Congress for its part in S.J.Res. 23 stated that this legislation constituted "specific statutory authorization within the meaning of section 5(b) of the War Powers Resolution." It also noted that "nothing" in S.J. Res. 23 "supercedes any requirement of the War Powers Resolution." The President and the Congress, in sum, maintained their respective positions on the constitutionality of the War Powers Resolution and the responsibilities of the President under it, while finding a legislative vehicle around which both branches could unite to support the President's response to the terrorist attacks on the United States.

Use of Force Against Iraq Resolution 2002: A Classic Application of the War Powers Resolution?

In the summer of 2002, the Bush Administration made public its views regarding what it deemed a significant threat to U.S. interests and security posed by the prospect that Iraq had or was acquiring weapons of mass destruction. Senior members of the Bush Administration cited a number of violations of U.N. Security Council resolutions by Iraq regarding the obligation imposed at the end of the Gulf War in 1991 to end its chemical, biological and nuclear weapons programs. On September 4, 2002, President Bush met with leaders from both Houses and parties at the White House. At that meeting the President stated that he would seek Congressional support, in the near future, for action deemed necessary to deal with the threat posed to the United States by the regime of Saddam Hussein of Iraq. The President also indicated that he would speak to the United Nations shortly and set out his concerns about Iraq.

On September 12, 2002, President Bush addressed the U.N. General Assembly and set out the history of Iraqi misdeeds over the last two decades and the numerous times that Iraq had not fulfilled its commitments to comply with various U.N. Security Council resolutions, including disarmament, since the Gulf War of 1991. He stated that the United States would work with the U.N. Security Council to deal with Iraq's challenge. However, he emphasized that if Iraq refused to fulfill its obligations to comply with U.N. Security Council resolutions, the United States would see that those resolutions were enforced.[83]

Subsequently, on September 19, 2002, the White House sent a "draft" joint resolution to House Speaker Dennis Hastert, House Minority Leader Richard Gephardt, Senate Majority Leader Thomas Daschle and Senate Minority Leader Trent Lott. This draft would have authorized the President to use military force not only against Iraq but "to restore international peace and security in the region." Subsequently introduced as S.J. Res. 45 on September 26, it served as the basis for an extensive debate over the desirability, necessity, and scope of a new Congressional authorization for the use of force. The Senate used this bill as the focus for a debate which began, after cloture was invoked, on October 3. The Senate debate continued from October 4 until October 11, 2002, and involved consideration of numerous amendments to the measure. In the end the Senate adopted H.J. Res. 114 in lieu of S.J. Res. 45.

The draft measure was not formally introduced in the House. Instead, the vehicle for House consideration of the issue was H.J. Res. 114. Cosponsored by Speaker Hastert and Minority Leader Gephardt and introduced on October 2, 2002, H.J.Res. 114 embodied modifications to the White House draft that were agreeable to the White House, most House and Senate Republicans, and the House Democratic leader. The House International Relations Committee reported out a slightly amended version of the joint resolution on October 7, 2002 (H. Report 107-721). The House adopted the rule governing debate on the joint resolution (H. Res. 474) on October 8, 2002; and debated the measure until October 10, when it passed H.J. Res. 114 by a vote of 296-133. Subsequently, the Senate passed the House version of H.J. Res 144 on October 11 by a vote of 77-23, and President Bush signed the "Authorization for Use of Military Force against Iraq Resolution of 2002" into law on October 16, 2002.[84]

---

83 See the White House website for comments by the President to the Congressional leaders and to the U.N. under news (September) at [http://www.whitehouse.gov/news/releases/2002/09/].

84 P.L. 107–243; 116 Stat. 1498. For a detailed side-by-side comparison of the House and Senate versions of the authorization of force against Iraq legislation and proposed amendments *see* CRS Report RL31596, *Authorization of Use of U.S. Armed Forces Against Iraq: Side-by-Side Comparison of Selected Legislative Proposals*, by Dianne E. Rennack.

In signing H.J. Res. 114 into law, President Bush noted that by passing this legislation the Congress had demonstrated that "the United States speaks with one voice on the threat to international peace and security posed by Iraq." He added that the legislation carried an important message that "Iraq will either comply with all U.N. resolutions, rid itself of weapons of mass destruction, and . . . its support for terrorists, or will be compelled to do so." While the President noted he had sought a "resolution of support" from Congress to use force against Iraq, and appreciated receiving that support, he also stated that:

> . . . my request for it did not, and my signing this resolution does not, constitute any change in the long-standing positions of the executive branch on either the President's constitutional authority to use force to deter, prevent, or respond to aggression or other threats to U.S. interests or on the constitutionality of the War Powers Resolution.

The President went on to state that on the "important question of the threat posed by Iraq", his views and goals and those of the Congress were the same. He further observed that he had extensive consultations with the Congress in the past months, and that he looked forward to "continuing close consultation in the months ahead." He stated his intent to submit written reports to Congress every 60 days on matters "relevant to this resolution."[85]

The central element of P.L. 107-243 is the authorization for the President to use the armed forces of the United States

> as he determines to be necessary and appropriate in order to (1) defend the national security of the United States against the continuing threat posed by Iraq; and (2) enforce all relevant United Nations Security Council resolutions regarding Iraq.

As predicates for the use of force, the statute requires the President to communicate to Congress his determination that the use of diplomatic and other peaceful means will not "adequately protect the United States . . . or . . . lead to enforcement of all relevant United Nations Security Council resolutions" and that the use of force is "consistent" with the battle against terrorism. Like P.L. 102-1 and P.L. 107-40, the statute declares that it is "intended to constitute specific statutory authorization within the meaning of section 5(b) of the War Powers Resolution." It also requires the President to make periodic reports to Congress "on matters relevant to this joint resolution." Finally, the statute expresses Congress' "support" for the efforts of the President to obtain "prompt and decisive action by the Security Council" to enforce Iraq's compliance with all relevant Security Council resolutions.

---

[85] Fortext of President Bush's signing statement for H.J.Res. 114 see the State Department's Washington File entry at [http://usinfo.state.gov/topical/pol/usandun/02101606.htm].

Public Law 107-243 clearly confers broad authority on the President to use force. In contrast to P.L. 102-1, the authority granted is not limited to the implementation of previously adopted Security Council resolutions concerning Iraq but includes "all relevant . . . resolutions." Thus, it appears to incorporate resolutions concerning Iraq that may be adopted by the Security Council in the future as well as those already adopted. The authority also appears to extend beyond compelling Iraq's disarmament to implementing the full range of concerns expressed in those resolutions. Unlike P.L. 107-40, the President's exercise of the authority granted is **not** dependent upon a finding that Iraq was associated in some direct way with the September 11, 2001, attacks on the U.S. Moreover, the authority conferred can be used for the broad purpose of defending "the national security of the United States against the continuing threat posed by Iraq." Nevertheless, P.L. 107-243 is narrower than P.L. 107-40 in that it limits the authorization for the use of force to Iraq. It also requires as a predicate for the use of force that the President determine that peaceful means cannot suffice and that the use of force against Iraq is consistent with the battle against terrorism. It further limits the force used to that which the President determines is "necessary and appropriate." Finally, as with P.L. 107-40, the statutory authorization for use of force granted to the President in P.L. 107-243 is not dependent for its exercise upon prior authorization by the U.N. Security Council. In the form that P.L. 107-243 is drafted, and given the context in which it was debated, one could argue that it is a classic example of an authorization vehicle contemplated by the original War Powers Resolution.

Proposed Amendments

After 30 years of experience with it in practice, controversy continues over the War Powers Resolution's effectiveness and appropriateness as a system for maintaining a congressional role in the use of armed forces in conflict. One view is that the War Powers Resolution is basically sound and does not need amendment.[86] Those who hold this opinion believe it has brought about better communication between the two branches in times of crisis, and has given Congress a vehicle by which it can act when a majority of Members wish to do so. The Resolution served as a restraint on the use of armed forces by the President in some cases because of awareness that certain actions might invoke its provisions. For example, the threat of invoking the War Powers Resolution may have been helpful in getting U.S. forces out of Grenada, in keeping the number of military advisers in El

[86] Fascell, Representative Dante B. Testimony. U.S. Congress. Senate. Committee on Foreign Relations. The War Powers after 200 years: Congress and the President at Constitutional Impasse. Hearings, July 13-September 29, 1988. P. 11.

Salvador limited to 55, and in prodding Congress to take a stand on authorizing the war against Iraq.

A contrary view is that the War Powers Resolution is an inappropriate instrument that restricts the President's effectiveness in foreign policy and should be repealed.[87] Those with this perspective believe that the basic premise of the War Powers Resolution is wrong because in it, Congress attempts excessive control of the deployment of U.S. military forces, encroaching on the responsibility of the President.[88] Supporters of repeal contend that the President needs more flexibility in the conduct of foreign policy and that the time limitation in the War Powers Resolution is unconstitutional and impractical. Some holding this view contend that Congress has always had the power, through appropriations and general lawmaking, to inquire into, support, limit, or prohibit specific uses of U.S. Armed Forces if there is majority support. The War Powers Resolution does not fundamentally change this equation, it is argued, but it complicates action, misleads military opponents, and diverts attention from key policy questions.

A third view is that the War Powers Resolution has not been adequate to accomplish its objectives and needs to be strengthened or reshaped.[89] Proponents of this view assert that Presidents have continued to introduce U.S. armed forces into hostilities without consulting Congress and without congressional authorization. Presidents have cited section 4(a)(1) on only one occasion—Mayaguez—and by the time the action was reported, it was virtually over.

Holders of this third view have proposed various types of amendments to the War Powers Resolution. These include returning to the version originally passed by the Senate, establishing a congressional consultation group, adding a cutoff of funds, and providing for judicial review. A general discussion of these categories of possible changes follows.

Return to Senate Version: Enumerating Exceptions for Emergency Use

In 1977, Senator Thomas Eagleton proposed that the War Powers Resolution return to the original language of the version passed by the Senate, and this proposal has been made several times since. This would require prior

[87] Examples of bills to repeal the War Powers Resolution include S. 2030 introduced by Senator Barry Goldwater on October 31, 1983, H.R. 2525, introduced by Representative Robert Dornan on May 27, 1987 and S. 5, introduced by Senator Robert Dole on January 4, 1995. See also the most recent major legislative floor debate on repeal of the War Powers Resolution, held on June 7, 1995. This debate centered on an amendment to H.R. 1561, offered by Representative Henry Hyde, which would have repealed most of the key elements of the War Powers Resolution. The amendment was defeated by a vote of 217–201. Congressional Record, June 7, 1995, pp. H5655–H5674[daily edition].

[88] Congressional Record, July 12, 1983, p. S9670.

[89] A broad-gauged proposal reflective of this view is S. 564, Use of Force Act, introduced by Senator Biden on March 15, 1995.

congressional authorization for the introduction of forces into conflict abroad without a declaration of war except to respond to or forestall an armed attack against the United States or its forces or to protect U.S. citizens while evacuating them. The amendment would eliminate the construction that the President has 60 to 90 days in which he can militarily act without authorization. Opponents fear the exceptions to forestall attacks or rescue American citizens abroad would serve as a blanket authorization and might be abused, yet might not allow the needed speed of action and provide adequate flexibility in other circumstances.

Shorten or Eliminate Time Limitation

Another proposal is to shorten the time period that the President could maintain forces in hostile situations abroad without congressional authorization from 60 to 30 days, or eliminate it altogether. Some proponents of this amendment contend the current War Powers Resolution gives the President 60 to 90 days to do as he chooses and that this provides too much opportunity for mischief or irreversible action. The original Senate version provided that the use of armed forces in hostilities or imminent hostilities in any of the emergency situations could not be sustained beyond 30 days without specific congressional authorization, extendable by the President upon certification of necessity for safe disengagement. Opponents of this and related measures argue that they induce military opponents to adopt strategies to win given conflicts in Congress that they could not win in the field over time.

Replace Automatic Withdrawal Requirement

The War Powers Resolution has an automatic requirement for withdrawal of troops 60 days after the President submits a section 4(a)(1) report. Some Members of Congress favor replacing this provision with expedited procedures for a joint resolution to authorize the action or require disengagement. One of the main executive branch objections to the War Powers Resolution has been that the withdrawal requirement could be triggered by congressional inaction, and that adversaries can simply wait out the 60 days. By providing for withdrawal by joint resolution, this amendment would also deal with the provision for withdrawal by concurrent resolution, under a cloud because of the *Chadha* decision. On the other hand, a joint resolution requiring disengagement could be vetoed by the President and thus would require a two-thirds majority vote in both Houses for enactment.

Cutoff of Funds

Some proposals call for prohibiting the obligation or expenditure of funds for any use of U.S. armed forces in violation of the War Powers Resolution or laws passed under it except for the purpose of removing troops.[90] Congress could enforce this provision by refusing to appropriate further funds to continue the military action. This has always been the case, some contend, and would not work because Congress would remain reluctant to withhold financial support for U.S. Armed Forces once they were abroad.

Elimination of Action by Concurrent Resolution

Many proposed amendments eliminate section 5(c) providing that U.S. forces engaged in hostilities abroad without congressional authorization are to be removed if Congress so directs by concurrent resolution, and section 7 providing priority procedures for a concurrent resolution. Those who hold this view contend the concurrent resolution section is invalid because of the *Chadha* decision.

Expedited Procedures

Several proposals call for new and more detailed priority procedures for joint resolutions introduced under the War Powers Resolution. These would apply to joint resolutions either authorizing a military action or calling for the withdrawal of forces, and to congressional action to sustain or override a Presidential veto of the joint resolution.[91]

Consultation Group

Several proposed amendments have focused on improving consultation under the War Powers Resolution, particularly by establishing a specific consultation group in Congress for this purpose. Senators Byrd, Nunn, Warner, and Mitchell have proposed the President regularly consult with an initial group of 6 Members—the majority and minority leaders of both Chambers plus the Speaker of the House and President pro tempore of the Senate. Upon a request from a majority of this core group, the President is to consult with a permanent consultative group of 18 Members consisting of the leadership and the ranking and minority members of the Committees on Foreign Relations, Armed Services, and Intelligence. The permanent consultative group would also be able to determine that the President

---

[90] S.J. Res. 323, introduced by Senators Byrd, Warner, and Nunn, May 19, 1988. On September 29, 1983, Senators Cranston, Eagleton, and Stennis introduced an amendment to this effect that had been proposed in the Senate Foreign Relations in July 1977 and known as Committee Print No. 2, July 1, 1977. In U.S. Congress. Senate. Committee on Foreign Relations. War Powers. Hearings, July 13,14 and 15, 1977. Wash., GPO, 1977. P.338. For a review of the use of funding cutoffs by Congress since 1970 see CRS Report RS20775, *Congressional Use of Funding Cutoffs Since 1970 Involving U.S. Military Forces and Overseas Deployments*, by Richard F. Grimmett.,and CRS Report RL33837, *Congressional Authority to Limit U.S. Military Operations in Iraq*, by Jennifer K. Elsea, Michael John Garcia, and Thomas J. Nicola.

[91] See Krotoski, Mark L. Essential Elements of Reform of the War Powers Resolution. Santa Clara Law Review. Vol. 28, Summer 1989, p. 609–750.

should have reported an introduction of forces and to introduce a joint resolution of authorization or withdrawal that would receive expedited procedures.[92]

Other Members have favored a consultation group, but consider that amendment of the War Powers Resolution is not required for Congress to designate such a group.[93] On October 28, 1993, House Foreign Affairs Chairman Lee Hamilton introduced H.R. 3405 to establish a Standing Consultative Group. Its purpose would be to facilitate improved interaction between the executive branch and Congress on the use of U.S. military forces abroad, including under the War Powers Resolution or United Nations auspices. Members of the Consultative Group would be appointed by the Speaker of the House and the Majority Leader of the Senate, after consultation with the minority leaders. The Group would include majority and minority representatives of the leadership and the committees on foreign policy, armed services, intelligence, and appropriations.

Another proposal would attempt to improve consultation by broadening the instances in which the President is required to consult. This proposal would cover all situations in which a President is required to report, rather than only circumstances that invoke the time limitation, as is now the case.[94]

Judicial Review

Proposals have been made that any Member of Congress may bring an action in the United States District Court for the District of Columbia for judgment and injunctive relief on the grounds that the President or the U.S. Armed Forces have not complied with any provision of the War Powers Resolution. The intent of this legislation is to give standing to Members to assert the interest of the House or Senate, but whether it would impel courts to exercise jurisdiction is uncertain. Most recent Federal court decisions have rejected War Powers lawsuits by Congressional litigants on the grounds they lacked standing to sue. Proposals have also called for the court not to decline to make a determination on the merits, on the grounds that the issue of compliance is a political question or otherwise nonjusticiable; to accord expedited consideration to the matter; and to prescribe judicial remedies including that the President submit a report or remove Armed Forces from a situation.[95]

---

92 S.J.Res. 323, introduced May 19, 1988.

93 Fascell, Representative Dante. Testimony before Foreign Relations Committee, July 13, 1988.

94 Strengthening Executive-Legislative Consultation on Foreign Policy. Foreign Affairs Committee Print, October 1983, p. 67.

95 H.J.Res. 95, War Powers Amendments of 1995, introduced by Representative DeFazio, June 16, 1995.

Change of Name

Other proposals would construct a Hostilities Act or Use of Force Act and repeal the War Powers Resolution.[96] A possible objection to invoking the War Powers Resolution is reluctance to escalate international tension by implying that a situation is war. Some would see this as a step in the wrong direction; in the Korean and Vietnam conflicts, some contend, it was self-deceptive and ultimately impractical not to recognize hostilities of that magnitude as war and bring to bear the Constitutional provision giving Congress the power to declare war.

United Nations Actions

With the increase in United Nations actions since the end of the Cold War, the question has been raised whether the War Powers Resolution should be amended to facilitate or restrain the President from supplying forces for U.N. actions without congressional approval. Alternatively, the United Nations Participation Act might be amended, or new legislation enacted, to specify how the War Powers Resolution is to be applied, and whether the approval of Congress would be required only for an initial framework agreement on providing forces to the United Nations, or whether Congress would be required to approve an agreement to supply forces in specified situations, particularly for U.N. peacekeeping operations.

[96] H.R. 3912, Introduced by Representative Lungren, February 4, 1988. Biden, Joseph R. Jr. and John B. Ritch. The War Power at a Constitutional Impasse: a "Joint Decision" Solution. Georgetown Law Journal, Vol. 77:367.

Appendix A. Instances Reported under the War Powers Resolution

This appendix lists reports Presidents have made to Congress as the result of the War Powers Resolution. Each entry contains the President's reference to the War Powers Resolution.[97] The reports generally cite the President's authority to conduct foreign relations and as Commander in Chief; each entry indicates any additional legislative authority a President cites for his action.

(1) **Danang, Vietnam.** On April 4, 1975, President Ford reported the use of naval vessels, helicopters, and Marines to transport refugees from Danang and other seaports to safer areas in Vietnam. His report mentioned section 4(a)(2) of the War Powers Resolution and authorization in the Foreign Assistance Act of 1961 for humanitarian assistance to refugees suffering from the hostilities in South Vietnam. Monroe Leigh, Legal Adviser to the Department of State, testified later that the President "advised the members of the Senate and House leadership that a severe emergency existed in the coastal communities of South Vietnam and that he was directing American naval transports and contract vessels to assist in the evacuation of refugees from coastal seaports."[98]

(2) **Cambodia.** On April 12, 1975, President Ford reported the use of ground combat Marines, helicopters, and supporting tactical air elements to assist with the evacuation of U.S. nationals from Cambodia. The report took note of both section 4 and section 4(a)(2) of the War Powers Resolution. On April 3, 1975, the day the President authorized the Ambassador to evacuate the American staff, he directed that the leaders of the Senate and House be advised of the general plan of evacuation. On April 11, the day he ordered the final evacuation, President Ford again directed that congressional leaders be notified.

(3) **Vietnam.** On April 30, 1975, President Ford reported the use of helicopters, Marines, and fighter aircraft to aid in the evacuation of U.S. citizens and others from South Vietnam. The report took note of section 4 of the War Powers Resolution. On April 10, the President had asked Congress to clarify its limitation on the use of forces in Vietnam to insure evacuation of U.S. citizens and to cover some Vietnamese nationals, but legislation to this effect was not completed. On April 28, the President directed that

[97] Two of the reports did not mention the War Powers Resolution but met the basic requirement of reporting specified deployments or uses of forces. For the text of the reports until April 12, 1994, and other key documents and correspondence see U.S. Congress. House. Committee on Foreign Affairs. Subcommittee on International Security, International Organizations and Human Rights. The War Powers Resolution, Relevant Documents, Reports, Correspondence. Committee Print., 103rd Congress, second session, May 1994. 267 p.

[98] U.S. Congress. House. Committee on International Relations. War Powers: A test of compliance relative to the Danang sealift, the evacuation of Phnom Penh, the evacuation of Saigon, and the Mayaguez incident. Hearings, May 7 and June 4, 1975. Washington, U.S. Govt. Printing Off., 1975. P. 3.

congressional leaders be notified that the final phase of the evacuation of Saigon would be carried out by military forces within the next few hours.[99]

(4) **Mayaguez.** On May 15, 1975, President Ford reported that he had ordered U.S. military forces to rescue the crew of and retake the ship Mayaguez that had been seized by Cambodian naval patrol boats on May 12, that the ship had been retaken, and that the withdrawal of the forces had been undertaken. The report took note of section 4(a)(1) of the War Powers Resolution. On May 13, Administration aides contacted ten Members from the House and 11 Senators regarding the military measures directed by the President.[100]

(5) **Iran.** On April 26, 1980, President Carter reported the use of six aircraft and eight helicopters in an unsuccessful attempt of April 24 to rescue the American hostages in Iran. The report was submitted "consistent with the reporting provision" of the War Powers Resolution. President Carter said the United States was acting in accordance with its right under Article 51 of the United Nations Charter to protect and rescue its citizens where the government of the territory in which they are located is unable or unwilling to protect them. The Administration did not inform congressional leaders of the plan on grounds that consultation could endanger the success of the mission.

(6) **Sinai.** The United States, Egypt, and Israel signed an executive agreement on August 3, 1981, outlining U.S. participation in a Multinational Force and Observers unit to function as a peacekeeping force in the Sinai after Israel withdrew its forces. In anticipation of this accord, on July 21, 1981, President Reagan requested congressional authorization for U.S. participation. Congress authorized President Reagan to deploy military personnel to the Sinai in the Multinational Force and Observers Participation Resolution, P.L. 97-132, signed December 29, 1981. On March 19, 1982, President Reagan reported the deployment of military personnel and equipment to the Multinational Force and Observers in the Sinai. The President said the report was provided "consistent with section 4(a)(2) of the War Powers Resolution" and cited the Multinational Force and Observers Participation Resolution.

(7) **Lebanon.** On August 24, 1982, President Reagan reported the dispatch of 800 Marines to serve in the multinational force to assist in the withdrawal of members of the Palestine Liberation force from Lebanon. The report was provided "consistent with" but did not cite any specific provision of the War Powers Resolution. President Reagan had begun discussions with congressional leaders on July 6, 1982 after the plan had been publicly

---

99 Ibid., p. 6.
100 Ibid., p. 78.

announced, and after leaks in the Israeli press indicated that he had approved the plan on July 2.[101]

(8) Lebanon. On September 29, 1982, President Reagan reported the deployment of 1,200 Marines to serve in a temporary multinational force to facilitate the restoration of Lebanese government sovereignty. He said the report was being submitted "consistent with the War Powers Resolution." On this second Multinational Force in Lebanon there was a considerable amount of negotiation between the executive branch and Congress, but most of it occurred after the decision to participate had been made and the Marines were in Lebanon.[102]

(9) **Chad.** On August 8, 1983, President Reagan reported the deployment of two AWACS electronic surveillance planes and eight F-15 fighter planes and ground logistical support forces to Sudan to assist Chad and other friendly governments helping Chad against Libyan and rebel forces. He said the report was being submitted consistent with Section 4 of the War Powers Resolution. On August 23, 1983, a State Department spokesman announced that the planes were being withdrawn.

(10) **Lebanon.** On August 30, 1983, after the Marines participating in the Multinational Force in Lebanon were fired upon and two were killed, President Reagan submitted a report "consistent with section 4 of the War Powers Resolution." In P.L.98-119, the Multinational Force in Lebanon Resolution, signed October 12, 1983, Congress determined section 4(a) had become operative on August 29, 1983, and authorized the forces to remain for 18 months.

(11) **Grenada.** On October 25, 1983, President Reagan reported that U.S. Army and Marine personnel had begun landing in Grenada to join collective security forces of the Organization of Eastern Caribbean States in assisting in the restoration of law and order in Grenada and to facilitate the protection and evacuation of U.S. citizens. He submitted the report "consistent with the War Powers Resolution." President Reagan met with several congressional leaders at 8 p.m. on October 24.[103] This was after the directive ordering the landing had been signed at 6 p.m., but before the actual invasion that began at 5:30 a.m., October 25.

(12) **Libya.** On March 26, 1986, President Reagan reported (without any mention of the War Powers Resolution) that, on March 24 and 25, U.S. forces conducting freedom of navigation exercises in the Gulf of Sidra had

[101] Oberdorfer, Don and John M. Goshko. Peace-keeping Force. Washington Post, July 7, 1982, p. 1.

[102] Gwetzman, Bernard. U.S. To Send Back Marines to Beirut. New York Times, September 21, 1982, p. 1.

[103] U.S. Declares Goal in to Protect Americans and Restore Order. Washington Post, October 26, 1983. P. A7.

been attacked by Libyan missiles. In response, the United States fired missiles at Libyan vessels and at Sirte, the missile site.

(13) **Libya.** On April 16, 1986, President Reagan reported, "consistent with the War Powers Resolution", that on April 14 U.S. air and naval forces had conducted bombing strikes on terrorist facilities and military installations in Libya. President Reagan had invited approximately a dozen congressional leaders to the White House at about 4 p.m. on April 14 and discussed the situation until 6 p.m. He indicated that he had ordered the bombing raid and that the aircraft from the United Kingdom were on their way to Libya and would reach their targets about 7 p.m.

(14) **Persian Gulf**[104]. On September 23, 1987, President Reagan reported that, on September 21, two U.S. helicopters had fired on an Iranian landing craft observed laying mines in the Gulf. The President said that while mindful of legislative- executive differences on the interpretation and constitutionality of certain provisions of the War Powers Resolution, he was reporting in a spirit of mutual cooperation.

(15) **Persian Gulf.** On October 10, 1987, President Reagan reported "consistent with the War Powers Resolution" that, on October 8, three U.S. helicopters were fired upon by small Iranian naval vessels and the helicopters returned fire and sank one of the vessels.

(16) **Persian Gulf.** On October 20, 1987, President Reagan reported an attack by an Iranian Silkworm missile against the U.S.-flag tanker Sea Isle City on October 15 and U.S. destruction, on October 19, of the Iranian Rashadat armed platform used to support attacks and mine-laying operations. The report was submitted "consistent with the War Powers Resolution."

(17) **Persian Gulf.** On April 19, 1988, President Reagan reported "consistent with the War Powers Resolution" that in response to the U.S.S. Samuel B. Roberts striking a mine on April 14, U.S. Armed Forces attacked and "neutralized" two Iranian oil platforms on April 18 and, after further Iranian attacks, damaged or sank Iranian vessels. The President called the actions "necessary and proportionate." Prior to this action, the President met with congressional leaders.

(18) **Persian Gulf.** On July 4, 1988, President Reagan reported that on July 3 the USS Vincennes and USS Elmer Montgomery fired upon approaching Iranian small craft, sinking two. Firing in self-defense at what it believed to be a hostile Iranian military aircraft, the Vincennes had shot down an

[104] Earlier, on September 21, 1987, Secretary of State George P. Shultz submitted a report concerning the Iraqi aircraft missile attack on the U.S.S. Stark in the Persian Gulf similar to reports in this list submitted by Presidents. The report did not mention the War Powers Resolution but said the U.S. presence had been maintained in the Gulf pursuant to the authority of the President as Commander-in-Chief.

Iranian civilian airliner. The President expressed deep regret. The report was submitted "consistent with the War Powers Resolution."

(19) **Persian Gulf.** On July 14, 1988, President Reagan reported that, on July 12, two U.S. helicopters, responding to a distress call from a Japanese-owned Panamanian tanker, were fired at by two small Iranian boats and returned the fire. The report was submitted "consistent with the War Powers Resolution."

(20) **Philippines.** On December 2, 1989, President George H. W. Bush submitted a report to congressional leaders "consistent with" the War Powers Resolution, describing assistance of combat air patrols to help the Aquino government in the Philippines restore order and to protect American lives. After the planes had taken off from Clark Air Base to provide air cover, Vice President Quayle and other officials informed congressional leaders. On December 7, House Foreign Affairs Committee Chairman Dante Fascell wrote President Bush expressing his concern for the lack of advance consultation. In reply, on February 10, 1990, National Security Adviser Brent Scowcroft wrote Chairman Fascell that the President was "committed to consultations with Congress prior to deployments of U.S. Forces into actual or imminent hostilities in all instances where such consultations are possible. In this instance, the nature of the rapidly evolving situation required an extremely rapid decision very late at night and consultation was simply not an option."

(21) **Panama.** On December 21, 1989, President George H.W. Bush reported "consistent with the War Powers Resolution" that he had ordered U.S. military forces to Panama to protect the lives of American citizens and bring General Noriega to justice. By February 13, 1990, all the invasion forces had been withdrawn. President Bush informed several congressional leaders of the approaching invasion of Panama at 6 p.m. on December 19, 1989. This was after the decision to take action was made, but before the operation actually began at 1:00 a.m., December 20.

(22) **Liberia.** On August 6, 1990, President George H. W. Bush reported to Congress that following discussions with congressional leaders, a reinforced rifle company had been sent to provide additional security to the U.S. Embassy in Monrovia and helicopter teams had evacuated U.S. citizens from Liberia. The report did not mention the War Powers Resolution or cite any authority.

(23) **Iraq.** On August 9, 1990, President George H. W. Bush reported to Congress "consistent with the War Powers Resolution" that he had ordered the forward deployment of substantial elements of the U.S. Armed Forces into the Persian Gulf region to help defend Saudi Arabia after the invasion of Kuwait by Iraq. The Bush Administration notified congressional leaders that it was deploying U.S. troops to Saudi Arabia on August 7, the date of

the deployment. After the forces had been deployed, President Bush held several meetings with congressional leaders and members of relevant committees, and committees held hearings to discuss the situation.

(24) **Iraq.** On November 16, 1990, President George H. W. Bush reported, without mention of the War Powers Resolution but referring to the August 9 letter, the continued buildup to ensure "an adequate offensive military option." Just prior to adjournment, Senate Majority Leader Mitchell and Speaker Foley designated Members to form a consultation group, and the President held meetings with the group on some occasions, but he did not consult the members in advance on the major buildup of forces in the Persian Gulf area announced November 8.

(25) **Iraq.** On January 18, 1991, President George H. W. Bush reported to Congress "consistent with the War Powers Resolution" that he had directed U.S. Armed Forces to commence combat operations on January 16 against Iraqi forces and military targets in Iraq and Kuwait. On January 12, Congress had passed the Authorization for Use of Military Force against Iraq Resolution (P.L. 102-1), which stated it was the specific statutory authorization required by the War Powers Resolution. P.L. 102-1 required the President to submit a report to the Congress at least once every 60 days on the status of efforts to obtain compliance by Iraq with the U.N. Security Council resolution, and Presidents submitted subsequent reports on military actions in Iraq "consistent with" P.L. 102-1. An exception is report submitted June 28, 1993, described below.

(26) **Somalia.** On December 10, 1992, President George H. W. Bush reported "consistent with the War Powers Resolution" that U.S. armed forces had entered Somalia on December 8 in response to a humanitarian crisis and a U.N. Security Council Resolution determining that the situation constituted a threat to international peace. He included as authority applicable treaties and laws, and said he had also taken into account views expressed in H.Con. Res. 370, S.Con.Res. 132, and the Horn of Africa Recovery and Food Security Act, P.L. 102-274. On December 4, the day the President ordered the forces deployed, he briefed a number of congressional leaders on the action.

(27) **Bosnia.** On April 13, 1993, President Clinton reported "consistent with Section 4 of the War Powers Resolution" that U.S. forces were participating in a NATO air action to enforce a U.N. ban on all unauthorized military flights over Bosnia-Hercegovina, pursuant to his authority as Commander in Chief. Later, on April 27, President Clinton consulted with about two dozen congressional leaders on potential further action.

(28) **Somalia.** On June 10, 1993, President Clinton reported that in response to attacks against U.N. forces in Somalia by a factional leader, the U.S. Quick Reaction Force in the area had participated in military action to quell

the violence. He said the report was "consistent with the War Powers Resolution, in light of the passage of 6 months since President Bush's initial report. . . ." He said the action was in accordance with applicable treaties and laws, and said the deployment was consistent with S.J.Res. 45 as adopted by the Senate and amended by the House. (The Senate did not act on the House amendment, so Congress did not take final action on S.J.Res. 45.)

(29) **Iraq.** On June 28, 1993, President Clinton reported "consistent with the War Powers Resolution" that on June 26 U.S. naval forces had launched missiles against the Iraqi Intelligence Service's headquarters in Baghdad in response to an unsuccessful attempt to assassinate former President Bush in Kuwait in April 1993.

(30) **Macedonia**[105]**.** On July 9, 1993, President Clinton reported "consistent with Section 4 of the War Powers Resolution" the deployment of approximately 350 U.S. armed forces to Macedonia to participate in the U.N. Protection Force to help maintain stability in the area of former Yugoslavia. He said the deployment was directed in accordance with Section 7 of the United Nations Participation Act.

(31) **Bosnia.** On October 13, 1993, President Clinton reported "consistent with the War Powers Resolution" that U.S. military forces continued to support enforcement of the U.N. no-fly zone in Bosnia, noting that more that 50 U.S. aircraft were now available for NATO efforts in this regard.

(32) **Haiti.** On October 20, 1993, President Clinton submitted a report "consistent with the War Powers Resolution" that U.S. ships had begun to enforce a U.N. embargo against Haiti.

(33) **Macedonia.** On January 8, 1994, President Clinton reported "consistent with the War Powers Resolution" that approximately 300 members of a reinforced company team (RCT) of the U.S. Army's 3rd Infantry Division (Mechanized) had assumed a peacekeeping role in Macedonia as part of the United Nations Protection Force (UNPROFOR) on January 6, 1994.

(34) **Bosnia.** On February 17, 1994, President Clinton reported "consistent with the War Powers Resolution" that the United States had expanded its participation in United Nations and NATO efforts to reach a peaceful solution in former Yugoslavia and that 60 U.S. aircraft were available for participation in the authorized NATO missions.

(35) **Bosnia.** On March 1, 1994, President Clinton reported "consistent with" the War Powers Resolution that on February 28 U.S. planes patrolling the "no-fly zone" in former Yugoslavia under the North Atlantic Treaty Organization (NATO) shot down 4 Serbian Galeb planes.

[105] See footnote 66 above discussing Macedonia.

(36) **Bosnia.** On April 12, 1994, President Clinton reported "consistent with" the War Powers Resolution that on April 10 and 11, U.S. warplanes under NATO command had fired against Bosnian Serb forces shelling the "safe" city of Gorazde.

(37) **Rwanda.** On April 12, 1994, President Clinton reported "consistent with" the War Powers Resolution that combat-equipped U.S. military forces had been deployed to Burundi to conduct possible non-combatant evacuation operations of U.S. citizens and other third-country nationals from Rwanda, where widespread fighting had broken out.

(38) **Macedonia.** On April 19, 1994, President Clinton reported "consistent with the War Powers Resolution" that the U.S. contingent in the former Yugoslav Republic of Macedonia had been augmented by a reinforced company of 200 personnel.

(39) **Haiti.** On April 20, 1994, President Clinton reported "consistent with the War Powers Resolution" that U.S. naval forces had continued enforcement in the waters around Haiti and that 712 vessels had been boarded.

(40) **Bosnia.** On August 22, 1994, President Clinton reported the use on August 5 of U.S. aircraft under NATO to attack Bosnian Serb heavy weapons in the Sarajevo heavy weapons exclusion zone upon request of the U.N. Protection Forces. He did not cite the War Powers Resolution but referred to the April 12 report that cited the War Powers Resolution.

(41) **Haiti.** On September 21, 1994, President Clinton reported "consistent with the War Powers Resolution" the deployment of 1,500 troops to Haiti to restore democracy in Haiti. The troop level was subsequently increased to 20,000.

(42) **Bosnia.** On November 22, 1994, President Clinton reported "consistent with the War Powers Resolution" the use of U.S. combat aircraft on November 21, 1994 under NATO to attack bases used by Serbs to attack the town of Bihac in Bosnia.

(43) **Macedonia.** On December 22, 1994, President Clinton reported "consistent with the War Powers Resolution" that the U.S. Army contingent in the former Yugoslav Republic of Macedonia continued its peacekeeping mission and that the current contingent would soon be replaced by about 500 soldiers from the 3rd Battalion, 5th Cavalry Regiment, 1st Armored Division from Kirchgons, Germany.

(44) **Somalia.** On March 1, 1995, President Clinton reported "consistent with the War Powers Resolution" that on February 27, 1995, 1,800 combat-equipped U.S. armed forces personnel began deployment into Mogadishu, Somalia, to assist in the withdrawal of U.N. forces assigned there to the United Nations Operation in Somalia (UNOSOM II).

(45) **Haiti.** On March 21, 1995, President Clinton reported "consistent with the War Powers Resolution" that U.S. military forces in Haiti as part of a U.N. Multinational Force had been reduced to just under 5,300 personnel. He noted that as of March 31, 1995, approximately 2,500 U.S. personnel would remain in Haiti as part of the U.N. Mission in Haiti (UNMIH).

(46) **Bosnia.** On May 24, 1995, President Clinton reported "consistent with the War Powers Resolution" that U.S. combat-equipped fighter aircraft and other aircraft continued to contribute to NATO's enforcement of the no-fly zone in airspace over Bosnia-Herzegovina. U.S. aircraft, he noted, are also available for close air support of U.N. forces in Croatia. Roughly 500 U.S. soldiers continue to be deployed in the former Yugoslav Republic of Macedonia as part of the U.N. Preventive Deployment Force (UNPREDEP). U.S. forces continue to support U.N. refugee and embargo operations in this region.

(47) **Bosnia.** On September 1, 1995, President Clinton reported "consistent with the War Powers Resolution," that "U.S. combat and support aircraft" had been used beginning on August 29, 1995, in a series of NATO air strikes against Bosnian Serb Army (BSA) forces in Bosnia-Herzegovina that were threatening the U.N.- declared safe areas of Sarajevo, Tuzla, and Gorazde." He noted that during the first day of operations, "some 300 sorties were flown against 23 targets in the vicinity of Sarajevo, Tuzla, Goradzde and Mostar."

(48) **Haiti.** On September 21, 1995, President Clinton reported "consistent with the War Powers Resolution" that currently the United States has 2,400 military personnel in Haiti as participants in the U.N. Mission in Haiti (UNMIH). In addition, 260 U.S. military personnel are assigned to the U.S. Support Group Haiti.

(49) **Bosnia**. On December 6, 1995, President Clinton notified Congress, "consistent with the War Powers Resolution," that he had "ordered the deployment of approximately 1,500 U.S. military personnel to Bosnia and Herzegovina and Croatia as part of a NATO 'enabling force' to lay the groundwork for the prompt and safe deployment of the NATO-led Implementation Force (IFOR)," which would be used to implement the Bosnian peace agreement after its signing. The President also noted that he had authorized deployment of roughly 3,000 other U.S. military personnel to Hungary, Italy, and Croatia to establish infrastructure for the enabling force and the IFOR.

(50) **Bosnia**. On December 21, 1995, President Clinton notified Congress "consistent with the War Powers Resolution" that he had ordered the deployment of approximately 20,000 U.S. military personnel to participate in the NATO-led Implementation Force (IFOR) in the Republic of Bosnia-Herzegovina, and approximately 5,000 U.S. military personnel would be

deployed in other former Yugoslav states, primarily in Croatia. In addition, about 7,000 U.S. support forces would be deployed to Hungary, Italy and Croatia and other regional states in support of IFOR's mission. The President ordered participation of U.S. forces "pursuant to" his "constitutional authority to conduct the foreign relations of the United States and as Commander-in-Chief and Chief Executive."

(51) **Haiti.** On March 21, 1996, President Clinton notified Congress "consistent with the War Powers Resolution" that beginning in January 1996 there had been a "phased reduction" in the number of United States personnel assigned to the United Nations Mission in Haiti (UNMIH). As of March 21, 309 U.S. personnel remained a part of UNMIH. These U.S. forces were "equipped for combat."

(52) **Liberia.** On April 11, 1996, President Clinton notified Congress "consistent with the War Powers Resolution" that on April 9, 1996 due to the "deterioration of the security situation and the resulting threat to American citizens" in Liberia he had ordered U.S. military forces to evacuate from that country "private U.S. citizens and certain third-country nationals who had taken refuge in the U.S. Embassy compound. . . ."

(53) **Liberia.** On May 20, 1996, President Clinton notified Congress, "consistent with the War Powers Resolution" of the continued deployment of U.S. military forces in Liberia to evacuate both American citizens and other foreign personnel, and to respond to various isolated "attacks on the American Embassy complex" in Liberia. The President noted that the deployment of U.S. forces would continue until there was no longer any need for enhanced security at the Embassy and a requirement to maintain an evacuation capability in the country.

(54) **Central African Republic.** On May 23, 1996, President Clinton notified Congress, "consistent with the War Powers Resolution" of the deployment of U.S. military personnel to Bangui, Central African Republic, to conduct the evacuation from that country of "private U.S. citizens and certain U.S. Government employees," and to provide "enhanced security" for the American Embassy in Bangui.

(55) **Bosnia.** On June 21, 1996, President Clinton notified Congress, "consistent with the War Powers Resolution" that United States forces totaling about 17,000 remain deployed in Bosnia "under NATO operational command and control" as part of the NATO Implementation Force (IFOR). In addition, about 5,500 U.S. military personnel are deployed in Hungary, Italy and Croatia, and other regional states to provide "logistical and other support to IFOR." The President noted that it was the intention that IFOR would complete the withdrawal of all troops in the weeks after December 20, 1996, on a schedule "set by NATO commanders consistent with the safety of troops and the logistical requirements for an orderly withdrawal."

He also noted that a U.S. Army contingent (of about 500 U.S. soldiers) remains in the Former Yugoslav Republic of Macedonia as part of the United Nations Preventive Deployment Force (UNPREDEP).

(56) **Rwanda and Zaire.** On December 2, 1996, President Clinton notified Congress "consistent with the War Powers Resolution," that in support of the humanitarian efforts of the United Nations regarding refugees in Rwanda and the Great Lakes Region of Eastern Zaire, he had authorized the use of U.S. personnel and aircraft, including AC-130U planes to help in surveying the region in support of humanitarian operations, although fighting still was occurring in the area, and U.S. aircraft had been subject to fire when on flight duty.

(57) **Bosnia.** On December 20, 1996, President Clinton notified Congress "consistent with the War Powers Resolution," that he had authorized U.S. participation in an IFOR follow-on force in Bosnia, known as SFOR (Stabilization Force), under NATO command. The President said the U.S. forces contribution to SFOR was to be "about 8,500" personnel whose primary mission was to deter or prevent a resumption of hostilities or new threats to peace in Bosnia. SFOR's duration was Bosnia is expected to be 18 months, with progressive reductions and eventual withdrawal.

(58) **Albania.** On March 15, 1997, President Clinton notified Congress "consistent with the War Powers Resolution," that on March 13, 1997, he had utilized U.S. military forces to evacuate certain U.S. Government employees and private U.S. citizens from Tirana, Albania, and to enhance security for the U.S. embassy in that city.

(59) **Congo and Gabon.** On March 27, 1997, President Clinton notified Congress "consistent with the War Powers Resolution," that on March 25, 1997, a standby evacuation force of U.S. military personnel had been deployed to Congo and Gabon to provide enhanced security for American private citizens, government employees and selected third country nationals in Zaire, and be available for any necessary evacuation operation.

(60) **Sierra Leone.** On May 30, 1997, President Clinton notified Congress "consistent with the War Powers Resolution," that on May 29 and May 30, 1997, U.S. military personnel were deployed to Freetown, Sierra Leone to prepare for and undertake the evacuation of certain U.S. Government employees and private U.S. citizens.

(61) **Bosnia.** On June 20, 1997, President Clinton notified Congress "consistent with the War Powers Resolution," that U.S. Armed Forces continued to support peacekeeping operations in Bosnia and other states in the region in support of the NATO-led Stabilization Force (SFOR). He reported that most U.S. military personnel then involved in SFOR were in Bosnia, near Tuzla, and about 2,800 U.S. troops were deployed in Hungary, Croatia,

Italy, and other regional states to provide logistics and other support to SFOR. A U.S. Army contingent of about 500 also remained deployed in the Former Yugoslav Republic of Macedonia as part of the U.N. Preventative Deployment Force (UNPREDEP).

(62) **Cambodia.** On July 11, 1997, President Clinton notified Congress "consistent with the War Powers Resolution," that in an effort to ensure the security of American citizens in Cambodia during a period of domestic conflict there, he had deployed a Task Force of about 550 U.S. military personnel to Utapao Air Base in Thailand. These personnel were to be available for possible emergency evacuation operations in Cambodia.

(63) **Bosnia.** On December 19, 1997, President Clinton notified Congress "consistent with the War Powers Resolution," that he intended "in principle" to have the United States participate in a security presence in Bosnia when the NATO SFOR contingent withdrew in the summer of 1998.

(64) **Guinea-Bissau.** On June 12, 1998 President Clinton reported to Congress "consistent with the War Powers Resolution" that, on June 10, 1998, in response to an army mutiny in Guinea-Bissau endangering the U.S. Embassy and U.S. government employees and citizens in that country, he had deployed a standby evacuation force of U.S. military personnel to Dakar, Senegal, to remove such individuals, as well as selected third country nationals, from the city of Bissau.

(65) **Bosnia.** On June 19, 1998, President Clinton reported to Congress "consistent with the War Powers Resolution" regarding activities in the last six months of combat-equipped U.S. forces in support of NATO's SFOR in Bosnia and surrounding areas of former Yugoslavia.

(66) **Kenya and Tanzania.** On August 10, 1998, President Clinton reported to Congress "consistent with the War Powers Resolution" that he had deployed, on August 7, 1998, a Joint Task Force of U.S. military personnel to Nairobi, Kenya to coordinate the medical and disaster assistance related to the bombings of the U.S. embassies in Kenya and Tanzania. He also reported that teams of 50-100 security personnel had arrived in Nairobi, Kenya and Dar es Salaam, Tanzania to enhance the security of the U.S. embassies and citizens there.

(67) **Albania.** On August 18, 1998, President Clinton reported to Congress, "consistent with the War Powers Resolution," that he had, on August 16, 1998, deployed 200 U.S. Marines and 10 Navy SEALS to the U.S. Embassy compound in Tirana, Albania to enhance security against reported threats against U.S. personnel.

(68) **Afghanistan and Sudan.** On August 21, 1998, by letter, President Clinton notified Congress "consistent with the War Powers Resolution" that he had authorized airstrikes on August 20th against camps and installations

in Afghanistan and Sudan used by the Osama bin Laden terrorist organization. The President did so based on what he termed convincing information that the bin Laden organization was responsible for the bombings, on August 7, 1998, of the U.S. embassies in Kenya and Tanzania.

(69) **Liberia.** On September 29, 1998, by letter, President Clinton notified Congress "consistent with the War Powers Resolution" that he had deployed a stand by response and evacuation force to Liberia to augment the security force at the U.S. Embassy in Monrovia, and to provide for a rapid evacuation capability, as needed, to remove U.S. citizens and government personnel from the country.

(70) **Bosnia.** On January 19, 1999, by letter, President Clinton notified Congress "consistent with the War Powers Resolution" that pursuant to his authority as Commander-in-Chief he was continuing to authorize the use of combat-equipped U.S. Armed Forces to Bosnia and other states in the region to participate in and support the NATO-led Stabilization Force (SFOR). He noted that U.S. SFOR military personnel totaled about 6,900, with about 2,300 U.S. military personnel deployed to Hungary, Croatia, Italy and other regional states. Also some 350 U.S. military personnel remain deployed in the Former Yugoslav Republic of Macedonia (FYROM) as part of the UN Preventative Deployment Force (UNPREDEP).

(71) **Kenya.** On February 25, 1999, President Clinton submitted a supplemental report to Congress "consistent with the War Powers Resolution" describing the continuing deployment of U.S. military personnel in Kenya to provide continuing security for U.S. embassy and American citizens in Nairobi in the aftermath of the terrorist bombing there.

(72) **Yugoslavia/Kosovo.** On March 26, 1999, President Clinton notified Congress "consistent with the War Powers Resolution," that on March 24, 1999, U.S. military forces, at his direction and acting jointly with NATO allies, had commenced air strikes against Yugoslavia in response to the Yugoslav government's campaign of violence and repression against the ethnic Albanian population in Kosovo.

(73) **Yugoslavia/Albania.** On April 7, 1999, President Clinton notified Congress, "consistent with the War Powers Resolution," that he had ordered additional U.S. military forces to Albania, including rotary wing aircraft, artillery, and tactical missiles systems to enhance NATO's ability to conduct effective air operations in Yugoslavia. About 2,500 soldiers and aviators are to be deployed as part of this task force.

(74) **Yugoslavia/Albania.** On May 25, 1999, President Clinton reported to Congress, "consistent with the War Powers Resolution" that he had directed "deployment of additional aircraft and forces to support NATO's ongoing efforts [against Yugoslavia], including several thousand additional

U.S. Armed Forces personnel to Albania in support of the deep strike force located there." He also directed that additional U.S. forces be deployed to the region to assist in "humanitarian operations."

(75) **Yugoslavia/Kosovo.** On June 12, 1999, President Clinton reported to Congress, "consistent with the War Powers Resolution," that he had directed the deployment of about "7,000 U.S. military personnel as the U.S. contribution to the approximately 50,000-member, NATO-led security force (KFOR)" currently being assembled in Kosovo. He also noted that about "1,500 U.S. military personnel, under separate U.S. command and control, will deploy to other countries in the region, as our national support element, in support of KFOR."

(76) **Bosnia.** On July 19, 1999, President Clinton reported to Congress "consistent with the War Powers Resolution" that about 6,200 U.S. military personnel were continuing to participate in the NATO-led Stabilization Force (SFOR) in Bosnia, and that another 2,200 personnel were supporting SFOR operations from Hungary, Croatia, and Italy. He also noted that U.S. military personnel remain in the Former Yugoslav Republic of Macedonia to support the international security presence in Kososo (KFOR).

(77) **East Timor.** On October 8, 1999, President Clinton reported to Congress "consistent with the War Powers Resolution" that he had directed the deployment of a limited number of U.S. military forces to East Timor to support the U.N. multinational force (INTERFET) aimed at restoring peace to East Timor. U.S. support had been limited initially to "communications, logistics, planning assistance and transportation." The President further noted that he had authorized deployment of the amphibious ship USS BELLEAU WOOD, together with its helicopters and her complement of personnel from the 31st Marine Expeditionary Unit (Special Operations Capable) (MEU SOC)) to the East Timor region, to provide helicopter airlift and search and rescue support to the multinational operation. U.S. participation was anticipated to continue until the transition to a U.N. peacekeeping operation was complete.

(78) **Yugoslavia/Kosovo.** On December 15, 1999, President Clinton reported to Congress "consistent with the War Powers Resolution" that U.S. combat-equipped military personnel continued to serve as part of the NATO-led security force in Kosovo (KFOR). He noted that the American contribution to KFOR in Kosovo was "approximately 8,500 U.S. military personnel." U.S. forces were deployed in a sector centered around "Urosevac in the eastern portion of Kosovo." For U.S. KFOR forces, "maintaining public security is a key task." Other U.S. military personnel are deployed to other countries in the region to serve in administrative and logistics support roles for U.S. forces in KFOR. Of these forces, about 1,500 U.S. military personnel are in Macedonia and Greece, and occasionally in Albania.

(79) **Bosnia.** On January 25, 2000, President Clinton reported to Congress "consistent with the War Powers Resolution" that the U.S. continued to provide combat-equipped U.S. Armed Forces to Bosnia and Herzegovina and other states in the region as part of the NATO led Stabilization Force (SFOR). The President noted that the U.S. force contribution was being reduced from "approximately 6,200 to 4,600 personnel," with the U.S. forces assigned to Multinational Division, North, centered around the city of Tuzla. He added that approximately 1,500 U.S. military personnel were deployed to Hungary, Croatia, and Italy to provide "logistical and other support to SFOR," and that U.S. forces continue to support SFOR in "efforts to apprehend persons indicted for war crimes."

(80) **East Timor.** On February 25, 2000, President Clinton reported to Congress "consistent with the War Powers Resolution" that he had authorized the participation of a small number of U.S. military personnel in support of the United Nations Transitional Administration in East Timor (UNTAET), with a mandate to maintain law and order throughout East Timor, facilitate establishment of an effective administration there, deliver humanitarian assistance, and support the building of self-government. The President reported that the U.S. contingent was small: three military observers, and one judge advocate. To facilitate and coordinate U.S. military activities in East Timor, the President also authorized the deployment of a support group (USGET), consisting of 30 U.S. personnel. U.S. personnel would be temporarily deployed to East Timor, on a rotational basis, and through periodic ship visits, during which U.S. forces would conduct "humanitarian and assistance activities throughout East Timor." Rotational activities should continue through the summer of 2000.

(81) **Sierra Leone.** On May 12, 2000, President Clinton, "consistent with the War Powers Resolution" reported to Congress that he had ordered a U.S. Navy patrol craft to deploy to Sierra Leone to be ready to support evacuation operations from that country if needed. He also authorized a U.S. C-17 aircraft to deliver "ammunition, and other supplies and equipment" to Sierra Leone in support of United Nations peacekeeping operations there.

(82) **Yugoslavia/Kosovo.** On June 16, 2000, President Clinton reported to Congress, "consistent with the War Powers Resolution," that the U.S. was continuing to provide military personnel to the NATO-led KFOR security force in Kosovo. U.S. forces were numbered at 7,500, but were scheduled to be reduced to 6,000 when ongoing troop rotations were completed. U.S. forces in Kosovo are assigned to a sector centered near Gnjilane in eastern Kosovo. Other U.S. military personnel are deployed to other countries to serve in administrative and logistics support roles, with approximately 1,000 U.S. personnel in Macedonia, Albania, and Greece.

(83) **Bosnia.** On July 25, 2000, President Clinton reported to Congress, "consistent with the War Powers Resolution," that combat-equipped U.S. military personnel continued to participate in the NATO-led Stabilization Force (SFOR) in Bosnia and Herzegovina, being deployed to Bosnia, and other states in the region in support of peacekeeping efforts in former Yugoslavia. U.S. military personnel levels have been reduced from 6,200 to 4,600. Apart from the forces in Bosnia, approximately 1,000 U.S. personnel continue to be deployed in support roles in Hungary, Croatia, and Italy.

(84) **East Timor.** On August 25, 2000, President Clinton reported to Congress," consistent with the War Powers Resolution," that the United States was currently contributing three military observers to the United Nations Transitional Administration in East Timor (UNTAET) that is charged by the UN with restoring and maintaining peace and security there. He also noted that the U.S. was maintaining a military presence in East Timor separate from UNTAET, comprised of about 30 U.S. personnel who facilitate and coordinate U.S. military activities in East Timor and rotational operations of U.S. forces there. U.S. forces currently conduct humanitarian and civic assistance activities for East Timor's citizens. U.S. rotational presence operations in East Timor are presently expected, the President said, to continue through December 2000.

(85) **Yemen.** On October 14, 2000, President Clinton reported to Congress, "consistent with the War Powers Resolution," that on October 12, 2000, in the wake of an attack on the USS COLE in the port of Aden, Yemen, he had authorized deployment of about 45 military personnel from U.S. Naval Forces Central Command to Aden to provide "medical, security, and disaster response assistance." The President further reported that on October 13, 2000 about 50 U.S. military security personnel arrived in Aden, and that additional "security elements" may be deployed to the area, to enhance the ability of the U.S. to ensure the security of the USS COLE and the personnel responding to the incident. In addition, two U.S. Navy surface combatant vessels are operating in or near Yemeni territorial waters to provide communications and other support, as required.

(86) **Yugoslavia/Kosovo.** On December 18, 2000, President Clinton reported to Congress, "consistent with the War Powers Resolution," that the United States was continuing to provide approximately 5,600 U.S. military personnel in support of peacekeeping efforts in Kosovo as part of the NATO-led international security force in Kosovo (KFOR). An additional 500 U.S. military personnel are deployed as the National Support Element in Macedonia, with an occasional presence in Albania and Greece. U.S. forces are assigned to a sector centered around Gnjilane in the eastern portion of Kosovo. The President noted that the mission for these U.S. military forces is maintaining a safe and secure environment through conducting "security patrols in urban areas and in the countryside throughout their sector."

(87) **Bosnia.** On January 25, 2001, President George W. Bush reported to Congress, "consistent with the War Powers Resolution," that about 4,400 combat-equipped U.S. Armed Forces continued to be deployed in Bosnia and Herzegovina, and other regional states as part of the NATO-led Stabilization Force (SFOR).Most were based at Tuzla in Bosnia. About 650 others were based in Hungary, Croatia, and Italy, providing logistical and other support.

(88) **East Timor.** On March 2, 2001, President George W. Bush reported to Congress, "consistent with the War Powers Resolution," that the U.S. armed forces were continuing to support the United Nations peacekeeping effort in East Timor aimed at providing security and maintaining law and order in East Timor, coordinating delivery of humanitarian assistance, and helping establish the basis for self-government in East Timor. The U.S. currently has three military observers attached to the United Nations Transitional Administration in East Timor (UNTAET). The United States also has a separate military presence, the U.S. Support Group East Timor (USGET), of approximately 12 U.S. personnel, including a security detachment, which "facilitates and coordinates" U.S. military activities in East Timor.

(89) **Yugoslavia/Kosovo.** On May 18, 2001, President George W. Bush reported to Congress, "consistent with the War Powers Resolution," that the United States was continuing to provide approximately 6,000 U.S. military personnel in support of peacekeeping efforts in Kosovo as part of the NATO-led international security force in Kosovo (KFOR). An additional 500 U.S. military personnel are deployed as the National Support Element in Macedonia, with an occasional presence in Greece and Albania. U.S. forces in Kosovo are assigned to a sector centered around Gnjilane in the eastern portion. President Bush noted that the mission for these U.S. military forces is maintaining a safe and secure environment through conducting security patrols in urban areas and in the countryside through their sector.

(90) **Bosnia.** On July 24, 2001, President George W. Bush reported to Congress, "consistent with the War Powers Resolution," about 3,800 combat-equipped U.S. Armed Forces continued to be deployed in Bosnia and Herzegovina, and other regional states as part of the NATO-led Stabilization Force (SFOR). Most were based at Tuzla in Bosnia. About 500 others were based in Hungary, Croatia, and Italy, providing logistical and other support.

(91) **East Timor.** On August 31, 2001, President George W. Bush reported to Congress, "consistent with the War Powers Resolution," that the U.S. armed forces were continuing to support the United Nations peacekeeping effort in East Timor aimed at providing security and maintaining law and order in East Timor, coordinating delivery of humanitarian assistance,

and helping establish the basis for self-government in East Timor. The U.S. currently has three military observers attached to the United Nations Transitional Administration in East Timor (UNTAET). The United States also has a separate military presence, the U.S. Support Group East Timor (USGET), of approximately 20 U.S. personnel, including a security detachment, which "facilitates and coordinates" U.S. military activities in East Timor, as well as a rotational presence of U.S. forces through temporary deployments to East Timor. The President stated that U.S. forces would continue a presence through December 2001, while options for a U.S. presence in 2002 are being reviewed, with the President's objective being redeployment of USGET personnel, as circumstances permit.

(92) **Anti-terrorist operations.** On September 24, 2001, President George W. Bush reported to Congress, "consistent with the War Powers Resolution," and "Senate Joint Resolution 23" that in response to terrorist attacks on the World Trade Center and the Pentagon he had ordered the "deployment of various combat-equipped and combat support forces to a number of foreign nations in the Central and Pacific Command areas of operations." The President noted in efforts to "prevent and deter terrorism" he might find it necessary to order additional forces into these and other areas of the world. . . ." He stated that he could not now predict "the scope and duration of these deployments," nor the "actions necessary to counter the terrorist threat to the United States."

(93) **Afghanistan.** On October 9, 2001, President George W. Bush reported to Congress, "consistent with the War Powers Resolution," and "Senate Joint Resolution 23" that on October 7, 2001, U.S. Armed Forces "began combat action in Afghanistan against Al Qaida terrorists and their Taliban supporters." The President stated that he had directed this military action in response to the September 11, 2001 attacks on U.S. "territory, our citizens, and our way of life, and to the continuing threat of terrorist acts against the United States and our friends and allies." This military action was "part of our campaign against terrorism" and was "designed to disrupt the use of Afghanistan as a terrorist base of operations."

(94) **Yugoslavia/Kosovo**. On November 19, 2001, President George W. Bush reported to Congress, "consistent with the War Powers Resolution," that the United States was continuing to provide approximately 5,500 U.S. military personnel in support of peacekeeping efforts in Kosovo as part of the NATO-led international security force in Kosovo (KFOR). An additional 500 U.S. military personnel are deployed as the National Support Element in Macedonia, with an occasional presence in Greece and Albania. U.S. forces in Kosovo are assigned to a sector centered around Gnjilane in the eastern portion. President Bush noted that the mission for these U.S. military forces is maintaining a safe and secure environment through conducting security patrols in urban areas and in the countryside through their sector.

(95) **Bosnia**. On January 21, 2002, President George W. Bush reported to Congress, "consistent with the War Powers Resolution," that about 3,100 combat- equipped U.S. Armed Forces continued to be deployed in Bosnia and Herzegovina, and other regional states as part of the NATO-led Stabilization Force (SFOR).Most were based at Tuzla in Bosnia. About 500 others were based in Hungary, Croatia, and Italy, providing logistical and other support.

(96) **East Timor.** On February 28, 2002, President George W. Bush reported to Congress, "consistent with the War Powers Resolution," that U.S. armed forces were continuing to support the United Nations peacekeeping effort in East Timor aimed at providing security and maintaining law and order in East Timor, coordinating delivery of humanitarian assistance, and helping establish the basis for self-government in East Timor. The U.S. currently has three military observers attached to the United Nations Transitional Administration in East Timor (UNTAET). The United States also has a separate military presence, the U.S. Support Group East Timor (USGET), comprised of approximately 10 U.S. personnel, including a security detachment, which "facilitates and coordinates" U.S. military activities in East Timor, as well as a rotational presence of U.S. forces through temporary deployments to East Timor. The President stated that U.S. forces would continue a presence through 2002. The President noted his objective was to gradually reduce the "rotational presence operations," and to redeploy USGET personnel, as circumstances permitted.

(97) **Anti-terrorist operations**. On March 20, 2002, President George W. Bush reported to Congress, "consistent with the War Powers Resolution," on U.S. efforts in the "global war on Terrorism." He noted that the "heart of the al-Qaeda training capability" had been "seriously degraded," and that the remainder of the Taliban and the al-Qaeda fighters were being "actively pursued and engaged by the U.S., coalition and Afghan forces." The United States was also conducting "maritime interception operations . . . to locate and detain suspected al-Qaeda or Taliban leadership fleeing Afghanistan by sea." At the Philippine Government's invitation, the President had ordered deployed "combat-equipped and combat support forces to train with, advise, and assist" the Philippines' Armed Forces in enhancing their "existing counterterrorist capabilities." The strength of U.S. military forces working with the Philippines was projected to be 600 personnel. The President noted that he was "assessing options" for assisting other nations, including Georgia and Yemen, in enhancing their "counterterrorism capabilities, including training and equipping their armed forces." He stated that U.S. combat-equipped and combat support forces would be necessary for these efforts, if undertaken.

(98) **Yugoslavia/Kosovo.** On May 17, 2002, President George W. Bush reported to Congress, "consistent with the War Powers Resolution," that

the U.S. military was continuing to support peacekeeping efforts of the NATO-led international security force in Kosovo (KFOR). He noted that the current U.S. contribution was about 5,100 military personnel, with an additional 468 personnel in Macedonia; and an occasional presence in Albania and Greece.

(99) **Bosnia.** On July 22, 2002, President George W. Bush reported to Congress, "consistent with the War Powers Resolution," that the U.S. military was continuing to support peacekeeping efforts of the NATO-led Stabilization Force (SFOR) in Bosnia and Herzegovina and other regional states. He noted that the current U.S. contribution was "approximately 2,400 personnel." Most U.S. forces in Bosnia and Herzegovina are assigned to the Multinational Division, North headquartered in Tuzla. An additional 60 U.S. military personnel are deployed to Hungary and Croatia to provide logistical and other support.

(100) **Anti-terrorist operations.** On September 20, 2002, President Bush reported to Congress "consistent with the War Powers Resolution," that U.S. "combat-equipped and combat support forces" have been deployed to the Philippines since January 2002 to train with, assist and advise the Philippines' Armed Forces in enhancing their "counterterrorist capabilities." He added that U.S. forces were conducting maritime interception operations in the Central and European Command areas to combat movement, arming, or financing of "international terrorists." He also noted that U.S. combat personnel had been deployed to Georgia and Yemen to help enhance the "counterterrorist capabilities" of their armed forces.

(101) **Cote d'Ivoire.** On September 26, 2002, President Bush reported to Congress "consistent with the War Powers Resolution," that in response to a rebellion in Cote d'Ivoire that he had on September 25, 2002 sent U.S. military personnel into Cote d'Ivoire to assist in the evacuation of American citizens and third country nationals from the city of Bouake; and otherwise assist in other evacuations as necessary.

(102) **Yugoslavia/Kosovo**. On November 15, 2002, the President reported to Congress "consistent with the War Powers Resolution" that the U.S. was continuing to deploy combat equipped military personnel as part of the NATO-led international security force in Kosovo (KFOR). Currently the U.S. has approximately 4,350 U.S. military personnel in Kosovo, with an additional 266 military personnel in Macedonia. The U.S. also has an occasional presence in Albania and Greece, associated with the KFOR mission.

(103) **Bosnia.** On January 21, 2003, President George W. Bush reported to Congress, "consistent with the War Powers Resolution," that about 1,800 U.S. Armed Forces personnel continued to be deployed in Bosnia and Herzegovina, and other regional states as part of the NATO-led Stabilization

Force (SFOR). Most were based at Tuzla in Bosnia. About 80 others were based in Hungary and Croatia, providing logistical and other support.

(104) **Anti-terrorist operations.** On March 20, 2003, President Bush reported to Congress, "consistent with the War Powers Resolution," as well as P.L. 107-40, and "pursuant to" his authority as Commander-in-Chief, that he had continued a number of U.S. military operations globally in the war against terrorism. These military operations included ongoing U.S. actions against al-Qaeda fighters in Afghanistan; collaborative anti-terror operations with forces of Pakistan in the Pakistan/Afghanistan border area; "maritime interception operations on the high seas" in areas of responsibility of the Central and European Commands to prevent terrorist movement and other activities; and military support for the armed forces of Georgia and Yemen in counter-terrorism operations.

(105) **War against Iraq.** On March 21, 2003, President Bush reported to Congress, "consistent with the War Powers Resolution," as well as P.L. 102-1 and P.L. 107-243, and "pursuant to" his authority as Commander-in-Chief, that he had "directed U.S. Armed Forces, operating with other coalition forces, to commence operations on March 19, 2003, against Iraq." He further stated that it was not possible to know at present the duration of active combat operations or the scope necessary to accomplish the goals of the operation—"to disarm Iraq in pursuit of peace, stability, and security both in the Gulf region and in the United States."

(106) **Yugoslavia/Kosovo**. On May 14, 2003, President Bush reported to Congress, "consistent with the War Powers Resolution," that combat-equipped U.S. military personnel continued to be deployed as part of the NATO-led international security force in Kosovo (KFOR). He noted that about 2,250 U.S. military personnel were deployed in Kosovo, and additional military personnel operated, on occasion, from Macedonia, Albania, and Greece in support of KFOR operations.

(107) **Liberia.** On June 9, 2003, President Bush reported to Congress, "consistent with the War Powers Resolution," that on June 8 he had sent about 35 combat-equipped U.S. military personnel into Monrovia, Liberia, to augment U.S. Embassy security forces, to aid in the possible evacuation of U.S. citizens if necessary. The President also noted that he had sent about 34 combat-equipped U.S. military personnel to help secure the U.S. embassy in Nouakchott, Mauritania, and to assist in evacuation of American citizens if required. They were expected to arrive at the U.S. embassy by June 10, 2003. Back-up and support personnel were sent to Dakar, Senegal, to aid in any necessary evacuation from either Liberia or Mauritania.

(108) **Bosnia.** On July 22, 2003, President Bush reported to Congress, "consistent with the War Powers Resolution," that the United States continued to provide about 1,800 combat-equipped military personnel in Bosnia and

Herzegovina in support of NATO's Stabilization Force (SFOR) and its peacekeeping efforts in this country.

(109) **Liberia.** On August 13, 2003, President Bush reported to Congress, "consistent with the War Powers Resolution," that in response to conditions in Liberia, on August 11, 2003, he had authorized about 4,350 U.S. combat-equipped military personnel to enter Liberian territorial waters in support of U.N. and West African States efforts to restore order and provide humanitarian assistance in Liberia.

(110) **Anti-terrorist operations.** On September 19, 2003, President Bush reported to Congress "consistent with the War Powers Resolution," that U.S. "combat-equipped and combat support forces" continue to be deployed at a number of locations around the world as part of U.S. anti-terrorism efforts. American forces support anti-terrorism efforts in the Philippines, and maritime interception operations continue on the high seas in the Central, European and Pacific Command areas of responsibility, to "prevent the movement, arming, or financing of international terrorists." He also noted that "U.S. combat equipped and support forces" had been deployed to Georgia and Djibouti to help in enhancing their "counterterrorist capabilities."

(111) **Yugoslavia/Kosovo.** On November 14, 2003, the President reported to Congress "consistent with the War Powers Resolution" that the United States was continuing to deploy combat equipped military personnel as part of the NATO-led international security force in Kosovo (KFOR). Currently the United States has approximately 2,100 U.S. military personnel in Kosovo, with additional American military personnel operating out of Macedonia, Albania, and Greece, in support of KFOR operations.

(112) On January 22, 2004, the President reported to Congress "consistent with the War Powers Resolution" that the United States was continuing to deploy combat equipped military personnel in Bosnia and Herzegovina in support of NATO's Stabilization Force (SFOR) and its peacekeeping efforts in this country. About 1,800 U.S. personnel are participating.

(113) On February 25, 2004, the President reported to Congress "consistent with the War Powers Resolution" that, on February 23, he had sent a combat- equipped "security force" of about "55 U.S. military personnel from the U.S. Joint Forces Command" to Port-au-Prince, Haiti to augment the U.S. Embassy security forces there and to protect American citizens and property in light of the instability created by the armed rebellion in Haiti.

(114) On March 2, 2004, the President reported to Congress "consistent with the War Powers Resolution" that on February 29 he had sent about "200 additional U.S. combat-equipped, military personnel from the U.S. Joint Forces Command" to Port- au-Prince, Haiti for a variety of purposes,

including preparing the way for a UN Multinational Interim Force, and otherwise supporting UN Security Council Resolution 1529 (2004).

(115) On March 20, 2004, the President sent to Congress "consistent with the War Powers Resolution," a consolidated report giving details of multiple ongoing United States military deployments and operations "in support of the global war on terrorism (including in Afghanistan)," as well as operations in Bosnia and Herzegovina, Kosovo, and Haiti. In this report, the President noted that U.S. anti- terror related activities were underway in Georgia, Djibouti, Kenya, Ethiopia, Yemen, and Eritrea. He further noted that U.S. combat-equipped military personnel continued to be deployed in Kosovo as part of the NATO-led KFOR (1,900 personnel); in Bosnia and Herzegovina as part of the NATO-led SFOR (about 1,100 personnel); and approximately 1,800 military personnel were deployed in Haiti as part of the U.N. Multinational Interim Force.

(116) On November 4, 2004, the President sent to Congress, "consistent with the War Powers Resolution," a consolidated report giving details of multiple ongoing United States military deployments and operations "in support of the global war on terrorism." These deployments, support or military operations include activities in Afghanistan, Djibouti, as well as Kenya, Ethiopia, Eritrea, Bosnia and Herzegovina, and Kosovo. In this report, the President noted that U.S. anti-terror related activities were underway in Djibouti, Kenya, Ethiopia, Yemen, and Eritrea. He further noted that U.S. combat-equipped military personnel continued to be deployed in Kosovo as part of the NATO-led KFOR (1,800 personnel); and in Bosnia and Herzegovina as part of the NATO-led SFOR (about 1,000 personnel). Meanwhile, he stated that the United States continues to deploy more than 135,000 military personnel in Iraq.

(117) On May 20, 2005, the President sent to Congress "consistent with the War Powers Resolution," a consolidated report giving details of multiple ongoing United States military deployments and operations "in support of the global war on terrorism," as well as operations in Iraq, where currently about 139,000 U.S. military personnel are stationed. U.S. forces are also deployed in Kenya, Ethiopia, Yemen, Eritrea, and Djibouti assisting in "enhancing counter-terrorism capabilities" of these nations. The President further noted that U.S. combat-equipped military personnel continued to be deployed in Kosovo as part of the NATO-led KFOR (1,700 personnel). Approximately 235 U.S. personnel are also deployed in Bosnia and Herzegovina as part of the NATO Headquarters-Sarajevo who assist in defense reform and perform operational tasks, such as counter-terrorism and supporting the International Criminal Court for the Former Yugoslavia.

(118) On December 7, 2005, the President sent to Congress "consistent" with the War Powers Resolution, a consolidated report giving details of

multiple ongoing United States military deployments and operations "in support of the global war on terrorism," and in support of the Multinational Force in Iraq, where about 160, 000 U.S. military personnel are deployed. U.S. forces are also deployed in the Horn of Africa region—Kenya, Ethiopia, Yemen, and Djibouti—assisting in "enhancing counter-terrorism capabilities" of these nations. The President further noted that U.S. combat-equipped military personnel continued to be deployed in Kosovo as part of the NATO-led KFOR (1,700 personnel). Approximately 220 U.S. personnel are also deployed in Bosnia and Herzegovina as part of the NATO Headquarters-Sarajevo who assist in defense reform and perform operational tasks, such as "counter-terrorism and supporting the International Criminal Court for the Former Yugoslavia."

(119) On June 15, 2006, the President sent to Congress "consistent" with the War Powers Resolution, a consolidated report giving details of multiple ongoing United States military deployments and operations "in support of the war on terror," and in Kosovo, Bosnia and Herzegovina, and as part of the Multinational Force (MNF) in Iraq. Presently, about 131, 000 military personnel were deployed in Iraq. U.S. forces were also deployed in the Horn of Africa region, and in Djibouti to support necessary operations against al-Qaida and other international terrorists operating in the region. U.S. military personnel continue to support the NATO-led Kosovo Force (KFOR). The current U.S. contribution to KFOR is about 1,700 military personnel. The NATO Headquarters-Sarajevo was established in November 22, 2004 as a successor to its stabilization operations in Bosnia-Herzegovina to continue to assist in implementing the peace agreement. Approximately 250 U.S. personnel are assigned to the NATO Headquarters-Sarajevo who assist in defense reform and perform operational tasks, such as "counter-terrorism and supporting the International Criminal Court for the Former Yugoslavia."

(120) On July 18, 2006, the President reported to Congress "consistent" with the War Powers Resolution, that in response to the security threat posed in Lebanon to U.S. Embassy personnel and citizens and designated third country personnel," he had deployed combat-equipped military helicopters and military personnel to Beirut to assist in the departure of the persons under threat from Lebanon. The President noted that additional combat-equipped U.S. military forces may be deployed "to Lebanon, Cyprus and other locations, as necessary." to assist further departures of persons from Lebanon and to provide security. He further stated that once the threat to U.S. citizens and property has ended, the U.S. military forces would redeploy.

(121) On December 15, 2006, the President sent to Congress "consistent" with the War Powers Resolution, a consolidated report giving details of multiple ongoing United States military deployments and operations

"in support of the war on terror," in Kosovo, Bosnia and Herzegovina, and as part of the Multinational Force (MNF) in Iraq. Presently, about 134, 000 military personnel are deployed in Iraq. U.S. forces were also deployed in the Horn of Africa region, and in Djibouti to support necessary operations against al-Qaida and other international terrorists operating in the region, including Yemen. U.S. military personnel continue to support the NATO-led Kosovo Force (KFOR). The current U.S. contribution to KFOR is about 1,700 military personnel. The NATO Headquarters-Sarajevo was established in November 22, 2004 as a successor to its stabilization operations in Bosnia-Herzegovina to continue to assist in implementing the peace agreement. Approximately 100 U.S. personnel are assigned to the NATO Headquarters-Sarajevo who assist in defense reform and perform operational tasks, such as "counter-terrorism and supporting the International Criminal Court for the Former Yugoslavia."

Appendix B. Instances Not Formally Reported to the Congress Under the War Powers Resolution

In some instances where U.S. Armed Forces have been deployed in potentially hostile situations abroad, Presidents did not submit reports to Congress under the War Powers Resolution and the question of whether a report was required could be raised. Representative examples of these instances since 1973 include:[106]

- evacuation of civilians from Cyprus in 1974
- evacuation of civilians from Lebanon in 1976
- Korean DMZ tree-cutting incident of 1976
- transport of European troops to Zaire in 1978
- dispatch of additional military advisers to El Salvador in 1981
- shooting down of two Libyan jets over the Gulf of Sidra on August 19, 1981, after one had fired a heat-seeking missile
- the use of training forces in Honduras after 1983
- dispatch of AWACS to Egypt after a Libyan plane bombed a city in Sudan March 18, 1983

[106] The list does not include military assistance or training operations generally considered routine, forces dispatched for humanitarian reasons such as disaster relief, or covert actions. War powers questions have not been raised about U.S. armed forces dispatched for humanitarian aid in peaceful situations, such as 8,000 marines and sailors sent to Bangladesh on May 12, 1991, to provide disaster relief after a cyclone. The War Powers Resolution applies only to the introduction of forces into situations of hostilities or imminent hostilities and to forces equipped for combat.

- shooting down of two Iranian fighter planes over Persian Gulf on June 5, 1984, by Saudi Arabian jet fighter planes aided by intelligence from a U.S. AWACS
- interception by U.S. Navy pilots on October 10, 1985, of an Egyptian airliner carrying hijackers of the Italian cruise ship *Achille Lauro*
- use of U.S. Army personnel and aircraft in Bolivia for anti-drug assistance on July 14, 1986
- buildup of fleet in Persian Gulf area in 1987
- force augmentations in Panama in 1988 and 1989
- shooting down 2 Libyan jet fighters over the Mediterranean Sea on January 4, 1989
- dispatch of military advisers and Special Forces teams to Colombia, Bolivia, and Peru, in the Andean initiative, announced September 5, 1989, to help those nations combat illicit drug traffickers
- transport of Belgian troops and equipment into Zaire September 25–27, 1991
- evacuation of non-essential U.S. government workers and families from Sierra Leone, May 3, 1992
- a bombing campaign against Iraq, termed Operation Desert Fox, aimed at destroying Iraqi industrial facilities deemed capable of producing weapons of mass destruction, as well as other Iraqi military and security targets, December 16–23, 1998.

Appendix C. Text of the War Powers Resolution

War Powers Resolution[107]

Public Law 93-148 [H.J.Res. 542], 87 Stat. 555, passed over President's veto November 7, 1973

JOINT RESOLUTION Concerning the war powers of Congress and the President.

Resolved by the Senate and House of Representatives of the United States of America in Congress assembled,

[107] As presented in *Legislation on Foreign Relations,* volume II, Joint Committee Print of the House Committee on International Relations and Senate Committee on Foreign Relations.

SHORT TITLE

Section 1. This joint resolution may be cited as the "War Powers Resolution".

PURPOSE AND POLICY

Sec. 2.[108] (a) It is the purpose of this joint resolution to fulfill the intent of the framers of the Constitution of the United States and insure that the collective judgment of both the Congress and the President will apply to the introduction of United States Armed Forces into hostilities, or into situations where imminent involvement in hostilities is clearly indicated by the circumstances, and to the continued use of such forces in hostilities or in such situations.

(b) Under article I, section 8, of the Constitution, it is specifically provided that the Congress shall have the power to make all laws necessary and proper for carrying into execution, not only its own powers but also all other powers vested by the Constitution in the Government of the United States, or in any department or officer thereof.

(c) The constitutional powers of the President as Commander-in-Chief to introduce United States Armed Forces into hostilities, or into situations where imminent involvement in hostilities is clearly indicated by the circumstances, are exercised only pursuant to (1) a declaration of war, (2) specific statutory authorization, or (3) a national emergency created by attack upon the United States, its territories or possessions, or its armed forces.

---

[108] 50 U.S.C. 1541.

See also the authorization for participation in a multinational force in Lebanon, 1983 (Public Law 98-119; 97 Stat. 805).

See also the sense of Congress regarding the possible introduction of U.S. Armed Forces into El Salvador, 1984 (Public Law 98–473; 98 Stat. 1904, 1942).

See also the introduction of U.S. Armed Forces into Central America for combat, 1984 (sec. 310 of Public Law 98-525; 98 Stat. 2516).

See also the authorization for use of U.S. military force against Iraq, 1991 (Public Law 102-1; 105 Stat. 3).

See also Congressional findings and conditional authorization for use of U.S. military force in Somalia, 1993 (sec. 8151 of Public Law 103–139; 107 Stat. 1475), and the sense of the Congress and a statement of Congressional policy on U.S. armed forces in Somalia, 1993 (sec. 1512 of Public Law 103-160; 107 Stat. 1840).

See also the Joint Resolution regarding U.S. policy toward Haiti, 1994 (Public Law 103-423; 108 Stat. 4358).

See also the limitation on deployment of U.S. Armed Forces in Haiti during Fiscal Year 2000 and congressional notification of deployments, 1999 (sec. 1232 of Public Law 106-65, 113 Stat. 788).

See also the authorization for use of military force in the global war against terrorism, 2001 (Public Law 107-40; 115 Stat. 224).

See also the authorization for use of military force against Iraq, 2002 (Public Law 107-243; 116 Stat. 1498).

CONSULTATION

SEC. 3.[109] The President in every possible instance shall consult with Congress before introducing United States Armed Forces into hostilities or into situations where imminent involvement in hostilities is clearly indicated by the circumstances, and after every such introduction shall consult regularly with the Congress until United States Armed Forces are no longer engaged in hostilities or have been removed from such situations.

REPORTING

SEC. 4.[110] (a) In the absence of a declaration of war, in any case in which United States Armed Forces are introduced—

(1) into hostilities or into situations where imminent involvement in hostilities is clearly indicated by the circumstances;

(2) into the territory, airspace of waters of a foreign nation, while equipped for combat, except for deployments which relate solely to supply, replacement, repair, or training of such forces; or

(3) in numbers which substantially enlarge United States Armed Forces equipped for combat already located in a foreign nation;

the President shall submit within 48 hours to the Speaker of the House of Representatives and to the President pro tempore of the Senate a report, in writing, setting forth—

(A) the circumstances necessitating the introduction of United States Armed Forces;

(B) the constitutional and legislative authority under which such introduction took place; and

(C) the estimated scope and duration of the hostilities or involvement.

(b) The President shall provide such other information as the Congress may request in the fulfillment of its constitutional responsibilities with respect to committing the Nation to war and to the use of United States Armed Forces abroad.

(c) Whenever United States Armed Forces are introduced into hostilities or into any situation described in subsection (a) of this section, the President shall, so long as such armed forces continue to be engaged in such hostilities or situation, report to the Congress periodically on the status of such hostilities or situation as well as on the scope and duration of such hostilities

[109] 50 U.S.C. 1542.
[110] 50 U.S.C. 1543.

or situation, but in no event shall he report to the Congress less often than once every six months.

CONGRESSIONAL ACTION

SEC. 5.[111] (a) Each report submitted pursuant to section 4(a)(1) shall be transmitted to the Speaker of the House of Representatives and to the President pro tempore of the Senate on the same calendar day. Each report so transmitted shall be referred to the Committee on Foreign Affairs[112] of the House of Representatives and to the Committee on Foreign Relations of the Senate for appropriate action. If, when the report is transmitted, the Congress has adjourned sine die or has adjourned for any period in excess of three calendar days, the Speaker of the House of Representatives and the President pro tempore of the Senate, if they deem it advisable (or if petitioned by at least 30 percent of the membership of their respective Houses) shall jointly request the President to convene Congress in order that it may consider the report and take appropriate action pursuant to this section.

(b) Within sixty calendar days after a report is submitted or is required to be submitted pursuant to section 4(a)(1), whichever is earlier, the President shall terminate any use of United States Armed Forces with respect to which such report was submitted (or required to be submitted), unless the Congress (1) has declared war or has enacted a specific authorization for such use of United States Armed Forces, (2) has extended by law such sixty-day period, or (3) is physically unable to meet as a result of an armed attack upon the United States. Such sixty-day period shall be extended for not more than an additional thirty days if the President determines and certifies to the Congress in writing that unavoidable military necessity respecting the safety of United States Armed Forces requires the continued

---

[111] 50 U.S.C. 1544.

Consider also sec. 1013 of the Department of State Authorization Act, Fiscal Years 1984 and 1985 (Public Law 98–164; 97 Stat. 1062; 50 U.S.C. 1546a) which provides:

"EXPEDITED PROCEDURES FOR CERTAIN JOINT RESOLUTION AND BILLS

"SEC. 1013. Any joint resolution or bill introduced in either House which requires the removal of United States Armed Forces engaged in hostilities outside the territory of the United States, its possessions and territories, without a declaration of war or specific statutory authorization shall be considered in accordance with the procedures of section 601(b) of the International Security Assistance and Arms Export Control Act of 1976, except that any such resolution or bill shall be amendable. If such a joint resolution or bill should be vetoed by the President, the time for debate in consideration of the veto message on such measure shall be limited to twenty hours in the Senate and in the House shall be determined in accordance with the Rules of the House."

For text of sec. 601(b) of the International Security Assistance and Arms Export Control Act of 1976, see *Legislation on Foreign Relations Through 2002*, vol. I-A.

[112] Sec. 1(a)(5) of Public Law 104-14 (109 Stat. 186) provided that references to the Committee on Foreign Affairs of the House of Representatives shall be treated as referring to the Committee on International Relations of the House of Representatives.

use of such armed forces in the course of bringing about a prompt removal of such forces.

(c) Notwithstanding subsection (b), at any time that United States Armed Forces are engaged in hostilities outside the territory of the United States, its possessions and territories without a declaration of war or specific statutory authorization, such forces shall be removed by the President if the Congress so directs by concurrent resolution.

CONGRESSIONAL PRIORITY PROCEDURES FOR JOINT RESOLUTION OR BILL

SEC. 6.[113] (a) Any joint resolution or bill introduced pursuant to section 5(b) at least thirty calendar days before the expiration of the sixty-day period specified in such section, shall be referred to the Committee on Foreign Affairs of the House of Representatives or the Committee on Foreign Relations of the Senate, as the case may be, and such committee shall report one such joint resolution or bill, together with its recommendations, not later than twenty-four calendar days before the expiration of the sixty-day period specified in such section, unless such House shall otherwise determine by the yeas and nays.

(b) Any joint resolution or bill so reported shall become the pending business of the House in question (in the case of the Senate the time for debate shall be equally divided between the proponents and the opponents), and shall be voted on within three calendar days thereafter, unless such House shall otherwise determine by yeas and nays.

(c) Such a joint resolution or bill passed by one House shall be referred to the committee of the other House named in subsection (a) and shall be reported out not later than fourteen calendar days before the expiration of the sixty-day period specified in section 5(b). The joint resolution or bill so reported shall become the pending business of the House in question and shall be voted on within three calendar days after it has been reported, unless such House shall otherwise determine by yeas and nays.

(d) In the case of any disagreement between the two Houses of Congress with respect to a joint resolution or bill passed by both Houses, conferees shall be promptly appointed and the committee of conference shall make and file a report with respect to such resolution or bill not later than four calendar days before the expiration of the sixty-day period specified in section 5(b). In the event the conferees are unable to agree within 48 hours, they shall report back to their respective House in disagreement. Notwithstanding any rule in either House concerning the printing of conference

[113] 50 U.S.C. 1545.

reports in the Record or concerning any delay in the consideration of such reports, such report shall be acted on by both Houses not later than the expiration of such sixty-day period.

CONGRESSIONAL PRIORITY PROCEDURES FOR CONCURRENT RESOLUTION

Sec. 7.[114] (a) Any concurrent resolution introduced pursuant to section 5(c) shall be referred to the Committee on Foreign Affairs of the House of Representatives or the Committee on Foreign Relations of the Senate, as the case may be, and one such concurrent resolution shall be reported out by such committee together with its recommendations within fifteen calendar days, unless such House shall otherwise determine by the yeas and nays.

(b) Any concurrent resolution so reported shall become the pending business of the House in question (in the case of the Senate the time for debate shall be equally divided between the proponents and the opponents) and shall be voted on within three calendar days thereafter, unless such House shall otherwise determine by yeas and nays.

(c) Such a concurrent resolution passed by one House shall be referred to the committee of the other House named in subsection (a) and shall be reported out by such committee together with its recommendations within fifteen calendar days and shall thereupon become the pending business of such House and shall be voted upon within three calendar days, unless such House shall otherwise determine by yeas and nays.

(d) In the case of any disagreement between the two Houses of Congress with respect to a concurrent resolution passed by both Houses, conferees shall be promptly appointed and the committee of conference shall make and file a report with respect to such concurrent resolution within six calendar days after the legislation is referred to the committee of conference. Notwithstanding any rule in either House concerning the printing of conference reports in the Record or concerning any delay in the consideration of such reports, such report shall be acted on by both Houses not later than six calendar days after the conference report is filed. In the event the conferees are unable to agree within 48 hours, they shall report back to their respective Houses in disagreement.

[114] 50 U.S.C. 1546.

INTERPRETATION OF JOINT RESOLUTION

SEC. 8.[115] (a) Authority to introduce United States Armed Forces into hostilities or into situations wherein involvement in hostilities is clearly indicated by the circumstances shall not be inferred—

(1) from any provision of law (whether or not in effect before the date of the enactment of this joint resolution), including any provision contained in any appropriation Act, unless such provision specifically authorizes the introduction of United States Armed Forces into hostilities or into such situations and states that it is intended to constitute specific statutory authorization within the meaning of this joint resolution; or

(2) from any treaty heretofore or hereafter ratified unless such treaty is implemented by legislation specifically authorizing the introduction of United States Armed Forces into hostilities or into such situations and stating that it is intended to constitute specific statutory authorization within the meaning of this joint resolution.

(b) Nothing in this joint resolution shall be construed to require any further specific statutory authorization to permit members of United States Armed Forces to participate jointly with members of the armed forces of one or more foreign countries in the headquarters operations of high-level military commands which were established prior to the date of enactment of this joint resolution and pursuant to the United Nations Charter or any treaty ratified by the United States prior to such date.

(c) For purposes of this joint resolution, the term "introduction of United States Armed Forces" includes the assignment of members of such armed forces to command, coordinate, participate in the movement of, or accompany the regular or irregular military forces of any foreign country or government when such military forces are engaged, or there exists an imminent threat that such forces will become engaged, in hostilities.

(d) Nothing in this joint resolution—

(1) is intended to alter the constitutional authority of the Congress or of the President, or the provisions of existing treaties; or

(2) shall be construed as granting any authority to the President with respect to the introduction of United States Armed Forces into hostilities or into situations wherein involvement in hostilities is clearly indicated by the circumstances which authority he would not have had in the absence of this joint resolution.

[115] 50 U.S.C. 1547.

SEPARABILITY CLAUSE

Sec. 9.[116] If any provision of this joint resolution or the application thereof to any person or circumstances is held invalid, the remainder of the joint resolution and the application of such provision to any other person or circumstance shall not be affected thereby.

EFFECTIVE DATE

Sec. 10.[117] This joint resolution shall take effect on the date of its enactment.

[116] 50 U.S.C. 1548.
[117] 50 U.S.C. 1541 note.

DOCUMENT NO. 3

WAR POWERS RESOLUTION: PRESIDENTIAL COMPLIANCE

CRS Report
RL33532

June 12, 2007

Richard F. Grimmett
Specialist in National Defense
Foreign Affairs, Defense, and Trade

Summary

Two separate but closely related issues confront Congress each time the President introduces armed forces into a situation abroad that conceivably could lead to their involvement in hostilities. One issue concerns the division of war powers between the President and Congress, whether the use of armed forces falls within the purview of the congressional power to declare war and the War Powers Resolution (WPR). The other issue is whether or not Congress concurs in the wisdom of the action. This report does not deal with the substantive merits of using armed forces in specific cases, but rather with congressional authorization for military action, and the application and effectiveness of the WPR. The purpose of the WPR (P.L. 93-148, passed over President Nixon's veto on November 7, 1973) is to ensure that Congress and the President share in making decisions that may get the United States involved in hostilities. Compliance becomes an issue whenever the President introduces U.S forces abroad in situations that might be construed as hostilities or imminent hostilities. Criteria for compliance include prior consultation with Congress, fulfillment of the reporting requirements, and congressional authorization. If the President has not complied fully, the issue becomes what action Congress should take to bring about compliance or to influence U.S. policy. A related issue has been congressional authorization of U.N. peacekeeping or other U.N.-sponsored actions.

For over three decades, war powers and the War Powers Resolution have been an issue in U.S. military actions in Asia, the Middle East, Africa,

Central America, and Europe. Presidents have submitted 121 reports to Congress as a result of the War Powers Resolution, although only one (the Mayaguez situation) cited Section 4(a)(1) or specifically stated that forces had been introduced into hostilities or imminent hostilities. Congress invoked the WPR in the Multinational Force in Lebanon Resolution (P.L. 98-119), which authorized the Marines to remain in Lebanon for 18 months. In addition, P.L. 102-1, enacted in January 1991, authorizing the use of U.S. armed forces in response to Iraqi aggression against Kuwait, stated that it constituted specific statutory authorization within the meaning of the WPR. On November 9, 1993, the House used a section of the WPR to state that U.S. forces should be withdrawn from Somalia by March 31, 1994; Congress had already taken this action in appropriations legislation. War powers have been at issue in former Yugoslavia/Bosnia/Kosovo, Iraq, and Haiti. Authorizing military actions in response to the terrorist attacks against the United States of September 11, 2001, through P.L. 107-40 directly involved war powers. The continued use of force to obtain Iraqi compliance with U.N. resolutions remained a war powers issue from the end of the Gulf war on February 28, 1991, until the enactment of P.L. 107-243, in October 2002, which explicitly authorized the President to use force against Iraq, an authority he exercised in March 2003, and continues to exercise for military operations in Iraq.

Debate continues on whether using the War Powers Resolution is effective as a means of assuring congressional participation in decisions that might get the United States involved in a significant military conflict. Proposals have been made to modify or repeal the resolution. None have been enacted to date. This report will be updated as events warrant.

Most Recent Developments

On December 15, 2006, the President sent to Congress "consistent" with the War Powers Resolution, a consolidated report giving details of multiple ongoing United States military deployments and operations "in support of the war on terror," in Kosovo, Bosnia and Herzegovina, and as part of the Multinational Force (MNF) in Iraq. Presently, about 134, 000 military personnel are deployed in Iraq. U.S. forces were also deployed in the Horn of Africa region, and in Djibouti to support necessary operations against al-Qaida and other international terrorists operating in the region, including Yemen. U.S. military personnel continue to support the NATO-led Kosovo Force (KFOR). The current U.S. contribution to KFOR is about 1, 700 military personnel. The NATO Headquarters-Sarajevo was established in November 22, 2004 as a successor to its stabilization operations in Bosnia-Herzegovina to continue to assist in implementing the peace agreement. Approximately 100 U.S. personnel are assigned to the NATO Headquarters-Sarajevo who assist in defense reform and perform operational tasks, such as "counter-terrorism and supporting the International Criminal Court for the Former Yugoslavia."

Background and Analysis

Under the Constitution, war powers are divided. Congress has the power to declare war and raise and support the armed forces (Article I, Section 8), while the President is Commander in Chief (Article II, Section 2). It is generally agreed that the Commander in Chief role gives the President power to repel attacks against the United States and makes him responsible for leading the armed forces. During the Korean and Vietnam wars, the United States found itself involved for many years in undeclared wars. Many Members of Congress became concerned with the erosion of congressional authority to decide when the United States should become involved in a war or the use of armed forces that might lead to war. On November 7, 1973, Congress passed the War Powers Resolution (P.L. 93-148) over the veto of President Nixon.

The War Powers Resolution (WPR) states that the President's powers as Commander in Chief to introduce U.S. forces into hostilities or imminent hostilities are exercised only pursuant to (1) a declaration of war; (2) specific statutory authorization; or (3) a national emergency created by an attack on the United States or its forces. It requires the President in every possible instance to consult with Congress before introducing American armed forces into hostilities or imminent hostilities unless there has been a declaration of war or other specific congressional authorization. It also requires the President to report to Congress any introduction of forces into hostilities or imminent hostilities, Section 4(a)(1); into foreign territory while equipped for combat, Section 4(a)(2); or in numbers which substantially enlarge U.S. forces equipped for combat already in a foreign nation, Section 4(a)(3). Once a report is submitted "or required to be submitted" under Section 4(a)(1), Congress must authorize the use of forces within 60 to 90 days or the forces must be withdrawn. (For detailed background, see CRS Report RL32267, *The War Powers Resolution: After Thirty-Three Years*, by Richard F. Grimmett, and CRS Report RL31133, *Declarations of War and Authorizations for the Use of Military Force: Historical Background and Legal Implications*, by Jennifer Elsea and Richard F. Grimmett.) It is important to note that since the War Powers Resolution's enactment, over President Nixon's veto in 1973, every President has taken the position that it is an unconstitutional infringement by the Congress on the President's authority as Commander in Chief. The courts have not directly addressed this question.

United Nations Actions

U.N. Security Council resolutions provide authority for U.S. action under international law. Whether congressional authorization is required under domestic law depends on the types of U.N. action and is governed by the Constitution, the U.N. Participation Act (P.L. 79-264, as amended), as well as by the War Powers Resolution. Section 8(b) of the War Powers Resolution exempts only participation in headquarters operations of joint military commands established prior to 1973.

For armed actions under Articles 42 and 43 of the U.N. Charter, Section 6 of the U.N. Participation Act authorizes the President to negotiate special agreements with the Security Council, subject to the approval of Congress, providing for the numbers and types of armed forces and facilities to be made available to the Security Council. Once the agreements have been concluded, further congressional authorization is not necessary, but no such agreements have been concluded. Some Members have sought to encourage negotiation of military agreements under Article 43 of the U.N. Charter. Questions include whether congressional approval is required only for an initial agreement on providing peacekeeping forces in general, or for each agreement to provide forces in specific situations, and how such approvals would relate to the War Powers Resolution.

Section 7 of the U.N. Participation Act authorizes the detail of up to 1, 000 personnel to serve in any noncombatant capacity for certain U.N. peaceful settlement activities. The United States has provided personnel to several U.N. peacekeeping missions, such as observers to the U.N. Truce Supervision Organization in Palestine. In these instances, controversy over the need for congressional authorization has not occurred because the action appeared to fall within the authorization in Section 7 of the Participation Act. Controversy has arisen when forces have been deployed in larger numbers or as possible combatants.

In the 103rd Congress, Members used several vehicles in seeking some control over future peacekeeping actions wherever they might occur. Both the Defense Appropriations Act for FY1994, P.L. 103-139 (Section 8153), and for FY1995, P.L. 103-335 (Section 8103), stated the sense of Congress that funds should not be used for U.N. peacekeeping or peace enforcement operations unless the President consulted with Congress at least 15 days in advance whenever possible. Section 1502 of the Defense Authorization for FY1994, P.L. 103-60, required the President to submit by April 1, 1994, a report on multinational peacekeeping including the requirement of congressional approval for participation and the applicability of the War Powers Resolution and the U.N. Participation Act.

Along similar lines, the conference report accompanying the Department of State Appropriations Act for FY1994, H.R. 2519 (P.L. 103-121, signed October 27, 1993), called for the Secretary of State to notify both Appropriations Committees 15 days in advance, where practicable, of a vote by the U.N. Security Council to establish any new or expanded peacekeeping mission. The Foreign Relations Authorization Act, P.L. 103-236, signed April 30, 1994, established new requirements for consultation with Congress on U.S. Participation in U.N. Peacekeeping Operations. Section 407 required monthly consultations on the status of peacekeeping operations and advance reports on resolutions that would authorize a new U.N. peacekeeping operation. It also required 15 days' advance notice of any U.S assistance to support U.N. peacekeeping operations and a quarterly report on all assistance that had been provided to the U.N. for peacekeeping operations. To permit presidential flexibility, conferees explained, the quarterly report need not include temporary duty assignments of U.S personnel in support of peacekeeping operations of less than 20 personnel in any one case.

The following discussion provides background on major cases of U.S. military involvement in overseas operations in recent years that have raised War Powers questions.

Former Yugoslavia/Bosnia

The issue of war powers and whether congressional authorization is necessary for U.S participation in U.N. action was also raised by efforts to halt fighting in the former territory of Yugoslavia, particularly in Bosnia. The United States participated without congressional authorization in airlifts into Sarajevo, naval monitoring of sanctions, aerial enforcement of a "no-fly zone," and aerial enforcement of safe havens.

Because some of the U.S. action has been taken within a NATO framework, action in Bosnia has raised the broader issue of whether action under NATO is exempt from the requirements of the War Powers Resolution or its standard for the exercise of war powers under the Constitution. Article 11 of the North Atlantic Treaty states that its provisions are to be carried out by the parties "in accordance with their respective constitutional processes," implying some role for Congress in the event of war. Section 8(a) of the War Powers Resolution states that authority to introduce U.S. forces into hostilities is not to be inferred from any treaty, ratified before or after 1973, unless implementing legislation specifically authorizes such introduction and says it is intended to constitute an authorization within the meaning of the War Powers Resolution. Section 8(b) states that nothing in the Resolution should be construed to require further authorization for U.S. participation in the headquarters operations of military commands established before 1973, such as NATO headquarters operations.

On August 13, 1992, the U.N. Security Council adopted Resolution 770 calling on all nations to take "all measures necessary" to facilitate the delivery of humanitarian assistance to Sarajevo. On August 11, 1992, the Senate passed S.Res. 330 urging the President to work for such a resolution and pledging funds for participation, but saying that no U.S. military personnel should be introduced into hostilities without clearly defined objectives. On the same day, the House passed H.Res. 554 urging the Security Council to authorize measures, including the use of force, to ensure humanitarian relief. Thus, both chambers of Congress supported action but not by legislation authorizing the use of U.S. forces. For details of congressional actions relating to Bosnia from 1993 through 1995, see CRS Report RL32267, *The War Powers Resolution: After Thirty-Three Years*, by Richard F. Grimmett.

In late 1995, the issue of war powers and Bosnia was raised again as President Clinton sent more than 20, 000 American combat troops to Bosnia as part of a NATO-led peacekeeping force. In December 1995, Congress considered and voted on a number of bills and resolutions, but the House and Senate could not come to consensus on any single measure. Subsequently, President Clinton in December 1996, agreed to provide up to 8, 500 ground troops to participate in a NATO-led follow-on force in Bosnia termed the Stabilization Force (SFOR). On March 18, 1998, the House defeated by a vote of 193-225, H.Con. Res. 227, a resolution directing the President, pursuant to section 5(c) of the War Powers Resolution to remove United States Armed Forces from the Republic of Bosnia and Herzegovina (H.Rept. 105-442). (For additional information, see CRS Report RL32392, *Bosnia and Herzegovina: Issues for U.S. Policy*, by Steven Woehrel, CRS Report RL32282, *Bosnia and Kosovo: U.S. Military Operations*, by Steve Bowman, and CRS Report RL32267, *The War Powers Resolution: After Thirty-Three Years*, by Richard F. Grimmett.)

Kosovo

The issue of presidential authority to deploy forces in the absence of congressional authorization, under the War Powers Resolution, or otherwise, became an issue of significant controversy in late March 1999 when President Clinton ordered U.S. military forces to participate in a NATO-led military operation in Kosovo. This action has become the focus of an ongoing policy debate over the purpose and scope of U.S. military involvement in Kosovo. The President's action to commit forces to the NATO Kosovo operation also led to a suit in Federal District Court for the District of Columbia by some Members of Congress seeking a judicial finding that the

President was violating the War Powers Resolution and the Constitution by using military forces in Yugoslavia in the absence of authorization from the Congress.

The Kosovo controversy began in earnest when on March 26, 1999, President Clinton notified the Congress "consistent with the War Powers Resolution," that on March 24, 1999, U.S. military forces, at his direction and in coalition with NATO allies, had commenced air strikes against Yugoslavia in response to the Yugoslav government's campaign of violence and repression against the ethnic Albanian population in Kosovo. Prior to the President's action, the Senate, on March 23, 1999, had passed, by a vote of 58-41, S.Con.Res. 21, a nonbinding resolution expressing the sense of the Congress that the President was authorized to conduct "military air operations and missile strikes in cooperation with our NATO allies against the Federal Republic of Yugoslavia (Serbia and Montenegro)."

Subsequently, the House voted on a number of measures relating to U.S. participation in the NATO operation in Kosovo. On April 28, 1999, the House of Representatives passed H.R. 1569, by a vote of 249-180. This bill would prohibit the use of funds appropriated to the Defense Department from being used for the deployment of "ground elements" of the U.S. Armed Forces in the Federal Republic of Yugoslavia unless that deployment is specifically authorized by law. On that same day the House defeated H.Con. Res. 82, by a vote of 139-290. This resolution would have directed the President, pursuant to section 5(c) of the War Powers Resolution, to remove U.S. Armed Forces from their positions in connection with the present operations against the Federal Republic of Yugoslavia. On April 28, 1999, the House also defeated H.J. Res. 44, by a vote of 2-427. This joint resolution would have declared a state of war between the United States and the "Government of the Federal Republic of Yugoslavia." The House on that same day also defeated, on a 213-213 tie vote, S.Con. Res. 21, the Senate resolution passed on March 23, 1999, that supported military air operations and missile strikes against Yugoslavia. On April 30, 1999, Representative Tom Campbell and 17 other members of the House filed suit in Federal District Court for the District of Columbia seeking a ruling requiring the President to obtain authorization from Congress before continuing the air war, or taking other military action against Yugoslavia.

The Senate, on May 4, 1999, by a vote of 78-22, tabled S.J. Res. 20, a joint resolution, sponsored by Senator John McCain, that would authorize the President "to use all necessary force and other means, in concert with United States allies, to accomplish United States and North Atlantic Treaty Organization objectives in the Federal Republic of Yugoslavia (Serbia and Montenegro)." The House, meanwhile, on May 6, 1999, by a vote of 117-301, defeated an amendment by Representative Istook to H.R. 1664, the FY1999 defense supplemental appropriations bill, that would have prohibited the expenditure of funds in the bill to implement any plan to use U.S. ground forces to invade Yugoslavia, except in time of war. Congress, meanwhile, on May 20, 1999, cleared for the President's signature, H.R. 1141, an emergency supplemental appropriations bill for FY1999, that provided billions in funding for the existing U.S. Kosovo operation.

On May 25, 1999, the 60th day had passed since the President notified Congress of his actions regarding U.S. participation in military operations in Kosovo. Representative Campbell, and those who joined his suit, noted to the Federal Court that this was a clear violation of the language of the War Powers Resolution stipulating a withdrawal of U.S. forces from the area of hostilities occur after 60 days in the absence of congressional authorization to continue, or a presidential request to Congress for an extra 30 day period to safely withdraw. The President did not seek such a 30-day extension, noting instead that the War Powers Resolution is constitutionally defective. On June 8, 1999, Federal District Judge Paul L. Friedman dismissed the suit of Representative Campbell and others that sought to have the court rule that President Clinton was in violation of the War Powers Resolution and the Constitution by conducting military activities in Yugoslavia without having received prior authorization from Congress. The judge ruled that Representative Campbell and others lacked legal standing to bring the suit (*Campbell v. Clinton*, 52 F. Supp. 2d 34(D.D.C. 1999)). Representative Campbell appealed the ruling on June 24, 1999, to the U.S. Court of Appeals for the District of Columbia. The appeals court agreed to hear the case. On February 18, 2000, the appeals court affirmed the opinion of the District Court that Representative Campbell and his co-plaintiffs lacked standing to sue the President. (Campbell v. Clinton, 203 F.3d 19 (D.C. Cir. 2000). On May 18, 2000, Representative Campbell and 30 other Members of Congress appealed this decision to the United States Supreme Court. On October 2, 2000, the United States Supreme Court, without comment, refused to hear the appeal of Representative Campbell thereby letting stand the holding of the U.S. Court of Appeals. (Campbell v. Clinton, *cert. denied*, 531U.S. 815 October 2, 2000). On May 18, 2000, the Senate defeated by, a vote of 47-53, an amendment to S. 2521, the Senate's version of the Military Construction Appropriations Act, FY2001, that would have, among other things, terminated funding for the continued deployment of U.S. ground combat troops in Kosovo after July 1, 2001 unless the President sought and received Congressional authorization to keep U.S troops in Kosovo. (For detailed discussion of major issues see CRS Report RL31053, *Kosovo and U.S. Policy*, by Steven J. Woehrel and Julie Kim; CRS Report RL30352, *War Powers Litigation Initiated by Members of Congress Since the Enactment of the War Powers Resolution*, by David M. Ackerman.)

Iraq: Post 1991

During the week of October 3, 1994, Iraq began sending two additional divisions to join regular forces in southern Iraq, close to the border of Kuwait. On October 8, President Clinton responded by sending about 30,000 additional U.S. forces and additional combat planes to join the forces already in the Gulf area. He said the United States would honor its commitment to defend Kuwait and enforce U.N. resolutions on Iraq. Congress recessed on October 8 until November 29, 1994, so it did not discuss the issue of congressional authorization. On October 28, President Clinton reported to Congress that by October 15 there were clear indications that Iraq had redeployed its forces to their original location. On November 7, the Defense Department announced 7,000 of the U.S. forces would be withdrawn before Christmas.

Earlier, three continuing situations in Iraq since the end of Desert Storm brought about the use of U.S. forces and thus raised war powers issues. The first situation resulted from the Iraqi government's repression of Kurdish and Shiite groups. U.N. Security Council Resolution 688 of April 5, 1991, condemned the repression of the Iraqi civilian population and appealed for contributions to humanitarian relief efforts. The second situation stemmed from the U.N. cease-fire resolution of April 3, 1991, Security Council Resolution 687, which called for Iraq to accept the destruction or removal of chemical and biological weapons, and international control of its nuclear materials.

The third situation was related to both of the earlier ones. On August 26, 1992, the United States, Britain, and France began a "no-fly" zone, banning Iraqi fixed wing and helicopter flights south of the 32nd parallel and creating a limited security zone in the south, where Shiite groups are concentrated. After violations of the no-fly zones and various other actions by Iraq, on January 13, 1993, the outgoing Bush Administration announced that aircraft from the United States and coalition partners had attacked missile bases in southern Iraq and that the United States was deploying a battalion task force to Kuwait to underline the U.S. continuing commitment to Kuwait's independence. On January 6, 1993, the United States gave Iraq an ultimatum to remove newly deployed missiles in the no-fly zone. On January 19, 1993, President George H.W. Bush reported to Congress that U.S. aircraft on December 27, 1992, had shot down an Iraqi aircraft that had entered the no-fly zone and had undertaken further military actions on January 13, 17, and 18.

President Clinton said on January 21, 1993, that the United States would adhere to the policy toward Iraq set by the former Bush Administration, and on January 22, 23, April 9 and 18, June 19, and August 19, 1993, U.S. aircraft fired at targets in Iraq after pilots detected Iraqi radar or anti-aircraft fire directed at them. A number of such incidents occurred while planes patrolled the no-fly zone. On June 6, 1994, President Clinton reported that over the previous two years, the northern no-fly zone had deterred Iraq from a military offensive in the northern zone. Iraqi forces had responded to the no-fly zone in the south, he reported, by continuing to use land-based artillery to shell marsh villages. In addition, Iraq was conducting a large search and destroy operation and razing and burning marsh villages, in violation of U.N. Security Council Resolution 688. Until Iraq fully complied with all relevant U.N. Security Council resolutions, he reported, the United States would maintain sanctions and other measures designed to achieve compliance.

A war powers issue for years was whether the use of U.S. force in Iraq in the period after the early 1991 Desert Storm conflict had been authorized by Congress. P.L. 102-1 authorized the President to use U.S. armed forces pursuant to U.N. Security Council Resolution 678 to achieve implementation of previous Security Council Resolutions; Security Council Resolution 687 was adopted after this. On August 2, 1991, the Senate adopted an amendment to the Defense Authorization bill for FY1992 supporting the use of all necessary means to achieve the goals of Resolution 687. Senator Dole said the amendment was not intended to authorize the use of force by the President, and that in his view in the current circumstances the President required no specific authorization from Congress. As enacted, Section 1095 of P.L. 102-190 states the sense of Congress that it supports the use of all necessary means to achieve the goals of Security Council Resolution 687 as being consistent with the Authorization for Use of Military Force Against Iraq Resolution. The bill (Section 1096) also included an amendment by Senator Pell supporting the use of all necessary means to protect Iraq's Kurdish minority, consistent with relevant U.N. resolutions and authorities contained in P.L. 102-1.

In addition to these continuing situations, on June 28, 1993, President Clinton reported to Congress that on June 26, U.S. naval forces had launched a Tomahawk cruise missile strike on the Iraqi Intelligence Service's main command and control complex in Baghdad and that the military action was completed. He said the Iraqi Intelligence Service had planned the failed attempt to assassinate former President Bush during his visit to Kuwait in April 1993. On September 5, 1996, President Clinton reported to Congress on U.S. military actions in Iraq to obtain compliance with U.N. Security Council Resolutions, especially in light of attacks by Iraqi military forces against the Kurdish-controlled city of Irbil. U.S. actions ordered by the President included extending the no-fly zone in southern Iraq from 32 to 33 degrees north latitude, and cruise missile attacks from B-52H bombers and ships in the USS Carl Vinson Battle Group against fixed, surface-to-air missile sites, command and control centers, and air defense control facilities south of the 33rd parallel in Iraq. Except for the report of June 28, 1993,

Presidents Bush and Clinton did not cite the War Powers Resolution in their reports related to military activities in Iraq in the period after the 1991 Gulf War. Rather, they submitted them "consistent with" P.L. 102-1, which required the President to submit a report to the Congress at least once every 60 days on the status of efforts to obtain compliance by Iraq with the U.N. Security Council resolution adopted in response to the Iraq aggression.

Starting in 1998 and through the end of the Clinton Administration, Iraq's refusal to permit U.N. weapons inspection teams access to various Iraqi sites, and Iraqi threats to U.S. aircraft policing the "no-fly zones" resulted in U.S. military action on numerous occasions against Iraqi military forces and targets in the "no-fly zones." President Clinton chose to report these actions under the requirements of P.L. 102-1, rather than the War Powers Resolution. In early February 2001, President George W. Bush authorized U.S. aircraft to attack Iraqi radar installations in Southern Iraq believed to threaten allied forces enforcing the "no-fly zone." Additional bombings of Iraqi sites were authorized and took place from the summer of 2001 into March 2003. Such actions, in the past, were reported under P.L. 102-1. Congress provided authorization for future military action, under specified conditions, through passage of P.L. 107-243 signed into law on October 16, 2002. In a report to Congress on January 20, 2003, pursuant to P.L. 107-243, President Bush stated that information required to be reported regarding actions taken against Iraq required by section 3 of P.L. 102-1 would in the future be included in the reports required by P.L. 107-243. On March 19, 2003, President Bush directed U.S. Armed Forces to commence combat operations against Iraq to enforce its disarmament. Since he announced the end of major combat operations against Iraq on May 1, 2003, the President has made periodic reports on the current situation in Iraq "consistent with" P.L. 107-243, which have become the equivalent of reports to Congress envisioned by the War Powers Resolution. For a recent example of these reports to Congress see House Document 108-231, 108th Congress, 2nd session, submitted November 4, 2004. (For related information, see CRS Report RL31701, *Iraq: U.S. Military Operations*, by Steve Bowman, and CRS Report RL31339, *Iraq: U.S. Regime Change Efforts and Post-Saddam Governance*, by Kenneth Katzman.)

Haiti

On July 3, 1993, Haitian military leader Raoul Cedras and deposed President Jean-Bertrand Aristide signed an agreement at Governors Island providing for the restoration of President Aristide on October 30. The United Nations and Organization of American States took responsibility for verifying compliance. Because the Haitian authorities did not comply with the agreement, on October 13, 1993, the U.N. Security Council voted to restore sanctions against Haiti. On October 20, President Clinton submitted a report "consistent with the War Powers Resolution" that U.S. ships had begun to enforce a U.N. embargo. Some Members of Congress complained that Congress had not been consulted about nor authorized the action. On October 18, 1993, Senator Dole said he would offer an amendment to the FY1994 Defense Appropriations bill (H.R. 3116) which would require congressional authorization for all deployments into Haitian waters and airspace unless the President made specified certifications. Congressional leaders and Administration officials negotiated the terms of the amendment. As enacted, Section 8147 of P.L. 103-139 stated the sense that funds should not be obligated or expended for U.S. military operations in Haiti unless the operations were (1) authorized in advance by Congress, (2) necessary to protect or evacuate U.S. citizens, (3) vital to the national security and there was not sufficient time to receive congressional authorization, or (4) the President submitted a report in advance that the intended deployment met certain criteria.

On May 6, 1994, the U.N. Security Council adopted Resolution 917 calling for measures to tighten the embargo. On June 10, 1994, President Clinton announced steps being taken to intensify the pressure on Haiti's military leaders that included assisting the Dominican Republic to seal its border with Haiti, using U.S. naval patrol boats to detain ships suspected of violating the sanctions, a ban on commercial air traffic, and sanctions on financial transactions. As conditions in Haiti worsened, President Clinton stated he would not rule out the use of force, and gradually the use of force appeared certain. Many Members continued to contend congressional authorization was necessary for any invasion of Haiti. On July 31, the U.N. Security Council authorized a multinational force to use "all necessary means to facilitate the departure from Haiti of the military leadership . . . on the understanding that the cost of implementing this temporary operation will be borne by the participating Member States" (Resolution 940, 1994).

On August 3, the Senate adopted an amendment to the Department of Veterans Affairs appropriation, H.R. 4624, by a vote of 100-0 expressing its sense that the Security Council Resolution did not constitute authorization for the deployment of U.S. forces in Haiti under the Constitution or the War Powers Resolution, but the amendment was not agreed to in conference. President Clinton said the same day that he would welcome the support of Congress but did not agree that he was constitutionally mandated to obtain it. On September 15, 1994, in an address to the Nation, President Clinton said he had called up the military reserve and ordered two aircraft carriers into the region. His message to the military dictators was to leave now or the United States would force them from power. The first phase of military action would remove the dictators from power and restore Haiti's democratically elected government. The second phase would involve a much smaller force joining with forces from other U.N. members which would leave Haiti after 1995 elections were held and a new government installed.

While the Defense Department continued to prepare for an invasion within days, on September 16 President Clinton sent to Haiti a negotiating team of former President Jimmy Carter, former Joint Chiefs of Staff Chairman Colin Powell, and Senate Armed Services Committee Chairman Sam Nunn. Again addressing the Nation on September 18, President Clinton announced that the military leaders had agreed to step down by October 15, and agreed to the immediate introduction of troops from the 15, 000 member international coalition beginning September 19. He said the agreement was only possible because of the credible and imminent threat of multinational force. He emphasized the mission still had risks and there remained possibilities of violence directed at U.S. troops, but the agreement minimized those risks. He also said that under U.N. Security Council resolution 940, a 25-nation international coalition would soon go to Haiti to begin the task of restoring democratic government. Also on September 18, President Clinton reported to Congress on the objectives in accordance with the sense expressed in Section 8147 (c) of P.L. 103-139, the FY1994 Defense Appropriations Act.

U.S. forces entered Haiti on September 19, 1994. On September 21, President Clinton reported "consistent with the War Powers Resolution" the deployment of 1, 500 troops, to be increased by several thousand. (At the peak in September there were about 21, 000 U.S. forces in Haiti.) He said the U.S. presence would not be open-ended but would be replaced after a period of months by a U.N. peacekeeping force, although some U.S. forces would participate in and be present for the duration of the U.N. mission. The forces were involved in the first hostilities on September 24 when U.S. Marines killed 10 armed Haitian resisters in a fire-fight.

On October 3, 1994, the House Foreign Affairs Committee reported H.J.Res. 416 authorizing the forces in Haiti until March 1, 1995, and providing procedures for a joint resolution to withdraw the forces. On October 6, the House adopted an amended text introduced by Representative Ron Dellums. As passed, H.J.Res. 416 stated the sense of the Congress that the President should have sought congressional approval before deploying U.S. forces to Haiti, supported a prompt and orderly withdrawal as soon as possible, and required a monthly report on Haiti as well as other reports. This same language was also adopted by the Senate on October 6 as S. J. Res. 229, and on October 7 the House passed S.J.Res. 229. President Clinton signed it on October 25, 1994 (P.L. 103-423).

After the U.S. forces began to disarm Haitian forces and President Aristide returned on October 15, 1994, the United States began to withdraw some forces. On March 31, 1995, U.N. peacekeeping forces assumed responsibility for missions previously conducted by U.S. military forces. By September 21, 1995, President Clinton reported the United States had 2, 400 military personnel in Haiti as participants in the U.N. Mission in Haiti (UNMIH), and 260 U.S. military personnel assigned to the U.S. Support Group Haiti. On December 5, 1997, President Clinton stated that he intended to keep some military personnel in Haiti, even though United Nations peacekeeping forces were withdrawing. The Pentagon stated that U.S. military personnel in Haiti would be about 500, consisting mainly of engineering and medical units, with a combat element responsible for protecting the U.S. contingent. On March 2, 2004, the President reported to Congress "consistent with the War Powers Resolution" that, on February 29, he had sent about "200 additional U.S. combat-equipped, military personnel from the U.S. Joint Forces Command" to Port-au-Prince, Haiti, for a variety of purposes, including preparing the way for a U.N. Multinational Interim Force, and otherwise supporting U.N. Security Council Resolution 1529 (2004). For further information on Haiti, see CRS Report RL32294, *Haiti: Developments and U.S. Policy Since 1991 and Current Congressional Concerns*, by Maureen Taft-Morales.

Somalia

In Somalia, the participation of U.S. military forces in a U.N. operation to protect humanitarian assistance, which began in December 1992, became increasingly controversial as fighting and casualties increased and objectives appeared to be expanding. On October 7, 1993, President Clinton announced that all U.S forces would be withdrawn by March 31, 1994, and most forces left by that date. The remaining 58 Marines, who had remained to protect U.S. diplomats, were withdrawn September 15, 1994.

A major issue for Congress was whether to authorize U.S. action in Somalia. On February 4, 1993, the Senate passed S.J. Res. 45 to authorize the President to use U.S armed forces pursuant to U.N. Security Council Resolution 794. S.J. Res. 45 stated it was intended to constitute the specific statutory authorization under Section 5(b) of the War Powers Resolution. On May 25, 1993, the House amended and passed S.J. Res. 45. The amendment authorized U.S. forces to remain for one year. S.J. Res. 45 was then sent to the Senate for its concurrence, but the measure did not reach the floor.

As sporadic fighting resulted in the deaths of Somali and U.N. forces, including Americans, controversy over the operation intensified. On September 9, 1993, the Senate adopted an amendment to S. 1298, the Defense Authorization Bill, expressing the sense of Congress that the President by November 15, 1993, should seek and receive congressional authorization for the continued deployment of U.S. forces to Somalia. It asked that the President consult with Congress and report the goals, objectives, and anticipated jurisdiction of the U.S. mission in Somalia by October 15, 1993. On September 29, the House adopted a similar amendment to its bill, H.R. 2401. On October 7, the President consulted with congressional leaders from both parties for over two hours on Somalia policy and also announced that U.S. forces would be withdrawn by March 31, 1994.

On October 15, 1993, the Senate adopted an amendment by Senator Byrd to H.R. 3116, the Defense Department Appropriations Act for FY1994, cutting off funds for U.S. military operations in Somalia after March 31, 1994, unless the President obtained further spending authority from Congress. The Senate approved the use of military operations only for the protection of American military personnel and bases and for helping maintain the flow of relief aid by giving the U.N. forces security and logistical support. The amendment, which became Section 8151 of P.L. 103-139, required U.S. forces in Somalia to remain under the command and control of U.S. commanders. In addition, on November 9, 1993, the House adopted H.Con.Res. 170, using Section 5(c) of the War Powers Resolution to direct the President to remove forces from Somalia by March 31, 1994; sponsors stated it was a non-binding measure, and the Senate did not act on the measure. The Defense Appropriations Act for FY1995 (P.L. 103-335, signed September 30, 1994) prohibited the use of funds for the continuous presence of U.S. forces in Somalia, except for the protection of U.S. personnel, after September 30, 1994.

On November 4, the U.N. Security Council decided to end the U.N. mission in Somalia by March 31, 1995. On March 3, 1995, U.S. forces completed their assistance to United Nations forces evacuating Somalia.

Instances Formally Reported Under the War Powers Resolution

Presidents have submitted 121 reports to Congress as a result of the War Powers Resolution. Of these, President Ford submitted 4, President Carter 1, President Reagan 14, President George H.W. Bush 7, President Clinton 60, and President George W. Bush 35. For a summary of the 111 reports submitted by the Presidents from 1975-2003, see CRS Report RL32267, *The War Powers Resolution: After Thirty-Three Years,* by Richard F. Grimmett. The following is a brief summary of reports submitted by President Bush George W. Bush since January 2004. The reports are submitted to the Speaker of the House as executive communications, and subsequently published on the U.S. government printing office website under House Documents. The full texts of these Presidential reports may be found at [http://www.gpoaccess.gov/serialset/cdocuments/index.html].

(112) On January 22, 2004, the President reported to Congress "consistent with the War Powers Resolution" that the United States was continuing to deploy combat equipped military personnel in Bosnia and Herzegovina in

support of NATO's Stabilization Force (SFOR) and its peacekeeping efforts in this country. About 1,800 U.S. personnel are participating.

(113) On February 25, 2004, the President reported to Congress "consistent with the War Powers Resolution" that, on February 23, he had sent a combat-equipped "security force" of about "55 U.S. military personnel from the U.S. Joint Forces Command" to Port-au-Prince, Haiti to augment the U.S. Embassy security forces there and to protect American citizens and property in light of the instability created by the armed rebellion in Haiti.

(114) On March 2, 2004, the President reported to Congress "consistent with the War Powers Resolution" that on February 29 he had sent about "200 additional U.S combat-equipped, military personnel from the U.S. Joint Forces Command" to Port-au-Prince, Haiti for a variety of purposes, including preparing the way for a UN Multinational Interim Force, and otherwise supporting UN Security Council Resolution 1529(2004).

(115) On March 20, 2004, the President sent to Congress "consistent with the War Powers Resolution," a consolidated report giving details of multiple ongoing United States military deployments and operations "in support of the global war on terrorism (including in Afghanistan)," as well as operations in Bosnia and Herzegovina, Kosovo, and Haiti. In this report, the President noted that U.S. anti-terror related activities were underway in Georgia, Djibouti, Kenya, Ethiopia, Yemen, and Eritrea. He further noted that U.S. combat-equipped military personnel continued to be deployed in Kosovo as part of the NATO-led KFOR (1, 900 personnel); in Bosnia and Herzegovina as part of the NATO-led SFOR (about 1,100 personnel); and approximately 1, 800 military personnel were deployed in Haiti as part of the U.N. Multinational Interim Force.

(116) On November 4, 2004, the President sent to Congress, "consistent with the War Powers Resolution," a consolidated report giving details of multiple ongoing United States military deployments and operations "in support of the global war on terrorism." These deployments, support or military operations include activities in Afghanistan, Djibouti, as well as Kenya, Ethiopia, Eritrea, Bosnia and Herzegovina, and Kosovo. In this report, the President noted that U.S. anti-terror related activities were underway in Djibouti, Kenya, Ethiopia, Yemen, and Eritrea. He further noted that U.S. combat-equipped military personnel continued to be deployed in Kosovo as part of the NATO-led KFOR (1, 800 personnel); and in Bosnia and Herzegovina as part of the NATO-led SFOR (about 1,000 personnel). Meanwhile, he stated that the United States continues to deploy more than 135,000 military personnel in Iraq.

(117) On May 20, 2005, the President sent to Congress "consistent with the War Powers Resolution," a consolidated report giving details of multiple ongoing United States military deployments and operations "in support of

the global war on terrorism," as well as operations in Iraq, where currently about 139,000 U.S. military personnel are stationed. U.S. forces are also deployed in Kenya, Ethiopia, Yemen, Eritrea, and Djibouti assisting in "enhancing counter-terrorism capabilities" of these nations. The President further noted that U.S. combat-equipped military personnel continued to be deployed in Kosovo as part of the NATO-led KFOR (1,700 personnel). Approximately 235 U.S. personnel are also deployed in Bosnia and Herzegovina as part of the NATO Headquarters-Sarajevo who assist in defense reform and perform operational tasks, such as counter-terrorism and supporting the International Criminal Court for the Former Yugoslavia.

(118) On December 7,2005, the President sent to Congress "consistent" with the War Powers Resolution, a consolidated report giving details of multiple ongoing United States military deployments and operations "in support of the global war on terrorism," and in support of the Multinational Force in Iraq, where about 160,000 U.S. military personnel are deployed. U.S. forces are also deployed in the Horn of Africa region—Kenya, Ethiopia, Yemen, and Djibouti—assisting in "enhancing counter-terrorism capabilities" of these nations. The President further noted that U.S combat-equipped military personnel continued to be deployed in Kosovo as part of the NATO-led KFOR (1,700 personnel). Approximately 220 U.S. personnel are also deployed in Bosnia and Herzegovina as part of the NATO Headquarters-Sarajevo who assist in defense reform and perform operational tasks, such as "counter-terrorism and supporting the International Criminal Court for the Former Yugoslavia."

(119) On June 15, 2006, the President sent to Congress "consistent" with the War Powers Resolution, a consolidated report giving details of multiple ongoing United States military deployments and operations "in support of the war on terror," and in Kosovo, Bosnia and Herzegovina, and as part of the Multinational Force (MNF) in Iraq. Presently, about 131,000 military personnel were deployed in Iraq. U.S. forces were also deployed in the Horn of Africa region, and in Djibouti to support necessary operations against al-Qaida and other international terrorists operating in the region. U.S. military personnel continue to support the NATO-led Kosovo Force (KFOR). The current U.S. contribution to KFOR is about 1,700 military personnel. The NATO Headquarters-Sarajevo was established in November 22,2004 as a successor to its stabilization operations in Bosnia-Herzegovina to continue to assist in implementing the peace agreement. Approximately 250 U.S. personnel are assigned to the NATO Headquarters-Sarajevo who assist in defense reform and perform operational tasks, such as "counter-terrorism and supporting the International Criminal Court for the Former Yugoslavia."

(120) On July 18,2006, the President reported to Congress "consistent" with the War Powers Resolution, that in response to the security threat posed in Lebanon to U.S Embassy personnel and citizens and designated third

country personnel," he had deployed combat-equipped military helicopters and military personnel to Beirut to assist in the departure of the persons under threat from Lebanon. The President noted that additional combat-equipped U.S. military forces may be deployed "to Lebanon, Cyprus and other locations, as necessary." to assist further departures of persons from Lebanon and to provide security. He further stated that once the threat to U.S. citizens and property has ended, the U.S. military forces would redeploy.

(121) On December 15, 2006, the President sent to Congress "consistent" with the War Powers Resolution, a consolidated report giving details of multiple ongoing United States military deployments and operations "in support of the war on terror," in Kosovo, Bosnia and Herzegovina, and as part of the Multinational Force (MNF) in Iraq. Presently, about 134,000 military personnel are deployed in Iraq. U.S. forces were also deployed in the Horn of Africa region, and in Djibouti to support necessary operations against al-Qaida and other international terrorists operating in the region, including Yemen. U.S. military personnel continue to support the NATO-led Kosovo Force (KFOR). The current U.S. contribution to KFOR is about 1,700 military personnel. The NATO Headquarters-Sarajevo was established in November 22, 2004 as a successor to its stabilization operations in Bosnia-Herzegovina to continue to assist in implementing the peace agreement. Approximately 100 U.S. personnel are assigned to the NATO Headquarters-Sarajevo who assist in defense reform and perform operational tasks, such as "counter-terrorism and supporting the International Criminal Court for the Former Yugoslavia."

Consultation with Congress

Section 3 of the War Powers Resolution requires the President "in every possible instance" to consult with Congress before introducing U.S. armed forces into situations of hostilities and imminent hostilities, and to continue consultations as long as the armed forces remain. A review of instances involving the use of armed forces since passage of the Resolution, noted in this report, indicates there has been very little consultation with Congress under the Resolution when consultation is defined to mean seeking advice prior to a decision to introduce troops. Presidents have met with congressional leaders after the decision to deploy was made but before commencement of operations.

One problem is the interpretation of when consultation is required. The War Powers Resolution established different criteria for consultation than for reporting. Consultation is required only before introducing armed forces into "hostilities or into situations where imminent involvement in hostilities is clearly indicated by the circumstances," the circumstances triggering the time limit. A second problem is the meaning of the term consultation. The executive branch has often taken the view that the consultation requirement has been fulfilled when from the viewpoint of some Members of Congress it has not. The House report on the War Powers Resolution said, "... consultation in this provision means that a decision is pending on a problem and that Members of Congress are being asked by the President for their advice and opinions and, in appropriate circumstances, their approval of action contemplated." A third problem is who represents Congress for consultation purposes. The House version specifically called for consultation between the President and the leadership and appropriate committees. This was changed to less specific wording in final House-Senate conference committee version, to provide some flexibility. Some critics of the existing statute have introduced proposals to specify a consultation group. But Congress has yet to act on such a proposal.

Issues for Congress

An immediate issue for Congress when the President introduces troops into situations of potential hostilities is whether to invoke Section 4(a)(1) of the War Powers Resolution and trigger a durational limit for the action unless Congress authorizes the forces to remain. If Congress concurs in a President's action, application of the Resolution may be desirable either to legitimize the action and strengthen it by making clear congressional support for the measure or to establish the precedent that the Resolution does apply in such a situation. On the other hand, some may believe it is preferable to leave the President more flexibility of action than is possible under the Resolution. Or some may not wish to have a formal vote on either the issue of applying the Resolution or the merits of utilizing armed forces in that case. If Congress does not concur in an action taken by a president, the Resolution offers a way to terminate it.

A longer-term issue is whether the War Powers Resolution is working or should be amended. Some contend that it has been effective in moderating the President's response to crisis situations because of his awareness that certain actions would trigger its reporting and legislative veto provisions. Or they suggest that it could be effective if the President would comply fully or Congress would invoke its provisions. Others believe it is not accomplishing its objectives and suggest various changes. Some have proposed that the Resolution return to the original Senate-passed version, which would enumerate circumstances in which the President needed no congressional authorization for use of armed forces (namely to respond to or forestall an armed attack against the United States or its forces or to protect U.S. citizens while evacuating them) but prohibit any other use or any permissible use for more than 30 days unless authorized by Congress.

Others would replace the automatic requirement for withdrawal of troops after 60 days with expedited procedures for a joint resolution authorizing the action or requiring disengagement. Still others would repeal the Resolution on grounds that it restricts the President's effectiveness in foreign policy or is unconstitutional.

Several Members have suggested establishing a consultative group to meet with the President when military action is being considered. Senators Byrd, Nunn, Warner, and Mitchell introduced S.J. Res. 323 in 1988 and S. 2 in 1989 to establish a permanent consultation group of 18 Members consisting of the leadership and the ranking and minority members of the Committees on Foreign Relations, Armed Services, and Intelligence. The bill would permit an initial consultative process to be limited to a core group of six Members—the majority and minority leaders of both chambers plus the Speaker of the House and President pro tempore of the Senate. On October 28, 1993, House Foreign Affairs Chairman Lee Hamilton introduced H.R. 3405 to establish a congressional consultative group equivalent to the National Security Council. No action was taken on this proposal.

Thus far, however, executive branch officials and congressional leaders, who themselves have varying opinions, have been unable to find mutually acceptable changes in the War Powers Resolution. President Clinton, in Presidential Decision Directive 25 signed May 3, 1994, supported legislation to amend the Resolution along the lines of the Mitchell, Nunn, Byrd, and Warner proposal of 1989, to establish a consultative mechanism and also eliminate the 60-day withdrawal provisions. Although many agreed on the consultation group, supporters of the legislation contended the time limit had been the main flaw in the War Powers Resolution, whereas opponents contended the time limit provided the teeth of the Resolution. The difficulty of reaching consensus in Congress on what action to take is reflected in the fact that in the 104th Congress, only one measure, S. 5, introduced January 4, 1995, by then Majority Leader Dole was the subject of a hearing. S. 5, if enacted, would have repealed most of the existing War Powers Resolution. An effort to repeal most of the War Powers Resolution in the House on June 7, 1995, through an amendment to the Foreign Assistance and State Department Authorization Act for FY1996-97 (H.R. 1561) by Representative Hyde, failed (201-217). Other than these instances, no other War Powers related legislation was even considered during the 104th Congress.

On March 18, 1998, the House defeated H.Con. Res. 227, a resolution that would have directed the President, pursuant to section 5(c) of the War Powers Resolution to remove United States Armed Forces from the Republic of Bosnia and Herzegovina (H.Rept. 105-442). It was the hope of Representative Tom Campbell, its sponsor, that passage of the resolution could lead to a court case that would address the constitutionality of the War

Powers Resolution. On March 31, 1998, the House passed a Supplemental Appropriations bill (H.R. 3579) that would ban use of funds for conduct of offensive operations against Iraq, unless such operations were specifically authorized by law. This provision was dropped in the conference with the Senate. On June 24, 1998, the House passed H.R. 4103, the Defense Department Appropriations bill for FY1999, with a provision by Representative Skaggs that banned the use of funds appropriated or otherwise made available by this act "to initiate or conduct offensive military operations by United States Armed Forces except in accordance with the war powers clause of the Constitution (Article 1, Section 8), which vests in Congress the power to declare and authorize war and to take certain specified, related actions." The Skaggs provision was stricken by the House-Senate conference committee on H.R. 4103. No further War Powers-related actions were taken by Congress by the adjournment of the 105th Congress.

During the 106th Congress, efforts were made to force the President to seek congressional authority for military operations in Kosovo, leading to votes in the House and Senate on that issue. Subsequently, Representative Tom Campbell and others sued the President in Federal Court in an effort to clarify congressional-Executive authority in this area. A Federal District Court and an Appeals Court refused to decide the case on the merits, instead holding that the plaintiffs lacked standing to sue. On October 2, 2000, the United States Supreme Court, let stand the holding of the U.S. Appeals Court.[1]

During the first session of the 107th Congress, the Congress passed S.J. Res. 23, on September 14, 2001, in the wake of the terrorist attacks against the World Trade Center in New York City, and the Pentagon building in Arlington, Virginia. This legislation, titled the "Authorization for Use of Military Force," passed the Senate by a vote of 98-0; the House of Representatives passed it by a vote of 420-1. This joint resolution authorizes the President "to use all necessary and appropriate force against those nations, organizations, or persons he determines planned, authorized, committed, or aided the terrorist attacks that occurred on September 11, 2001, or harbored such organizations or persons, in order to prevent any future acts of international terrorism against the United States by such nations, organizations or persons." Congress further declared in the joint resolution that "Consistent with section 8(a)(1) of the War Powers resolution," the above language is "intended to constitute specific statutory authorization within the meaning of section 5(b) the War Powers Resolution." S.J. Res. 23 further stated that "Nothing in this resolution supersedes any requirement of the

[1] Campbell v. Clinton, 52 F. Supp. 2d 34 (D.D.C. 1999), *aff'd*, 203 F.3d 19 (D.C. Cir. 2000), *cert. denied*, 531 U.S. 815 (2000).

War Powers Resolution." President George W. Bush signed S.J. Res. 23 into law on September 18, 2001 (P.L. 107-40, 115 Stat. 224).

During the second session of the 107th Congress, the Congress passed H.J. Res. 114, the Authorization for the Use of Force Against Iraq Resolution of 2002 (P.L. 107-243). On October 16, 2002, President Bush signed this legislation into law. This statute authorizes the President to use the armed forces of the United States

> as he determines to be necessary and appropriate in order to (1) defend the national security of the United States against the continuing threat posed by Iraq; and (2) enforce all relevant United Nations Security Council resolutions regarding Iraq.

Prior to using force under this statute the President is required to communicate to Congress his determination that the use of diplomatic and other peaceful means will not "adequately protect the United States . . . or . . . lead to enforcement of all relevant United Nations Security Council resolutions" and that the use of force is "consistent" with the battle against terrorism. The statute also stipulates that it is "intended to constitute specific statutory authorization within the meaning of section 5(b) of the War Powers Resolution." It further requires the President to make periodic reports to Congress "on matters relevant to this joint resolution." Finally, the statute expresses Congress's "support" for the efforts of the President to obtain "prompt and decisive action by the Security Council" to enforce Iraq's compliance with all relevant Security Council resolutions.

P.L. 107-243 clearly confers broad authority on the President to use force. The authority granted is **not limited** to the implementation of **previously adopted** Security Council resolutions concerning Iraq but includes "all relevant . . . resolutions." Thus, it appears to incorporate resolutions concerning Iraq that may be adopted by the Security Council in the future as well as those already adopted. The authority also appears to extend beyond compelling Iraq's disarmament to implementing the full range of concerns expressed in those resolutions. The President's exercise of the authority granted is **not** dependent upon a finding that Iraq was complicit in the attacks of September 11, 2001. Moreover, the authority conferred can be used for the purpose of defending "the national security of the United States against the continuing threat posed by Iraq." On March 19, 2003, President Bush used the authority granted in P.L. 107-243 by launching a military attack against Iraq. The President continues to use that authority for ongoing military operations in Iraq.

DOCUMENT NO. 4

CONGRESSIONAL AUTHORITY TO LIMIT U.S. MILITARY OPERATIONS IN IRAQ

CRS Report
RL33837

July 11, 2007

Jennifer K. Elsea, Michael John Garcia, and Thomas J. Nicola
Legislative Attorneys
American Law Division

Summary

On October 16, 2002, President Bush signed the Authorization for Use of Military Force Against Iraq Resolution of 2002. Since the March 2003 invasion of Iraq, Congress has enacted appropriation bills to fund the continuation of the Iraq war, including military training, reconstruction, and other aid for the government of Iraq. In April, 2007, however, Congress passed a supplemental appropriations bill to fund the war that contained conditions and a deadline for ending some military operations. The President vetoed the bill, arguing in part that some of its provisions are unconstitutional. The current dispute is centered on whether Congress has the constitutional authority to legislate limits on the President's authority to conduct military operations in Iraq, even though it did not initially provide express limits. Specific issues include whether Congress may, through limitations on appropriations, set a ceiling on the number of soldiers or regulate which soldiers the President may assign to duty in Iraq, and whether an outright repeal or expiration of the authorization for use of military force (AUMF) against Iraq would have any effect.

It has been suggested that the President's role as Commander in Chief of the Armed Forces provides sufficient authority for his deployment of troops, and any efforts on the part of Congress to intervene could represent an unconstitutional violation of separation-of-powers principles. While even proponents of strong executive prerogative in matters of war appear to concede that it is within Congress's authority to cut off funding entirely for a military operation, it has been suggested that spending measures that restrict but do not end financial support for the war in Iraq would amount to an "unconstitutional condition." The question may turn on whether specific proposals involve purely operational decisions committed to the President in his role as Commander in Chief, or whether they are instead valid exercises of Congress's authority to allocate resources using its war powers and power of the purse.

This report begins by providing background, discussing constitutional provisions allocating war powers between Congress and the President, and presenting a historical overview of relevant court cases. It discusses Congress's power to rescind prior military authorization, concluding, in light of relevant jurisprudence and the War Powers Resolution, that the repeal of the AUMF, absent the further denial of appropriations or the establishment of a specific deadline for troop withdrawal, would likely have little, if any, legal effect on the continuation of combat operations. The report discusses Congress's ability to limit funding for military operations in Iraq, examining relevant court cases and prior measures taken by Congress to restrict military operations, as well as possible alternative avenues to fund operations if appropriations are cut. There follows a summary of relevant measures included in the vetoed FY2007 supplemental appropriations bill, H.R. 1591, and the enacted act, H.R. 2206. The report provides historical examples of measures that restrict the use of particular personnel, and concludes with a brief analysis of arguments that might be brought to bear on the question of Congress's authority to limit the availability of troops to serve in Iraq. Although not beyond debate, such a restriction appears to be within Congress's authority to allocate resources for military operations.

Introduction

On May 1, 2007, President George W. Bush vetoed the U.S. Troop Readiness, Veterans' Care, Katrina Recovery, and Iraq Accountability Appropriations Act, H.R. 1591, in part because of measures designed to limit the U.S. military role in Iraq. He called the bill "unconstitutional because it purports to direct the conduct of operations of war in a way that infringes upon the powers vested in the presidency by the Constitution, including as commander in chief of the Armed Forces."[1] The next day, the House of Representatives voted to approve the bill by a vote of 222 to 203, fail-ing to muster the two-thirds majority necessary to override the veto.[2] Congress then

[1] 153 Cong. Rec. H4315 (daily ed. May 2, 2007) (President's veto message), *also available at* [http://www.whitehouse.gov/news/releases/2007/05/20070502-1.html].
[2] *Id.* at H4326.

passed a new version of the supplemental appropriations bill, H.R. 2206 (P.L. 110-128), without providing timetables for withdrawal from Iraq, but conditioning the release of reconstruction assistance to Iraq on achievement of certain benchmarks by the Iraqi government, unless the President waives the requirements.[3] The House of Representatives agreed to vote on a withdrawal deadline when it takes up FY2008 supplemental appropriations, which is expected in September.

As Congress considers defense authorization and appropriations bills for FY2008, there may be a renewed focus on whether or to what extent Congress has the constitutional authority to legislate limits on the President's authority to conduct military operations in Iraq. Congress may consider measures, for example, to repeal the authorization to use force in Iraq, to set deadlines for the withdrawal of most troops from Iraq, to set requirements for unit rotations into Iraq, or to make other requirements that could affect the deployment of armed forces to Iraq.

It has been suggested that the President's role as Commander in Chief of the Armed Forces provides sufficient authority for his deployment of additional troops, and any efforts on the part of Congress to intervene could represent an unconstitutional violation of separation-of-powers principles. While even proponents of strong executive prerogative in matters of war appear to concede that it is within Congress's authority to cut off funding entirely for a military operation, it has been suggested that spending measures that restrict but do not end financial support for the war in Iraq would amount to an "unconstitutional condition."[4] The question may turn on whether the President's decisions on troop deployment and mission assignment are purely operational decisions committed to the President in his role as Commander in Chief, or whether congressional action to limit the availability of troops and the missions they may perform is a valid exercise of Congress's authority to allocate resources using its war powers and power of the purse.

Background

On October 16, 2002, Congress passed and President Bush signed the Authorization for Use of Military Force Against Iraq Resolution of 2002.[5]

---

[3] For a detailed analysis of the FY2007 supplemental appropriations bills, see CRS Report RL33900, *FY2007 Supplemental Appropriations for Defense, Foreign Affairs, and Other Purposes,* by Stephen Daggett *et al.*

[4] *See, e.g.,* David B. Rivkin Jr. and Lee A. Casey, *What Congress Can (And Can't) Do on Iraq,* WASH. POST (January 16, 2007) at A19; *see also* Charles Tiefer, *Can Appropriation Riders Speed Our Exit from Iraq?,* 42 STAN. J. INT'LL. 291(2006)(predicting arguments that would be made to oppose congressional funding restrictions).

[5] P.L. 107-243; 116 Stat. 1498. For more background, see CRS Report RL31133, *Declarations of War and Authorizations for the Use of Military Force: Historical Background and Legal Implications,* by Richard F.

While the President noted he had sought a "resolution of support" from Congress to use force against Iraq, and appreciated receiving that support, he also stated that:

> . . . my request for it did not, and my signing this resolution does not, constitute any change in the long-standing positions of the executive branch on either the President's constitutional authority to use force to deter, prevent, or respond to aggression or other threats to U.S. interests or on the constitutionality of the War Powers Resolution.[6]

The President indicated he would continue to consult with Congress and to submit written reports to Congress every 60 days on matters relevant to the resolution to use force,[7] which authorizes the President to use the armed forces of the United States

> as he determines to be necessary and appropriate in order to (1) defend the national security of the United States against the continuing threat posed by Iraq; and (2) enforce all relevant United Nations Security Council resolutions regarding Iraq.

The statute required certain conditions to be met prior to the initiation of military operations and made periodic reports to Congress mandatory, but did not set a timetable or any criteria for determining when to withdraw troops from Iraq. It appears to incorporate future UN Security Council resolutions concerning Iraq that may be adopted by the Security Council as well as those adopted prior to its enactment, effectively authorizing military force not only to compel disarmament but to carry out other functions necessary for achieving the goals adopted or that may be adopted by the Security Council. Thus, it appears that the resolution authorizes force deemed necessary by the President for so long as Iraq poses a continuing threat to the United States and the U.S. military presence is not inconsistent with relevant U.N. resolutions.

The resolution does not itself stipulate limitations with respect to the amount of force that may be used or the resources that may be expended to accomplish the authorized objectives; however, Congress may set limits by means of legislation or the budgeting process. The Department of Defense has some latitude regarding how it allocates funds for various operations, and may have additional statutory authority to obligate funds without additional prior express authorization from Congress.

Grimmett and Jennifer K. Elsea.

[6] *See* President's Statement on Signing H.J.Res. 114, October 16, 2002, *available at* [http://usinfo.state.gov/dhr/Archive/2003/Oct/09-906028.html].

[7] *Id.*

I. Constitutional Provisions

At least two arguments support the constitutionality of Congress's authority to limit the President's ability to increase or maintain troop levels in Iraq. First, Congress's constitutional power over the nation's armed forces provides ample authority to legislate with respect to how they may be employed. Under Article I, § 8, Congress has the power "To lay and collect Taxes . . . to . . . pay the Debts and provide for the common Defence,""To raise and support Armies," "To provide and maintain a Navy," "To make Rules for the Government and Regulation of the land and naval Forces," and "To declare War, grant letters of Marque and Reprisal, and make Rules concerning Captures on Land and Water," as well as "To provide for calling forth the Militia to execute the Laws of the Union, suppress Insurrections and repel Invasions" and "To provide for organizing, arming, and disciplining, the Militia, and for governing such Part of them as may be employed in the Service of the United States." Further, Congress is empowered "To make all Laws which shall be necessary and proper for carrying into Execution the foregoing Powers . . ." as well as "all other Powers vested by this Constitution in the Government of the United States, or in any Department or Officer thereof."

Secondly, Congress has virtually plenary constitutional power over appropriations, one that is not qualified with reference to its powers in section 8. Article I, § 9 provides that "No Money shall be drawn from the Treasury, but in Consequence of Appropriations made by Law." It is well established, as a consequence of these provisions, that "no money can be paid out of the Treasury unless it has been appropriated by an act of Congress"[8] and that Congress can specify the terms and conditions under which an appropriation may be used,[9] so long as it does not impose an unconstitutional condition on the use of the funds.[10]

On the executive side, the Constitution vests the President with the "executive Power," Article II, § 1, cl. 1, and appoints him "Commander in Chief of the Army and Navy of the United States," *id.*, § 2, cl. 1. The President is empowered, "by and with the Advice and Consent of the Senate, to make Treaties," authorized "from time to time [to] give to the Congress Information on the State of the Union, and [to] recommend to their Consideration such Measures as he shall judge necessary and expedient,"

[8] Cincinnati Soap Co. v. United States, 301 U.S. 308, 321 (1937).

[9] Fullilove v. Klutznick, 448 U.S. 448, 474 (1980); South Dakota v. Dole, 483 U.S. 203, 206–07 (1987). For a scholarly treatment of the Appropriations Clause, see Kate Stith, *Congress' Power of the Purse*, 97 Yale L. J. 1343 (1988).

[10] United States v. Klein, 80 U.S. (8 Wall.) 128 (1872) (holding invalid an appropriations proviso that effectively nullified some effects of a presidential pardon and that appeared to prescribe a rule of decision in court cases); United States v. Lovett, 328 U.S. 303 (1946)(invalidating as a bill of attainder an appropriations provision denying money to pay salaries of named officials).

and bound to "take Care that the Laws be faithfully executed." *Id.*, § 3. He is bound by oath to "faithfully execute the Office of President of the United States," and, to the best of his "Ability, preserve, protect and defend the Constitution of the United States." *Id.*, § 1, cl. 8.

It is clear that the Constitution allocates powers necessary to conduct war between the President and Congress. While the ratification record of the Constitution reveals little about the meaning of the specific war powers clauses, the importance of preventing all of those powers from accumulating in one branch appears to have been well understood,[11] and vesting the powers of the sword and the purse in separate hands appears to have been part of a careful design.[12]

It is generally agreed that some aspects of the exercise of those powers are reserved to the Commander in Chief, and that Congress could conceivably legislate beyond its authority in such a way as to intrude impermissibly into presidential power. The precise boundaries separating legislative from executive functions, however, remain elusive. There can be little doubt that Congress would exceed its bounds if it were to confer exclusive power to direct military operations on an officer not subordinate to the President,[13] or to purport to issue military orders directly to subordinate officers.[14] At the same time, Congress's power to make rules for the government and regulation of the armed forces provides it wide latitude for restricting the nature of orders the President may give. Congress's power of appropriations gives it ample power to supply or withhold resources, even if the President deems them necessary to carry out planned military operations.[15]

---

[11] *See* Louis Fisher, Presidential War Power 7 (2d ed. 2004)(noting that allocation of war powers to Congress was a break with monarchial theories, under which all such powers belonged to the executive); *id.* at 8–12.

[12] *See* William C. Banks and Peter Raven-Hansen, National Security Law and the Power of the Purse 27–32(1994).

[13] Congress has by statute provided that the President must issue orders to subordinate military commands through the appropriate chain of command rather than directly. *See* Francis D. Wormuth and Edwin B. Firmage, To Chain the Dog of War: The War Power of Congress in History and Law 93(2nd ed. 1989)(citing the Command of the Army Act of 1867, 14 Stat. 485, 486–87, which required that "all orders and instructions relating to military operations" be "issued through the General of the Army," and made orders issued contrary to the provision punishable by prison sentence from two to twenty years). Congress has also authorized judges to issue orders directed to military commanders requiring them to provide military aid to marshals for the arrest of persons accused of crimes against the United States who were on board foreign ships in U.S. harbors. 2 Stat. 339(1805).

[14] *But see id.* at 93–94 (asserting that during the Reconstruction period following the Civil War, the "army was given its orders directly by Congress," and that President Andrew Johnson's efforts to circumvent the statute were cited in the ninth article of impeachment against him, although no proof was offered at trial).

[15] For a discussion of theories asserting the presidential prerogative to spend without appropriations when necessary for military operations, see generally Colonel Richard D. Rosen, *Funding "Non-traditional" Military Operations: The Alluring Myth of a Presidential Power of the Purse,* 155 Mil. L. Rev. 1 (1998); *see also* Major Brian A. Hughes, *Uses and Abuses of O&M Funded Construction: Never Build on a Foundation of Sand,* 2005-AUG Army Law. 1 (describing how fiscal law constrains military spending, sometimes impeding military operations).

Congress's War Powers

The power "To Declare War" has long been construed to mean not only that Congress can formally take the nation into war but also that it can authorize the use of the armed forces for military expeditions that may not amount to war.[16] While a restrictive interpretation of the power "To declare War" is possible, for example, by viewing the Framers' use of the verb "to declare" rather than "to make"[17] as an indication of an intent to limit Congress's ability to affect the course of a war once it is validly commenced,[18] Congress's other powers over the use of the military would likely fill any resulting void. In practice, courts have not sought to delineate the boundaries of each clause relating to war powers or identify gaps between them to find specific powers that are denied to Congress.[19]

Early exercises of Congress's war powers may shed some light on the original understanding of how the war powers clauses might empower Congress to limit the President's use of the armed forces. In the absence of a standing army, early presidents were constrained to ask Congress for support in advance of undertaking any military operations.[20] Congress generally provided the requested support and granted the authority to raise the necessary troops to defend the frontiers from deprivations by hostile Indians[21] and to build a navy to protect U.S. commerce at sea.[22]

---

16 Bas v. Tingy, 4 U.S. 37(1800).

17 The Framers' decision to substitute "declare" for "make" has generally been interpreted to allow the President the authority to repel sudden attacks. 2 Max Farrand, The Records of the Federal Convention of 1787, 318–19 (rev. ed. 1937)(explanation of James Madison and Elbridge Gerry on their motion to amend text).

18 *Cf.* John C. Yoo, *War and the Constitutional Text*, 69 U. Chi. L. Rev. 1639, 1669–71 (2002)(arguing that "to declare" means to formally recognize rather than to authorize or commence).

19 *See* 3 Joseph Story, Commentaries on the Constitution §§ 1170–71 (1833) (stating that the powers to issue letters of marque and reprisal and to authorize captures are incidental to the power to declare war, implying their express mention was unnecessary, but noting that these "incidental" powers may also be employed during peace). *But see, e.g.*, J. Terry Emerson, *War Powers Legislation*, 74 W. Va. L. Rev. 53, 62 (1972)(arguing that early opinions related to the Quasi-War with France, often advanced for the proposition that Congress is empowered to regulate military operations that do not amount to war, should be read as strict interpretations of Congress's power to make rules for captures).

20 *See* Abraham Sofaer, War, Foreign Affairs and Constitutional Power 116-17 (1976) (describing President Washington's efforts to obtain support for military efforts, including a build-up of military strength to preserve peace and maintain U.S. stature among nations).

21 *See*, e.g., Act of March 3d, 1791, for raising and adding another Regiment to the Military Establishment of the United States, and for making further provision for the protection of the frontier, 1 Stat. 222; Act of March 5, 1792, 1 Stat. 241 (adding three regiments for three years or until peace with Indian tribes was established); Act of July 16, 1798, 1 Stat. 604 (authorizing the President to raise twelve additional regiments of infantry and six troops of light dragoons during the continuance of differences with the French Republic).

22 *See, e.g.*, Act of March 27, 1794, To provide a naval armament, 1 Stat. 351 ("Whereas the depredations committed by Algerine corsairs render it necessary. . ." authorizing the building and manning of six ships of specific types, until the establishment of peace with the Regency of Algiers)(amended in 1796 to remove restrictions so that vessels could be used for other purposes, 1 Stat. 453); Act of April 27, 1798, To provide an additional Armament for the protection of the Trade of the United States. . ., 1 Stat. 552; Act of June 22, 1798, 1 Stat. 569 (authorizing the President "to increase the strength of any revenue cutter, for the purposes of defence, against hostilities near the sea coast" by manning the vessels with up to 70 seamen and marines).

Congress, in exercising its authority to raise the army and navy, sometimes raised forces for specific purposes, which may be viewed as both an implicit authorization to use the forces for such purposes and as an implicit limitation on their use.[23] On the other hand, Congress often delegated broad discretion to the President within those limits, and appears to have acquiesced to military actions that were not explicitly authorized.[24]

In several early instances, Congress authorized the President to use military forces for operations that did not amount to a full war. Rather than declaring a formal war with France, Congress authorized the employment of the naval forces for limited hostilities. The Third Congress authorized the President to lay and enforce embargoes of U.S. ports, but only while Congress was not in session (and embargo orders were to expire 15 days after the commencement of the next session of Congress).[25] The Fifth Congress authorized the President to issue instructions to the commanders of public armed ships to capture certain French armed vessels and to recapture ships from them,[26] and to retaliate against captured French citizens who had seized U.S. citizens and subjected them to mistreatment.[27] Congress also authorized U.S. merchant vessels to defend themselves against French vessels.[28] The Supreme Court treated these statutes as authorizing a state of "partial war" between the United States and France.[29] Such an undeclared war was described as an "imperfect" war, as distinguished from a "Solemn" or "perfect" war, declared as such, in that, in the first case, all members of one nation are at war with all members of the other nation; in the second case, those who are authorized to commit hostilities act "under special authority."[30] This suggests an early understanding that Congress's war powers extend to establishing the scope of hostilities to be carried out by the armed forces.

In the majority of cases, however, it appears that Congress has given broad deference to the President to decide how much of the armed forces to

---

[23] Some proposals explicitly to limit how the vessels could be employed were stricken prior to enactment, but the congressional debates left unclear whether the majority of members thought the restrictions unconstitutional or merely unwise, or whether the absence of specific authority was meant to be a limitation. *See* SOFAER, *supra* note 20, at 147–54. The John Adams Administration interpreted the legislation restrictively, and instructed naval commanders accordingly that their authority was to be "partial and limited." *See id.* at 156.

[24] *See id.* at 129 (noting that offensive actions against Wabash Indians and against a British fort may have exceeded express statutory authorization but were authorized by implication through appropriations).

[25] Act of June 4, 1794, 1 Stat. 372. *See also* Act of June 5, 1794 §§ 7–8, 1 Stat. 381, 384 (authorizing the President to use armed forces to detain violators and compel foreign ships to depart).

[26] Act of May 28, 1798, 1 Stat. 561. *See also* Act of July 9, 1798, 1 Stat. 578.

[27] Act of March 3, 1799, 1 Stat. 743 (empowering and requiring the President to "cause the most rigorous retaliation to be executed on [French suspects who] have been or hereafter may be captured in pursuance of any of the laws of the United States").

[28] 1 Stat. 572.

[29] Bas v. Tingy, 4 U.S.(Dall.) 37 (1800).

[30] *Id.* at 40. *See also* Talbot v. Seeman, 5 U.S.(Cranch) 1, 28 (1801)("Congress may authorize general hostilities . . . or partial hostilities'").

employ in a given situation. After Tripoli declared war against the United States in 1801 and U.S. vessels were already engaged in defensive actions against them, Congress did not enact a full declaration of war. Rather, it issued a sweeping authorization for the commissioning of privateers, captures, and other actions to "equip, officer, man, and employ *such of the armed vessels of the United States as may be judged requisite by the President of the United States,* for protecting effectually the commerce and seamen thereof on the Atlantic ocean, the Mediterranean and adjoining seas," as well as to "cause to be done *all such other acts of precaution or hostility as the state of war will justify, and may, in his opinion, require.*"[31] In declaring war against Great Britain in 1812, Congress authorized the President to "use the whole land and naval force of the United States to carry the same into effect, and to issue to private armed vessels of the United States commissions or letters of marque and general reprisal, in such form as he shall think proper. . . ."[32]

That Congress has traditionally left it up to the President to decide how much of the armed forces to employ in a given conflict need not imply that such deference is constitutionally mandated. The fact that Congress has seen fit to include such language may just as easily be read as an indication that Congress believes that the decision is its to delegate. Under this view, even in the case of a declaration of war, Congress retains the power to authorize the President to use only a portion of the armed forces to engage in a particular conflict. On the other hand, some have argued that the President is authorized to deploy all of the armed forces as he sees fit, with or without an express authorization to use force or a declaration of war.[33] According to this theory, in essence, Congress can stop the deployment of military forces only by cutting appropriations and discharging the troops.

Congress has also used its authority to provide for the organization and regulation of the armed forces to regulate how military personnel are to be organized and employed. The earliest statutes prescribed in fairly precise terms how military units were to be formed and commanded. For example, the 1798 act establishing the Marine Corps mandated the raising of a corps to consist of "one major, four captains, sixteen first lieutenants, twelve second lieutenants, forty-eight sergeants, forty-eight corporals, thirty-two

---

[31] Act of February 6, 1802, 2 Stat. 129 (emphasis added). For more examples of authorizations to use force and declarations of war, see CRS Report RL31133, *Declarations of War and Authorizations for the Use of Military Force: Historical Background and Legal Implications,* by Richard F. Grimmett and Jennifer K. Elsea.

[32] Act of June 18, 1812, ch. 102, 2 Stat 755.

[33] *See, e.g.,* Bradley Larschan, *The War Powers Resolution: Conflicting Constitutional Powers, The War Powers, and U.S. Foreign Policy,* 16 Denver J. Int'l L. & Pol'y 33, 45 (1987) (arguing that once Congress has raised an army and appropriated funds for it, "it falls to the President to use the armed forces in his capacity to conduct foreign policy in situations short of war"). The author states that it is "clear that the Congress may prohibit the use of U.S. forces in certain areas by statute," but that "it is the President who orders deployment of the troops." *Id.* at 49.

drums and fifes, and seven hundred and twenty privates. . . ."[34] Congress authorized the President to appoint certain other officers as necessary if he were to assign the Marine Corps or any part of it to shore duty, and to assign the detachment to duty in "forts and garrisons of the United States, on the sea-coast, or any other duty on shore." Officers of the Marine Corps could be detached to serve on board frigates and other armed vessels. The Marine Corps was increased in size and reorganized in 1834 to be commanded by a colonel, with the proviso that no Marine Corps officer could be placed in command of a navy yard or vessel of the United States.[35]

It appears to have been understood that personnel and units authorized to perform certain duties could not be assigned to perform other duties without authorization from Congress. In 1808, when Congress authorized eight new regiments of specific types and composition, it felt compelled to include language making members of the light dragoon regiment liable to "serve on foot as light infantry" until sufficient horses and other accouterments could be provided.[36] The Supreme Court later interpreted an 1802 statute providing for the establishment of the Corps of Engineers, although broadly worded to permit the President to direct that its members serve such duty in such places as he saw fit, to authorize only engineering duties:

> But, however broad this enactment is in its language, it never has been supposed to authorize the President to employ the corps of engineers upon any other duty, except such as belongs either to military engineering, or to civil engineering.[37]

The Commander-in-Chief Clause

Early in the nation's history, the Commander-in-Chief power was understood to connote "nothing more than the supreme command and direction of the military and naval forces, as first general and admiral of the confederacy."[38] Concurring in that view in 1850, Chief Justice Taney stated:

> [The President's] duty and his power are purely military. As Commander-in-Chief, he is authorized to direct the movements of the naval and military forces placed by law at his command, and to employ them in the manner he may deem most effectual to harass and conquer and subdue the enemy.[39]

This formula, taken alone, provides only an approximate demarcation of the line separating Congress's role from the President's. Advocates of a

34 1 Stat. 594, 595 (1798).
35 4 Stat. 712, 713 (1834).
36 2 Stat. 481, 483 (1808).
37 Gratiot v. United States, 40 U.S. (15 Pet.) 336, 371 (1841)(finding that the President could contract for other services but must pay an additional stipend for them from other funds).
38 *The Federalist*, No. 69 (Alexander Hamilton).
39 Fleming v. Page, 50 U.S. (9 How.) 603, 615 (1850).

strong role for Congress might characterize a legislative effort to limit the number of troops available in Iraq as placing troops "by law" under the President's command, while proponents of a strong executive would likely view it as a limitation on the President's ability to "employ them in the manner" he sees fit. With respect to the latter argument, however, it should be noted that the particular question before the *Fleming* Court did not call into question the extent to which Congress could restrict the manner of employing troops once placed at the command of the President.

Other early cases demonstrate Congress's authority to restrict the President's options for the conduct of war. In *Little v. Barreme,*[40] Chief Justice Marshall had occasion to recognize congressional war power and to deny the exclusivity of presidential power. There, after Congress had authorized limited hostilities with France, a U.S. vessel under orders from the President had seized what its commander believed was a U.S. merchant ship bound from a French port, allegedly carrying contraband material. Congress had, however, provided by statute only for seizure of such vessels bound *to* French ports.[41] Upholding an award of damages to the ship's owners for wrongful seizure, the Chief Justice said:

> It is by no means clear that the president of the United States whose high duty it is to 'take care that the laws be faithfully executed,' and who is commander in chief of the armies and navies of the United States, might not, without any special authority for that purpose in the then existing state of things, have empowered the officers commanding the armed vessels of the United States, to seize and send into port for adjudication, American vessels which were forfeited by being engaged in this illicit commerce. But when it is observed that [an act of Congress] gives a special authority to seize on the high seas, and limits that authority to the seizure of vessels bound or sailing to a French port, the legislature seems to have prescribed that the manner in which this law shall be carried into execution, was to exclude a seizure of any vessel not bound to a French port.[42]

Accordingly, the Court held, the President's instructions exceeded the authority granted by Congress and were not to be given force of law, even in the context of the President's military powers and even though the instructions might have been valid in the absence of contradictory legislation.

In *Bas v. Tingy,*[43] the Court looked to congressional enactments rather than plenary presidential power to uphold military conduct related to the limited war with France. The following year, in *Talbot v. Seeman,*[44] the Court upheld as authorized by Congress a U.S. commander's capture of a neutral

[40] 6 U.S. (2 Cr.) 170 (1804).
[41] 1 Stat. 613 (1799).
[42] 6 U.S. (2 Cr.) at 177–178.
[43] 4 U.S. (4 Dall.) 37 (1800).
[44] 5 U.S. (1 Cr.) 1,28 (1801).

ship, saying that "[t]he whole powers of war being, by the constitution of the United States, vested in congress, the acts of that body can alone be resorted to as our guides in this inquiry." During the War of 1812, the Court recognized in *Brown v. United States*,[45] that Congress was empowered to authorize the confiscation of enemy property during wartime, but that absent such authorization, a seizure authorized by the President was void.

The onset of the Civil War provided some grist for later assertions of unimpeded presidential prerogative in matters of war. In the *Prize Cases*,[46] the Supreme Court sustained the blockade of Southern ports instituted by President Lincoln in April, 1861, at a time when Congress was not in session. Congress had at the first opportunity ratified the President's actions,[47] so that it was not necessary for the Court to consider the constitutional basis of the President's action in the absence of congressional authorization or in the face of any prohibition. Nevertheless, the Court approved the blockade five-to-four as an exercise of presidential power alone, on the basis that a state of war was a fact and that, the nation being under attack, the President was bound to take action without waiting for Congress.[48] The case has frequently been cited to support claims of greater presidential autonomy by reason of his role as Commander in Chief.

However, it should be recalled that where Lincoln's suspension of the Writ of Habeas Corpus varied from legislation enacted later to ratify it, the Court looked to the statute[49] rather than to the executive proclamation[50] to determine the breadth of its application.[51] The Chief Justice described the allocation of war powers as follows:

> The power to make the necessary laws is in Congress; the power to execute in the President. Both powers imply many subordinate and auxiliary powers. Each includes all authorities essential to its due exercise. But neither can the President, in war more than in peace, intrude upon the proper authority of Congress, nor Congress upon the proper authority of the President. . . .[52]

---

45 12 U.S. (8 Cr.) 110 (1814).

46 67 U.S. (2 Bl.) 635 (1863).

47 12 Stat. 326 (1861)(ratifying all "acts, proclamations, and orders" done by the President "respecting the army and navy. . . and calling out or relating to the militia").

48 67 U.S. (2 Bl.) at 668 ("[The President] does not initiate war, but is bound to accept the challenge without waiting for any special legislative authority."). The minority argued that only congressional authorization could stamp an insurrection with the character of war. Later, a unanimous Court adopted the majority view. The Protector, 79 U.S. (12 Wall.) 700 (1872).

49 Act of March 3d, 1863, 12 Stat. 755 (authorizing the suspension of habeas corpus, but with limitations in Union states to those held as prisoners of war; all others were to be indicted or freed.)

50 Proclamation of September 15, 1863, 13 Stat. 734 (suspending habeas corpus with respect to those in federal custody as military offenders or "as prisoners of war, spies, or aiders and abettors of the enemy").

51 *Ex parte* Milligan, 71 U.S. (4 Wall.) 2 (1866).

52 *Id.* at 139 (Chase, C.J., concurring).

The Chief Justice described the Commander-in-Chief power as entailing "the command of the forces and the conduct of campaigns,"[53] but nevertheless agreed that military trials of civilians accused of violating the law of war in Union states were invalid without congressional approval, despite the government's assertion that the "[Commander in Chief's] power to make an effectual use of his forces [must include the] power to arrest and punish one who arms men to join the enemy in the field against him."[54]

On the other hand, the Supreme Court has also suggested that the President has some independent authority to employ the armed forces, at least in the absence of contrary congressional action. In the 1890 case of *In re Neagle,* the Supreme Court suggested, in dictum, that the President has the power to deploy the military abroad to protect or rescue persons with significant ties to the United States. Discussing examples of the executive lawfully acting in the absence of express statutory authority, Justice Miller approvingly described the Martin Koszta affair, in which an American naval ship intervened to prevent a lawful immigrant from being captured by an Austrian vessel, despite the absence of clear statutory authorization.[55] Only one federal court, in an 1860 opinion, has clearly held that in the absence of congressional authorization, the President has authority to deploy military forces abroad to protect U.S. persons (and property).[56] Nevertheless, there historically appears to be some support for this view by both the executive

[53] *Id.* at 139 ("Congress cannot direct the conduct of campaigns, nor can the President, or any commander under him, without the sanction of Congress, institute tribunals for the trial and punishment of offences, either of soldiers or civilians, unless in cases of a controlling necessity. . .").

[54] *Id.* at 17 (government argument).

[55] *In re* Neagle, 135 U.S. 1, 64 (1890) (describing the incident and rhetorically asking, "Upon what act of congress then existing can any one lay his finger in support of the action of our government in this matter?"). For further discussion, see Louis Henkin, Foreign Affairs and the U.S. Constitution 347-348 (2nd ed. 2002); Wormuth & Firmage, *supra* note 13, at 154 (stating that the U.S. captain had acted against the President's orders, but that President Pierce justified the action to Congress, which later awarded the captain a medal). In an earlier opinion, the Court had also stated in dictum that one of the privileges of a U.S. citizen is "to demand the care and protection of the Federal government over his life, liberty, and property when on the high seas or within the jurisdiction of a foreign government." *Slaughter-House Cases,* 83 U.S. 36, 79 (1872). It should be noted that Koszta was not a U.S. citizen, but a legal immigrant who had declared an intention to apply for citizenship. Accordingly, an 1868 statute authorizing the use of any means "not amounting to acts of war" to obtain the release of U.S. *citizens* was likely inapplicable. Expatriation Act of July 27, 1868, 15 Stat. 223.

[56] Durand v. Hollins, 8 Fed. Cas. 111 (C.C.S.D.N.Y. 1860) (Nelson, Circuit Justice) (holding that a Navy commander was not civilly liable for damages caused by his forces during an 1854 action to protect U.S. citizens and property in Greytown, Nicaragua). In an opinion by Circuit Justice Nelson, the Court held that the Commander was not liable because the military action was pursuant to a valid exercise of federal authority to be exercised by the President:

> . . . as it respects the interposition of the executive abroad, for the protection of the lives or property of the citizen, the duty must, of necessity, rest in the discretion of the president. Acts of lawless violence, or of threatened violence to the citizen or his property, cannot be anticipated and provided for; and the protection, to be effectual or of any avail, may, not unfrequently, require the most prompt and decided action. Under our system of government, the citizen abroad is as much entitled to protection as the citizen at home. *Id.* at 112.

and legislative branches.[57] However, the scope of any such authority remains unclear, as does the degree to which it may be limited by an act of Congress.

The expansion of presidential power related to war, asserted as a combination of Commander-in-Chief authority and the President's inherent authority over the nation's foreign affairs, began in earnest in the twentieth century. In *United States v. Curtiss-Wright Export Corp*,[58] the Supreme Court confirmed that the President enjoys greater discretion when acting with respect to matters of foreign affairs than may be the case when only domestic issues are involved. In that case, Congress, concerned with the outside arming of the belligerents in the war between Paraguay and Bolivia, had authorized the President to proclaim an arms embargo if he found that such action might contribute to a peaceful resolution of the dispute. President Franklin Roosevelt issued the requisite finding and proclamation, and Curtiss-Wright and associate companies were indicted for violating the embargo. They challenged the statute, arguing that Congress had failed adequately to elaborate standards to guide the President's exercise of the power thus delegated.[59] Justice Sutherland concluded that the limitations on delegation in the domestic field were irrelevant where foreign affairs are involved, a result he based on the premise that foreign relations is exclusively an executive function combined with his constitutional model positing that internationally, the power of the federal government is not one of enumerated but of inherent powers, emanating from concepts of

---

[57] *See* GAO, Office of Compt. Gen., *President Authority Protection of American Lives and Property Abroad*, 55 Comp. Gen. 1081 (1975) (describing historical practice and the weight of scholarly authority as supporting the power of the President to order military rescue operations in the absence of congressional authorization); Dept. of Justice, Office of Legal Counsel, 4A U.S. Op. Off. Legal Counsel 185, *Presidential Power to Use the Armed Forces Abroad Without Statutory Authorization* (1980) (alleging presidential authority to deploy forces to protect, and retaliate for injuries suffered by, U.S. persons and property). For discussion of the deployment of military forces to protect U.S. persons or property, see FISHER, *supra* note 11, at 57-58 (describing historical practice, and noting mid-20th century study listing 148 examples of this occurrence); Arthur M. Schlesinger, Jr., The Imperial Presidency 54-57 (rev. ed. 2004)(discussing mid-nineteenth century instances where presidents unilaterally committed forces to protect U.S. persons or property). The number and degree to which these actions occurred without congressional authorization is the subject to some debate. *See* Wormuth & Firmage, *supra* note 13, at 135-51 (discussing and disputing validity of various lists of military actions compiled to demonstrate historical prevalence of presidential war-making). For example, some argue that President Jefferson's ordering of the Navy to protect American shipping from Barbary pirates was done without congressional approval, while others view these orders as having been issued pursuant to legislation providing for a "naval peace establishment." *Compare* Dept. of Justice, Off. of Legal Counsel, *supra*, at 187 (describing Jefferson's use of the Navy as a "famous early example" of President's acting without congressional authorization to protect U.S. interests) *with* Fisher, *supra* note 11, at 35–36 (characterizing the orders as being issued pursuant to congressional authorization, and noting that Jefferson denied having inherent authority to commit such acts). Whether such usage would legitimate the authority is also subject to debate. *See* Wormuth & Firmage, *supra* note 13, at 135.

[58] 299 U.S. 304 (1936).

[59] The Supreme Court had recently held that the Constitution required Congress to elaborate standards when delegating authority to the President. Schechter Poultry Corp. v. United States, 295 U.S. 495 (1935).

sovereignty rather than the Constitution. The Court affirmed the convictions, stating that:

> It is important to bear in mind that we are here dealing not alone with an authority vested in the President by an exertion of legislative power, but with such an authority plus the very delicate, plenary and exclusive power of the President as the sole organ of the federal government in the field of international relations—a power which does not require as a basis for its exercise an act of Congress, but which, of course, like every other governmental power, must be exercised in subordination to the applicable provisions of the Constitution. It is quite apparent that if, in the maintenance of our international relations, embarrassment—perhaps serious embarrassment—is to be avoided and success for our aims achieved, congressional legislation which is to be made effective through negotiation and inquiry within the international field must often accord to the President a degree of discretion and freedom from statutory restriction which would not be admissible were domestic affairs alone involved. Moreover, he, not Congress, has the better opportunity of knowing the conditions which prevail in foreign countries, and especially is this true in time of war.[60]

The case is cited frequently to support a theory of presidential power not subject to restriction by Congress, although the case in fact involved an exercise of authority delegated by Congress. *Curtiss-Wright* remains precedent admonishing courts to show deference to the President in matters involving international affairs, including by interpreting ambiguous statutes in such a manner as to increase the President's discretion.[61] The case has also been cited in favor of broad presidential discretion to implement statutes related to military affairs.[62] To the extent, however, that Justice Sutherland interpreted presidential power as being virtually plenary in the realms of foreign affairs and national defense, the case has not been followed to establish that Congress lacks authority in these areas.

The constitutional allocation of war powers between the President and Congress, where Congress had not delegated the powers exercised by the President, was described by Justice Jackson, concurring in the *Steel Seizure* Case[63]:

> The Constitution expressly places in Congress power "to raise and support Armies" and "to provide and maintain a Navy." This certainly lays upon Congress primary responsibility for supplying the armed forces. Congress alone controls the raising of revenues and their appropriation and may

[60] 299 U.S. at 319-20.

[61] *See* Haig v. Agee, 453 U.S. 280, 291, 293-294 & n. 24, 307-308 (1981); Sale v. Haitian Centers Council, Inc., 509 U.S. 155 (1993)(construing treaty and statutory provisions as not limiting presidential discretion in interdicting refugees on high seas in the light of the President's "unique responsibility" in foreign and military affairs, citing *Curtiss-Wright*).

[62] *See* Loving v. United States, 517 U.S. 748 (1996).

[63] Youngstown Sheet and Tube Co. v. Sawyer, 343 U.S. 579, 641 (1952).

> determine in what manner and by what means they shall be spent for military and naval procurement . . .
>
> There are indications that the Constitution did not contemplate that the title Commander in Chief of the Army and Navy will constitute him also Commander in Chief of the country, its industries and its inhabitants. He has no monopoly of "war powers," whatever they are. While Congress cannot deprive the President of the command of the army and navy, only Congress can provide him any army or navy to command.

The Jackson opinion is commonly understood to establish that whatever powers the President may exercise in the absence of congressional authorization, the President may act contrary to an act of Congress only in matters involving exclusive presidential prerogatives.[64]

Presidents from Truman to George W. Bush have claimed independent authority to commit U.S. armed forces to involvements abroad absent any Congressional participation other than consultation and after-the-fact financing. In 1994, for example, President Clinton based his authority to order the participation of U.S. forces in NATO actions in Bosnia-Herzegovina on his "constitutional authority to conduct U.S. foreign relations" and as his role as Commander in Chief,[65] and protested efforts to restrict the use of military forces there and elsewhere as an improper and possibly unconstitutional limitation on his "command and control" of U.S. forces.[66] Ever since Congress passed the War Powers Resolution over President Nixon's

---

[64] Justice Jackson's concurrence took note of the fact that *Curtiss-Wright* did not involve a case in which the President took action contrary to an act of Congress. *Id.* at 635-36 &n.2. *Curtiss-Wright,* he said:

> involved, not the question of the President's power to act without congressional authority, but the question of his right to act under and in accord with an Act of Congress. The constitutionality of the Act under which the President had proceeded was assailed on the ground that it delegated legislative powers to the President. Much of the Court's opinion is *dictum,* but the *ratio decidendi* is contained in the following language:
>
> > When the President is to be authorized by legislation to act in respect of a matter intended to affect a situation in foreign territory, the legislator properly bears in mind the important consideration that the form of the President's action—or, indeed, whether he shall act at all—may well depend, among other things, upon the nature of the confidential information which he has or may thereafter receive, or upon the effect which his action may have upon our foreign relations. This consideration, in connection with what we have already said on the subject, discloses the unwisdom of requiring Congress in this field of governmental power to lay down narrowly definite standards by which the President is to be governed. As this court said in Mackenzie v. Hare, 239 U.S. 299, 311, 'As a government, the United States is invested with all the attributes of sovereignty. As it has the character of nationality it has the powers of nationality, especially those which concern its relations and intercourse with other countries. *We should hesitate long before limiting or embarrassing such powers.*' (Italics supplied [by Justice Jackson])*Id.*, at 321–322.
>
> That case does not solve the present controversy. It recognized internal and external affairs as being in separate categories, and held that the strict limitation upon congressional delegations of power to the President over internal affairs does not apply with respect to delegations of power in external affairs. It was intimated that the President might act in external affairs without congressional authority, but not that he might act contrary to an Act of Congress.

[65] 30 Weekly Comp. Pres. Doc. 406 (March 2, 1994).

[66] *See* Interview with Radio Reporters, 1993 Pub. Papers 1763–64; *see also* Fisher, *supra* note 11, at 184.

veto, all Presidents have regarded it as an unconstitutional infringement on presidential powers.[67]

In the context of what it terms the "Global War on Terror," the Bush Administration has claimed that the President's commander-in-chief authority entails inherent authority with respect to the capture and detention of suspected terrorists, authority he has claimed cannot be infringed by legislation.[68] In 2004, the Supreme Court avoided deciding whether Congress could pass a statute to prohibit or regulate the detention and interrogation of captured suspects, which the Administration had asserted would unconstitutionally interfere with core commander-in-chief powers, by finding that Congress had implicitly authorized the detention of enemy combatants when it authorized the use of force in the aftermath of the September 11, 2001, terrorist attacks.[69] However, the Supreme Court in 2006 invalidated President Bush's military order authorizing trials of aliens accused of terrorist offenses by military commission, finding that the regulations promulgated to implement the order did not comply with relevant statutes.[70] The Court did not expressly pass on the constitutionality of any statute or discuss possible congressional incursion into areas of exclusive presidential authority, which was seen by many as implicitly confirming Congress's authority to legislate in such a way as to limit the power of the Commander in Chief.[71]

II. Repeal of Prior Authorization to Use Military Force

While it is well-established that Congress and the President each possess authority on ending a military conflict, issues may arise if the political branches are in disagreement as to whether or how to end a military conflict. Inter-branch disagreement regarding the cessation of hostilities has been a rare occurrence, but it is not unprecedented. In the 110th Congress, a number of proposals have been introduced that would repeal or establish

[67] P.L. 93-148, 87 Stat. 555, codified at 50 U.S.C. § 1541 *et seq. See* CRS Report RL33532, *The War Powers Resolution: Presidential Compliance,* by Richard F. Grimmett.

[68] *See, e.g. Oversight of the Department of Justice: Hearing Before the Senate Judiciary Committee,* 107th Cong. (2002) (testimony of Attorney General John Ashcroft)(arguing that Congress has no constitutional authority to interfere with the President's decision to detain enemy combatants); *see also* Reid Skibell, *Separation-of-Powers and the Commander in Chief—Congress's Authority to Override Presidential Decisions in Crisis Situations,* 13 GEO. MASON L. REV. 183 (2004)(documenting Bush Administration claims with respect to Congress's lack of power to legislate in matters related to the conduct of the war and arguing that these represent an expansion over prior administrations' claims).

[69] *See* Hamdi v. Rumsfeld, 542 U.S. 507, 517 (2004).

[70] Hamdan v. Rumsfeld, 126 S.Ct. 2749 (2006).

[71] The Court adopted Chief Justice Chase's formulation for allocating war powers, *see id.* at 2773, and Justice Jackson's framework for determining separation-of-powers disputes between the President and Congress, *see id.* at 2774 n.24 ("Whether or not the President has independent power, absent congressional authorization, to convene military commissions, he may not disregard limitations that Congress has, in proper exercise of its own war powers, placed on his powers. The Government does not argue otherwise.")(citation omitted).

an expiration date for the Authorization for Use of Military Force against Iraq Resolution of 2002.[72] The following sections discuss the constitutional authority implicated by a repeal of military authorization, procedural, and other considerations involved in rescinding prior military authorization as compared to limiting appropriations, and the legal effect that a repeal would have on continuing hostilities.

Historical Practice

Although the U.S. Constitution expressly empowers Congress to declare war, it is notably silent regarding which political body is responsible for returning the United States to a state of peace. Some evidence suggests that this omission was not accidental.[73] During the Constitutional Convention, a motion was made by one of the delegates to modify the draft document by adding the words "and peace" after the words "to declare war."[74] This motion, however, was unanimously rejected. Convention records do not clearly evidence the framers' intent in rejecting the motion.

Some early constitutional commentators suggested that the motion failed because the framers believed that the power to make peace more naturally belonged to the treaty-making body, as conflicts between nations were typically resolved through treaties of peace.[75] Although the framers did not specifically empower Congress to make peace, they also did not expressly locate the power with the treaty-making body, perhaps because of a recognition that peace might sometimes be more easily achieved through means other than treaty.[76]

---

[72] *See* H.R. 1460 (repealing 2002 resolution); H.R. 1262 (same); S. 679 (declaring that objectives of 2002 resolution have been achieved, and requiring redeployment of forces from Iraq); S.J. Res. 3 (establishing expiration date for 2002 resolution); S. 670 (requiring new military authorization unless certain objectives are met); H.R. 930 (repealing 2002 resolution); H.R. 508 (same); H.R. 413 (same).

[73] Up to that point, the shared American and English tradition suggested that the institution with the power to instigate war was also the body with the power to end it. Blackstone believed that under the English system, "wherever the right resides of beginning a national war, there also must reside the right of ending it, or the power of making peace." 1 WILLIAM BLACKSTONE, COMMENTARIES ON THE LAWS OF ENGLAND 250 (1756). When America declared its independence, it also rejected the monarchial form of government. Nevertheless, the legal document that the Constitution was intended to replace, the Articles of Confederation, expressly accorded the national legislative body with "the sole and exclusive right and power of determining on peace and war." ARTICLES OF CONFEDERATION, art. IX, § 1. Under the Articles, there was neither a national executive nor judicial body.

[74] FARRAND, *supra* note 17, at 319; *see also* 3 JAMES MADISON, THE PAPERS OF JAMES MADISON 1352 (Henry Gilpin, ed. 1840).

[75] 3 JOSEPH STORY, COMMENTARIES ON THE CONSTITUTION § 1173 (1833); WILLIAM RAWLE, A VIEW OF THE CONSTITUTION OF THE UNITED STATES, 110-111 (2nd ed. 1929). It should be noted that at the time the proposal was rejected, the framers had designated the Senate as the treaty-making body. The President was made part of the treaty-making body several weeks later. FARRAND, *supra* note 17, at 538.

[76] As a practical matter, a requirement that peace be achieved through a treaty between the warring parties would, in certain circumstances, lead to odd results:

> The President, who is the Commander-in-Chief . . . and a majority of both branches of Congress, which declares war and maintains the forces necessary for its prosecution, might desire peace yet be unable to obtain it because a third of the Senate plus one Senator were contrary minded. Or our erstwhile antagonist might be the contrary minded one. Or the war might have resulted

It has been suggested that the framers did not allocate an exclusive body with peace-making authority because they believed "it should be more easy to get out of a war than into it."[77] Given the framers' failure to designate a single political branch responsible for returning the country from a state of war to a state of peace, the power to make peace was likely understood to be a shared power, with each branch having the authority on terminating a military conflict.[78] The executive could return the country to a state of peace through a treaty with the warring party, subject to the Senate's advice and consent. Congress could declare peace or rescind a previous authorization to use military force pursuant to its plenary authority to repeal prior enactments, its power to regulate commerce with foreign nations, or its power to make laws "necessary and proper" to effectuate its constitutional powers.[79]

Regardless of the framers' intent, the legislative and executive branches have historically treated peace-making as a shared power. Peace has been declared in one of three ways: (1) via legislation terminating a conflict, (2) pursuant to a treaty negotiated and signed by the executive and ratified following the advice and consent of the Senate, and (3) through a presidential proclamation.[80] All three methods have been recognized as constitutionally legitimate by the Supreme Court,[81] including most clearly in the 1948 case of *Ludecke v. Watkins,* where the Court plainly stated, "The state of war may be terminated by treaty or legislation or Presidential proclamation."[82] Notably, the Court has recognized that the termination of a military conflict is a "political act,"[83] and it has historically refused

> in the extinction of said antagonist. Such, in fact, was the situation at the close of the Civil War, which accordingly could not be brought to an end in the legal sense by a treaty of peace . . .

Edward S. Corwin, *Power of Congress to Declare Peace,* 18 MICH. L. REV. 669, 672–673 (1920).

77 *Id.* at 669. *See also* MADISON, *supra* note 74, at 1352 (quoting delegate Oliver Ellsworth in debate to give Congress the power to "make war").

78 *See* Corwin, *supra* note 76, at 673.

79 *Id.* at 674.

80 A listing of all instances where the U.S. has formally declared war or authorized the use of military force, along with the date and means by which peace was declared or military authorization was terminated, can be found in CRS Report RL31133, *Declarations of War and Authorizations for the Use of Military Force: Historical Background and Legal Implications,* by Richard F. Grimmett and Jennifer K. Elsea.

81 E.g., Hijo v. United States, 194 U.S. 315 (1904) (recognizing state of war with Spain as ending with ratification of peace treaty); The Protector, 79 U.S. 700 (1871) (relying on presidential proclamations to determine the beginning and ending date of the Civil War); Commercial Trust v. Miller, 262 U.S. 51, 57 (1923) (recognizing congressional act as ending war with Germany). It should be noted that the Civil War is the only "war" which was ended by presidential proclamation. It could be argued that the methods by which the political branches may signal the termination of a domestic insurrection are different than those by which they may end a conflict with a foreign nation.

82 335 U.S. 160, 168 (1948) (internal quotations omitted). There are potentially other ways in which peace could be made that were not contemplated by the *Ludecke* Court. *See* CLINTON ROSSITER, THE SUPREME COURT AND THE COMMANDER IN CHIEF 79-80 (1970) (suggesting that a war could also be ended by, among other things, an executive agreement with or without specific congressional authorization).

83 *Ludecke,* 335 U.S. at 168-169.

to review the political branches' determinations of when a conflict has officially ended.[84]

Rescinding Military Authorization Versus Cutting Appropriations: Procedural and Other Considerations

As a procedural matter, it is more difficult for Congress to terminate authorization for a military conflict than to limit appropriations necessary for the continuation of hostilities. As in the case of ordinary legislation, congressional declarations of peace and rescissions of military authorization have historically taken the form of a bill or joint resolution passed by both Houses and presented to the President for signature.[85] Like other legislation, such measures are subject to presidential veto, which Congress may override only with a two-thirds majority of each House.[86]

In contrast, Congress's ability to deny funds for the continuation of military hostilities is not contingent upon the enactment of a positive law, though such a denial may take the form of a positive enactment.[87] Although the President has the power to veto legislative proposals, he cannot compel Congress to pass legislation, including bills to appropriate funds necessary for the continuation of a military conflict. Thus, while a majority of both Houses would be necessary to terminate military authorization, and a super-majority of both Houses would be required to override a presidential veto, a simple majority of a single House could prevent the appropriation of funds necessary for the continuation of a military conflict. [88]It should be noted, however, that legislation probably would be required to prevent the President from exercising statutory authority to transfer certain funds appropriated to other operations for use in support of the military conflict that Congress was attempting to limit. Like other positive legislation, such a measure would be subject to presidential veto.

---

84 Baker v. Carr, 369 U.S 186, 213-214 (1962) (describing the Court's refusal to review the political branches' determination of when or whether a war has ended). *See generally* ROSSITER, *supra* note 82, at 83-89 (discussing Supreme Court jurisprudence upholding political branches' determinations as to the official end of a war, including in cases where actual hostilities ceased several years beforehand).

85 *See* CRS Report RL31133, *Declarations of War and Authorizations for the Use of Military Force: Historical Background and Legal Implications*, by Richard F. Grimmettand Jennifer K. Elsea; *see also* J. Gregory Sidak, *To Declare War*, 41 DUKE L.J. 27, 81-86 (discussing historical operation of bicameralism and presentment in the war-making context, along with scholarly views concerning whether presentment is necessary).

86 U.S. CONST., art. I, § 7, cl. (2)-(3).

87 *See, e.g.*, P.L. 91-652, § 7(a) (1971) (prohibiting funds appropriated from being used to introduce U.S. ground troops into Cambodia); P.L. 93-50, § 307 (1973) (prohibiting appropriated funds from being used in U.S. combat activities in Indochina after August15, 1973); P.L. 103-139, § 8135 (1993) (barring appropriations from being used for combat forces in Somalia after March 31, 1994). For additional examples, see CRS Report RS20775, *Congressional Use of Funding Cutoffs Since 1970 Involving U.S. Military Forces and Overseas Deployments*, by Richard F. Grimmett, and CRS Report RL33803, *Congressional Restrictions on U.S. Military Operations in Vietnam, Cambodia, Laos, Somalia, and Kosovo: Funding and Non-Funding Approaches*, by Amy Belasco, Lynn J. Cunningham, Hannah Fischer, and Larry A. Niksch.

88 *See* Sidak, *supra* note 85, at 104–105.

While it may be procedurally easier for Congress to refuse appropriations for a military conflict than to rescind military authorization, policy considerations may sometimes make the latter option more appealing. For example, some Members of Congress who support the winding down of a military operation might nevertheless be reluctant to reduce the funds for troops on the battlefield. There might also be concerns over potential effects that a denial of appropriations might have on unrelated military operations. Although appropriations legislation can be crafted to effectively terminate hostilities while permitting funding of force protection measures during the orderly redeployment of troops from the battlefield, such legislation, like other positive enactments, would be subject to presidential veto.

In certain circumstances, a President may be more willing to agree to a rescission of military authorization than to an appropriations bill that limits the funding of military operations, particularly if the rescission does not include a deadline for troop withdrawal. Indeed, during the Vietnam War, Congress was able to rescind military authorization at an earlier date than it was able to cut off appropriations. In 1971, Congress passed and President Nixon signed a measure rescinding the 1964 Gulf of Tonkin resolution, which had provided congressional authorization for U.S. military operations against North Vietnam.[89] The Mansfield Amendment, enacted later that year, called for the "prompt and orderly" withdrawal of U.S. troops from Indochina at the "earliest possible date."[90] However, these measures did not include a deadline for troop withdrawal. Although U.S. troop presence in South Vietnam diminished considerably pursuant to the Nixon Administration's "Vietnamization" strategy even prior to these enactments, the United States continued significant air bombing campaigns in the years following the rescission of military authorization. During this same period, President Nixon vetoed or threatened to veto a number of appropriations bills that would have either prohibited funds from being used for certain military operations in Southeast Asia or required a complete withdrawal of U.S. troops from Vietnam. In 1973, two years after rescinding military authorization, Congress was finally able to enact appropriations limitations, signed by the President, that barred combat operations in Indochina.[91] These appropriations measures were approved only after the signing of a cease-fire agreement with North Vietnam and the withdrawal of U.S. troops from South Vietnam, and served primarily to

[89] P.L. 91-672, § 12(1971).

[90] P.L. 92-156, §601(a) (1971).

[91] *E.g.*, P.L. 93-50, §§ 304-307 (1973) (preventing funding expenditures from being used "in or over . . . or off the shores of" Cambodia, Laos, North Vietnam and South Vietnam after August 15, 1973). For further background and examples of funding restrictions proposed and enacted, see CRS Report RS20775, *Congressional Use of Funding Cutoffs Since 1970 Involving U.S. Military Forces and Overseas Deployments*, by Richard F. Grimmett, and CRS Report RL33803, *Congressional Restrictions on U.S. Military Operations in Vietnam, Cambodia, Laos, Somalia, and Kosovo: Funding and Non-Funding Approaches*, by Amy Belasco, Lynn J. Cunningham, Hannah Fischer, and Larry A. Niksch.

end the aerial bombing campaign in Cambodia and prevent U.S. forces from being reintroduced into hostilities.

In sum, in situations where Congress seeks to prevent the executive's continuation of military combat operations, it may be procedurally easier for Congress to deny appropriations than it would be to statutorily compel a withdrawal from hostilities. However, past experience suggests that, at least in certain circumstances, policy considerations may cause the two branches to view the rescission of military authorization as a more appealing alternative—postponing an inter-branch conflict on appropriations for a later date, enabling Congress to signal its interest in winding down a conflict, and (at least temporarily) preserving the President's discretion as to how the conflict is waged.

Legal Consequences of Congressional Rescission of Military Authorization, Absent Additional Congressional Action

Although Congress has the power to rescind authorization of a military conflict or enact a declaration of peace, the practical effect that such an action might have on the President's ability to continue a military conflict may nevertheless remain difficult to predict. Historically, courts have been unwilling to interpret a congressional rescission of military authorization as barring the executive from continuing to wage a military campaign, *at least so long as Congress continues to appropriate money in support of such operations.* Although the War Powers Resolution establishes procedures by which Congress may direct the withdrawal of U.S. troops from military conflicts that lack statutory authorization, the constitutionality and practical effects of these requirements have been questioned. Finally, even in the absence of express congressional authorization, the President may possess some inherent or implied power as Commander in Chief to continue to engage in certain military operations. The following sections explain these points in greater detail.

Judicial Interpretation

Jurisprudence suggests that courts would not necessarily view a repeal of prior authorization, by itself, as compelling the immediate withdrawal of U.S. forces. As an overarching matter, courts have been highly reluctant to act in cases involving national security, especially when they require a pronouncement as to the legality of a military conflict or the strategies used therein.[92] Many such cases have been dismissed without reaching the

[92] This is not to say that every legal challenge to a wartime activity is doomed to failure. In some circumstances, the courts have found unlawful certain military activities involving the seizure of property or the detention of enemy combatants, at least in instances such action was deemed to lack sufficient congressional authorization. *See, e.g.*, Little v. Barreme, 6 U.S. (2 Cr.) 170 (1804) (upholding damage award to owners of U.S. merchant ship seized during quasi-war with France, when Congress

merits of the arguments at issue, including when they involve a political question that the judiciary considers itself ill-suited to answer.[93] Legal actions brought by Members of Congress challenging the lawfulness of military actions have had no greater success than suits brought by private citizens.[94] While the courts have suggested a willingness to intervene in disputes between the two branches that reach a legal (as opposed to political) impasse, they have yet to find an impasse on matters of war that has required judicial settlement. In other words, as long as Congress retains options for bringing about a military disengagement but has not exercised them, courts are unlikely to get involved.[95]

The Vietnam conflict is the lone instance where Congress repealed military authorization while major combat operations were still ongoing. Although the Nixon Administration significantly decreased the number of U.S. troops present in South Vietnam following the repeal of the Gulf of Tonkin Resolution and enactment of the Mansfield Amendment in 1971,[96] major

---

had not authorized such seizures); Youngstown Sheet and Tube Co. v. Sawyer, 343 U.S. 579, 641 (1952) (finding unlawful the government seizure of property to settle labor dispute during Korean War); Rasul v. Bush, 542 U.S. 466 (2004) (finding that federal habeas statute applied to persons detained in Guantanamo Bay pursuant to the "war on terror"); Hamdi v. Rumsfeld, 542 U.S. 507(2004) (persons deemed "enemy combatants" in the "war on terror" have right to challenge detention before a neutral decision-maker); Hamdan v. Rumsfeld, 126 S.Ct. 2749 (2006) (finding that military tribunals convened by presidential order did not comply with the Uniform Code of Military Justice).

93 In *Baker v. Carr,* 369 U.S. 186 (1962), the Supreme Court described situations where the political question doctrine was implicated:

> It is apparent that several formulations which vary slightly according to the settings in which the questions arise may describe a political question, although each has one or more elements which identify it as essentially a function of the separation of powers. Prominent on the surface of any case held to involve a political question is found a textually demonstrable constitutional commitment of the issue to a coordinate political department; or a lack of judicially discoverable and manageable standards for resolving it; or the impossibility of deciding without an initial policy determination of a kind clearly for nonjudicial discretion; or the impossibility of a court's undertaking independent resolution without expressing lack of respect due coordinate branches of government; or an unusual need for unquestioning adherence to a political decision already made; or the potentiality of embarrassment from multifarious pronouncements by various departments on one question.

Id. at 217.

94 For background and examples, see CRS Report RL30352, *War Powers Litigation Initiated by Members of Congress Since the Enactment of the War Powers Resolution*, by David. M. Ackerman.

95 *See, e.g,* Campbell v. Clinton, 52 F. Supp.2d 34 (D. D.C. 1999) (dismissing action seeking declaration that the President acted unlawfully in ordering air strikes in Kosovo and Yugoslavia without congressional authorization, because impasse had not been reached, as Congress had not barred introduction of U.S. forces or barred appropriations from being used for such purpose).

96 In a statement upon signing into law legislation containing the Mansfield Amendment, President Nixon claimed that its instructions were non-binding and pledged to continue his own policies for ending the war. Courts reached different conclusions as to the binding nature of the Mansfield Amendment's instructions for withdrawal. In 1972, a district court in the Second Circuit concluded, in an opinion affirmed without opinion by the court of appeals, that the Amendment "had binding force and effect on every officer of the Government... [and] illegalized the pursuit of an inconsistent executive or administration policy." DaCosta v. Nixon, 55 F.R.D. 145 (E.D.N.Y., 1972), *aff'd without opinion,* 456 F.2d 1335 (2nd Cir. 1972). A year later, however, the Second Circuit Court of Appeals, while not deciding the issue, suggested that the binding nature of the Amendment was unsettled, and noted that "weighty constitutional considerations which support the President in his duties as

combat operations continued into 1973, when Congress cut off all funding for military operations in Indochina.

During this period, federal courts heard a number of suits challenging the legality of continued hostilities in the absence of congressional authorization. None of these challenges proved successful, in large part because Congress continued to appropriate money for military operations. It is a well-established principle that Congress's appropriation of funds may serve in some circumstances to confer authority for executive action.[97] Reviewing courts have found this principle no less applicable concerning matters of war. The appropriation of billions of dollars in support of U.S. combat operations in Indochina, even after the repeal of the Gulf of Tonkin resolution, was viewed as congressional authorization for continued U.S. participation in hostilities,[98] regardless of whether some Members of Congress had a motivation for approving continued appropriations other than that reflected in the express language of the enacted legislation.[99]

Courts have also declined on political question grounds to examine the motives of Congress in choosing to appropriate funds after rescinding direct authorization for U.S. military activities. [100]In the words of one court,

---

Commander-in-Chief preclude too hasty an adoption of the view" that the Amendment was binding. DaCosta v. Laird, 471 F.2d 1146, 1156-1157 (2nd Cir. 1973).

97 Fleming v. Mohawk Wrecking & Lumber Co., 331 U.S. 111, 116 (1947). *See also* Berk v. Laird 317 F. Supp. 715, 727-728 (D.C.N.Y. 1970) (discussing Supreme Court jurisprudence recognizing congressional appropriations as authorizing executive activity, and concluding that Congress's appropriations for ongoing military operations in Indochina constituted authorization of those activities). Dept. of Justice, Office of Legal Counsel, 2000 OLC LEXIS 16, *Authorization for Continuing Hostilities in Kosovo* (2000), at* 14-33 (discussing judicial and scholarly recognition of appropriations statutes serving to authorize combat operations) *[hereinafter* "OLC Opinion on Hostilities in Kosovo"].

98 *See* DaCosta v. Laird, 448 F.2d 1368, 1369 (2nd Cir. 1971), *cert. denied,* 405 U.S. 979 ("In other words, there was sufficient legislative action in extending the Selective Service Act and in appropriating billions of dollars to carry on military and naval operations in Vietnam to ratify and approve the measures taken by the Executive, even in the absence of the Gulf of Tonkin Resolution."); Orlando v. Laird, 443 F.2d 1039, 1043 (2nd Cir. 1971), *cert. denied,* 404 U.S. 869 ("The framers' intent to vest the war power in Congress is in no way defeated by permitting an inference of authorization from legislative action furnishing the manpower and materials of war for the protracted military operation in Southeast Asia."); Massachusetts v. Laird, 451 F.2d 26, 34 (1st Cir. 1971) (finding that Constitution had not been breached when President acted with support of Congress, including through the appropriation of billions of dollars to support ongoing combat operations); *see also* Berk v. Laird, 317 F. Supp. 715 (E.D.N.Y.1970) (decided prior to repeal of Gulf of Tonkin resolution, but recognizing that continued appropriation of funds as authorization of conflict's continuation).

99 *See* Holtzmanv. Schlesinger, 484 F.2d 1307, 1313-1314 (2nd Cir. 1973), *cert. denied, 416* U.S. 936 (1974) (finding appropriations legislation gave President sufficient authority to order the bombing of Cambodia, despite claim by some Members of Congress that legislation was "coerced" by presidential veto of appropriations bills that would have immediately cut off funding of such acts); Drinan v. Nixon, 364 F. Supp. 854 (D.C.Mass. 1973) (same).

100 *Orlando,* 443 F.2d at 1043 (the decision to endorse military action through appropriations rather than direct authorization was "committed to the discretion of the Congress and outside the power and competency of the judiciary, because there are no intelligible and objectively manageable standards by which to judge such actions"); Sarnoff v. Connally, 457 F.2d 809, 810 (9th Cir. 1972), *cert. denied,* 409 U.S. 929 ("Whether a plaintiff challenges the selective service system or the foreign aid and appropriations aspects of congressional cooperation in the present conflict, he presents a political question which we decline to adjudicate."); *Berk,* 317 F. Supp. at 728-729 (recognizing that method that Congress chooses to endorse or authorize action is a political question).

any attempt to assess Congress's intentions in appropriating funds, and determining whether such appropriations were truly meant to further continuing hostilities, would necessarily "require the interrogation of members of Congress regarding what they intended by their votes, and then synthesization of the various answers. To do otherwise would call for gross speculation in a delicate matter pertaining to foreign relations."[101] Such an examination of Congress's motivations was deemed beyond the scope of appropriate judicial scrutiny.[102]

Some argued that Congress's termination of statutory authorization for ongoing hostilities and instruction that the conflict end at the soonest practical date barred the President, at the very least, from "escalating" hostilities. Though the Court of Appeals for the Second Circuit suggested in a 1971 case that this argument might be valid,[103] subsequent rulings indicated that the court would only be willing to consider this argument in very limited circumstances. Notably, in the 1973 case of *DaCosta v. Laird*,[104] the Second Circuit Court of Appeals dismissed a challenge to the President's order to mine the harbors of North Vietnam, where it was argued that this order represented an unlawful escalation of hostilities in light of congressional enactments ordering the withdrawal of U.S. troops at the earliest practicable date. The circuit court dismissed this challenge because it raised a nonjusticiable political question. Deciding such a case would require the court to assess the strategy and tactics used by the executive to wind down a conflict, an assessment it was ill-equipped to make:

> Judges, deficient in military knowledge, lacking vital information upon which to assess the nature of battlefield decisions, and sitting thousands of miles from the field of action, cannot reasonably determine whether a specific military operation constitutes an "escalation" of the war or is merely a new tactical approach within a continuing strategic plan. What if, for example, the war "de-escalates" so that it is waged as it was prior to the mining of North Vietnam's harbors, and then "escalates" again? Are the courts required to oversee the conduct of the war on a daily basis, away from the scene of action? In this instance, it was the President's view that the mining of North Vietnam's harbor was necessary to preserve the lives of American soldiers in South Vietnam and to bring the war to a close. History will tell whether or not that assessment was correct, but without the benefit of such extended hindsight we are powerless to know.[105]

Though the circuit court did not completely rule out the possibility that a further escalation of hostilities could be deemed unlawful, the court suggested it would be willing to consider such arguments only in the most

[101] Atlee v. Laird, 347 F.Supp. 689, 706 (D.C.Pa. 1972), *aff'd without opinion*, 411 U.S. 911 (1973).
[102] *Id.*; *Holtzman*, 484 F.2d at 1314 &n.4.
[103] *DaCosta*, 448 F.2d at 1370.
[104] DaCosta v. Laird, 471 F.2d 1146 (2nd Cir. 1973).
[105] *Id.* at 1155.

limited of circumstances. For example, the court suggested that a "radical change in the character of war operations—as by an intentional policy of indiscriminate bombing of civilians without any military objective—*might* be sufficiently measurable judicially to warrant a court's consideration."[106]

In *Holtzman v. Schlesinger,* decided later that year, the Second Circuit Court of Appeals reversed a lower court decision that had declared unlawful the continued bombing of Cambodia following the removal of U.S. troops and prisoners of war from Vietnam. The circuit court held that it was a nonjusticiable political question as to whether the bombing violated the Mansfield Amendment's instruction that hostilities be terminated at the "earliest practicable date." Comparing the situation with that at issue *in DaCosta,* the court found that the challenge raised "precisely the questions of fact involving military and diplomatic expertise not vested in the judiciary."[107] Further, even assuming *arguendo* that the military and diplomatic issues raised by the bombing were judicially manageable, the circuit court found that Congress had authorized the bombing through continued appropriations.[108]

Taken together, these cases suggest that a reviewing court would probably not interpret a repeal of prior military authorization as requiring the immediate withdrawal of U.S. forces from ongoing hostilities in Iraq. Further, courts may be reluctant to assess whether specific military tactics or strategies pursued by the executive constitute an impermissible "escalation" of a conflict in the aftermath of such a repeal.[109] Accordingly, it does not appear that the termination of direct authorization to use force, absent additional action such as the denial of appropriations or possibly the inclusion of an unambiguous deadline for troop withdrawal, would be interpreted by a reviewing court as constraining the executive's ability to continue U.S. combat operations.

Implications of the War Powers Resolution

The consequences of a repeal of an authorization to use military force were arguably made more significant with the enactment of the War Powers Resolution (WPR).[110] Enacted in 1973 over President Nixon's veto, the

---

106 *Id.* at 1156 (italics added).

107 *Holtzman,* 484 F.2d at 1309-1310 (2nd Cir. 1973), *cert. denied,* 416 U.S. 936 (1974).

108 *Id.* at 1313. Specifically, the court noted the language of § 108 of the Joint Resolution Continuing Appropriations for Fiscal 1974, P.L. 93-52, which barred funding for military operations in and around Indochina after August 15, 1973. The Court inferred from this language that military activities at issue in the case before it, occurring before this deadline, were authorized.

109 *See, e.g.,* Mottola v. Nixon, 318 F. Supp. 538, 540 (1970) (characterizing the extension of the conflict in Vietnam into Cambodia as a "necessary incidental, tactical incursion ordered by the Commander in Chief" that would be authorized so long as the military operations in Vietnam were found to be authorized), *rev'd on other grounds,* 464 F.2d 178 (9th Cir. 1972)(ordering district court to dismiss for lack of standing).

110 P.L. 93-148 (1973) *[hereinafter* "War Powers Resolution" or "WPR"]. For further background and explanation of the War Powers Resolution, see CRS Report RL32267, *The War Powers Resolution: After Thirty Years,* by Richard F. Grimmett.

WPR was an effort by Congress to reassert its role in matters of war—a role that many Members believed had been allowed to erode during the Korean and Vietnam conflicts. Among other things, the WPR establishes a procedure by which Congress may (theoretically) compel the President to withdraw U.S. forces from foreign-based conflicts when a declaration of war or authorization to use military force has been terminated. Specifically, WPR § 5(c) provides that

> at any time that United States Armed Forces are engaged in hostilities outside the territory of the United States, its possessions and territories without a declaration of war or specific statutory authorization, such forces shall be removed by the President if the Congress so directs by concurrent resolution.

While § 5(c) offers a mechanism by which Congress might compel presidential compliance with a law that had rescinded statutory authorization to use military force,[111] its constitutional validity is doubtful given the Supreme Court's ruling in the 1983 case *of INS v. Chadha.*[112] In *Chadha,* the Court held that for a resolution to become a law, it must go through the bicameral and presentment process in its entirety.[113] Accordingly, a concurrent or simple resolution could not be used as a "legislative veto" against executive action. Although the *Chadha* Court did not expressly find WPR § 5(c) to be unconstitutional, it was listed in Justice White's dissent as one of nearly 200 legislative vetoes for which the majority had sounded the "death knell,"[114] and most commentators have agreed with this assessment.[115]

---

[111] The wording of the War Powers Resolution makes clear that appropriations in support of military operations does not in itself constitute "specific statutory authorization" of those operations for purposes of WPR requirements. *See* WPR § 8(a) (noting that authorization is not to be inferred from provisions "contained in any appropriation Act, unless such provision specifically authorizes the introduction of United States Armed Forces into hostilities . . . [and states] that it is intended to constitute specific statutory authorization. . .").

[112] 462 U.S. 919(1983).

[113] *Id.* at 951.

[114] *Id.* at 967, 1003 (White, J., dissenting).

[115] *See, e.g.,* Senate Foreign Relations Comm. Rep., Persian Gulf and the War Powers Resolution, S.Rept. No. 106, 100th Cong., 1st Sess., at 6 (1987) (describing § 5(c) as being "effectively nullified" by the *Chadha* decision); Henkin, *supra* note 55, at 126-127 (recognizing invalidation of § 5(c) by *Chadha* and describing arguments to the contrary as "plausible but not compelling"); Wormuth and Firmage, *supra* note 13, at 222 (noting that the reasoning of *Chadha* "apparently invalidates secion 5(c) of the War Powers Resolution"); Ronald D. Rotunda, *the War Powers Act in Perspective,* 2 Mich. L. & Pol'y Rev. 1, 8 (1997) (claiming that most "scholars have concluded that. . . [§ 5(c)] is unconstitutional ever since *INS v. Chadha).* In contrast, some have argued that neither a declaration of war nor a subsequent rescission of authorization to use force constitutes an "ordinary" act of legislation falling under the requirements of the Presentment Clause. *See* Stephen L. Carter, *The Constitutionality of the War Powers Resolution,* 70 Va.L. Rev. 101, 130-132 (1984). The legitimacy of this argument is untested and highly controversial, as Congress has always presented a declaration of war or authorization to use military force to the president. Further, even assuming *arguendo* that a declaration of war does not need to be presented to the President, it is not necessarily clear that legislation ending hostilities would also not require presentment. *See* Henkin, *supra* note 55, at 127, 379; Carter, *supra,* at 130-132 (describing weaknesses of argument against presentment requirement); *see also* Sidak, *supra* note 85, at 84-85 (discussing historical and scholarly view that presentment is necessary).

Thus, it seems highly unlikely that the WPR could be used to enforce a congressional repeal of an authorization to use military force in Iraq.

Section 5(b) of the WPR establishes a requirement for the withdrawal of U.S. troops 60 days after armed forces are *introduced without* congressional authorization into a situation where hostilities are imminent, unless Congress enacts legislation providing authority for the use of force or extends the deadline.[116] This provision would not appear to supply a means by which Congress could compel the withdrawal of U.S. forces from Iraq, as the introduction of those forces was done pursuant to congressional authorization.[117] Even if Congress were to rescind that authorization, the legality of actions taken pursuant to it would not be nullified.[118] Arguably, however, a substantial increase in troop levels that takes place subsequent to any repeal of the authorization for use of military force against Iraq could trigger the requirements of WPR § 5(b),[119] although it is unclear how large such an increase would need to be before it would be sufficiently "substantial."[120] Congress has in the past enacted or considered legislation declaring the 60-day limit to have taken effect, although apparently with little practical effect.[121] In any case, it appears that WPR section 5(c), which permits Congress to compel the withdrawal of U.S. troops via concurrent resolution, was intended to address situations where Congress desired an end to previously authorized hostilities.

---

[116] The requirement in § 5(b) does not apply in cases in which Congress "is physically unable to meet as a result of an armed attack upon the United States." 50 U.S.C. § 1554. The 60-day deadline is automatically extended for thirty days "if the President determines and certifies to the Congress in writing that unavoidable military necessity respecting the safety of United States Armed Forces requires the continued use of such armed forces in the course of bringing about a prompt removal of such forces."

[117] P.L. 107-243, § 5 (c) ("Congress declares that this section is intended to constitute specific authorization within the meaning of section 5(b) of the War Powers Resolution.").

[118] *See DaCosta*, 448 F.2d at 1369 (the repeal of Gulf of Tonkin resolution " did not wipe out its history nor could it have the effect of a *nunc pro tunc* action").

[119] P.L. 93-148, §§ 4(a), 5(b). The reporting requirement in § 4(a), which begins the sixty-day withdrawal deadline, also comes into effect in the event troops are introduced in "numbers which substantially enlarge United States Armed Forces equipped for combat already located in a foreign nation." However, it appears that the deadline only applies if the report was made necessary due to circumstances described in § 4(a)(1), where troops are initially introduced into hostilities. *See* MICHAEL J. GLENNON, CONSTITUTIONAL DIPLOMACY 103(1990)(explaining that the omission of a requirement for the President to specify whether a report is submitted pursuant to § 4(a)(1) or § 4(a)(2) or (3) makes it impossible to know whether the sixty-day time period has been triggered).

[120] In addition, it could be argued that even if Congress repealed the AUMF, the subsequent appropriation of funds in support of military operations would constitute legal authorization for such activity — at least in circumstances where Congress intended appropriations to support further hostilities, rather than simply to protect troops already in the field. *See* OLC Opinion on Hostilities in Kosovo, *supra* note 97, at * 33-52 (discussing instances in which appropriations suggest a clear intent by Congress to authorize further hostilities, and arguing that the WPR " cannot be read to deny legal effect to . . . [the] clear intent" of Congress to use appropriations measures to authorize further hostilities).

[121] *See* GLENNON, *supra* note 119, at 104 (noting efforts with respect to Lebanon in 1983, P.L. 98-119, and Grenada, in which case no such final triggering legislation emerged, despite both Houses having passed measures to that effect). The necessity for separate legislation to trigger the triggering provision, subject as it is to presidential veto, seems to defeat the purpose for § 5(b). *See id.* at 105 (opining that the provision's "central objective was to create a self-activating mechanism to control abuse of presidential discretion in the event Congress lacked the backbone to do so").

Inherent Presidential Authority to Use Military Force Absent Congressional Authorization

Even in the absence of express congressional authorization, it is well-recognized that the President may still employ military force in *some* circumstances pursuant to his powers as Commander in Chief and his inherent authority in the area of foreign affairs,[122] at least so long as no statute stands in his way. A President would likely argue that this inherent authority would permit him to instruct U.S. forces to engage in certain military operations related to an ongoing conflict, even if statutory authorization for U.S. participation in that conflict had been rescinded. Further, even if Congress were to enact legislation requiring the cessation of military operations after a specified date, it is highly unlikely that this measure would be interpreted to prohibit any and all military operations, specifically as they relate to rescue and evacuation missions. It appears well-understood, at least as a matter of historical practice, that such missions are not intended to be covered under legislation otherwise barring future participation in hostilities.[123]

III. Use of the Power of the Purse to Restrict Military Operations

Congress has used its spending power to restrict the deployment and use of the armed forces in the past.[124] In 1973, for instance, after other legislative efforts failed to draw down U.S. participation in combat operations in Indochina,[125] Congress effectively ended it by means of appropriations riders prohibiting use of funds. Section 307 of the Second Supplemental Appropriations Act for Fiscal Year 1973, P.L. 93-50 (1973), stated that, "None of the funds herein appropriated under this act may be expended to support directly or indirectly combat activities in or over Cambodia, Laos,

---

[122] *See supra* at 9–15.

[123] For example, even after Congress enacted legislation cutting off funding for all combat operations in Indochina, President Ford's subsequent use of military forces to evacuate U.S. citizens and third country nationals was not seriously questioned, nor was a subsequent authorization of an operation to rescue the crew of the *Mayaguez* from Cambodian territory (a mission which was reported to Congress following the procedures of the War Powers Resolution, but only after the operation was completed). For background on congressional attitudes towards these rescue missions, see FISHER, *supra* note 11, at 157–158. *See also* Rappenecker v. United States, 509 F. Supp. 1024, 1030 (D.C. Cal. 1980). The *Rappenecker* case involved a civil suit by former crewmen of the *Mayaguez* for injuries they received during their rescue. Although the President ordered their rescue in the absence of prior congressional authorization, the Court assumed that the order was constitutionally valid. *Id.*

[124] For examples of such measures and a discussion of the context in which they were enacted, see CRS Report RS20775, *Congressional Use of Funding Cutoffs Since 1970 Involving U.S. Military Forces and Overseas Deployments,* by Richard F. Grimmett, and CRS Report RL33803, *Congressional Restrictions on U.S. Military Operations in Vietnam, Cambodia, Laos, Somalia, and Kosovo: Funding and Non-Funding Approaches,* by Amy Belasco, Lynn J. Cunningham, Hannah G. Fischer, and Larry A. Niksch. *See also, e.g.,* Louis Fisher, *How Tightly Can Congress Draw the Purse Strings?,* 83 AM.J.INT'L. L. 758 (1989), and Tiefer, *supra* note 4.

[125] *See* P.L. 91-672, § 12, 84 Stat. 2053 (repealing Gulf of Tonkin Resolution); P.L. 92-156, § 601(a), 85 Stat. 423, 430 (Mansfield Amendment); *see also* P.L. 92-156, § 501(a), 85 Stat. 423, 427 (1971) (Fullbright proviso).

North Vietnam, and South Vietnam, and after August 15, 1973, no other funds heretofore appropriated under any other act may be expended for such purpose." Section 108 of the Continuing Appropriations Resolution for Fiscal Year 1974, P.L. 93-52 (1973), provided that, "Notwithstanding any other provision of law, on or after August 15, 1973, no funds herein or heretofore appropriated may be obligated or expended to finance directly or indirectly combat activities by United States military forces in or over or from off the shores of North Vietnam, South Vietnam, Laos or Cambodia." A year later, Congress passed an authorizing statute, section 38(f)(1) of the Foreign Assistance Act of 1974, P.L. 93-559 (1974), which set a total ceiling of U.S. civilian and military personnel in Vietnam of 4,000 six months after enactment and a total ceiling of 3,000 within one year of enactment.

A provision of an authorization act, section 404 of the International Security Assistance and Arms Export Control Act of 1976, P.L. 94-329 (1976), comprehensively prohibited using funds for military and paramilitary operations in Angola. It stated that:

> Notwithstanding any other provision of law, no assistance of any kind may be provided for the purpose, or which would have the effect, of promoting, augmenting, directly or indirectly, the capacity of any nation, group, organization, movement, or individual to conduct military or paramilitary operations in Angola, unless and until Congress expressly authorizes such assistance by law enacted after the date of enactment of this section.

This section added that if the President determined that the prohibited assistance to Angola should be furnished, he should submit to the Speaker of the House and the Senate Committee on Foreign Relations a report describing recommended amounts and categories of assistance to be provided and identities of proposed aid recipients. This report also was to include a certification of his determination that furnishing such assistance was important to U.S. national security interests and an unclassified detailed statement of reasons supporting it.

Section 109 of the Foreign Assistance and Related Programs Appropriations Act for Fiscal Year 1976, P.L. 94-330 (1976), signed the same day as P.L. 94-329, provided that, "None of the funds appropriated or made available pursuant to this act shall be obligated to finance directly or indirectly any type of military assistance to Angola."

In the 1980s, various versions of the Boland Amendment were enacted to prohibit using funds for various military activities in or around Nicaragua.[126] For example, section 8066 of the Department of Defense Appropriations Act included in the Continuing Appropriations Resolution for Fiscal Year,

[126] *E.g.*, P.L. 98-473, § 8066, 98 Stat. 1904, 1935 (1984); *see* 133 Cong Rec. 15664-15701 (June 15, 1987) (detailing various forms of the Boland Amendment that were enacted).

1985, P.L. 98-473, 98 Stat. 1935 (1984), for example, stated that "During Fiscal Year 1985, no funds available to the Central Intelligence Agency, the Department of Defense, or any other agency or entity of the United States involved in intelligence activities may be obligated or expended for the purpose, or which would have the effect of supporting, indirectly or indirectly, military or paramilitary operation in Nicaragua by any nation, group, organization, movement or individual." This provision stated that after February 28, 1985, the President could expend $14 million in funds if the President made a report to Congress which specified certain criteria, including the need to provide further assistance for military or paramilitary operations prohibited by the Boland Amendment, and if Congress passed a joint resolution approving such action.

In the 1990s, Congress enacted section 8151 of the DOD Appropriations Act for Fiscal Year 1994, P.L. 103-139 (1993), which approved using armed forces for certain purposes including combat in a security role to protect United Nations units in Somalia, but cut off funding after March 31, 1994, except for a limited number of military troops to protect American diplomatic personnel and American citizens unless further authorized by Congress. Section 8135 of the DOD Appropriations Act for Fiscal Year 1995, P.L. 103-335 (1994), provided that, "None of the funds appropriated in this act may be used for the continuous presence in Somalia of United States military personnel, except for the protection of United States personnel, after September 30, 1994." In title IX of the DOD Appropriations Act for Fiscal Year 1995, P.L. 103-335 (1994), Congress provided that, "No funds provided in this act are available for United States military participation to continue Operation Support Hope in or around Rwanda after October 7, 1994, except for any action that is necessary to protect the lives of United States citizens."

These examples reveal the approaches that Congress has employed to prohibit or restrict using military force. They have ranged from the least comprehensive "none of the funds appropriated in this act may be used" to the most comprehensive "notwithstanding any other provision of law, no funds may be used." The phrase "none of the funds appropriated in this act" limits only funds appropriated and made available in the act that carries the restriction, but not funds, if any, that may be available pursuant to other appropriations acts or authorizing statutes. To restrict funds appropriated and made available not only in the act that carries the restriction, but also pursuant to other appropriations acts, Congress has used the phrase "none of the funds appropriated in this act or any other act may be used." The most comprehensive restriction is "notwithstanding any other provision of law, no funds may be used." This language precludes using funds that have been appropriated in any appropriations acts as well as any funds that may be made available pursuant to any authorizing statutes including laws that authorize transfers of appropriated or nonappropriated funds.[127]

Procedural Considerations

There is a parliamentary impediment to including the phrases "none of the funds appropriated in this act or any other act may be used" or "notwithstanding any other provision of law, no funds may be used" in a general appropriations bill. House Rule XXI, clause 2, makes subject to a point of order language that changes existing law (i.e., legislation) in a general appropriations bill (i.e., one providing appropriations for several agencies). A bill that appropriates funds for a single purpose or a single agency is not a general appropriations bill to which this restriction applies. The intent of Rule XXI, clause 2 is to separate the authorizing and appropriating functions and place them in separate committees.

Nonetheless, a practice has developed that just as the House may decline to appropriate funds for a purpose that has been authorized by law, it may by limitation prohibit appropriating money in a general appropriations bill for part of a purpose while appropriating funds for the remainder of it. Such a limitation ". . . may apply solely to the money of the appropriation under consideration" and ". . . may not apply to money appropriated in other acts."[128] Thus, the phrase "none of the funds appropriated *in this act* may be used" is not subject to a point of order, but the phrase "none of the funds appropriated *in this act or any other act* may be used" and the phrase "notwithstanding any other provision of law, no funds may be used" do not appear to qualify as permissible limitations in a general appropriations bill and would be subject to points of order under Rule XXI, clause 2 because they are considered legislation. To avoid a point of order, a limitation in a general appropriations bill may not impose new or additional duties on an executive official, may not restrict authority to incur obligations, and may not make an appropriation contingent upon (i.e., "unless" or "until") the occurrence of an event not required by law.[129] If a Member raises a point of order that language in a general appropriations bill violates Rule XXI, clause 2, and the point of order is sustained by the chair, the legislative language is stricken.

---

[127] *See, e.g.,* 31 U.S.C. chap. 15, subchap. III "Transfers and Reimbursements" for provisions that authorize transfers of funds, including the Economy Act, 31 U.S.C. §§ 1535 and 1536, which allows an agency to transfer funds to another agency if the receiving agency can provide or get by contract goods or services less expensively or more conveniently than the ordering agency can get goods or services by a contract with a commercial enterprise. Transfer authority also is included in some other provisions of the United States Code that apply to individual departments and agencies and sometimes in appropriations acts.

[128] *See* John V. Sullivan, House Parliamentarian, Constitution, *Jefferson's Manual, and Rules of the House of Representatives One Hundred Ninth Congress*, H. Doc. 108-241, at § 1053 (2005).

[129] *See id.* at §§ 1053-57 for an explanation of limitations.

Although legislation in a general appropriations bill is subject to a point of order under Rule XXI, clause 2, a restriction in a House rule is not self-enforcing. Consequently, legislation may be included in a general appropriations bill and become law if no point of order is raised, if a point of order is overruled, or if the House either suspends the rules or agrees to a special order known as a rule reported from the Committee on Rules that waives the point of order against including such legislation.[130]

Like House Rule XXI, clause 2, Senate Standing Rule XVI also prohibits including legislation in a general appropriations bill, but the Senate rule permits legislation to be included if it is germane to the subject matter of the bill under consideration. If a point of order that language constitutes legislation on an appropriations bill is raised, the proponent of the language may defend it by asserting that it is germane. The question of germaneness is not decided by the presiding officer; it is submitted to the Senate. If a majority of Senators vote that the language in question is germane, it remains in the bill and the point of order that it constitutes legislation is dismissed and is not presented to the presiding officer for a ruling. If a majority of the Senate votes that language is not germane, the presiding officer then rules on whether it constitutes legislation. If the point of order is sustained, the language is removed; if it is overruled, the language remains in the bill and can be enacted.[131]

As mentioned earlier, the intent of these House and Senate rules is to separate authorizing and appropriating functions by constraining the bodies from enacting legislation in appropriations bills, but prohibiting use of funds for a purpose or purposes does not contravene the House or Senate rule provided that the prohibition applies only to funds appropriated in the bill being considered.

Because an appropriations act generally funds programs for a fiscal year, each provision contained in the act is presumed to be in effect only until the end of the fiscal year. "A provision contained in an annual appropriation act is not to be construed as permanent legislation unless the language used therein or the nature of the provision makes it clear that Congress intended it to be permanent. The presumption can be overcome if the provision uses language indicating futurity or if the provision is of a general character bearing no relation to the object of the appropriation. . . . The most common word of futurity is 'hereafter' and provisions using this term have often been construed to be permanent."[132] Other words of futurity include

---

130 *Id.* at § 1058.

131 Floyd M. Riddick, Senate Parliamentarian Emeritus, and Alan S. Frumin, Senate Parliamentarian, *Riddick's Senate Procedure: Precedents and Practices*, S. DOC. 101-28, at 101et seq. (1992).

132 Government Accountability Office, Office of General Counsel, I Principles of Appropriations Law 2-34 (3d ed. 2006) (footnotes omitted).

"after the date of approval of this act,""henceforth," and specific references to future fiscal years.[133]

While including a word or words of futurity has the effect of making a provision extend beyond the fiscal year covered by an appropriations act, such a provision would constitute legislation that would appear to be subject to a point of order under House Rule XXI, clause 2 and Senate Standing Rule XVI during congressional consideration. If the parliamentary impediments can be overcome, however, such legislation may be enacted and become valid law.

Availability of Alternative Funds

A fundamental principle in appropriations law is that appropriations may not be augmented with funds from outside sources without statutory authority.

> As a general proposition, an agency may not augment its appropriations from outside sources without specific statutory authority. When Congress makes an appropriation, it also is establishing an authorized program level. In other words, it is telling the agency that it cannot operate beyond the level that it can finance under its appropriation. To permit an agency to operate beyond this level with funds derived from some other source without specific congressional sanction would amount to a usurpation of the congressional prerogative. Restated, the objective of the rule against augmentation of appropriations is to prevent a government agency from undercutting the congressional power of the purse by circuitously exceeding the amount Congress has appropriated for that activity.[134]

While no statute in precise terms expressly prohibits augmenting appropriations, the concept is based on some appropriations laws. The Miscellaneous Receipts Statute, 31 U.S.C. § 3302(b), requires that a government official who receives money for the government from any source must deposit it in the U.S. Treasury as soon as practicable without deduction for any charge or claim. Under the Purpose Statute, 31 U.S.C. § 1301, appropriated funds may be used only for the purposes for which they are appropriated. A criminal provision, 18 U.S.C. § 209, prohibits supplementing the salary of an officer or employee of the government from any source other than the United States government.[135]

An example of a statute permitting gift funds from other countries to finance a war is section 202 of the Continuing Resolution for Fiscal Year 1991, P.L. 101-403 (1990), passed before the first Gulf war. Section 202 added

---

133 *Id.* at 2-36.

134 Government Accountability Office, Office of General Counsel, II Principles of Appropriations Law, 6-162 (3d ed. 2006).

135 *Id.* at 6-163.

a new section 2608 to title 10 of the United States Code to authorize any person, foreign government, or international organization to contribute money or real or personal property for use by the Department of Defense. However, before the Department of Defense could spend the funds, they had to be first appropriated by Congress.

The Purpose Statute states that funds may be used only for purposes for which they have been appropriated; by implication it precludes using funds for purposes that Congress has prohibited. When Congress states that no funds may be used for a purpose, an agency would violate the Purpose Statute if it should use funds for that purpose; it also in some circumstances could contravene a provision of the Antideficiency Act, 31 U.S.C. § 1341. Section 1341 prohibits entering into obligations or expending funds in advance of or in excess of an amount appropriated unless authorized by law. If Congress has barred using funds for a purpose, entering into an obligation or expending any amount for it would violate the act by exceeding the amount—zero—that Congress has appropriated for the prohibited purpose.[136]

To determine whether an agency has violated the Antideficiency Act, it would be necessary to review the language in an appropriations act or authorizing statute that includes a prohibition on using funds for a specific purpose. If an appropriations act prohibits using funds "in this act" for a purpose, for example, expending any amount from that act for the prohibited purpose would appear to contravene the Antideficiency Act because Congress has appropriated zero funds for it. Entering into obligations or expending funds, if any, that may be available from a different appropriations act or other fund for that purpose, however, would not appear to be prohibited by the Antideficiency Act; an agency would be able to use funds from sources other than the appropriations act that contains the prohibition or limitation.

Violating the Antideficiency Act would be significant because it has notification and penalty provisions not found in the Purpose Statute. The Purpose Statute does not expressly provide for penalties; it generally is enforced by imposing administrative sanctions on the officer or employee who violates the statute.[137] The Antideficiency Act, by contrast, contains a provision that not only provides for administrative discipline, including, when circumstances warrant, suspension from duty without pay or removal from office, 31 U.S.C. § 1349, but also one that requires an immediate report of a violation to the President and Congress, 31 U.S.C. § 1351. Moreover, the Antideficiency Act has a criminal penalty provision: Section 1350 of title 31 provides that an officer or employee who "knowingly and willfully"

[136] *Id.* at 6-62.
[137] *Id.* at 6-78.

violates the act "shall be fined not more than $5,000, imprisoned for not more than two years, or both." Although the act has a criminal provision, no one appears to have been prosecuted or convicted for violating it.[138] Another criminal provision, 18 U.S.C. § 435, not part of the Antideficiency Act, makes punishable by a fine of $1,000, imprisonment of not more than one year, or both, knowingly contracting to erect, repair, or furnish any public building or for any public improvement for an amount more than the amount appropriated for that purpose.

The Antideficiency Act prohibits entering into obligations or expending funds in advance of or in excess of an amount appropriated *unless authorized by law.* One law that authorizes entering into obligations in advance of appropriations is the Feed and Forage Act. Also referred to as Revised Statute 3732, the Feed and Forage Act is part of and an express exception to the Adequacy of Appropriations Act, 41 U.S.C. § 11. Section 11 generally states that no government contract or purchase may be made unless it is authorized by law or is under an appropriation adequate to its fulfillment. The Feed and Forage Act exception authorizes the Department of Defense and the Department of Transportation[139] with respect to the Coast Guard when it is not operating as service in the Navy to make contracts in advance of appropriations for clothing, subsistence, forage, fuel, quarters, transportation, or medical and hospital supplies. Obligations entered into pursuant to Feed and Forage Act authority must not exceed the necessities of the current year. The Secretary of Defense and the Secretary of Transportation immediately must advise Congress of the exercise of this authority and report quarterly on the estimated obligations incurred pursuant to it.[140] Although the Feed and Forage Act authorizes *entering into obligations* such as contracts, *actual expenditures* are not permitted pursuant to this authority until Congress appropriates the necessary funds.[141]

Redeployment from Iraq: Provisions in the Vetoed Supplemental

On May 1, 2007, President George W. Bush vetoed the U.S. Troop Readiness, Veterans' Care, Katrina Recovery, and Iraq Accountability Appropriations Act, H.R. 1591.[142] In his veto message, the President said that the bill was

---

138 *Id.* at 6-141.

139 6 U.S.C. § 468 transfers the Coast Guard to the Department of Homeland Security, but a corresponding change to 41 U.S.C. § 11 has not been enacted.

140 *See* Louis Fisher, Presidential Spending Power 238-247 (1975) for an explanation of the Feed and Forage Act.

141 *See* Secretary of Defense (Comptroller), *Budget Execution Flexibilities, Fiscal Year 2005* (2004), *available at* [http://www.dod.mil/comptroller/execution/Final_Budget_Execution.pdf].

142 The House agreed to its version of H.R. 1591 by a vote of 218 to 212 on March 23, 2007. 153 Cong. Rec. H2999 (daily ed. March 23, 2007). On March 29, 2007, the Senate agreed to its version of H.R. 1591 by a vote of 51 to 47. 153 Cong. Rec. S4093 (daily ed. March 29, 2007). The House agreed to the conference report to accompany H.R. 1591 onApril25, 2007, by a vote of 218 to 208. 153 Cong. Rec. H4157-H4158 (daily ed. April 25, 2007). See 153 Cong. Rec. H3823 (daily ed. April 24, 2007) for a

objectionable because it would set an arbitrary date to begin withdrawing American forces from Iraq and would micromanage commanders in the field by restricting their ability to fight. He also objected to the inclusion of billions of dollars of spending and other provisions not related to the war. Finally, he asserted that the bill was unconstitutional because it "purport[ed] to direct the conduct of operations of war in a way that infringes upon the powers vested in the presidency by the Constitution, including as commander in chief of the Armed Forces."[143] The next day, the House of Representatives, by a vote of 222 to 203—two-thirds not voting in the affirmative—failed to override the veto.[144]

Criteria Relating to Troops

Section 1901 of H.R. 1591, had it become law, would have provided that none of the funds appropriated or made available in the supplemental appropriations bill or in any other act could be used to deploy any armed forces unit unless the chief of the military department concerned certified in writing to the Committees on Appropriations and the Committees on Armed Services in advance of deployment that the unit was "fully mission capable" (i.e., "capable of performing assigned mission essential tasks to prescribed standards under the conditions expected in the theater of operations, consistent with the guidelines set forth in the Department of Defense readiness reporting system"). The President would have had the authority to waive the capability requirement on a unit-by-unit basis if he certified in writing to the appropriate committees that deploying a unit that is not fully mission-capable were required for reasons of national security and transmitted a report detailing the reason or reasons.

Under section 1902, no funds appropriated or made available in the supplemental or in any other act would have been permitted to be obligated or expended to initiate developing, to continue developing, or to execute any order that would have the effect of extending the deployment of any Army, Army Reserve, or Army National Guard unit beyond 365 days or of any Marine Corps or Marine Corps Reserve unit beyond 210 days. This limitation was not to be construed to require force levels in Iraq to be decreased below the total U.S. force levels in Iraq prior to January 10, 2007. The President would have had the authority to waive this limitation on a unit-by-unit basis

reprint of the conference report, H.Rept. 110-107. The Senate agreed to the conference report on April 26, 2007, by a vote of 51 to 46. 153 CONG. REC. S5153 (daily ed. April 26, 2007). For a comprehensive discussion of H.R. 1591 and the status of followup legislation, see CRS Report RL33900, *FY2007 Supplemental Appropriations for Defense, Foreign Affairs, and Other Purposes*, by Stephen Daggett, Amy Belasco, Pat Towell, Susan B. Epstein, Connie Veillette, Curt Tarnoff, Rhoda Margesson, and Bart Elias.

143 See 153 CONG. REC. H4315 (daily ed. May 2, 2007) for a reprint of the veto message.

144 *Id.* at H4326.

by certifying in writing national security reasons and reporting details to the Committees on Appropriations and the Committees on Armed Services.

Pursuant to section 1903, no funds in the supplemental or in any other act were to be available for deploying Army, Army Reserve, or Army National Guard units for Operation Iraqi Freedom if such unit had been deployed within the previous 365 days, or for deploying any Marine Corps or Marine Corps Reserve unit if such unit had been deployed within the previous 210 days. This limitation was not to be construed to require force levels in Iraq to be decreased below the levels in that country prior to January 10, 2007. Like the limitations in sections 1901 and 1902, this one would have been subject to waiver by the President on a unit-by unit basis under the certification and notification procedures prescribed in the earlier limitations.

Benchmarks for Iraqi Government and Dates for Redeployment

Section 1904 modified House and Senate language relating to Iraqi benchmarks and timetables. It would have required the President by July 1, 2007, to make and report to Congress determinations relating to progress that the government of Iraq is making in meeting benchmarks taken from the House and Senate bills. The President's inability to make any of the determinations relating to the benchmarks was to have resulted in the commencement of troop redeployment from Iraq no later than July 1, 2007, with a goal of completing redeployment within 180 days. If the President were able to make the determinations, the Secretary of Defense would have been required to commence redeploying forces from Iraq not later than October 1, 2007, with a goal of completing redeployment within 180 days. In either case, funds appropriated or otherwise made available in the bill or any other act were to be immediately available to plan and execute a safe and orderly redeployment of the Armed Forces from Iraq.

Section 1904(a) of H.R. 1591 would have directed the President to determine and report findings to Congress on or before July 1, 2007, that relate to several matters including whether the Iraqi government—

- has given U.S. and Iraqi forces authority to pursue all extremists and is making substantial progress in delivering Iraqi forces to Baghdad and protecting them from political interference;
- is making substantial progress in meeting its commitment to pursue reconciliation initiatives, including enacting a hydro-carbon law, adopting legislation for conducting provincial and local elections, reforming current laws governing the de-Baathification process, amending the Iraqi constitution, and allocating Iraqi revenues for reconstruction projects;

- is making, with U.S. armed forces, substantial progress in reducing the level of sectarian violence in Iraq; and
- is ensuring the rights of minority political parties in the Iraqi Parliament are protected.

Under section 1904(e), after the conclusion of the 180-day redeployment period specified above, the Secretary of Defense would not be permitted to deploy or maintain members of the U. S. armed forces for any purpose other than the following:

- protecting American diplomatic facilities and American citizens, including U.S. armed forces;
- serving in roles consistent with customary diplomatic positions;
- engaging in targeted special actions limited in duration and scope to killing or capturing members of al-Qaeda and other terrorist organizations with global reach; or
- training members of the Iraqi security forces.

Section 1904(f) would have required that 50% of funds for assistance to Iraq under the headings "Economic Support Fund" and "International Narcotics Control and Law Enforcement" was to be withheld from obligation until the President had made a determination that the government of Iraq has met certain benchmarks.

Finally, Section 1904(h) would have required that, beginning on September 1, 2007, and every 60 days thereafter, the Commander of the Multi-National Forces, Iraq, and the U.S. Ambassador to Iraq were jointly to submit to Congress a report describing and assessing in detail the progress that the government of Iraq is making regarding benchmarks listed in section 1904(a).

Other Restrictions

Section 1311 would have prohibited the use of funds in the supplemental or in any other act to establish any military installation or base for the permanent stationing of U.S. military forces in Iraq or to exercise U.S. control over oil revenues in Iraq. Section 1312 would have denied authority to use funds in the supplemental to contravene several conventions and laws, including the United Nations Convention Against Torture and Other Cruel, Inhuman or Degrading Treatment or Punishment and 18 U.S. Code section 2340A. This limitation also applied to renditions. Section 1313 contained a requirement for the Secretary of Defense, within 30 days of enactment and every 90 days thereafter, to submit to the congressional defense committees a classified report assessing the individual transition readiness of units of Iraqi and Afghan security forces.

Provisions from the Enacted Supplemental, P.L. 110-28

The House and Senate agreed to H.R. 2206, the U.S. Troop Readiness, Veterans' Care, Katrina Recovery, and Iraq Accountability Act Appropriations Act, P.L. 110-28, on May 24, 2007,[145] and the President signed it on May 25. This act provides supplemental funding through September 30, 2007, with no timetable for withdrawing troops. Section 1314 contains the major provisions relating to Iraq; it establishes 18 political and security benchmarks for the Iraqi government to meet. These benchmarks, similar to those that were included in the vetoed H.R. 1591, include enacting and implementing legislation on de-Baathification and on ensuring equitable distribution of hydrocarbon resources, increasing the number of Iraqi security forces units capable of operating independently, and allocating $10 billion in Iraqi revenues for reconstruction projects, including delivering essential services, on an equitable basis.

The President is required to submit reports to Congress by July 15, 2007, and by September 15, 2007, on whether the Iraqi government is making sufficient progress in achieving these benchmarks. Obligation of reconstruction assistance to Iraq in the Economic Support Fund, about $1.6 billion, is prohibited unless the President certifies in both reports that Iraq is making progress on all the benchmarks or waives this requirement with a detailed rationale. The act requires an assessment of progress by the Iraqi government in meeting the benchmarks from the Government Accountability Office and an assessment of combat readiness of Iraqi security forces from an independent private sector entity selected by the Department of Defense.

P.L. 110-28 does not include criteria relating to United States forces including mission readiness, periods between deployments, and duration of deployments, which were a part of the vetoed H.R. 1591 and could have been waived on a unit-by-unit basis by the President for national security reasons.

An earlier version of H.R. 2206, passed by the House, would have split the total amount into two portions. The first portion, about $47.6 billion, would have been available immediately to fund about two additional months of military operations. The second portion, about $53.2 billion, would have been available only if the President on or before July 13, 2007, submitted a report to Congress detailing progress of the Iraqi government in meeting

[145] The House divided the question and held two votes; the first one on $10.8 billion in congressional additions to the request by the Department of Defense passed by a vote of 348 to 73, and the second one on $88.5 billion requested by DOD passed by a vote of 280 to 142. See 153 Cong. Rec. H5909-5911 (daily ed. May 25, 2007, which continued proceedings of May 24) for these votes and 153 Cong. Rec. H5776-H5800 and H5801-5805 (daily ed. May 25, 2007) for the text of the first and second amendments, respectively. The Senate agreed to H.R. 2206 by a vote of 80 to 14. 153 Cong. Rec. S6823 (daily ed. May 24, 2007).

political and security benchmarks, similar to those that were included in the vetoed H.R. 1591, and a joint resolution of approval was enacted into law.[146] The Senate passed on May 17, 2007, a version of H.R. 2206 that expressed the sense of Congress in support of United States forces and requested a conference with the House.[147] The House earlier rejected by a vote of 171 to 255 H.R. 2337, a bill to require the Department of Defense to redeploy servicemembers and contractors from Iraq within 180 days.[148]

The rule reported by the Committee on Rules which provided for consideration of H.R. 2206 in the House of Representatives, H.Res. 486, 110th Cong., 1st Sess., makes in order as an amendment the text of H.R. 2451, which requires withdrawing most United States forces from Iraq by June 28, 2008, when the House considers supplemental appropriations for military operations in Iraq or Afghanistan for FY2008.[149]

IV. Limiting Deployment of Military Personnel

The Constitution accords Congress with ample authority to regulate the use of military personnel. Among other things, Congress is designated with the power "To raise and support Armies;" "To provide and maintain a Navy;" "To make Rules for the Government and Regulation of the land and naval Forces;" and "To provide for organizing, arming, and disciplining, the Militia, and for governing such Part of them as may be employed in the Service of the United States."[150] In the 110th Congress, several legislative proposals have been introduced that would limit the deployment of certain military personnel to Iraq.[151] Some have argued that congressional action limiting the use of particular troops during wartime would, at least in certain circumstances, infringe upon the President's authority as commander in chief to conduct a military campaign in a manner that he deems appropriate.[152]

---

146 The House agreed to its May 10 version of H.R. 2206 by a vote of 221 to 205. See 153 Cong. Rec. H4831-H4854 and H4866-H4867 (daily ed. May 11, 2007) for the text and vote on H.R. 2206, respectively.

147 The Senate agreed to its May 17 version of H.R. 2206 by a vote of 94 to 1. See 153 Cong. Rec. S6218-6219 (daily ed. May 17, 2007) for the text and vote on H.R. 2206, respectively.

148 See 153 Cong. Rec. H4796 and H4807 (daily ed. May 10, 2007) for the text and vote on H.R. 2337, respectively.

149 The House agreed to H.Res. 438 by a vote of 218 to 201. See 153 Cong. Rec. H 5730 and 5748 for the text and vote on H.Res. 438, respectively.

150 U.S. CONST. art. I, § 8.

151 *See, e.g.*, H.R. 1591 (as passed by both Houses and vetoed by the President), §§ 1902-1903 (limiting deployment of U.S. troops to Iraq); S.Amdt. 2012 to H.R. 1585 (requiring minimum periods between deployment for units and members of the armed forces for Operation Iraqi Freedom and Operation Enduring Freedom); H.R. 1234 (barring funds from being appropriated for further deployment of U.S. military personnel to Iraq); S. 670 (limiting funds for deployment of additional U.S. troops to Iraq unless Secretary of Defense certifies that troops are adequately trained and prepared).

152 *See* Rivkin and Casey, *supra* note 4 ("Congress cannot, in other words, act as the president's puppet master, and so long as currently authorized and appropriated funding lasts, the president can dispatch additional troops to Iraq with or without Congress's blessing.").

As a matter of historical practice, Congress has occasionally imposed limitations and other requirements on the deployment of U.S. troops, including during wartime. These limitations have been effectuated either through the statutory prohibition on the use of military personnel for a particular purpose, or via the denial of appropriations in support of a particular operation. The following are examples in which Congress has limited the President's ability to use particular military personnel for certain purposes:

- **1915**—The Army appropriations act restricted Army tours of duty in the Philippines to two years and tours in the Canal Zone to three years, unless the servicemember requested otherwise or in cases of insurrection or actual or threatened hostilities.[153] The restriction was amended in 1934 to provide for two-year tours and in both areas as well as certain other foreign duty stations.[154] The restriction was repealed in 1945,[155] and replaced with a requirement for the Secretary of Defense to report twice annually to the Armed Services committees regarding regulations governing the lengths of tours of duty for the Army and Air Force outside the continental United States.
- **1933**—The Treasury and Post Office Appropriation Act for FY1934,[156] provided that "Assignments of officers of the Army, Navy, or Marine Corps to permanent duty in the Philippines, on the Asiatic Station, or in China, Hawaii, Puerto Rico, or the Panama Canal Zone shall be for not less than three years. No such officer shall be transferred to duty in the continental United States before the expiration of such period unless the health of such officer or the public interest requires such transfer, and the reason for the transfer shall be stated in the order directing such transfer."
- **1940**—The Selective Training and Service Act of 1940 provided that "Persons inducted into the land forces of the United States under this Act shall not be employed beyond the limits of the Western Hemisphere except in the Territories and possessions of the United States, including the Philippine Islands."[157]
- **1945**—In an act extending the Selective Training and Service Act until the end of World War II, as determined by the earlier of dates proclaimed by the President or by concurrent resolution by both Houses of Congress, provided that no inductee under the age of nineteen

---

[153] 38 Stat. 1078.
[154] P.L. 73-266, 48 Stat. 815, 816.
[155] P.L. 80-436, 62 Stat. 70-71.
[156] 47 Stat. 1516, § 12.
[157] P.L. 76-783, § 3(e), 54 Stat. 885, 886.

"shall be ordered into actual combat service until after he has been given at least six months of [appropriate] military training. . . ."[158]

- **1948**—The Selective Service Act of 1948 provided that eighteen-and nineteen-year old enlistees for one-year tours could not be assigned to land bases outside the continental United States.[159]
- **1951**—The Universal Military Training and Service Act of 1951 required inductees, enlistees, and other persons called to active duty to receive at least four months' "full and adequate" training prior to deployment overseas, and prohibited the expenditure of funds to transport or maintain a servicemember overseas in violation of the provision.[160]
- **1956**—10 U.S.C. § 6015 prohibited assignment of female servicemembers to duty on combat aircraft and all vessels of the Navy.[161] 10 U.S.C. § 6018 prohibited the assignment of Navy officers to shore duty not explicitly authorized by law.[162]
- **1985**—The National Defense Authorization Act, 1985 prohibited the expenditure of funds to support an end strength of U.S. Armed Forces personnel stationed in NATO countries above a level of 326,414.[163] The measure was later modified to reduce the level further but to provide waiver authority to the President to increase the force level to up to 311,855, upon notification to Congress, if he determined the national security interests required exceeding the ceiling.[164]
- **1992**—The National Defense Authorization Act for FY1992 prohibited the use of appropriated funds to support an end strength level of members of the Armed Forces of the United States assigned to permanent duty ashore in nations outside the United States at any level in excess of 60 percent of the end strength level of such members on September 30, 1992, with exceptions in the event of declarations of war or emergency.[165]

The precise scope of Congress's ability to limit the deployment of U.S. military forces has not been ruled upon by the courts, and it is therefore unclear whether legislative measures limiting the use of particular military personnel during wartime would ever be deemed to be an unconstitutional

158 P.L. 79-54, § 2, 59 Stat. 166-67.
159 P.L. 80-759, § 4(h), 62 Stat. 604, 608.
160 P.L. 82-51, § 1(d), 65 Stat. 75, 78.
161 70A Stat. 375-76.
162 70A Stat. 376.
163 98 P.L. 525, § 1002(c)(1), 98 Stat. 2575.
164 P.L. 101-510, 104 Stat. 1546 (1990).
165 P.L. 102-484, § 1302, 106 Stat. 2545.

infringement upon the President's authority as Commander in Chief.[166] Nonetheless, historical practice suggests that, at least in some circumstances, Congress may oblige the President to comply with certain requirements on the deployment of particular military personnel, including during periods of armed conflict.

Analysis and Conclusion

Much of the historical debate over war powers has taken place in the context where a President has initiated the use of military force with ambiguous or no congressional authorization, which is not the case here. There is no obvious reason, however, to suppose that Congress's constitutional power to limit hostilities depends on whether the hostilities were initiated with Congress's express approval at the outset.[167] Likewise, it does not seem consistent to suggest that Congress's authority to limit the scope of hostilities may be exercised validly only at the initiation of hostilities, without opportunity for changing course once troops are engaged.

In modern times, federal courts have been reticent to decide cases involving war powers on the merits,[168] including those involving appropriations measures.[169] However, in discussing whether a particular challenge raises non-justiciable political questions involving matters textually committed to the political branches by the Constitution,[170] courts have generally reiterated the understanding of a shared allocation of war powers.[171] That is, it is generally agreed that Congress cannot "direct campaigns," but that

[166] For example, some have suggested that Congress could not bar the President from using military force to respond to a foreign invasion. *See* Sidak, *supra* note 85, at 51–55.

[167] *See* Tiefer, *supra* note 4, at 310–12 (outlining possible arguments for differentiating between authorized and unauthorized wars).

[168] *See* Jonathan L. Entin, *The Dog That Rarely Barks: Why the Courts Won't Resolve the War Powers Debate,* 47 Case W. Res. L. Rev. 1305 (1997)(explaining paucity of court decisions regarding war powers).

[169] *See* Stith, *supra* note 9, at 1387 (noting that courts have declined to enforce executive compliance with appropriations limitations, "particularly in areas where the Executive's powers constitutional are significant").

[170] Baker v. Carr, 369 U.S. 186, 211-12 (1962) (noting that justiciability of a foreign affairs matter is determined "in terms of the history of its management by the political branches, of its susceptibility to judicial handling in the light of its nature and posture in the specific case, and of the possible consequences of judicial action"); Powell v. McCormack, 395 U.S. 486, 521 (1969)(making "a textually demonstrable constitutional commitment of the issue to a coordinate political department" the dominant factor for determining justiciability).

[171] Massachusetts v. Laird, 451 F.2d 26, 31-32 (1st Cir. 1971)("The Congress may without executive cooperation declare war, thus triggering treaty obligations and domestic emergency powers. The executive may without Congressional participation repel attack, perhaps catapulting the country into a major conflict. But beyond these independent powers, each of which has its own rationale, the Constitutional scheme envisages the joint participation of the Congress and the executive in determining the scale and duration of hostilities."). Another court found justiciable the question of whether military operations were constitutional, proclaiming the test to be "whether there is any action by the Congress sufficient to authorize or ratify the military activity in question," Orlando v. Laird, 443 F.2d 1039 (2d Cir. 1971), *cert. denied,* 404 U.S. 869 (1971). The same court, however, found a determination of the effects of Congress's repeal of the Gulf of Tonkin Resolution to be a non-justiciable political question. DaCosta v. Laird, 448 F.2d 1368 (2d Cir. 1971), *cert. denied 405* U.S. 979 (1972).

Congress can regulate the conduct of hostilities, at least to some degree, and that Congress can limit military operations without the risk of a presidential veto by refusing to appropriate funds.

In 1970, in response to a challenge related to the Vietnam conflict, a federal district court[172] expanded on the theme of congressional authority, with particular reference to Congress's appropriations power:

> The power to commit American military forces under various sets of circumstances is shared by Congress and the Executive. . . . The Constitutional expression of this arrangement was not agreed upon by the Framers without considerable debate and compromise. A desire to facilitate the independent functioning of the Executive in foreign affairs and as commander-in-chief was tempered by a widely shared sentiment opposing the concentration of unchecked military power in the hands of the president. Thus, while the president was designated commander-in-chief of the armed forces, Congress was given the power to declare war. However, it would be shortsighted to view Art. I, § 8, cl. 11 as the only limitation upon the Executive's military powers. . . . [I]t is evident that the Founding Fathers envisioned congressional power to raise and support military forces as providing that body with an effective means of controlling presidential use thereof. Specifically, the House of Representatives . . . was viewed by the Framers as the bulwark against encroachment by the other branches. In *The Federalist No.* 58 (Hamilton or Madison), we find:
>
>> The House of Representatives cannot only refuse, but they alone can propose, the supplies requisite for the support of government. They, in a word, hold the purse—that powerful instrument by which we behold in the history of the British Constitution, an infant and humble representation of the people gradually enlarging the sphere of its activity and importance, and finally reducing, as far as it seems to have wished, all the overgrown prerogatives of the other branches of the government. This power over the purse may, in fact, be regarded as the most complete and effectual weapon with which any constitution can arm the immediate representatives of the people, for obtaining a redress of every grievance, and for carrying into effect every just and salutary measure.

Despite Congress's well-established authority over appropriations, it has been argued that the power of the purse cannot be wielded in such a way as to fetter the discretion of the Commander in Chief.[173] Congress's power of the purse is subject to the same constitutional restrictions as any other legislative enactment, including those that affect allocation of powers among the three branches.[174] That is, Congress cannot use appropriations

[172] Davi v. Laird, 318 F.Supp. 478, 480 (W.D. Va. 1970).

[173] *See* Rivkin and Casey, *supra* note 4; *see also* Rosen, *supra* note 15, at 14-18 (outlining theories but questioning their validity).

[174] Marbury v. Madison, 5 U.S. (1 Cr.) 137 (1803)(Congress may not enlarge the original jurisdiction of the Supreme Court); United States v. Klein, 80 U.S. (8 Wall.) 128 (1872) (Congress may not nullify effects of a presidential pardon or prescribe a rule of decision in a court case); United States v.

measures to achieve unconstitutional results, although it might, in some circumstances, achieve a similar result simply by failing to appropriate money.[175] The doctrine of "unconstitutional conditions," most frequently applicable to laws conditioning benefits for states or private citizens on their relinquishment of constitutional rights, is said to apply as well to legislation authorizing presidential action.[176] This notion, however, adds little to the analysis. Congress has ample constitutional authority to enact legislation that restricts the scope of military operations. If Congress can enact a limitation on the conduct of military operations directly, it can do so through appropriations. The larger question remains whether the limitation enacted amounts to an unconstitutional usurpation of the actual conduct of war.

Some commentators agree that Congress has the authority to cut off funds for military operations entirely, but assert that a partial cut-off or limitation on the use of funds would amount to an unconstitutional condition by interfering with the President's authority to conduct battlefield operations.[177] There has been some suggestion in the past that the President's responsibility to provide for troops in the field justifies further deployments without prior authorization from Congress,[178] with some arguing that the President has an independent implied spending power to carry out these responsibilities.[179] These arguments do not easily square with Congress's established prerogative to limit the scope of wars through its war powers, and do not conform with Congress's absolute authority to appropriate funds.

Congress has frequently, although not invariably, acceded to presidential initiatives involving the use of military force. While a history of congres-

Lovett, 328 U.S. 303 (1946)(Congress may not create a bill of attainder by means of an appropriations measure denying money to pay salaries of named officials); Reid v. Covert, 354 U.S. 1 (1957) (Congress may not displace judicial role by subjecting civilians to military courts-martial during time of peace); INS v. Chadha, 462 U.S. 919 (1983)(Congress may not invalidate executive decisions by one-house "legislative veto").

175 For example, in *United States v. Klein,* the Supreme Court invalidated a statute that prohibited the Court of Claims from receiving evidence of a presidential pardon in support of a claim against the government, finding the law interfered with the judicial power and the President's pardon power. However, the Court upheld a statute that prohibited payment of the same claims out of the Treasury. Hart v. United States, 118 U.S. 62 (1886). Congress's failure to appropriate funds for constitutionally mandated activities might itself be unconstitutional, but neither the courts nor the President would have the authority in such a case to mandate the expenditure of funds from the Treasury for the activity. *See* Stith, *supra* note 9, at 1351.

176 *See, e.g.,* John Norton Moore, *Do We Have an Imperial Congress?,* 43 U. Miami L. Rev. 139, 145 & n25 (1988)("Congress cannot condition funding or authority for the President to act in the foreign affairs arena upon the President's surrender of his own constitutionally grounded duties and privileges.").

177 *See* Rivkin and Casey, *supra* note4 ("Under our constitutional system . . . the power to cut off funding does not imply the authority to effect lesser restrictions, such as establishing benchmarks or other conditions on the president's direction of the war.").

178 *See* Tiefer, *supra* note4, at 314-15 (describing the Nixon Administration's legal rationale for expanding the Vietnam conflict into Cambodia and Laos).

179 *See* Rosen, *supra* note 15, at 14-18 (summarizing theories).

sional acquiescence may create a gloss on the Constitutional allocation of powers,[180] such a gloss will not necessarily withstand an express statutory mandate to the contrary. It does not appear that Congress has developed a sufficiently consistent or lengthy historical practice to have abandoned either its war power or its authority over appropriations. The executive branch has objected to legislative proposals it views as intrusive into presidential power, including conditions found in appropriations measures.[181] And it remains possible to construe the function of "conducting military operations" broadly to find impermissible congressional interference in even the most mundane statutes regulating the armed forces. To date, however, no court has invalidated a statute passed by Congress on the basis that it impinges the constitutional authority of the Commander in Chief,[182] whether directly or indirectly through appropriations. In contrast, presidential assertions of authority based on the Commander-in-Chief Clause, in excess of or contrary to congressional authority, have been struck down by the courts.[183]

On the other hand, Presidents have sometimes deemed such limitations to be unconstitutional or merely precatory, and have at times not given them

---

180 *See* Dames & Moore v. Regan, 453 U.S. 654 (1981) (executive agreements settling claims with Iran subsequent to the 1979-1981 hostage crisis held to be within President's power, in part because of unbroken historical practice of Congress acceding to Presidential settlement of foreign claims by executive agreement).

181 *See* H. Jefferson Powell, *The President's Authority over Foreign Affairs: An Executive Branch Perspective,* 67 GEO. WASH. L. REV. 527, 565-75 (1999)(surveying historical examples of disagreements involving commander-in-chief powers).

182 In one case, the Supreme Court agreed with the Court of Claims that a law passed pursuant to Congress's authority to regulate the armed forces could not restrict a President's commander-in-chief powers, and interpreted the statute accordingly. In *Swaim v. United States,* 165 U.S. 553 (1897), an officer challenged his court-martial on the grounds that it had been ordered by the President himself, where contemporary statute provided for the convening of courts-martial by certain commanders. The Court held the President had the inherent authority to convene courts-martial, citing with approval the legislative record describing the Articles of War as "not [intended] to exclude the inherent power residing in the president of the United States under the Constitution." *Id.* at 557. The Senate Committee explained further:

> In this state of the history of legislation and practice, and in consideration of the nature of the office of commander in chief of the armies of the United States, the committee is of opinion that the acts of congress which have authorized the constitution of general courts-martial by an officer commanding an army, department, etc., are, instead of being restrictive of the power of the commander in chief, separate acts of legislation, and merely provide for the constitution of general courts-martial by officers subordinate to the commander in chief, and who, without such legislation, would not possess that power, and that they do not in any manner control or restrain the commander in chief of the army from exercising the power which the committee think, in the absence of legislation expressly prohibitive, resides in him from the very nature of his office, and which, as has been stated, has always been exercised.

Id at 557-58. Even recognizing the inherent power of the president to convene courts-martial, however, the Court proceeded to explore whether the Articles of War had been properly applied. The case appears to demonstrate that Congress may regulate the exercise of inherent commander-in-chief powers as long as it does not extinguish them completely.

183 *See* Little v. Barreme, 6 U.S. (2 Cr.) 170 (1804); *Ex parte* Milligan, 71 U.S. (4 Wall.) 2 (1866); Youngstown Sheet and Tube Co. v. Sawyer, 343 U.S. 579 (1952); Hamdan v. Rumsfeld, 126 S.Ct. 2749 (2006).

the force of law.[184] In other words, Administrations have relied on an argument based on the doctrine of "unconstitutional conditions" to justify the President's authority to reject a limitation on national security spending while continuing to spend the funds.[185] Whether or not the President is constitutionally entitled to spend funds without adhering to relevant legislative conditions appears to be an issue unlikely to be resolved by the courts.

In sum, it seems that under the constitutional allocation of powers Congress has the prerogative of placing a legally binding condition on the use of appropriations to regulate or end the deployment of U.S. armed forces to Iraq. Such a prohibition seems directly related to the allocation of resources at the President's disposal, and would therefore not appear to interfere impermissibly with the President's ability to exercise command and control over the U.S. armed forces. Although not beyond question, such a prohibition would arguably survive challenge as an incident both of Congress's war power and of its power over appropriations.

[184] *See* Powell, *supra* note 181, at 552–53.

[185] *See* Tiefer, *supra* note 4, at 312 (providing examples of the "say no, but keep the dough" approach for circumventing appropriations limitations viewed as unconstitutional); Powell, *supra* note 181, at 553 (describing executive branch formula for determining the effect on an appropriation of an invalid condition to be based on "whether Congress's main purpose in enacting the appropriation was to create a means of forcing the congressional policy embodied in the condition on the President").

B. EXECUTIVE POWERS IN THE GLOBAL WAR AGAINST TERRORISTS

EXECUTIVE POWERS IN THE GLOBAL WAR AGAINST TERRORISTS

National Security Letters, Intelligence Surveillance, Protect America Act, and the Restore Act

Commentary

This second section of Volume 90 provides and discusses primary source documents that inform readers of the continued accretion of powers to the Executive Branch, as it wages the Global War Against Terrorists. The section begins by returning to the topic of National Security Letters (NSLs) introduced in Volumes 80 and 81 of this series. The section then moves to a presentation and analysis of the *Protect America Act of 2007*. Although a relatively short piece of legislation with a fairly narrow scope, it generated considerable controversy. The section concludes with a discussion of the *Restore Act of 2007*, which as of this writing has not become law, but can be reasonably considered as pending legislation that embodies the sense of Congress.

National Security Letters

Volumes 80 and 81 of this series presented congressional testimony concerning the Office of the Inspector General's (OIG) March 2007 report, *A Review of the Federal Bureau of Investigation's Use of National Security Letters*. The testimony of both proponents and opponents of the more liberal use of NSLs witnessed during the period covered by the report, 2003 through 2005, helped explain the issues raised in the report. The actual March 2007 report was not provided in Volumes 80 and 81 (because of its length) and in the interest of brevity will be discussed but not presented in this volume. Nonetheless, the documents presented in this section, *National Security Letters in Foreign Intelligence Investigations: Legal Background and Recent Amendments*; *Response to the DOJ Inspector General's Report on FBI's Use of National Security Letters*; *A Review of the FBI's Use of National Security Letters: Assessment of Corrective Actions and Examination of NSL Usage in 2006*, and *DOJ Statement Regarding OIG Report on National Security Letters* provide readers and researchers up-to-date, authoritative primary source documentation that explains the history and contemporary use of NSLs.

The USA PATRIOT Act significantly expanded the FBI's preexisting authority to obtain information through national security letters. Information sought no longer must pertain to a foreign power or an agent of a foreign power. It only needs to be relevant to an investigation to protect against international terrorism or espionage, provided that the investigation of a United States person is not conducted "solely on the basis of activities protected by the First Amendment of the Constitution of the United States." In other words, NSLs may request information about persons other than the subjects of FBI national security investigations, so long as the requested information has some relevance to an authorized investigation.

Four federal statutes authorize intelligence officials to issue five types of NSLs to request business record information, to assist in national security investigations: The Right to Financial Privacy Act; The Electronic Communications Privacy Act; The Fair Credit Reporting Act; and The National Security Act. The NSLs are issued much like administrative subpoenas. The USA Patriot Act permitted special agents in charge of field offices to sign NSLs, authorized the FBI to use NSLs to obtain consumer full credit reports in international terrorism investigations pursuant to an amendment to the *Fair Credit Reporting Act* (FCRA), and provided that issuance of NSLs will be governed by Attorney General guidelines. Not long following the USA PATRIOT Act's expansion of the authority to issue NSLs, suspected abuse of the various authorities brought increased scrutiny of the Executive Branch's use of NSLs.

The USA PATRIOT Improvement and Reauthorization Act sought to remedy the apparent flaws in the USA PATRIOT Act, by providing for judicial review of the NSLs and for attendant confidentiality requirements. The Reauthorization Act also made the authorities enforceable and provided sanctions for failure to comply with an NSL or for violating confidentiality requirements with the intent to obstruct justice. Additionally, in the Reauthorization Act, Congress directed the Department of Justice (DOJ) Office of the Inspector General (OIG) to review "the effectiveness and use, including any improper or illegal use, of national security letters issued by the DOJ." It was quite clear that by the summer of 2006, many members of the U.S. Congress, as well as the general public, harbored significant reservations about how the administration was wielding its formidable NSL power. Civil rights attorneys began to ask, "Is this constitutional or is it Ashcroft?" These attorneys felt similar concern about his successor, Alberto Gonzales.

The first NSL document in this section, *National Security Letters in Foreign Intelligence Investigations*, provides the legal background and recent changes to NSL law. It reviews judicial and legislative action, compares NSL attributes, and addresses other topics, such as certifying officials, information covered, confidentiality, enforceability, dissemination, liability, and oversight. It also briefly addresses the DOJ's Inspector General's report, which is thoroughly discussed in the two documents that follow.

The OIG's report, *A Review of the FBI's Use of National Security Letters: Assessment of Corrective Actions and Examination of NSL Usage in 2006*, like its March 2007 predecessor, *A Review of the Federal Bureau of Investigation's Use of National Security Letters*, authoritatively addressed several issues and extended the DOJ IG's examination of the FBI's use of NSLs into 2006. The 2007 report examined the use of NSLs by the DOJ from 2003 through 2005, specifically addressing any improper or illegal use of such authority. The report also assessed the effectiveness of national security letters as an investigative tool. In assessing effectiveness, the report compared the importance of the information acquired to that available from other sources; how the information is collected, retained, analyzed, and disseminated; the extent to which the DOJ utilized the information to produce analytical intelligence products for distribution; and the extent to which the DOJ provided such information to law enforcement authorities for use in criminal proceedings.

The 2007 OIG report presented some startling findings, demonstrating that fears of NSL abuse were at least partially founded. The FBI had no written policy or directive requiring the retention of signed copies of NSL requests and had no uniform system for tracking responses. Even though the FBI was required to file semiannual classified reports to Congress describing the total number of NSL requests issued pursuant to three of the five NSL authorities, it was unable to do so accurately, due to an incomplete and erroneous database, as well as analytical inadequacies associated with the database. As a result, the OIG determined that from 2003 through 2005 almost 4,600 out of 143,074 NSL requests were not reported to Congress.

In its 2007 report, the OIG found that the types of NSL requests changed in a significant aspect, during the three-year period. The percentage of NSLs involving U.S. persons increased from about 39 percent of all NSL requests in 2003 to about 53 percent CY 2005. The 2008 OIG report shows the percentage of NSLs involving U.S. persons reached 57 percent in 2006. The apparent targeting shift is troubling, in that it increases the likelihood that private information about innocent Americans will be inappropriately collected and stored. The 2007 report showed that approximately 73 percent of the total number of NSLs during the period covered by the report were issued in counterterrorism investigations, approximately 26 percent were issued in counterintelligence investigations, and less than 1 percent were issued in foreign computer intrusion cyber investigations. About 43.7 percent were issued during preliminary investigations and 56.3 percent were issued during full investigations. The significant shift toward issuing NSLs on U.S. persons coupled with the greatly expanded use of NSLs attracted the attention of many civil rights groups and led to the impassioned congressional testimony provided in Volumes 80 and 81 of this series.

As to the effectiveness of National Security Letters as an investigative tool, the OIG found that FBI investigators considered the NSLs to be absolutely critical to the success of investigations. Once they were provided with increased and more liberal NSL powers, investigators fell into the "salted peanuts syndrome"; the more NSLs they used, the more they wanted. That desire is quite understandable for a field investigator and the agent-in-charge, who not only wants to support and facilitate the efforts of his subordinates, but also has the power to sign the NSLs.

Another use of NSLs that is important to investigators is for obtaining financial records of suspected terrorists and terrorist organizations. Tracking the movement of funds through financial institutions assists in identifying and locating individuals who provide financial support to terrorists. Additionally, NSLs are used to obtain credit requests and grant information from financial institutions, which in turn leads to useful information such as the subject's name, address and former addresses, places of employment, and former places of employment. Still, the tracking of funds and requests for credit led, in many instances, to the collection and storage of information on innocent third parties who were not subjects of the investigations. In some instances, the NSLs led to a dragnet of sorts that collected useful and relevant information, but also personal information on people who were not suspected of wrongdoing.

The civil liberties argument against the use of NSLs is essentially that the present suite of NSL powers granted to the Executive Branch are too broad, rely too much on the discretion of agents-in-charge, and cause even well-intentioned investigators to sweep up and retain personal information on an unacceptable number of innocent citizens. What is an acceptable number depends, of course, on one's perception of the severity of the threat of terrorism, and perceptions vary widely between the Executive and Legislative Branches, as well as within the American public.

The OIG found that while the FBI disseminated information derived from NSLs to other members of the intelligence community and to a variety of federal, state, and local law enforcement agencies, it could not determine the number of analytical intelligence products containing NSL-derived data that were actually disseminated from 2003 through 2005, because the products did not reference NSLs as the source of the information. The principal non-DOJ entities to which NSL-derived information was disseminated are members of the intelligence community and joint terrorism task forces. Additionally, information derived from NSLs was provided to law enforcement authorities for use in criminal proceedings. While the sharing of NSL-derived information is more of a government efficiency concern than an investigative effectiveness measure, it does raise the protection of privacy/investigative effectiveness balance issue.

Although the OIG found that NSL-generated information was shared with prosecutors in the U.S. Attorneys' offices, DOJ officials did not know how often. The OIG did learn that about half of the FBI's field divisions referred one or more counterterrorism investigation targets to law enforcement authorities for possible prosecution. However, the sources and sensitive details of the information were not necessarily readily shared. Anti-Terrorism Advisory Councils (ATACs), other terrorism prosecutors, and intelligence research specialists in the U.S. Attorneys' offices may have seen the NSL-derived information in the investigative files or through access to the FBI's databases. Notably, information derived from national security letters is not required to be marked or tagged as coming from NSLs when it is entered in FBI databases or when it is shared with law enforcement authorities outside the FBI. Consequently, once the information is entered into the FBI's database, it may be accessed and handled with no greater degree of sensitivity than other information. That would be less of a problem if NSLs were issued only in appropriate and necessary situations. As we will see, however, that was not always the case.

The 2007 OIG report also presents information on the improper or illegal use of NSL authority divided into two groups: those that were reported by FBI employees (26 possible violations) and those that were not (22 possible violations). Both the 26 possible violations reported by the FBI and the 22 discovered by the OIG were purportedly the result of error. However, some raise the issue of due diligence in learning and supervising the proper application of the various authorities, including properly preparing third parties for legal compliance. Notably, the FBI did not issue comprehensive guidance about NSL-related infractions until November 2006, more than 5 years after the USA PATRIOT Act was enacted. The OIG correctly assessed that the lack of guidance contributed to the high rate of unreported possible violations.

The more worrying aspect of the unreported possible violations is that they were found in 22 percent (17 of 77) of the investigative files the OIG reviewed, pointing to an unacceptably high error rate. If that error rate were applicable to the 143,074 NSL requests during the period, a truly disturbing number of improper uses of NSLs would result and suggest that drastic remedial action is required. That is probably the single greatest concern of those who believe additional controls on the use of NSLs are imperative, including returning to Federal Intelligence Surveillance Court (FISC) approval. The FBI, for its part, has already begun implementation of remedial action. Nonetheless, it is unclear if the FBI will be able to overcome the trust deficit it has accrued.

The 2007 OIG report goes on to explain two ways in which the FBI Headquarters Counterterrorism Division circumvented the requirements of NSL authorities or issued NSLs contrary to the AG's guidelines and internal FBI policy. First, the FBI obtained telephone toll billing records or subscriber information from telephone companies using "exigent letters" instead of issuing NSLs or grand jury subpoenas. The exigent letters were signed by FBI Headquarters Counterterrorism Division personnel who were not authorized to sign NSLs. The letters stated the records were requested due to exigent circumstances and that subpoenas had been submitted to the U.S. Attorney's Office for processing and service.

However, in most instances, the FBI could not document the relationship of the requests to pending national security investigations, and many of the letters were not necessitated by exigent circumstances. In any event, due to poor recordkeeping, the FBI could not tell which letters were sent in emergency circumstances. The FBI also used after-the-fact NSLs to "cover" information improperly obtained, often months after the fact. The FBI needs to better explain to investigators, and codify in writing with examples, what constitutes an exigent circumstance and who is authorized to make that determination.

The OIG also was concerned that the FBI issued exigent letters that contained factual misstatements indicating that subpoenas requesting the information had been submitted to the U.S. Attorney's Office which was to process and serve them formally and as expeditiously as possible. The OIG's concern centers on the fact that in many, if not most instances, a subpoena request had not been submitted to any U.S. Attorney's Office before the exigent letter was sent to the telephone companies. By using exigent letters to acquire telephone toll billing records and subscriber information from three telephone companies without first issuing NSLs or grand jury subpoenas, the FBI circumvented statutory requirements as well as DOJ guidelines and internal FBI policies.

The OIG reports that those missteps were exacerbated by the use of exigent letters in non-emergency circumstances, failure to ensure that there were duly authorized investigations to which the requests could be tied, and failure to ensure that NSLs were issued promptly after the fact, pursuant to existing or new counterterrorism investigations. Whether this OIG observation can be attributed to simple neglect or intentionally misleading assurances made by investigators, it still erodes the trust Congress and the public have in the FBI to properly use its NSL powers.

The 2007 OIG report addresses other noteworthy facts and circumstances related to the FBI's use of national security letters. First, Executive Order 12333 § 2.4 provides that, "the least intrusive collection techniques feasible" are to be used, but that the FBI should not avoid using a more intrusive technique, if required, to gather the information needed. The FBI failed to provide clear guidance to FBI agents on how to determine when more intrusive techniques are authorized. Some of the thorny issues include whether investigators should gather NSL information about parties two or three steps removed from their subjects, without determining if the contacts reveal suspicious connections; whether there is an evidentiary threshold beyond "relevance to an authorized investigation" that should be considered before financial records or full credit histories are obtained on persons who are not investigative subjects; and whether NSLs are more or less intrusive than other investigative techniques authorized for use during national security investigations, such as physical surveillance. These are difficult issues, to be sure. Still, they pose critical questions that must be addressed, if individual rights and civil liberties are to be properly safeguarded.

Concluding that the FBI's use of national security letters has grown dramatically since enactment of the USA PATRIOT Act in October 2001—the overwhelming majority of the NSLs sought telephone toll billing records information, subscriber information, or electronic communication transactional records, most NSLs were issued during counterterrorism investigations, and the percentage of requests generated from investigations of U.S. persons increased significantly—the 2007 OIG report highlighted the need for a review of NSL procedures that may well lead to increased scrutiny.

The OIG's conclusions are extraordinarily troublesome. The FBI's use of an incomplete and inaccurate database that underreports the number of NSL requests; lack of knowledge of how much NSL-derived information is shared; numerous instances of improper uses of NSLs, reflecting an unacceptably high error rate; improper use of "exigent letters; and failure to provided clear guidance describing how case agents and supervisors should apply the AG guidelines' requirement to use the "least intrusive collection techniques feasible" combine to sound a clarion call for remedial action. To that end, the OIG report offers several promising recommendations to the FBI to assist it in better managing the use of NSLs.

Not surprisingly, the FBI seemed to take the 2007 OIG report in stride and accepted its criticisms in the spirit in which they were provided. The FBI Director informed the Inspector General that he fully supported all the recommendations set forth in the 2007 report, some of which are currently being implemented. The 2008 OIG report noted that the FBI and the DOJ have made significant progress in implementing the recommendations from the 2007 report and in adopting other corrective actions to address serious problems identified in the use of NSLs.

Furthermore, the 2008 report observes that the FBI has issued needed guidance on the use of NSLs, provided mandatory training to FBI employees on the proper use of NSLs, developed a new data system to facilitate the issuance of NSLs and improve the accuracy of NSL data in required congressional reports, issued specific NSL guidance on critical topics, issued a prohibition on use of exigent letters, established a requirement for sufficient and independent supervisory and legal reviews, and reinforced procedures for identifying and reporting possible intelligence violations. The FBI also has reorganized to address the deficiencies by creating the Office of Integrity and Compliance (OIC). But, the 2008 report states that there is more to be done.

The 2008 report makes 17 recommendations regarding the FBI's continued use of NSLs. Additionally, the OIG continues its investigation of the improper use of exigent letters. It remains unclear, therefore, whether further debate will continue to surround authority issues in the future, possibly calling for a direct role for the FISC in the NSL approval process. A credible argument can be made that the FISC, or another federal court can now be sufficiently responsive to issue timely NSL approvals. The issue of maintenance of recorded information on innocent citizens may also lead to further discourse. Clearly, the FBI should have a process for destroying such information as soon as it is determined it is no longer needed (or was never needed) for an investigation. Finally, there must be a national debate that determines the severity of the threat posed by terrorists and the extent to which the American public is willing to sacrifice civil liberties in response to that threat.

DOCUMENT NO. 5

NATIONAL SECURITY LETTERS IN FOREIGN INTELLIGENCE INVESTIGATIONS: LEGAL BACKGROUND AND RECENT AMENDMENTS

CRS Report
RL33320

March 20, 2007

Charles Doyle
Senior Specialist
American Law Division

Summary

Five federal statutes authorize intelligence officials to request certain business record information in connection with national security investigations. The authority to issue these national security letters (NSLs) is comparable to the authority to issue administrative subpoenas. The USA PATRIOT Act expanded the authority under four of the NSL statutes and created the fifth. Thereafter, the authority has been reported to have been widely used. Prospects of its continued use dimmed, however, after two lower federal courts held the lack of judicial review and the absolute confidentiality requirements in one of the statutes rendered it constitutionally suspect.

The USA PATRIOT Improvement and Reauthorization Act (H.R. 3199), P.L. 109-177, and its companion P.L. 109-178, amended the five NSL sections to expressly provide for judicial review of both the NSLs and the confidentiality requirements that attend them. The sections have also been made explicitly judicially enforceable and sanctions recognized for failure to comply with an NSL request or to breach NSL confidentiality requirements with the intent to obstruct justice. The use of the authority has been made subject to greater Congressional oversight.

The text of the five provisions—section 1114(a)(5) of the Right to Financial Privacy Act (12 U.S.C. 3414(a)(5)); sections 626 and 627 of the Fair Credit

Reporting Act (15 U.S.C. 1681u, 1681v); section 2709 of title 18 of the United States Code; and section 802 of the National Security Act (50 U.S.C. 436)—in their amended form have been appended.

A report by the Department of Justice's Inspector General found that in its early use of its expanded USA PATRIOT Act authority the FBI had "used NSLs in violation of applicable NSL statutes, Attorney General Guidelines, and internal FBI policies," but that no criminal laws had been broken.

This report is available abridged—without footnotes, appendices, and most of the citations to authority—as CRS Report RS22406, *National Security Letters in Foreign Intelligence Investigations: A Glimpse of the Legal Background and Recent Amendments,* by Charles Doyle.

Introduction

Five statutory provisions vest government agencies responsible for certain foreign intelligence investigations (principally the Federal Bureau of Investigation (FBI)) with authority to issue written commands comparable to administrative subpoenas.[1] A National Security Letter (NSL) seeks customer and consumer transaction information in national security investigations from communications providers, financial institutions and credit agencies. Section 505 of the USA PATRIOT Act expanded the circumstances under which an NSL could be used.[2] Subsequent press accounts suggested that their use had become wide-spread.[3] Two lower federal courts, however, found the uncertainties, practices and policies associated with the use of NSL authority contrary to the First Amendment right of freedom of speech, and thus brought into question the extent to which NSL authority could be used in the future.[4] The USA PATRIOT Improvement and Reauthorization Act,[5]

[1] 18 U.S.C. 2709; 12 U.S.C. 3414; 15 U.S.C. 1681v; 15 U.S.C. 1681u; 50 U.S.C. 436; the text of each is appended.

Federal administrative subpoena authority is discussed in U.S. Department of Justice, Office of Legal Policy, *Report to Congress on the Use of Administrative Subpoena Authorities by Executive Branch Agencies and Entities* [2002], available on March 6, 2006 at [http://www.usdoj.gov/olp/intro.pdf]; see also CRS Report RL33321, *Administrative Subpoenas in Criminal Investigations: A Brief Legal Analysis,* abridged as CRS Report RS22407, *Administrative Subpoenas in Criminal Investigations: A Sketch,* both by Charles Doyle.

[2] P.L. 109-56, 115 Stat. 365 (2001).

[3] From calendar year 2003 through 2005, the FBI issued approximately 44,000 NSLs containing 143,074 requests. In one investigation, it issued 9 NSLs requesting information relating to 11,000 telephone numbers. U.S. Department of Justice, Office of the Inspector General, *A Review of the Federal Bureau of Investigation's Use of National Security Letters (IG Report)* at xviii-xix (March 2007), available on March 12, 2007 at [www.usdoj.gov/oig/special/s0703b/final.pdf].

[4] *Doe v. Ashcroft,* 334 F.Supp.2d 471, 526-27 (S.D.N.Y. 2004)("the Court concludes that the compulsory, secret, and unreviewable production of information required by the FBI's application of 18 U.S.C. 2709 violates the Fourth Amendment and that the non-disclosure provision of 18 U.S.C. 2709(c) violates the First Amendment"); *Doe v. Gonzales,* 386 F.Supp.2d 66, 78-82 (D.Conn. 2005)(the court did not reach the Fourth Amendment issue). Justice Ginsburg declined to lift the stay of Connecticut court's injunction pending appeal in the Second Circuit, 126 S.Ct. 1 (2005).

[5] P.L. 109-177 (H.R. 3199), 120 Stat. 192 (2006).

and Public Law 109-178 (S. 2271) amend the NSL statutes and related law to address some of the concerns raised by critics and the courts.[6]

Background

The ancestor of the first NSL letter provision is an exception to privacy protections afforded by the Right to Financial Privacy Act (RFPA).[7] Its history is not particularly instructive and consists primarily of a determination that the exception in its original form should not be too broadly construed.[8] But the exception was just that, an exception. It was neither an affirmative grant of authority to request information nor a command to financial institutions to provided information when asked. It removed the restrictions on the release of customer information imposed on financial institutions by the Right to Financial Privacy Act, but it left them free to decline to comply when asked to do so.

> [I]n certain significant instances, financial institutions [had] declined to grant the FBI access to financial records in response to requests under Section 1114(a). The FBI informed the Committee that the problem occurs particularly in States which have State constitutional privacy protection provisions or State banking privacy laws. In those States, financial institutions decline to grant the FBI access because State law prohibits them from granting such access and the RFPA, since it permits but does not mandate such access, does not override State law. In such a situation, the concerned financial institutions which might otherwise desire to grant the FBI access to a customer's record will not do so, because State law does not allow such cooperation, and cooperation might expose them to liability to the customer whose records the FBI sought access. H.Rept. 99-690, at 15-6 (1986).

Congress responded with passage of the first NSL statute as an amendment to the Right to Financial Privacy Act, affirmatively giving the FBI access to financial institution records in certain foreign intelligence cases.[9] At the same time in the Electronic Communications Privacy Act, it afforded

---

[6] The appended statutes note the amendments and additions.

[7] Section 1114, P.L.95-630, 92 Stat. 3706 (1978); now codified at 12 U.S.C. 3414(a)(1) (A), (B): "Nothing in this chapter (except sections 3415, 3417, 3418, and 3421 of this title) shall apply to the production and disclosure of financial records pursuant to requests from–(A) a Government authority authorized to conduct foreign counter- or foreign positive-intelligence activities for purposes of conducting such activities; [or] (B)the Secret Service for the purpose of conducting its protective functions (18 U.S.C. 3056; 3 U.S.C. 202, P. L. 90-331, as amended)."

[8] "Section 1114 provides for special procedures in the case of foreign intelligence. . . . though the committee believes that some privacy protections may well be necessary for financial records sought during a foreign intelligence investigation, there are special problems in this area which make consideration of such protections in other congressional forums more appropriate. Nevertheless, the committee intends that this exemption be used only for legitimate foreign intelligence investigations: investigations proceeding only under the rubric of "national security" do not qualify. Rather this exception is available only to those U.S. Government officials specifically authorized to investigate the intelligence operations of foreign governments," H.Rept. 95-1383, at 55 (1978).

[9] P.L.99-569, § 404, 100 Stat. 3197 (1986); 12 U.S.C. 3414(a)(5)(A)(1988 ed.).

the FBI comparable access to the telephone company and other communications service provider customer information.[10] Together the two NSL provisions afforded the FBI access to communications and financial business records under limited circumstances—customer and customer transaction information held by telephone carriers and banks pertaining to a foreign power or its agents relevant to a foreign counter-intelligence investigation.[11]

Both the communications provider section and the Right to Financial Privacy Act section contained nondisclosure provisions[12] and limitations on further dissemination except pursuant of guidelines promulgated by the Attorney General.[13] Neither had an express enforcement mechanism nor identified penalties for failure to comply with either the NSL or the nondisclosure instruction.

In the mid-90's, Congress added two more NSL provisions—one permits NSL use in connection with the investigation of government employee leaks of classified information under the National Security Act;[14] and the other grants the FBI access to credit agency records pursuant to the Fair Credit Reporting Act, under much the same conditions as apply to the records of financial institutions.[15] The FBI asked for the Fair Credit Reporting Act amendment as a threshold mechanism to enable it to make more effective use of its bank record access authority:

> FBI's right of access under the Right of Financial Privacy Act cannot be effectively used, however, until the FBI discovers which financial institutions are being utilized by the subject of a counterintelligence investigation. Consumer reports maintained by credit bureaus are a ready source of such information, but, although such report[s] are readily available to the private sector, they are not available to FBI counterintelligence investigators. . . .
>
> FBI has made a specific showing . . . that the effort to identify financial institutions in order to make use of FBI authority under the Right to Financial Privacy Act can not only be time-consuming and resource-intensive, but can also require the use of investigative techniques—such as physical and electronic surveillance, review of mail covers, and canvassing of all banks in an area–that would appear to be more intrusive than the review of credit reports. H.Rep.No.. 104-427, at 36 (1996).[16]

---

[10] 18 U.S.C. 2709 (1988 ed.); *see also,* S.Rept. 99-541, at 43 (1986)("This provision is substantially the same as language recently reported by the Intelligence Committee as section 503 of the Intelligence Authorization Act for Fiscal Year 1987, [P.L. 99-569]").

[11] 18 U.S.C. 2709 (1988 ed.); 12 U.S.C. 3414(a)(5)(A).

[12] 18 U.S.C. 2709(c)("No wire or electronic communication service provider, or officer, employee, or agent thereof, shall disclose to any person that the Federal Bureau of Investigation has sought or obtained access to information or records under this section"); *see also,* 12 U.S.C. 3414(a)(5)(D). Note that unlike section 3486, the prohibition is neither temporary nor judicially supervised.

[13] 18 U.S.C. 2709(d)(1988 ed.); 12 U.S.C. 3414(a)(5)(B)(1988 ed.).

[14] 50 U.S.C. 436.

[15] 15 U.S.C. 1681u.

[16] The Senate Intelligence Committee had made similar observations in a prior Congress when considering legislation that ultimately became the National Security Amendment, S.Rep.No. 103-256, at 17-22 (1994).

The National Security Act NSL provision authorized access to credit and financial institution records of federal employees with security clearances who were required to give their consent as a condition for clearance.[17] Passed in the wake of the Ames espionage case, it is limited to investigations of classified information leaks. As noted at the time, "The Committee believes section 801 will serve as a deterrent to espionage for financial gain without burdening investigative agencies with unproductive recordkeeping or subjecting employees to new reporting requirements.... The Committee recognizes that consumer credit records have been notoriously inaccurate, and expects that information obtained pursuant to this section alone will not be the basis of an action or decision adverse to the interest of the employee involved."[18]

Both the Fair Credit Reporting Act section and the National Security Act section contain dissemination restrictions;[19] as well as safe harbor (immunity),[20] and nondisclosure provisions.[21] Neither has an explicit penalty for improper disclosure of the request, but the Fair Credit Reporting Act section expressly authorizes judicial enforcement.[22]

The USA PATRIOT Act amended three of the four existing NSL statutes and added a fifth. In each of the three NSL statutes available exclusively to the FBI—the Electronic Communications Privacy Act section (18 U.S.C. 2709), the Right to Financial Privacy Act section (12 U.S.C. 3414(a)(5)), and the Fair Credit Reporting Act section (15 U.S.C. 1681u)—Section 505 of the USA PATRIOT Act:

- expanded FBI issuing authority beyond FBI headquarter officials to include the heads of the FBI field offices (i.e., Special Agents in Charge (SAC));
- eliminated the requirement that the record information sought pertain to a foreign power or the agent of a foreign power;
- required instead that the NSL request be relevant to an investigation to protect against international terrorism or foreign spying;
- added the caveat that no such investigation of an American can be predicated exclusively of First Amendment protected activities.[23]

The amendments allowed NSL authority to be employed more quickly (without the delays associated with prior approval from FBI headquarters)

---

17 50 U.S.C. 456 (1994 ed.).
18 H.Rep.No. 103-541 at 53-4 (1994).
19 15 U.S.C. 1681u(f), 50 U.S.C. 436(e).
20 15 U.S.C. 1681u(k), 50 U.S.C. 436(c).
21 15 U.S.C. 1681u(d); 50 U.S.C. 436(b).
22 15 U.S.C. 1681u(c).
23 P.L. 107-56, § 505, 115 Stat. 365-66 (2001).

and more widely (without requiring that the information pertain to a foreign power or its agents).[24]

Subsection 358(g) of the USA PATRIOT Act amended the Fair Credit Reporting Act to add a fifth and final NSL section; the provision had one particularly noteworthy feature, it was available not merely to the FBI but to any government agency investigating or analyzing international terrorism:

> Notwithstanding section 1681b of this title or any other provision of this subchapter, a consumer reporting agency shall furnish a consumer report of a consumer and all other information in a consumer's file to a government agency authorized to conduct investigations of, or intelligence or counterintelligence activities or analysis related to, international terrorism when presented with a written certification by such government agency that such information is necessary for the agency's conduct or such investigation, activity or analysis.[25]

Although the subsection's legislative history treats it as a matter of first impression,[26] Congress' obvious intent was to provide other agencies with the national security letter authority comparable to that enjoyed by the FBI under the Fair Credit Reporting Act. The new section had a nondisclosure

---

[24] "The information acquired through NSLs is extremely valuable to national security investigations. . . . Unfortunately; however, NSLs were of limited utility prior to the PATRIOT Act. While records held by third parties may generally be subpoenaed by a grand jury in a criminal investigation so long as those records are relevant, the standard for obtaining such records through an NSL was much higher before October of 2001.

"The FBI had to have specific and articulable facts that the information requested pertained to a foreign power or an agent of a foreign power. This requirement often prohibited the FBI from using NSLs to develop evidence at the early stage of an investigation, which is precisely when they are the most useful.

"The prior standard, Mr. Chairman, put the cart before the horse. Agents trying to determine whether or not there were specific and articulable facts that a certain individual was a terrorist or spy were precluded from using an NSL in this inquiry because, in order to use an NSL, they first had to be in possession of such facts.

"Suppose, for example, investigators were tracking a known al-Qaeda operative and saw him having lunch with three individuals. A responsible agent would want to conduct a preliminary investigation of those individuals and find out, among other things, with whom they had recently been in communication.

"Before the passage of the PATRIOT Act, however, the FBI could not have issued an NSL to obtain such information. While investigators could have demonstrated that this information was relevant to an ongoing terrorism investigation, they could not have demonstrated sufficient specific, and articulable facts that the individuals in question were agents of a foreign power," *Material Witness Provisions of the Criminal Code, and the Implementation of the USA PATRIOT Act: Section 505 That Addresses National Security Letters, and Section 804 That Addresses Jurisdiction Over Crimes Committed at U.S. Facilities Abroad: Hearing Before the Subcomm. on Crime, Terrorism, and Homeland Security of the House Comm. on the Judiciary*, 109th Cong., 1st Sess. at 9-10 (testimony of Counselor Matthew Berry, Office of Legal Policy, U.S. Department of Justice).

[25] P.L. 107-56, § 358(g), 115 Stat. 327 (2001).

[26] E.g.,H.Rept. 107-250, at 60-1 ("this section facilitates government access to information contained in suspected terrorists' credit reports when the government inquiry relates to an investigation, of or intelligence activity or analysis relating to, domestic or international terrorism. Even though private entities such as lender and insurers can access an individual's credit history, the government is strictly limited in its ability under current law to obtain the information. This section would permit those investigating suspected terrorists prompt access to credit histories that may reveal key information about the terrorist's plan or source of refunding—without notifying the target").

and a safe harbor subsection, 15 U.S.C. 1681v(c), (e), but no express means of judicial enforcement or penalties for improper disclosure of a request under the section.

In the 108th Congress, the scope of the Right to Financial Privacy Act NSL was enlarged by defining the financial institutions subject to the authority to include not only banks and credit unions but also car dealers, jewelers, and real estate agents, among others.[27] The same Congress saw a number of proposals introduced to exempt libraries from the reach of the communications NSL,[28] to increase Congressional oversight over the use of NSL authority,[29] and to add the USA PATRIOT Act section 505 NSL amendments to the list of those temporary sections scheduled to expire on December 31, 2005.[30] The 108th also witnessed the introduction of proposals that ultimately evolved into the NSL amendments in the USA PATRIOT Improvement and Reauthorization Act. H.R. 3179, introduced by Representative Sensenbrenner, would have reenforced the five national security letter provisions with explicit authority for judicial enforcement[31] and with criminal penalties for improper disclosure of the issuance of such letters. The penalties were to be the same as those proposed under the general

[27] P.L. 108-177, § 374, 117 Stat. 2628 (2004), 12 U.S.C. 3414(d), adopts the definition of financial institution found in 31 U.S.C. 5312(a)(2) and (c)(1), i.e.: (A) an insured bank (as defined in 12 U.S.C. 1813(h)); (B) a commercial bank or trust company; (C) a private banker; (D) an agency or branch of a foreign bank in the United States; (E) any credit union; (F) a thrift institution; (G) a broker or dealer registered with the Securities and Exchange Commission; (H) a broker or dealer in securities or commodities; (I) an investment banker or investment company; (J) a currency exchange; (K) an issuer, redeemer, or cashier of travelers' checks, checks, money orders, or similar instruments; (L) an operator of a credit card system; (M) an insurance company; (N) a dealer in precious metals, stones, or jewels; (O) a pawnbroker; (P) a loan or finance company; (Q) a travel agency; (R) a licensed sender of money or any other person who engages as a business in the transmission of funds, including any person who engages as a business in an informal money transfer system or any network of people who engage as a business in facilitating the transfer of money domestically or internationally outside of the conventional financial institutions system; (S) a telegraph company; (T) a business engaged in vehicle sales, including automobile, airplane, and boat sales; (U) persons involved in real estate closings and settlements; (V) the United States Postal Service; (W) an agency of the United States Government or of a State or local government carrying out a duty or power of a business described in this paragraph; (X) a casino, gambling casino, or gaming establishment with an annual gaming revenue of more than $1,000,000 which–(i) is licensed as a casino, gambling casino, or gaming establishment under the laws of any State or any political subdivision of any State; or (ii) is an Indian gaming operation conducted under or pursuant to the Indian Gaming Regulatory Act other than an operation which is limited to class I gaming (as defined in section 4(6) of such Act); (Y) any business or agency which engages in any activity which the Secretary of the Treasury determines, by regulation, to be an activity which is similar to, related to, or a substitute for any activity in which any business described in this paragraph is authorized to engage; (Z) any other business designated by the Secretary whose cash transactions have a high degree of usefulness in criminal, tax, or regulatory matters; or (*A*) any futures commission merchant, commodity trading advisor, or commodity pool operator registered, or required to register, under the Commodity Exchange Act.

[28] H.R. 3352, § 5 (Rep. Otter); S. 1158, § 3 (Sen. Boxer); S. 1507, § 2 (Sen. Feingold); S. 1552, § 4(b) (Sen. Murkowski); and S. 1709, § 5 (Sen. Craig).

[29] S. 436, §3 (Sen. Leahy).

[30] H.R. 3171, § 4 (Rep. Kucinich); H.R. 3352, § 7 (Rep. Otter); S. 1695, § 2 (Sen. Leahy); and S. 1709, § 6 (Sen. Craig).

[31] In *Doe v. Ashcroft*, 334 F.Supp.2d 471, 496-501 (S.D.N.Y. 2004), the Government argued unsuccessfully that the NSL statutes should be understood to include an implicit judicial enforcement component.

administrative subpoena bills offered in the 108th—imprisonment for not more than five years when committed with the intent to obstruct and for not more than one year otherwise, proposed 18 U.S.C. 1510(e). A Justice Department witness explained that, "Oftentimes, the premature disclosure of an ongoing terrorism investigation can lead to a host of negative repercussions, including the destruction of evidence, the flight of suspected terrorists, and the frustration of efforts to identify additional terrorist conspirators. For these reasons, the FBI has forgone using NSLs in some investigations for fear that the recipients of those NSLs would compromise an investigation by disclosing the fact that they had been sent an NSL."[32] The enforcement provision would have been backed by the court's contempt power, proposed 18 U.S.C. 2332h.[33] It had no explicit provisions, however, to permit the recipient to file a motion to quash or modify the NSL request.

NSLs in Court

Legislation in the 108th Congress did not enjoy the benefit of two court decisions that colored the debate over NSL authority during the 109th Congress. *Doe v. Ashcroft*[34] and *Doe v. Gonzales*[35] suggested that the NSL statutes could not withstand constitutional scrutiny unless more explicit provisions were made for judicial review and permissible disclosure by recipients. In essence, *Doe v. Ashcroft* found that the language of 18 U.S.C. 2709 and the practices surrounding its use offended (1) the Fourth Amendment because "in all but the exceptional case it has the effect of authorizing coercive searches effectively immune from any judicial process," 334 F. Supp.2d at 506, and (2) the First Amendment because its sweeping, permanent gag order provision applies "in every case, to every person, in perpetuity, with no vehicle for the ban to ever be lifted from the recipient or other persons affected under any circumstances, either by the FBI itself, or pursuant to judicial process," *id.* at 476.

---

[32] *Anti-Terrorism Intelligence Tools Improvement Act of 2003: Hearing Before the Subcomm. on Crime, Terrorism, and Homeland Security (House Hearing)*, 108th Cong. 2d Sess. 7-8 (2004)(prepared statement of United States Assistant Attorney General Daniel J. Bryant).

[33] Proposed 18 U.S.C. 2332h ("In the case of a refusal to comply with a request for records, a report, or other information made to any person under section 2709(b) of this title, section 625 (a) or (b) or 626 of the Fair Credit Reporting Act [15 U.S.C. 168 1u, 168 1v], section 1114(a)(5)A) of the right to Financial Privacy Act [12 U.S.C. 3414, or section 802(a) of the National Security Act of 1947 [50 U.S.C. 436(a)], the Attorney General may invoke the aid of any court of the United States within the jurisdiction of which the investigation is carried on or the person resides, carries on business, or may be found, to compel compliance with the request. The court may issue an order requiring the person to comply with the request. Any failure to obey the order of the court may be punished by the court as contempt thereof. Any process under this section may be served in any judicial district in which the person maybe found").

[34] 334 FSupp.2d 471 (S.D.N.Y. 2004).

[35] 386 F.Supp.2d 66 (D.Conn. 2005).

The court concluded that the national security letters before it differed from administrative subpoenas by want of judicial review either before or after "the seizure":

> While the Fourth Amendment reasonableness standard is permissive in the context of the administrative subpoenas, the constitutionality of the administrative subpoena is predicated on the availability of a neutral tribunal to determine, after a subpoena issued, whether the subpoena actually complies with the Fourth Amendment's demands. In contrast to an actual physical search, which must be justified by the warrant and probable cause requirements occurring *before* the search, an administrative subpoena "is regulated by and its justification derives from, [judicial] process" available *after* the subpoena is issued.
>
> Accordingly, the Supreme Court has held that an administrative subpoena "may not be made and enforced" by the administrative agency; rather, the subpoenaed party must be able to "obtain judicial review of the reasonableness of the demand prior to suffering penalties for refusing to comply." In sum, longstanding Supreme Court doctrine makes clear that an administrative subpoena statute is consistent with the Fourth Amendment when it is subject to "judicial supervision" and "surrounded by every safeguard of judicial restraint." 334 F.Supp.2d at 495, quoting *inter alia, Oklahoma Press Pub. Co. v. Walling,* 327 U.S. at 217; *See v. City of Seattle,* 387 U.S. 541, 544-45 (1967).

With regard to the First Amendment question, the court concluded section 2709(c) constituted both a prior restraint and a content-based limit on speech. As such, it could only survive if it were "narrowly tailored to promote a compelling governmental interest," 334 F.Supp.2d at 511, quoting *inter alia, United States v. Playboy Entertainment Group, Inc.,* 529 U.S. 803, 813 (2000). Compelling governmental interest there was, the court conceded, but narrowly tailored did not describe the facially all-encompassing, permanent nondisclosure requirement, 334 F. Supp.2d at 514. By way of emphasizing the troubling sweep of the nondisclosure ban found in 18 U.S.C. 2709(c), the court pointed to legislative proposals in the 108th Congress that might serve as one of several possible models for a more narrowly tailored means of protecting the legitimate governmental interests upon which section 2709 rested:

> Bills pending in the House and Senate would require the Attorney General to certify, before ordering secrecy, that disclosure would present a "danger to the national security," and the non-disclosure order could later be terminated by the Attorney General or a court, if the danger expires. 334 F.Supp.2d at 521, *citing,* H.R. 3037 (108th Cong.) and S. 2555 (108th Cong.).

Although it did not address the Fourth Amendment issue, *Doe v. Gonzales* reached much the same conclusion on the First Amendment issue: narrowly defined, the government's interest was not compelling; broadly defined, the restraints and restrictions of section 2709(c) which served that interest lacked the narrow tailoring necessary to survive constitutional strict scrutiny, 386 F.Supp.2d at 82.

The Doe cases addressed only section 2709 NSLs, but the characteristics which tripped the court's suspicions were common to all.

NSL Amendments in the 109th Congress

Both USA PATRIOT Act reauthorization statutes—P.L. 109-177(H.R. 3199) and P.L. 109-178 (S. 2271)[36]—amend the NSL statutes.[37] They provide for judicial enforcement of the letter requests and for judicial review of both the requests and accompanying nondisclosure requirements.[38] They establish specific penalties for failure to comply or to observe the nondisclosure requirements.[39] They make it clear that the nondisclosure requirements do not preclude a recipient from consulting an attorney.[40] They provide a mechanism to lift the nondisclosure requirement.[41] They expand Congressional oversight and call for an Inspector General's audit of use of the authority.[42]

Comparison of NSL Attributes

Addressees and Certifying Officials

The five NSL statutes share a number of common attributes but each has its own individual features as well. They are most distinctive with respect to the nature of the businesses to whom they may be addressed. Electronic Communication Privacy Act NSLs are addressed to communications providers.[43] Those issued under the authority of the Right to Financial Privacy Act may be directed to any financial institution, which as noted earlier, includes not only banks and credit unions, but credit card companies, car dealers, jewelers and a number of entities that are likely the scene of large cash transactions.[44] The Fair Credit Reporting Act NSLs may be addressed to consumer credit reporting agencies.[45] Recipients of the National

---

36 120 Stat. 192 (2006) and 120 Stat. 278 (2006), respectively.

37 Other proposals in the 109th Congress include H.R. 1526 (Rep. Otter) (sunset for section 505, excluding libraries from NSLs); H.R. 2715 (Rep. Nadler) (limits availability of NSLs and related gag orders); S. 3 (Sen. Gregg)(vests the Attorney General with authority to set NSL information sharing guidelines); S. 317 (Sen. Feingold) (exempts libraries and booksellers from communications NSLs); S. 737 (Sen. Craig) (SAFE Act); S. 693/S. 1680 (Sen. Cornyn) (judicial review and enforcement); S. 1266 (Sen. Roberts) (S.Rept. 109-85)(replaces NSLs with administrative subpoena powers); (S. 2369) (Sen. Specter)(sunsets the P.L. 109-177, P.L. 109-178 NSL provisions after December 31, 2009).

38 28 U.S.C. 3511.

39 28 U.S.C. 3511(c), 18 U.S.C. 1510(e).

40 12 U.S.C. 3414((a)(3)(A); 15 U.S.C. 1681v(c)(1), 1681u(d)(1); 18 U.S.C. 2709(c)(1); 50 U.S.C. 436(B)(1).

41 28 U.S.C. 3511(b).

42 P.L. 109-177, §§ 118, 119.

43 18 U.S.C. 2709.

44 12 U.S.C. 3414(a),(d).

45 15 U.S.C. 1681u(a), 1681v(a).

Security Act NSLs may include either financial institutions or consumer credit reporting agencies as well as any commercial entity with information concerning an agency employee's travel.[46]

FBI officials are authorized to provide the initial certification required for issuance of an NSL under any of the five statutes. In three instances, the authority is exclusive; in the other two it is enjoyed by other federal officials as well. In the case of the Electronic Communications Privacy Act NSL section, the Right to Financial Privacy Act section and one of the Fair Credit Report Act NSL sections, issuance requires the certification of either the Director of the FBI, a senior FBI official (no lower than the Deputy Assistant Director), or the Special Agent in Charge of an FBI field office.[47]

Certifying officials under the other statutes are described more broadly. The National Security Act NSL section contemplates certification by officials from a wider range of agencies; the second Fair Credit Reporting Act NSL section allows certification by both a wider range of agencies and a wider range of officials. Senior officials no lower than Assistant Secretary or Assistant Director of an agency whose employee with access to classified material is under investigation may certify a National Security Act NSL request.[48] A designated supervisory official of any agency "authorized to conduct investigations of, or intelligence or counterintelligence activities and analysis related to, international terrorism" may certify a NSL request under the second, more recent Fair Credit Reporting Act section.[49]

Purpose, Standards, Information Covered

Although variously phrased, the purpose for each of the NSLs is to acquire information related to the requesting agency's national security concerns. The most common statement of purpose is "to protect against international terrorism or clandestine intelligence activities."[50] The more recent of the Fair Credit Reporting Act NSL sections simply indicates that the information must be sought for the requesting intelligence agency's investigation, activity or analysis.[51] The National Security Act NSL authority is available to conduct law enforcement investigations, counterintelligence inquiries, and security determinations.[52] As to standards, the Electronic Communications Privacy Act authorizes NSLs for relevant information.[53] The same standard may apply to the others which are a little more cryptic, authorizing NSLs

[46] 50 U.S.C. 436(a).
[47] 18 U.S.C. 2709 (b); 12 U.S.C. 3414(a)(5)(A); 15 U.S.C. 1681u(b).
[48] 50 U.S.C. 436 (a)(3).
[49] 15 U.S.C. 1681v(a).
[50] 18 U.S.C. 2709(b); 12 U.S.C. 3414(a)(5)(A); 15 U.S.C. 1681u(b).
[51] 15 U.S.C. 1681v(a).
[52] 50 U.S.C. 436(a)(1).
[53] 18 U.S.C. 2709(b).

when the information is "sought for"[54] or "is necessary"[55] for the statutory purpose.

The communications NSL provision and the earlier of the two credit agency NSL statutes are fairly specific in their descriptions of the information that may be requested through an NSL. An Electronic Communications Privacy Act NSL may request a customer's name, address, length of service and billing records.[56] The older of the two Fair Credit Report Act sections authorizes a NSL to acquire name, address or former address, place or former place of employment, and the name and address of any financial institution with which the consumer has or once had an account.[57] The Right to Financial Privacy Act NSL provision covers the financial records of a financial institution's customers;[58] the second and more recent Fair Credit Reporting Act NSL provision covers a consumer reporting agency's consumer reports and "all other" consumer information in its files.[59] The National Security Act provision is at once the most inclusive and the most restricted. It authorizes NSLs for financial information and records and consumer reports held by any financial agency, institution, holding company or consumer reporting agency, and for travel information held by any commercial entity.[60] On the other hand, it is the only provision that limits the information provided to that pertaining to the target of the agency's investigation and to information of a kind whose disclosure the target has previously approved.[61]

Confidentiality

Prior to their amendment in the 109th Congress, the NSL statutes generally featured an open ended confidentiality clause. The communications NSL provision for example declared, "No wire or electronic communication service provider, or officer, or employee, or agent thereof, shall disclose to any person that the Federal Bureau of Investigation has sought or obtained access to information or records under this section."[62] The statutes did not indicate whether a recipient might consult an attorney in order to ascertain his rights and obligations nor whether it might ever be lifted. It was this silence in the face of a seemingly absolute, permanent nondisclosure command that the *Doe* courts found constitutionally unacceptable[63] and

54 15 U.S.C. 1681u(a); 12 U.S.C. 3414(a)(5)(A).
55 15 U.S.C. 1681v; 50 U.S.C. 436(a).
56 18 U.S.C. 2709(b).
57 15 U.S.C. 1681u(a),(b).
58 12 U.S.C. 3414(a)(5)(A).
59 15 U.S.C. 1681v(a)
60 50 U.S.C. 436(a)(1).
61 50 U.S.C. 436(a)(2),(3).
62 18 U.S.C. 2709(c) (2000 ed.); see also, 12 U.S.C. 3414(a)(5)(D) (2000 ed.); 15 U.S.C. 1681u(d) (2000 ed.); 15 U.S.C. 1681v(c) (2002 Supp.); 50 U.S.C. 436(b) (2000 ed.).
63 *Doe v. Ashcroft*, 334 F.Supp.2d 471, 522 (S.D.N.Y. 2004). and *Doe v. Gonzales*, 386 F.Supp.2d 66, 78-81 (D.Conn. 2005).

that perhaps led to the reconstruction of the NSL confidentiality requirements in their current form.

As NSL statutes now read, secrecy is not absolutely required. Instead NSL recipients are bound to secrecy only upon the certification of the requesting agency that disclosure of the request or response may result in a danger to national security; may interfere with diplomatic relations or with a criminal, counterterrorism, or counterintelligence investigation; or may endanger the physical safety of an individual. A recipient may disclose the request to those necessary to comply with the request and to an attorney the recipient consults for related legal advice or assistance. In doing so, the recipient must advise them of the secrecy requirements. Aside from its attorney and at the agency's election, the recipient must also identify those to whom it has disclosed the request. A recipient may petition the court to modify or extinguish any NSL secrecy requirement within a year of issuance.[64] Thereafter, it may petition to have the veil of secrecy lifted, although it may resubmit a rejected request only once a year.[65] In all instances, the standards used for the original secrecy certification govern—danger to national security, interference with diplomatic relations or ongoing investigations, and personal safety—and a good faith agency certification that disclosure would create such a risk is conclusive.[66] A breach of a confidentiality requirement committed knowingly and with the intent to obstruct an investigation or related judicial proceedings is punishable by imprisonment for not more than five years and/or a fine of not more than $250,000 (not more than $500,000 for an organization).[67]

Judicial Review and Enforceability

In addition to authority to review and set aside NSL nondisclosure requirements, the federal courts also enjoy jurisdiction to review and enforce the underlying NSL requests. Recipients may petition and be granted an order modifying or setting aside an NSL, if the court finds that compliance would be unreasonable, oppressive, or otherwise unlawful.[68] Subpoenas issued under the Federal Rules of Criminal Procedure may be modified or quashed if compliance would be unreasonable or oppressive.[69] The Rule affords protection against undue burdens and protects privileged communications.[70] Compliance with a particular NSL might be unduly burdensome in some situations, but the circumstances under which NSLs are used suggest few

64 28 U.S.C. 3511(b)(2).
65 28 U.S.C. 3511(b)(3).
66 28 U.S.C. 3511(b)(2), (30).
67 18 U.S.C. 1510(e), 3571,3559.
68 28 U.S.C. 3511.
69 F.R.Crim.P. 17(c)(2).
70 2 Wright, Federal Practice and Procedure § 275 (Crim. 3d ed. 2000).

federally recognized privileges. The Rule also imposes a relevancy requirement, but in the context of an investigation a motion to quash will be denied unless it can be shown that "there is no reasonable possibility that the category of materials the Government seeks will produce information relevant" to the investigation.[71] The authority to modify or set aside a NSL that is unlawful affords the court an opportunity to determine whether the NSL in question complies with the statutory provisions under which it was issued. On the other hand, the court's authority may be invoked to enforce the NSL against a recalcitrant recipient and failure to comply thereafter is punishable as contempt of court.[72]

Dissemination

Attorney General guidelines govern the sharing of information acquired in response to NSLs under two statutes.[73] A third, the older of the two Fair Credit Report Act sections limits dissemination to sharing within the FBI, with other agencies to the extent necessary to secure approval of a foreign counterintelligence investigation, or with military investigators when the information concerns a member of the Armed Forces.[74] The National Security Act authorizes dissemination of NSL information to the agency of the employee under investigation, to the Justice Department for law enforcement or counterintelligence purposes, or to another federal agency if the information is clearly relevant to its mission.[75] The more recent Fair Credit Reporting Act NSL section has no explicit provision on restricting dissemination.[76]

Liability, Fees and Oversight

Since judicial enforcement is a feature new to all but one of the NSL statutes,[77] they might be expected to include other incentives to overcome recipient resistance. Three do offer immunity from civil liability for recipients who comply in good faith,[78] and two offer fees or reimbursement to defer the costs of compliance.[79]

---

71 *United States v. R. Enterprises, Inc.*, 498 U.S. 292, 301 (1991).
72 28 U.S.C. 3511(c).
73 12 U.S.C. 3414(a)(5)(B)("The Federal Bureau of Investigation may disseminate information obtained pursuant to this paragraph only as provided in guidelines approved by the Attorney General for foreign intelligence collection and foreign counterintelligence investigations conducted by the Federal Bureau of Investigation, and, with respect to dissemination to an agency of the United States, only if such information is clearly relevant to the authorized responsibilities of such agency"); see also, 18 U.S.C. 2709(d).
74 15 U.S.C. 1681u(f).
75 50 U.S.C. 436(e).
76 15U.S.C. 1681v.
77 In addition to the newly added judicial enforcement mechanism in 28 U.S.C. 3511, the earlier Fair Credit Report Act NSL sections had a limited judicial enforcement subsection, as it had for some time, 15 U.S.C. 1681u(c).
78 15 U.S.C. 1681u(k), 1681v(e); 50 U.S.C. 436(c)(2).
79 15 U.S.C. 1681u(e); 50 U.S.C. 4356(d).

The confidentiality that necessarily surrounds NSL requests could give rise to concerns of governmental overreaching. Consequently, regular reports on the use of NSL authority must be made to the Congressional intelligence and judiciary committees and in some instances to the banking committees.[80] Moreover, section 119 of the USA PATRIOT Improvement and Reauthorization Act instructs the Inspector General of the Department of Justice to audit and to report to the judiciary and intelligence committees as to the Department's use of the authority in the years following expansion of the authority in the USA PATRIOT Act. The section also directs the Attorney General and the Director of National Intelligence to report to Congress on the feasibility of establishing minimization requirements for the NSLs.

The chart that follows summarizes the differences among the five NSL sections:

NSL statute	18 U.S.C. 2709	12 U.S.C. 3414	15 U.S.C. 1681u	15 U.S.C. 1681v	50 U.S.C. 436
Addressee	communications providers	financial institutions	consumer credit agencies	consumer credit agencies	financial institutions, consumer credit agencies, travel agencies
Certifying officials	senior FBI officials and SACs	senior FBI officials and SACs	senior FBI officials and SACs	supervisory official of an agency investigating, conducting intelligence activities relating to or analyzing int'l terrorism	senior officials no lower than Ass't Secretary or Ass't Director of agency w/ employees w/ access to classified material
Information covered	identified customer's name, address, length of service, and billing info	identified customer financial records	identified consumer's name, address, former address, place and former place of employment	all information relating to an identified consumer	all financial information relating to consenting, identified employee

80 P.L. 109-177, § 118(a)(adding the judiciary committees as recipients of all NSL required reports); 12 U.S.C. 3414(a)(5)(C)(intelligence committees); 18 U.S.C. 2709 (intelligence and judiciary committees); 15 U.S.C. 1681u(h)(intelligence and banking committees), 1681v(judiciary, intelligence, and banking committees).

NSL statute	18 U.S.C. 2709	12 U.S.C. 3414	15 U.S.C. 1681u	15 U.S.C. 1681v	50 U.S.C. 436
Standard/ Purpose	relevant to an investigation to protect against int'l errorism or clandestine intelligence activities	sought for foreign counter-intelligence purposes to protect against int'l terrorism or clandestine intelligence activities	sought for an investigation to protect against int'l terrorism or clandestine intelligence activities	necessary for the agency's investigation, activities, or analysis relating to int'l terrorism	necessary to conduct a law enforcement investigation, counter-intelligence inquiry or security determination
Dissemination	only per Att'y Gen. guidelines	only per Att'y Gen. guidelines	w/i FBI, to secure approval for intell. investigation, to military investigators when inform. relates to military member	no statutory provision	only to agency of employee under investigation, DoJ for law enforcement or intell. purposes, or fed. agency when clearly relevant to mission
Immunity/ fees	no provisions	no provisions	fees; immunity for good faith compliance with a NSL	immunity for good faith compliance with a NSL	reimbursement; immunity for good faith compliance with a NSL

Inspector General's Report

Section 119 of the USA PATRIOT Improvement and Reauthorization Act, P.L. 109-177, 120 Stat. 219 (2006), instructed the Department of Justice's Inspector General to review and report on the FBI's use of NSLs. In early March 2007, the Inspector General released the first of two required reports that covered calendar years 2003 through 2005. The second, covering the time period through the end of calendar year 2006 is due before the end of this year (P.L. 109-177, §119(c)(2), 120 Stat. 220 (2006)).

The report notes that FBI use of NSLs has increased dramatically, expanding from 8,500 requests in 2000 to 47,000 in 2005, *IG Report* at 120. Seventy-four percent were issued in conjunction with counterterrorism investigations, most of the rest in connection with counterintelligence investigations, and less than 1 percent as part of a foreign computer intrusion investigation, *Id.* During the 3 years under review, the percentage of NSLs used to investigate Americans ("U.S. persons") increased from 39% in 2003 to 53%

in 2005.[81] A substantial majority of the requests involve records relating to telephone or e-mail communications, *IG Report* at 120.

The report is somewhat critical of the FBI's initial performance:

> [W]e found that the FBI used NSLs in violation of applicable NSL statutes, Attorney General Guidelines, and internal FBI policies. In addition, we found that the FBI circumvented the requirements of the ECPA NSL statute when it issued at least 739 "exigent letters" to obtain telephone toll billing records and subscriber information from three telephone companies without first issuing NSLs. Moreover, in a few other instances, the FBI sought or obtained telephone toll billing records in the absence of a national security investigation, when it sought and obtained consumer full credit reports in a counterintelligence investigation, and when it sought and obtained financial records and telephone toll billing records without first issuing NSLs. *Id.* at 124.

More specifically, the Report found that:

the only FBI data collection system produced "inaccurate" results

- a "significant number of NSL-related possible violations are not being identified or reported" as required
- the FBI issued over 700 exigent letters acquiring information in a manner that "circumvented the ECPA NSL statute and violated the Attorney General's Guidelines . . . and internal FBI policy"
- the FBI's Counterrorism Division initiated over 300 NSLs in a manner that precluded effective review prior to approval
- 60% of the individual files examined showed violations of FBI internal control policies
- the FBI does not retain signed copies of the NSLs it issues
- the FBI has not provided clear guidance on the application of the Attorney General's least-intrusive-feasible-investigative-technique standard in the case of NSLs
- the precise interpretation of toll billing information as it appears in the ECPA NSL statute is unclear
- SAC supervision of the attorneys responsible for review of the legal adequacy of proposed NSLs made some of the attorneys reluctant to

[81] *Id.* A "U.S. person" is generally understood to mean "a citizen of the United States, an alien lawfully admitted for permanent residence (as defined in section 1101(a)(2) of title 8), an unincorporated association a substantial number of members of which are citizens of the United States or aliens lawfully admitted for permanent residence, or a corporation which is incorporated in the United States, but does not include a corporation or an association which is a foreign power, as defined in subsection(a) (1), (2), or (3) of this section," 50 U.S.C. 1801.

question the adequacy of the underlying investigation previously approved by the SAC

- there was no indication that the FBI's misuse of NSL authority constituted criminal conduct
- personnel both at FBI headquarters and in the field consider NSL use indispensable
- information generated by NSLs is fed into a number of FBI systems. IG *Report* at 121-24

Exigent Letters

Prior to enactment of the ECPA, the Supreme Court held that customers had no Fourth Amendment protected privacy rights in the records the telephone company maintained relating to their telephone use.[82] Where a recognized expectation of privacy exists for Fourth Amendment purposes, the Amendment's usual demands such as those of probable cause, particularity, and a warrant may be eased in the face of exigent circumstances. For example, the Fourth Amendment requirement that officers must knock and announce their purpose before forcibly entering a building to execute a warrant can be eased in the presence of certain exigent circumstances such as the threat of the destruction of evidence or danger to the officers.[83] Satisfying Fourth Amendment requirements, however, does not necessary satisfy statutory demands.

The ECPA prohibits communications service providers from supplying information concerning customer records unless one of the statutory exceptions applies.[84] There are specific exceptions for disclosure upon receipt of a grand jury subpoena[85] or an NSL.[86] A service provider who knowingly or intentionally violates the prohibition is subject to civil liability,[87] but there are no criminal penalties for the breach.

The Inspector General found that contrary to assertions that "the FBI would obtain telephone records only after it served NSLs or grand jury subpoenas, the FBI obtained telephone bill records and subscriber information prior to serving NSLs or grand jury subpoenas."[88] The FBI responded that it had barred the use of exigent letters, but emphasized that the term "exigent letter" does not include emergency disclosures under the exception now

[82] *Smith v. Maryland*, 442 U.S. 735, 745 (1979).
[83] *Richards v. Wisconsin*, 520 U.S. 385, 391 (1997); *Wilson v. Arkansas*, 514 U.S. 927, 936 (1995).
[84] 18 U.S.C. 2702(c).
[85] 18 U.S.C. 2703(c)(2).
[86] 18 U.S.C. 2709(a).
[87] 18 U.S.C. 2707(a).
[88] *IG Report* at 90.

found in 18 U.S.C. 2702(c) (4). Thus, the FBI might request that a service provider invoke that exception to the record disclosure bar "if the provider reasonably believes that an emergency involving immediate danger of death or serious physical injury to any person justifies disclosure of the information," 18 U.S.C. 2702(c)(4).

Appendix

(Language added by P.L. 109-177(H.R. 3199): in italics)
(Language repealed: struck out)
(Language added by P.L. 109-178 (S. 2271): underlined)

12 U.S.C. 3414

(a)(1) Nothing in this chapter (except sections 3415, 3417, 3418, and 3421 of this title) shall apply to the production and disclosure of financial records pursuant to requests from:

(A) a Government authority authorized to conduct foreign counter- or foreign positive-intelligence activities for purposes of conducting such activities;

(B) the Secret Service for the purpose of conducting its protective functions (18 U.S.C. 3056; 3 U.S.C. 202, Public Law 90-331, as amended); or

(C) a Government authority authorized to conduct investigations of, or intelligence or counterintelligence analyses related to, international terrorism for the purpose of conducting such investigations or analyses.

(2) In the instances specified in paragraph (1), the Government authority shall submit to the financial institution the certificate required in section 3403(b) of this title signed by a supervisory official of a rank designated by the head of the Government authority.

~~(3) No financial institution, or officer, employee, or agent of such institution, shall disclose to any person that a Government authority described in paragraph (1) has sought or obtained access to a customer's financial records.~~

(3) (A) If the Government authority described in paragraph (1) or the Secret Service, as the case may be, certifies that otherwise there may result a danger to the national security of the United States, interference with a criminal, counterterrorism, or counterintelligence investigation, interference with diplomatic relations, or danger to the life or physical safety of any person, no financial institution, or officer, employee, or agent of such institution, shall disclose to any person (other than those to whom such disclosure is necessary to comply with the request or an attorney to obtain legal advice or legal assistance with respect to the request) that the Government authority or the Secret Service has sought or obtained access to a customer's financial records.

(B) The request shall notify the person or entity to whom the request is directed of the nondisclosure requirement under subparagraph (A).

(C) Any recipient disclosing to those persons necessary to comply with the request or to an attorney to obtain legal advice or legal assistance with respect to the request shall inform such persons of any applicable nondisclosure requirement. Any person who receives a disclosure under this subsection shall be subject to the same prohibitions on disclosure under subparagraph (A).

(D) At the request of the authorized Government agency or the Secret Service, any person making or intending to make a disclosure under this section shall identify to the requesting official of the authorized Government agency or the Secret Service the person to whom such disclosure will be made or to whom such disclosure was made prior to the request, ~~*[but in no circumstance shall a person be required to inform such requesting official that the person intends to consult an attorney to obtain legal advice or legal assistance]*~~ except that nothing in this section shall require a person to inform the requesting official of the authorized Government authority or the Secret Service of the identity of an attorney to whom disclosure was made or will be made to obtain legal advice or legal assistance with respect to the request for financial records under this subsection.

(4) The Government authority specified in paragraph (1) shall compile an annual tabulation of the occasions in which this section was used.

(5)(A) Financial institutions, and officers, employees, and agents thereof, shall comply with a request for a customer's or entity's financial records made pursuant to this subsection by the Federal Bureau of Investigation when the Director of the Federal Bureau of Investigation (or the Director's designee in a position not lower than Deputy Assistant Director at Bureau headquarters or a Special Agent in Charge in a Bureau field office designated by the Director) certifies in writing to the financial institution that such records are sought for foreign counter intelligence purposes to protect against international terrorism or clandestine intelligence activities, provided that such an investigation of a United States person is not conducted solely upon the basis of activities protected by the first amendment to the Constitution of the United States.

(B) The Federal Bureau of Investigation may disseminate information obtained pursuant to this paragraph only as provided in guidelines approved by the Attorney General for foreign intelligence collection and foreign counterintelligence investigations conducted by the Federal Bureau of Investigation, and, with respect to dissemination to an agency of the United States, only if such information is clearly relevant to the authorized responsibilities of such agency.

(C) On the dates provided in section 415b of Title 50, the Attorney General shall fully inform the congressional intelligence committees (as defined in section 401a of Title 50) concerning all requests made pursuant to this paragraph.

~~(D) No financial institution, or officer, employee, or agent of such institution, shall disclose to any person that the Federal Bureau of Investigation has sought or obtained access to a customer's or entity's financial records under this paragraph.~~

(i) If the Director of the Federal Bureau of Investigation, or his designee in a position not lower than Deputy Assistant Director at Bureau headquarters or a Special Agent in Charge in a Bureau field office designated by the Director, certifies that otherwise there may result a danger to the national security of the United States, interference with a criminal, counterterrorism, or counterintelligence investigation, interference with diplomatic relations, or danger to the life or physical safety of any person, no financial institution, or officer, employee, or agent of such institution, shall disclose to any person (other than those to whom such disclosure is necessary to comply with the request or an attorney to obtain legal advice or legal assistance with respect to the request) that the Federal Bureau of Investigation has sought or obtained access to a customer's or entity's financial records under subparagraph (A).

(ii) The request shall notify the person or entity to whom the request is directed of the nondisclosure requirement under clause (i).

(iii) Any recipient disclosing to those persons necessary to comply with the request or to an attorney to obtain legal advice or legal assistance with respect to the request shall inform such persons of any applicable nondisclosure requirement. Any person who receives a disclosure under this subsection shall be subject to the same prohibitions on disclosure under clause (i).

(iv) At the request of the Director of the Federal Bureau of Investigation or the designee of the Director, any person making or intending to make a disclosure under this section shall identify to the Director or such designee the person to whom such disclosure will be made or to whom such disclosure was made prior to the request, ~~*[but in no circumstance shall a person be required to inform the Director or such designee that the person intends to consult an attorney to obtain legal advice or legal assistance]*~~ except that nothing in this section shall require a person to inform the Director or such designee of the identity of an attorney to whom disclosure was made or will be made to obtain legal advice or legal assistance with respect to the request for financial records under subparagraph (A).

(b)(1) Nothing in this chapter shall prohibit a Government authority from obtaining financial records from a financial institution if the Government authority determines that delay in obtaining access to such records would create imminent danger of—

(A) physical injury to any person;

(B) serious property damage; or

(C) flight to avoid prosecution.

(2) In the instances specified in paragraph (1), the Government shall submit to the financial institution the certificate required in section 3403(b) of this title signed by a supervisory official of a rank designated by the head of the Government authority.

(3) Within five days of obtaining access to financial records under this subsection, the Government authority shall file with the appropriate court a signed, sworn statement of a supervisory official of a rank designated by the head of the Government authority setting forth the grounds for the emergency access. The Government authority shall thereafter comply with the notice provisions of section 3409(c) of this title.

(4) The Government authority specified in paragraph (1) shall compile an annual tabulation of the occasions in which this section was used.

[there is no subsection (c)]

(d) For purposes of this section, and sections 1115 and 1117 [12 U.S.C. 3415, 3417 relating to cost reimbursement and civil penalties respectively] insofar as they relate to the operation of this section, the term "financial institution" has the same meaning as in subsections (a)(2) and (c)(1) of section 5312 of title 31, United States Code, except that, for purposes of this section, such term shall include only such a financial institution any part of which is located inside any State or territory of the United States, the District of Columbia, Puerto Rico, Guam, American Samoa, the Commonwealth of the Northern Mariana Islands, or the United States Virgin Islands. [Subsection (d) was added by subsection 374(a)of the Intelligence Authorization Act for Fiscal Year 2004, P.L. 108-177, 117 Stat. 2628 (2003).]

18 U.S.C. 2709

(a) Duty to provide.—A wire or electronic communication service provider shall comply with a request for subscriber information and toll billing records information, or electronic communication transactional records in its custody or possession made by the Director of the Federal Bureau of Investigation under subsection (b) of this section.

(b) Required certification.—The Director of the Federal Bureau of Investigation, or his designee in a position not lower than Deputy Assistant Director at Bureau headquarters or a Special Agent in Charge in a Bureau field office designated by the Director, may—

(1) request the name, address, length of service, and local and long distance toll billing records of a person or entity if the Director

(or his designee) certifies in writing to the wire or electronic communication service providerto which the request is made that the name, address, length of service, and toll billing records sought are relevant to an authorized investigation to protect against international terrorism or clandestine intelligence activities, provided that such an investigation of a United States person is not conducted solely on the basis of activities protected by the first amendment to the Constitution of the United States; and

(2) request the name, address, and length of service of a person or entity if the Director (or his designee) certifies in writing to the wire or electronic communication service provider to which the request is made that the information sought is relevant to an authorized investigation to protect against international terrorism or clandestine intelligence activities, provided that such an investigation of a United States person is not conducted solely upon the basis of activities protected by the first amendment to the Constitution of the United States.

(c) Prohibition of certain disclosure.—~~No wire or electronic communication service provider, or officer, employee, or agent thereof, shall disclose to any person that the Federal Bureau of Investigation has sought or obtained access to information or records under this section.~~

(1) If the Director of the Federal Bureau of Investigation, or his designee in a position not lower than Deputy Assistant Director at Bureau headquarters or a Special Agent in Charge in a Bureau field office designated by the Director, certifies that otherwise there may result a danger to the national security of the United States, interference with a criminal, counterterrorism, or counterintelligence investigation, interference with diplomatic relations, or danger to the life or physical safety of any person, no wire or electronic communications service provider, or officer, employee, or agent thereof, shall disclose to any person (other than those to whom such disclosure is necessary to comply with the request or an attorney to obtain legal advice or legal assistance with respect to the request) that the Federal Bureau of Investigation has sought or obtained access to information or records under this section.

(2) The request shall notify the person or entity to whom the request is directed of the nondisclosure requirement under paragraph (1).

(3) Any recipient disclosing to those persons necessary to comply with the request or to an attorney to obtain legal advice or legal assistance with respect to the request shall inform such person of any applicable nondisclosure requirement. Any person who receives a disclosure under this subsection shall be subject to the same prohibitions on disclosure under paragraph (1).

(4) At the request of the Director of the Federal Bureau of Investigation or the designee of the Director, any person making or intending to make a disclosure

under this section shall identify to the Director or such designee the person to whom such disclosure will be made or to whom such disclosure was made prior to the request, [~~but in no circumstance shall a person be required to inform the Director or such designee that the person intends to consult an attorney to obtain legal advice or legal assistance~~] <u>except that nothing in this section shall require a person to inform the Director or such designee of the identity of an attorney to whom disclosure was made or will be made to obtain legal advice or legal assistance with respect to the request under subsection (a).</u>

(d) Dissemination by bureau.—The Federal Bureau of Investigation may disseminate information and records obtained under this section only as provided in guidelines approved by the Attorney General for foreign intelligence collection and foreign counterintelligence investigations conducted by the Federal Bureau of Investigation, and, with respect to dissemination to an agency of the United States, only if such information is clearly relevant to the authorized responsibilities of such agency.

(e) Requirement that certain congressional bodies be informed.—On a semiannual basis the Director of the Federal Bureau of Investigation shall fully inform the Permanent Select Committee on Intelligence of the House of Representatives and the Select Committee on Intelligence of the Senate, and the Committee on the Judiciary of the House of Representatives and the Committee on the Judiciary of the Senate, concerning all requests made under subsection (b) of this section.

<u>(f) Libraries- A library (as that term is defined in section 213(1) of the Library Services and Technology Act (20 U.S.C. 9122(1)), the services of which include access to the Internet, books, journals, magazines, newspapers, or other similar forms of communication in print or digitally by patrons for their use, review, examination, or circulation, is not a wire or electronic communication service provider for purposes of this section, unless the library is providing the services defined in section 2510(15) ('electronic communication service') of this title.</u>

15 U.S.C. 1681v.

(a) Disclosure

Notwithstanding section 1681b of this title or any other provision of this subchapter, a consumer reporting agency shall furnish a consumer report of a consumer and all other information in a consumer's file to a government agency authorized to conduct investigations of, or intelligence or counterintelligence activities or analysis related to, international terrorism when presented with a written certification by such government agency that such information is necessary for the agency's conduct or such investigation, activity or analysis.

(b) Form of certification

The certification described in subsection (a) shall be signed by a supervisory official designated by the head of a Federal agency or an officer of a Federal agency whose appointment to office is required to be made by the President, by and with the advice and consent of the Senate.

(c) Confidentiality

~~No consumer reporting agency, or officer, employee, or agent of such consumer reporting agency, shall disclose to any person, or specify in any consumer report, that a government agency has sought or obtained access to information under subsection (a).~~

(1) If the head of a government agency authorized to conduct investigations of intelligence or counterintelligence activities or analysis related to international terrorism, or his designee, certifies that otherwise there may result a danger to the national security of the United States, interference with a criminal, counterterrorism, or counterintelligence investigation, interference with diplomatic relations, or danger to the life or physical safety of any person, no consumer reporting agency or officer, employee, or agent of such consumer reporting agency, shall disclose to any person (other than those to whom such disclosure is necessary to comply with the request or an attorney to obtain legal advice or legal assistance with respect to the request), or specify in any consumer report, that a government agency has sought or obtained access to information under subsection (a).

(2) The request shall notify the person or entity to whom the request is directed of the nondisclosure requirement under paragraph (1).

(3) Any recipient disclosing to those persons necessary to comply with the request or to any attorney to obtain legal advice or legal assistance with respect to the request shall inform such persons of any applicable nondisclosure requirement. Any person who receives a disclosure under this subsection shall be subject to the same prohibitions on disclosure under paragraph (1).

(4) At the request of the authorized Government agency, any person making or intending to make a disclosure under this section shall identify to the requesting official of the authorized Government agency the person to whom such disclosure will be made or to whom such disclosure was made prior to the request~~*, [but in no circumstance shall a person be required to inform such requesting official that the person intends to consult an attorney to obtain legal advice or legal assistance]*~~ except that nothing in this section shall require a person to inform the requesting official of the identity of an attorney to whom disclosure was made or will be made to obtain legal advice or legal assistance with respect to the request for information under subsection (a).

(d) Rule of construction

Nothing in section 1681u of this title shall be construed to limit the authority of the Director of the Federal Bureau of Investigation under this section.

(e) Safe harbor

Notwithstanding any other provision of this subchapter, any consumer reporting agency or agent or employee thereof making disclosure of consumer reports or other information pursuant to this section in good-faith reliance upon a certification of a governmental agency pursuant to the provisions of this section shall not be liable to any person for such disclosure under this subchapter, the constitution of any State, or any law or regulation of any State or any political subdivision of any State.

(f) Reports to Congress- (1) On a semi-annual basis, the Attorney General shall fully inform the Committee on the Judiciary, the Committee on Financial Services, and the Permanent Select Committee on Intelligence of the House of Representatives and the Committee on the Judiciary, the Committee on Banking, Housing, and Urban Affairs, and the Select Committee on Intelligence of the Senate concerning all requests made pursuant to subsection (a).

(2) In the case of the semiannual reports required to be submitted under paragraph (1) to the Permanent Select Committee on Intelligence of the House of Representatives and the Select Committee on Intelligence of the Senate, the submittal dates for such reports shall be as provided in section 507 of the National Security Act of 1947 (50 U.S.C. 415b).

15 U.S.C. 1681u

(a) Identity of financial institutions

Notwithstanding section 1681b of this title or any other provision of this subchapter, aconsumer reporting agency shall furnish to the Federal Bureau of Investigation the names and addresses of all financial institutions (as that term is defined in section 3401 of Title 12) at which a consumer maintains or has maintained an account, to the extent that information is in the files of the agency, when presented with a written request for that information, signed by the Director of the Federal Bureau of Investigation, or the Director's designee in a position not lower than Deputy Assistant Director at Bureau headquarters or a Special Agent in Charge of a Bureau field office designated by the Director, which certifies compliance with this section. The Director or the Director's designee may make such a certification only if the Director or the Director's designee has determined in writing, that such information is sought for the conduct of an authorized investigation to protect against international terrorism or clandestine intelligence activities, provided that such an investigation of a United States person is not conducted solely upon the basis of activities protected by the first amendment to the Constitution of the United States.

(b) Identifying information

Notwithstanding the provisions of section 1681b of this title or any other provision of this subchapter, a consumer reporting agency shall furnish identifying information respecting a consumer, limited to name, address, former addresses, places of employment, or former places of employment, to the Federal Bureau of Investigation when presented with a written request, signed by the Director or the Director's designee in a position not lower than Deputy Assistant Director at Bureau headquarters or a Special Agent in Charge of a Bureau field office designated by the Director, which certifies compliance with this subsection. The Director or the Director's designee may make such a certification only if the Director or the Director's designee has determined in writing that such information is sought for the conduct of an authorized investigation to protect against international terrorism or clandestine intelligence activities, provided that such an investigation of a United States person is not conducted solely upon the basis of activities protected by the first amendment to the Constitution of the United States.

(c) Court order for disclosure of consumer reports

Notwithstanding section 1681b of this title orany other provision of this subchapter, if requested in writing by the Director of the Federal Bureau of Investigation, or a designee of the Director in a position not lower than Deputy Assistant Director at Bureau headquarters or a Special Agent in Charge in a Bureau field office designated by the Director, a court may issue an order ex parte directing a consumer reporting agency to furnish a consumer report to the Federal Bureau of Investigation, upon a showing in camera that the consumer report is sought for the conduct of an authorized investigation to protect against international terrorism or clandestine intelligence activities, provided that such an investigation of a United States person is not conducted solely upon the basis of activities protected by the first amendment to the Constitution of the United States.

The terms of an order issued under this subsection shall not disclose that the order is issued for purposes of a counterintelligence investigation.

(d) Confidentiality

~~No consumer reporting agency or officer, employee, or agent of a consumer reporting agency shall disclose to any person, other than those officers, employees, or agents of a consumer reporting agency necessary to fulfill the requirement to disclose information to the Federal Bureau of Investigation under this section, that the Federal Bureau of Investigation has sought or obtained the identity of financial institutions or a consumer report~~

~~respecting any consumer under subsection (a), (b), or (c) of this section, and no consumer reporting agency or officer, employee, or agent of a consumer reporting agency shall include in any consumer report any information that would indicate that the Federal Bureau of Investigation has sought or obtained such information or a consumer report.~~

(1) If the Director of the Federal Bureau of Investigation, or his designee in a position not lower than Deputy Assistant Director at Bureau headquarters or a Special Agent in Charge in a Bureau field office designated by the Director, certifies that otherwise there may result a danger to the national security of the United States, interference with a criminal, counterterrorism, or counterintelligence investigation, interference with diplomatic relations, or danger to the life or physical safety of any person, no consumer reporting agency or officer, employee, or agent of a consumer reporting agency shall disclose to any person (other than those to whom such disclosure is necessary to comply with the request or an attorney to obtain legal advice or legal assistance with respect to the request) that the Federal Bureau of Investigation has sought or obtained the identity of financial institutions or a consumer report respecting any consumer under subsection (a), (b), or (c), and no consumer reporting agency or officer, employee, or agent of a consumer reporting agency shall include in any consumer report any information that would indicate that the Federal Bureau of Investigation has sought or obtained such information on a consumer report.

(2) The request shall notify the person or entity to whom the request is directed of the nondisclosure requirement under paragraph (1).

(3) Any recipient disclosing to those persons necessary to comply with the request or to an attorney to obtain legal advice or legal assistance with respect to the request shall inform such persons of any applicable nondisclosure requirement. Any person who receives a disclosure under this subsection shall be subject to the same prohibitions on disclosure under paragraph (1).

(4) At the request of the Director of the Federal Bureau of Investigation or the designee of the Director, any person making or intending to make a disclosure under this section shall identify to the Director or such designee the person to whom such disclosure will be made or to whom such disclosure was made prior to the request, ~~*[but in no circumstance shall a person be required to inform the Director or such designee that the person intends to consult an attorney to obtain legal advice or legal assistance]*~~ except that nothing in this section shall require a person to inform the Director or such designee of the identity of an attorney to whom disclosure was made or will be made to obtain legal advice or legal assistance with respect to the request for the identity of financial institutions or a consumer report respecting any consumer under this section.

(e) Payment of fees

The Federal Bureau of Investigation shall, subject to the availability of appropriations, pay to the consumer reporting agency assembling or providing report or information in accordance with procedures established under this section a fee for reimbursement for such costs as are reasonably necessary and which have been directly incurred in searching, reproducing, or transporting books, papers, records, or other data required or requested to be produced under this section.

(f) Limit on dissemination

The Federal Bureau of Investigation may not disseminate information obtained pursuant to this section outside of the Federal Bureau of Investigation, except to other Federal agencies as may be necessary for the approval or conduct of a foreign counterintelligence investigation, or, where the information concerns a person subject to the Uniform Code of Military Justice, to appropriate investigative authorities within the military department concerned as may be necessary for the conduct of a joint foreign counterintelligence investigation.

(g) Rules of construction

Nothing in this section shall be construed to prohibit information from being furnished by the Federal Bureau of Investigation pursuant to a subpoena or court order, in connection with a judicial or administrative proceeding to enforce the provisions of this subchapter. Nothing in this section shall be construed to authorize or permit the withholding of information from the Congress.

(h) Reports to Congress

(1) On a semiannual basis, the Attorney General shall fully inform the Permanent Select Committee on Intelligence and the Committee on Banking, Finance and Urban Affairs of the House of Representatives, and the Select Committee on Intelligence and the Committee on Banking, Housing, and Urban Affairs of the Senate concerning all requests made pursuant to subsections (a), (b), and (c) of this section.

(2) In the case of the semiannual reports required to be submitted under paragraph (1) to the Permanent Select Committee on Intelligence of the House of Representatives and the Select Committee on Intelligence of the Senate, the submittal dates for such reports shall be as provided in section 415b of Title 50.

(i) Damages

Any agency or department of the United States obtaining or disclosing any consumer reports, records, or information contained therein in violation of this section is liable to the consumer to whom such consumer reports, records, or information relate in an amount equal to the sum of—

(1) $100, without regard to the volume of consumer reports, records, or information involved;

(2) any actual damages sustained by the consumer as a result of the disclosure;

if the violation is found to have been willful or intentional, such punitive damages as a court may allow; and

(4) in the case of any successful action to enforce liability under this subsection, the costs of the action, together with reasonable attorney fees, as determined by the court.

(j) Disciplinary actions for violations

If a court determines that any agency or department of the United States has violated any provision of this section and the court finds that the circumstances surrounding the violation raise questions of whether or not an officer or employee of the agency or department acted willfully or intentionally with respect to the violation, the agency or department shall promptly initiate a proceeding to determine whether or not disciplinary action is warranted against the officer or employee who was responsible for the violation.

(k) Good-faith exception

Notwithstanding any other provision of this subchapter, any consumer reporting agency or agent or employee thereof making disclosure of consumer reports or identifying information pursuant to this subsection in good-faith reliance upon a certification of the Federal Bureau of Investigation pursuant to provisions of this section shall not be liable to any person for such disclosure under this subchapter, the constitution of any State, or any law or regulation of any State or any political subdivision of any State.

(l) Limitation of remedies

Notwithstanding any other provision of this subchapter, the remedies and sanctions set forth in this section shall be the only judicial remedies and sanctions for violation of this section.

(m) Injunctive relief

In addition to any other remedy contained in this section, injunctive relief shall be available to require compliance with the procedures of this section. In the event of any successful action under this subsection, costs together with reasonable attorney fees, as determined by the court, maybe recovered.

50 U.S.C. 436

(a) Generally

(1) Any authorized investigative agency may request from any financial agency, financial institution, or holding company, or from any consumer reporting agency, such financial records, other financial information, and consumer reports as may be necessary in order to conduct any authorized law enforcement investigation, counterintelligence inquiry, or security determination. Any authorized investigative agency may also request records maintained by any commercial entity within the United States pertaining to travel by an employee in the executive branch of Government outside the United States.

(2) Requests may be made under this section where—

(A) the records sought pertain to a person who is or was an employee in the executive branch of Government required by the President in an Executive order or regulation, as a condition of access to classified information, to provide consent, during a background investigation and for such time as access to the information is maintained, and for a period of not more than three years thereafter, permitting access to financial records, other financial information, consumer reports, and travel records; and

(B)(i) there are reasonable grounds to believe, based on credible information, that the person is, or may be, disclosing classified information in an unauthorized manner to a foreign power or agent of a foreign power;

(ii) information the employing agency deems credible indicates the person has incurred excessive indebtedness or has acquired a level of affluence which cannot be explained by other information known to the agency; or

(iii) circumstances indicate the person had the capability and opportunity to disclose classified information which is known to have been lost or compromised to a foreign power or an agent of a foreign power.

(3) Each such request—

(A) shall be accompanied by a written certification signed by the department or agency head or deputy department or agency head concerned, or by a senior official designated for this purpose by the department or agency head concerned (whose rank shall be no lower than Assistant Secretary or Assistant Director), and shall certify that—

(i) the person concerned is or was an employee within the meaning of paragraph (2)(A);

(ii) the request is being made pursuant to an authorized inquiry or investigation and is authorized under this section; and

(iii) the records or information to be reviewed are records or information which the employee has previously agreed to make available to the authorized investigative agency for review;

(B) shall contain a copy of the agreement referred to in subparagraph (A)(iii);

(C) shall identify specifically or by category the records or information to be reviewed; and

(D) shall inform the recipient of the request of the prohibition described in subsection (b) of this section.

(b) Disclosure of requests

~~Notwithstanding any other provision of law, no governmental or private entity, or officer, employee, or agent of such entity, may disclose to any person, other than those officers, employees, or agents of such entity necessary to satisfy a request made under this section, that such entity has~~ ~~*received or satisfied a request made by an authorized investigative agency under this section.*~~

(1) If an authorized investigative agency described in subsection (a) certifies that otherwise there may result a danger to the national security of the United States, interference with a criminal, counterterrorism, or counterintelligence investigation, interference with diplomatic relations, or danger to the life or physical safety of any person, no governmental or private entity, or officer, employee, or agent of such entity, may disclose to any person (other than those to whom such disclosure is necessary to comply with the request or an attorney to obtain legal advice or legal assistance with respect to the request) that such entity has received or satisfied a request made by an authorized investigative agency under this section.

(2) The request shall notify the person or entity to whom the request is directed of the nondisclosure requirement under paragraph (1).

(3) Any recipient disclosing to those persons necessary to comply with the request or to an attorney to obtain legal advice or legal assistance with respect to the request shall inform such persons of any applicable nondisclosure requirement. Any person who receives a disclosure under this subsection shall be subject to the same prohibitions on disclosure under paragraph (1).

(4) At the request of the authorized investigative agency, any person making or intending to make a disclosure under this section shall identify to the requesting official of the authorized investigative agency the person to whom such disclosure will be made or to whom such disclosure was made prior to the request, ~~*[but in no circumstance shall a person be required to inform such official that*~~

~~the person intends to consult an attorney to obtain legal advice or legal assistance]~~ except that nothing in this section shall require a person to inform the requesting official of the identity of an attorney to whom disclosure was made or will be made to obtain legal advice or legal assistance with respect to the request under subsection (a).

(c) Records or information; inspection or copying

(1) Notwithstanding any other provision of law (other than section 6103 of Title 26), an entity receiving a request for records or information under subsection (a) of this section shall, if the request satisfies the requirements of this section, make available such records or information within 30 days for inspection or copying, as may be appropriate, by the agency requesting such records or information.

(2) Any entity (including any officer, employee, or agent thereof) that discloses records or information for inspection or copying pursuant to this section in good faith reliance upon the certifications made by an agency pursuant to this section shall not be liable for any such disclosure to any person under this subchapter, the constitution of any State, or any law or regulation of any State or any political subdivision of any State.

(d) Reimbursement of costs

Any agency requesting records or information under this section may, subject to the availability of appropriations, reimburse a private entity for any cost reasonably incurred by such entity in responding to such request, including the cost of identifying, reproducing, or transporting records or other data.

(e) Dissemination of records or information received

An agency receiving records or information pursuant to a request under this section may disseminate the records or information obtained pursuant to such request outside the agency only—

(1) to the agency employing the employee who is the subject of the records or information;

(2) to the Department of Justice for law enforcement or counterintelligence purposes; or

(3) with respect to dissemination to an agency of the United States, if such information is clearly relevant to the authorized responsibilities of such agency.

(f) Construction of section

Nothing in this section may be construed to affect the authority of an investigative agency to obtain information pursuant to the Right to Financial Privacy Act (12 U.S.C. 3401 et seq.) or the Fair Credit Reporting Act (15 U.S.C. 1681 et seq.).

18 U.S.C. 1510

(e) Whoever, having been notified of the applicable disclosure prohibitions or confidentiality requirements of section 2709(c)(1) of this title, section 626(d)(1) or 627(c)(1) of the Fair Credit Reporting Act (15 U.S.C. 1681u(d)(1) or 1681v(c)(1)), section 1114(a)(3)(A) or 1114(a)(5)(D)(i) of the Right to Financial Privacy Act (12 U.S.C. 3414(a)(3)(A) or3414(a)(5)(D)(i)), or section 802 (b)(1) of the National Security Act of 1947 (50 U.S.C. 436(b)(1)), knowingly and with the intent to obstruct an investigation or judicial proceeding violates such prohibitions or requirements applicable by law to such person shall be imprisoned for not more than five years, fined under this title, or both.

P.L. 109-177, Sec. 118

Reports on National Security Letters

(a) Existing Reports—Any report made to a committee of Congress regarding national security letters under section 2709(c)(1) of title 18, United States Code, sections 626(d) or 627 (c) of the Fair Credit Reporting Act (15 U.S.C. 1681u(d) or 1681v(c)), section 1114(a)(3) or 1114(a)(5)(D) of the Right to Financial Privacy Act (12 U.S.C. 3414(a)(3) or 3414(a)(5)(D)), or section 802(b) of the National Security Act of 1947 (50 U.S.C. 436(b)) shall also be made to the Committees on the Judiciary of the House of Representatives and the Senate.

* * *

(c) Report on Requests for National Security Letters—

(1) IN GENERAL—In April of each year, the Attorney General shall submit to Congress an aggregate report setting forth with respect to the preceding year the total number of requests made by the Department of Justice for information concerning different United States persons under—

(A) section 2709 of title 18, United States Code (to access certain communication service provider records), excluding the number of requests for subscriber information;

(B) section 1114 of the Right to Financial Privacy Act (12 U.S.C. 3414) (to obtain financial institution customer records);

(C) section 802 of the National Security Act of 1947 (50 U.S.C. 436) (to obtain financial information, records, and consumer reports);

(D) section 626 of the Fair Credit Reporting Act (15 U.S.C. 1681u) (to obtain certain financial information and consumer reports); and

(E) section 627 of the Fair Credit Reporting Act (15 U.S.C. 1681v) (to obtain credit agency consumer records for counterterrorism investigations).

(2) UNCLASSIFIED FORM—The report under this section shall be submitted in unclassified form.

(d) National Security Letter Defined—In this section, the term "national security letter' means a request for information under one of the following provisions of law:

(1) Section 2709(a) of title 18, United States Code (to access certain communication service provider records).

(2) Section 1114(a)(5)(A) of the Right to Financial Privacy Act (12 U.S.C. 3414(a)(5)(A)) (to obtain financial institution customer records).

(3) Section 802 of the National Security Act of 1947 (50 U.S.C. 436) (to obtain financial information, records, and consumer reports).

(4) Section 626 of the Fair Credit Reporting Act (15 U.S. C. 1681u) (to obtain certain financial information and consumer reports).

(5) Section 627 of the Fair Credit Reporting Act (15 U.S.C. 1681v) (to obtain credit agency consumer records for counterterrorism investigations).

P.L. 109- 177, Sec. 119

Audit of Use of National Security Letters

(a) Audit— The Inspector General of the Department of Justice shall perform an audit of the effectiveness and use, including any improper or illegal use, of national security letters issued by the Department of Justice.

(b) Requirements—The audit required under subsection (a) shall include—

(1) an examination of the use of national security letters by the Department of Justice during calendar years 2003 through 2006;

(2) a description of any noteworthy facts or circumstances relating to such use, including any improper or illegal use of such authority; and

(3) an examination of the effectiveness of national security letters as an investigative tool, including—

(A) the importance of the information acquired by the Department of Justice to the intelligence activities of the Department of Justice or to any other department or agency of the Federal Government;

(B) the manner in which such information is collected, retained, analyzed, and disseminated by the Department of Justice, including any direct access to such information (such as access to "raw data') provided to any other department, agency, or instrumentality of Federal, State, local, or tribal governments or any private sector entity;

(C) whether, and how often, the Department of Justice utilized such information to produce an analytical intelligence product for distribution within

the Department of Justice, to the intelligence community (as such term is defined in section 3(4) of the National Security Act of 1947 (50 U.S.C. 401a(4))), or to other Federal, State, local, or tribal government departments, agencies, or instrumentalities;

(D) whether, and how often, the Department of Justice provided such information to law enforcement authorities for use in criminal proceedings;

(E) with respect to national security letters issued following the date of the enactment of this Act, an examination of the number of occasions in which the Department of Justice, or an officer or employee of the Department of Justice, issued a national security letter without the certification necessary to require the recipient of such letter to comply with the nondisclosure and confidentiality requirements potentially applicable under law; and

(F) the types of electronic communications and transactional information obtained through requests for information under section 2709 of title 18, United States Code, including the types of dialing, routing, addressing, or signaling information obtained, and the procedures the Department of Justice uses if content information is obtained through the use of such authority.

(c) Submission Dates—

(1) PRIOR YEARS—Not later than one year after the date of the enactment of this Act, or upon completion of the audit under this section for calendar years 2003 and 2004, whichever is earlier, the Inspector General of the Department of Justice shall submit to the Committee on the Judiciary and the Permanent Select Committee on Intelligence of the House of Representatives and the Committee on the Judiciary and the Select Committee on Intelligence of the Senate a report containing the results of the audit conducted under this subsection for calendar years 2003 and 2004.

(2) CALENDAR YEARS 2005 AND 2006—Not later than December 31, 2007, or upon completion of the audit under this subsection for calendar years 2005 and 2006, whichever is earlier, the Inspector General of the Department of Justice shall submit to the Committee on the Judiciary and the Permanent Select Committee on Intelligence of the House of Representatives and the Committee on the Judiciary and the Select Committee on Intelligence of the Senate a report containing the results of the audit conducted under this subsection for calendar years 2005 and 2006.

(d) Prior Notice to Attorney General and Director of National Intelligence; Comments—

(1) NOTICE—Not less than 30 days before the submission of a report under subsections (c)(1) or (c) (2), the Inspector General of the Department of Justice shall provide such report to the Attorney General and the Director of National Intelligence.

(2) COMMENTS—The Attorney General or the Director of National Intelligence may provide comments to be included in the reports submitted under subsections (c)(1) or (c)(2) as the Attorney General or the Director of National Intelligence may consider necessary.

(e) Unclassified Form—The reports submitted under subsections (c)(1) or (c)(2) and any comments included under subsection (d)(2) shall be in unclassified form, but may include a classified annex.

(f) Minimization Procedures Feasibility—Not later than February 1, 2007, or upon completion of review of the report submitted under subsection (c) (1), whichever is earlier, the Attorney General and the Director of National Intelligence shall jointly submit to the Committee on the Judiciary and the Permanent Select Committee on Intelligence of the House of Representatives and the Committee on the Judiciary and the Select Committee on Intelligence of the Senate a report on the feasibility of applying minimization procedures in the context of national security letters to ensure the protection of the constitutional rights of United States persons.

(g) National Security Letter Defined—In this section, the term snational security letter' means a request for information under one of the following provisions of law:

(1) Section 2709 (a) of title 18, United States Code (to access certain communication service provider records).

(2) Section 1114(a)(5)(A) of the Right to Financial Privacy Act (12 U.S.C. 3414(a)(5)(A)) (to obtain financial institution customer records).

(3) Section 802 of the National Security Act of 1947 (50 U.S.C. 436) (to obtain financial information, records, and consumer reports).

(4) Section 626 of the Fair Credit Reporting Act (15 U.S. C. 1681u) (to obtain certain financial information and consumer reports).

(5) Section 627 of the Fair Credit Reporting Act (15 U.S.C. 1681v) (to obtain credit agency consumer records for counterterrorism investigations).

28 U.S.C. 3511

(a) The recipient of a request for records, a report, or other information under section 2709(b) of this title, section 626(a) or (b) or 627(a) of the Fair Credit Reporting Act, section 1114(a)(5)(A) of the Right to Financial Privacy Act, or section 802(a) of the National Security Act of 1947 may, in the United States district court for the district in which that person or entity does business or resides, petition for an order modifying or setting aside the request. The court may modify or set aside the request if compliance would be unreasonable, oppressive, or otherwise unlawful.

(b)(1) The recipient of a request for records, a report, or other information under section 2709(b) of this title, section 626(a) or (b) or 627(a) of the Fair Credit Reporting Act, section 1114(a)(5)(A) of the Right to Financial Privacy Act, or section 802(a) of the National Security Act of 1947, may petition any court described

in subsection (a) for an order modifying or setting aside a nondisclosure requirement imposed in connection with such a request.

(2) If the petition is filed within one year of the request for records, a report, or other information under section 2709(b) of this title, section 626(a) or (b) or 627(a) of the Fair Credit Reporting Act, section 1114(a)(5)(A) of the Right to Financial Privacy Act, or section 802(a) of the National Security Act of 1947, the court may modify or set aside such a nondisclosure requirement if it finds that there is no reason to believe that disclosure may endanger the national security of the United States, interfere with a criminal, counterterrorism, or counterintelligence investigation, interfere with diplomatic relations, or endanger the life or physical safety of any person. If, at the time of the petition, the Attorney General, Deputy Attorney General, an Assistant Attorney General, or the Director of the Federal Bureau of Investigation, or in the case of a request by a department, agency, or instrumentality of the Federal Government other than the Department of Justice, the head or deputy head of such department, agency, or instrumentality, certifies that disclosure may endanger the national security of the United States or interfere with diplomatic relations, such certification shall be treated as conclusive unless the court finds that the certification was made in bad faith.

(3) If the petition is filed one year or more after the request for records, a report, or other information under section 2709(b) of this title, section 626(a) or (b) or 627(a) of the Fair Credit Reporting Act, section 1114 (a)(5)(A) of the Right to Financial Privacy Act, or section 802(a) of the National Security Act of 1947, the Attorney General, Deputy Attorney General, an Assistant Attorney General, or the Director of the Federal Bureau of Investigation, or his designee in a position not lower than Deputy Assistant Director at Bureau headquarters or a Special Agent in Charge in a Bureau field office designated by the Director, or in the case of a request by a department, agency, or instrumentality of the Federal Government other than the Federal Bureau of Investigation, the head or deputy head of such department, agency, or instrumentality, within ninety days of the filing of the petition, shall either terminate the nondisclosure requirement or re-certify that disclosure may result in a danger to the national security of the United States, interference with a criminal, counterterrorism, or counterintelligence investigation, interference with diplomatic relations, or danger to the life or physical safety of any person. In the event of re-certification, the court may modify or set aside such a nondisclosure requirement if it finds that there is no reason to believe that disclosure may endanger the national security of the United States, interfere with a criminal, counterterrorism, or counterintelligence investigation, interfere with diplomatic relations, or endanger the life or physical safety of any person. If the recertification that disclosure may endanger the national security of the United States or interfere with diplomatic relations is made by the Attorney General, Deputy Attorney General, an Assistant Attorney General, or the Director of the Federal Bureau of Investigation, such

certification shall be treated as conclusive unless the court finds that the recertification was made in bad faith. If the court denies a petition for an order modifying or setting aside a nondisclosure requirement under this paragraph, the recipient shall be precluded for a period of one year from filing another petition to modify or set aside such nondisclosure requirement.

(c) In the case of a failure to comply with a request for records, a report, or other information made to any person or entity under section 2709(b) of this title, section 626(a) or (b) or 627(a) of the Fair Credit Reporting Act, section 1114(a)(5)(A) of the Right to Financial Privacy Act, or section 802(a) of the National Security Act of 1947, the Attorney General may invoke the aid of any district court of the United States within the jurisdiction in which the investigation is carried on or the person or entity resides, carries on business, or may be found, to compel compliance with the request. The court may issue an order requiring the person or entity to comply with the request. Any failure to obey the order of the court may be punished by the court as contempt thereof. Any process under this section may be served in any judicial district in which the person or entity may be found.

(d) In all proceedings under this section, subject to any right to an open hearing in a contempt proceeding, the court must close any hearing to the extent necessary to prevent an unauthorized disclosure of a request for records, a report, or other information made to any person or entity under section 2709(b) of this title, section 626(a) or (b) or 627(a) of the Fair Credit Reporting Act, section 1114(a)(5)(A) of the Right to Financial Privacy Act, or section 802(a) of the National Security Act of 1947. Petitions, filings, records, orders, and subpoenas must also be kept under seal to the extent and as long as necessary to prevent the unauthorized disclosure of a request for records, a report, or other information made to any person or entity under section 2709(b) of this title, section 626(a) or (b) or 627(a) of the Fair Credit Reporting Act, section 1114(a)(5)(A) of the Right to Financial Privacy Act, or section 802(a) of the National Security Act of 1947.

(e) In all proceedings under this section, the court shall, upon request of the government, review ex parte and in camera any government submission or portions thereof, which may include classified information.

DOCUMENT NO. 6

FBI'S USE OF NATIONAL SECURITY LETTERS: RESPONSE TO DOJ INSPECTOR GENERAL'S REPORT

Press Release
FBI National Press Office

March 9, 2007

Washington, D.C.—In the post-9/11 world, the National Security Letter (NSL) remains an indispensable investigative tool. NSLs contribute significantly to the FBI's ability to carry out its national security responsibilities by directly supporting its counterterrorism, counterintelligence, and intelligence missions. NSLs also allow the FBI to obtain information to eliminate concerns about individuals and close down investigations with a high degree of confidence there is no terrorism or adverse intelligence-gathering threat. We are pleased the Inspector General concurs with the FBI concerning the value of the NSL tool.

"The Inspector General conducted a fair and objective review of the FBI's use of a proven and useful investigative tool," said Director Robert S. Mueller, III, "and his finding of deficiencies in our processes is unacceptable. We strive to exercise our authorities consistent with the privacy protections and civil liberties that we are sworn to uphold. Anything less will not be tolerated. While we've already taken some steps to address these shortcomings, I am ordering additional corrective measures to be taken immediately," Mueller said.

Importantly, the OIG found no deliberate or intentional misuse of authorities, whether NSL statutes or Attorney General Guidelines. Nevertheless, the OIG review identified several areas of inadequate auditing and oversight of these vital investigative tools, as well as inappropriate processes, and these are findings of significant concern.

As a result, Director Mueller is implementing reforms to the process designed to correct those deficiencies identified—with accountability. Those steps include strengthening internal controls, changing policies and procedures to improve oversight of the NSL approval process, barring certain practices identified in the Inspector General's report, and ordering an expedited inspection.

The FBI will work together with DOJ's National Security Division and the Privacy and Civil Liberties Office to implement these reforms. Throughout this process, the FBI will continue to work closely with the OIG to gauge progress and consider any additional reforms.

In its review, the OIG took into consideration the environment in which the Bureau has functioned over the last five years. Since September 11, 2001, as the report noted, the FBI has undergone major reorganization. The men and women of the Bureau's Counterterrorism Division, in particular, have carried an extraordinary workload, transforming operations while working at a breakneck pace to protect Americans. The OIG also recognized the importance of NSLs, citing a number of instances in which they have been used by the FBI to gather the basic building blocks of its counterterrorism and counterintelligence investigations.

The deficiencies identified, however, require the FBI to redouble its efforts to ensure we do not repeat the mistakes in the use of these authorities, however lacking in intent. Any report of possible violations of legal authorities will continue to be carefully reviewed, and, if warranted, referred to the appropriate entities. If we determine that we obtained any information to which we were not legally entitled, whether due to FBI or third-party error, that information will be sealed, sequestered, and where appropriate, destroyed. In addition, employee conduct related to these violations will be reviewed and, if appropriate, employees will be disciplined.

The OIG report made ten recommendations in response to its findings, designed to provide both the necessary controls over the issuance of NSLs and the creation and maintenance of accurate records. Director Mueller assured the Inspector General, in a detailed response included in the report, that the FBI fully supports each recommendation.

The FBI concurs with the Inspector General that, when implemented, these reforms can improve the accuracy of the reporting of the use of NSLs and ensure compliance with the requirements governing their use. Along with those already put in place, these reforms will ensure full compliance with both the letter and the spirit of the authorities entrusted to the Bureau, and will strengthen the process, alleviate concerns, and ensure the confidence of the Congress and the American public, while allowing the FBI to continue to protect the nation from those who would do us harm.

DOCUMENT NO. 7

FBI'S USE OF NATIONAL SECURITY LETTERS: ASSESSMENT OF CORRECTIVE ACTIONS AND EXAMINATION OF NSL USAGE IN 2006

U.S. Department of Justice Report
Office of the Inspector General

March 2008

List of Acronyms

ACS	Automated Case Support System
ADC	Assistant Division Counsel
CAU	Communications Analysais Unit
CDC	Chief Division Counsel
CTD	Counterterrorism Division
DNI	Director of National Intelligence
EAD	Executive Assistant Director
EC	Electronic Communication
ECPA	Electronic Communications Privacy Act
FBI	Federal Bureau of Investigation
FCRA	Fair Credit Reporting Act
FISA	Foreign Intelligence Surveillance Act of 1978
IIS	Internal Investigations Section
IOB	Intelligence Oversight Board
ISP	Internet Service Provider
JTTF	Joint Terrorism Task Force
NARA	National Archives and Records Administration

NSB	National Security Branch
NSD	National Security Division
NSI	National Security Investigations
NSL	National Security Letter
NSLB	National Security Law Branch
OGC	Office of the General Counsel
OIC	Office of Integrity and Compliance
OIG	Office of the Inspector General
OIPR	Office of Intelligence Policy and Review
OLC	Office of Legal Counsel
OPR	Office of Professional Responsibility
RFPA	Right to Financial Privacy Act
SAC	Special Agent in Charge
TFOS	Terrorist Financing Operations Section

Chapter One:
Introduction

The *USA PATRIOT Improvement and Reauthorization Act of 2005* (Patriot Reauthorization Act or the Act) directed the Department of Justice (Department or DOJ) Office of the Inspector General (OIG) to review, among other things, "the effectiveness and use, including any improper or illegal use, of national security letters issued by the Department of Justice."[1] The Act required the OIG to conduct reviews on the Federal Bureau of Investigation's (FBI) use of national security letters (NSL) for two separate time periods.[2]

The OIG's first report on the FBI's use of NSLs, issued on March 9, 2007, covered calendar years 2003 through 2005.[3] This is the OIG's second report on the FBI's use of NSLs. In this report we describe and assess the response by the FBI and the Department to the serious misuse of NSL authorities that our first report described. In addition, as required by the Patriot Reauthorization Act, this report describes the FBI's use of NSLs in calendar year 2006.

We are also in the process of completing an investigation of the FBI's use of exigent letters, a practice that we described generally in our first NSL report. This investigation also will assess responsibility for the improper use of these exigent letters. We are nearing the end of that investigation on the use of exigent letters, and we intend to issue a report covering this subject in the near future.

I. Provisions of the Patriot Act and Patriot Reauthorization Act

In the Introduction of our first NSL report, we described the expansion of the FBI's national security letter authorities in the USA PATRIOT Act (Patriot Act) and do not repeat that description here.[4] However, for this report on the

[*] This report includes information that the Department of Justice considered to be classified and therefore could not be publicly released. To create this public version of the report, the OIG redacted (deleted) the portions of the report that the Department considered to be classified, and we indicated where those redactions were made. In addition, the OIG has provided copies of the full classified report to the Department, the Director of National Intelligence, and Congress. Editor's Note: Classified text has been marked [Text not available] throughout the document.

[1] *USA PATRIOT Improvement and Reauthorization Act of 2005*, Pub. L. No. 109-177, § 119(a), 120 Stat. 192 (2006).

[2] The Patriot Reauthorization Act also directed the OIG to conduct reviews on the use and effectiveness of Section 215 orders for business records, another investigative authority that was expanded by the Patriot Act. The results of the OIG's first review on Section 215 orders are contained in a report issued on March 9, 2007. The OIG's second review of Section 215 orders in 2006 is contained in a separate report issued in conjunction with this report.

[3] U.S. Department of Justice Office of the Inspector General, *Review of the Federal Bureau of Investigation's Use of National Security Letters* (March 9, 2007) (NSL I), available at www.doj.gov/oig. We refer to the unclassified version of that report as the first NSL report. Although the Act required the OIG to include only calendar years 2003 through 2004 in the first report, we elected to also include 2005 in that report.

[4] NSL I, 10-16. The term "USA PATRIOT Act" is an acronym for the law entitled the *Uniting and Strengthening America by Providing Appropriate Tools Required to Intercept and Obstruct Terrorism Act of 2001*, Pub. L. No. 107-56 (2001). This law is commonly referred to as "the Patriot Act."

FBI's use of NSL authorities in 2006, we first identify the issues that the Patriot Reauthorization Act directed the OIG to review:

(1) an examination of the use of national security letters by the Department of Justice during calendar year 2006;

(2) a description of any noteworthy facts or circumstances relating to such use, including any improper or illegal use of such authority; and

(3) an examination of the effectiveness of national security letters as an investigative tool, including—

(A) the importance of the information acquired by the Department of Justice to the intelligence activities of the Department of Justice or to any other department or agency of the Federal Government;

(B) the manner in which such information is collected, retained, analyzed, and disseminated by the Department of Justice, including any direct access to such information (such as access to "raw data") provided to any other department, agency, or instrumentality of Federal, State, local, or tribal governments or any private sector entity;

(C) whether, and how often, the Department of Justice utilized such information to produce an analytical intelligence product for distribution within the Department of Justice, to the intelligence community . . ., or to other Federal, State, local, or tribal government departments, agencies or instrumentalities;

(D) whether, and how often, the Department of Justice provided such information to law enforcement authorities for use in criminal proceedings; . . . .[5]

With respect to national security letters issued following the date of enactment of the Patriot Reauthorization Act (March 9, 2006), the Act also directed the OIG to examine:

(E) the number of occasions in which the Department of Justice, or an officer or employee of the Department of Justice, issued a national security letter without the certification necessary to require the recipient of such letter to comply with the nondisclosure and confidentiality requirements potentially applicable under law.

[5] Patriot Reauthorization Act, § 11903).

II. Methodology of the OIG Review

To describe and assess the status of the FBI's implementation of its response to the recommendations made in our first NSL report, additional corrective actions taken by the FBI and other Department components, and the FBI's use of national security letters in 2006, the OIG conducted interviews of over 30 current and former FBI and Department employees, including personnel at FBI Headquarters in the Office of the General Counsel (FBI OGC), Counterterrorism Division, Counterintelligence Division, and Cyber Division; and personnel in 3 field offices: Baltimore, Miami, and Washington, D.C. We examined over 18,000 FBI documents and pieces of digital information provided by FBI Headquarters operational and support divisions and the 3 field divisions. Among the documents we analyzed were FBI Headquarters guidance memoranda; correspondence; national security letters; reports by the FBI's Inspection Division, the FBI OGC, and the Department's Office of Professional Responsibility; information posted on the FBI's Intranet; e-mails; and training materials on the use of NSLs.

To examine the progress of the FBI's implementation of the 11 recommendations in our first NSL report, we analyzed the FBI's memoranda describing the status of its corrective actions. We also interviewed FBI officials from the FBI OGC and Inspection Division, other senior FBI officials including the FBI Director and Deputy Director, and field personnel responsible for issuing and reviewing NSLs including the Special Agents in Charge (SAC), Chief Division Counsels (CDC), Supervisory Special Agents, and Special Agents. Additionally, we reviewed all NSL-related guidance issued by the FBI since our first report was issued, reviewed the types of NSL training provided and to whom it was provided, and observed a demonstration of the new NSL data system that was designed to manage and track NSLs.

We also examined other corrective actions and new oversight measures implemented in 2007 by the FBI, the Department's National Security Division (NSD), and the Office of the Deputy Attorney General relating to the use of NSLs. These measures included the FBI's establishment of an Office of Integrity and Compliance (OIC) and the NSD's new compliance reviews, called "national security reviews," which review the FBI's use of NSL authorities and other intelligence techniques in national security investigations. We interviewed NSD and FBI personnel responsible for these reviews and examined relevant documents describing the establishment of the OIC and the national security reviews. In addition, we evaluated the August 2007 report and proposal to the Attorney General by the Department's Chief Privacy and Civil Liberties Officer which recommended how the FBI should use and retain NSL-derived information.

The OIG also visited three field offices to assess the accuracy of the FBI's review of NSLs issued by these field offices, initiated after the issuance of our March 2007 report. The FBI's review assessed a random sample of 10 percent of all national security investigations active at any time from 2003 through 2006. We re-examined case files that had been reviewed by FBI inspectors during the FBI's March 2007 field review to verify the accuracy of the data collected by the FBI's review and compared our findings to the FBI's findings.

In addition, in response to the statutory directive to identify the number of occasions in which the Department issued national security letters without the applicable certification necessary to require the recipients to comply with the non-disclosure and confidentiality requirements of the Patriot Reauthorization Act, we reviewed a random sample of all NSLs issued from March 10, 2006, through December 31, 2006, to determine whether these NSLs complied with this requirement. For purposes of assessing compliance with the new legislation, we also analyzed 11 so-called "blanket" national security letters issued after March 9, 2006, that were not part of the random sample but which we identified in the course of another part of our review and which will be described in our forthcoming NSL report.

Finally, to document the FBI's usage of NSLs in calendar year 2006, as required by the Patriot Reauthorization Act, we analyzed data in the FBI OGC database. We also examined the Department's annual public reports to evaluate NSL requests in 2006 and to analyze trends in NSL usage from 2003 through 2006.

III. Organization of the Report

This report is divided into eight chapters. This first chapter contains the background to this report, the organization and methodology of the report, and a summary of the report's findings.

Chapter Two evaluates the FBI's specific responses to the 11 recommendations we made in our first NSL report. In this chapter, we also examine the FBI's new OIC, the NSD's new procedures for auditing compliance with NSL authorities and other techniques used in national security investigations, and the report by the Department's Chief Privacy and Civil Liberties Officer regarding the use and retention of information obtained through NSLs.

Chapter Three describes steps taken by the FBI in response to our March 2007 report, including three reviews the FBI initiated following release of our first NSL report:

(1) its review of NSLs issued by FBI field offices from a random sample of 10 percent of all national security investigations active at any time from 2003 through 2006;

(2) a separate review of 10 percent of NSLs issued by FBI Headquarters divisions during the same period; and

(3) a review of NSLs issued in FBI counterintelligence investigations pursuant to the *Fair Credit Reporting Act* (FCRA) from 2002 through 2006.

Chapter Four presents the data on the FBI's use of national security letters in 2006. This information is based on data derived from the FBI OGC national security letter tracking database and the Department's semiannual classified reports to Congress on NSL usage.

Chapter Five addresses the effectiveness of national security letters in 2006.

Chapter Six presents our findings on the number of occasions in which the Department issued national security letters without the certifications necessary to require the recipients of such letters to comply with the non-disclosure and confidentiality requirements of the Patriot Reauthorization Act.

Chapter Seven describes several instances of improper or illegal use of national security letter authorities in 2006. These include the matters self-reported by FBI Headquarters and field personnel to the FBI OGC in 2006.

Chapter Eight contains our conclusions and recommendations.

The Unclassified Appendix to the report contains comments on the report by the Attorney General, the Director of National Intelligence, the Assistant Attorney General for the National Security Division, and the FBI. The classified report also contains a Classified Appendix.

As noted above, the OIG will soon issue another NSL report that will describe the results of our investigation of the FBI's use of exigent letters to obtain telephone records from three communication service providers from 2002 through 2006. The report, which will expand on the general findings in our first NSL report on the use of exigent letters in 2003 through 2005, will examine the practice of using exigent letters rather than NSLs or other legal process to obtain records from the three communication service providers, the types of investigations for which records were sought, the process used to obtain the records, and inaccurate statements in many of the letters. The report also will describe the types of records obtained from the three communication service providers and how FBI agents and analysts handled and used the information obtained in response to these letters. The report will describe the FBI's efforts to issue legal process after the fact to cover information previously obtained from the exigent letters; the issuance of 11 "blanket" NSLs in 2006, and other improper NSLs; and the use of less formal types of requests to obtain records from the three communication service providers, such as verbal requests, e-mails, and telephone calls—only some of which were later documented in exigent letters or legal process. In addition, the report will evaluate the responsibility of FBI personnel who signed exigent letters and blanket NSLs and the responsibility of their supervisors and FBI officials. Finally, we will evaluate the processes that led to the issuance of exigent letters, improper blanket NSLs, and other improper NSLs and improper requests for information.

IV. Summary of OIG Findings

Our review concluded that, since issuance of our March 2007 report, the FBI and the Department have made significant progress in implementing the recommendations from that report and in adopting other corrective actions to address serious problems we identified in the use of national security letters. The FBI has also devoted significant energy, time, and resources toward ensuring that its field managers and agents understand the seriousness of the FBI's shortcomings in its use of NSLs and their responsibility for correcting these deficiencies.

Our interviews of senior FBI officials, including the Director, the Deputy Director, and the General Counsel, indicate that the FBI's senior leadership is committed to correcting the serious deficiencies in the FBI's use of NSLs identified in our first report. They have attempted to reinforce throughout all levels of the FBI the necessity of adhering to the rules governing the use of NSL authorities.

For example, among other measures the FBI has issued needed guidance on the use of NSLs, provided mandatory training to FBI employees on the proper use of NSLs, and developed a new data system to facilitate the issuance of NSLs and improve the accuracy of NSL data in required congressional reports. The FBI has issued numerous NSL policies and guidance memoranda on topics that include the proper usage of NSLs and statutory and procedural authorizations and restrictions; a prohibition on use of exigent letters; the requirement for sufficient and independent supervisory and legal reviews; and the procedures for identifying and reporting possible intelligence violations.

The FBI has also created a new Office of Integrity and Compliance (OIC), modeled after private sector compliance programs, to ensure that national security investigations and other FBI activities are conducted in a manner consistent with appropriate laws, regulations, and policies. We believe this office can perform a valuable function by providing a process for identifying compliance requirements and risks, assessing existing control mechanisms, and developing and implementing better controls to ensure proper use of NSLs. However, we recommend that the FBI consider providing the OIC with a larger permanent staffing level so that it can develop the skills, knowledge, and independence to lead or directly carry out the critical elements of this new compliance program.

In addition to the FBI's efforts to address the OIG's recommendations, the Department's National Security Division (NSD) has implemented additional measures to promote better compliance with NSL authorities and to address other issues raised by our first report. For example, in 2007 the NSD began reviews to examine whether the FBI is using various intelligence techniques, including NSLs, in accordance with applicable laws, guidelines, and policies.

Also, the Department's Office of the Chief Privacy and Civil Liberties Officer and the Civil Liberties Protection Officer of the Office of the Director of National Intelligence convened a working group to examine how NSL-derived information is used and retained by the FBI, with special emphasis on the protection of privacy interests, and in August 2007 sent a report and proposal to the Attorney General on minimization procedures with respect to NSL-derived data. However, after review of this proposal, we concluded that the NSL Working Group's report did not adequately address measures to label or tag NSL-derived information and to minimize the retention and dissemination of such information. In February 2008, the Acting Chief Privacy and Civil Liberties Officer told us that the proposal had been withdrawn and that he intends to reconvene the NSL Working Group to reconsider the August 2007 report and proposal. We examine the August 2007 report of the NSL Working Group and make recommendations for the NSL Working Group to consider as it revises that proposal.

In this report, we also examine the three reviews conducted by the FBI in 2007 following release of our first report. The FBI's reviews confirmed that the types of deficiencies identified in our first NSL report had occurred throughout the FBI from 2003 through 2006. The FBI's field review was important because it covered a larger, statistically valid sample of NSLs and case files. The FBI reviews confirmed similar types of possible intelligence violations in the FBI's use of NSLs that we found. However, the FBI's field review found a higher overall possible IOB violation rate (9.43 percent) than the OIG found (7.5 percent) in the sample we examined in our first NSL report.

However, we examined in detail the FBI's field review and determined that it did not capture all NSL-related possible intelligence violations in the files it reviewed, and therefore did not provide a fully accurate baseline from which to measure future improvement in compliance with NSL authorities. For example, during our re-examination of case files that FBI inspectors determined had no NSL-related possible intelligence violations in three field offices, we identified 15 additional NSL-related possible intelligence violations. In addition, because FBI inspectors were unable to locate information provided in response to a significant number of NSLs chosen for review in its sample, the results of the FBI's field review likely understated the rate of possible intelligence violations.

In short, despite the significant challenges facing the FBI in eliminating fully shortcomings in its use of NSLs, we believe the FBI and the Department have evidenced a commitment to correcting the problems we found in our first NSL report and have made significant progress in addressing the need to improve compliance in the FBI's use of NSLs. However, because only 1 year has passed since the OIG's first NSL report was released and some measures are not fully implemented or tested, we believe it is too early to definitively state whether the new systems and controls developed by the FBI and the Department will eliminate fully the problems with NSLs that we identified. We believe the FBI must implement all of our recommendations in the first NSL report, demonstrate sustained commitment to the steps it has taken and committed to take to improve compliance, implement additional recommendations described in this second report, consider additional measures to enhance privacy protections for NSL-derived information, and remain vigilant in holding FBI personnel accountable for properly preparing and approving NSLs and for handling responsive records appropriately.

Finally, as required by the Patriot Reauthorization Act, this report details the FBI's use of national security letters in calendar year 2006. It is important to note that the FBI's use of NSLs in 2006 occurred before we issued our first NSL report in March 2007, which identified the serious deficiencies in the FBI's use of and oversight of NSLs, and before the FBI began to implement corrective actions. Therefore, not surprisingly, this report contains similar findings to our March 2007 report regarding deficiencies in the FBI's use of NSLs.

As shown in Chart 4.5, we determined that the FBI's use of national security letters in 2006 continued the upward trend we identified in our first NSL report that covered the period 2003 through 2005. In 2006, the FBI issued 49,425 NSL requests, a 4.7-percent increase over NSL requests issued in 2005. For the 4-year period 2003 through 2006, the FBI issued a total of 192,499 NSL requests.

As shown in Chart 4.6, the percentage of NSL requests generated from investigations of U.S. persons continued to increase significantly, from approximately 39 percent of all NSL requests issued in 2003 to approximately 57 percent of all NSL requests issued in 2006.

In our interviews, FBI field and Headquarters personnel told us that NSLs continued to be an indispensable investigative tool in major terrorism and espionage investigations conducted in 2006. They reported that NSLs were used to identify the financial dealings of investigative subjects, confirm the

Chart 4.5: NSL Requests (2003 through 2006)

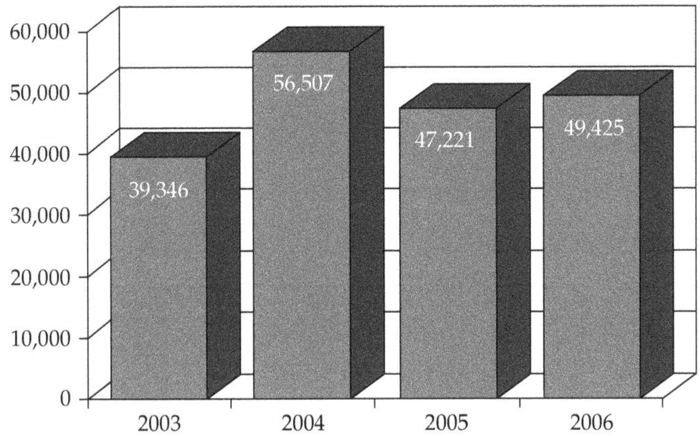

Sources: DOJ semiannual classified reports to Congress and FBI OGC database as of May 2006 (for 15 U.S.C. S 1681v NSL requests in 2003 through 2005)

Chart 4.6: NSL Requests Relating to U.S. Persons and non-U.S. Persons (2003 through 2006)

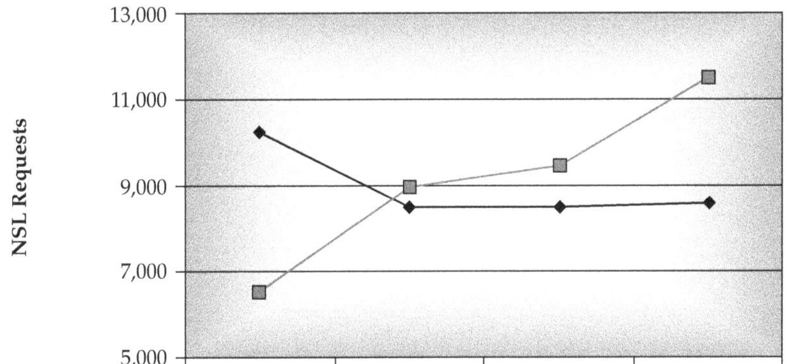

	2003	2004	2005	2006
Non-U.S. Persons	10,232	8,494	8,536	8,605
U.S. Persons	6,519	8,943	9,475	11,517

Source: DOJ semiannual classified reports to Congress

identity of subjects, support the use of sophisticated intelligence techniques, and establish predication for the initiation of preliminary and full counterterrorism and counterintelligence investigations.

As directed by the Patriot Reauthorization Act, we also conducted an audit of the number of occasions in which NSLs issued after the effective date of the Act did not contain the certifications necessary to require the recipients to comply with applicable non-disclosure and confidentiality requirements.

The vast majority of the NSLs and approval memoranda we examined, which are known as electronic communications (EC), substantially complied with the Patriot Reauthorization Act certification requirement and FBI policy. We believe this compliance record was largely due to the prompt guidance the FBI OGC issued on the date the Act was signed, the availability of new NSL forms on its Intranet website, and periodic guidance FBI OGC attorneys provided to the field as questions arose. We found that only 10 NSLs (3 percent of a random sample of 375 NSLs we examined) were issued without the required certifications. Our audit also determined that 97 percent of the NSLs in the random sample imposed non-disclosure and confidentiality obligations on recipients.

However, we also determined that 17 NSL approval memoranda (5 percent of the random sample) contained insufficient explanations to justify imposition of these obligations. We identified eight NSLs in our sample that contained recitals about non-disclosure that were inconsistent with the corresponding approval memoranda, signifying that case agents, their supervisors, and Chief Division Counsels were not careful in reviewing and approving these documents to ensure consistency. In addition to these non-compliant NSLs that were part of the random sample, we identified eight "blanket" NSLs issued by senior Counterterrorism Division officials in 2006 that did not contain the required certifications.

To assess any "improper or illegal use" of NSLs in 2006, as required by the Patriot Reauthorization Act, we examined the reports of possible intelligence violations involving the use of NSLs that were sent to the FBI OGC from January 1, 2006, through December 31, 2006. We identified 84 possible intelligence violations involving the use of NSLs, of which the FBI determined that 34 needed to be reported to the President's Intelligence Oversight Board (IOB).[6] The 34 matters included the same types of errors identified in our first NSL report that was completed in March 2007, such as the issuance of NSLs without proper authorization, improper requests, and unauthorized collection of telephone or Internet e-mail records. Of these 34 intelligence violations, 20 were the result of FBI errors, while 14 resulted initially from mistakes by recipients of the national security letters. We generally agreed with the FBI's decisions on which violations needed to be reported to the IOB, except for six that we believed should have been reported to the IOB but were not. We concluded that the decisions not to report these were inconsistent with prior FBI OGC decisions or that the reasons for not reporting them to the IOB were unpersuasive.

[6] Of the 84 possible intelligence violations, 52 involved the FBI's acquisition of information it had not requested in the NSLs (referred to as "initial third party errors"). Since the FBI OGC has not yet determined whether the FBI compounded the third party errors by using or uploading the unauthorized information, we could not reach a conclusion as to whether these 52 matters involved improper use of NSL-derived information.

As we did in our first NSL report, we determined whether the FBI would have been entitled to the information provided under applicable NSL statutes, Attorney General Guidelines, and internal policies. We found that of the 84 possible intelligence violations identified and reported to the FBI OGC in 2006, the FBI received information it was not entitled to receive in 14 matters. In one of the matters the FBI requested information it was not entitled to under the applicable NSL statute. In the other 13 matters, the FBI made proper requests but, due to third party errors, obtained information it was not entitled to receive under the pertinent NSL statutes.

This report makes 17 recommendations regarding the FBI's continued use of NSLs. For example, two recommendations are designed to remind FBI case agents and supervisors to carefully examine the circumstances surrounding the issuance of each NSL to determine whether there is adequate justification for imposing non-disclosure and confidentiality requirements on the NSL recipient and to ensure that NSL approval memoranda and the associated NSLs contain consistent information and certifications.

Three additional recommendations are designed to reinforce the FBI's obligation to provide timely reports of possible intelligence violations, ensure that these reports detail the precise remedial measures employed to handle unauthorized NSL-derived information, and provide case agents and supervisors with examples of common errors in the use of NSLs. We address the last recommendation to the Department regarding the NSL Working Group's proposal to the Attorney General.

Finally, as noted above, we are continuing our investigation of the FBI's previous use of exigent letters, the blanket NSLs, and other improper NSLs and requests for telephone records. The findings and recommendations in this NSL report should be considered in conjunction with the findings of that forthcoming report.

Chapter Two: Status of the FBI'S and DOJ'S Corrective Actions in Response to the OIG'S First NSL Report

In our first NSL report, we made 11 recommendations to the FBI to help improve its use and oversight of national security letters. In a letter to the OIG dated March 6, 2007, that was included as an appendix to that report, the FBI stated that it agreed with each of the recommendations and would work with the Department's National Security Division (NSD) and the Office of the Chief Privacy and Civil Liberties Officer (Privacy Officer) to implement the recommended reforms.[7]

In May 2007 and September 2007, the FBI provided memoranda to the OIG describing the status of the FBI's efforts to implement these recommendations. The FBI Inspection Division and the FBI Office of the General Counsel (FBI OGC) have also provided updates to the OIG on the FBI's progress in implementing specific recommendations. Further, the Department's NSD has implemented additional measures to address the serious concerns we uncovered regarding the use of national security letters.

In this chapter, we assess the progress of the FBI's and the Department's efforts to address the problems that our first report found with the use of national security letters. To assess these efforts, we analyzed the FBI's memoranda describing the status of its corrective actions; interviewed FBI officials from the OGC and Inspection Division; interviewed other senior FBI officials, including the FBI Director and Deputy Director; and interviewed field personnel responsible for issuing and reviewing NSLs such as the Special Agents in Charge (SAC), Chief Division Counsels (CDC), Supervisory Special Agents, and Special Agents. In addition, to assess the Department's actions, we reviewed all new NSL-related guidance issued by the FBI to the field and Headquarters divisions since our first report was issued, reviewed the types of NSL training provided and to whom it was provided, and observed a demonstration of the new data system that was designed to manage and track NSLs.

In Section I of this chapter, we provide an overview of the FBI's and the Department's efforts to implement our recommendations and the additional steps it has taken to promote compliance with the NSL statutes, applicable Attorney General Guidelines, and internal FBI policies governing the use of NSLs. In Section II, after listing each of our 11 recommendations and the background for each, we summarize the FBI's responses to the recommendations and analyze the FBI's efforts to date to implement the recommendations.

---

[7] See NSL I, Unclassified Appendix.

In Section III of this chapter, we describe other corrective measures implemented in 2007 by the FBI, the Department's NSD, and the Privacy Officer. We also describe the FBI's creation of a new Office of Integrity and Compliance (OIC). In addition, we assess a proposal from a working group led by the Privacy Officer that relates to the retention of NSL-derived information.

I. Overview of the FBI's and Department's Corrective Measures

In the year since the OIG issued its first report on NSLs, the FBI and other Department components have implemented a series of measures designed to promote stricter compliance with NSL statutes, Attorney General Guidelines, and internal FBI policies governing use of NSL authorities. Some of these measures directly respond to the OIG's specific recommendations, while others were additional measures proposed or implemented by the FBI, NSD, or the Attorney General.

In this follow-up review, we examined the FBI's and the Department's actions, as of December 2007, in response to the OIG's recommendations. Some of these actions are one-time measures (such as the FBI's statistical reviews of NSLs issued by field and Headquarters divisions in 2003 through 2006 and the FBI's review of NSLs issued in counterintelligence investigations pursuant to the *Fair Credit Reporting Act* (FCRA) from 2002 through 2006). Others are longer-term actions that require sustained commitment by the FBI's senior leadership, attorneys, CDCs, and other FBI and Department personnel to be fully implemented.

Our recommendations in our first NSL report fell into four broad categories.

- Four recommendations (numbers 1, 2, 3, and 6) focused on enhancements in FBI recordkeeping and information technology supporting the use of NSLs. These recommendations were intended to improve the FBI's ability to capture accurate, complete, and timely information on NSLs for congressional and public reporting; to render NSLs subject to effective internal and external reviews; and to identify when NSL-derived information was used in analytical intelligence products or provided to law enforcement authorities for use in criminal proceedings.
- Three recommendations (numbers 4, 7, and 8) addressed the need for additional guidance and training to ensure that FBI personnel use NSLs in accordance with pertinent authorities, to reduce or eliminate common mistakes in the issuance of NSLs, to clarify distinctions among the different NSL statutes, to identify possible Intelligence Oversight Board (IOB) violations arising from the use of NSLs, and to eliminate the use of exigent letters.

- Three recommendations (numbers 9, 10, and 11) focused on the role of attorneys in the FBI OGC and the CDCs in providing advice about NSLs. These recommendations were designed to promote better oversight by the FBI OGC's National Security Law Branch (NSLB) at FBI Headquarters, close and independent review of NSLs by CDCs, and clear guidance about the use and sequencing of NSLs in accordance with the requirement in the Attorney General Guidelines to use the "least intrusive collection techniques feasible."
- One recommendation (number 5) suggested that the FBI consider seeking a legislative amendment to the *Electronic Communications Privacy Act* (ECPA) to clarify the information the FBI is entitled to obtain through ECPA NSLs.

OIG Findings on the FBI's and Department's Corrective Actions

Our review found that the FBI and the Department have made significant progress in implementing our recommendations and in adopting other corrective actions to address problems we uncovered in the use of national security letters. We also found that the FBI has devoted significant energy, time, and resources toward ensuring that its field managers and agents understand the seriousness of the FBI's shortcomings in its use of NSLs and their responsibility for correcting these deficiencies. However, there are additional steps that the FBI is still considering and needs to take, and we believe that ensuring full compliance will require the continual attention, vigilance, and reinforcement by the FBI and the Department. We also believe it is too soon to definitively state whether the new systems and controls developed by the FBI and the Department will eliminate fully the problems with the use of NSLs that we and the FBI have identified.

It is important to first note that the FBI's leadership has made it a top priority for the FBI to correct the serious deficiencies in the use of NSLs. In our interviews with Director Mueller, Deputy Director Pistole, and General Counsel Caproni, it was clear to us that they appreciated the importance of this issue, the significance of the problems that we had uncovered, and the critical need to correct these problems.

For example, Director Mueller said he believes that the FBI's shortcomings in complying with NSL authorities resulted from the FBI's previous lack of focus on the procedures necessary to ensure that all legal requirements were satisfied. He attributed the problems to several factors, including inadequate infrastructure at FBI Headquarters to ensure that all legal requirements were followed, organizational "stove piping" under which FBI personnel did not fully communicate across division lines, rotation of FBI middle management so that they did not always "take ownership" of problems they encountered, the significant pressure to respond to any terrorist threat, and inadequate staffing in the FBI's Counterterrorism Division (CTD) in the period following the September 11 attacks.

Director Mueller also emphasized his commitment to address problems in the FBI's use of NSLs, and, as one example, pointed to the establishment of the FBI's OIC (discussed in Section III of this chapter). He stated that he believes this office will assist him and other members of the FBI's senior leadership in identifying and addressing areas of weakness as well as other compliance issues. He also stated that he believes that he has been successful in driving down through the organization the necessity of adhering to NSL authorities and that SACs are "on board" with the NSL compliance and training initiatives and are communicating this message throughout the ranks of the FBI.

FBI Deputy Director Pistole similarly told the OIG that the FBI is devoting significant time and attention to ensuring that SACs understand the substantive legal requirements for NSLs. One of the venues he said he is using to reinforce these requirements is the Strategy Performance Sessions he chairs each quarter via teleconference with the SACs in the FBI's 56 field offices. Each of the ten sessions is held with approximately 6 SACs each and lasts approximately 90 minutes. The second quarter 2007 sessions, which also were attended by the FBI General Counsel, were called, "Preserve Civil Liberties." These sessions focused on the OIG's findings in our first NSL report and the FBI's findings on NSL compliance problems identified in its field office reviews (described in Chapter Three of this report).

Deputy Director Pistole also stated that he is stressing NSL compliance in conjunction with mid-year progress reviews and annual performance appraisals of SACs. During these reviews, he asks the SACs individually what they are doing to ensure compliance with NSL requirements and requires them to cite examples. As the rating official for all SACs, he said that he expects SACs to know the substantive legal requirements for NSLs and regularly stresses in their progress reviews that they cannot assume that their personnel are following FBI guidance on NSLs.

FBI General Counsel Caproni stated that she has devoted significant time and attention to addressing the OIG's recommendations and implementing other measures to improve NSL compliance. Following release of the OIG's report, Caproni held a conference call in March 2007 with all CDCs to review the OIG's most significant findings, describe the FBI's response, and underscore the role of CDCs in reviewing and approving NSLs and ensuring that any unauthorized information obtained from NSLs is handled appropriately. She also discussed these issues at the CDC conference in July 2007 and the SAC conference in October 2007. Caproni emphasized at the CDC conference that it is "clearly and unequivocally" the duty of CDCs to review predication for NSLs.

Caproni also noted that the FBI OGC had issued or was preparing to issue additional guidance on NSLs based on the OIG's findings and the additional findings developed from the FBI's reviews in 2007. Among the new guidance issued were memoranda directing FBI case agents to review NSL-derived records prior to uploading them into FBI databases to ensure that they correspond to the NSLs and have not generated unauthorized information; prohibiting the use of exigent letters; reiterating the distinctions between the NSL authorities in the FCRA; clarifying the role of CDCs in conducting independent reviews of NSLs; and describing procedures for redacting NSL-derived information that is beyond the scope of the NSL to prevent unauthorized dissemination. In June 2007, the FBI OGC issued a comprehensive 24-page memorandum on the use of NSL authorities that covered these topics.[8]

Caproni also stated that the FBI OGC has devoted additional resources to support the NSL-related activities of FBI Headquarters divisions, including the assignment of additional NSLB attorneys to either be co-located with or to support all the CTD sections. She believes that these additional resources will assist the FBI OGC in identifying and avoiding potential problems before they occur. In March 2007, Caproni also ordered all NSLB attorneys to provide live training any time they visit a field office.

In addition to the FBI's efforts to address the OIG's recommendations, the Department's NSD has implemented additional measures to promote better compliance with NSL authorities and to address the privacy issues raised by our first report. For example, in 2007 the NSD began national security reviews to examine whether the FBI is using various intelligence techniques, including NSLs, in accordance with applicable laws, guidelines, and policies.

Also, the Privacy Officer convened a working group to examine how NSL-derived information is used and retained by the FBI, with special emphasis on the protection of privacy interests, and sent a proposal to the Attorney

---

[8] These memoranda are described in more detail in Section II of this chapter in conjunction with our analysis of the FBI's implementation of recommendations 4, 7, 8, and 10.

Caproni also noted that in August 2007, the FBI OGC requested a legal opinion from the Department's Office of Legal Counsel (OLC) on three issues that arose in the course of the FBI's 2007 NSL reviews. The three questions were: (1) whether, in response to *Electronic Communication Privacy Act* (ECPA) NSLs, the FBI may obtain Social Security Numbers, dates of birth, and other information used by the communication provider to identify or maintain a profile of a customer or subscriber; (2) whether the term "toll billing records information" in the ECPA NSL statute includes records of incoming/outgoing calls upon which a fee could be assessed regardless of whether a fee is actually assessed and regardless of whether the information must be culled from aggregate data; and (3) whether the government may obtain information verbally regarding the existence of an account in connection with a given telephone number or person from an electronic communication service provider without additional legal process. As of February 11, 2008, OLC had not provided its opinion on these questions. Caproni stated that once OLC issues its opinion, the FBI OGC will determine what steps it must take to address the appropriateness of retaining NSL-derived information in the categories covered by the opinion.

General for review on minimization procedures with respect to NSL-derived data.

Based on our review, we believe the FBI and the Department have taken significant steps to address the findings of the OIG's first report on NSLs and have made significant progress in implementing corrective actions. However, we also believe it is too soon to state with full confidence whether the steps the FBI and the Department have taken will eliminate fully the problems we identified in our first report on NSLs. Some measures, such as the FBI's new NSL data system and the OIC are positive steps but are not fully implemented or tested. Other measures, such as the NSD's reviews and the recent FBI OGC guidance on the responsibility of case agents to ensure that information obtained from NSLs has not generated unauthorized collections, have not been in place long enough to gauge their effectiveness.

Yet, despite the multiple challenges facing the FBI to eliminate fully problems in the use of NSLs, we believe the FBI and the Department have evidenced a commitment to correcting the problems we found in our first NSL report and have made significant progress in addressing the need to improve compliance in the FBI's use of NSLs.

In the next section of this chapter, we discuss in greater detail the specific steps that have been taken or are planned to address each of the OIG's 11 recommendations. After that, we examine other initiatives implemented by the FBI and the Department regarding NSL use.

II. Status of the FBI's Implementation of the OIG's Recommendations in Our First NSL Report

We set forth below each of our recommendations in our first NSL report, describe the background for the recommendations, summarize the actions taken by the FBI to date to address the recommendations, and provide our analysis.

Recommendation No. 1

Require all Headquarters and field personnel who are authorized to issue national security letters to create a control file for the purpose of retaining signed copies of all national security letters they issue.

Background: In our first NSL report, we found that the FBI did not have policies requiring the retention of signed copies of NSLs or the uploading of NSLs into the FBI's principal investigative database, the Automated Case Support (ACS) system. This meant that the FBI did not have a reliable audit trail tracking the issuance of NSLs, which prevented internal and external reviews of compliance with NSL statutes, applicable Attorney General Guidelines, and internal FBI policies governing the use of NSLs.

FBI Actions Taken to Address the Recommendation: The FBI issued three communications to field and Headquarters divisions to address this recommendation. On March 6, 2007, the FBI OGC sent an e-mail message to all CDCs and SACs directing that copies of signed NSLs be maintained both in the investigative file and a field office "drop" file so that all NSLs issued by each field and Headquarters division are maintained and can be located in one place. This was superseded by the FBI Records Management Division's memorandum dated March 9, 2007, requiring that signed copies of NSLs be retained in the relevant investigative file by the issuing division. This requirement is reiterated in the FBI OGC's Comprehensive Guidance on National Security Letters (Comprehensive Guidance EC) issued on June 1, 2007 (also discussed in connection with Recommendation Nos. 3,4, and 8 through 11).

OIG Analysis: We believe that the steps taken by the FBI will help ensure that copies of all issued NSLs are retained in a file created by field and Headquarters divisions. Maintaining signed copies of the NSLs in the pertinent investigative files should ensure that all NSLs issued by a field office or Headquarters division are collected in one location and are available for internal or external audits or reviews.

Recommendation No. 2

Improve the FBI OGC NSL tracking database to ensure that it captures timely, complete, and accurate data on NSLs and NSL requests.

Background: In our first NSL report, we found the FBI OGC NSL tracking database (OGC database) did not contain accurate and complete information about NSL requests. This occurred because of flaws and structural problems in the database. In addition, since the FBI relied upon the OGC database in preparing the Department's semiannual classified reports to Congress, the flaws and structural problems in the database affected the accuracy of the Department's reports to Congress. For example, in the 77 case files we examined in 4 field offices in connection with our first NSL report, we found that for the period 2003 through 2005, the OGC database underreported the total number of NSLs and NSL requests by 17 percent and 22 percent, respectively.

We also identified circumstances in which certain data fields in the OGC database were left blank, had typographical errors or other erroneous entries, or contained default settings—all of which resulted in errors or understatements in reporting to Congress on NSLs. We also found that delays by FBI field and Headquarters personnel in entering data into the ACS system contributed to additional discrepancies in the data reported to

Congress, including the failure to report almost 4,600 NSL requests for the period 2003 through 2005. Other structural problems or flaws in the database resulted in discrepancies affecting the Department's reporting of the total number of NSL requests, the total number of "investigations of different U.S. persons", and the total number of "investigations of different non-U.S. persons" that were reported to Congress over the 3-year period.

In light of these flaws and structural problems with the OGC database, we recommended that the FBI improve its database to ensure the collection of timely, complete, and accurate data on NSL usage for purposes of congressional and public reporting and to facilitate internal and external audits or reviews.

FBI Actions Taken to Address the Recommendation: The FBI OGC issued an EC dated March 19, 2007, mandating that field offices conduct monthly counts of NSLs issued by their offices in order to reconcile NSL data contained in the OGC database. In April 2007, personnel in the FBI OGC instituted a process for comparing these monthly NSL counts to data in the OGC database to check for inaccuracies in the database. According to the EC, any discrepancies identified by the FBI OGC are being reconciled and will be used to improve guidance and training on NSL reporting. The FBI told the OIG that it will continue requiring these monthly counts and reconciliations until the new database for tracking NSL data is implemented. This database, discussed below, known as the NSL subsystem to the Foreign Intelligence Surveillance Act (FISA) Management System (NSL data system), has replaced the OGC database. While the new data system does not correct historical information, it is designed to improve the accuracy of NSL data in the future.

FBI OGC personnel reported that the FISA Unit of the FBI OGC's NSLB developed the NSL data system to facilitate the approval and issuance of NSLs and support data collection for congressional and public reporting. The NSL data system prompts the drafter of an NSL to enter information about the subject, the predication for the NSL, the type of NSL, the NSL recipients, and the specific information sought by the NSL (such as telephone numbers or e-mail addresses). The NSL data system will route the NSL request through the required levels of review and approval similar to the manner in which applications for use of FISA authorities are routed in the FBI. Upon completion of all approvals, the NSL data system will generate the approval EC and the NSLs for signature by the field or Headquarters approving officials. As a result, the accuracy of NSLs and the efficiency of issuing NSLs should improve, and there also should be fewer discrepancies between the approval ECs and the NSLs. The FBI established an automatic link between the NSL data system and the ACS system that facilitates automatic uploading of approval ECs and NSLs into the ACS system. In addition, FBI OGC personnel said that all information necessary to generate the

Department's congressional and public reporting will be collected as part of the new NSL data system. The FBI informed us that on January 1, 2008, this system was deployed throughout the FBI.

The Records Management Division's March 9, 2007, directive noted previously also mandated that NSLs be uploaded into the ACS system as an NSL "Document Type" to facilitate recordkeeping and reporting. As a result, NSLs issued after March 9, 2007, can now be sorted and counted by field office in the ACS system, which will help verify the accuracy of information used in the Department's congressional and public reports on NSLs and will assist in facilitating internal and external NSL reviews.[9]

In addition, in an attempt to correct deficiencies in the existing OGC database, the NSLB has modified the database so that FBI personnel making entries about NSLs must complete all fields required for congressional and public reporting. The FBI also changed the default setting in the OGC database on the status of the NSL target from "non-U.S. person" to "U.S. person" and changed the default number of NSL requests from "0" to "1." The FBI told us that it believes these changes should reduce errors caused by the previous default settings.

The FBI OGC assigned additional personnel to enter data into the OGC database and conducted training for all personnel who entered NSL data to ensure they understand the data being entered and recognized when incorrect data had been provided. These measures were designed to improve the old database before the new NSL data system was implemented. Now, all reporting of NSLs is done through the new system.

OIG Analysis: We believe that the steps taken by the FBI to create a central database for generating and approving NSLs and for collecting data pertinent to congressional and public reporting on NSL usage should improve the collection of timely, complete, and accurate data on NSLs. This new NSL data system will enable field agents to insert case-specific information into a standardized NSL request form, automatically track the progress of each NSL, identify delays in the process, send automatic reminders to advance the review and approval process, and facilitate the transmission of NSL documents among participants in the NSL approval process.

Now that the NSL data system is fully operational, it should eliminate the need for FBI OGC personnel to manually re-enter NSL data into the antiquated OGC database after the information has been uploaded into the ACS system by field and Headquarters personnel. Using the new data system, FBI field personnel will need to enter NSL data only once—when the

---

[9] The "Document Types" are Telephone Subscriber Information; Telephone Toll Records; E-Mail Subscriber Records; E-Mail Transactional Records; Financial Records, *Right to Financial Privacy Act* (RFPA) § 3414 (a)(5); Financial Institution Listings, FCRA; Consumer Identifying Information; and Full Credit Report.

NSL is created—because the data system will automatically upload the approval EC and NSL into the ACS system. The FBI stated that all the information necessary to produce required congressional reports on NSLs will be collected as part of this process, which should improve the timely, complete, and accurate collection of NSL data.

The FBI also stated that the NSL data system contains controls to minimize the risk of data entry errors, such as setting the default to U.S. person, prohibiting an entry of "0" for the number of requests, and preventing the use of consumer full credit reports in counterintelligence cases. However, the OIG disagrees that changing the default setting status from a "non-U.S. person" to a "U.S. person" is the best way to ensure accurate data entry. As we noted in our first NSL report, from 2003 through 2005 the OGC database contained a default setting of "non-U.S. person" for the investigative subject of NSL requests for *Right to Financial Privacy Act* (RFPA) and ECPA toll billing/electronic communication transaction records. As a result, known or presumed U.S. persons could be misidentified if the default setting was not corrected (from "non-U.S. person" to "U.S. person") during data entry. This resulted in an understatement of the number of investigations of U.S. persons who were the targets of NSLs. The OIG believes that an error is just as likely to occur if the default is changed to "U.S. person" because personnel entering the data may fail to correct the default setting when the target of the investigation is a "non-U.S. person." We believe the appropriate way to minimize the risk of error would be to create a blank mandatory field and require FBI personnel to make an affirmative selection before the data system allows the user to proceed to the next entry.

Similarly, as described in our first NSL report, the OGC database was programmed to provide a default setting of "0" for the number of NSL requests. Since every NSL generates at least one NSL request, a "0" entry for NSL requests is erroneous. However, since one NSL can generate more than one request, FBI personnel may fail to correct the new default "1" setting just as they previously failed to correct the previous default "0" setting." According to the FBI, the new NSL data system corrects this deficiency because it assigns the number of NSL requests automatically.

We believe that the FBI's decision to assign additional NSLB personnel to enter data into the database and provide additional training for these personnel should help reduce the frequency of data entry errors. However, we also believe that the FBI OGC should require periodic reviews of a sample of NSLs in the new NSL data system to ensure that the training provided is successfully applied in practice and has reduced or eliminated data entry errors.

The OIG also notes that the NSL data system does not capture the date when the SAC (or other approving official) signs the NSL; rather, it includes the date that the SAC electronically certifies approval of the EC and NSL. Until the FBI implements electronic signature capability, this may create a possible variance between the two dates.

Recommendation No. 3

Improve the FBI OGC NSL database to include data reflecting NSL requests for information about individuals who are not the investigative subjects but are the targets of NSL requests.

Background: We determined in our first NSL report that the OGC database did not include data on whether the target of the NSL is the subject of the underlying investigation or another individual. The target of an NSL is frequently not the same person as the subject of the underlying investigation. Since the database did not distinguish between the target of the NSL and subject of the investigation, the FBI did not know and was unable to estimate the number of NSL requests relating to persons who are not investigative subjects. In light of the Patriot Act's expansion of the FBI's authority to collect information on individuals who are not subjects of its investigations, we recommended that the OGC database be modified to capture this information from NSL approval ECs so that the information is subject to internal and external oversight.

FBI Actions Taken to Address the Recommendation: The new NSL data system will prompt the user to enter information about the subject, the predication for the NSL, the type of NSL, the NSL recipient, and specific targets of the NSL, including targets other than the subject of the investigation.

In 2006, the FBI modified its NSL guidance to require, with the exception of NSLs seeking subscriber information, that agents indicate in the NSL approval EC whether the request is for a person other than the subject of the investigation or in addition to that subject and to state the U.S. person or non-U.S. person status of those individuals.[10] That guidance was reiterated in the Comprehensive Guidance EC issued by the FBI OGC in June 2007.

OIG Analysis: Our review indicates that the steps taken by the FBI will help ensure that the new NSL data system contains accurate data about individuals who are not investigative subjects but are the targets of NSL requests. We reviewed a demonstration of the NSL data system, which indicated that, when fully implemented, the new data system should satisfy our recommendation by capturing data on the U.S. person/non-U.S. person status of targets of NSLs, not just the status of the investigative subjects.

[10] There is no statutory requirement in the ECPA to report the U.S. person status of NSL requests for subscriber information. In many cases, the identity of the subscriber is unknown.

Recommendation No. 4

Consider issuing additional guidance to field offices that will assist in identifying possible IOB violations arising from use of national security letter authorities, such as (a) measures to reduce or eliminate typographical and other errors in national security letters so that the FBI does not collect unauthorized information; (b) best practices for identifying the receipt of unauthorized information in the response to national security letters due to third party errors; (c) clarifying the distinctions between the two NSL authorities in the *Fair Credit Reporting Act* (15 U.S.C. §§ 1681u and 1681v); and (d) reinforcing internal FBI policy requiring that NSLs must be issued from investigative files, not from control files.

Background: Our first NSL report noted that the majority of the possible intelligence violations that were self-reported by FBI personnel to the FBI OGC by field offices, 22 of 26, arose from FBI errors. Most of these involved typographical errors or the case agent's good faith but erroneous belief that the information requested related to an investigative subject. Moreover, many NSL-related possible intelligence violations throughout the FBI were not identified or reported by FBI personnel.

Some of the possible intelligence violations we identified resulted from typographical errors in the telephone number or e-mail address in the NSLs. We also determined that the FBI entered unauthorized information in an FBI database because agents and intelligence analysts did not verify that the information supplied by the NSL recipients matched the information requested in the NSLs. Additionally, we found that some FBI personnel were confused about the two NSL authorities available under FCRA NSL statutes and, as a result, either requested or obtained unauthorized information.

We also identified two circumstances in which the FBI relied exclusively on control files rather than investigative files to initiate approval for NSLs in violation of internal FBI policy. In one instance, the FBI issued at least 300 NSLs in connection with a classified special project overseen by FBI Headquarters. The second instance involved the issuance of six NSLs by the Electronic Surveillance Operations and Sharing Unit in the Counterterrorism Division. In addition to violating FBI policy, when NSLs are issued exclusively from control files it is difficult to determine if the statutory and Attorney General's Guidelines requirements for issuing NSLs have been satisfied.

Unless the errors in the use of NSLs are identified by the FBI promptly and any improperly obtained information is sequestered or returned, unauthorized information obtained in response to improper NSLs may result in additional problems. In some instances, agents and analysts upload digital responses to NSLs into the ACS system and the Investigative Data

Warehouse, which makes the data available to other agents, Headquarters personnel, and other law enforcement and intelligence agencies. Accordingly, we recommended that the FBI consider issuing additional guidance that would assist FBI personnel in identifying possible intelligence violations arising from these types of errors.

FBI Actions Taken to Address the Recommendation: **4(a) measures to reduce or eliminate typographical and other errors in national security:** In a Comprehensive Guidance EC, the FBI General Counsel mandated that the model NSL approval ECs and model NSLs posted on the NSLB website be used by FBI personnel when drafting the NSLs. The FBI believes that mandatory use of these models will help reduce typographical errors in NSLs and approval ECs. The FBI also provided new NSL training to field and Headquarters personnel that emphasized the potential for collection of unauthorized information due to typographical errors and the need to ensure that information is appropriately requested. In addition, as described in Chapter Three of this report, several reviews of the FBI's use of NSL authorities conducted in 2007 by the FBI's Inspection Division and national security reviews conducted by the NSD will assist the FBI in developing additional guidance to reduce these and other types of errors.

OIG Analysis: **4(a)** The OIG believes that the steps taken by the FBI will help reduce typographical and other errors in NSLs so that the FBI does not collect unauthorized information.

We believe that mandating the use of the model NSL approval ECs and model NSLs in conjunction with the new NSL data system (in which data elements such as case numbers, type of NSL, subject and target names, and telephone numbers must be typed only once) should help to reduce typographical and other data entry errors. Once typed, the information becomes part of the electronically generated approval EC and accompanying NSL. These steps will avoid the electronic "cutting and pasting" that created errors as we noted in our first NSL report. However, case agents and supervisors will still need to verify that the initial data entries are made correctly. To verify this, we recommend that the information in the NSL be checked by the case agent or the supervisor against any serialized source document to verify that the data extracted from the source document and used in the NSL (such as the telephone number or e-mail address) is accurately entered.[11] This would enable FBI personnel and internal and external auditors to compare the data in the source document with the particulars described in the NSL to ensure consistency and accuracy.

[11] Under FBI internal procedures, each document that is placed in an investigative file must be numbered in sequence. This number is known as the serial number, and the document is known as the serial. Federal Bureau of Investigation, Manual of Administrative Operations and Procedures, 2-4.1.1.

The OIG also believes that periodic training of FBI personnel responsible for generating, reviewing, and approving NSLs that emphasizes the need to ensure that information is appropriately requested in NSLs and identifies the potential for unauthorized collections due to typographical and other errors is essential to the success of these corrective actions.

FBI Actions Taken to Address the Recommendation: **4(b) best practices for identifying the receipt of unauthorized information in the response to national security letters due to third party errors:** On January 3, 2007, the FBI OGC issued a memorandum entitled, Legal Advice and Opinions; Uploading of NSL Return Information. The memorandum directed that information obtained in response to NSLs be reviewed before it is uploaded into Telephone Applications and other FBI databases to ensure that the information is responsive to the NSL request and that there has been no unauthorized collection. The Comprehensive Guidance EC issued on June 1, 2007, reiterated this policy and states that any improper information obtained in response to NSLs may not be retained or uploaded into any FBI database and must immediately be sequestered. It further stated that a report to the FBI OGC of a potential intelligence violation must be prepared by the case agent. The January 3 memorandum also stated that when the NSLB adjudicates the matter, it is to confirm whether the information is relevant. If the information is not relevant, the NSLB will direct that the information either be returned or destroyed. If unauthorized information is collected that is relevant to the investigation, the memorandum directs that it be sequestered and not uploaded into any FBI database or utilized in any manner until another NSL has been issued to address the overproduction.

The Comprehensive Guidance EC includes as an attachment an NSL Review Checklist for use by personnel who review or upload NSL-derived information. The checklist has a check box indicating that the case agent has confirmed that the information is relevant and there has not been an unauthorized collection. There also is a check box indicating that if the information is not relevant to the investigation the user has contacted the CDC or the NSLB for advice on how to proceed with a potential IOB report and that the CDC will sequester the information and determine the appropriate action.

The Comprehensive Guidance EC also differentiated between two categories of unauthorized collections: production of information not relevant to the investigation and "overproduction" of information that was not requested by the NSL but is relevant to the investigation. Information not relevant to the investigation would include data on a telephone number other than the telephone number listed in the NSL due to a typographical error in the NSL. In addition, an NSL recipient may generate unauthorized collections by providing information on the subscriber associated with the telephone number referenced in the NSL for a time period greater than was requested. The Comprehensive Guidance EC directs that supervisors are required to monitor compliance with this policy, recommending that during quarterly file reviews squad supervisors conduct spot checks of information obtained in response to NSLs to ensure that case agents are following these procedures.

The FBI OGC also issued a memorandum on April 4, 2007, regarding procedures for redacting information obtained in response to, but beyond the scope of, an NSL and for disseminating the information to case agents while awaiting adjudication of the potential intelligence violation. The method of redaction is left to the discretion of the CDC. However, the procedures require that no matter what method is used, the redacted information should not be visible or accessible, should not be uploaded into any FBI database, and should remain sequestered with the CDC.[12]

New NSL training also addresses the need to review NSL-derived information prior to uploading it to FBI databases. In addition, we were informed that the FBI OGC and the NSLB are reviewing the findings of the Inspection Division's 2007 review of NSLs to determine if additional measures or training would improve compliance on the handling of unauthorized information obtained in response to NSLs.

OIG Analysis: **4(b)** We believe that the steps thus far taken by the FBI will assist FBI personnel in identifying possible intelligence violations arising from use of NSL authorities. The FBI OGC guidance memoranda dated January 3, 2007, and April 4, 2007, and the Comprehensive Guidance EC provide specific instructions for handling unauthorized records obtained in response to NSLs and direct that such records not be uploaded into any FBI databases.

The new NSL data system also requires case agents reviewing NSL-derived information to identify the receipt of any unauthorized information. When case agents receive records in response to NSLs, they must complete several steps, including entering an electronic certification stating that the responsive records have been reviewed for unauthorized collection. The data system has a comment field that must be completed if an unauthorized collection occurs. If the person entering data does not complete all required tasks, the data system sends electronic reminders until all required entries are made.

In its response to our recommendations that address potential errors by the FBI or NSL recipients, the FBI noted its implementation of new training, issuance of new guidance, and development of the new NSL data system.

[12] When a portion of NSL-derived information is redacted by a "strike-though" or by "blacking out" using a black marker or other similar marking device, the information must not be legible through the blackened/redacted portion.

While we believe these measures are important, we also believe the FBI needs to proactively and regularly scrutinize national security investigations and the use of NSLs. In light of the FBI's increasing reliance on NSLs as a primary investigative technique employed in both terrorism and espionage investigations (discussed in Chapter Five of this report), the FBI should examine the preparation of NSL-related documents and the handling of NSL-derived information with periodic reviews and inspections. Any recurring problems that suggest continuing confusion or uncertainty about the proper use of NSLs, or inadequate field supervision and review, should be promptly discussed with FBI attorneys and addressed. We also believe that the FBI OGC should establish mechanisms for spot checking entries into the new NSL data system using resources available from the FBI Inspection Division and the FBI's new OIC. Moreover, FBI personnel authorized to request information pursuant to the NSL authorities must know that the use of these authorities imposes requirements and responsibilities for which they will be held accountable.

FBI Actions Taken to Address the Recommendation: **4(c) clarifying the distinctions between the two NSL authorities in the *Fair Credit Reporting Act*:** A memorandum dated March 5, 2007, issued to all field offices and the Counterintelligence Division by the FBI National Security Branch (NSB), clarified the distinction between 15 U.S.C. § 1681u and 15 U.S.C. § 1681v of the FCRA and mandated a review of NSLs issued under the FCRA. The distinction between the two NSL authorities also is highlighted in the Comprehensive Guidance EC.

As we describe in Chapter Three of this report, on March 5, 2007, the FBI's Executive Assistant Director for the NSB also directed all 56 field offices to review all NSLs issued pursuant to the FCRA in counterintelligence case files from 2002 through 2006. The purpose of the review was to determine if any of these NSLs requested consumer full credit reports in violation of 15 U.S.C. § 1681v or resulted in the improper collection of such reports in response to NSL requests for limited credit information pursuant to 15 U.S.C. § 1681u. The directive stated that all such incidents must be reported to the FBI OGC as potential intelligence violations regardless of whether the information was requested by the FBI or erroneously produced by the credit reporting agency. The memorandum directed that any improperly obtained consumer full credit reports be removed from the files and that any possible intelligence violations identified through the review be reported. We describe the results of the FCRA review in Chapter Three of this report. In sum, the review showed that the FBI issued at least 33 NSLs seeking consumer full credit reports in counterintelligence cases in violation of the FCRA NSL statute and internal FBI policy. In 29 of these 33 matters, the FBI obtained the consumer full credit reports. The unauthorized information was sequestered in 23 instances, returned to the third party provider in 1 instance, and in 5 instances the ECs did not state what was done with the information.

The FBI General Counsel also provided training at the counterintelligence conferences for SACs in January and February 2007 regarding NSLs, the SACs' responsibilities prior to authorizing NSLs, and the fact that an NSL for a consumer full credit report is not authorized in a counterintelligence investigation absent an international terrorism nexus.

In addition, new NSL training addresses the distinction between the two FCRA NSL authorities and emphasizes the need to identify a nexus to international terrorism before generating an NSL pursuant to 15 U.S.C. § 1681v in a counterintelligence investigation.

OIG Analysis: **4(c)** The FBI's FCRA review revealed that 20 percent of the FBI's field offices (11 of 56) issued a total of 33 improper FCRAv NSLs during 2002 through 2006, the 5-year period covered by the review. In 29 of these instances, the FBI improperly obtained consumer full credit reports. The review determined that only two of these matters had previously been reported to the FBI OGC pursuant to the mandatory self-reporting requirement. The review also showed that 64 percent of the FBI's field offices (35 of 56) issued a total of 233 NSLs seeking limited credit information pursuant to 15 U.S.C. § 1681u during the review period, in response to which the credit reporting agencies improperly produced consumer full credit reports. Only 6 of the 233 unauthorized collections had previously been reported to the FBI OGC pursuant to the mandatory self-reporting requirement. Thus, only 6 percent of the improper requests and 3 percent of the unauthorized collections were self-reported to the FBI OGC.

The results of the FBI's review demonstrated continued confusion or inadequate knowledge about the statutory requirements for FCRA NSLs among case agents, supervisors, and CDCs throughout 2006. Moreover, the results demonstrated the ineffectiveness of the FBI's mandatory self-reporting requirements. The case agents, their supervisors, their attorneys, and the SACs did not recognize that they had made improper requests under the FCRA. Similarly, the case agents and analysts who reviewed the responsive records did not recognize the receipt of the unauthorized collections.

The OIG believes that the steps thus far taken by the FBI will help clarify the distinctions between the two types of FCRA NSLs. In addition, the new NSL data system is programmed so that FBI personnel cannot generate an NSL request for a consumer full credit report from a counterintelligence case file. Also, as demonstrated in the new NSL data system training module, when the statute under which the records are requested is selected, the language of the statute appears in a textbox. The text of the NSL statute informs the requester what records the FBI is authorized to obtain under each NSL statute. The results of the FBI's review of FCRA NSLs will also assist the FBI in developing further training to assist agents and supervisors in distinguishing the two types of FCRA NSLs.

However, successful implementation of this recommendation will require review by case agents, their supervisors, and CDCs and Headquarters attorneys of all FCRAv NSLs to verify the required nexus to international terrorism exists. To identify any unauthorized collection of records obtained in response to any type of FCRA NSL, the responsive records must be carefully and consistently reviewed upon receipt. Case agents and their supervisors must be vigilant to ensure that any unauthorized collections are promptly identified and reported in accordance with FBI policies.

FBI Actions Taken to Address the Recommendation: **4(d) reinforcing internal FBI policy requiring that NSLs must be issued from investigative files, not from control files:** In an EC dated February 23, 2007, the FBI OGC mandates that NSLs be issued from open investigative files and that the NSL approval EC must not refer solely to a control file number. The Comprehensive Guidance EC also prohibits NSLs from being issued solely from a control file. The EC notes that absent reference to an authorized investigation it is difficult for the FBI to ensure for purposes of congressional reporting and auditing that the requirements of the NSL statute are met.

The new NSL data system incorporates the requirements of the February 23, 2007, EC in its programming by precluding case agents from generating an NSL solely from a control file.

OIG Analysis: **4(d)** The steps taken by the FBI reinforce internal policy requiring that NSLs be issued only from investigative files, not solely from control files. The clear guidance contained in the February 23, 2007, EC mandates that NSLs be issued from open investigative cases and further states that: (1) the NSL approval EC must refer to the investigative case file or sub-file number of the investigation to which the NSL relates; (2) NSLs should not be issued under control file numbers; and (3) investigative activity requiring an open investigation, such as issuing NSLs, may not be conducted solely from a control file. This policy was reiterated in the Comprehensive Guidance EC and also is referenced in the FBI's mandatory NSL training provided for field agents assigned to counterterrorism or counter-intelligence squads. Additionally, the new NSL data system will ensure that NSLs are not being requested solely from control or administrative files.

Both the Attorney General's Guidelines for FBI National Security Investigations and Foreign Intelligence Collection (NSI Guidelines) and FBI policy require that an NSL issued in a national security investigation be issued from an open investigative file. Regular monitoring that includes file reviews and periodic reminders will help ensure that NSLs are issued only from open national security investigation case files.

Recommendation No. 5

Consider seeking legislative amendment to the *Electronic Communications Privacy Act* to define the phrase "telephone toll billing records information."

Background: We found in our first NSL report that FBI agents and attorneys frequently had questions regarding the types of records they could obtain when requesting "toll billing records information," a term that is not defined in the ECPA NSL statute. The imprecision of the statutory language and sparse case law generated multiple inquiries by CDCs to NSLB attorneys and confusion on the part of communication service providers who provided different types of information in response to the FBI's ECPA NSLs. Accordingly, we recommended that the FBI consider seeking legislative revision of the ECPA NSL statute to clarify the records the FBI is permitted to obtain and ensure consistent interpretation of the statute.

FBI Action Taken to Address the Recommendation: Based on recommendations from the FBI, the Department has drafted a proposed amendment to clarify the phrase "telephone toll billing records information" in the ECPA. The proposed amendment specifies the types of information the FBI can obtain pursuant to the ECPA NSL statute. The proposed amendment was cleared by the Office of Management and Budget and was sent to Congress on July 13, 2007.[13] The proposed amendment would authorize the FBI to obtain the following records in response to ECPA NSLs:

- name;
- address;
- local and long distance telephone connection records, or records of session times and durations;
- length of service (including start date) and types of service utilized;
- telephone or instrument number or other subscriber number or identity, including any temporarily assigned network address;
- means and source of payment for such service (including any credit card or bank account number); and
- records identifying the origin, routing, or destination of electronic communications.

OIG Analysis: The OIG agrees that, if enacted, the proposed amendment to the ECPA NSL statute would clarify the meaning of the phrase "telephone toll billing records information" by specifying the types of records and information that the FBI can obtain in counterterrorism and counterintelligence

[13] The FBI OGC had no additional information on the status of the proposed legislation as of February 2008.

investigations from electronic communication service providers and remote computing services.

Recommendation No. 6

Consider measures that would enable FBI agents and analysts to (a) label or tag their use of information derived from national security letters in analytical intelligence products and (b) identify when and how often information derived from NSLs is provided to law enforcement authorities for use in criminal proceedings.

Background: We found in our first NSL report that the FBI generates a variety of analytical intelligence products using information derived from NSLs. These include analyses of communication and financial links between investigative subjects and others, as well as analyses of NSL-derived data in relation to information developed from other intelligence techniques that are stored in other FBI databases, such as the Investigative Data Warehouse. NSL-derived data also is used to generate more formal intelligence products, such as Intelligence Information Reports, Intelligence Assessments, and Intelligence Bulletins. These products are stored in various FBI databases, shared within the Department and with Joint Terrorism Task Forces (JTTF), and disseminated to other federal agencies and other members of the Intelligence Community. The FBI also provides information derived from NSLs to law enforcement authorities for use in criminal proceedings. However, because NSL-derived information is not marked, tagged, or otherwise identified as coming from NSLs when it is entered in FBI databases or when it is shared with law enforcement authorities or other Intelligence Community members, it is impossible to determine when and how often the FBI provided NSL-derived information to law enforcement authorities for use in criminal proceedings (one of the topics the Patriot Reauthorization Act directed the OIG to address in our NSL reports). Accordingly, we recommended that the FBI consider measures to label or tag NSL-derived information so that the FBI's use of the information can be better tracked in intelligence products and in criminal proceedings.

FBI Actions Taken to Address the Recommendation: At the direction of the Attorney General, in July 2007 the Department's Chief Privacy and Civil Liberties Officer convened a National Security Letter Working Group (NSL Working Group) to examine issues regarding retention of NSL-derived information. The Attorney General directed the NSL Working Group to evaluate how NSL-derived information is used, stored, and disseminated, with a particular focus on the retention of NSL-derived information.[14] The NSL Working Group considered information provided to it by the FBI

[14] We provide further analysis of the NSL Working Group's recommendations in Section III of this chapter.

about enhancements to the FBI's information technology systems designed to support agents when handling NSL-derived data.[15]

The NSL Working Group concluded that tagging of NSL-derived information was not feasible at the time, but it recommended that the FBI require NSL-derived information to be placed in a specific sub-file of the pertinent investigative file. In a draft memorandum to the Attorney General, dated August 17, 2007 (NSL Working Group August 2007 Draft), the NSL Working Group stated:

> Because the [FBI's] new systems provide for the structured storage of information and NSL information can be segregated in the database, the Working Group concluded that the individual tagging of NSL-derived data did not provide any measurable value for privacy protections at this time. That said, and as explained in more detail in the FBI's proposed directive, ensuring that information derived from NSLs is appropriately labeled as such and tied to a specific NSL does function as a form of tagging. The benefit to privacy of requiring additional tagging, such as through meta-tags, was determined to place an undue burden on the operation of such an important tool.

In brief, the NSL Working Group concluded that additional measures requiring the tagging or labeling of NSL-derived information would "place an undue burden on the operation [of NSLs.]"

As an alternative to tagging, the NSL Working Group recommended that the FBI label all NSL-derived information and place the paper copies or electronic media in an investigative case sub-file specifically designated for NSL-derived information. The NSL Working Group also recommended that the FBI implement minimization procedures for NSL-derived information that were developed by the NSL Working Group. Several of these proposed procedures replicated procedures that the FBI had already developed and implemented in response to the OIG's recommendations in our first NSL report.

The NSL Working Group also concluded that existing controls and enhanced guidelines established by the FBI on the acquisition and use of NSL-derived information, if properly followed, could protect privacy interests. The NSL Working Group also stated that the FBI has made significant progress in responding to and rectifying previous concerns about its compliance with statutory and guidelines limitations regarding the use of NSLs, has a better mechanism for tracking its use of NSLs, and is subject to additional oversight through the NSD.

---

[15] The enhancements included improved processes for: (1) approving and authorizing the issuing of NSLs; (2) reviewing and identifying the responsiveness of records produced pursuant to NSL requests; and (3) ensuring that only NSL-derived information deemed to have investigative value be uploaded into any FBI database.

OIG Analysis: As discussed later in this chapter, while we agree that the FBI has made significant progress in addressing our concerns about compliance with NSL authorities, we believe it is too soon to say that the FBI has "rectified" many of the problems we identified in our first NSL report and too early to fully assess whether the new systems and controls will reduce or eliminate these concerns.

The OIG believes that the NSL Working Group's analysis of the tagging issue does not take into consideration the FBI's existing process for labeling NSL-derived information in the ACS system and Telephone Applications database, and whether that process can be adapted-without undue burden and cost to follow NSL-derived information as it travels through other databases and uses. The OIG recommends the FBI and the NSL Working Group give additional consideration to whether the FBI could build upon existing databases without undue burden or cost to label or tag NSL-derived information and to identify when and how often information derived from NSLs is used in analytical intelligence products and provided to law enforcement authorities for use in criminal proceedings.

Recommendation No. 7

Take steps to ensure that the FBI does not improperly issue exigent letters.

Background: In our first NSL report, we found that on over 700 occasions the FBI obtained telephone toll billing records or subscriber information from 3 communication service providers without first issuing NSLs or grand jury subpoenas as the statute requires. Instead, the FBI obtained the records with "exigent letters" that were signed by FBI Headquarters Counterterrorism Division personnel who were not authorized to sign NSLs. We also found through interviews of the Counterterrorism Division's Communications Analysis Unit (CAU) personnel and a review of FBI documents that there sometimes were no pending national security investigations associated with the requests at the time the exigent letters were sent. In addition, we found that due to inadequate recordkeeping, the FBI was unable to provide reliable documentation to substantiate that NSLs or other legal process was issued to cover the records obtained in response to a sample of exigent letters for which we requested such documentation. We also determined that exigent letters sometimes were used in non-emergency circumstances.

We identified additional problems with respect to the CAU's efforts to issue after-the-fact NSLs to cover records obtained from the three communication service providers under contract with the FBI. Among these problems were that the CAU generally: (1) did not inform field division personnel who they asked to issue the NSLs that the information had already been acquired by the FBI and (2) did not consistently provide information establishing predication for the requests necessary to satisfy the ECPA NSL statute, the Attorney General's NSI Guidelines, and internal FBI policy. As a result, the approval ECs issued in connection with the after-the-fact NSLs sometimes violated the Attorney General's NSI guidelines and FBI internal policy.

We concluded that by issuing exigent letters rather than NSLs, the FBI circumvented the requirements of the ECPA NSL statute and violated the Attorney General's NSI Guidelines and internal FBI policy. We were not convinced by the legal justifications offered by FBI attorneys for acquiring the records through exigent letters: (1) to reconcile the strict requirements of the ECPA NSL statute with the FBI's mission to prevent terrorist attacks and (2) that use of exigent letters could be defended as a use of the ECPA's emergency voluntary disclosure authority for acquiring non-content information (18 U.S.C. § 2702(c)(4)). Accordingly, we recommended that the FBI take steps to ensure that the FBI does not issue exigent letters.

FBI Actions Taken to Address the Recommendation: In an EC dated March 1, 2007, the FBI OGC issued a directive prohibiting the use of exigent letters that promise future legal process and reiterated the authorized procedures for obtaining telephone records pursuant to the emergency voluntary disclosure provision of the ECPA, 18 U.S.C. § 2702 (c)(4). The Comprehensive Guidance EC and mandatory NSL training provided to field and Headquarters personnel reiterated the prohibition on the use of exigent letters. In the course of the FBI's review of field and Headquarters NSLs, the Inspection Division included questions designed to ascertain whether exigent letters were used by FBI personnel outside the CAU. The inspectors found no instances in which exigent letters were used by the field in the case files they reviewed.

The FBI OGC also told us it is meeting regularly with the NSD to address issues previously identified by the OIG in our first NSL report. In addition, as discussed further in Recommendation No. 9, NSLB attorneys regularly attend operational meetings of the Headquarters Counterterrorism units that had previously issued exigent letters and Counterintelligence units to provide legal advice, spot legal issues, and provide oversight on national security matters, including issuance of NSLs. The NSLB has also assigned two NSLB attorneys, one each to the New York and Los Angeles field divisions to provide advice on the use of intelligence techniques, including NSLs, authorized by the Attorney General's NSL Guidelines. Additionally, the FBI OGC said it has added two Senior Executive Service positions within the NSLB to oversee national security matters.

OIG Analysis: The OIG agrees with the FBI's actions to prohibit use of exigent letters. Since our first NSL report, the FBI OGC has sent several communications and reiterated in periodic mandatory NSL training that exigent letters promising legal process in the future are prohibited. The FBI also has clarified the methods by which it may obtain certain non-content telephone and e-mail transactional data in emergency circumstances in accordance with authority in the ECPA, 18 U.S.C. § 2702(c)(4).

The OIG believes that by issuing two ECs, providing mandatory NSL training prohibiting use of exigent letters, requiring NSLB attorneys to regularly attend counterterrorism and counterintelligence operational meetings, placing NSLB attorneys in the New York and Los Angeles field divisions, and adding two Senior Executive Service positions within NSLB, the FBI has taken the steps necessary to provide needed oversight of national security letter matters. While we have no knowledge of additional exigent letters being issued in 2007 subsequent to the March 1, 2007, and June 1, 2007, guidance memoranda, the FBI must continue to emphasize in mandatory NSL training for all personnel assigned to programs overseen by the National Security Branch and to FBI managers the prohibition against using exigent letters and other circumventions of the NSL statutes. In our forthcoming report, we will provide additional recommendations designed to address the findings of our investigation of the FBI's use of exigent letters.

Recommendation No. 8

Take steps to ensure that, where appropriate, the FBI makes requests for information in accordance with the requirements of national security letter authorities.

Background: In the course of our first NSL review, we identified a variety of instances in which the FBI used NSLs contrary to statutory limitations, Attorney General Guidelines, or internal guidance or policies. In addition to the use of exigent letters (discussed above in connection with Recommendation No. 7), the instances of improper or illegal use of NSL authorities in 2003 through 2005 generally fell into the following categories:

- issuing NSLs after the investigative authority to conduct the underlying investigation lapsed;
- obtaining telephone toll billing records and e-mail subscriber information concerning the wrong individuals;
- obtaining information that was not requested in the NSL;
- obtaining information beyond the time period referenced in the NSL;
- issuing FCRA NSLs seeking records that the FBI was not authorized to obtain, such as issuing FCRAv NSLs seeking consumer full credit reports for counterintelligence investigations with no international terrorism nexus;
- issuing an ECPA NSL seeking an investigative subject's educational records, including applications for admission, emergency contact information, and associations with campus organizations; and

- issuing NSLs exclusively out of control files rather than from investigative files in violation of FBI policy.

In our first NSL report, we also identified repeated failures to adhere to internal FBI OGC guidance regarding the documentation necessary for approval of NSLs. In our review of 77 investigative files and 293 NSLs in 4 FBI field offices, we found that 60 percent of the investigative files contained one or more of the following infractions:

- NSL approval ECs that were not reviewed and initialed by one or more of the required field supervisors or CDC;
- NSL approval ECs that did not contain all of the required information; and
- NSLs that did not contain the recitals or other information required by the authorizing statutes.

While these infractions did not rise to the level of possible intelligence violations, they were violations of the FBI's internal control policies established to ensure the proper review, use, and tracking of NSLs. For example, review of the NSL package is designed to ensure that errors or inadequate predication are identified and corrected before an NSL is issued. If elements of the approval EC or the NSL are missing, the FBI official signing the NSL cannot be assured that the required predication, specifications of items sought, and statutory authority are correct.

FBI Actions Taken to Address the Recommendation:

New Guidance: The June 2007 Comprehensive Guidance EC provides guidance on the use, requirements, and reporting of NSLs by reminding FBI personnel of the statutory and procedural authorizations and restrictions; requiring sufficient and independent supervisory and legal reviews; requiring that FBI personnel use "model" NSL and approval EC forms posted on the NSLB's website to ensure all statutory requirements are met and decrease the likelihood of errors; providing checklists for use in drafting the approval EC and NSL, for reviewing responses to NSLs, and prior to disseminating NSL-derived information; and identifying what constitutes a possible intelligence violation and specifying required actions in the event a possible intelligence violation is discovered.

The Comprehensive Guidance EC described the four NSL statutes and the specific types of information that can be obtained from third parties using NSLs. It also emphasized that the content of communications cannot be obtained with an NSL. It clarified that the [Text not available] may not be requested through an NSL as a matter of policy, even though these elements have not been determined to be "content" under the ECPA NSL statute.

The guidance cautioned drafters of approval ECs and NSLs to review them carefully to ensure that the information requested by the EC (such as telephone, e-mail, or other account numbers) match those in the NSL and that there are no typographical errors that could result in unauthorized collection and a possible intelligence violation. The guidance also directed that all approval ECs and NSLs must be reviewed for legal sufficiency by the CDC at the field office or by NSLB attorneys at Headquarters before being forwarded to the appropriate designated approving official.

On March 5, 2007, the FBI NSB issued a separate guidance memorandum clarifying the distinctions between the two NSL authorities in the FCRA.

Training: The NSLB has developed a new NSL training module incorporating the findings in the OIG's first NSL report and addressing the common errors discussed in the report such as typographical errors, confusion regarding the two FCRA NSL authorities, and legal review and approval of NSLs. The training refers to the FBI's March 2007 prohibition on the use of exigent letters that promise future legal process and establishes procedures for properly obtaining information in emergency situations in accordance with 18 U.S.C. § 2702. FBI OGC officials told us that the FBI OGC and the NSLB will review the findings of the Inspection Division's review of NSLs in the field and Headquarters divisions to determine if additional procedures or training would improve compliance with this authority.

The FBI OGC has mandated that all NSLB attorneys visiting field offices conduct NSL training during their visits. From March 2007 through February 2008, 45 of the FBI's 56 field offices and at least 3,042 FBI field and Headquarters personnel involved in preparing and reviewing NSLs received live NSL training from NSLB attorneys.[16] While some Headquarters units had already received NSL training following the release of our first NSL report, mandatory training for personnel in the Counterterrorism, Counterintelligence, and Cyber Divisions was conducted in early May 2007. The NSLB and the Training Division developed an online virtual academy course on NSLs that will be required for all personnel involved in drafting and approving NSLs and will supplement live training. NSL training also has been provided to non-FBI agents serving on the JTTFs nationwide.

On August 21, 2007, the FBI stated in a written response to an OIG request for information, that all FBI employees must complete mandatory training related to NSLs. According to the memorandum, NSL training is offered to new professional staff and to all new Special Agents. A mandatory 2-hour

[16] Attendees at these training sessions included Secretaries, Paralegals, Intelligence Analysts, Linguists, Special Agents, Supervisory Special Agents, Section and Unit Chiefs, non-FBI Task Force Officers, Supervisory Resident Agents, Assistant Division Counsels and Chief Division Counsels, Assistant Special Agents in Charge, Special Agents in Charge, FBI OGC attorneys, and Deputy Assistant Directors.

block of instruction is provided during the 17th week of New Agent Training.

Management Meetings, SAC Conferences, and the Annual CDC Conference: As noted above, the FBI Deputy Director told us that NSLs were a major topic of discussion at quarterly Strategy Performance Sessions he chaired via teleconference that were attended by SACs from the FBI's 56 field offices. At the second quarter 2007 sessions, the Deputy Director discussed the findings from the OIG's first NSL report and the steps that the FBI has taken to resolve the OIG recommendations and to implement procedures directed by the Attorney General.

Also, SACs told us that NSL compliance was discussed at the annual SAC conference held in October 2007. NSLB attorneys also provided a presentation on use of NSLs at the CDC conference in July 2007, which included an overview of the findings in the OIG's first NSL report; a discussion of each of the NSL statutes; an overview of the NSLB's guidance on standards and approvals for NSLs; and the required elements of the NSLs, model NSLs, and approval ECs. NSLs also were discussed at squad meetings within field offices, and field office personnel told us that they received numerous e-mails from FBI OGC attorneys and CDCs providing guidance on NSLs.

Office of Integrity and Compliance: As described more fully in Section III of this chapter, the FBI has created a new Office of Integrity and Compliance (OIC) that reports to the Deputy Director. The mission of the OIC is to develop and oversee a program that develops compliance standards and training programs; identifies compliance risks in FBI operations and makes sure that necessary audits are performed; and ensures that national security investigations and other FBI activities are conducted in a manner consistent with laws, regulations, and policies. The OIC is also required to deliver an annual report on compliance issues.[17]

Enhancements to Information Technology: As described in connection with Recommendations Nos. 2 and 4, the new NSL data system is designed to guide the user to more accurately and completely prepare NSLs and route the NSL through the required levels of review. Upon completion of all approvals, the system will generate approval ECs and NSLs for signature by field or Headquarters approving officials. The new NSL data system also is programmed to preclude users from preparing an NSL seeking a consumer full credit report in a counterintelligence investigation that lacks an international terrorism nexus. For each type of NSL, the data system generates a link to the text of the statute to inform the requester what records are authorized to be requested.

[17] Deputy Director's Office, Federal Bureau of Investigation, electronic communication to Director's Office, Finance Division, and Inspection Division, Establishment of New FBI HQ Divisions; Director's Office Creation of the Office of Integrity and Compliance, June 5, 2007.

Additional Support for the FBI OGC: The FBI OGC has been assigned two new Senior Executive Service positions within the NSLB. One position will head a new section overseeing operational aspects of national security law while the other will head a National Security Law Training and Policy Section. The FBI told us that these positions were filled in February 2008.

FBI OGC officials told us that they are meeting regularly with the NSD and consulting with it on the development of new policy regarding NSLs to address issues identified in our first NSL report. In addition, the NSD and the NSLB conducted 15 national security reviews in 2007, which included a review of the use of NSLs. These reviews were accompanied by NSL training if such training had not recently been given.

OIG Analysis: These initiatives are positive steps that will help the FBI ensure NSLs are issued in accordance with the requirements of national security letter authorities. The Comprehensive Guidance EC compiled in one document NSL guidance and memoranda that had previously been issued piecemeal over several years. This guidance also addressed several of the major findings in our first NSL report, clarified the NSL process, and resolved prior conflicting guidance. We found that the Comprehensive Guidance EC was favorably received by field personnel, who described it during our interviews as "very comprehensive," "very helpful," "a very worthwhile resource," and "thorough and well done."

The FBI has also identified additional opportunities and methods for providing NSL training so all FBI personnel assigned to national security investigations will be aware of the contents of the guidance, including the requirements of the statutes and the required steps in the NSL preparation and approval process.

By issuing the Comprehensive Guidance EC, providing additional training on NSL procedures to field and Headquarters personnel, adding two senior level positions in the FBI OGC to oversee legal issues arising in national security investigations, participating in the NSD's national security reviews, and creating a new NSL data system, we believe that the FBI's ability to comply with NSL authorities will improve significantly.

Recommendation No. 9

Implement measures to ensure that the FBI OGC is consulted about activities undertaken by FBI Headquarters National Security Branch, including its operational support activities, that could generate requests for records from third parties that the FBI is authorized to obtain exclusively though the use of its national security letter authorities.

Background: In our first NSL report, we noted our concern about the ability of NSLB attorneys to obtain accurate and complete information about the

FBI's use of NSL authorities. Our review of the FBI's use of exigent letters used by the CAU and "certificate letters" used by the Terrorist Financing Operations Section (TFOS) determined that FBI OGC attorneys were not consulted in advance about tools used by Headquarters CTD units.[18] For example, we determined that NSLB attorneys responsible for providing guidance on the FBI's use of NSL authorities were unaware of the CAU's practice of using exigent letters until late 2004, although CAU personnel had been using these letters as early as 2003.

We also determined that the TFOS issued at least 19 certificate letters to a Federal Reserve Bank seeking financial records concerning 244 named individuals instead of issuing NSLs pursuant to the *Right to Financial Privacy Act* (RFPA). We also found that the TFOS continued to issue certificate letters despite an August 2004 restriction on this type of request by the FBI Assistant General Counsel. As a matter of policy, the Federal Reserve Bank requires that the FBI issue RFPA NSLs to obtain its records. Accordingly, Federal Reserve attorneys later stated that the Federal Reserve Bank should not have provided the bank records in response to the certificate letters because they were not duly authorized RFPA NSLs.

In our first NSL report, we also found that FBI Headquarters personnel regularly issued NSLs seeking electronic communication transactional records exclusively from "control files" rather than from investigative files, a practice not permitted by FBI policy. This practice prevents a reviewing or approving authority from determining whether the NSLs were issued in the course of authorized investigations or whether the information sought in the NSLs was relevant to those investigations. Documentation of this information is necessary to establish compliance with NSL statutes, the Attorney General's NSI Guidelines, and internal FBI policy.

Accordingly, to ensure that FBI OGC attorneys are consulted about activities undertaken by the NSB, we recommended that the FBI implement measures to promote timely consultation about the NSB's activities, including its operational support activities.

FBI Actions Taken to Address the Recommendation: The FBI OGC mandated in April 2007 that NSLB attorneys involved in national security law matters regularly attend operational meetings to provide legal advice and oversight. Attorneys in the two NSLB units that provide legal advice to counterterrorism operations regularly attend meetings of the CAU, the Electronic Surveillance Operations and Sharing Unit, and the Communication Exploitation Section at Headquarters. The NSLB attorneys that provide

[18] These certificate letters were used instead of issuing NSLs pursuant to the *Right to Financial Privacy Act* (RFPA). The letters contained certifications that there were "specific and articulable facts giving reason to believe that the customer or entity whose records are sought is a foreign power or an agent of a foreign power as defined in 50 U.S.C. § 1801."

legal advice to counterintelligence operations now also regularly attend operational meetings to play a more active legal role. Additionally, NSLB Unit Chiefs regularly attend operational meetings and have daily contact with their units to provide legal advice, to spot legal issues, and to provide guidance and oversight on national security matters, including NSLs. The NSLB has also assigned an NSLB attorney to each of two large field offices, New York and Los Angeles, to support the national security law program in those offices.

NSLB attorneys also have provided new NSL training to operational units in the CTD and the Counterintelligence Division. The FBI OGC has posted an NSL training presentation on the NSLB's website and has posted online a virtual academy training course.

The Comprehensive Guidance EC mandates that all NSLs and NSL approval ECs issued by Headquarters components be reviewed and approved by NSLB attorneys. Prior to this mandate, Headquarters officials authorized to sign NSLs were encouraged but not required to consult with the NSLB.

OIG Analysis: The OIG believes that the requirement that all Headquarters-issued NSLs be reviewed by NSLB attorneys, the attendance of NSLB attorneys at meetings of the CTD and the Counter-intelligence Division sections to which they are assigned, and mandatory attendance by NSLB attorneys at certain CTD operational meetings should help identify use of new intelligence tools or unconventional requests that may implicate NSL authorities or other intelligence techniques. In addition, mandatory quarterly training of personnel from the specified CTD units should help to ensure that FBI OGC attorneys are consulted about the CTD's activities.

However, we believe the FBI should also have NSLB attorneys similarly participate in operational meetings of other units in the CTD and the Counterintelligence Division in addition to the units that already have been associated with improper use of NSLs. By participating in these operational meetings, it is more likely that the FBI OGC will be in a position to identify and address requests for information that may be inconsistent with the FBI's obligations under the NSL statutes, applicable Attorney General Guidelines, and internal policies governing the use of NSLs.

Recommendation No. 10

Ensure that Chief Division Counsel and Assistant Division Counsel provide close and independent review of requests to issue national security letters.

Background: In our first NSL report, we identified circumstances in which some CDCs and Assistant Division Counsels (ADC) were reluctant to provide an unbiased, independent legal review of NSLs for fear of antagonizing or second-guessing their supervisors, the Special Agents in Charge, who had already approved the underlying investigation. While recognizing that review of NSLs is only one of many issues on which CDCs' independent legal advice is critical, we recommended that the FBI consider measures to ensure that CDCs and ADCs provide thorough and independent oversight of NSL requests.

FBI Actions Taken to Address the Recommendation: The Comprehensive Guidance EC mandates that CDCs and ADCs provide independent legal review of NSLs. The EC stated that the CDCs' and ADCs' legal reviews are separate from and independent of the investigative reviews conducted by SACs or Headquarters approving authorities. The guidance stated that a legal review should consider whether:

- the information sought in the NSL is relevant to an authorized national security investigation (an investigation to protect against international terrorism or clandestine intelligence activities);
- there is an open and authorized FBI preliminary or full investigation from which the NSL is being issued; and
- there is sufficient predication for the underlying investigation and that predication is sufficiently detailed in the approval EC.

The guidance also stated that if the CDCs, ADCs, or NSLB attorneys determine that legal sufficiency does not exist, they must return the NSL document to the requesting employee for revision. Similarly, if the attorney determines that less intrusive means of obtaining the information are feasible, the NSL will not be approved.

On March 15, 2007, the FBI General Counsel held a conference call with all CDCs and on March 30, 2007, sent an e-mail to all CDCs and ADCs reminding them of the need to provide independent legal review of NSLs. The FBI Director stressed at a conference of all SACs the importance of CDCs providing independent legal advice and stressing the role of the head of the office in creating an environment that would foster such advice. The Deputy Director said that at the October 2007 SAC conference and during quarterly Strategy Performance Sessions, he also informed SACs of the need for them to recognize the independence of the CDCs and ADCs. NSL training also emphasizes the requirement that legal review be conducted by CDCs, ADCs, or NSLB attorneys.

The FBI General Counsel and the FBI's senior leadership are still considering how to address the issues identified in our first NSL report arising from the current reporting chain for CDCs. While CDCs continue to report to field division SACs, the General Counsel told us that she is considering whether the CDCs are assigned an unreasonable level of collateral duties that distract them from focusing on their legal duties. If she concludes this is the case, she will discuss the matter with the SACs. As we noted in our first NSL report, this issue involves difficult institutional questions beyond the issue of compliance with NSL authorities.

OIG Analysis: The actions taken by the FBI reinforced that CDCs and ADCs should provide independent legal review of requests to issue NSLs. The Deputy Director of the FBI and the Assistant Director of the CTD both told us that they believe CDCs exercise independent judgment in evaluating NSLs and could not identify any circumstances in which they had not done so. The Deputy Director stated that it is in the best interest of the SACs to have the CDCs' best, candid advice—even if such advice is not what SACs want to hear. He said he has discussed this issue with SACs during his quarterly meetings with them.

However, further action in response to this recommendation is still being considered by the FBI. We believe it is important for the FBI to resolve the factors weighing for and against modification of the CDCs' reporting chain within the FBI. Review of NSLs is only one of the many oversight functions exercised by CDCs, and the FBI needs the CDCs' independent judgment in ensuring that field agents and supervisors scrupulously observe statutory authorities, Attorney General's Guidelines, and FBI policies governing national security investigations and other authorities.

Recommendation No. 11

Provide guidance and training to Special Agents, Chief Division Counsel, and all FBI officials authorized to sign NSLs on the meaning and application of the Attorney General's Guidelines' proviso calling for use of the "least intrusive collection techniques feasible" to the FBI's use of national security letter authorities.

Background: The Attorney General's NSI Guidelines provide that:

> Choice of Methods. The conduct of investigations and other activities authorized by these Guidelines may present choices between the use of information collection methods that are more or less intrusive, considering such factors as the effect on the privacy of individuals and potential damage to reputation. As Executive Order 12333 § 2.4 provides, "the least intrusive collection techniques feasible" are to be used in such situations. The FBI shall not hesitate to use any lawful techniques consistent with these Guidelines, even if intrusive, where the degree of intrusiveness is warranted in light of the seriousness of a threat to the national security or the strength of the information indicating its existence. This point is to be particularly observed in investigations relating to terrorism.[19]

[19] NSI Guidelines, § I(B)(2).

We found that the FBI had not provided clear guidance describing how case agents and supervisors should apply the Attorney General Guidelines' requirement to use the "least intrusive techniques feasible" when deciding how to use and sequence NSLs. While we recognized that there cannot be one model regarding the use of NSLs in all types of national security investigations, and that the FBI cannot issue definitive guidance addressing when and what types of NSLs should be issued at each stage of investigations, we recommended that the FBI provide guidance and training on the use and sequencing of NSLs. In providing such guidance and training, the FBI could highlight and reconcile the important privacy considerations that underlie the Attorney General Guidelines' proviso with the FBI's mission to detect and deter terrorist attacks and espionage threats.

FBI Actions Taken to Address the Recommendation: The Comprehensive Guidance EC requires that as part of their independent legal reviews of NSLs for legal sufficiency, CDCs, ADCs, or NSLB attorneys must not approve an NSL if a less intrusive means of obtaining the information is feasible.

On December 20, 2007, the FBI OGC issued guidance to all divisions titled Least Intrusive Techniques in National Security and Criminal Investigations that further addressed this recommendation. The FBI General Counsel told us that a draft of this guidance had previously been provided to civil liberties groups for comment.

OIG Analysis: By providing guidance on application of the Attorney General Guidelines' proviso on the review of NSLs in its Comprehensive Guidance EC, and by issuing the December 20, 2007, guidance on Least Intrusive Techniques in National Security and Criminal Investigations, the FBI has taken significant steps toward addressing this recommendation. However, because the guidance includes many factors to consider when deciding when and how to employ a particular technique, the FBI also needs to provide training on the practical application of this guidance for agents and supervisors.

OIG Conclusions on FBI's Corrective Actions

Based on our analysis of the steps that the FBI has taken, as well as our interviews with FBI leadership, field managers, and personnel involved in the NSL process, we believe that the FBI has made significant progress in addressing the serious problems and deficiencies identified by the OIG in our first NSL report. The FBI's executive leadership, including the Director, Deputy Director, and General Counsel, have expressed their commitment to ensuring that Headquarters and field managers, supervisors, agents, analysts, and support staff understand the seriousness of the FBI's shortcomings in its use of NSLs, the proper use of NSLs, and each of their responsibilities for correcting the deficiencies. The Deputy Director and the

General Counsel continue to emphasize and discuss critical NSL topics at meetings and conferences of executive managers and CDCs.

Since our first NSL report was provided to the FBI, the FBI has issued approximately nine NSL policies and sent numerous other ECs to the field and Headquarters divisions providing guidance on topics that include proper usage of NSLs and statutory and procedural authorizations and restrictions; prohibition on the use of exigent letters; review and redaction of NSL-responsive information; the requirement for sufficient and independent supervisory and legal reviews; and identification of and procedures for submitting possible intelligence violations. The FBI also has developed a new NSL data system with model NSLs and approval ECs that are required to be used when issuing and reviewing NSLs. These measures should eliminate or reduce the types of typographical errors found in the past. To reinforce the new policies and guidelines, FBI OGC attorneys provided NSL training to 45 FBI field offices and at least 3,042 field and Headquarters personnel involved in preparing and reviewing NSLs from March through February 2008. An online virtual academy course on NSLs has also been developed and will be mandatory for all personnel involved in drafting and approving NSLs.

Beyond responding to the OIG's specific recommendations, the FBI has conducted three field reviews on NSL usage to make an independent assessment of the seriousness of the problem and to determine what additional measures were needed. (These reviews are more fully discussed in Chapter Three of this report.)

However, several actions that are necessary to fully satisfy our recommendations are still under development or are in need of additional work by the FBI or the Department. Specifically, the FBI needs to continue to work on:

- providing periodic training to all 56 field offices for those involved in the NSL process. This mandatory training needs to continue indefinitely to address the constant rotation of staff into positions that involve NSL-related work;
- meeting and working with the Chief Privacy and Civil Liberties Officer's NSL Working Group to give additional consideration to label or tag NSL-derived information and to identify when and how often this information is used in analytical intelligence products and provided to law enforcement authorities for use in criminal proceedings;
- fully addressing the current reporting chain for CDCs; and
- providing training on "least intrusive collection techniques" in national security and criminal investigations" to the field.

We believe it is too soon to conclude whether the new guidance, training, and systems put in place by the FBI in response to our first NSL report will fully eliminate the problems with the use of NSLs that we identified and that the FBI confirmed in its own reviews. At the same time, we believe that the FBI has made significant progress in addressing these issues and that the FBI's senior leadership is committed to addressing misuse of NSLs. However, to ensure that adherence to NSL authorities remains permanently embedded in FBI culture and practice, the FBI—and the Department—must be aggressive and vigilant in monitoring compliance with NSL authorities by reinforcing the rules governing the use of NSLs, implementing a sustained process for field and Headquarters verification that NSLs are being handled properly, and ensuring that any violations are identified and reported in a timely manner.

III. Other Corrective Measures Implemented by the FBI and Other Department Components

In this section we describe additional oversight measures implemented in 2007 by the FBI, the NSD, and the Office of the Deputy Attorney General relating to the use of national security letters. We describe the FBI's establishment of a new Office of Integrity and Compliance (OIC) and the NSD's new compliance reviews, termed national security reviews, which review compliance with NSL authorities and other intelligence techniques used by the FBI in national security investigations. In addition, we examine an August 2007 proposal to the Attorney General by the Department's Chief Privacy and Civil Liberties Officer that addresses how the FBI uses and retains NSL-derived information.

A. The FBI's Office of Integrity and Compliance

On July 13, 2007, the FBI announced creation of the OIC.[20] The FBI Director stated that the OIC was established to ensure that national security investigations and other FBI activities are conducted in a manner consistent with appropriate laws, regulations, and policies. According to the FBI's description of the OIC, its mission is "to develop, implement, and oversee a program that ensures there are processes and procedures in place that promote FBI compliance with both the letter and spirit of all applicable laws, regulations, and policies."[21] The OIC is charged with developing compliance standards, training programs, and risk assessments; ensuring that necessary

[20] Letter from the Attorney General and FBI Director to Richard B. Cheney, President of the Senate, July 13, 2007.

[21] Deputy Director's Office, Federal Bureau of Investigation, electronic communication to Director's Office, Finance Division, and Inspection Division, Establishment of New FBI HQ Divisions; Director's Office Creation of the Office of Integrity and Compliance, June 5, 2007.

audits are performed; and delivering an annual report on compliance issues.

1. Organization Structure and Operations

Under the organization plan, the Head of the OIC reports to the FBI's Deputy Director. Organizationally, the Integrity and Compliance Program consists of a steering committee (the "FBI Integrity and Compliance Council") that is chaired by the FBI Director and includes as members the Deputy Director; the Associate Deputy Director; the Executive Assistant Director (EAD) of the National Security Branch; the EAD of the Criminal, Cyber, Response, and Services Branch; the EAD of the Science and Technology Branch; the EAD of the Human Resources Branch; the Chief Information Officer; the Head of the OIC; the FBI's Chief Financial Officer; and the General Counsel. The Council is supported by the Executive Management Committees that are responsible for identifying compliance risks in five different functional areas of the FBI's operations: the National Security Branch, criminal investigations, investigative support, administration, and information technology.

Each Executive Management Committee is chaired by the EAD responsible for the functional area and includes as members the Assistant Director from the functional area; a Deputy General Counsel from the FBI OGC; representatives from the OIC; and other members as the chair finds necessary. The Executive Management Committees are required to meet at least four times a year to analyze the nature of the compliance risks facing their functional areas; identify specific risk areas; and assess and establish policies, procedures, and training to mitigate those risks. Within 2 days of an Executive Management Committee meeting, the committee chair is required to assess and rank the compliance risks, designate a "risk owner," and document the results with the OIC. The risk owner is responsible for further assessing the risk, determining whether corrective actions are warranted, and developing mitigation plans.

To conduct the risk assessments, the most significant risks identified by the Executive Management Committees are to be subjected to a detailed analysis by a compliance risk assessment team (called a Red Team) created by the risk owner with the assistance of the OIC. The Red Teams are staffed with a representative from the OIC, two subject matter experts from the organization having primary responsibility for the risk area, and a representative from the FBI OGC. The Red Teams will review the law, FBI policies, training, and monitoring requirements related to the issue. The Red Teams were directed to produce within 60 days of receiving the tasking a report analyzing the risks and developing a risk mitigation plan. Those reports will be provided to the risk owner and the pertinent Executive Management Committee chair for review and implementation of measures to mitigate the risks. In addition to reports of individual risks, the FBI planned to require the OIC to prepare a consolidated annual report on compliance risks throughout the FBI. In February 2008, the FBI informed us that it had decided to eliminate the requirements that Red Teams develop risk mitigation plans (but did not eliminate the risk assessment report) and that the Executive Management Committees prepare a consolidated annual report on compliance risks throughout the FBI. In addition, the FBI stated that the Executive Management Committees are to provide an annual report on "the state of the Integrity and Compliance program." Although it is not clear that the revised annual report will include a consolidated assessment of compliance risks, we believe that such a consolidated assessment listing all identified risks will be valuable to the FBI and the Attorney General.

FBI officials told the OIG that they also plan to divide personnel assigned to the OIC into two units: the Compliance Operations Unit and the Compliance Policy and Analysis Unit. According to the FBI, the Compliance Operations Unit will support implementation of compliance policy and standards within FBI divisions, including analyzing operations and legal requirements; identifying specific compliance risk areas; prioritizing the risks; and establishing policies, procedures, and training to ensure compliance. The OIC's Compliance Policy and Analysis Unit will establish compliance policy, including a methodology for assessing risk (described below), compliance standards, and monitoring and auditing procedures. The Compliance Policy and Analysis Unit also will develop and provide training and monitor the overall compliance program.

The OIC is designed to be independent from, but expected to work closely with, the FBI's Inspection Division to identify high-risk areas. The Head of the OIC said that the Inspection Division would include monitoring of identified compliance risks (which will be incorporated into the Inspection Division's inspection protocols) in its inspections of Headquarters and field divisions. According to OIC documents, the Inspection Division is expected to provide the OIC with inspection data gathered during its inspections to support the OIC's compliance monitoring and will conduct audits as needed to support the compliance oversight program.

As of January 2008, the Attorney General and the Office of Management and Budget had approved the establishment of the OIC. Congressional committees were notified on November 21, 2007. According to the Head of the OIC, the FBI's Corporate Resource Planning Board (which approves the establishment of positions) and the FBI's Position Review Board (which determines whether positions are staffed with Special Agents or support staff) authorized 12 positions for the OIC, including a Senior Executive Service position, 1 Secretary, 1 Special Agent (on a detail/rotation), 5 Attorneys, and

4 Management and Program Analysts.[22] In addition, two attorneys from the FBI's Office of General Counsel were later transferred to the OIC, along with the ethics/standards of conduct function that they support. As of February 2008, the OIC had 12 personnel on board. The FBI told us that the OIC will re-evaluate its staffing and organizational structure as the program continues to mature. As of January 2008, each of the five Executive Management Committees had met three times, and Red Teams were conducting reviews to analyze the top compliance risks in each of the five functional areas.

2. Risk Assessment Process

The procedures describing the OIC's operations were still in development during the OIG's review. However, the Head of the OIC provided information to the OIG on the assessment tool that the Executive Management Committees intended to use to assess and rank identified risks. The assessment tool allows the Executive Management Committees to assign a numerical value to internal and external factors associated with each risk, including such considerations as the complexity of the program or activity, environmental factors (such as whether the program is a new activity or involves new technology), workforce factors (such as whether training related to the activity is available), and potential privacy and civil liberty impacts. The tool also includes "weighting" factors, such as the frequency and potential magnitude of any potential harm associated with the risk.[23] Using the numerical values assigned to all the factors, the assessment tool calculates an overall score that enables the Executive Management Committees to rank the risks. The chair of each committee provides independent judgment regarding the recommended rankings and approves the ordering of the potential risks. The committee Chairs are to provide the FBI Deputy Director and the OIC with their committee's assessment of the five highest-ranked risks. The FBI Director, as chair of the FBI Integrity and Compliance Council, is responsible for determining whether the risk identification and rankings are "sound."

After the most important risks have been identified, Red Teams will use an OIC-developed draft compliance checklist to guide their reviews. In addition, the OIC developed a compliance risk assessment report format for

[22] Initially, the OIC was authorized to have two Special Agent positions, but one of the positions was subsequently converted to a support position.

[23] NSLs will not be subjected to the risk assessment process. The Head of the OIC told the OIG that the OIC risk identification process will not be used to assess risks associated with NSLs because the reviews conducted by the OIG in 2006 and 2007 and by the FBI Inspection Division in 2007 already identified those risks and corrective actions (including updating policy and guidance and providing training) are being taken in response to those reviews.

compiling the Red Teams' findings that addresses specific elements related to the risk. The risk assessment report format includes:

- a summary of the risk;
- a review of the legal authorities relevant to the operations being reviewed;
- an assessment of the internal policies, procedures, and cost controls in place;
- an assessment of the training provided related to the at-risk activity;
- a listing and assessment of the existing data that management has available to identify or assess potential compliance failures related to the risk;
- a discussion of potential compliance failures that already have been identified; and
- a brief assessment of potential corrective actions identified by the Red Team to ameliorate the risk under review.

As noted above, the Red Teams' reports should be provided to the risk owner and the responsible Executive Management Committee within 60 days after the initial Red Team meeting. The risk owner is then expected to develop and implement a mitigation plan for ameliorating the compliance risks.

3. OIG Analysis

While the OIC is in the developmental stages and its procedures and expected outcomes are not yet fully defined, we believe it can be a valuable tool for the FBI. As planned, the OIC can provide the FBI with a structured process for identifying compliance requirements and risks, assessing existing control mechanisms, and developing and implementing better controls to ensure compliance with law, regulations, and policies. Senior FBI management, including the FBI Director, told us that they are committed to supporting the successful implementation of the compliance program.

However, we believe that the OIC faces significant challenges in fulfilling its mission. One challenge for an internal compliance program—particularly one staffed with technical experts from the program or office under review—is to identify unknown or emerging risks. Consequently, such a compliance program may unduly focus on risks that are already known and are already being addressed. However, the Head of the OIC told the OIG that the FBI is attempting to meet this challenge by involving individuals at all levels of the program or office in the risk identification process. Additionally, the FBI stated that the OIC staff, through internal and external contacts and reviews, provides advice to the Executive Management Committees on information it develops concerning possible compliance concerns.

We also note that a compliance oversight process in which the subject program or office that "owns" a set of identified compliance risks also rates the severity of the risks may introduce a tendency or bias toward focusing on risks or activities most important to the risk owner. These activities may be different from those risk-sensitive activities viewed as most significant by an independent entity conducting a compliance review. While the OIG recognizes that the Executive Management Committees that identify and prioritize risks include members from the FBI OGC and FBI executive management who are expected to provide objective compliance expertise (as opposed to operational or technical expertise), the final determination of how risks are ranked lies with the "risk owning" office. According to the FBI, having the owning office rank the risks will provide "buy in" on the need to address the risk. However, we believe that objective ranking of risks for further assessment and remediation is a critical component of a successful compliance program. Consequently, although the rankings are reviewed by the Director and Deputy Director, we believe that the FBI must be vigilant to ensure that the ranking of risks by the risk owners is objective.

In addition, we note that the OIC currently has an authorized permanent staffing level of only 14 positions and will depend on FBI personnel in other offices to carry out many functions critical to the success of the new compliance program.[24] As presently envisioned, the OIC appears to serve as a coordinator rather than an entity with sufficient independent resources and a capability to identify and assess compliance risks. For example, as described above, the Red Teams responsible for conducting the detailed risk assessments are composed primarily of personnel from the risk-owning office and the FBI OGC, while the OIC's role is to facilitate the assessment process and receive the results for the Executive Management Committees. According to the FBI, this structure is modeled on corporate practices. Similarly, to conduct compliance monitoring, the OIC will rely on Inspection Division personnel to conduct the monitoring or inspections. However, we believe this can place FBI agents in a difficult position when they are only temporarily assigned the responsibility to inspect and potentially criticize the actions of FBI colleagues and units since after their rotation in the Inspection Division, they often return to work alongside the FBI employees and supervisors whose actions they reviewed during their rotation. Accordingly, to make the difficult judgment calls regarding weaknesses and compliance problems that will arise in the course of the OIC's work, we believe that the FBI should consider providing the OIC with a substantial permanent staffing level so that it can develop the skills, knowledge, and independence to lead or directly carry out the critical elements of a new compliance program.

[24] The number of permanently assigned OIC staff is much lower than the number of employees in the Inspection Division, which currently is assigned 30 employees.

B. National Security Division

In September 2006 the Department established the National Security Division (NSD) to consolidate the supervision of the Department's primary national security elements within a single division. The NSD was created by combining the Office of Intelligence Policy and Review (OIPR) and the Counterterrorism and Counterespionage Sections that were formerly part of the Criminal Division. In July 2007 the Department announced that it would reorganize the NSD and, as a part of the reorganization, would create within the NSD an Office of Intelligence to replace the OIPR. The mission of the Office of Intelligence is "to ensure that national security investigations are conducted in a manner consistent with the nation's laws, regulations, and policies, including those designed to protect the privacy interests and civil liberties of [U.S.] citizens."[25] On September 24, 2007, the Assistant Attorney General for the NSD issued a memorandum that detailed the structure and operations of the three sections that comprise the new Office of Intelligence.[26] However, in February 2008, the NSD informed the OIG that the reorganizations announced in September 2007 had not been completed, as the Office of Intelligence had not yet been created. We describe below the operations of the Office of Intelligence and the roles of each of the three sections as they were announced in September 2007.

1. Office of Intelligence

The Office of Intelligence will consist of three sections: the Oversight Section, the Operations Section, and the Litigation Section (see Chart 2.1). The Oversight Section will oversee all aspects of the FBI's national security program and its use of intelligence techniques to support that program, including NSLs. The Operations Section will conduct intelligence operations work, such as representing the government in presenting applications to the Foreign Intelligence Surveillance Court. The Litigation Section will supervise and coordinate criminal and civil litigation matters related to the FISA and other intelligence issues.

Attorney staffing levels for the Office of Intelligence will remain the same as its predecessor offices—approximately 85 attorneys—and it was anticipated that the attorneys would rotate among various units and sections within the Office of Intelligence. The majority of the attorneys are to be assigned to the Operations Section and may serve on rotating assignments among the three units that comprise that section (the Counterterrorism

[25] Letter from the Attorney General and FBI Director to Richard B. Cheney, President of the Senate, July 13, 2007, 1.

[26] Assistant Attorney General, National Security Division, memorandum to all National Security Division Employees, September 24, 2007.

Chart 2.1: Organization of the Office of Intelligence

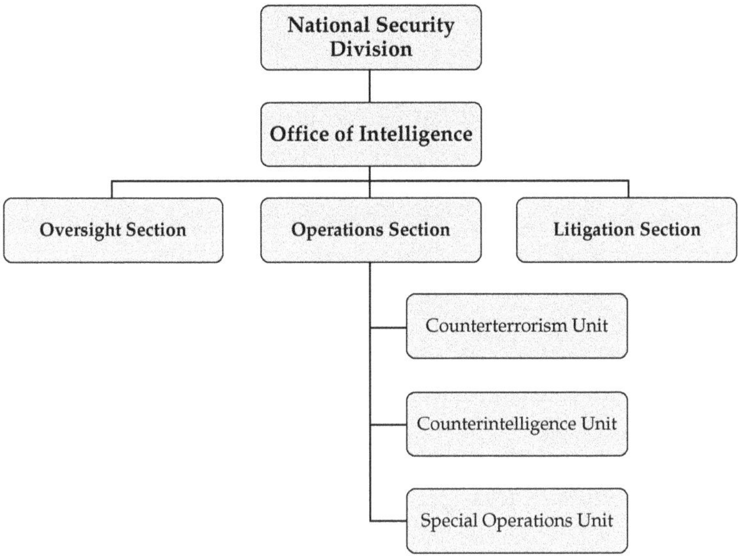

Source: Department of Justice, National Security Division

Unit, the Counterintelligence Unit, and the Special Operations unit). In addition, some attorney positions in the Oversight and Litigation Sections will be filled by attorneys from the Operations Section on a rotating basis. Attorneys also will be expected to provide support to other sections where appropriate. For example, Operations Section attorneys that prepare FISA applications would be expected to provide support to the Litigation Section if the FISA applications are at issue in related criminal trials.

2. Oversight Section

According to NSD officials, the mission of the Oversight Section will include functions previously exercised by OIPR as well as several new oversight functions that represent a significant expansion of the Department's oversight of the FBI's investigative operations. OIPR's oversight was focused primarily on the FBI's use of FISA authorities and included "accuracy reviews" to ensure the accuracy of FBI declarations to the Foreign Intelligence Surveillance Court and "minimization reviews" to ensure that FISA information was handled appropriately. These minimization reviews are conducted to assess the FBI's compliance with the FISA requirement that the FBI implement procedures "reasonably designed . . . to minimize the acquisition and retention, and prohibit the dissemination, of nonpublicly available information concerning unconsenting United States persons. . . ."[27] OIPR also previously conducted reviews of FBI notices related to national security investigations to ensure compliance with the Attorney General Guidelines.

In April 2007 OIPR expanded its oversight functions to include most. aspects of the FBI's national security program and its use of national security tools, including national security letters.[28] These oversight functions were implemented under OIPR; the NSD did not wait for the establishment of the Oversight Section. According to the NSD's September 24, 2007, reorganization memorandum, the Oversight Section will take over the responsibility of reviewing national security investigation case files in FBI field offices and Headquarters divisions to provide guidance on a wide range of issues, including compliance with Attorney General Guidelines, the use of NSLs, and the predication for national security investigations. In 2007, OIPR began reviewing all FBI referrals to the IOB and will report to the Attorney General any recurring problems or trends. In addition, as a part of the NSD's overall mission, Office of Intelligence attorneys will provide training on legal and regulatory compliance issues. Each of these oversight activities, which OIPR began conducting in 2007, is discussed further in the following sections.

a. National Security Reviews

In response to the OIG's March 2007 report on NSLs, the NSD instituted what it terms national security reviews to examine whether the FBI is using a variety of intelligence techniques, including NSLs, in accordance with applicable laws, guidelines, and policies.

From the time the review process was established in April 2007 through December 30, 2007, the NSD completed national security reviews at 14 FBI field offices and 1 Headquarters division. The national security reviews focused on the initiation and maintenance of national security investigations to verify compliance with laws, guidelines and policies, as well as the FBI's use of NSLs. According to NSD personnel, the scope of the reviews will expand over time to encompass other elements of the national security investigative program, such as undercover operations, and how

[27] 50 U.S.C. §§ 1801(h)(l) and 1821(4)(A). During the minimization audits, attorneys from OIPR visited FBI field offices to assess the FBI's minimization of the results of FISA-approved electronic surveillance and physical searches; counsel case agents, intelligence analysts, and linguists on specific issues; and provide training to those involved in the minimization process.

[28] According to an NSD Associate Counsel, because intelligence investigations typically focus more on identifying and addressing threats than on prosecuting criminals, Department attorneys previously had been less involved in the FBI's national security investigations than they had been in traditional criminal investigations. In traditional criminal investigations, Department attorneys approve some investigative steps, obtain search warrants, and guide the conduct of the investigation in preparation for prosecution. In contrast, the primary involvement of Department attorneys in national security investigations resulted from their role as representatives to the Foreign Intelligence Surveillance Court.

information related to national security investigations has been disseminated outside of the FBI.

The NSD worked with the FBI to select the 15 offices to be reviewed in 2007. The FBI OGC selected as the first field office to be reviewed one that had received a particularly favorable review in its last inspection by the FBI's Inspection Division. The NSD selected the remaining 13 field offices and 1 Headquarters division with the FBI OGC's concurrence based on several considerations. To gain experience before reviewing a large field office, the NSD scheduled the reviews so that the first reviews were of small and medium-sized FBI field offices. Two larger field offices were scheduled for review in the last quarter of 2007. For 2008, the NSD plans to conduct reviews at 14 additional FBI field offices and 1 Headquarters' division. In 2008, the NSD plans to select for national security reviews offices that have higher numbers of national security investigations about which the NSD has had questions (identified in its review of FBI initiation notices of national security investigations) and also to continue to conduct FISA minimization and accuracy reviews.[29]

The national security reviews are conducted by teams consisting of NSD attorneys with intelligence experience and representatives from the FBI OGC. Personnel from the Office of the Chief Privacy and Civil Liberties Officer may also attend reviews but they are not considered part of the review team. The teams conducting the national security reviews typically consist of six members: three NSD attorneys, two FBI OGC attorneys, and one FBI Special Agent.

During each of the 15 reviews completed as of December 31, 2007, the team members worked in pairs to review approximately 25 selected case files. The case files were selected to include: (1) case files that had already been identified as being of interest based on OIPR's review of national security investigation notices; (2) case files generated in both counterintelligence and counterterrorism investigations; and (3) case files that included NSLs. For most case files, the team reviewed each NSL issued since January 1, 2006, but selected only a sample from case files that contained a large number of NSLs.

To guide the reviews, attorneys in OIPR developed a checklist that identified the information to be collected from each case file. The checklist was modeled on the data collection instrument used by the OIG for our first NSL report. It contained additional data points to capture information on the initiation and maintenance of national security investigations and on the use of other intelligence techniques and procedures.

[29] FBI is required to provide the NSD with approval memoranda signifying the initiation of national security investigations.

According to an NSD Associate Counsel, prior to on-site visits OIPR attorneys provided training to team members on how to conduct the reviews and record their results. On October 8, 2007, the NSD issued a memorandum setting forth details of its process for conducting future national security reviews and for communicating results to the NSD's senior leadership.

At the conclusion of each national security review, the team prepared a narrative report of its findings. A summary of these reports follows.

The NSD provided the OIG with reports of its reviews of national security investigations in 13 FBI field and Headquarters offices that it conducted from April 2007 through November 2007.[30] The reviews focused on three areas: examinations of the initiations, extensions, and conversions of national security investigations; evaluations of all aspects of the use of NSLs issued between January 1, 2006, and the date of NSD's review; and determinations as to whether possible IOB violations had been reported to the FBI OGC. The NSD generated separate reports for each review that included overall observations, along with specific findings regarding each investigation and NSL it reviewed.

During its reviews, which ranged from 2 to 5 days in length, the NSD reviewed a total of 1,047 NSLs in 276 investigations. The NSD reviewed as few as 4 NSLs in 2 investigations in 1 office and as many as 130 NSLs in 23 investigations in another office. The reviewed investigations included 150 counterterrorism matters and 126 counterintelligence matters. We were not able to determine from the NSD reports the statute under which all the NSLs that it reviewed were issued. However, approximately 80 percent of the NSLs for which we were able to identify the statute were issued under ECPA.

The NSD's findings were consistent with those identified in our first NSL report on the FBI's use of national security letters. The NSD reviews examined overcollections, errors in approval ECs and NSLs, inconsistencies between approval ECs and NSLs, the inability to locate responsive records, failure to include the U.S. person status of the subject of the investigation or the target of the NSL, and failure to describe in the approval EC the relevance of the records sought to the investigation. The NSD found that:

- The FBI obtained information it did not request or that it was not entitled to receive. The NSD observed that a mismatch between the FBI's requested date range and the manner in which third parties maintained their records often caused the overcollections. Additionally, there was little documentation of overcollections or documentation of the disposition of these matters.

[30] The OIG reviewed the first report that was finalized, along with 12 draft reports. After completion of our analysis, the NSD told us that it has finalized all 13 reports.

- Errors occurred in the NSLs and approval ECs because case agents relied on previously drafted documents that were outdated or no longer valid.
- There were "disconnects" between the NSL and approval ECs, including approval ECs that did not specifically state the information being requested or that differed from the records requested in the NSLs.
- The information provided by third parties to the FBI was not always retained in the investigative case files because the original documents were provided to analysts or FBI Headquarters.
- The approval ECs did not consistently reference the U.S. person status of individuals, which is required for purposes of congressional reporting.
- The relevance of information requested in the NSLs to the underlying investigations was not consistently explained in approval ECs.

In addition to these issues, the NSD reviews identified other noteworthy matters. In our first NSL report, we noted that a field office reported to the FBI OGC that it had obtained information from an asset and had not issued an NSL to obtain that information. The FBI OGC did not report the matter to the IOB—a decision that we disagreed with and the FBI later changed. In its reviews, the NSD found instances in two field offices in which assets provided financial records to the FBI, but the FBI did not issue NSLs to obtain the records, as required by the *Right to Financial Privacy Act* NSL statute. Neither of these matters had been reported to the FBI OGC prior to the NSD review. The NSD also found instances in which the current Patriot Reauthorization Act non-disclosure and confidentiality models were not being used, the required certifications were missing, or there was no stated basis in the approval ECs for imposing these obligations. In addition, the NSD identified instances in which NSLs were served during lapses in investigations, contrary to the NSL statutes and the Attorney General Guidelines; consumer full credit reports obtained in response to *Fair Credit Report Act* NSLs seeking limited credit information were not successfully redacted and the reports were fully readable; and a field office uploaded into the ACS system unauthorized information obtained in response to NSLs.

The NSD made several recommendations to address issues that it determined warranted further examination. To address unauthorized collections, the NSD recommended that the FBI develop guidance that more specifically provides instruction on:

- overcollected information;
- sequestration of information with the CDCs;
- destruction or other disposition of improperly obtained information;
- uploading of information into FBI databases; and

- verification of removal (of overcollected information) from FBI electronic files and databases.

To prevent the receipt of unauthorized information, the NSD also recommended that the FBI work more closely with NSL recipients by revising the standard language used in NSLs in describing the time periods for which records are requested.[31]

To address errors and inconsistencies between the NSLs and approval ECs, as well as missing required language, certifications, or an established nexus between the investigation and the records requested, the NSD recommended that:

- standardized NSL forms from the FBI OGC website be used;
- case agents be provided instruction and training to ensure that the information requested in the NSLs matches what is requested in the approval ECs; and
- case agents be provided instruction and training on the importance of describing in NSL approval ECs a sufficient nexus or relevance between the investigation and the information requested.

To address the FBI's inability to locate records received in response to NSLs, the NSD recommended that:

- case agents keep original results in the investigative case files and provide copies to analysts and FBI headquarters; and
- the FBI OGC initiate a tracking system so case agents can determine whether NSLs have been served and whether the NSL recipients have provided responses to the FBI.

The NSD also recommended that the Department establish a working group of representatives from the NSD, the FBI, and the Office of the Deputy Attorney General to review the results of the NSD's national security reviews. The NSD suggested that the NSL Working Group recommend changes to guidelines, practices, and training to establish clear, concise, well-documented, and consistent procedures for implementing the NSL statutes and Attorney General Guidelines.

b. Reviews of FBI Reports to the IOB

As directed by the Attorney General in March 2007, the NSD also is responsible for reviewing all FBI reports of possible intelligence violations to the

[31] This NSD recommendation may have already been addressed when, in May 2006, the FBI OGC revised the model attachment for ECPA toll record NSLs. The NSD reviewed NSLs issued on or after January 1, 2006. Since we are unable to determine the dates of the NSLs that the NSD reviewed, we are unable to determine whether the unauthorized collections occurred prior to or after the issuance of the new model attachment.

IOB in order to identify recurring problems and assess the FBI's response to such violations. According to NSD officials, the review process focuses on whether these reports indicate that a change in policy, training, or oversight mechanisms is warranted. The Oversight Section also will report to the Attorney General twice a year and inform the Department's Chief Privacy and Civil Liberties Officer of any referrals that raise "serious civil liberties or privacy issues."

As of November 30, 2007, the NSD had forwarded its initial semiannual report to the Attorney General. The report provided a statistical summary and description of reports to the IOB from January 1, 2007, through June 30, 2007, and reported the NSD's observations regarding trends and patterns in the notices of reports to the IOB. Chief among these were observations relating to the reporting of national security investigations by FBI field offices, compliance with Foreign Intelligence Surveillance Court orders, and maintaining current investigative authority for ongoing operations. The NSD report recommended that existing policy regarding reporting by the FBI to the NSD of the initiation of national security investigations needed to be modified. In addition, the NSD recommended additional guidance and training to avoid lapses in investigative authority and to clarify the scope of records that may be obtained through ECPA NSLs.

c. Training and Outreach

In addition to conducting national security reviews, the NSD plans to provide training on legal and regulatory compliance issues for its attorneys and for FBI agents and analysts and to conduct outreach to other members of the Intelligence Community.

3. OIG Analysis

Based on our review of documents describing the NSD's national security reviews, our interviews of NSD officials, the data collection instrument, and the report of the results of the first national security review, we believe the national security reviews are important additions to other audits and oversight measures implemented by the FBI (described in this chapter and in Chapter Three of this report). In particular, we believe the experience of NSD attorneys and other personnel in the new Office of Intelligence will bring important expertise to the oversight of NSLs and other intelligence techniques.

We also believe that the scope of the NSD's reviews is reasonable. These reviews examine compliance with laws, guidelines, and policies relating to the FBI's use of various intelligence techniques, including NSLs. Further, the NSD's plan to shift the focus of its reviews over time to encompass other aspects of the FBI's national security investigations seems reasonable and appropriate.

However, it is important that sufficient resources be allocated, both in the FBI and NSD, to keep pace with the plans to complete approximately 15 national security reviews per year. Moreover, as the results of the FBI's three 2007 NSL reviews (discussed in Chapter Three of this report) are fully evaluated, the NSD should re-evaluate whether adjustments to the scope and focus of the national security reviews are warranted.

C. National Security Letter Working Group

In response to a directive in the Patriot Reauthorization Act and our first NSL report, the Attorney General directed the Department's Privacy Officer, working with the Civil Liberties Protection Officer of the Office of the Director of National Intelligence (DNI), to convene a working group (NSL Working Group) to examine how NSL-derived information is used and retained by the FBI.[32] In addition to the Privacy Officer and the DNI's Civil Liberties Protection Officer, the NSL Working Group included the senior privacy official of the FBI and representatives from the Department's Office of Legal Policy, NSD, and the Office of the DNI Director.

In our first NSL report, the OIG noted the proviso in the Attorney General's NSI Guidelines that national security investigations should use the "least intrusive collection techniques feasible" to carry out the investigations.[33] The OIG reported that we found no clear guidance on how Special Agents should reconcile the Attorney General Guidelines' limitations with the expansive authority provided in the NSL statutes. Our concerns over the lack of formal guidance were magnified because of the volume of NSLs generated by the FBI each year and because the information collected is retained for long periods in databases available to many authorized law enforcement personnel. To better identify NSL-derived data retained by the FBI, we recommended, among other things, that the FBI consider measures to label or tag NSL-derived information in its databases.

In August 2007 the NSL Working Group completed a proposal for minimization and retention of certain NSL-derived information and sent the proposal to the Attorney General for approval.[34] The proposed policy and

---

32 Section 119(f) of the Patriot Reauthorization Act, states:

> Minimization Procedures Feasibility—Not later than February 1, 2007, or upon completion of review of the report submitted under subsection (c)(l), whichever is earlier, the Attorney General and the Director of National Intelligence shall jointly submit to the Committee on the Judiciary and the Permanent Select Committee on Intelligence of the House of Representatives and the Committee on the Judiciary and the Select Committee on Intelligence of the Senate a report on the feasibility of applying minimization procedures in the context of national security letters to ensure the protection of the constitutional rights of United States persons.

33 NSI Guidelines, § I(B)(2).

34 The NSL Working Group adopted the definition of "minimization procedures" as it is used in FISA 50 U.S.C. § 1801(h):

> (1) specific procedures . . . that are reasonably designed in light of the purpose and technique of [NSLs] to minimize the acquisition and retention, and prohibit the dissemination,

recommendations relate to data obtained by the FBI in response to NSLs seeking financial and consumer credit information as well as data obtained in response to NSLs seeking telephone billing records, telephone and e-mail subscriber information, and electronic communication transactional records.[35] However, the recommendations of the NSL Working Group were not acted upon by the Attorney General. In February 2008, the Privacy Officer told the OIG that the proposal had been withdrawn from the Office of the Attorney General and that the Privacy Officer intended to reconvene the Working Group. According to the Privacy Officer, the Working Group needs to make specific enhancements to both the proposal and related procedures to describe more fully the research, clarify the Working Group's findings, and potentially strengthen its recommendations. Below, we describe the findings, reasoning, and recommendations contained in the proposal submitted to the Attorney General by the NSL Working Group, followed by our analysis and recommendations. We offer these comments for the NSL Working Group to consider as it prepares to re-examine these important issues.

1. Evaluation of Existing Controls and Guidelines

The NSL Working Group initially examined existing controls and guidelines that protect privacy interests regarding the acquisition and use of NSL-derived information. The report of the NSL Working Group noted that NSLs can only be used in connection with national security investigations, must be approved by a senior FBI official, and provide access only to limited information. Further, the report noted that NSL-derived information is subject to standard agency records retention rules, must be disseminated and retained only in accordance with applicable Attorney General Guidelines, and can only be accessed through FBI databases by authorized individuals for official purposes. Based on this evaluation, the NSL Working Group concluded that "significant limitations already exist governing the proper use of NSLs."[36]

---

of non-publicly available information concerning unconsenting United States persons consistent with the need of the United States to obtain, produce, and disseminate foreign intelligence information; (2) procedures that require that non-publicly available information, which is not foreign intelligence information . . . shall not be disseminated in a manner which identifies any United States person, without such person's consent, unless such person's identity is necessary to understand foreign intelligence information or assess its importance.

Chief Privacy and Civil Liberties Officer, U.S. Department of Justice, memorandum to the Attorney General, U.S. Department of Justice, August 17, 2007, 6. (NSL Working Group Memorandum).

35 The report stated that the Department planned to use the findings of the NSL Working Group in preparing the report to Congress required by § 119(f) of the Patriot Reauthorization Act on the "feasibility of applying minimization procedures in the context of national security letters to ensure the protection of the constitutional rights of United States persons." NSL Working Group Memorandum, 1.

36 Id. at 5.

The NSL Working Group's report concluded that the FBI has made "significant progress in identifying and rectifying concerns about the FBI's compliance" with NSL authorities.[37] For example, the NSL Working Group cited the FBI OGC's June 1, 2007, Comprehensive Guidance EC that directs Special Agents to review information received in response to NSL requests; improvements to the FBI's electronic data systems; the establishment of the FBI OIC; and the new oversight activities of the NSD.

The NSL Working Group report concluded that controls provided by existing statutes and guidelines, if properly followed, effectively minimize the collection of information on U.S. persons and protect privacy interests. However, the NSL Working Group also stated that further enhancements to privacy safeguards, which we discuss in the next section, would be appropriate.

2. Additional Privacy Enhancements Recommended by the NSL Working Group

To improve privacy safeguards for information acquired with NSLs, the NSL Working Group proposed initial minimization procedures applicable to information derived from RFPA, FCRA, and ECPA NSLs. Some of the proposed procedures amplify recently implemented requirements imposed by the FBI in response to the OIG's first NSL report. The NSL Working Group stated that its recommendations recognized that "information that appears to be of little value today" may later become significant. It also stated that private business practices calling for routine destruction of older records helped guide the group's recommendations.[38]

a. Financial and Credit Information

According to the NSL Working Group's recommendation, NSL-derived financial and credit information should initially be reviewed by the case agent or analyst to determine whether the information has "investigative value." The NSL Working Group defined information as having "investigative value" if the information "contributes to a national security investigation or to an authorized intelligence collection requirement."[39] The determination of whether information has investigative value is to be made by "the case agent or other employee familiar with the scope of the investigation and its objectives."[40]

The NSL Working Group noted that information requested in an NSL may be produced in paper or electronic form and therefore established slightly

[37] Id. at 6.
[38] id. at 6-7.
[39] NSL Working Group Memorandum, Attachment, 1.
[40] Id.

different procedures for making the "investigative value" determination given the different formats. The NSL Working Group stated that financial or credit information received in electronic form should be uploaded onto a desktop computer and reviewed to identify non-responsive data and to determine if it has investigative value. Under the proposal, data from responsive financial or credit paper documents may also be temporarily entered into a desktop computer – but not into an FBI-wide database—so that it may be more easily reviewed to determine if it has investigative value.

Under the NSL Working Group's proposal, FBI personnel may upload into FBI databases and include in analytical products only financial and credit information that is determined to have "current or reasonably potential" investigative value. The electronic media and paper copies of all responsive documents, whether determined to have investigative value or not, are to be retained in designated sections of the investigative file.

b. Electronic Communication Transactional Data

Under the proposal, information derived from ECPA NSLs (telephone toll billing records, telephone and e-mail subscriber information, and electronic communication transactional records) need only be determined to be responsive to the NSL in order to be uploaded into any appropriate FBI-wide database (such as the ACS system or Telephone Applications database). Unlike the limitations imposed on NSL-derived financial and credit information (requiring an initial determination that the information has "investigative value"), the NSL Working Group's proposal would not restrict the initial uploading of these records into FBI databases. The NSL Working Group concluded that electronic communication transactional information cannot be evaluated in isolation, but must be uploaded so that link analysis and other analytical measures can be used to determine its investigative value. The NSL Working Group also stated that it based its recommendation on reduced privacy interests associated with ECPA NSL records. As with financial and credit data, the NSL Working Group's proposal requires retention of the electronic media containing the data in designated sections of the investigative file.

3. Other Enhancements Considered but Not Recommended

According to its report, the NSL Working Group also considered but decided not to recommend additional minimization procedures. The NSL Working Group also recommended against applying any time limitation on the retention of NSL-derived information beyond the existing routine agency data retention protocols relating to investigative files. Instead, the NSL Working Group stated that information found to have investigative value should remain available for unrestricted access by authorized users of the ACS system or the Investigative Data Warehouse until it is archived in accordance with applicable National Archives and Records Administration disposition schedules.[41]

In addition, the NSL Working Group recommended against "tagging" NSL-derived information so that it would be identifiable as such if it is used in analytical intelligence products or transferred to other Intelligence Community-wide computer systems, concluding this would cause "an undue burden on the operation of such an important tool." Further, the NSL Working Group stated that planned enhancements to the FBI's information technology systems will allow NSL-derived information to be segregated in the FBI OGC's NSL tracking database. Consequently, the NSL Working Group concluded that "tagging" NSL-derived data would not provide "any measurable value for privacy protections. . . . "

The NSL Working Group decided against recommending that the FBI delete NSL-derived data from its data systems when cases are closed. According to the NSL Working Group's report, requiring the deletion of NSL-derived data upon case closing would have potential negative impacts on the investigative process because closing a case is not necessarily indicative of a subject's innocence. For example, the FBI sometimes closes counterintelligence cases when the subject leaves the country, but may reopen the case if the subject returns. Further, the NSL Working Group stated that information gathered during an investigation that is closed could have investigative value in other cases.

4. OIG Analysis of the NSL Working Group's Report and Recommendations

The OIG believes that the NSL Working Group should consider further whether and how to provide additional privacy safeguards and measures for minimizing the retention of NSL-derived information.

First, the NSL Working Group's conclusion that "significant limitations already exist governing the proper use of NSLs" could easily have been written in March 2006 when the Patriot Reauthorization Act directed the OIG to review the FBI's use of NSLs. At that time, the NSL statutes, Attorney General Guidelines, and internal FBI policies established a highly regulated system for controlling the approval process and for identifying violations of these statutes, guidelines, and policies. Yet, notwithstanding these

[41] The length of time that the FBI retains investigative information, whether in paper or electronic format, depends on several factors, including the case type (for example, intelligence or criminal investigations) and other characteristics of the case (for example, if it involved a "most wanted" suspect). In general, information related to intelligence investigations is retained in the FBI's files (either in the paper case file or in the FBI's electronic systems) for 30 years after a case is closed, and information related to criminal investigations is retained for 20 years after a case is closed. After that time, the case information is reviewed, and information that is identified for permanent retention is transferred to the National Archives and Records Administration (NARA) for storage. Any cases not meeting the criteria for permanent retention and transfer to the NARA are destroyed.

controls, we found serious abuses of national security letter authorities, which we described in our first NSL report. These included improperly obtaining consumer full credit reports, obtaining information beyond the time period specified in the NSLs, and issuing improper requests under the cited NSL statutes. Accordingly, contrary to the NSL Working Group's conclusions, we do not believe that existing controls are a sufficient basis upon which to rely in evaluating the need for additional privacy protections for NSL-derived information.

Second, as we elaborated earlier in this chapter and elsewhere in this report, while we agree that the FBI has made significant progress in addressing the findings in our first NSL report, we believe it is too soon to say that the FBI has rectified all of the problems we identified. Moreover, we believe it is too early to fully assess whether the new systems and controls developed by the FBI and the Department (including mandatory NSL training, the creation of the new NSL data system, the establishment of the OIC, and the NSD's national security reviews) will eliminate fully the improper or illegal uses of NSLs that we and the FBI have identified. Therefore, we believe the NSL Working Group should not base its recommendations on new and untested measures, some of which have only recently been implemented, some that are not yet implemented, and none of which have been evaluated by internal or external evaluators.

Third, the NSL Working Group's proposal does not explain the basis for two of its major conclusions. First, it does not explain how the new FBI data system for tracking issuance of NSLs relates to the principal FBI databases that store NSL-derived information. The memorandum does not explain how the "structured storage of information and NSL information can be segregated in the database" and the reasons for its conclusion that "individual tagging, as that term is commonly understood . . . did not provide any measurable value for privacy protections at this time." Second, the memorandum does not explain what options, including use of "meta tags," the NSL Working Group considered and rejected or the basis for its conclusion that such measures would "place an undue burden" on the operation of NSLs. In later discussions, the Privacy Officer indicated that these matters would be more fully explained in the revised NSL Working Group report and recommendations.

Fourth, we are concerned that the NSL Working Group's proposed standard for uploading and retaining NSL-derived financial and credit information provides no meaningful constraint and requires no balancing of privacy interests against genuine investigative needs. The NSL Working Group's proposal would allow any information that a Special Agent believes "contributes" to an investigation to be uploaded and retained. As described by the NSL Working Group, it is difficult to conceive of responsive information that a Special Agent could not find "contributes" to an investigation in some way. Consequently, we believe the standard is so broad as to be meaningless. When we discussed the standard with the Privacy Officer, the Privacy Officer stated that the standard was intended to be limiting, although he stated that the August 17 memorandum did not provide appropriate clarity to ensure that the intended protections were real and not illusory.

Fifth, we are concerned that the NSL Working Group did not sufficiently assess whether to establish any time limits on the retention of NSL-derived data, sufficiently explain its reasoning for its conclusion, or at least consider more modest measures such as requiring that information derived from NSLs be reviewed during annual case reviews, when cases are closed, or after a reasonable period following the closing of investigations (for example, 3 or 5 years after closure). While we understand the NSL Working Group's rationale regarding the difficulty in predicting at a fixed point in time the investigative value of certain information, we are not convinced from the analysis contained in the NSL Working Group's memorandum that measures short of retention for 30 years are not feasible or workable. In particular, we do not find the NSL Working Group protocols sufficiently protective of the privacy interests of individuals who have been determined not to be of investigative interest.

For example, according to OIG interviews with FBI Special Agents, a primary use of NSLs is to close leads and eliminate suspects. Yet, information from NSLs for which the primary investigative value is to eliminate a suspect or close a lead falls within the NSL Working Group's broad definition of information having "investigative value" and may be uploaded and retained for many years. Under this approach, information related to individuals determined not to be of interest or concern to law enforcement also would be retained on the chance that the information could become relevant in the future. However, the argument that large amounts of data from NSLs that eliminated a suspect or closed leads should be retained for many years because it *may* not be available in the future should be weighed against the individual's privacy interests. It is not clear that the NSL Working Group did this, and we do not believe it adequately explained its reasoning for rejecting alternatives other than the FBI's general retention policy regarding investigative information. In light of the vast amounts of digital information that the FBI can collect on communication, financial, and credit transactions, we believe the NSL Working Group did not give sufficient weight to the valid privacy interests that weigh against retention and accessibility of such data for 30 years. We believe the NSL Working Group should reconsider this significant concern when it reconvenes.

For the above reasons, we believe the NSL Working Group should reconsider its reasoning and conclusions that there should be no periodic review of data to determine whether the investigative value overcomes reasonable privacy interests. While we acknowledge that in many, and perhaps most, instances under such a review, the Special Agent or other official reviewing the case file may determine that the data should be retained, we believe that determination should be made only after a considered judgment rather than by application of a low standard that almost always will result in retention.

We also believe that the NSL Working Group should reconsider its proposal to allow unlimited uploading and retention of electronic communication transactional data regardless of its investigative value. We understand that information derived from ECPA NSLs must be uploaded into appropriate databases for link analysis and other examination to determine if it has investigative value. However, we are concerned that the NSL Working Group did not adequately consider or explain why it rejected a proposal that the FBI remove information that, upon analysis, is determined to have no investigative value after some reasonable period of time.

We also are not convinced by the NSL Working Group's initial assessment that the reduced privacy concerns associated with electronic communication transactional data, as compared with financial or credit data, justify rejection of any limits on uploading all responsive information. To the contrary, we believe that the volume of electronic communication transactional data collected, as well as the wide accessibility of that data, should be given more weight in balancing the need for additional privacy protections. As we describe elsewhere in this report, the vast majority of the FBI's NSLs are requests for electronic communication records under the ECPA. Further, much of the information in FBI databases is periodically transferred to the Investigative Data Warehouse. According to the FBI, the Investigative Data Warehouse contains data from 53 different sources and is available to over 13,000 Special Agents, analysts, and law enforcement partners around the world.[42] Consequently, the Working Group should identify ways to establish meaningful controls to ensure that NSL-derived electronic communication transactional data, including information that has no identified investigative value, is not made widely available to the world-wide law enforcement community.

In sum, we believe it was premature for the NSL Working Group to conclude that current mechanisms to control the use and retention of NSL-derived information are adequate to protect the privady and civil liberties of U.S. citizens. The NSL Working Group's preliminary conclusions are based in part on corrective measures that have not been fully implemented or demonstrated to be effective. We therefore believe that the NSL Working Group's recommendations related to the retention of NSL-derived information

[42] Federal Bureau of Investigation, "By the Numbers—FBI Transformation Since 2001," September 6, 2006, http://www.fbi.gov/page2/september 06/numbers090606.htm (accessed November 30, 2007).

require further examination and explanation regarding how to balance the legitimate privacy interests of individuals against potential investigative needs. The NSL Working Group should consider whether and how to extend additional privacy safeguards to data obtained in response to the thousands of NSL requests issued each year that result in the collection of data on how U.S. citizens communicate, bank, and spend their money.

IV. OIG Conclusions and Recommendations

In conclusion, we believe the FBI and the Department have made significant progress in implementing the recommendations from our first NSL report and in adopting other corrective actions to address problems we and the FBI identified in the use of national security letters. We also found that the FBI has devoted significant energy, time, and resources toward ensuring that its field managers and agents understand the seriousness of the FBI's shortcomings in its use of NSLs and their responsibility for correcting these deficiencies.

For example, the FBI Director and Deputy Director have underscored the significance of the OIG's findings with senior Headquarters officials, SACs, and other personnel throughout the ranks of the FBI; stressed that compliance with NSL authorities is a major priority; and emphasized that personnel involved in drafting, reviewing, and approving NSLs will be held accountable for infractions. The Deputy Director and the General Counsel have reinforced these messages with SACs and CDCs. The FBI also has generated comprehensive legal guidance on use of NSLs; provided mandatory NSL training to Assistant Special Agents in Charge, Supervisory Special Agents, Special Agents, and Intelligence Analysts; underscored the responsibility of CDCs in reviewing and approving NSLs and of case agents in ensuring that NSLs do not generate unauthorized records; and developed enhanced information technology tools that should facilitate the preparation of NSLs, reduce or eliminate errors, and improve the accuracy of congressional and public reporting on NSL usage. We believe that these and other steps taken in the last year underscore the FBI's commitment to addressing the problems we identified in our first NSL report.

The FBI's efforts to promote better compliance with NSL authorities also have been enhanced by other FBI initiatives and by the national security reviews conducted by the NSD and the FBI. The information developed from the FBI's 2007 NSL audits and the NSD's national security reviews is also likely to provide additional insights into problem areas and form the basis for additional guidance and compliance measures.

However, because only a year has passed since the OIG's first NSL report was released and some measures are not fully implemented, we also believe it is too early to definitively state whether the new systems and controls developed by the FBI and the Department will eliminate fully the problems with the uses of NSLs that we and the FBI have identified. We believe the FBI must implement all of our recommendations in the first NSL report, demonstrate sustained commitment to the steps it has taken and committed to take to improve compliance, implement additional recommendations in this second report, consider additional measures to enhance privacy protections for NSL-derived information, and remain vigilant in holding FBI personnel accountable for properly preparing and approving NSLs and for handling responsive records appropriately.

In addition to the steps taken to date to address the recommendations in our first NSL report, we recommend that the FBI:

1. Create blank mandatory fields in the database supporting the NSL data system for entering the U.S. person/non-U.S. person status of the targets of NSLs and for entering the number of NSL requests in order to prevent inaccuracies that may otherwise result from the current default settings.
2. Implement measures to verify the accuracy of data entry into the new NSL data system by including periodic reviews of a sample of NSLs in the database to ensure that the training provided on data entry to the support staff of the FBI OGC National Security Law Branch (NSLB), other Headquarters divisions, and field personnel is successfully applied in practice and has reduced or eliminated data entry errors. These periodic reviews should also draw upon resources available from the FBI Inspection Division and the FBI's new Office of Integrity and Compliance (OIC).
3. Implement measures to verify that data requested in NSLs is checked against serialized source documents to verify that the data extracted from the source document and used in the NSL (such as the telephone number or e-mail address) is accurately recorded on the NSL and the approval EC.
4. Regularly monitor the preparation of NSL-related documents and the handling of NSL-derived information with periodic reviews and inspections. This includes requiring that during quarterly file reviews, squad supervisors conduct, at a minimum, spot checks of NSL-related documents in investigative files to ensure adherence to NSL authorities, Attorney General Guidelines, and internal FBI policies governing use of NSL authorities.
5. Assign NSLB attorneys to participate in pertinent meetings of operational and operational support units in the Counterterrorism and Counterintelligence Divisions.

6. Consider increasing the staffing level of the OIC so that it can develop the sufficient skills, knowledge, and independence to lead or directly carry out critical elements of the OIC's work.

We also recommend that the Department:

7. Direct that the NSL Working Group, with the FBI's and the NSD's participation, re-examine measures for (a) addressing the privacy interests associated with NSL-derived information, including the benefits and feasibility of labeling or tagging NSL-derived information, and (b) minimizing the retention and dissemination of such information.

Chapter Three: The FBI'S 2007 Reviews of National Security Letters in Response to the OIG'S First NSL Report

In this chapter, we describe additional efforts undertaken by the FBI in response to the OIG's 2007 report to review the FBI's compliance with statutes, guidelines, and internal policies governing the use of national security letters. Section I describes three FBI reviews of NSLs conducted in 2007 in response to the OIG's findings. These three FBI reviews were undertaken to assess the extent of the errors in NSL usage. The FBI conducted: (1) a review of NSLs issued by FBI field offices from a random sample of 10 percent of all national security investigations active at any time from 2003 through 2006; (2) a separate review of 10 percent of NSLs issued by Headquarters divisions during the same period; and (3) a review of NSLs issued in counterintelligence investigations pursuant to the *Fair Credit Reporting Act* (FCRA) from 2002 through 2006.

The OIG analyzed the results of these three reviews to assess their methodology and accuracy. Section II describes the results of the OIG's analysis.

The FBI's reviews were initiated soon after the issuance of the OIG's first NSL report in March 2007. In that report, the OIG had examined a judgmental sample of 293 NSLs from 77 national security investigation case files. In our sample, we identified 22 NSL-related possible intelligence violations, which represented a possible intelligence violation rate of 7.5 percent.[43] These errors included both improper requests from the FBI and unauthorized collections due to third party errors.

As discussed later in this chapter, the findings of the FBI's three NSL reviews generally confirmed the OIG's findings as to the types of errors made by FBI agents in their use of NSL authorities as well as the unauthorized collections caused by third parties that provided the FBI with information that was not requested. Current FBI policy requires that substantive errors in the use of NSL authorities by FBI personnel as well as errors caused by third parties resulting in overproduction of information to the FBI be reported to the FBI OGC and the FBI Inspection Division as potential Intelligence Oversight Board (IOB) violations (PIOBs). The FBI OGC reviews these reports and determines if the FBI has reason to believe that such conduct "may be unlawful or contrary to Executive Order or Presidential Directive," the IOB's reporting standard under Executive Order 12863. Although the types of possible IOB violations identified by the OIG in our first NSL report and in the FBI's NSL reviews were similar, the FBI's

[43] The FBI OGC concluded that only 5 of the 22 matters identified by the OIG's first NSL report as possible intelligence violations should be reported to the IOB.

field review of a larger sample, [Text not available] case files, found a higher overall possible violation rate (9.43 percent) than the OIG found in its sample (7.5 percent).[44]

However, when we analyzed the FBI's 10-percent field office review, the OIG identified additional possible intelligence violations missed by the FBI. Moreover, inspectors were unable to locate records obtained in response to 6.8 percent of the NSLs selected for the field review.[45] Consequently, we believe that the rate of possible violations identified by the FBI in its 2007 field review is still understated, and therefore the FBI's field review does not provide a fully reliable baseline from which to measure improvement in compliance with NSL authorities in the future.

The OIG's review also found that the FBI reclassified as "administrative errors" some issues that initially were reported as possible intelligence violations during the field review. For some of these deficiencies, we are concerned that use of the phrase "administrative error" appears to understate the severity of the possible violation.

The FBI's 2007 reviews also identified two issues involving the use of NSLs that previously had not been fully addressed by the FBI. The FBI's reviews determined that: (1) FBI field offices received and retained Social Security Numbers and date of birth information in response to NSLs seeking subscriber information pursuant to the *Electronic Communications Privacy Act* (ECPA), even though this information was not requested in the NSLs; and (2) field offices and Headquarters operating divisions were often unable to locate records obtained in response to NSLs.

The FBI's 2007 reviews further demonstrated that the FBI's mechanism for identifying and self-reporting possible intelligence violations had been ineffective in the years since enactment of the Patriot Act in October 2001.[46]

In sum, we credit the FBI for using a reasonably sound methodology in conducting its reviews of NSL activities, for committing significant resources to the reviews, and for making the examination and analysis of the results a high priority. Its reviews confirmed the problems that the OIG's first NSL report identified. Although our analysis of the FBI's field and Headquarters reviews shows that the FBI was not able to ascertain the

---

44 The FBI used a statistically valid sample that allowed its results to be projected to the universe of all NSLs issued by the FBI during the 2003 through 2006 review period. In our first NSL report, the OIG used a judgmental sample, and the results could not be statistically projected to the universe of all NSLs issued during the review period.

45 The problems locating responsive records likewise affected the FBI's other reviews: records provided in response to 28 percent of NSLs examined in the Headquarters review were not initially located, and, in the FCRA review, 13 of the 56 field offices (23 percent) reported being unable to locate responsive records for 1 or more FCRA NSLs.

46 The term "USA PATRIOT Act" is an acronym for the *United and Strengthening America by Providing Appropriate Tools Required to Intercept and Obstruct Terrorism Act of 2001*, Pub. L. No. 107-56, 115 Stat. 272 (2001). It is commonly referred to as "the Patriot Act."

full extent of the possible violations of NSL authorities in national security investigations, the OIG nonetheless believes that the results of the FBI's reviews can help guide the corrective action that the FBI is implementing to enhance compliance with NSL authorities. These reviews again demonstrate that the additional remedial measures being implemented by the FBI are necessary and should remain a priority.

In the following sections, we discuss in more detail the FBI's 2007 reviews and our analysis of them.

I. The FBI's 2007 Reviews of National Security Letters

In this section, we examine the methodology and findings of three reviews conducted in 2007 by the FBI's Inspection Division in response to the OIG's first NSL report: (1) a review of NSLs issued by FBI field offices from a random sample of 10 percent of all national security investigations active at any time from 2003 through 2006; (2) a separate review of 10 percent of NSLs issued by Headquarters divisions during the same period; and (3) a review of NSLs issued in all counterintelligence investigations pursuant to the FCRA from 2002 through 2006.

A. The FBI's 2007 Field Review of National Security Letters

In response to the OIG's first NSL report, the FBI conducted a special review to assess whether FBI field offices complied with NSL statutes, Attorney General Guidelines, and internal FBI policies governing the use of NSLs and whether certain field offices had higher than average PIOB violation rates. The FBI assigned a large number of senior inspectors to conduct the reviews quickly, and the FBI made the review and analysis of the results a high priority. The FBI used a statistically valid sample and audit methodology that allowed its results to be projected beyond the sample of NSLs it reviewed to the universe of NSLs issued by the FBI during the review period.

1. Methodology of the FBI's 2007 Field Review

To conduct its field review, the FBI selected a random sample of 10 percent of the case files in the three types of investigations in which NSLs may lawfully be issued: counterterrorism, counterintelligence, and foreign computer intrusion cyber investigations. The FBI determined that [Text not available] of these types of investigations were active at any time between January 1, 2003, and December 31, 2006, and randomly selected [Text not available] case files for review.[47] The FBI assigned 170 inspectors to review

[47] The FBI sample was proportional by case type (counterterrorism, counterintelligence, and cyber investigations) and field office. The [Text not available] cases included investigations for which the

the case files at 56 field offices over a 5-day period (March 16, 2007, to March 20, 2007). The inspectors were instructed to review every NSL and related document in each selected file to determine if any possible intelligence violations occurred. When the review was completed, the inspectors had reviewed 7,863 NSLs issued during the 4 years covered by the review.[48]

Because many of the inspectors conducting the field review had no training or experience in issuing NSLs or with national security investigations, the FBI provided training and guidance on conducting the review. Inspection Division supervisors and FBI OGC attorneys told us that they repeatedly instructed the inspectors to "err on the side of over-reporting" possible intelligence violations even if they did not involve an NSL-related violation.[49] Also, the Chief Division Counsels (CDC) at each field office were made available to answer questions from the inspectors while they were on site at the field offices.

When the inspectors noted possible violations during the field review, they were instructed to give a paper copy of the NSL, the associated approval memorandum (referred to as the approval Electronic Communication or EC), and a PIOB violation form to the field office's CDC. The inspectors also transmitted the results of their reviews to the Inspection Division on a daily basis. The Inspection Division aggregated this information into a consolidated database for analysis.

For each possible intelligence violation the FBI inspectors identified and reported to the Inspection Division the CDCs were instructed to make a preliminary decision as to whether the matter should be reported to the FBI OGC as a possible intelligence violation based on guidance issued by the FBI OGC in November 2006. These preliminary decisions were forwarded to the Inspection Division. Regardless of these initial decisions, the CDCs were instructed to then make an "official" determination in writing

FBI OGC NSL tracking database showed that one or more NSLs had been issued as well as investigations in which the database showed no NSLs. The inspectors found NSLs in [Text not available] of the case files. The number of case files reviewed at each field office ranged from [Text not available] in the El Paso and Anchorage field offices to [Text not available] in the New York field office. The number of NSLs reviewed in each field office ranged from [Text not available] in Knoxville to [Text not available] in the Washington, D.C., field offices. The FBI's random sample included [Text not available] cases that were designated as FBI Headquarters investigations. There were 16 NSLs within these case files, and these NSLs were reviewed as a part of the FBI's field audit, not the Headquarters audit.

48 However, the FBI inspectors could not locate records in response to 532 NSLs, and 1,175 NSLs (including these 532) were not fully reviewed because the inspectors could not find all relevant documents (approval electronic communication (EC)), NSL, and responsive records) or were unable to make a determination as to whether a possible intelligence violation had occurred. We did not include in our calculations of the unauthorized collection portion of the PIOB error rates NSLs for which responsive records could not be located.

49 Inspection Division personnel supervising the audit told us that they instructed the inspectors not to search case files for infractions unrelated to national security letter authorities (for example, if investigative activity unrelated to NSLs occurred after authorization for the investigation had lapsed). However, if they encountered such violations, referred to as "other" reportable possible intelligence violations, they were instructed to document the possible violations.

and forward those decisions, along with all NSL-related documentation, to the FBI OGC[50] As of February 2008, the FBI OGC was in the process of adjudicating which matters in fact were reportable to the FBI OGC and determining which matters should be reported to the IOB.

2. The FBI's Post-Field Work Analysis

Upon completion of the field review, supervisors in the Inspection Division analyzed the results reported by the inspectors to identify the extent of the NSL-related possible intelligence violations in each FBI field office. During their preliminary review of the results, the supervisors discovered that:

- some information entered by the inspectors was incomplete or contradictory;
- some forms reported possible intelligence violations that the supervisors did not believe rose to the level of being reportable; and
- certain field offices had significantly lower rates of possible intelligence violations compared with other field offices.

To resolve contradictions in information submitted by inspectors and determine whether possible intelligence violations had occurred, Inspection Division supervisors performed what they termed a "scrubbing process" during which they examined each form to identify and resolve any discrepancies. Specifically, the supervisors reviewed the PIOB forms to determine why some forms were submitted without identifying a possible intelligence violation and to resolve contradictions between possible violations noted and the inspectors' comments.

Simultaneously, the Inspection Division supervisors requested guidance from the FBI OGC regarding violations that the supervisors did not believe rose to the level of a possible intelligence violation, such as instances in which inspectors were unable to locate the signed copy of an NSL.[51] The FBI OGC agreed with the supervisors that certain types of errors noted by the inspectors did not constitute an NSL-related possible intelligence violation. Consequently, the FBI OGC attorneys created a list of 11 NSL-related infractions they termed "administrative errors." Table 3.1 provides

[50] As of December 4, 2007, an Inspection Division supervisor told us that all 56 CDCs had forwarded documentation of the reported possible intelligence violations to the FBI OGC. However, some CDCs did not make official determinations of whether the matters reported to them were possible intelligence violations; instead, these CDCs merely forwarded the facts and documents related to the potential intelligence violations to the FBI OGC for its review and determination.

[51] As we reported in our first NSL report, FBI policy did not require retention of signed copies of NSLs. In March 2007, in response to the OIG's recommendations, the FBI directed that signed copies of NSLs must be retained in the investigative file to which the request relates. See Records Management Division, Federal Bureau of Investigation (FBI), electronic communication to all Divisions, Procedural and Operational Issuances, March 9, 2007. As described fully in Chapter Two of this report, FBI policy now requires that the NSL itself must be uploaded as an NSL document into the Automated Case Support (ACS) system. Id.

a list of the infractions the FBI OGC deemed NSL-related administrative errors. Using the FBI OGC's list, the Inspection Division supervisors re-examined the entries on the PIOB forms and determined whether they were reportable NSL-related possible intelligence violations or administrative errors.

Finally, regarding the variation in PIOB violation rates between field offices, the Inspection Division supervisors were concerned that the inspectors who reported low PIOB violation rates for the field offices to which they were assigned may have missed possible intelligence violations. To determine whether that had occurred, the Inspection Division conducted follow-up visits to six field offices to re-review the files examined during the initial inspection. The supervisors' concerns proved correct. During the initial field visits, the inspectors had identified one NSL-related possible intelligence violation in these six offices. Inspectors assigned to the follow-up visits found 83 additional possible intelligence violations that were missed by the first inspection teams.

Table 3.1: NSL-Related Infractions Identified in the FBI's 2007 Field Review Later Classified by the FBI as "Administrative Errors"

Nature of NSL Infraction	Number of Infractions
Unable to locate NSL results/records submitted by the NSL recipient	532
Approval EC lacked detailed information on specific records requested compared with details in the NSL	433
Approval EC did not cite specific statutory authority for issuing the NSL	136
Unable to locate signed NSL	102
Unable to determine if the NSL was served	**81**
Unable to locate initialed/approval EC requesting issuance of NSL	**71**
Approval EC requesting issuance of NSL lacked appropriate approvals	**50**
Records requested in approval EC differed from records requested in the NSL	**33**
Statutory authority cited in the approval EC differed from the citation in the NSL	**33**
Error in typing/recording of NSL date	**20**
Error in typing/recording of approval EC date	**7**
Total	**1,498**

3. The FBI's Findings

After the Inspection Division supervisors completed the scrubbing process, they reported to the OIG that as of November 2007, they had identified 640 NSL-related possible intelligence violations in 634 NSLs.[52] These 640 matters included:

- **Improper Authorizations.** Approximately 6 percent involved violations of internal FBI policy designed to ensure appropriate supervisory and legal review. These included instances in which NSLs were issued from investigations that were inactive or had not been properly authorized, lacked documentation of predication, lacked documentation of required approvals, or did not document the relevance of the requested information to the underlying investigation in the approval ECs.
- **Improper Requests.** Approximately 4 percent involved NSLs that requested information the FBI was not authorized to request.
- **Unauthorized Collections.** The majority (90 percent) involved the receipt of records not requested in the NSL or the receipt of information not relevant to an FBI investigation.

"Unauthorized collections" is a phrase used by the FBI and the OIG to describe several circumstances in which the FBI receives information in response to NSLs that was not requested or was mistakenly requested. For example, many unauthorized collections occur due to errors on the part of NSL recipients when they provide more information than was requested (such as records for a longer period of time or records on additional persons). The FBI sometimes also refers to these matters as "over collections" or "overproductions." We refer to these as "initial third party errors" because, while the NSL recipient may initially have provided more information than requested, the FBI may or may not have compounded the initial error by using or uploading the information. Other unauthorized collections can result from FBI errors, such as when a typographical error in the telephone number or e-mail address results in the acquisition of data on the wrong person or e-mail address. When we present data on "unauthorized collections" in this report we note whether the infraction occurred due to initial third party error or FBI error.

Table 3.2 provides more specific information on the types of NSL-related possible intelligence violations identified during the FBI's field review and

[52] The data presented below describing the 640 NSL violations is a summary of the initial decisions made by CDCs during the FBI's field review and does not reflect the final decisions that will be made by the FBI OGC. As we previously noted, as of February 2008 the FBI OGC had not completed reviewing and adjudicating all of the possible intelligence violations identified during the FBI's field review. The FBI OGC will make the determination as to the types of potential intelligence violations that the field should report to the FBI OGC as well as the violations the FBI determines are reportable to the IOB.

Table 3.2: Possible NSL-Related IOB Violations Identified in the FBI's 2007 Field Review (2003 through 2006)

Category	Possible NSL-Related IOB Violation	Number	Percentage
Improper Authorizations (FBI error)	NSL issued with no authorized investigation (no case ever opened)	2	-
	NSL lacked predication or sufficient justification, or information sought not relevant to the investigation	5	-
	NSL issued in a preliminary investigation prior to January 16, 2003	0	-
	NSL issued in a preliminary investigation under FCRA between January 16, 2003, and December 31, 2003	2	-
	NSL. lacked approval of Senior Executive Service official	28	-
	NSL requested before or after authorized period of investigation	3	-
	Total Improper Authorizations	**40**	**6.25%**
Improper Requests (FBI error)	NSL issued under FCRAv for a consumer full credit report in a counterintelligence case with no nexus to international terrorism	14	-
	NSL-requested information beyond the scope permissible by statute	10	-
	Total Improper Requests	**24**	**3.75%**
Unauthorized Collections (FBI error or initial third party error)	The NSL recipient provided data in excess of the NSL request (initial third party error)	364	-
	The NSL recipient furnished records or information not requested in the NSL (initial third party error)	312	-
	NSL issued with typographical mistakes in names, addresses, telephone numbers, account numbers, etc. (FBI error)	19	-
	Note: The total of the three rows above must be adjusted to account for NSLs that had violations reported in more than one category	(119)	-
	Total Unauthorized Collections	**576**	**90.00%**
	Total NSL PIOB Violations	**640**	**100.00%**

Note: We derived the percentage of violations by dividing the number of occurrences by 640, the total number of NSL-related PIOB violations.

shows how many times each type occurred. In the table below and elsewhere in this report, we use the phrase "initial third party error" to describe a mistake initially attributable to the NSL recipient of providing more information than requested by the FBI. In some instances, FBI employees identified such overproductions and segregated the information, rather than using it or uploading the information into FBI databases. However, we found that in all but 1 percent of the instances identified by the FBI's field review (4 of 557), FBI personnel failed to identify the improperly provided information and thereby failed to take required steps for sequestering the information from the case file and ensuring that the information was not used or uploaded into FBI databases.[53] Because these 553 matters were not identified by field agents or supervisors, they were not self-reported to the FBI OGC as required.

As shown in Table 3.2, 576 of 640 (90 percent) possible intelligence violations were the result of the unauthorized collection of telephone or e-mail transactional records, financial records, and credit records pursuant to the ECPA, RFPA, and FCRA NSL statutes. These unauthorized collections occurred due to errors made either by NSL recipients (initial third party error) or by the FBI. For example, these included instances in which:

1. The NSL recipient erred by providing data in excess of the NSL request, such as providing information for a full billing cycle rather than providing records for the shorter period requested in the NSL.[54]
2. The NSL recipient erred by furnishing records or information not requested in the NSL, such as information on individuals who used a particular telephone number or e-mail address during dates before or after the subject of the FBI investigation.[55] Certain NSL recipients also produced Social Security Numbers and dates of birth in response to ECPA NSLs seeking subscriber information, even though this information was not requested in the NSL.[56]

---

[53] As discussed in Chapter Seven, On August 1, 2007, the IOB directed the FBI OGC to report third party errors that are compounded by the FBI. After this direction, FBI OGC officials told us that they began evaluating third party errors to determine if the FBI compounded the errors by using the inappropriately provided information or uploading it into FBI databases. If the FBI compounded a third party error, FBI OGC officials told us they would report the matter to the IOB.

[54] In May 2006, the FBI OGC approved use of a revised attachment for ECPA toll record NSLs that included information "which encompasses the billing cycle that is used with respect to the account(s) information requested" among the types of records that may be considered by the recipients to be "toll billing records."

[55] FBI OGC attorneys told us that if the date range in the NSL was reasonable when the NSL was issued, and the records received were within the date range of the NSL, the FBI OGC does not consider such records to be unauthorized collections.

[56] As discussed in Chapter Two of this report, in August 2007 the FBI OGC requested a legal opinion from the Department's Office of Legal Counsel (OLC) on whether the FBI may lawfully retain Social Security Numbers and date of birth information provided to the FBI in response to NSLs seeking subscriber information pursuant to the *Electronic Communications Privacy Act* (ECPA), 18 U.S.C. § 2709(c). As of February 2008, the OLC had not issued its opinion.

3. The FBI erred by requesting information on the wrong telephone number, e-mail account, or Internet Protocol address in the NSL due to FBI typographical errors.

4. Comparison of Findings in the FBI's 2007 NSL Field Review and the OIG's First NSL Report

The findings of the FBI's 2007 NSL field review were generally consistent with the OIG's findings in our March 2007 NSL report as to the types of errors made by FBI agents in their use of NSL authorities. Although the types of possible intelligence violations identified by the OIG and in the FBI's 2007 field review were similar, the FBI's review found a higher overall violation rate and a higher rate of errors attributable to third party unauthorized collections than the OIG found.

In the OIG's judgmental sample of 77 national security investigation case files maintained by 4 field offices, we identified 22 possible violations in the 293 NSLs we examined that we believed should have been reported to the FBI OGC.[57] Of those 22 violations, 10 involved unauthorized collections due to third party error. In its 2007 field review, FBI inspectors reviewed 6,688 NSLs for which all relevant NSL documents were available, (approval EC, NSL, and responsive records) and found 634 NSLs that contained 640 possible violations. Of those 640 violations, 557 involved unauthorized collections attributable to initial third party errors. A comparison of these findings for the two reporting periods is illustrated in Chart 3.1.

B. The FBI's 2007 Headquarters Review of NSLs

As a result of the OIG's findings in our first NSL report, the FBI Inspection Division also conducted a special review of NSLs issued by Headquarters divisions to determine the nature and extent of any problems associated with these NSLs. In this section, we describe the Inspection Division's review of NSLs issued by Headquarters divisions from 2003 through 2006, including the FBI's methodology, findings, and subsequent recommendations.

---

[57] Following issuance of our first NSL report, the FBI OGC instructed pertinent field offices to report the 22 potential IOBs to the FBI OGC. The FBI OGC determined that only five were reportable to the IOB. The five matters that were reported to the IOB were issuance of an NSL without obtaining required approval to extend the investigation; issuance of an NSL for material that arguably constituted prohibited content; issuance of an NSL citing the ECPA NSL statute that requested the *Right to Financial Privacy Act* (RFPA) financial records associated with e-mail accounts; and issuance of two NSLs requesting consumer full credit reports pursuant to 15 U.S.C. § 1681v in a counterintelligence case with no international terrorism nexus.

Chart 3.1: Comparison of Possible NSL-Related IOB Violations Identified in the OIG's First NSL Report and the FBI's 2007 Field Review

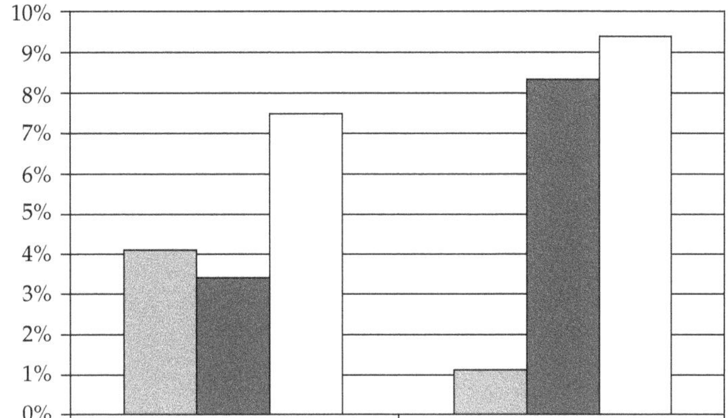

	OIG NSL I (2003 - 2005)	FBI Field Review (2003 - 2006)
FBI NSL PIOBs	4.10%	1.10%
Third Party NSL PIOBs	3.41%	8.33%
Total NSL PIOB Rate	7.51%	9.43%

1. Background

In our first NSL report, the OIG found that FBI Headquarters personnel issued approximately 300 NSLs exclusively from control files rather than from investigative files. If NSLs are issued exclusively from control files, case agents and their supervisors cannot determine whether the requests are tied to substantive investigations that have established the required evidentiary predicate for issuing NSLs. Issuing NSLs from control files is contrary to internal FBI policies.

2. FBI Methodology

To determine the extent of NSL-related possible intelligence violations in FBI Headquarters divisions, in April and May 2007 the FBI Inspection Division reviewed a random sample of approximately 10 percent of 2,440 NSLs (249 were selected for review) issued between January 1, 2003, and December 31, 2006, by FBI Headquarters divisions.[58] The FBI searched the Automated Case Support (ACS) system to identify the universe of NSLs issued from Headquarters.[59] Once the universe of NSLs was identified and

[58] The Inspection Division's review of the Headquarters-issued NSLs consisted of a 10-percent sample of NSLs issued from Headquarters. This was a different methodology than that used in the field review, which consisted of a review of all NSLs contained within the 10-percent sample of randomly selected national security investigation case files.

[59] The Inspection Division used a keyword search on approval ECs in the ACS system to identify its universe of NSLs. However, this search would have missed those NSLs issued without approval

the sample was selected, the process used to conduct the Headquarters review was similar to that used for the field review: inspectors manually and electronically (through the ACS system) reviewed documentation, including the approval ECs, the NSLs, and information received in response to the NSLs for compliance with NSL statutes, Attorney General Guidelines, and internal FBI policies.

3. The FBI's Headquarters Findings

The Inspection Division's review of Headquarters-issued NSLs produced much higher violation rates than those the FBI reported in the field review. In total, the FBI inspectors identified 165 possible violations in the 249 Headquarters NSLs they reviewed. The 249 Headquarters NSLs were tied to 25 case files, of which 15 were investigative files and 10 were control files. The Headquarters review also identified a type of error—issuance of NSLs solely from control files—that was not identified in the FBI's field review and that accounted for a significant proportion of the possible intelligence violations. Over 50 percent (125) of the NSLs in the FBI's Headquarters review sample were issued exclusively from control files, in violation of internal FBI policy. As a result of these NSLs, the overall PIOB violation rate for Headquarters-issued NSLs was 71.5 percent, compared with a 9.4-percent violation rate in the FBI's field review.[60]

Even if the 125 NSLs issued from control files are not included, the resulting violation rate of 22.4 percent would place Headquarters among those field offices having the highest violation rates. Only 3 of 56 field offices had higher violation rates than Headquarters.

Table 3.3 provides specific information on the types of possible violations found during the FBI's Headquarters review and identifies how many times each violation occurred.

The FBI inspectors reviewing Headquarters-issued NSLs had greater difficulty locating signed copies of NSLs and records provided by NSL recipients than inspectors who reviewed NSLs during the field review. During the review of Headquarters-issued NSLs, inspectors were unable to locate signed copies of 225 of the 249 NSLs identified for the review and were unable to locate the records provided by the NSL recipients in response to

ECs. Additionally, the NSLs selected for the review of Headquarters' case files could not be identified by case file number through the ACS system because NSLs issued by Headquarters officials did not always have a case file associated with the NSLs.

60 The FBI's Headquarters review found NSLs issued from control files because the FBI had not issued specific guidance on this issue until 2007. As discussed in our first NSL report, many of the NSLs issued from Headquarters control files related to classified special projects. See NSL I, 98-103. The FBI Inspection Division reported that 88 of these 125 NSLs (70 percent) were generated from these classified special projects.

Table 3.3: Possible NSL-Related IOB Violations Identified in the FBI's 2007 Headquarters Review (2003 through 2006)

Category	Number of Errors	Rate of Error
NSL issued from control file with no open investigation (FBI error)	125	50.2%
NSL lacked predication or sufficient justification, or information sought not relevant to the investigation (FBI error)	5	2.0%
NSL requested information beyond the scope permissible by statute (FBI error)	2	0.8%
NSL issued with typographical mistakes in names, addresses, telephone numbers, account numbers (FBI error)	1	0.6%
NSL recipients provided data in excess of the NSL request, or furnished records or information not requested in the NSLs (initial third party error)	32	17.9%*
Total	**165**	**71.5%**

*The rate of third party error is based only on the 179 NSLs for which inspectors were able to locate and review records obtained in response to the NSLs. When responsive information could not be located during the Headquarters review, the OIG eliminated those NSLs from the third party error rate calculation.

70 NSLs (28 percent).[61] In addition, the inspectors found 168 approval ECs that did not reference preliminary or full investigations, which made it difficult to determine if the NSLs were issued from authorized investigations as required by the NSL statutes and the Attorney General's Guidelines for FBI National Security Investigations and Foreign Intelligence Collection (NSI Guidelines).

To address the deficiencies identified in its review of Headquarters-issued NSLs, the Inspection Division recommended that: (1) the Assistant Director for the Counterterrorism Division (CTD) perform a file review every 90 days of all Headquarters national security investigation case files to ensure NSL compliance, and (2) internal controls should be strengthened to ensure that each Headquarters NSL can be verified and associated with its responsive records. The Inspection Division also recommended that the Assistant Director for the CTD and the FBI General Counsel provide appropriate training to CTD personnel on the proper use of NSLs and that the Assistant Director for the CTD take action to facilitate the appropriate reporting of possible NSL-related intelligence violations to the FBI OGC.

[61] At the time of the Headquarters review, responsive records could not be located. Inspection Division personnel told us that these records were later located in Headquarters closed files and were reviewed to determine if there were overcollection.

As of October 2007, a draft e-mail had been prepared for the signature of the Assistant Director instructing the FBI Headquarters divisions to review the possible intelligence violations identified by the Inspection Division's review of Headquarters-issued NSLs. The Headquarters division personnel were also instructed to provide a written response to the Inspection Division with specific information on each possible intelligence violation, stating whether they agreed that a possible violation existed and to report those findings to the Internal Investigation Section, to the CTD, and to the FBI OGC.

C. The FBI's Review of FCRA NSLs Seeking Consumer Full Credit Reports in Counterintelligence Investigations

In response to the findings of the OIG in the first NSL report, the FBI recognized that some of its employees did not understand that a FCRA NSL could not be used to obtain a consumer full credit report in a counterintelligence investigation that does not have a nexus to international terrorism. Accordingly, to ensure that no such credit reports were in its files, the FBI ordered a review of all FCRA NSLs that had been issued in counterintelligence matters from January 1, 2002 through December 31, 2006, in all 56 field offices. In this section, we provide a brief summary of the OIG's findings in our first NSL report on the FBI's use of FCRA NSLs from 2003 through 2005. We then describe the results of the FBI's 2007 review of FCRA NSLs issued in counterintelligence investigations during the 5-year period the FBI reviewed.

1. The OIG's Findings on FCRA NSLs in Our First NSL Report

In our first NSL report, the OIG examined the potential intelligence violations self-reported by FBI personnel to the FBI OGC in 2003 through 2005 and found that only one involved an improper request for a consumer full credit report in a counterintelligence investigation with no nexus to international terrorism.[62] This matter subsequently was reported to the IOB.[63] However, during our review of investigative case files in four FBI field offices, we identified two additional improper requests for consumer full credit reports in counterintelligence investigations. These improper requests were not reported to the FBI OGC pursuant to the mandatory

[62] The FCRA was enacted in 1970 to protect personal information collected by credit reporting agencies. In 2001, the Patriot Act amended the FCRA to add a new national security letter authority, referred to as FCRAv NSLs, which authorizes the FBI to obtain a credit reporting agency's reports and "all other" consumer information in its files. Thus, the FBI can now obtain full credit reports on individuals during national security investigations upon certification that the information is "necessary for" the FBI's "investigations of, or intelligence or counterintelligence activities or analysis related to, international terrorism . . . ." See NSL I, 14-15.

[63] Id. at 70-72.

self-reporting requirement.[64] After examining these two additional matters, the FBI reported both to the IOB in 2007.

In addition to noting the potential intelligence violations involving use of FCRA NSLs summarized above, we found in our first NSL report that FBI field personnel sometimes confused the two NSL authorities under the FCRA. Although the National Security Law Branch (NSLB) attorneys sent periodic guidance and e-mails to all CDCs to clarify the distinctions between the two FCRA NSLs, we found that problems and confusion persisted. Accordingly, we recommended that the FBI issue additional guidance to field offices to clarify the two authorities and improve the identification of possible intelligence violations arising from the use of FCRA NSLs.[65]

2. The FBI's 2007 Review of FCRA NSLs

a. Directive to the Field

On March 5, 2007, the FBI's Executive Assistant Director for the National Security Branch (EAD NSB) directed the FBI's 56 field offices and the Counterintelligence Division to review all FCRA NSLs issued from January 1, 2002, through December 31, 2006, in counterintelligence investigations.[66] The purpose of the review was to determine whether any of these NSLs requested consumer full credit reports or resulted in the receipt of such reports in violation of the NSL statutes, Attorney General Guidelines, or internal FBI policies. The directive stated that if any such reports were requested or obtained in the absence of the required nexus to international terrorism, the incidents were to be reported to the FBI OGC as possible intelligence violations regardless of whether the information was requested by the FBI or was erroneously produced by the credit reporting agency. The directive also stated that the consumer full credit reports must be sequestered with the field office's CDC pending the issuance of the FBI OGC's opinion as to whether the matter should be sent to the IOB.[67]

b. Summary of Findings

In response to the directive, 41 FBI field offices reported that they had identified one or more FCRA NSLs that constituted improper requests or

---

[64] Id. at 79-81.

[65] We discuss this guidance in Chapter Two of this report in connection with Recommendation 4 in our first NSL report.

[66] National Security Branch, FBI, electronic communication to all Field Offices and Counterintelligence, Guidance on Use of Fair Credit Reporting Act NSLs in Counterintelligence Investigations; Review of Fair Credit Reporting Act NSLs Issued in CY 2006 in Counterintelligence Investigations, March 5, 2007. In response to the directive from the EAD NSB, each of the 56 field offices reported their results via EC. These are the documents the OIG reviewed in order to perform its analysis of the results of the FBI's FCRA NSL review. The Counterintelligence Division responded that it had not issued any FCRA NSLs during the review period.

[67] Id.

resulted in unauthorized collections. The two types of unauthorized collections included instances in which the response to the FCRA. request exceeded the scope of the request by providing the following:

- The NSL requested FCRAu(a) financial institution-identifying information or FCRAu(b) consumer-identifying information but the response included a consumer full credit report.
- The NSL requested FCRAu(b) consumer-identifying information but the response included financial institution-identifying information.

Thirteen of the 56 field offices (23 percent) reported being unable to locate the results of at least 1 FCRA NSL. One office reported being unable to locate the results of 97 FCRA NSLs. Table 3.4 summarizes the potential violations reported by the FBI field offices to the FBI OGC in response to the EAD NSB's directive. Each type of violation is described further in the following section.

Table3.4: Possible FCRA IOB Violations Identified in the FBI's 2007 Review of NSLs Issued in Counterintelligence Investigations (2002 through 2006)

FCRA PIOBs Reported by FBI Field Offices	No. of Field Offices	No. of NSLs	No. of Consumer Full Credit Reports Provided to the FBI	No. of PIOBs Previously Self-Reported
NSL requests for consumer full credit reports in counterintelligence investigations with no nexus to international terrorism (FBI error)	11	33	29	2
NSL requests for limited credit information for which consumer full credit reports were provided (initial third party error)	35	233	233	6
NSL requests for consumer-identifying information for which financial institution-identifying information was provided (initial third party error)	1	1	N/A	0

c. Improper Requests

Of the 56 FBI field offices, 11 reported that they had issued a total of 33 FCRAv NSLs in counterintelligence investigations with no nexus to international terrorism.[68] However, in one instance, a case agent and supervisor thought that the original FCRAv request was justified because the investigation later developed a nexus to international terrorism.[69] In another four instances, the requesting field offices did not receive the consumer full credit reports that they had improperly requested. Consequently, of the 33 FCRAv NSLs reported by the field offices, 33 were improper requests and 29 were improper requests for which the FBI obtained unauthorized information (consumer full credit reports). Of the 33 improper FCRAv NSLs identified in the review, only 2 had previously been reported to the FBI OGC pursuant to the mandatory self-reporting requirement.

d. Unauthorized Collections

Thirty-five of the FBI's 56 field offices reported that they had obtained unauthorized collections in response to NSLs seeking limited credit information pursuant to 15 U.S.C. § 1681u(a). These field offices had issued a total of 233 FCRAu NSLs requesting limited credit information, in response to which credit reporting agencies had produced consumer full credit reports.[70] During the review period, the FBI had issued a total of [Text not available] FCRAu NSLs of which [Text not available] were issued in counterintelligence cases. Thus, [Text not available] percent of these [Text not available] NSLs resulted in unauthorized collections. Of these 233 unauthorized collections, only 6 (3 percent) had previously been reported to the FBI OGC pursuant to the mandatory self-reporting requirement.

In another type of unauthorized collection, one FBI field office reported that it had obtained financial institution-identifying information (permissible in response to 15 U.S.C. § 1681u(a) NSLs) in response to an NSL seeking consumer-identifying information pursuant to 15 U.S.C. § 1681u(b).[71]

---

68 Three of these 33 FCRAv NSLs contained a reference to the FCRAu NSL statute, but the text of the NSL requested "credit reports" or "all information in the file." The FBI categorized these as improper requests.

69 FBI OGC attorneys told the OIG that the nexus to international terrorism must exist at the time the NSL is issued.

70 Among the 233 unauthorized collections was one instance in which the case agent could easily read the text of the consumer full credit report, even though the credit reporting agency attempted to redact this information. Moreover, the case agent relied on the poorly redacted information received from the credit reporting agency to later issue two NSLs seeking financial information pursuant to the *Right to Financial Privacy Act* (RFPA) NSL statute.

71 The FCRAu(a) NSL statute, 15 U.S.C. § 1681u(a), authorizes the FBI to obtain the names and addresses of all financial institutions at which a consumer maintains or has maintained an account. The FCRAu(b) NSL statute, 15 U.S.C. § 1681u(b), authorizes the FBI to obtain the consumer's name, address, former addresses, places of employment, or former places of employment.

II. The OIG's Analysis of the FBI's 2007 NSL Reviews

In this section, we provide the OIG's analysis of the three NSL reviews conducted by the FBI in 2007, described above.

A. The OIG's Verification of the FBI's 2007 Field Review of NSLs

To assess the accuracy of the FBI's field review, the OIG visited three field offices and re-examined case files that had been reviewed by FBI inspectors during the field review. We found that the FBI's field review used a sound sampling methodology but that FBI inspectors missed a significant number of NSL-related possible intelligence violations as they were reviewing the case files, thereby understating the actual rate of possible intelligence violations. In this section, we describe the methodology of our review, our findings, and our analysis.

1. The OIG's Methodology

The OIG reviewed a judgmental sample of the case files examined by FBI inspectors at three field offices during the FBI's March 2007 field review. The OIG's review was not designed to question the judgments of the CDCs or the Inspection Division determinations regarding whether violations identified by the inspectors were reportable to the IOB. Instead, our objective was to determine if the inspectors had identified all of the NSL-related possible intelligence violations in the files. Therefore, in selecting our sample for review, the OIG did not include any NSLs that were previously identified by the FBI's inspectors as containing possible NSL-related intelligence violations.

The three field offices we selected for our review had an average NSL violation rate below the FBI field review's overall 9.43-percent violation rate.[72] Just as the Inspection Division did when selecting its field offices for revisits, the OIG selected field offices with NSL violation rates below the overall average to test the assumption that these lower-than-average rates were the result of FBI inspectors missing violations in some of the NSLs they reviewed.

Using a judgmental sample, the OIG selected 15 case files in each of the 3 field offices, and from those files identified up to 60 NSLs in each field office to review.[73] The OIG selected case files that contained possible intelligence

[72] At the 3 field offices we visited, the FBI inspectors had previously reviewed a total of 1,114 NSLs and identified 33 NSL-related possible intelligence violations in those NSLs, for a PIOB violation rate of 2.96 percent for the 3 offices. Individually, the PIOB violation rates for the three offices were 2.56 percent, 2.47 percent, and 6.30 percent.

[73] The OIG selected sufficient samples to allow for cases that were not available for review. We ultimately reviewed 13 files in Field Office 1, 14 files in Field Office 2, and 15 files in Field Office 3, for a total of 42 files. From those 42 files, we reviewed a total of 169 different NSLs.

violations previously identified by the FBI inspectors during their review (and later confirmed by the CDCs), as well as case files in which no possible intelligence violations were identified by the inspectors. We reviewed the NSLs using the same criteria that the FBI inspectors were instructed to use during the FBI field review.

2. Findings of the OIG's Review

The OIG's review found that the FBI's field review did not identify a significant number of NSL-related possible intelligence violations. In the 42 case files re-examined by the OIG, the FBI's inspectors had previously reviewed 396 NSLs and identified 13 possible intelligence violations, for a violation rate of 3.28 percent. The OIG re-examined 169 of the NSLs in which the FBI inspectors had identified no possible intelligence violations, and we identified an additional 15 possible intelligence violations, for a violation rate of 8.88 percent.[74] Overall, the violation rate identified by the OIG was almost 3 times higher than the violation rate found by the FBI in these 42 case files. Table 3.5 describes the type and number of violations identified by the OIG in these case files. As noted above, we use the phrase "initial third party error" to describe instances in which the NSL recipient provided records beyond those requested in the NSLs. However, the FBI may at times have compounded the initial third party error by using or uploading the improperly provided information.

Chart 3.2 compares the error rates identified in the 42 case files at the 3 field offices visited by both the FBI and the OIG. The chart illustrates the rate of errors attributable to the FBI or initial third party error.

Table 3.6 illustrates the number of NSLs reviewed, the number of possible intelligence violations found in the 42 case files reviewed by the FBI and re-checked by the OIG, and the rate (occurrence of errors) at which the FBI and the OIG found possible intelligence violations within the sample reviewed.

Most of the possible intelligence violations identified by the OIG should have been identified by FBI inspectors if the inspectors compared the data provided by the NSL recipient with the data requested in the NSL and determined whether the data provided was relevant to the investigation. The violations were readily apparent to the OIG upon a review of the case files. For example, we identified instances in which the dates on the information provided by the NSL recipients did not match the dates requested on the NSLs.

[74] The OIG was unable to locate records responsive to 15 of the 169 NSLs we reviewed. The 8.88 percent violation rate therefore did not include possible intelligence violations that may have resulted from records obtained in response to these 15 NSLs.

Table 3.5: Possible NSL-Related IOB Violations Identified by the OIG Not Identified by FBI Inspectors at Three Field Offices During the FBI's 2007 Field Review

Category	NSL-Related PIOB Violations	Number
Improper Authorization	NSL lacked predication, sufficient justification, or documentation of relevance to the investigation (FBI error)	2
	Subtotal	**2**
Unauthorized Collection	NSL issued with typographical mistakes in names, addresses, telephone numbers, account numbers, etc. (FBI error)	2
	NSL resulted in collection of data requested in the NSL but for a longer (or different) period than was designated in the NSL (initial third party error)	6
	NSL resulted in collection of data not requested in the NSL or which was not relevant to the investigation (initial third party error)	5
	Subtotal	**13**
	Total	**15**

The five most serious possible intelligence violations identified by the OIG that were missed by the FBI's inspectors were:

- The receipt of telephone toll billing records for the "family plan" (multiple telephone numbers) of individuals who were not relevant to an authorized investigation; these telephone toll billing records were not sequestered and were maintained in an FBI case file. They were not uploaded into FBI data systems.[75]
- The NSL requested data on a wrong telephone number due to an FBI typographical error in the area code; these telephone toll billing records were not sequestered and were maintained in an FBI case file. They were not uploaded into FBI data systems.
- The NSL recipient provided telephone toll billing records for 1 year earlier than the time period requested by the FBI.

[75] The records obtained from the provider showed that the individual who was relevant to an authorized investigation was associated with the telephone number for the last 21 days of the 7-month period requested by the NSL. The FBI received additional telephone records related to two previous subscribers of the telephone number identified in the NSL. There was no indication that either of the previous subscribers were subjects of, or relevant to, any FBI investigation. The records of one of the previous subscribers included toll billing records for the telephone number listed in the NSL as well as multiple "family plan" lines for a period of 2 1/2 months within the 7-month period. During its review of the case file, the OIG identified these records for the two prior subscribers more than a year after the records were provided to the case agent.

Chart 3.2: Comparison of Possible NSL-Related IOB Violations Identified by the FBI and the OIG (by category) in NSLs Reviewed in Three Field Offices

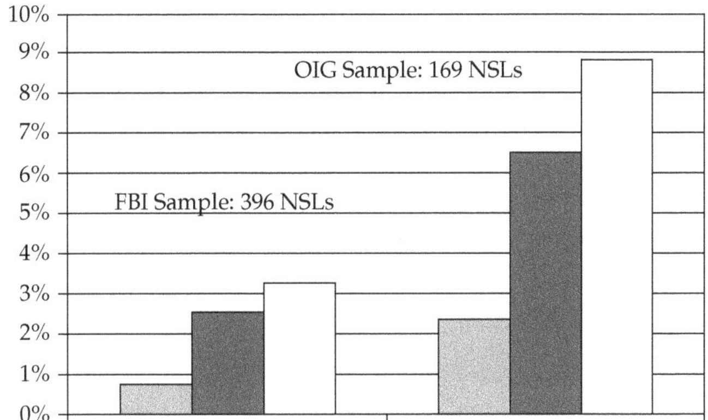

	FBI	OIG
PIOB Rate Due to FBI Error	0.76%	2.37%
PIOB Rate Due to Initial Third Party Error	2.52%	6.51%
Total PIOB Rate	3.28%	8.88%

Table 3.6: Comparison of Possible NSL-Related IOB Violations Identified by the FBI and the OIG at Three Field Offices

Field Office	NSLs Reviewed by FBI	PIOB Violations Identified by FBI	FBI PIOB Violation Rate	NSLs Re-Reviewed by OIG	PIOB Violations Identified by OIG	OIG PIOB Violation Rate
#1	210	5	**2.38%**	57	2	**3.51%**
#2	121	3	**2.48%**	56	3	**5.36%**
#3	65	5	**7.69%**	56	10	**17.86%**
Totals	**396**	**13**	**3.28%**	**169**	**15**	**8.88%**

- Two instances in which documents reflecting receipt of responsive records specifically incorporated Social Security Numbers and date of birth information on individuals who were not relevant to the underlying investigation; the error was compounded when these documents were electronically uploaded into the ACS system by the field office that served the NSL.[76]

[76] The case agent in the field office that issued the NSL had noted on the responsive records: "individual account records not relevant to this matter. New subscriber not related to subject. Don't upload."

The OIG's re-examination of case files in three FBI field offices demonstrated that the procedures implemented by the FBI for reviewing case files were not effective in ensuring that all NSL-related possible intelligence violations were identified. While the OIG is unable to calculate a revised NSL-related PIOB violation rate for all field offices, our determination that the FBI's possible intelligence violation totals are understated is also supported by additional data from the FBI's field review. Specifically, in the FBI's follow-up reviews of NSLs in 6 field offices in which FBI inspectors had initially identified only 1 possible intelligence violation during the field review, the FBI identified 83 additional NSL-related possible intelligence violations.

B. OIG Analysis

1. The OIG's Conclusions Regarding the Field and Headquarters Reviews

Despite the short period of time that the FBI devoted to planning and conducting its nationwide NSL field review, we believe the FBI used a reasonable methodology in conducting the review, committed significant resources to the effort, and made examination and analysis of the results a high priority. The FBI's 2007 field and Headquarters NSL reviews confirmed that the types of deficiencies identified by the OIG in our first NSL report occurred throughout the FBI from 2003 through 2006. Moreover, the FBI's 2007 reviews demonstrated that these deficiencies occurred in even greater numbers than the OIG found in our first NSL report.

However, we also concluded that the FBI's field review did not provide a fully reliable baseline from which to measure future improvement in compliance with NSL authorities. The OIG's re-examination of case files in three field offices that were included in the FBI's March 2007 field review demonstrated that the FBI's review missed a significant number of possible intelligence violations and therefore understated the percentage of possible violations. We believe this occurred because of:

- the short time period devoted to planning the review,
- the inspectors' lack of prior experience in conducting national security investigations or handling NSLs, and
- the Inspection Division's inability to conduct effective quality control during the review at the field offices due to time constraints it imposed on the review.

In addition, we believe the results of the FBI's field review likely understated the rate of possible intelligence violations because of the extent to which the FBI's inspectors were unable to locate information provided in response to NSLs. The inspectors were unable to locate or properly analyze the responsive records (such as financial records, credit reports, or telephone toll billing records) for almost 15 percent of the FBI's sample of NSLs issued within the 2003 to 2006 review period.[77] Without finding or fully reviewing the responsive records, FBI inspectors could not determine whether an unauthorized collection had occurred.[78] Given that unauthorized collections represented the substantial majority (576 of 640, or 90 percent) of NSL-related possible intelligence violations identified during the FBI's field review, it is likely that more possible intelligence violations would have been identified if all the responsive data for the NSLs reviewed by the FBI inspectors had been located and reviewed.[79]

Also, we note the FBI's categorization of 557 of the 576 instances of unauthorized collections (97 percent) as third party errors rather than FBI errors.[80] While the initial mistakes may be attributable to NSL recipients who provided more information than was requested in the NSLs, the FBI compounded the errors by the manner in which it handled the information. Significantly, upon receiving unauthorized information from third parties, case agents did not consistently recognize that they had received unauthorized information or, if they did, they did not take appropriate steps to sequester the information and self-report the violations to the FBI OGC.[81] As noted above, of the 557 identified possible intelligence violations that resulted initially from third party errors, case agents self-reported only 4 (less than 1 percent).[82] We determined in our field office reviews that

[77] As noted previously, the FBI inspectors could not locate records in response to 532 NSLs, and 1,175 NSLs (including the 532) were not fully reviewed because the inspectors could not find all relevant documents (approval EC, NSL, and responsive records) or were unable to make determinations as to whether a possible intelligence, violation had occurred.

[78] The FBI was able to identify only one instance of unauthorized collection without reviewing the NSL-responsive records.

[79] In light of the OIG's findings in our first NSL report that NSL-derived information could not consistently be located in the four field offices we visited, the FBI OGC issued guidance in January 2007 requiring that NSL-derived records be reviewed before uploading into FBI databases. This requirement was reiterated and expanded in the June 1, 2007, Comprehensive Guidance EC requiring that case agents ensure the NSL-derived information is responsive to the request and stored in the appropriate investigative file, and that receipt is documented. This and other recent NSL guidance are described in Chapter Two of this report.

[80] As shown in Table 3.2, FBI inspectors identified 676 third party errors (these matters are included in the 364 and 312 totals). However, in 117 instances, the same violation was reported in both third party error unauthorized collection totals and, in 2 additional instances, were also reported as FBI typographical errors. When the duplicate entries are removed, the balance is 557 violations due to initial third party errors.

[81] Guidance to the field issued by the FBI OGC on November 16, 2006, stated that if the field improperly or unintentionally acquires information through an NSL, the case agent should sequester the information with the CDC pending resolution of the potential intelligence violation by the FBI OGC. The FBI OGC thereafter advises the field whether the information may be used or whether the information must be returned to the carrier or be destroyed with appropriate documentation to the file. On November 30, 2006, the FBI OGC issued internal guidance stating that case agents are required to report to the FBI OGC the unauthorized collection of information obtained in response to NSLs, but that these matters are not reportable to the IOB. National Security Law Branch (NSLB), Federal Bureau of Investigation, memorandum to NSLB Attorneys, Guidance for Drafting IOB Opinions, November 30, 2006, 6–7. However, on August 1, 2007, the IOB directed the FBI to report instances in which the FBI "compounds a third party error by utilizing the inappropriately provided information or uploading the information into Bureau databases. . . . "

[82] The FBI's failure to self-report violations was not limited to unauthorized collections. Only 2 of the other 64 possible intelligence violations (640 minus 576) determined to be improper requests or

because the unauthorized information was not identified and sequestered, FBI agents incorporated the information into their case files. Additionally, in some cases, according to an FBI Inspection Division supervisor, this information was uploaded into the FBI's Telephone Applications database, which in turn is shared with other members of the Intelligence Community. Pursuant to the IOB's August 1, 2007, directive, the FBI OGC will be assessing whether the FBI compounded initial third party errors in the matters reported to it from the FBI's 2007 reviews.

The OIG also is concerned with the FBI's characterization of various infractions as "administrative errors." Many of these matters involved violations of internal controls designed to ensure appropriate supervisory and legal review of the use of NSL authorities. As we noted in our first NSL report, adherence to these internal controls is necessary to ensure that the FBI's NSL authorities are used appropriately and to facilitate appropriate supervisory and legal review of NSLs.[83] By calling these "administrative errors," the FBI diminishes their seriousness and fosters a perception that compliance with FBI policies governing the FBI's use of its NSL authorities is annoying paperwork. We believe that proper supervisory and legal review of all NSL-related documents are required to ensure compliance with NSL statutes, the Attorney General's NSI Guidelines, as well as internal FBI policies. We discussed this issue with senior FBI officials during the course of our review, and they agreed that the administrative error label could send the wrong message regarding the seriousness of violations of statutes, guidelines, or policies governing the use of NSLs. These officials agreed to consider using a different label, such as "lapses in internal controls," to describe these types of deficiencies.

2. The OIG's Conclusions Concerning the FBI's FCRA Review

In our first NSL report the OIG identified instances in which consumer full credit reports were obtained or requested through an NSL issued pursuant to the FCRAv NSL authority in counterintelligence investigations unrelated to international terrorism, a violation of the FCRAv NSL statute. The FBI responded by undertaking a comprehensive review of all such FCRA NSLs issued from January 1, 2002, through December 31, 2006, to determine whether these NSLs improperly requested 1681v consumer full credit reports or resulted in the receipt of unauthorized collections of consumer full credit reports in the absence of an international terrorism nexus. The review confirmed that such violations of the FCRA statutory requirements had occurred. For example, the FBI review identified 33 improper requests

improperly authorized NSLs had previously been reported to the FBI OGC through mandatory self-reporting.

[83] NSL I, 103-107.

seeking consumer full credit reports and 233 unauthorized collections of these reports.

To put these violations of the FCRA in perspective, we calculated the number of violations identified in the FBI's 2007 FCRA review in relation to the total number of FCRA NSLs issued in counterintelligence investigations during the 2002 through 2006 review period:

- The 33 improper FCRAv requests represent an error rate of [Text not available] percent since the FBI issued [Text not available] FCRAv NSLs in counterintelligence investigations during the 5-year review period.[84]
- The 233 unauthorized collections obtained in response to FCRAu NSLs represent an error rate of [Text not available] percent since the FBI issued [Text not available] FCRAu NSLs in counterintelligence investigations during the review period.[85]

The results of the FBI's FCRA review demonstrate that confusion or lack of knowledge of the statutory requirements was present among case agents, supervisors, and CDCs throughout 2006. Consequently, the FBI's mandatory self-reporting mechanism was not effective: only [Text not available] of the [Text not available] FCRA NSLs issued in counterintelligence investigations that were either improper requests or resulted in unauthorized collections—3 percent—were self-reported to the FBI OGC.[86] It appears that case agents, their supervisors, the CDCs, and the Special Agents in Charge did not recognize that they made improper requests under the FCRA. Similarly, neither the case agents nor the analysts who reviewed records responsive to these NSLs recognized that they had received unauthorized information in response to FCRA NSLs. For the most part, FBI field offices offered no explanation for the results they reported to the FBI OGC.

III. OIG Conclusions and Recommendations

In conclusion, we found that the violations identified during the FBI's 2007 Headquarters and field reviews, as well as the OIG's 2006 and 2007 field reviews, demonstrate that the additional remedial measures being implemented by the FBI are necessary and should remain a priority. These measures

[84] This calculation is based on data we analyzed from the FBI OGC's NSL tracking database.

[85] We compared the 13 possible FCRAv intelligence violations identified in the field review to the 33 possible FCRAv intelligence violations that the FBI identified in its 100-percent review of counterintelligence investigations between 2002 and 2006 in which FCRAv NSLs were issued without a nexus to international terrorism. We assumed that all 13 FCRAv matters would be among the 33 FCRAv identified in the 100-percent review. We had sufficient information to definitely match 11 of the 13. We could not match the other two matters. In one, the field office reporting in the 100-percent review did not include sufficient identifying information. In the other matter, the field review reported that a FCRAv NSL was issued but the responsive records could not be located.

[86] The 266 total is composed of 33 improper requests plus 233 unauthorized collections.

are required to ensure that: (1) the FBI adheres to national security letter authorities, Attorney General Guidelines, and internal FBI policies; (2) supervisors and CDCs provide close and independent reviews of NSLs; and (3) possible intelligence violations arising from the use of NSL authorities are promptly identified and accurately reported to the FBI OGC and, when required, to the IOB. Based on the results of the FBI's FCRA NSL review and other information about FCRA NSLs discussed elsewhere in this report, and the high percentage of instances in which the NSL-derived information could not be located by FBI and OIG inspectors, we believe the FBI must continue to reinforce the distinctions among the FBI's FCRA NSL authorities and ensure that any improperly obtained information is identified, sequestered, and reported as appropriate, and develop guidelines to improve the ability to locate NSL-derived information.

We therefore recommend that the FBI:

1. Reinforce the distinction between the FBI's NSL authorities pursuant to the *Fair Credit Reporting Act* (FCRA) throughout all levels of the FBI's National Security Branch at FBI Headquarters, in new agent training, in advanced training provided to agents and supervisors assigned to counterterrorism and counterintelligence programs, and in training provided to Assistant Special Agents in Charge and Special Agents in Charge.

2. Add procedures to include reviews of FCRA. NSLs issued in counterintelligence investigations in the FBI Inspection Division's periodic reviews and in the National Security Division's national security reviews (described in Chapter Two of this report).

3. Reiterate in its continuing discussions with major credit reporting agencies that the agencies should not provide consumer full credit reports in response to FCRAu NSLs and should ensure that they provide only requested information in response to all FCRA NSLs.

4. Ensure that guidance and training continue to identify the circumstances under which FCRA NSL matters must be reported to the FBI OGC as possible intelligence violations.

5. Issue additional guidance addressing the filing and retention of NSL-derived information that will improve the ability to locate NSL-derived information. The guidance should require that all NSL-derived information be appropriately documented, stored, easily identified, and readily available for internal and external review.

6. Include in its routine case file reviews and the National Security Division's national security reviews an analysis of the FBI's compliance with requirements governing the filing and retention of NSL-derived information.

Chapter Four:
National Security Letter Requests Issued by the FBI in 2006

In this chapter, we describe the FBI's data on the use of national security letters during calendar year 2006. However, for reasons discussed in our previous report on NSLs, we believe that the data provided by the FBI from the Department's semiannual classified reports to Congress and the FBI Office of the General Counsel (FBI OGC) national security letter tracking database (OGC database) do not accurately reflect the total number of NSL requests issued in 2006.

In our first NSL report we documented various technical and structural problems with the OGC database that resulted in inaccuracies and a significant understatement of NSL requests in the Department's reports to Congress. While noting the limitations of the OGC database, we provided in our first NSL report a summary and analysis of data derived in large part from the database because that database was the only centralized repository of data reflecting the FBI's use of national security letter authorities.

Moreover, in our investigation of the FBI's use of exigent letters, which will be described in our forthcoming NSL report, we found additional inaccuracies in the Department's semiannual classified reports to Congress and the OGC database. We determined that the FBI sought or obtained records or other information on thousands of telephone numbers outside the normal approval process, some of which were associated with improper NSLs, exigent letters, or other informal requests. Among these non-routine NSLs were 11 "blanket" NSLs that sought telephone data on approximately 3,860 telephone numbers (8 percent of all NSL requests captured by the OGC database in 2006). These NSLs were issued in an attempt to validate the FBI's earlier acquisition of data from three communication service providers pursuant to contracts with the FBI. The requests contained in these NSLs were not uploaded into the OGC database because they were not documented by electronic communications (EC) with leads sent to FBI OGC for purposes of compiling data for congressional reporting. The FBI told us that, after eliminating duplicates, there were 2,196 unique telephone numbers in the 11 blanket NSLs.

Our forthcoming NSL report will describe in more detail the circumstances surrounding issuance of these NSLs, including the fact that the FBI did not generate approval ECs before these NSLs were signed by senior FBI officials; some of the NSLs were signed by FBI personnel who were not authorized to sign NSLs; and some NSLs did not comply with the Patriot Reauthorization Act requirements regarding non-disclosure provisions.

With these caveats, we discuss in the balance of this chapter the data on NSL usage that was contained in the OGC database and in the 2006 semiannual classified reports to Congress. In Section I we discuss the methodology we used to collect and analyze the FBI data on NSL use in 2006. In Section II we report on the number of NSL requests issued in 2006. In Section III we present data on overall trends in the FBI's NSL usage from 2003 through 2006.

I. Methodology

For this review, the OIG analyzed data in the FBI OGC database related to NSLs issued during calendar year 2006.[87] The FBI used this database to collect the data it needed to prepare the Department's annual public reports and semiannual classified reports to Congress on NSL usage. We also examined these annual public reports to evaluate NSL requests in 2006 and to analyze trends in NSL usage from 2003 through 2006.

We examined the NSLS and NSL requests issued during the three types of investigations in which NSLs are authorized: counterterrorism, counterintelligence, and foreign computer intrusion cyber investigations. In our analysis, we refer to the number of national security letter requests rather than the number of national security letters because one NSL may include more than one request. For example, one NSL to a telephone company may request information on many telephone numbers. The data presented in the Department's semiannual classified reports to Congress and in its annual public reports are the numbers of requests made, not the number of letters issued. In this report, we follow that same approach. Chart 4.1 shows the relationship between the numbers of investigations, NSLs, and NSL requests in 2006.

Chart 4.1: Relationship between the numbers of investigations, NSLs, and NSL requests in 2006.
[Chart not available]

Source: FBI OGC database as of May 2007.

We used the OGC database for this information because it was the only centralized source on the Department's use of NSLs during 2006. As noted above, our first NSL report documented flaws in the internal reporting of NSLs and structural problems with the OGC database that affected the accuracy and reliability of the Department's semiannual classified reports to Congress.[88] Since the OIG issued its first NSL report, the FBI has taken steps to upgrade the technology it uses to generate NSLs and related documents.[89]

---

[87] After we completed our analysis of the FBI OGC NSL database, the FBI provided the OIG with an updated database in January 2008 that included a small amount of additional data for the third and fourth quarters of the semiannual classified reports to Congress for 2006. The January 2008 version of the database included [Text not available] (0.5 percent) more NSLs and [Text not available] (4 percent) more NSL requests than the May 2007 database that we used for our analyses. We determined that this small amount of additional NSLs and NSL requests would not materially change our analyses.

[88] See NSL I, 31-36.

[89] In Chapter Two of this report, we provide a description and our analysis of the FBI's efforts to improve the accuracy of the OGC database and the public and classified reports to Congress that are generated using this data.

The Department was required to file semiannual classified reports to Congress describing the total number of NSL requests issued pursuant to four of the five NSL authorities: *Right to Financial Privacy Act* (financial records), *Electronic Communications Privacy Act* (telephone toll billing records, electronic communication transactional records and subscriber information (telephone or e-mail)), and two *Fair Credit Reporting Act* authorities (for consumer and financial institution-identifying information and consumer full credit reports).[90] In addition, beginning in March 2006 pursuant to amendments to the NSL authorities in the Patriot Reauthorization Act, the Department was required to provide annual public reports on certain aspects of its NSL usage.

In its classified reports, the Department described:

(1) the number of investigations of different persons or organizations that generated NSL requests and

(2) the number of requests made in those investigations.

Based on data uploaded into the OGC database and the semiannual classified reports to Congress, we separated these totals into different categories for investigations of "U.S. persons or organizations" and "non-U.S. persons or organizations."[91]

II. National Security Letter Requests Issued in 2006

In this section, we describe the FBI's use of NSLs in 2006 as documented in the OGC database. We describe the total number of NSL requests as well as NSL requests relating to investigations of U.S. persons and non-U.S. persons. We also include a breakdown of the proportion of NSL requests issued during counterterrorism, counterintelligence, and foreign computer intrusion cyber investigations.

In 2006, the FBI issued a total of 48,106 NSL requests pursuant to four of the five national security letter authorities.[92] As shown in Chart 4.2, the

---

[90] Prior to the Patriot Reauthorization Act, the Department was required to provide reports to Congress only on its use of its NSL authorities under the *Right to Financial Privacy Act* (RFPA), the *Electronic Communications Privacy Act* (ECPA), and under the *Fair Credit Reporting Act* (FCRA) for consumer and financial institution-identifying information. The Patriot Reauthorization Act requires the Department also to report on use of its NSL authority pursuant to the FCRA for consumer full credit reports. See § 118(b) of the Patriot Reauthorization Act. The Department is not required to report the number of NSL requests issued pursuant to the *National Security Act* NSL statutes (authorizing the FBI to obtain financial records, other financial information, and consumer reports).

[91] 50 U.S.C. § 1801(i) defines a "United States Person" as:

> a citizen of the United States, an alien lawfully admitted for permanent residence . . . , an unincorporated association a substantial number of members of which are citizens of the United States or aliens lawfully admitted for permanent residence, or a corporation which is incorporated in the United States. . . .

[92] FBI records show that [Text not available] national security letters were issued pursuant to the *National Security Act* NSL statute in 2006.

overwhelming majority of these requests sought telephone toll billing records information, subscriber information (telephone or e-mail), or electronic communication transactional records under the *Electronic Communications Privacy Act* (ECPA) NSL statute.[93] The second most frequently used NSL authority, accounting for approximately [Text not available] percent of the total, sought records from financial institutions, such as banks, credit card companies, and finance companies under the *Right to Financial Privacy Act* (RFPA) authority. These records include open and closed checking and savings accounts. The remaining [Text not available] percent of the NSL requests were issued pursuant to the two *Fair Credit Reporting Act* (FCRA) NSL authorities and sought either financial institution- or consumer-identifying information or consumer full credit reports.[94]

Chart 4.2: NSL Requests (2006)
[Chart not available]

Source: FBI OGC NSL database as of May 2007.

As shown in Chart 4.3, the majority of NSL requests issued in 2006 were generated from investigations of U.S. persons.

Chart 4.3: NSL Requests Relating to Investigations of U.S. Persons and non-U.S. Persons (2006)

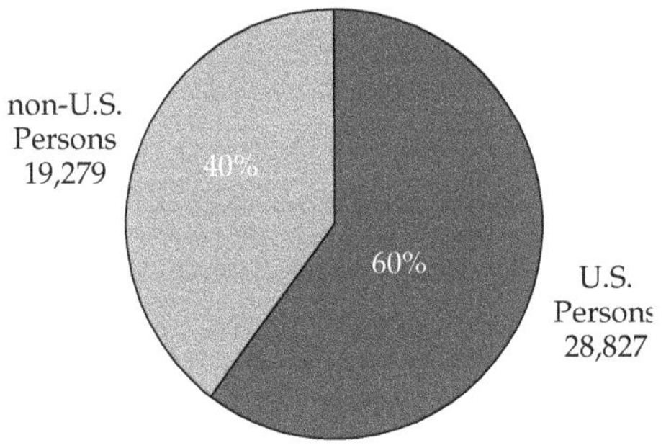

Source: FBI OGC NSL database as of May 2007

FBI data showed that in 2006 approximately [Text not available] percent of all NSL requests were issued during counterterrorism investigations, approximately [Text not available] percent were issued in counterintelligence investigations, and approximately [Text not available] percent were issued in foreign computer intrusion cyber investigations (Chart 4.4).

93 Electronic communication transactional records (e-mails) may include e-mail addresses associated with the account, screen names, and billing records and method of payment for the account.

94 A detailed description of the number of NSL requests for each of the four types of NSLs in counterterrorism and counterintelligence investigations is included in the Classified Appendix to this report.

Chart 4.4: NSL Requests in Counterterrorism, Counterintelligence, and Foreign Computer Intrusion Cyber Investigations (2006)
[Chart not available]
Source: FBI OGC NSL database as of May 2007.

FBI data showed that on average approximately one third of all counterterrorism, counterintelligence, and cyber investigations that were open at any time during 2006 used NSLs. NSLs were used in [Text not available] counterintelligence investigations ([Text not available] percent) than in counterterrorism investigations ([Text not available] percent) or cyber investigations ([Text not available] percent) in 2006, as shown in more detail in the Classified Appendix to this report.

III. Trends in National Security Letter Usage from 2003 through 2006

In this section, we describe the general levels and trends in the FBI's NSL requests from 2003 through 2006 as documented in the Department's semiannual classified reports to Congress and the OGC database, when applicable.

According to the Department's semiannual classified reports to Congress from 2003 through 2006 and information in the OGC database, the FBI issued a total of 192,499 NSL requests pursuant to its RFPA, ECPA, and FCRA NSL authorities during this 4-year period.[95] The total number of NSL requests issued by the FBI rose slightly (approximately 5 percent) in 2006 over the 2005 levels. Chart 4.5 illustrates the total number of NSL. requests issued during each of the years from 2003 through 2006.

FBI data showed that from 2003 through 2006, the overwhelming majority (about [Text not available] percent) of the FBI's NSL requests sought telephone toll billing records information, subscriber information (telephone or e-mail), or electronic communication transactional records under the ECPA NSL statute. The second most frequently used type of NSL request, accounting for approximately [Text not available] percent of the total, sought financial records (for example, open and closed checking and savings accounts) from financial institutions such as banks, credit card companies, and finance companies under the RFPA authority. The remaining [Text not available] percent of the NSL requests were issued pursuant to the two FCRA NSL authorities and sought either financial institution- or consumer-identifying information or consumer full credit reports.[96]

[95] As we reported in our first NSL report, this total includes [Text not available] NSL requests for consumer full credit reports issued from 2003 through 2005 that the Department was not required to include in its reports to Congress. See NSL I, 36.

[96] We provide a more detailed analysis of trends in the FBI's use of each of the four types of NSLs over the 4-year period in the Classified Appendix to this report.

Chart 4.5: NSL Requests (2003 through 2006)

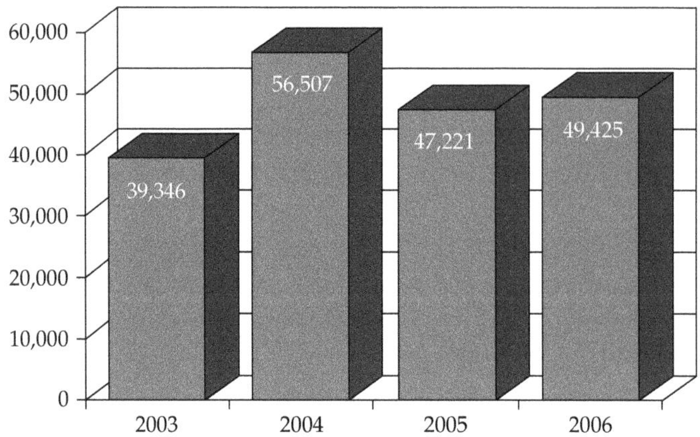

Sources: DOJ semiannual classified reports to Congress and FBI OGC database as of May 2006 (for 1681v NSL requests in 2003 through 2005)

NSL Requests Relating to U.S. Persons and non-U.S. Persons: FBI data also showed that the percentage of NSL requests generated from investigations of U.S. persons versus non-U.S. persons shifted over the 4-year period. In 2003, approximately 39 percent of NSL requests were generated in the course of investigations of U.S. persons. However, the number of NSL requests generated from investigations of U.S. persons almost doubled from 6,519 in 2003 to 11,517 in 2006, which represented 57 percent of all NSL requests in that year. During the same period, the number of NSL requests generated from investigations of non-U.S. persons declined from 10,232 in 2003 to 8,605 in 2006.

The Executive Assistant Director of the FBI's National Security Branch (NSB) provided several reasons for the increase in NSLs involving U.S. persons over the 4-year period. He stated that as the FBI has moved forward from the investigations of the September 11 attacks, it has focused on investigations of possible sleeper cells in the United States and conducted follow-up investigations of terrorist activities in the United Kingdom and elsewhere to determine if there is a U.S. nexus to those events. He also pointed to the FBI's interactions with state and local law enforcement agents, the work of the FBI's Field Intelligence Groups, and the investigations conducted by Joint Terrorism Task Forces, all of which have generated leads involving U.S. persons that result in the initiation of national security investigations and the issuance of NSLs.

Chart 4.6 depicts the number of NSL requests generated from investigations of U.S. persons and non-U.S. persons from 2003 through 2006.[97]

[97] Chart 4.6 does not contain the same totals as Chart 4.5 because the FBI is not required to report the U.S. person status of targets of subscriber NSLs. Specifically, 117,111 NSL requests seeking

Chart 4.6: NSL Requests Relating to U.S. Persons and non-U.S. Persons (2003 through 2006)

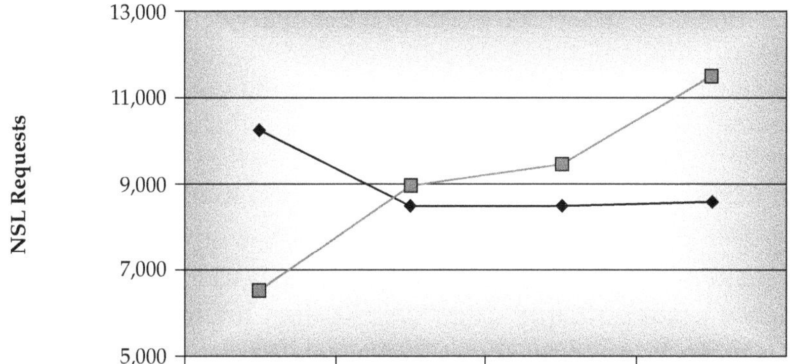

	2003	2004	2005	2006
Non-U.S. Persons	10,232	8,494	8,536	8,605
U.S. Persons	6,519	8,943	9,475	11,517

Source: DOJ semiannual classified reports to Congress

NSL Requests Issued During Counterterrorism, Counterintelligence, and Foreign Computer Intrusion Cyber Investigations: Chart 4.7 shows the distribution of NSL requests issued from the three types of investigations during the 4-year period. Overall, NSL requests issued in counterterrorism investigations accounted for a substantial majority of all requests. The proportion of NSL requests issued in counterintelligence investigations was [Text not available] in 2004 ([Text not available] Percent) than in 2003, 2005, and 2006 (ranging from [Text not available] percent in 2003 to [Text not available] percent in 2006).[98] The data also showed that the proportion of NSL requests issued in foreign computer intrusion cyber investigations was [Text not available] in 2006 ([Text not available] percent) than in previous years ([Text not available] percent).

Chart 4.7: NSL Requests in Counterterrorism, Counterintelligence, and Foreign Computer Intrusion Cyber Investigations (2003 through 2006)
[Chart not available]

Source: FBI OGC NSL database as of May 2006 and May 2007.

---

subscriber information for telephone numbers and Internet e-mail accounts in 2003 through 2006 did not identify the subject's status as a U.S. person or non-U.S. person. Similarly, while the FBI captured data on the status of persons who were the targets of consumer full credit reports issued in 2003 through 2005, the Department was not required to include this data in its reports. Beginning in 2006, the Patriot Reauthorization Act required the Department to report to Congress the status of targets of its NSL requests for consumer full credit reports. Thus, we do not include in Chart 4.6 the [Text not available] NSL requests that the OGC database identified as having been issued in 2003 through 2005 and the [Text not available] NSL requests reported to Congress in 2006 for consumer full credit reports pursuant to 15 U.S.C. § 1681v.

98 In 2004, the FBI issued 9 NSLs seeking subscriber information on 11,100 telephone numbers in connection with a single investigation.

Chapter Five
The Effectiveness of National Security Letters as an Investigative Tool

In our first NSL report we examined the effectiveness of national security letters in different types of national security investigations conducted between 2003 and 2005. Based on our interviews of Headquarters and field personnel and our examination of case files in four FBI field offices, we described the value of each type of NSL as well as the analyses developed from NSLs that enable the FBI to identify communication and financial links between subjects of its investigations and others.[99]

Our first NSL report also described the principal uses of NSLs: to develop evidence to support applications for Foreign Intelligence Surveillance Act orders; assess communication or financial links between investigative subjects or others; collect information sufficient to fully develop national security investigations; generate leads for other field divisions, members of Joint Terrorism Task Forces (JTTF), or other federal agencies, or to pass to foreign governments; develop analytical products for distribution within the FBI, other Department components, other federal agencies, and the intelligence community; develop information that is provided to law enforcement authorities for use in criminal proceedings; collect information sufficient to eliminate concerns about investigative subjects and thereby close national security investigations; and corroborate information derived from other investigative techniques.

We reported that the FBI uses information derived from NSLs (and other investigative tools) to generate a variety of analytical intelligence products, including Intelligence Information Reports, Intelligence Assessments, and Intelligence Bulletins. Information derived from NSLs is stored in various FBI databases, shared within the Department and with JTTFs, and disseminated to other federal agencies and the intelligence community. The FBI also provides information derived from NSLs to law enforcement authorities for use in criminal proceedings.

In this review, our examination of case files and interviews of FBI Headquarters officials and personnel in three FBI field offices confirmed that NSLs continued to be important tools in the FBI's national security investigations conducted in 2006. Many FBI personnel told us that NSLs are an essential and indispensable intelligence tool.

FBI personnel provided the following examples of the value of NSLs issued pursuant to the *Right to Financial Privacy Act* (RFPA), the *Fair Credit Reporting*

[99] See NSL I, 45-65.

Act (FCRA), and the *Electronic Communications Privacy Act* (ECPA) in advancing national security investigations they conducted in 2006:

- A field office reported that information from national security letters enabled case agents to identify pertinent e-mail addresses, telephone numbers, and bank accounts that were used to support a subject's terrorist activities. The investigators used information derived from the ECPA and RFPA NSLs to identify the extent of a subject's circle of associates and his financial network. Case agents stated that information on the subject's financial network was essential in developing the money laundering portion of the case.
- In 2006, while investigating a plot to conduct terrorist activities, a field office served ECPA and RFPA NSLs to obtain financial, telephone subscriber, and telephone toll records for the subjects and their associates. Using this information, investigators identified the financial associates of several of the investigation's subjects while ruling out the possibility that a larger terrorist organization was financing the plot.
- A field office opened a counterterrorism investigation in the spring of 2006 and issued numerous ECPA and RFPA NSLs to communications providers and financial institutions. These NSLs assisted the investigators in confirming the identities of the subjects and were used in support of an application for authority to use additional investigative techniques. NSLs also identified financial institutions that the subjects used, which in turn led to the discovery of certain purchases.
- In the summer of 2005, the FBI received information suggesting that individuals associated with two e-mail addresses were in contact with known extremists. The FBI issued ECPA NSLs to two Internet service providers (ISP) associated with these e-mail addresses to determine the identity of the users. This information was insufficient to positively identify the users of the e-mail accounts. However, information received indicated that the majority of log-ins for both e-mail accounts could be traced to two different ISPs. The FBI served ECPA NSLs on these ISPs. Responsive records enabled the FBI to determine where the users of the e-mail addresses were located.
- In June 2006, the U.S. mill [Text not available] Because of the potential threat, the FBI initiated preliminary investigations on the U.S.-based subscribers of two telephone numbers and issued ECPA NSLs to identify the subscribers. The investigation is continuing.
- Two individuals in possession of weapons were stopped by law enforcement officials and an FBI national security investigation was initiated. Over the next few months a source reported that one of the subjects was planning to travel abroad to engage in armed jihad against

U.S. and Coalition troops. A number of RFPA and ECPA NSLs were issued seeking financial information, credit reports, toll records, and e-mail account information on the primary subjects in this group.

- The FBI is investigating the foreign intelligence activities of a subject involved with a foreign government. An NSL has been served to assist the FBI in investigating a network for procuring illicit dual-use technology for use in a weapons of mass destruction program.
- In an FBI national security investigation, the FBI has issued NSLs that have helped to identify two FBI assets who were in contact with the subject of the investigation – contacts previously unknown to the FBI. The NSLs identified the subject's e-mail accounts, which in turn led to the issuance of additional NSLs. FBI counterintelligence personnel said that the imposition of the non-disclosure provisions in the NSLs has been critical in keeping the FBI's interest in the subject from coming to the attention of the foreign government involved in the matter.

Chapter Six:
OIG Findings on the FBI'S Compliance with the Patriot Reauthorization Act's Non-Disclosure and Confidentiality Provisions

Section 119(b)(3)(E) of the Patriot Reauthorization Act directed the OIG to perform an audit of national security letters issued after the Act became effective in March 2006 to determine the number of occasions in which NSLs were issued "without the certification necessary to require the recipient of such letter to comply with the nondisclosure and confidentiality requirements potentially applicable under law."

In Section I of this chapter we describe the new certification requirement in the Patriot Reauthorization Act, the steps taken by the FBI to implement the new measures, and the methodology of the OIG's audit of the FBI's compliance with the certification requirements. Section II provides our findings and analysis, and Section III contains our conclusions and recommendation.

I. Background

A. The Patriot Reauthorization Act

As initially drafted, the NSL statutes imposed non-disclosure and confidentiality obligations on all NSL recipients.[100] The national security letter provisions of the *Right to Financial Privacy Act* (RFPA), *Electronic Communications Privacy Act* (ECPA), and the *Fair Credit Reporting Act* (FCRA) authorized the FBI to advise recipients that they were prohibited by statute from disclosing to anyone that the FBI had sought or obtained access to the requested records.[101]

The non-disclosure and confidentiality provisions of the three NSL statutes provoked significant public controversy and generated the first judicial challenge to any of the Patriot Act amendments to the NSL statutes. See *Doe v. Ashcroft*, 334 F. Supp. 2d 471 (S.D.N.Y. 2004), *vacated by Doe v. Gonzales*, 449 F.3d 415 (2d Cir. 2006) *Doe v. Gonzales*, 386 F. Supp. 2d 669 (D. Conn. 2005), *dismissed as moot, Doe v. Gonzales*, 449 F.3d 415 (2d Cir. 2006), upon remand *Doe v. Gonzales*, 500 F. Supp. 2d 379 (S.D.N.Y. 2007) (holding non-disclosure provision in the Patriot Reauthorization Act, 18 U.S.C. § 2709, to be unconstitutional under the First Amendment).

---

[100] Throughout the national security letter statutes and Sections 116 and 117 of the Patriot Reauthorization Act, the terms "non-disclosure" and "confidentiality" are used interchangeably.

[101] Prior to the Patriot Act, the ECPA and the RFPA provided that no wire or electronic communication service provider or financial institution "shall disclose to any person that the Federal Bureau of Investigation has sought or obtained access to information or records." 18 U.S.C. § 2709(c)(2000); 12 U.S.C. § 3414(a)(3)(2000). The FCRA authorized disclosure only to "those officers, employees, or agents of a consumer reporting agency necessary to fulfill the requirement to disclose information to the Federal Bureau of Investigation. . . ." 15 U.S.C. § 1681u(d)(2000).

The Patriot Reauthorization Act modified the non-disclosure and confidentiality obligations on NSL recipients. The Act authorized the FBI to impose these obligations only upon certification of specified harm that might arise in the underlying investigation if a disclosure occurred. Specifically, after March 9, 2006, if the FBI seeks to impose non-disclosure and confidentiality disclosure requirements on an NSL recipient, the Patriot Reauthorization Act requires the FBI Director or his designee to certify that disclosure of the FBI's demand for information might result in:

- danger to the national security of the United States;
- interference with criminal, counterterrorism, or counterintelligence investigations;
- interference with diplomatic relations; or
- danger to the life or physical safety of any person.[102]

If the certifying official determines that confidentiality is necessary, Section 116 of the Patriot Reauthorization Act requires that recipients be notified of three specific obligations:

(1) that receipt of the NSL must remain confidential and cannot be disclosed except as required to comply with the NSL or to obtain legal advice from an attorney;

(2) if the recipients disclose the existence of the request to anyone (either to comply with the request or to obtain legal advice from an attorney), they must inform those individuals of the non-disclosure and confidentiality requirements; and

(3) upon request of the FBI Director or his designees, the recipients must reveal the identities of the individuals to whom they disclosed the existence of the NSLs.[103]

B. The FBI's Implementation of the Patriot Reauthorization Act Non-Disclosure and Confidentiality Requirements

On March 9, 2006, the date the President signed the Patriot Reauthorization Act, the FBI OGC notified all Special Agents in Charge (SAC) and Chief Division Counsels (CDC) that the NSL models that had been posted on FBI OGC's National Security Law Branch (NSLB) Intranet website could no longer be used to generate NSLs. The FBI OGC advised FBI personnel that

[102] Patriot Reauthorization Act, § 116 (2006). The Act provides that the Director's designee must not be in a position lower than a Headquarters Deputy Assistant Director or field division Special Agent in Charge designated by the Director. Id.

[103] NSL recipients are not required to divulge to the FBI that they intend to consult an attorney to obtain legal advice or legal assistance about the NSL. Patriot Reauthorization Act, § 116 (2006).

all NSLs that had been prepared but not yet served would have to be redrafted to conform to the new requirement in the law.

To implement the new law, on March 9, 2006, the FBI Director delegated certification authority to all SACs and other designated senior officials.[104] In the delegation memorandum, the FBI OGC advised that non-disclosure certifications "should not and may not be made in a perfunctory manner." The delegation also stated that the individual signing the NSL must make an assessment that there is "a genuine need for non-disclosure" based on one of the possible dangers listed in the statute that could result from disclosure.[105]

The FBI OGC concurrently disseminated guidance on the provisions of the new law to FBI Headquarters and field divisions. Also on March 9, the FBI OGC distributed revised NSL approval ECs and NSL models to all SACs and CDCs and posted the new models on the FBI OGC's Intranet website.[106] The FBI OGC advised that the non-disclosure provision could no longer automatically be included in NSLs and explained the certification process. The FBI OGC repeatedly emphasized through e-mails to all CDCs, communications with individual CDCs, and the new models it generated that certifications for imposing the non-disclosure obligation were not to be perfunctory or automatic.

On March 15, 2006, the FBI OGC issued further guidance reiterating that the non-disclosure provision was "no longer automatically included in the NSL" and that the FBI must ensure that there is a "genuine need" for non-disclosure prior to use. To amplify the statutory directive noted above, the FBI OGC guidance explained that when the non-disclosure provision is sought, the approval EC must provide a factual predicate to justify imposition of

---

[104] In addition to the SACs, the Director delegated certification signature authority, non-disclosure certification authority, and non-disclosure recertification authority for NSLs to the following FBI senior officials: Deputy Director; Executive Assistant Director and Assistant Executive Assistant Director for the National Security Branch; Assistant Directors and all Deputy Assistant Directors of the Counterterrorism, Counterintelligence, and Cyber Divisions; General Counsel and Deputy General Counsel for the National Security Law Branch; and Assistant Directors in Charge of the New York, Washington, D.C., and Los Angeles field offices.

[105] Office of the General Counsel, Federal Bureau of Investigation, electronic communication to all Divisions, Delegation of Non-Disclosure Certification Authority, March 9, 2006, at 4.

[106] FBI policy requires that all NSLs and approval ECs contain certain information. NSL approval ECs must provide "predication" for the NSL by explaining why the information sought is relevant to an authorized investigation; document approval of the NSL by appropriate personnel; certify the necessity for non-disclosure and confidentiality when applicable; include information needed to fulfill congressional reporting requirements; and document transmittal information for the NSLB, the responsible Headquarters division, and the division that is asked to serve the NSL. The NSL must identify the statutory authority for the request and types of records requested; contain identifying information for the targeted individual or account; certify that the records are relevant to an authorized investigation; certify, when applicable, that disclosure may result in an adverse consequence; and provide the notifications listed above to the recipient. For a more detailed description of these requirements, see NSL I, 22-27.

the provision.[107] The guidance listed the 4 potential harms noted in the Act (quoted above) and suggested the following 13 adverse consequences that case agents should consider in articulating the factual predicate justifying non-disclosure:

1. Disclosure may [Text not available]
2. Disclosure may [Text not available]
3. Disclosure may [Text not available]
4. Disclosure may [Text not available]
5. Disclosure may [Text not available]
6. Disclosure may [Text not available]
7. Disclosure may [Text not available]
8. Disclosure may [Text not available]
9. Disclosure may [Text not available]
10. Disclosure may [Text not available]
11. Disclosure may [Text not available]
12. Disclosure may [Text not available]
13. Disclosure may [Text not available]

The FBI OGC also advised case agents to identify in their approval ECs any other reasons for imposing non-disclosure and confidentiality requirements if they were not on the list.

C. Methodology of the OIG Review

1. Random Sample of NSLs Issued After March 9, 2006

To perform our audit of the FBI's compliance with the non-disclosure and confidentiality provisions of the Patriot Reauthorization Act, we identified a statistically valid random sample of all NSLs issued from March 10, 2006, through December 31, 2006. By reviewing those NSLs to determine the number of NSLs that imposed non-disclosure and confidentiality obligations, we could project how many NSLs issued throughout the FBI during that period imposed these conditions.

The FBI provided us with the FBI OGC NSL tracking database for calendar year 2006, which we used to determine the universe of national security letters issued during the relevant time period. The database contained 15,187 records, each representing one national security letter issued from

[107] According to the NSLB Intranet website, "[if] a non-disclosure provision is sought, the EC must set forth a factual predicate to require such a provision."

March 10, 2006, through December 31, 2006. We determined that a sample size of 375 NSLs would permit us to project from the sample to the universe of all NSLs issued from March 10, 2006, through December 31, 2006, at a 95 percent confidence level. We then sequentially numbered the 15,187 records and used a random number generator to produce a list of 500 numbers (to ensure an adequate list of NSLs if the FBI was unable to produce every NSL we requested). We used the first 375 random numbers to locate the corresponding NSL in the OGC database, and we obtained copies of the NSLs and corresponding approval ECs.[108]

Our random sample included NSLs from 51 different FBI field offices and Headquarters divisions. The number of NSLs from each office ranged from 1 to 37.[109] Counterterrorism investigations generated 243 of the 375 NSLs in the sample, counter-intelligence investigations generated 127 NSLs, and foreign computer intrusion cyber investigations generated 5 NSLs.[110]

For purposes of evaluating compliance with applicable non-disclosure and confidentiality requirements in the Act and other FBI policies, we reviewed both the NSL approval ECs and the NSLs. We examined the approval ECs to determine whether they:

- identified a national security investigation or foreign computer intrusion cyber investigation file number; and
- contained either a certification that disclosure that the FBI sought the requested information would result in the adverse consequences listed in the statute or a determination that the case did not warrant activation of the non-disclosure provision.[111]

---

[108] As we noted in our first NSL report, during the period 2003 through 2005 the FBI did not require case agents or others to retain copies of signed NSLs. As described in Chapter Three of this report, the directive to retain signed copies of NSLs was issued in March 2007 in conformity with one of our recommendations in our first NSL report. Accordingly, to perform this audit we had to use unsigned copies of NSLs that we obtained from a query of the FBI Automated Case Support (ACS) system.

For a variety of reasons, the FBI was unable to provide 56 NSL approval ECs and corresponding NSLs from our original list in response to our request. These reasons included instances in which NSLs were not electronically uploaded into the FBI ACS system, the requested documents were subject to access restrictions or had been permanently "charged out" or removed from the database, or the case file or serial numbers did not exist. When this occurred, we requested replacement records based on the random numbers we had generated.

[109] Three NSLs in our random sample were issued from FBI Headquarters case files.

[110] The distribution of NSLs among the counterterrorism, counterintelligence, and cyber investigative programs in our random sample was [Text not available] to the distribution recorded in the FBI NSL tracking database for NSLs issued throughout 2006, an issue we address in Chapter Four of this report. Our analysis of the OGC database found that [Text not available] of all NSLs issued during calendar year 2006 were generated from counterterrorism investigations, [Text not available] from counterintelligence investigations, and [Text not available] from cyber investigations. This is [Text not available] to the distribution we found in our random sample: [Text not available] generated from counterterrorism investigations, [Text not available] from counterintelligence investigations, and [Text not available] from cyber investigations.

[111] The Attorney General's Guidelines for FBI National Security Investigations and Foreign Intelligence Collection require that NSLs be issued only in connection with national security investigations. FBI policy requires that NSLs be issued from investigative files, not from control files. See NSL I, 100-104.

We then determined whether the approval EC included a justification for non-disclosure and confidentiality. If a justification was included, we next determined whether that justification referenced any of the 13 possible adverse consequences listed on the FBI OGC Intranet website or identified other adverse consequences. We also examined the NSLs to determine whether they included non-disclosure and confidentiality obligations.

2. Other 2006 NSLs Identified During the Review

In addition to our analysis of the random sample of 375 NSLs, we identified 8 "blanket" NSLs issued after March 9, 2006, that we found did not comply with the Patriot Reauthorization Act non-disclosure and confidentiality requirements. We identified these blanket NSLs in our investigation of the FBI's use of exigent letters. In that investigation, we learned that the FBI's Counterterrorism Division issued at least 11 follow-up blanket NSLs to "cover" information obtained by personnel in the FBI's Communications Analysis Unit at FBI Headquarters in response to exigent letters or other informal requests. These NSLs sought telephone toll billing records for 3,860 telephone numbers (which corresponded to approximately 2,196 unique telephone numbers) pursuant to the ECPA NSL statute. None of these NSLs was accompanied by approval ECs, a violation of FBI policy. As a result, we were unable to determine whether the senior FBI officials who signed these NSLs considered whether there was adequate predication to impose the non-disclosure and confidentiality obligations that were referenced in 8 of the 11 NSLs. We will provide more details and our analysis of these NSLs in our forthcoming NSL report.

II. OIG Findings and Analysis

A. NSLs That Invoked Non-Disclosure and Confidentiality Obligations

Of the 375 NSLs we examined in our random sample, 365, or 97 percent imposed the non-disclosure and confidentiality obligation established in the Patriot Reauthorization Act. Based on that result, we projected that of the 15,187 NSLs the FBI issued from March 10, 2006, through December 31, 2006, 14,782 NSLs imposed the non-disclosure and confidentiality obligations.

As noted above, we examined approval ECs to determine whether the recitals required to be made when seeking to impose the non-disclosure and confidentiality obligations matched the text of the NSLs. We found

We reviewed the approval ECs accompanying the 375 NSLs to determine whether they complied with this requirement. Of the 375 approval ECs we examined, we found 1 instance in which an approval EC indicated that the FBI relied exclusively on an FBI Headquarters control file rather than an investigative file to initiate approval for the issuance of an NSL.

Chart 6.1: NSLs that Imposed Non-Disclosure and Confidentiality Obligations (March 10, 2006 through December 31, 2006)

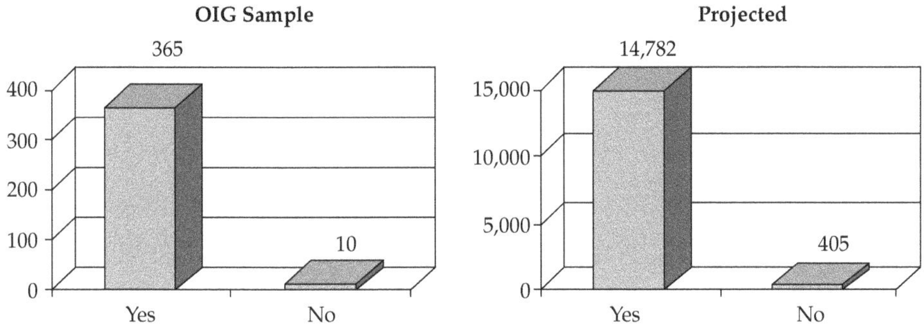

that the language of the approval ECs was not consistent with the corresponding NSLs in only 2 of the 365 instances. In one instance, the approval EC did not include the SAC's certification of the need for the requirements, and in the other the approval EC contained internally inconsistent recitals about the necessity for invoking the provisions.

Of the 364 NSL approval ECs that included justifications for imposing the obligations, 225, or 62 percent, included 1 of the 13 justifications listed in the FBI OGC's March 15, 2006, guidance discussed above. Of these 225 approval ECs, 184, or 82 percent, stated that disclosure could prematurely reveal a national security investigation to the target or persons affiliated with the target or the subject matter of the national security investigation and cause them to change their behavior patterns and circumvent detection. This justification also was cited in 23 additional approval ECs in conjunction with 7 other justifications from FBI OGC's list. The remaining 18 approval ECs cited other justifications suggested by the FBI OGC.

The balance of the approval ECs (139 of 364, or 38 percent) referred to adverse consequences from premature disclosures that were not specifically referenced on the FBI OGC's list. The adverse consequences described in the certifications ranged from perfunctory justifications to detailed descriptions of the specific consequences that might result from disclosure. The detailed descriptions included how disclosure would affect the behavior of suspects or the effectiveness of the FBI's investigative techniques and overall investigations.

Of the 364 approval ECs we examined that sought approval to impose the non-disclosure and confidentiality obligations, all but 17 (5 percent) contained justifications for imposing the non-disclosure and confidentiality obligations that complied with the FBI OGC's guidance. The remaining approval ECs contained justifications for imposing the obligations that were case-specific. Examples of these justifications were that disclosure:

> will have a detrimental effect on the instant investigation for a number of reasons. First, [Text not available] and his associates would likely conceal their activities from the FBI and therefore frustrate FBI efforts to collect evidence of terrorist activity. Second, [Text not available] would refrain from using the telephone to discuss [Text not available] matters which would undermine FBI efforts [Text not available] Third, premature exposure of an FBI interest in [Text not available] would jeopardize the terrorist financing investigation of [Text not available] and possible FBI recruitment efforts.
>
> * * *
>
> Due to [Text not available] communications with subjects in [Text not available] who've been detained on terrorism related charges since [Text not available] and his communication and association with subjects of several [full investigations], disclosure of this request may detrimentally effect [sic] the outcome of the foreign prosecutorial efforts of charged terrorists in [Text not available] and ongoing intra-divisional counterterrorism investigations.

Examples of perfunctory justifications that we found to be insufficient were:

> You should remind [Text not available] Bank that it is prohibited from disclosing that the FBI has made this request since it may interfere with an [sic] counterterrorism investigation.
>
> * * *
>
> A Preliminary international terrorism investigation of subject, a Non-U.S. Person, was authorized in accordance with Attorney General Guidelines because the subject is or may be engaging, or has or may have engaged, in activities constituting a threat to the national security for or on behalf of a foreign power. The subject may or may not be involved with international terrorist activities, or knowingly conspired with or aids and abets such a person in such activities.

B. NSLs That Did Not Invoke Non-Disclosure and Confidentiality Obligations

Our review determined that 10 of the 375 NSLs we examined, or 3 percent, were issued "without the certification necessary to require the recipient of such letter[s] to comply with the nondisclosure and confidentiality requirements potentially applicable under law."[112] We reviewed the approval ECs associated with these 10 NSLs and found that 4 of these approval ECs contained representations that the facts of the cases did not warrant imposition of the non-disclosure and confidentiality obligations under the applicable NSL statute. Therefore, it appears that the absence of the non-disclosure

[112] Patriot Reauthorization Act, § 119 (b)(3)(E).

and confidentiality provisions in the NSLs was deliberate in these four cases and not an oversight.

In contrast, 6 of the 10 approval ECs were inconsistent with the corresponding NSLs. In five instances, the non-disclosure and confidentiality provisions were not included in the NSL despite the fact that the SAC had certified the need for the requirements in the approval ECs.[113] In one instance, the approval EC failed to address the basis for the SAC's determination that the facts did not warrant imposition of the non-disclosure and confidentiality obligations.[114]

Based on our sample, we project that, in total, the FBI issued 405 NSLs from March 10, 2006, through December 31, 2006, that did not impose the non-disclosure and confidentiality obligations.

C. "Blanket" NSLs Issued in 2006

As noted above, in the course of our exigent letters investigation we examined 11 NSLs issued by FBI Headquarters officials in the Counterterrorism Division in connection with efforts to issue legal process to cover information already acquired through exigent letters and other informal requests.

Eight of these 11 improper NSLs imposed non-disclosure and confidentiality requirements on the recipients that did not comply with the Patriot Reauthorization Act certification requirement for invoking these provisions.[115] The individuals who prepared these NSLs appear to have relied upon outdated NSL models that did not include the required certification. These eight NSLs included the pre-Patriot Reauthorization Act language to the effect that the recipient was prohibited under 18 U.S.C. § 2709(c) from disclosing that the FBI had sought or obtained access to information or records under the ECPA.[116]

---

[113] We determined that in three of the five instances the approval ECs contained the certifications justifying imposition of the non-disclosure and confidentiality obligations, but the case agents used outdated NSL models that did not contain the appropriate provisions. In two other instances, the approval ECs contained the certifications justifying imposition of the non-disclosure and confidentiality obligations, but the provisions were missing from the associated NSLs.

[114] We determined that the case agent used an outdated approval EC that did not provide options for including or omitting the non-disclosure and confidentiality provisions in the NSL.

[115] The other three blanket NSLs imposed a non-disclosure requirement on the recipients that complied with the Patriot Reauthorization Act certification requirement for invoking these provisions.

As we will describe in detail in our next NSL report, we determined that five of the eight NSLs that failed to contain the required ECPA certification violated the ECPA NSL statute for two additional reasons: two of the five NSLs were signed by FBI personnel who were not authorized to sign NSLs and at least four of the five sought records that were not relevant to an investigation of international terrorism.

[116] The FBI officials who signed these NSLs were an Assistant Director, a Deputy Assistant Director, two Acting Deputy Assistant Directors, and a SAC. In addition to being non-compliant with the non-disclosure and confidentiality requirements, these NSLs were improper for other reasons that will be discussed in the OIG's forthcoming NSL report. We determined that none of these NSLs was reviewed by FBI OGC attorneys.

In addition, none of these 11 blanket NSLs complied with internal FBI policy requiring the preparation and approval of memoranda establishing the existence of an open investigation and the relevance of the information sought to the underlying investigation. FBI policy requires that such memoranda accompany the submission of NSLs for approval; be approved by the squad supervisor and Assistant Special Agent in Charge; and contain a statement by the official signing the NSL that non-disclosure is necessary, together with facts to justify the non-disclosure and confidentiality obligations. Since November 28, 2001, FBI policy stated that NSLs should also be reviewed by CDCs to ensure legal sufficiency.[117]

III. OIG Conclusions and Recommendation

The vast majority of the NSLs and approval ECs we examined in our random sample substantially complied with the Patriot Reauthorization Act certification requirement and FBI policy related to non-disclosure and confidentiality requirements. We believe this compliance record was largely due to the prompt guidance the FBI OGC issued on the date the Act was signed, the availability of new NSL forms on its Intranet website, and periodic guidance FBI OGC attorneys provided to the field as questions arose.

Our analysis also showed that at least 97 percent of the NSLs we examined in the random sample imposed the non-disclosure and confidentiality obligations on recipients. The majority of the approval ECs supporting these NSL's referenced the assertion that disclosure of the NSL could [Text not available]. Case agents seeking approval of these NSLs for the most part adopted suggestions by the FBI OGC as to the possible adverse consequences that could result from disclosure.

In general, FBI employees complied with the requirement to provide substantive justifications for the non-disclosure certifications. We found that only 5 percent of the approval ECs in the random sample contained perfunctory justifications for invoking the requirements. In these instances, the case agents apparently failed to read or to follow FBI guidance plainly stating that such perfunctory reasons were not satisfactory. In addition, the

[117] The November 28, 2001, FBI OGC memorandum states that "[p]rior to certification, every NSL and cover EC issued by the field division should be reviewed by. . . the Office of the Chief Division Counsel. . . ." The memorandum provides that "[l]awyers reviewing NSL packages should use the checklists provided with this communication to ensure legal sufficiency." Office of General Counsel, National Security Law Unit, Federal Bureau of Investigation (FBI), electronic communication to all Field Offices, National Security Letter Matters, November 28, 2001. The FBI Director's March 9, 2006, delegation memorandum authorized the NSLB to issue guidance regarding the revisions of the national security letter statutes. NSLB's Intranet website stated in 2006 that "NSLs are reviewed by CDCs at the field office level." On June 1, 2007, the FBI OGC issued a comprehensive guidance EC to all divisions for the first time stating that "all Field Office NSLs must be reviewed by CDCs or ADCs for legal sufficiency" prior to forwarding the NSLs to the SAC for approval. The comprehensive guidance EC is described in Chapter Two of this report.

case agents' squad supervisors, CDCs, and SACs accepted and approved these insufficient justifications. While the number of non-compliant NSLs in our random sample was small, we are concerned that some case agents and their supervisors failed to adhere to FBI policy requiring sufficient justification for imposing non-disclosure and confidentiality requirements on NSL recipients.

Although we did not seek to verify whether the facts cited to support imposition of the non-disclosure and confidentiality obligations were accurate, we note that many of the approval ECs seeking to impose these obligations recited one of the FBI OGC's rationales without providing additional supporting details.[118] The FBI's comprehensive guidance EC dated June 1, 2007, directed that "FBI officials must make a case by case determination whether disclosure of the NSL" may cause one of the enumerated dangers to arise. We recommend that the FBI reiterate that case agents and supervisors must give individualized scrutiny to the circumstances of each case before seeking to invoke the non-disclosure and confidentiality requirements and that the FBI's Inspection Division and the Department's National Security Division consider including whether these justifications are factually supported in their periodic audits.[119]

We found that a small number of NSLs and approval ECs in our random sample (8 of 375) contained inconsistent recitals with respect to the need for invoking the non-disclosure and confidentiality obligations. Case agents and their supervisors, as well as CDCs, failed to identify and correct these errors. To address this and other data entry discrepancies, the FBI has implemented several corrective measures, including a new NSL data system that FBI officials believe will eliminate this and other data entry errors in the creation of NSLs and approval ECs.[120]

More troubling, 11 blanket NSLs issued by Headquarters officials in 2006 that sought telephone data on 3,860 telephone numbers did not comply with the Patriot Reauthorization Act requirements respecting these provisions, internal FBI policy, or both. We are concerned by the failure of senior Counterterrorism Division officials to comply with statutory requirements and internal policy regarding the issuance of NSLs and their failure to consult legal counsel. As noted previously, we will examine the circumstances

---

[118] We believe the justification required by FBI policy should be described in the approval EC and that it is not sufficient that the justification is documented elsewhere in the investigative file. Squad supervisors and CDCs (or internal and external auditors) should not be expected to search through multi-volume investigative files to locate reasons for invoking non-disclosure and confidentiality obligations. In light of the FBI OGC's June 1, 2007, comprehensive guidance EC, approval ECs must now contain facts supporting imposition of these obligations.

[119] These periodic audits are described in Chapter Two of this report.

[120] The corrective measures implemented by the FBI in response to our first NSL report are described in Chapter Two of this report.

that led to the issuance of these blanket NSLs in the OIG's forthcoming NSL report.

Based on our review and to ensure that non-disclosure and confidentiality provisions are imposed only when appropriate, we recommend that the FBI:

1. Periodically reissue guidance and training materials reminding case agents and supervisors assigned to national security investigations that they must carefully examine the circumstances surrounding the issuance of each NSL to determine whether there is adequate justification for imposing non-disclosure and confidentiality requirements on the NSL recipient.

Chapter Seven: Improper or Illegal Use of National Security Letters Reported by FBI Personnel in 2006

The Patriot Reauthorization Act directed the OIG to describe "improper or illegal uses" of the NSL authorities in 2006, similar to the requirement in our first NSL report. In this chapter, we report some of our findings on improper or illegal use of NSL authorities that were identified and reported to the FBI Office of the General Counsel (FBI OGC) by FBI personnel in 2006. However, our main findings on the most serious improper or illegal uses of NSL authorities will be described in our next NSL report, which will include the results of our detailed investigation of the FBI's use of exigent letters. That investigation expanded on the results of our exigent letter review in our first NSL report by examining, among other topics, the scope of the practice; the FBI's efforts to issue legal process after the fact to cover the information obtained from the exigent letters and other improper requests; our assessment of the accountability of FBI personnel, including agents who signed exigent letters and their supervisors, for the improper use of exigent letters; and the results of our examination of improper NSLs served on three communication service providers.

As we will fully describe in our next NSL report, from 2002 through 2006, we found that the FBI obtained telephone data on approximately 3,764 domestic and international telephone numbers (which correspond to approximately 2,032 unique telephone numbers) pursuant to exigent letters and other informal requests rather than through NSLs or other legal process served in advance of obtaining the records. We also found that the FBI issued 11 "blanket" NSLs in 2006 that sought retroactively to justify the FBI's acquisition of data through the exigent letters or other informal requests. All 11 of these blanket NSLs were improper for one or more reasons. Some sought records that the FBI was not authorized to obtain through the *Electronic Communications Privacy Act* (ECPA) NSL statute; many were issued in violation of the Attorney General's Guidelines for FBI National Security Investigations and Foreign Intelligence Collection (NSI Guidelines); and all were issued in violation of internal FBI policy. Following consultation with FBI OGC attorneys, the FBI issued new NSLs in 2007 to correct some of the improper blanket NSLs and also generated for the first time documentation explaining the predication for these NSLs.[121] In light of our findings of significant improper or illegal use of NSLs in 2006 through the use of exigent letters, other informal requests, improper blanket NSLs,

[121] We will describe and evaluate in our forthcoming NSL report the FBI OGC's adjudication of any possible intelligence violations that were reported as a result of exigent letters, blanket NSLs, and other improper requests.

and other improper NSLs, our findings in this chapter should be considered in conjunction with our forthcoming NSL report.

Chapter Three of this report describes additional improper NSLs identified through three reviews conducted by the FBI in 2007 in response to the OIG's first NSL report:

(1) a review of NSLs issued by FBI field offices from a random sample of 10 percent of all national security investigations active at any time from 2003 through 2006;

(2) a review of a random sample of 10 percent of all NSLs issued by Headquarters divisions during the same period; and

(3) a review of all NSLs issued pursuant to the *Fair Credit Reporting Act* (FCRA) in counterintelligence investigations from 2002 through 2006.

In this chapter, we address the matters that were self-reported by FBI field personnel in 2006 to the FBI OGC as possible intelligence violations. These violations occurred before the OIG issued its first NSL report and before the FBI began taking corrective action in response to our report (described in Chapter Two of this report). It is therefore not surprising that we found possible NSL-related intelligence violations in 2006 comparable to our findings in our first NSL report. Moreover, compared with the number of possible intelligence violations associated with the FBI's 2007 reviews, exigent letters and other informal requests, and the 11 blanket NSLs and other improper NSLs issued in 2006, the number of matters discussed in this chapter is relatively small.

It is important to note, however, as described in Chapter Three of this report, that the overwhelming majority of possible NSL-related intelligence violations that occurred since the Patriot Act significantly expanded the FBI's NSL authorities were not reported by FBI personnel to the FBI OGC through the self-reporting mechanism established 25 years ago to identify and address such violations.[122]

As described in Chapter Two of this report, the FBI is in the process of implementing the recommendations in our first NSL report that were intended to improve its compliance with NSL statutes, Attorney General Guidelines, and internal FBI policy. Moreover, the FBI and other components of the Department are taking additional steps to promote compliance with NSL statutes and policies governing other investigative techniques used in national security investigations. Once implemented, the FBI believes that many of the errors categorized as possible intelligence violations in our

[122] Possible intelligence violations can be reported by case agents, the case agents' supervisors who approve the issuance of the NSLs, or the Chief Division Counsels (CDC). They also can be reported as a result of a supervisor's file review or an audit.

first NSL report, in the FBI's 2007 reviews, and in this chapter will be significantly reduced.

In Section I of this chapter, we describe the FBI's procedures for reporting possible Intelligence Oversight Board (IOB) violations to the FBI OGC and the FBI OGC's process for deciding whether to report the violation to the IOB. In Section II, we discuss violations triggered by the use of NSLs that were reported in 2006 by case agents to the FBI OGC as possible violations that should be reported to the IOB. In Section III, we summarize our conclusion and provide our recommendations.

As we did in our first NSL report, we determined whether the FBI would have been entitled to the information under applicable NSL statutes, Attorney General Guidelines, and internal policies. We found that of the 84 possible intelligence violations identified and reported to the FBI OGC in 2006, the FBI received information it was not entitled to receive in 14 matters. In one of the matters the FBI requested information it was not entitled to under the applicable NSL statute. In this matter the case agent modified the standard language used for requesting information pursuant to the ECPA NSL statute by requesting publicly available content information. The FBI OGC concluded that the alteration of the ECPA NSL statutory language to request and obtain the information was beyond the scope of the ECPA.[123]

In the other 13 matters, the FBI made proper requests but, due to third party errors, obtained information it was not entitled to receive under the pertinent NSL statutes.

I. The FBI Process for Reporting Possible Violations Involving Intelligence Activities in the United States

In this section we briefly summarize the FBI's procedures for reporting possible intelligence violations to the FBI OGC and the manner in which the FBI OGC decides whether to report possible intelligence violations to the IOB. We then describe the November 2006 FBI OGC guidance to the field on reporting possible intelligence violations to the FBI OGC and separate guidance to the FBI OGC attorneys assigned to evaluate possible intelligence violations.

[123] We could not conclude whether the FBI compounded the errors involved in 52 matters in which it received unauthorized information as a result of third party errors because the FBI OGC has not yet adjudicated whether the FBI used the inappropriately obtained information or uploaded it into FBI databases. Prior to November 13, 2006, case agents were required to report to the FBI OGC unauthorized collections from third party errors. Effective November 13, 2006, the IOB agreed that such third party errors did not have to be reported to the IOB. However, as discussed later in this chapter, on August 1, 2007, the IOB directed that the FBI report unauthorized collections due to third party errors if the FBI compounded the errors by using information inappropriately provided or uploading it into FBI databases. We consider matters in which the FBI compounded third party errors to be an "improper" use of NSL-derived information.

A. The Process for Reporting Possible Intelligence Violations

Executive Order 12863 designates the IOB as a standing committee of the President's Foreign Intelligence Advisory Board and directs the IOB to inform the President of any activities that "may be unlawful or contrary to Executive Order or Presidential Directive."[124] This directive has been interpreted by the Department and the IOB during the period covered by our review to include reports of possible violations of provisions of Attorney General's NSI Guidelines or other guidelines or regulations approved by the Attorney General in accordance with Executive Order 12333, dated December 4, 1981, if the provision was designed to ensure the protection of individual rights.

To comply with the Executive Order 12863 directive, the FBI has developed an internal process for reporting possible intelligence violations to the FBI OGC that begins with the duty of FBI personnel to self-report to the FBI OGC possible intelligence violations within 14 days of discovery. These reports must include the identification of the substantive investigation in which the questionable activity occurred, the names of the relevant FBI personnel, the identification of the investigation's subject's status as a U.S. person or non-U.S. person, the legal authority for the investigation, a complete and thorough explanation of the error believed to have been committed, and the date of the incident. FBI OGC attorneys review the reports, prepare a written opinion as to whether the matter should be reported to the IOB, and draft the written communication to the IOB for those matters the FBI OGC determines meet the reporting requirements of Executive Order 12863.

In November 2006, the FBI OGC issued guidance to the field on the types of infractions involving the use of NSLs that must be reported to the FBI OGC as possible intelligence violations. The FBI OGC also issued revised guidance for attorneys assigned to its National Security Law Branch (NSLB) who evaluate possible intelligence violations. These guidance memoranda are described below.

B. FBI Guidance on Reporting and Adjudicating Possible Intelligence Violations

1. November 16, 2006, Guidance on Reporting Possible IOB Violations to the FBI OGC

On November 16, 2006, the FBI OGC issued a memorandum to all FBI divisions regarding revised procedures for reporting possible intelligence violations.[125] Although the FBI OGC previously had issued general guidance

[124] For a more detailed description of the IOB reporting process, see Office of the Inspector General, *Report to Congress on Implementation of Section 1001 of the USA PATRIOT Act* (March 8, 2006).

[125] Office of the General Counsel, National Security Law Branch (NSLB), Federal Bureau of Investigation, electronic communication to all divisions, Revised Procedures for the Submission of Reports of Potential Intelligence Oversight Board Matters, November 16, 2006.

on reporting possible intelligence violations and responded informally to questions that arose from the field about matters that should be reported, it had not previously identified in a comprehensive manner what infractions relating to the use and approval of NSLs (or other investigative techniques) were required to be reported to the FBI OGC and the Inspection Division's Internal Investigations Section as possible intelligence violations.[126] The November 16, 2006, guidance also addressed the FBI's retention practices for handling improperly or unintentionally acquired information and reporting such matters to the FBI OGC. As we noted in our first NSL report, prior to the 2006 guidance, FBI practices regarding these issues were not uniform, and the guidance for FBI employees was not clearly articulated.[127]

The memorandum identified the following types of NSL-related incidents that must be reported to the FBI OGC as possible intelligence violations and cautioned that the list was not exhaustive:

> Serving a National Security Letter (NSL) that contains a substantive typographical error that results in the acquisition of data that is not relevant to an authorized investigation (i.e., numbers in telephone number transposed).
>
> Serving an NSL that requests information that is beyond the scope permissible by statute (i.e., content information).
>
> Receiving information from a carrier beyond the scope of an NSL resulting in the unintentional acquisition of data.

The memorandum also directed FBI personnel to sequester with each field division's Chief Division Counsel (CDC) any information improperly received or unintentionally acquired using an NSL.[128] The memorandum stated that as part of its IOB adjudication process, the National Security Law Branch (NSLB) will advise the field whether the information may be used or whether it must be returned to the carrier or be destroyed with appropriate documentation to the file.

2. November 30, 2006, Guidance to FBI OGC NSLB Attorneys Adjudicating Possible IOB Violations

On November 30, 2006, the FBI OGC issued guidance to FBI OGC attorneys assigned to draft opinions based on reports of possible intelligence violations.[129] The memorandum described whether certain matters reportable to

[126] On April 7, 2006, the FBI OGC sent an e-mail to all CDCs and NSLB attorneys stating that unauthorized collections due to third party errors should be reported to the FBI OGC as possible intelligence violations. That policy was formalized and disseminated to all FBI divisions on November 16, 2006.

[127] See NSL I, 29.

[128] National Security Law Branch, electronic communication to all divisions, November 16, 2006. The FBI OGC further directed that information unintentionally acquired under the *Foreign Intelligence Surveillance Act* be sequestered, sealed, and delivered to the responsible FBI Headquarters unit to be submitted to the Foreign Intelligence Surveillance Court for appropriate disposition. Id.

[129] Julie Thomas, Deputy General Counsel, NSLB, Federal Bureau of Investigation, memorandum to NSLB Attorneys, Guidance for Drafting IOB Opinions, November 30, 2006.

the FBI OGC in turn should be reported to the IOB. The categories addressed in the guidance were certain violations of the Attorney General's NSI Guidelines, conduct involving NSLs, mistakes involving information obtained pursuant to orders of the Foreign Intelligence Surveillance Court, and conduct pertaining to other investigative techniques authorized by the Attorney General's NSI Guidelines.

With respect to the use of NSLs, the guidance directed FBI OGC attorneys to review the attachment to the NSL to determine whether there had been an unauthorized collection.[130] The guidance further stated that if the information obtained in response to an NSL was referenced in the attachment to the NSL, it was not necessary for the field to report the matter to the FBI OGC and the Inspection Division. If the information was. not referenced in the attachment but was relevant to the investigation, the CDCs in the field office that issued the NSL were directed to sequester the information until a new NSL was issued for the information. However, the guidance directed that such matters were to be reported to the FBI OGC and the Inspection Division as possible intelligence violations.

The most significant issue addressed in the guidance memorandum was whether information obtained by the FBI that was beyond the scope of the NSL due to third party error—referred to as "unauthorized collections" - had to be reported to the IOB. The memorandum advised that "if the FBI properly issues an NSL, and the carrier provided the information outside the scope of the NSL, the matter is not reportable to the IOB."[131] However, the memorandum did not address whether the FBI's handling of the unauthorized information could in some circumstances trigger the need to report to the IOB. For example, guidance did not address whether, if case agents received and uploaded unauthorized information provided to the FBI due to third party error, the mishandling of such information should be reported to the IOB.

On August 1, 2007, the IOB directed the FBI OGC to report third party errors that are compounded by the FBI.[132] Upon such direction, FBI OGC officials told us that they began evaluating third party errors to determine if the FBI compounded the errors by using the inappropriately provided

[130] FBI practice is to list on an attachment to the NSL—rather than in the body of the NSL itself—the types of records that the recipient may consider to be within the scope of the statute.

[131] The November 30, 2006, memorandum noted that the IOB had agreed that third party errors that resulted in the unauthorized collection of information pursuant to an NSL must be reported to the FBI OGC but were not required to be reported to the IOB. See General Counsel, Intelligence Oversight Board, letter to Julie F. Thomas, Deputy General Counsel, NSLB, Federal Bureau of Investigation, November 13, 2006.

[132] See General Counsel, Intelligence Oversight Board, letter to Julie F. Thomas, Deputy General Counsel, NSLB, Federal Bureau of Investigation, August 1, 2007.

information or uploading it into FBI databases. As a result of the new directive, the FBI OGC said it would reevaluate reports of unauthorized collections to determine if the FBI compounded the initial third party errors. If so, FBI OGC officials told us they would report the matters to the IOB.

II. Possible Intelligence Violations Arising From National Security Letters Reported to the FBI OGC in 2006

We determined that in 2006 FBI field divisions reported 84 possible intelligence violations to the FBI OGC arising from the use of NSL authorities in 75 different national security investigations.[133] As shown in Chart 7.1, this compares with 26 possible intelligence violations reported to the FBI OGC over a 3-year period (2003 through 2005) as we reported in our first NSL report.[134]

We believe the overall increase in the reports of possible intelligence violations may be explained in large part by the attention that our first NSL review focused on the FBI's obligation to examine information obtained in response to NSLs and report possible intelligence violations and closer scrutiny of NSLs and NSL-derived information by case agents, supervisors, and CDCs.

FBI Headquarters divisions, which issued approximately 450 NSLs in 2006, reported, in conjunction with a field office, one possible NSL-related intel

Chart 7.1: Possible NSL-Related IOB Violations Reported to the FBI OGC (2003 through 2006)

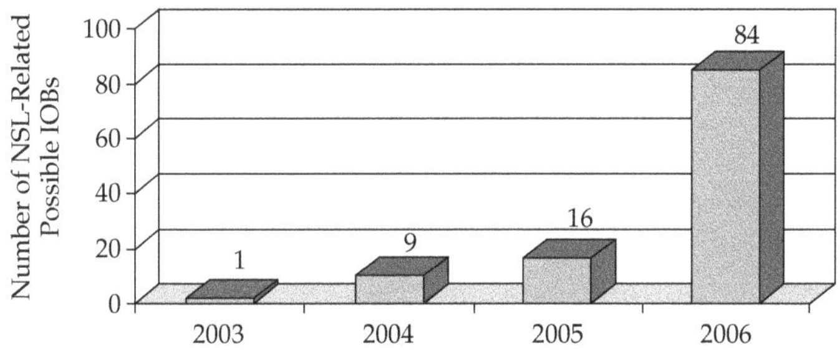

Source: FBI

[133] We considered the universe of possible NSL-related intelligence violations in 2006 to include all matters reported to the FBI OGC between January 1, 2006, and December 31, 2006. We reviewed all such matters for which we received documentation by August 1, 2007.

[134] See NSL I, 70.

ligence violation to the FBI OGC in 2006.[135] Headquarters divisions did not report any such violations from 2003 through 2005.

In this section we describe the possible intelligence violations regarding the use of NSL authorities that were reported to the FBI OGC in 2006, the number and nature of the possible intelligence violations, and our analysis of these matters compared with the 26 possible intelligence violations reported by the FBI from 2003 through 2005 and described in our first NSL report. Table 7.1 lists the categories of the possible intelligence violations reported in 2006 and whether they initially resulted from FBI or third party errors.[136]

Table 7.1: Summary of 84 Possible NSL-Related IOB Violations Reported to the FBI OGC (2006)

Category of Possible IOB Violations	Possible IOB Violations Reported to the FBI OGC		IOB Violations Reported to the IOB	
	FBI Error	Initial Third Party Error	FBI Error	Initial Third Party Error
Improper authorization	3	0	3	0
Improper request	3	0	1	0
Unauthorized investigative activity during lapse in investigation	8	0	1	0
Unauthorized dissemination	1	0	0	0
Unauthorized collection	18	52	15	14
Total Possible IOB Violations Reported to the FBI OGC in 2006		**84**[137]		**34**

[135] Based on the results of the FBI Inspection Division's review of 10 percent of the NSLs issued by Headquarters during the period 2003 through 2006, described in Chapter Three of this report, we believe that FBI Headquarters divisions were not recognizing or reporting possible NSL-related intelligence violations throughout this period. The Inspection Division review identified, based on guidance provided by the FBI OGC, at least 130 possible NSL-related intelligence violations from FBI Headquarters divisions in investigations open from 2003 through 2006. These included NSLs that exceeded statutory authority, NSLs issued solely out of control files, NSLs issued despite the lack of predication in the approval memoranda, and NSLs that resulted in unauthorized collections due to FBI or third party errors.

[136] In Table 7.1 and elsewhere in this chapter we use the phrase "initial third party error" because, as noted above, the FBI OGC has not yet determined whether the FBI compounded the NSL recipients' errors by using the information or uploading it into FBI databases.

[137] One matter included an initial third party error that resulted in both an unauthorized collection and an improper request by the FBI. Both possible intelligence violations are reflected in Table 7.1.

A. Possible NSL-Related IOB Violations Reported to the IOB in 2006

In 2006, the FBI OGC reported 34 of the 84 possible intelligence violations to the IOB, or 40 percent of the total.[138] Twenty of the possible intelligence violations reported to the IOB were attributable to FBI errors, while 14 were initially attributable to third party errors.

Table 7.2 provides additional details on these matters.

Table 7.2: Summary of 34 NSL-Related IOB Violations Reported to the IOB by the FBI OGC (2006)

Category of IOB Violations	Number of Violations Reported to the IOB
Improper Authorization (FBI Error)	
Issuing ECPA NSL without obtaining required Special Agent in Charge authorization to extend preliminary investigation after 6 months	1
Issuing Right to Financial Privacy Act (RFPA) NSL without obtaining required Headquarters authorization to extend preliminary investigation after 1 year	1
Serving ECPA NSLs before preliminary investigation was properly reauthorized by Special Agent in Charge	1
Improper Request (FBI Error)	
Issuing ECPA NSL to an Internet service provider in a manner that was deemed an improper request under pertinent NSL statute	1
Unauthorized Investigative Activity During Lapse in Investigation After NSL Was Properly Issued (FBI Error)	
Obtaining and analyzing RFPA records without obtaining required FBI Headquarters authorization to extend preliminary investigation after 1 year[139]	1
Unauthorized Collection (FBI Error)	
Obtaining ECPA telephone subscriber information not relevant to an authorized national security investigation	3
Obtaining ECPA telephone toll billing information not relevant to an authorized national security investigation	10

[138] Possible intelligence violations reported to the FBI OGC are also reported to the Inspection Division's Internal Investigations Section (IIS). If IIS determines that the conduct of an FBI employee is more than a performance issue, the FBI OGC refers the matter to the FBI's Office of Professional Responsibility (FBI OPR). The FBI Inspection Division reported that it did not refer any reports of these possible violations to the FBI OPR in 2006.

[139] In November 2007, the FBI OGC advised the OIG that it intends to issue a corrected adjudication memorandum stating that this violation is not reportable to the IOB.

Category of IOB Violations	Number of Violations Reported to the IOB
Obtaining ECPA e-mail subscriber information not relevant to an authorized national security investigation	1
Obtaining ECPA electronic communication transactional records not relevant to an authorized national security investigation	1
Total FBI Errors	**20**[140]
Unauthorized Collection (Initial Third Party Error)[141]	
Obtaining ECPA telephone subscriber information not relevant to an authorized national security investigation	2
Obtaining ECPA telephone toll billing information not relevant to an authorized national security investigation	4
Obtaining ECPA telephone toll billing information outside the time frame requested in the NSL	
Obtaining subject line or full content in response to an electronic communication transactional record ECPA NSL	3
Obtaining ECPA e-mail subscriber information not relevant to an authorized national security investigation	1
Obtaining RFPA financial records not relevant to authorized national security investigation	2
Total Initial Third Party Errors	**14**
Total Number of Violations	
Reported by the FBI OGC to the IOB	**34**

Nature of IOB Violations: The 34 intelligence violations reported by the FBI to the IOB in 2006 involved the following categories of violations.

140 The four possible NSL-related intelligence violations in Table 7.2 that are categorized as improper authorizations and improper requests also resulted in unauthorized collections. However, we did not "double count" these matters by including them in the "unauthorized collection" category.

141 As noted previously, "unauthorized collections" is a phrase used by the FBI and the OIG to describe several circumstances in which the FBI receives information in response to NSLs that was not requested or was mistakenly requested. For example, many unauthorized collections occur due to errors on the part of NSL recipients when they provide more information than was requested (such as records for a longer period of time or records on additional persons). The FBI sometimes also refers to these matters as "over collections" or "overproductions." We refer to these as "initial third party errors" because, while the NSL recipient may initially have provided more information than requested, the FBI may or may not have compounded the initial error by using or uploading the information. Other unauthorized collections can result from FBI errors, such as when a typographical error in the telephone number or e-mail address results in the acquisition of data on the wrong person or e-mail address. When we present data on "unauthorized collections" in this report we note whether the infraction occurred due to initial third party error or FBI error.

- In three matters NSLs were signed by appropriate field officials but the underlying investigations had not been approved or extended by the appropriate Headquarters or field supervisors.
- In one matter an NSL was served on an Internet service provider (ISP) in a manner that that was deemed an improper request under the pertinent NSL statute.
- In one matter the NSL was appropriately issued but the NSL recipient provided the records after the preliminary investigation had lapsed.
- In 29 matters the NSL recipient provided information that was not requested in the NSL or provided information on the wrong person due either to FBI typographical errors or initial errors by the NSL recipients.[142]

Three of the 14 initial third party errors noted in Table 7.2 resulted in the FBI's acquisition of either full e-mail content (two matters) or e-mail subject line content (one matter) from ISPs in response to ECPA electronic communication transactional record NSLs. In the two matters that resulted in acquisition of full e-mail content, an ISP mistakenly provided on the same disk the full message content of the e-mails for the requested account and for the account of an associated subscriber in the same investigation whose records had been requested in another NSL. On instruction from the FBI OGC, the disk and paper copies of the records were sealed and sequestered by the field division's CDC, and a new NSL was issued. In response, the ISP improperly sent the same full content information, which was thereafter again sequestered.

In the matter involving acquisition of e-mail subject line content, the ISP included the subject field for each e-mail transaction along with the e-mail header information for the requested 2-year time period. The NSL specifically directed that the ISP not include subject fields in its response. The FBI OGC directed that the information that exceeded the scope of the NSL be sealed and sequestered and await further direction from the FBI OGC.

Status of Investigative Subject and Target of NSL: We also attempted to determine whether the subject of the investigation in these 34 matters was a U.S. person and if the investigative subject was the same as the target of the NSL.[143]

---

142 Of the 15 unauthorized collections resulting from FBI errors, 12 were due to typographical errors, 2 were due to inadvertent misidentification of telephone numbers, and 1 was due to a computer software mistake.

143 50 U.S.C. § 1801(i) defines a "United States Person" as:

> a citizen of the United States, an alien lawfully admitted for permanent residence. . . . an unincorporated association a substantial number of members of which are citizens of the United States or aliens lawfully admitted for permanent residence, or a corporation which is incorporated in the United States . . . ."

- In 25 of the 34 matters, the subject of the investigation was a U.S. person, in 8 matters the subject was a non-U.S. person, and in 1 matter the status of the subject could not be determined.
- In 27 of the matters, the NSLs sought information about the subject of the underlying national security investigation, 3 NSLs sought information on a person other than the subject, 1 NSL sought information on both the subject and a non-subject; and 3 NSL targets could not be determined.

Timeliness of Reporting: We determined that 19 of the 34 possible intelligence violations reported to the IOB (56 percent) were reported within 14 days of discovery to the FBI OGC in accordance with FBI policy. However, 12 (35 percent) were not reported in a timely fashion.[144] Seven of these 12 took between 17 and 46 days to report and 5 took between 145 and 418 days. In two of these five matters, the agents did not realize the matters were reportable as possible intelligence violations until they attended NSL training a year after the violations occurred.[145] In the other three, no reason was given for the delay in reporting. We could not determine how long it took to report the remaining 3 of the 34 violations.

We also calculated the time it took for FBI personnel to identify possible intelligence violations. From our examination of reports to the FBI OGC, we determined that 26 of the 34 violations were discovered within approximately 2 months of the occurrence. Five of the possible intelligence violations were discovered between approximately 2 months and 8 months after they occurred. In one instance, discovery was delayed because the case agent mistakenly believed the underlying preliminary investigation had been extended. In the second case, discovery did not occur until the data was being uploaded into an FBI database. In the third, the case was reassigned and the violation not discovered until the new case agent took over. In the two remaining cases, field reports to the FBI OGC did not specify reasons for the delay. We could not determine how long it took for FBI personnel to discover the remaining three possible violations.

Remedial Actions: Twenty-nine of the 34 possible NSL-related intelligence violations reported to the IOB in 2006 involved unauthorized collections. We examined the 29 matters to determine whether case agents handled the unauthorized information in conformity with FBI guidance. FBI field and

---

On June 1, 2007, the FBI OGC issued comprehensive guidance that reiterated earlier guidance instructing agents to identify in NSL approval documents the status of persons associated with all NSL requests. See National Security Law Policy and Training Unit, Federal Bureau of Investigation, electronic communication to all divisions, Comprehensive Guidance on National Security Letters, June 1, 2007, at 13, which we described in detail in Chapter Two of this report.

144 This compares with 6 of the 26 possible intelligence violations (23 percent) reported in 2003 through 2005 that were not reported to the FBI OGC within 14 days of discovery, described in our first NSL report. See NSL I, 74.

145 In both matters, the agents made typographical errors in the NSLs and discovered the errors when they received the records from the NSL recipients.

Chart 7.2: Timeliness of 34 FBI Field Reports to the FBI OGC of Possible NSL-Related IOB Violations Reported to the IOB (2006)

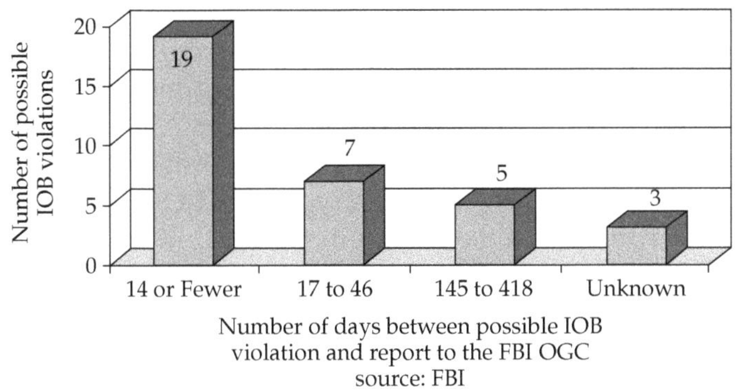

FBI OGC documentation stated that the inappropriately obtained records received in response to 20 of these 29 matters were sealed and sequestered while they were awaiting final dispositions by the field offices or further instructions from the NSLB. In field reports to the FBI OGC for the remaining nine matters, documentation indicated that a variety of remedial steps were taken: issuing a new NSL for the records; forwarding the unauthorized material to FBI Headquarters for appropriate action; offering the records back to the NSL recipient; removing telephone data from Telephone Applications, the FBI's principal database for storing telephone records, and from other FBI records; and destroying the records.

Twenty-one of the 29 matters reported to the FBI OGC involving unauthorized collections resulted in the FBI's acquisition of telephone subscriber or toll billing records. We examined the field reports to the FBI OGC to determine whether the inappropriately obtained data was uploaded into FBI databases. While 17 of the 21 reports stated that the information was not uploaded, we found that field reports for 4 matters did not address the issue.

B. OIG Analysis Regarding Possible NSL-Related IOB Violations Reported to the IOB

As we found in our first NSL report, the severity of the possible intelligence violations reported to the IOB varied. We believe the most serious were those in which the FBI obtained full e-mail content. In 2 of the 14 instances in which the unauthorized collection was initially attributable to third party errors, the FBI received full content e-mail information.[146] Among the 15 matters in which the FBI collected unauthorized information due to

[146] According to FBI records, FBI personnel did not compound the third party errors in either of these matters.

FBI error, 10 were due to typographical errors or misidentification of telephone 2 numbers that resulted in the FBI collecting telephone toll records on the wrong person.

Our examination of the 34 possible NSL-related intelligence violations reported by the FBI to the IOB in 2006 did not evidence deliberate or intentional violations of NSL statutes, Attorney General Guidelines, or internal FBI policy. Although the majority of the possible intelligence violations — 20 of 34, or 59 percent—arose from FBI errors, most were a consequence of errors in the telephone number listed in the NSL. In all but one instance, the FBI would have been entitled to obtain the information under the NSL statutes had it followed the requirements of those statutes, Attorney General Guidelines, and internal FBI policies. In one matter, the case agent modified the standard language used for requesting information pursuant to the ECPA NSL statute by requesting publicly available content information. The FBI OGC concluded that the alteration of the ECPA NSL statutory language to request and obtain the information was beyond the scope of the ECPA. The FBI OGC concluded that the matter should be reported to the IOB because the ECPA "does not have a 'catch-all' authority, nor does it allow for content as requested in the NSL."

However, although the 14 unauthorized collections were reported to the IOB, the FBI OGC has not yet adjudicated whether case agents compounded the errors by using the inappropriately provided information or uploading it into FBI databases.[147]

C. Possible NSL-Related IOB Violations Not Reported to the IOB in 2006

In 2006, FBI field offices reported 50 possible intelligence violations to the FBI OGC that were not reported to the IOB. Of these 50 that were not reported to the IOB, 13 resulted from FBI errors and 38 resulted from initial third party errors.[148]

Table 7.3 provides additional details on the nature and source of these possible intelligence violations:

We determined that 30 of the 50 possible intelligence violations that were not reported to the IOB (60 percent) were reported to the FBI OGC within 14 days of discovery in accordance with FBI policy. We could not determine how long it took to report 4 of the 50 possible intelligence violations. However, the remaining 16 possible intelligence violations (32 percent) were not reported to the FBI OGC in a timely fashion. Eight of these 16 took between 16 and 51 days to report, and 8 took between 71 and 268 days to report.

[147] The FBI OGC has been adjudicating over 1,200 possible IOB violations reported to it as a result of the three reviews the FBI conducted in response to the OIG's first NSL report. These reviews are described in Chapter Three of this report.

[148] One of the 50 violations included both an initial third party error and a subsequent FBI error.

Table 7.3: Summary of 50 Possible NSL-Related IOB Violations Not Reported to the IOB (2006)

Category of Possible IOB Violations	Number of Possible Violations Reported to the FBI OGC
Unauthorized Investigative Activity During Lapse in Investigation After NSL Properly Issued (FBI Error)	
Reviewing records obtained from an ECPA NSL after the national security investigation had lapsed	1
Requesting (but not issuing or serving) an NSL after the national security investigation had lapsed	1
Allowing the national security investigations to lapse before records sought in the NSLs were received	3
Allowing the national security investigations to lapse before analyzing records obtained from RFPA or ECPA NSLs	2
Improper Request (FBI Error)	
Issuing ECPA NSL without language regarding non-disclosure and confidentiality requirements pursuant to the Patriot Reauthorization Act	1
Issuing ECPA NSLs based on an unauthorized collection	1
Unauthorized Collection (FBI Error)	
Obtaining ECPA telephone subscriber information not relevant to an authorized national security investigation	1
Obtaining ECPA telephone toll information not relevant to an authorized national security investigation	2
Unauthorized Dissemination (FBI Error)	
Providing ECPA telephone subscriber and toll information to a third party not authorized to receive such information	1
Total FBI Errors	13
Unauthorized Collection (Initial Third Party Error)	
Obtaining ECPA telephone subscriber information not relevant to an authorized national security investigation	1
Obtaining ECPA telephone subscriber information outside the time frame or not requested in the NSL	2
Obtaining ECPA telephone toll information not relevant to an authorized national security investigation	12
Obtaining ECPA telephone toll information outside the time frame or not requested in the NSL	4
Obtaining ECPA telephone toll information when subscriber information was requested and obtaining toll records outside the time frame requested	1

Category of Possible IOB Violations	Number of Possible Violations Reported to the FBI OGC
Obtaining subject line or full content in response to ECPA electronic communication transactional records NSL	6
Obtaining ECPA electronic communication transactional records outside the time frame or not requested in the NSL	4
Obtaining RFPA financial records not relevant to an authorized national security investigation	3
Obtaining FCRAv full credit information in response to a FCRAu NSL in a counterintelligence investigation	4
Obtaining electronic communication transactional records in response to a preservation letter (not an NSL)	1
Total Initial Third Party Errors	**38**
Total Numher of Possible NSL-Related Violations Reported to the FBI OGC and not reported to IOB	**51**[149]

In 12 of the 16 matters that were not reported on a timely basis, no reason was given for the delay in reporting. In 3 of the 16, the reason for the delay was that the case agents did not realize the matters were reportable as possible intelligence violations until they were informed later or until they attended NSL training.[150] In the final instance, the case agent stated that he could not ask about the possible intelligence violation until the CDC returned to the office.

D. OIG Analysis of Possible NSL-Related IOB Violations Not Reported to the IOB

Similar to possible intelligence violations reported to the IOB in 2006, the matters not reported to the IOB in 2006 varied in seriousness. Among the three possible intelligence violations not reported to the IOB in which the FBI collected information not associated with an investigation due to FBI errors, two were matters in which the FBI in good faith requested telephone records on persons they believed were associated with the telephone numbers. However, after the records were received, the case agent discovered that the two sources had provided the wrong numbers. The third

[149] One matter included both an unauthorized collection error by the NSL recipient and a subsequent improper request error by the FBI. Both errors are reflected in Table 7.3.

[150] In each of these three instances, the NSL recipient provided records not requested in the NSL, which the case agents discovered when they received the records from the NSL recipient.

possible intelligence violation was the result of a mistranslation of a foreign name. In 6 of the 38 instances in which the unauthorized collection initially was attributable to third party errors, the NSL recipients sent the FBI subject line or full content e-mail information, which is prohibited by the ECPA NSL statute. In three matters the NSL recipients sent the FBI information well beyond the time frame requested in the NSL, which resulted in collection of records 1 year, 3 years, and 4 years outside the requested time frame.

In our examination of FBI OGC decisions that resulted in determinations not to report possible intelligence violations to the IOB, we agreed with the FBI OGC's reasoning for not reporting 44 of the 50 matters. Among the six other matters, we identified four FBI OGC decisions in which the rationale for not reporting the possible intelligence violation to the IOB was inconsistent with prior FBI OGC decisions and two FBI OGC decisions that were unpersuasive. Three of these possible intelligence violations were attributable to FBI error, two resulted from third party errors, and one involved both a third party error and an FBI error.

We concluded that the FBI OGC's decision not to report the following four matters to the IOB was inconsistent with other FBI OGC decisions in 2006 that involved similar facts. The four matters were:

- two third party errors in which properly served NSLs for ECPA telephone subscriber and electronic communication transactional records resulted in the acquisition of records outside the time period requested (in one instance resulting in the acquisition of records 4 years prior to the initial date noted in the NSL);[151] and
- two FBI errors in which the records obtained from properly issued NSLs (ECPA and another statute not identified) were received and analyzed prior to an authorized extension of the investigation.

For each of these four possible intelligence violations, the OIG found at least one nearly identical matter that the FBI OGC decided to report to the IOB in 2006.[152] The FBI OGC decision memoranda did not identify any

[151] Although, as noted above, third party errors did not have to be reported to the IOB from November 13, 2006, to August 1, 2007. The two possible intelligence violations involving third party errors were adjudicated prior to those dates (October 3, 2006, and October 7, 2006). Therefore, we believe both of these should have been reported to the IOB in accordance with applicable standards at the time. The FBI OGC advised the OIG in December 2007 that it is re-evaluating these two opinions in accordance with the IOB's November 13, 2006, letter and the August 1, 2007, directive. Under the new standard, one of these two matters would be reportable to the IOB because the FBI compounded the error, and the FBI OGC told us that it will issue a corrected opinion.

[152] Similar matters that were reported to the IOB included receiving records outside the time period requested and analyzing records prior to a required extension of the investigation. In November 2007, FBI OGC officials advised the OIG that it reconsidered one of its prior decisions to report a violation to the IOB that the OIG used to contrast FBI OGC decisions not to report similar matters to the IOB. The FBI OGC stated that it had erroneously analyzed and reported a matter to the IOB in which investigative activity (specifically, analyzing records) was performed after the preliminary

facts or circumstances that distinguished these matters from similar matters that the FBI reported to the IOB in 2006.

We also identified two other matters that we believe should have been reported to the IOB under the applicable reporting standard:

- improperly disseminating records to a communication service provider received in response to an ECPA NSL seeking telephone toll billing records; and
- using data obtained through an unauthorized collection to improperly generate ECPA NSLs for telephone toll billing and electronic communication subscriber records.

In the first matter, an FBI field office obtained ECPA telephone toll billing records with the intent of sending the records to the field office that issued the NSL. Instead, the FBI field office inadvertently disseminated the records to another communication service provider rather than the field office that initiated the NSL. Documentation of the incident states that the communication service provider that received the records recognized the error and contacted the original communication service provider, which then contacted the FBI. The FBI OGC reasoned that improper dissemination to a private communication service provider did not damage national security and had no impact on the rights of the subscriber.

Although the dissemination was inadvertent and the communication service provider did not further disseminate the information, we believe any dissemination to a party not authorized to receive the records, absent the consent of the person who the records concern or in specified emergency situations, should be reported to the IOB.[153] The ECPA states that the FBI may disseminate information only as specified in the Attorney General's NSI Guidelines. The Attorney General's NSI Guidelines provide standards and procedures for the sharing and dissemination of information obtained in national security investigations. The dissemination that took place in this matter was not among the specified types of dissemination permitted

---

investigation had expired. In contrast to the reasoning of a June 2006 decision, the FBI OGC reasoned that investigative activity undertaken after the expiration of a preliminary investigation is permissible if that activity is permissible under a threat assessment pursuant to the Attorney General's NSI Guidelines. FBI OGC officials told us that they consider the NSL- derived information to be FBI records because the field office had received the records in response to a properly issued NSL. The FBI OGC's rationale is reflected in the November 30, 2006, guidance to NSLB attorneys.

[153] The *Electronic Communications Privacy Act*, 18 U.S.C.§ 2709(d), provides:

> The Federal Bureau of Investigation may disseminate information and records obtained under this section only as provided in guidelines approved by the Attorney General for foreign intelligence collection and foreign counterintelligence investigations conducted by the Federal Bureau of Investigation, and, with respect to dissemination to an agency of the United States, only if such information is clearly relevant to the authorized responsibilities of such agency.

by the Attorney General's NSI Guidelines, and the matter should have been reported to the IOB.[154]

In the second matter, the FBI properly served an NSL for electronic communication (e-mail) subscriber records. In response, the NSL recipient provided the subscriber records and, in addition, electronic communication transactional records that were not requested in the NSL. Using information contained in the records that were not requested in the NSL and to which it therefore was not entitled, the FBI issued NSLs for ECPA telephone toll billing and electronic communication subscriber records (e-mail records) to two other NSL recipients. The first NSL recipient responded that it had no information, and the second NSL recipient furnished subscriber information. The FBI realized the error and issued two new NSLs to cover the information provided in response to the NSLs based on the inappropriately collected information. The field office reported the unauthorized collection and the issuance of the NSLs to the FBI OGC.

However, in its decision memorandum the FBI OGC addressed only the third party unauthorized collection, stating that the field office should contact the ISP and ask whether unintentionally acquired information should be returned or destroyed or, alternatively, issue a new NSL for the electronic communication transactional records. The FBI OGC reasoned that the original NSL was properly served, but that the provider furnished records that were not requested. Yet, the FBI OGC decision did not address the FBI's issuance of the two ECPA NSLs based on e-mail address information that the FBI had not requested in the original NSL but that was produced as a result of the NSL recipient's error. Since the FBI was not authorized to obtain the electronic communication transactional records in response to the initial NSL, we believe that the FBI's use of these records to generate additional NSLs should have been reported to the IOB as improper requests. We also believe the FBI's issuance of the NSLs that were based on the unauthorized information should also have been reported to the FBI OGC

---

[154] The Attorney General's NSI Guidelines provide:

a. Information may be disseminated with the consent of the person whom the information concerns, or where necessary to protect life or property from threatened force or violence, otherwise necessary for the safety or security of persons or property or for the prevention of crime, or necessary to obtain information for the conduct of a lawful investigation by the FBI.

b. Information that is publicly available or does not identify United States persons may be disseminated for any lawful purpose.

c. Dissemination of information provided to the FBI by other Intelligence Community agencies is subject to applicable agreements and understandings with such agencies concerning the dissemination of such information.

NSI Guidelines, § V1I(B)(1).

and in turn to the IOB as improper requests because the FBI compounded the third party error by using the information in its investigation.[155]

In addition to the matter described above, there were 37 other possible intelligence violations for a total of 38 matters that involved unauthorized collection due to third party errors in which the case agents may have compounded the errors. As noted in the previous section on possible intelligence violations reported to the IOB, the FBI OGC has not yet determined whether case agents compounded the third party errors in these 38 unauthorized collections.

We also examined the remedial actions taken regarding the unauthorized collections that took place in the matters that were not reported to the IOB, similar to our examination of the unauthorized collections that took place in the matters that were reported to the IOB. We found that the field reports of unauthorized collections that were not reported to the IOB did not consistently address whether telephone toll billing records were uploaded into FBI databases. Of the 41 field reports of unauthorized collections that were not reported to the IOB, 19 involved receipt of telephone toll billing records. While 12 of these 19 reports indicated that records were not uploaded into FBI databases, 7 of the reports did not address whether information inappropriately obtained was uploaded into FBI databases.[156]

E. Comparison of Possible NSL-Related IOB Violations Reported to the FBI OGC in 2006 and from 2003 through 2005

To determine whether there were noteworthy trends in the reporting of possible NSL-related intelligence violations to the FBI OGC from 2003 through 2006, we compared the 84 possible intelligence violations reported to the FBI OGC in 2006 with the 26 possible violations reported to the FBI OGC from 2003 through 2005, which we described in our first NSL report.[157] Table 7.4 compares the data in both periods.

As shown in Table 7.4, the number of possible intelligence violations reported to the FBI OGC rose dramatically in 2006 compared with matters reported in 2003 through 2005, from 26 for the 3 years to 84 in 1 year (2006).

155 The FBI improperly requested the two ECPA NSLs between March 2006 and May 2006.

As noted above, prior to August 1, 2007, the FBI OGC was not required to report to the IOB instances in which the FBI compounded third party errors such as in this matter. In light of the new reporting standard, the FBI OGC is in the process of reviewing previous adjudications of matters involving third party errors to determine if the FBI compounded these errors. In January 2008, the FBI OGC decided to "rewrite" its initial decision in this matter, and the rewrite concluded that the matter was reportable to the IOB under the new reporting standard because the agent had "inadvertently compounded the third party error by issuing NSLs based on information derived from over-produced data."

156 The FBI OGC November 16, 2006, guidance memorandum required that improperly obtained information be sequestered pending the FBI OGC's determination of whether the material can be used.

157 See NSL I, 70.

Table 7.4: Comparison of Possible NSL-Related IOB Violations Reported to the FBI OGC (2003 through 2005 and 2006)

	2003 through 2005			2006		
	Possible IOB Violations Reported to the FBI OGC			Possible IOB Violations Reported to the FBI OGC		
Category of Possible IOB Violation	FBI Error	Initial Third Party Error	Possible Violations Reported to the IOB	FBI Error	Initial Third Party Error	Possible Violations Reported to the IOB
Improper authorization	3	0	3	3	0	3
Improper request	4	0	3	3	0	1
Unauthorized investigative activity during lapse in investigation	0	0	0	8	0	1
Unauthorized dissemination	0	0	0	1	0	0
Unauthorized collection	15	4	13	18	52	29
Total FBI or third party errors	22	4	19	33	52	34
Total Possible IOB Violations	26		19	85[158]		34

The data also shows a marked increase in matters reported involving unauthorized collection.

Overall Number of Violations: The fact that the field reported to the FBI OGC over three times the number of possible intelligence violations in 2006 that it reported for the 3-year period from 2003 through 2005 appears primarily due to a significantly higher incidence of reported third party errors involving unauthorized collection. It also is likely that case agents, supervisors, and CDCs began to more closely scrutinize NSLs and NSL-derived information when the OIG was conducting its first NSL review from December 2005 until March 2007.

158 One matter included an initial third party error that resulted in both an unauthorized collection, and an improper request by the FBI. Both possible intelligence violations are reflected in Table 7.4.

Nature of Violations: In 2006, the possible intelligence violations resulting from unauthorized collections were similar to those we reported in our first NSL report, but in 2006, a much higher number of these matters were reported (19 in 2003 through 2005 compared with 70 in 2006). We believe the higher incidence of such reports is attributable to the FBI's closer scrutiny of records obtained in response to NSLs to verify that the responsive data matched the NSL requests. We believe that this heightened scrutiny of adherence to NSL authorities was likely attributable to the FBI's appropriate response to the OIG's first NSL review.

Source of Errors: The increase in the number of reported matters involving third party errors was particularly striking. From 2003 through 2005, FBI errors accounted for 85 percent of the errors, while in 2006 FBI errors accounted for only 39 percent of the errors. With regard to the source of the errors in just the unauthorized collections, from 2003 through 2005, the FBI was responsible for 79 percent of unauthorized collections, while in 2006 the FBI was responsible for only 27 percent of the unauthorized collections. As noted above, this trend suggests that FBI agents, their supervisors, and CDCs were scrutinizing NSLs and NSL- derived information more closely in 2006 than in the past.

Matters Reported to the IOB: While FBI field personnel reported to the FBI OGC in 2006 over three times the number of possible intelligence violations that were reported from 2003 through 2005, the percentage of matters reported to the IOB in 2006 was smaller. From 2003 through 2005, the FBI reported 73 percent of possible intelligence violations to the IOB. In 2006, only 40 percent of the matters reported to the FBI OGC were reported to the IOB. The lower percentage reported to the IOB in 2006 is attributable to the significant number of matters involving unauthorized collections resulting from initial third party errors that the FBI OGC adjudicated after November 13, 2006. After November 13, 2006, under agreement with the IOB, these matters were no longer required to be reported to the IOB.

However, following communications between the FBI OGC and the IOB in August 2007, these matters are now reported to the IOB when the FBI compounds the initial third party error by improperly utilizing the unauthorized information or uploading the unauthorized information into FBI databases. The FBI OGC instructed all CDCs to address whether the initial third party errors were compounded by the FBI when reporting possible intelligence violations to the FBI OGC. The NSLB Deputy General Counsel also advised the IOB's General Counsel that the FBI OGC would review its previous decisions on possible intelligence violations arising from third party errors to determine whether application of the August 2007 directive required further reporting to the IOB. The NSLB's Deputy General Counsel told the OIG that the FBI OGC will adjudicate these matters after the FBI

OGC has completed its adjudications of matters arising from the FBI's three 2007 NSL reviews (described in Chapter Three of this report). In light of the increased reporting of initial third party errors, we believe the FBI must take aggressive steps to ensure that when it obtains information not requested in NSLs discrepancies are promptly identified; that records are sequestered, returned, or otherwise handled in conformity with the FBI OGC's guidance; and that the FBI does not compound the error by using or uploading the improperly provided information.

III. OIG Conclusions and Recommendations

FBI field reports of possible intelligence violations arising from the use of NSLs in 2006 were similar to the reports we examined in our first NSL report covering 2003 through 2005. While there was a notable increase in reports of unauthorized collections in 2006, the percentage of reports of possible intelligence violations attributable to FBI error decreased in 2006. However, in August 2007 the IOB's General Counsel notified the FBI that it would require third party errors to be reported as possible intelligence violations when the FBI compounds such third party errors by utilizing the inappropriately provided information or uploading the information into FBI databases.

We believe the overall increase in the reports of possible intelligence violations may be explained in large part by the attention that our first NSL review focused on the FBI's obligation to examine information obtained in response to NSLs and report possible intelligence violations and to increased scrutiny of NSLs and NSL-derived information by case agents, supervisors, and CDCs.

As discussed in Chapter Two of this report, after the issuance of our first NSL report in March 2007, the FBI and other Department components took a variety of steps to promote compliance with NSL authorities. These include mandatory training of FBI personnel on statutes and rules governing the use of NSLs, as well as several reviews conducted by the FBI's Inspection Division and the National Security Division in conjunction with NSLB attorneys. The FBI also is incorporating technological improvements designed to simplify the preparation of NSL documents and minimize errors in generating these documents. While these efforts are ongoing, we recommend that the FBI:

1. Periodically reinforce in training and guidance provided to case agents and supervisors assigned to national security investigations the FBI OGC directive to report on a timely basis to the FBI OGC possible intelligence violations arising from the use of NSL authorities.

2. Require case agents and supervisors assigned to national security investigations to specify in any reports to the FBI OGC the precise remedial measures employed to handle any unauthorized information they obtain in response to NSLs and to address whether the inappropriately provided information was used or uploaded into FBI databases.
3. Periodically provide case agents and supervisors assigned to national security investigations with examples of common errors in the use of NSLs, such as the examples used in the November 30, 2006, FBI OGC guidance memorandum regarding possible NSL-related intelligence violations.

Chapter Eight: Conclusions and Recommendations

We believe the FBI and the Department have made significant progress in implementing the recommendations from our first NSL report and in adopting other corrective actions to address problems we identified in the use of national security letters. We found that the FBI has devoted significant time, energy, and resources toward ensuring that its field managers and agents understand the seriousness of the FBI's shortcomings in its use of NSLs and their responsibility for correcting these deficiencies.

For example, the FBI Director and Deputy Director have underscored the significance of the OIG's findings with senior Headquarters officials, Special Agents in Charge (SAC), and other personnel throughout the ranks of the FBI; stressed that compliance with NSL authorities is a major priority; and emphasized that personnel involved in drafting, reviewing, and approving NSLs will be held accountable for infractions. The Deputy Director and the General Counsel have reinforced these messages with SACs and Chief Division Counsels (CDC). The FBI also has generated comprehensive legal guidance on use of NSLs; provided mandatory NSL training to SACs, Assistant Special Agents in Charge, Supervisory Special Agents, Special Agents, Intelligence Analysts, and Headquarters personnel; underscored the responsibility of CDCs in reviewing and approving NSLs and of case agents in ensuring that NSLs do not generate unauthorized records; and developed enhanced information technology tools that should facilitate the preparation of NSLs, reduce or eliminate errors, and improve the accuracy of congressional and public reporting on NSL usage. We believe that these and other steps taken in the last year indicate that the FBI is committed to addressing the problems we identified in our first NSL report.

The FBI's efforts to promote better compliance with NSL authorities also have been enhanced by other FBI initiatives and by the national security reviews conducted by the National Security Division (NSD) and the FBI. The FBI has also created a new Office of Integrity and Compliance (OIC), modeled after private sector compliance programs, to ensure that national security investigations and other FBI activities are conducted in a manner consistent with appropriate laws, regulations, and policies. We believe this office can perform a valuable function by providing a process for identifying compliance requirements and risks, assessing existing control mechanisms, and developing and implementing better controls to ensure proper use of NSLs. However, we recommend that the FBI consider providing the OIC with a larger permanent staffing level so that it can develop the skills, knowledge, and independence to lead or directly carry out the critical elements of this new compliance program.

In addition to the FBI's efforts to address the OIG's recommendations, the Department's NSD has implemented additional measures to promote better compliance with NSL authorities and to address other issues raised by our first report. For example, in 2007 the NSD began reviews to examine whether the FBI is using various intelligence techniques, including NSLs, in accordance with applicable laws, guidelines, and policies.

In this report, we also examined the FBI's 2007 field and Headquarters NSL reviews, which confirmed that the types of deficiencies identified in our first NSL report had occurred throughout the FBI from 2003 through 2006. The FBI's field review was important because it covered a larger, statistically valid sample of NSLs and case files. The FBI reviews confirmed similar types of possible intelligence violations in the FBI's use of NSLs. However the FBI's field review found a higher overall violation rate (9.43 percent) than the OIG found (7.5 percent) in the sample we examined in our first NSL report.

However, we examined in detail the FBI's reviews and determined that they did not capture all NSL violations in the files they reviewed and therefore did not provide a fully accurate baseline from which to measure future improvement in compliance with NSL authorities. For example, during our re-examination of case files that FBI inspectors determined had no intelligence violations in three field offices, we discovered 15 NSL-related possible intelligence violations. In addition, because FBI inspectors were unable to locate information provided in response to a significant number of NSLs chosen for review in the FBI's random sample, the results of the FBI's field review likely understated the rate of possible intelligence violations.

In its review, the FBI categorized most instances of unauthorized collections as third party errors rather than as FBI errors. Yet, while the initial mistake may have been attributable to NSL recipients who provided more information than was requested in the NSLs, the FBI may have compounded the recipients' error by not taking appropriate steps to identify the overproduction, sequester the information, and report the violation to the FBI Office of the General Counsel (FBI OGC). We also noted that of the 557 identified possible intelligence violations that resulted initially from third party errors, case agents self-reported only 4 (less than 1 percent).

Finally, as required by the Patriot Reauthorization Act, this OIG review examined the FBI's use of national security letters in calendar year 2006.

Our review found that the FBI's use of national security letter requests in 2006 continued the upward trend we identified in our first NSL report, which covered the period 2003 through 2005. In 2006, the FBI issued 49,425 NSL requests, a 4.7 percent increase over NSL requests issued in 2005. For the 4-year period, 2003 through 2006, the FBI issued a total of 192,499 NSL requests.

Most NSL usage (about [Text not available] percent of all NSL requests) in 2006 occurred during counterterrorism investigations (compared to [Text not available] percent n 2005). About [Text not available] percent of all 2006 NSL requests were issued during counterintelligence investigations, and less than [Text not available] percent of the requests were generated during foreign computer intrusion cyber investigations. In addition, the use of NSLs in FBI counterterrorism investigations increased from approximately [Text not available] percent of investigations opened during 2003 to approximately [Text not available] percent of the counterterrorism investigations opened during 2006.

We also found that the percentage of NSL requests related to investigations of "U.S. persons" increased in 2006 compared with the corresponding percentage of such requests in 2005, from 53 percent to 57 percent. We also found that the percentage of NSL requests related to investigations of non-U.S. persons decreased from approximately 47 percent of all NSL requests issued in 2005 to approximately 43 percent of all NSL requests issued in 2006.

With respect to the effectiveness of national security letters, FBI Headquarters and field personnel reported that they continue to believe national security letters are indispensable investigative tools that serve as building blocks in many counterterrorism and counterintelligence investigations. National security letters have various uses, including obtaining evidence to support Foreign Intelligence Surveillance Act applications for electronic surveillance, pen register/trap and trace devices, or physical searches; developing communication or financial links between subjects of FBI investigations and between those subjects and others; providing evidence to initiate new investigations, expand investigations, or enable agents to close investigations; providing investigative leads; and corroborating information obtained by other investigative techniques. FBI officials told us that information derived from NSLs was a significant factor that contributed to the progress of major terrorism and espionage investigations conducted in 2006.

In addition, as required by the Patriot Reauthorization Act, we examined national security letters issued from March 10, 2006, through December 3 1, 2006, to determine if they were issued without the certification necessary to require the recipients to comply with potentially applicable non-disclosure and confidentiality requirements. The vast majority of the NSLs and approval ECs we examined substantially complied with the certification requirement and FBI policy. We believe this compliance record was largely due to the prompt guidance the FBI OGC issued on the date the Act was signed, the availability of new NSL forms on its Intranet website, and periodic guidance FBI OGC attorneys provided to the field as questions arose.

Our analysis showed that at least 97 percent of the NSLs we examined in a random sample imposed the non-disclosure and confidentiality obligations on recipients. The majority of the approval memoranda supporting these NSLs asserted that disclosure of the NSLs could prematurely reveal a national security investigation to the targets, persons affiliated with the targets, or the investigative subjects. We found that only 17 of 364 (5 percent) NSL approval memoranda in the random sample contained perfunctory or conclusory justifications for invoking the non-disclosure and confidentiality requirements. While the number of non-compliant NSLs in our random sample was small, we are concerned that some case agents and their supervisors did not follow FBI policy that requires sufficient justification for imposing non-disclosure and confidentiality requirements on NSL recipients.

A small number of NSLs and approval memoranda in our random sample (8 of 375) also contained inconsistent recitals with respect to the need for invoking the non-disclosure and confidentiality obligations, and case agents and their supervisors, as well as CDCs, failed to identify and correct these errors. FBI officials believe that a new NSL data system implemented in 2007 will eliminate this and other data entry discrepancies. However, apart from the random sample, we identified 8 (of the 11) blanket NSLs issued by Counterterrorism Division officials in 2006 that did not comply with the Patriot Reauthorization Act requirements respecting these provisions. These eight NSLs included the pre-Patriot Reauthorization Act language to the effect that the recipient was prohibited from disclosing that the FBI had sought or obtained access to information or records under the *Electronic Communications Privacy Act*. The senior Counterterrorism Division officials who signed these NSLs failed to ensure that the NSLs complied with statutory requirements and that the NSLs and related documents were reviewed by FBI attorneys prior to signing.

As required by the Patriot Reauthorization Act, our review also examined instances of improper or illegal use of national security letters in 2006. First, our review analyzed possible NSL-related intelligence violations that the FBI was required to report to the President's Intelligence Oversight Board (IOB). We identified 84 possible intelligence violations involving the use of national security letter authorities that were reported to the FBI OGC from January 1, 2006, through December 31, 2006, of which 34 were reported to the IOB. These 34 matters included the same types of intelligence violations reported to the IOB in 2003 through 2005, including NSLs without proper authorization, improper requests, and unauthorized collection of telephone or Internet e-mail records. Of these 34 intelligence violations, 20 were the result of FBI errors, while 14 resulted initially from mistakes by recipients of the national security letters. Of the 84 possible intelligence violations involving the use of NSL authorities identified and reported to the FBI OGC in 2006, the FBI received information it was not entitled to receive in 14 matters. In one of the matters the FBI requested information it was not entitled to under the applicable NSL statute. In the other 13 matters, the FBI made proper requests but, due to third party errors, obtained information it was not entitled to receive under the pertinent NSL statutes.

In sum, despite the significant challenges facing the FBI to eliminate fully shortcomings in its use of NSLs, we believe the FBI and the Department have evidenced a commitment to correcting the problems we found in our first NSL report and have made significant progress in addressing the need to improve compliance in the FBI's use of NSLs. The FBI's executive leadership, including the Director, Deputy Director, and General Counsel, expressed their commitment to ensure that Headquarters and field personnel understand the seriousness of the FBI's shortcomings in its use of NSLs, the proper use of NSLs, and their individual responsibilities for correcting the deficiencies.

However, because only 1 year has passed since the OIG's first NSL report was released and some measures are not fully implemented, we believe it is too early to definitively state whether the new systems and controls developed by the FBI and the Department will eliminate fully the problems with NSLs that we identified. We believe the FBI must implement all of our recommendations in the first NSL report, demonstrate sustained commitment to the steps it has taken and committed to take to improve compliance, implement additional recommendations described in this second report, consider additional measures to enhance privacy protections for NSL-derived information, and remain vigilant in holding FBI personnel accountable for properly preparing and approving NSLs and for handling responsive records appropriately.

As a result, in this report, we make 17 additional recommendations to the FBI to further improve its oversight and use of national security letters. We recommend that the FBI:

1. Create blank mandatory fields in the database supporting the NSL data system for entering the U.S. person/non-U.S. person status of the target of NSLs and for entering the number of NSL requests in order to prevent inaccuracies that may otherwise result from the current default settings.
2. Implement measures to verify the accuracy of data entry into the new NSL data system by including periodic reviews of a sample of NSLs in the database to ensure that the training provided on data entry to the support staff of the FBI OGC National Security Law Branch (NSLB), other Headquarters divisions, and field personnel is successfully applied in practice and has reduced or eliminated data entry errors.

These periodic reviews should also draw upon resources available from the FBI Inspection Division and the FBI's new Office of Integrity and Compliance (OIC).

3. Implement measures to verify that data requested in NSLs is checked against serialized source documents to verify that the data extracted from the source document and used in the NSL (such as the telephone number or e-mail address) is accurately recorded on the NSL and the approval EC.
4. Regularly monitor the preparation of NSL-related documents and the handling of NSL-derived information with periodic reviews and inspections. This includes requiring that during quarterly file reviews, squad supervisors conduct, at a minimum, spot checks of NSL-related documents in investigative files to ensure adherence to NSL authorities, Attorney General Guidelines, and internal FBI policies governing use of NSL authorities.
5. Assign NSLB attorneys to participate in pertinent meetings of operational and operational support units in the Counterterrorism and Counterintelligence Divisions.
6. Consider increasing the staffing level of the OIC so that it can develop the sufficient skills, knowledge, and independence to lead or directly carry out critical elements of the OIC's work.
7. Reinforce the distinction between the FBI's two NSL authorities pursuant to the *Fair Credit Reporting Act* throughout all levels of the FBI's National Security Branch at FBI Headquarters, in new agent training, in advanced training provided to agents and supervisors assigned to counterterrorism and counterintelligence programs, and in training provided to Assistant Special Agents in Charge and Special Agents in Charge.
8. Add procedures to include reviews of FCRA NSLs in counterintelligence investigations in the FBI Inspection Division's periodic reviews and in the NSD's national security reviews.
9. Reiterate in its continuing discussions with major credit reporting agencies that the agencies should not provide consumer full credit reports in response to FCRAu NSLs and should ensure that they provide only requested information in response to all FCRA NSLs.
10. Ensure that guidance and training continue to identify the circumstances under which FCRA. NSL matters must be reported to the FBI OGC as possible intelligence violations.
11. Issue additional guidance addressing the filing and retention of NSL-derived information that will improve the ability to locate NSL-derived information. The guidance should require that all

NSL-derived information be appropriately documented, stored, easily identified, and readily available for internal and external review.

12. Include in its routine case file reviews and the NSD's national security reviews an analysis of the FBI's compliance with requirements governing the filing and retention of NSL-derived information.
13. Periodically reissue guidance and training materials reminding case agents and supervisors assigned to national security investigations that they must carefully examine the circumstances surrounding the issuance of each NSL to determine whether there is adequate justification for imposing non-disclosure and confidentiality requirements on the NSL recipient.
14. Periodically reinforce in training and guidance provided to case agents and supervisors assigned to national security investigations the FBI OGC directive to timely report to the FBI OGC possible intelligence violations arising from the use of NSL authorities.
15. Require case agents and supervisors assigned to national security investigations to specify in any reports to the FBI OGC the precise remedial measures employed to handle any unauthorized information they obtain in response to NSLs and to address whether the inappropriately provided information was used or uploaded into FBI databases.
16. Periodically provide case agents and supervisors assigned to national security investigations with examples of common errors in the use of NSLs, such as the examples used in the November 30, 2006, FBI OGC guidance memorandum regarding possible NSL-related intelligence violations.

We also recommend that the Department:

17. Direct that the NSL Working Group, with the FBI's and the NSD's participation, re-examine measures for (a) addressing the privacy interests associated with NSL-derived information, including the benefits and feasibility of labeling or tagging NSL-derived information, and (b) minimizing the retention and dissemination of such information.

Finally, our forthcoming report will describe in detail the FBI's use of exigent letters, the issuance of 11 improper "blanket" NSLs and other improper NSLs, and other improper requests for telephone records, and will include additional recommendations. Therefore, the FBI should consider the findings and recommendations in our forthcoming NSL report together with the recommendations in this report in addressing measures to continue to improve the FBI's compliance with NSL authorities.

Unclassified Appendix

The Attorney General
Washington, D.C.

February 29, 2008

The Honorable Glenn A. FineInspector General
United States Department of Justice
950 Pennsylvania Avenue, NW
Washington, DC 20530

Dear Mr. Fine:

Thank you for your report entitled "A Review of the FBI's Use of National Security Letters: Corrective Actions and Use in 2006."

When you issued your report last year identifying concerns about the Federal Bureau of Investigation's use of national security letters during the years 2003-2005, Attorney General Gonzales and Director Mueller directed that significant resources be dedicated to improving oversight of this important national security tool. I appreciate your positive assessment of the Department's and the Bureau's efforts in this area, including your conclusion that the Department has made "significant progress" in implementing the recommendations outlined in your report. In particular, I am pleased that your report highlights the Bureau's important work in establishing an Office of Integrity and Compliance and the significant efforts of the National Security Division to create an Oversight Section within the Office of Intelligence, as well as their work to jointly complete 15 national security reviews in FBI field offices and headquarters components in 2007. Your report also correctly emphasizes the need for sustained focus on the Bureau's use of national security letters, and the institutional changes the Department has put in place will help ensure that we continue to devote sufficient resources to the oversight of our national security investigations.

I appreciate your continued recognition that national security letters are an important investigative tool, and that they have contributed to many counterterrorism and counterintelligence investigations. As the substantial efforts of the past year should make clear, the Department is committed to using this critical tool responsibly and in a manner consistent with the law.

Again, my thanks to you and to your staff for your efforts in preparing this report.

Sincerely
[Signature]
Michael B. Mukasey

Director of National Intelligence
Washington, DC 20511

MAR 07 2008

The Honorable Glenn A. Fine
Inspector General
United States Department of Justice
950 Pennsylvania Avenue, N.W.
Washington, D.C 20530

Dear Mr. Fine:

(U) Thank you for providing us a copy of your draft report dated February 14, 2008 titled, "A Review of the Federal Bureau of Investigation's Use of National Security Letters: Assessment of Corrective Actions and Examination of NSL Usage in 2006." We have reviewed your report and appreciate the opportunity to provide comment.

(U) As your report makes clear, National Security Letters are an invaluable tool the Federal Bureau of Investigation (FBI) uses to obtain information in national security investigations. We thank you for the extensive review your office has conducted, and look forward to receiving the forthcoming additional recommendations. We believe your report demonstrates the many improvements the FBI and Department of Justice have made to ensure compliance with National Security Letter laws, and applicable guidelines and procedures. While it is critical that our intelligence professionals have the authorities they need to detect and prevent threats to the national security, it is equally imperative that these authorities be executed with due care to the protection of civil liberties and with effective compliance and oversight mechanisms in place.

Sincerely,

[Signature]

J.M. McConnell

U.S. Department of Justice
National Security Division
Washington, D.C. 20530

February 29, 2008

The Honorable Glenn A. FineInspector General
United States Department of Justice
950 Pennsylvania Avenue, NW
Washington, DC 20530

Dear Mr. Fine:

Thank you for the opportunity to provide the views of the National Security Division on your report entitled "A Review of the FBI's Use of National Security Letters: Corrective Actions and Use in 2006."

As you know, following the issuance of your initial report identifying concerns about the Federal Bureau of Investigation's (FBI) use of national security letters (NSLs) in 2003–2005, Attorney General Gonzales and Director Mueller directed the implementation of a series of corrective actions, including implementation of all of the recommendations in your initial report. In addition, the Attorney General directed the National Security Division (NSD) and the Department's Privacy and Civil Liberties Office to work with the FBI to implement these corrective actions. These efforts were aimed at ensuring that the FBI uses NSLs in an appropriate manner in compliance with all applicable laws and policy requirements.

This direction and the actions taken pursuant to it, as well as the continuing efforts of the Department, demonstrate the commitment of senior Department leadership to addressing the serious issues identified in your earlier report. As your report notes, the Department has made significant progress and continues to devote significant energy, time, and resources to this effort.

For example, as your report states, the FBI has issued comprehensive guidance concerning the proper use of NSLs and has conducted training in field offices across the country. The FBI has also taken steps to improve the accuracy of its reporting of NSL statistics to Congress by developing a new NSL tracking database that is now available across the FBI. Further, with respect to the use of so-called "exigent letters," the FBI issued a Bureau-wide directive prohibiting the use of the type of letters described in your reports. In addition, in March 2007, the FBI Director ordered a one-time review of ten percent of all national security cases in the 56 FBI field offices and headquarters. This review was a substantial undertaking, requiring the deployment of over 100 inspectors and the review of thousands of investigative files.

Finally, as you discuss in your report, the Attorney General requested the Department of Justice's Chief Privacy and Civil Liberties Officer and the Office of the DNI to convene a working group to examine how NSL-derived information is used and retained by the FBI. The working group has made important progress in this area aimed at the protection of privacy and civil liberties, and the Attorney General has directed the group to continue its efforts. As part of this process, the working group will take into account the recommendations made in your new report.

I also want to highlight the progress of the Department's significant new national security oversight and compliance effort that was publicly announced in July 2007. This effort encompasses substantial changes within the Department of Justice to improve the Department's controls over its national security activities. The effort includes the implementation of a dedicated Oversight Section within NSD and the establishment of an Office of Integrity and Compliance within the FBI. The oversight and compliance programs run by these offices are at the forefront of the Department's ongoing effort to ensure that national security investigations are conducted in a manner consistent with our laws, regulations, and policies, including those designed to protect the privacy and civil liberties of our citizens.

For the first time, DOJ attorneys have been given the clear mandate to examine all aspects of the FBI's national security program for compliance with law, regulations, and policies. As part of this effort, the NSD is conducting regular National Security Investigation reviews at FBI field offices and headquarters units, working with the helpful input of the FBI. These reviews, which were developed in consultation with representatives of the Office of the Inspector General, represent a substantial new level and type of oversight of national security investigations by career Justice Department lawyers with years of intelligence experience. The reviews are not limited to areas where shortcomings have already been identified; instead, they are intended to enhance compliance across the national security investigative spectrum. NSD completed 15 such reviews in 2007 and plans to conduct a similar number on an annual basis. In addition, the Attorney General directed NSD to review all violations that the FBI refers to the Intelligence Oversight Board (IOB) in order to identify recurring problems and to assess the FBI's response to such violations. NSD is reporting regularly to the Attorney General on its review in this area.

The innovations and corrective actions described above reflect a new level of oversight and an appreciation of the need for strong measures to improve compliance in our national security investigations. We appreciate the very fine work that went into this NSL review, and we look forward to working with you as we implement all of the recommendations in your report. As your reports have noted, NSLs are an indispensible investigative tool and have contributed significantly to many counterterrorism and counterintelligence investigations. We are committed to using this critical tool in an appropriate manner that protects the privacy and civil liberties of all Americans.

Sincerely,
[Signature]
Kenneth L. Wainstein
Assistant Attorney General

U.S. Department of Justice
Federal Bureau of Investigation
Office of the Director
Washington, D.C. 20535

February 28, 2008

Honorable Glenn A. Fine
Inspector General
United States Department of Justice
Suite 4706
950 Pennsylvania Avenue, N.W.
Washington, DC 20530

Re: U.S. Department of Justice, Office of Inspector General "A Review of the Federal Bureau of Investigation's Use of National Security Letters: Corrective Actions and Use in 2006"

Dear Mr. Fine:

The FBI appreciates this opportunity to respond to the findings and recommendations made in the Office of the Inspector General's ("OIG's") review of corrective actions taken by the FBI in response to an OIG report published last year regarding the FBI's usage of National Security Letters ("NSLs")("NSL 1") and your review of the FBI's usage of NSLs in 2006 ("NSL 2" or "Report") as required by the USA PATRIOT Improvement and Reauthorization Act of 2005 ("Patriot Reauthorization Act"). This letter conveys our response, and I request that it be appended to the Report.

The Report begins with the first external review that has been conducted of the extensive actions taken by the FBI following the publication of NSL 1 in March 2007 and notes that FBI executive leadership has made correcting the problems identified in NSL 1 a "top priority" (Report at 15).

We appreciate the Report's finding that by devoting "significant time, energy and resources," we have made "significant progress" in correcting the deficiencies discussed in NSL 1 *(Id.* at 6). As detailed in the Report, these actions include policy changes, increased mandatory training and the creation of a new NSL automated workflow system that will help ensure compliance with laws, guidelines and policies and will improve the accuracy of our Congressional reporting regarding NSL usage. In addition to the actions recommended in NSL 1, we have conducted extensive internal reviews to ascertain fully the scope and nature of our compliance problems and to guide corrective action. Moreover, we have – in what may be unique within a federal government agency ~ created a new Office of Integrity and Compliance ("OIC"), which is modeled after private sector compliance programs. Further, in conjunction with the Department of Justice ("DOJ")'s National Security Division ("NSD"), we have instituted a program of systematic reviews of FBI national security investigations as a way both to ensure compliance with statutory schemes like those that govern NSLs and to serve as a warning system if there are other areas in which our compliance efforts can be strengthened. Although we have made substantial progress, we concur that we must — and will — sustain our commitment to ensuring compliance with the laws and policies governing usage of NSLs.

In addition to providing a review of corrective actions taken in response to NSL 1, the Report also responds to the Congressional mandate that the OIG examine the use of NSLs in 2006. We appreciate the Report recognizing "that the FBI's use of NSLs in 2006 [discussed in the Report] occurred before" NSL 1 and before extensive FBI corrective actions were implemented (Report at 8). Therefore, it is "not surprising[]" that NSL 2 contains findings similar to NSL 1 *(Id.).* NSLs remain an indispensable investigative tool that significantly advance the progress of national security investigations, as the Report details in Chapter 5, and, in almost all cases, potential errors or policy violations involving NSLs relate to information that the FBI was lawfully entitled to obtain (Report at 137).

The Report also reviewed compliance with the non-disclosure and confidentiality provisions of the Patriot Reauthorization Act and found that, thanks to prompt and recurring guidance, the "vast majority" of sampled NSLs (97 percent) complied with the Act in imposing non-disclosure and confidentiality obligations on NSL recipients (Report at 10).

As noted above, the FBI took very substantial corrective actions in the wake of NSL 1, including policy changes, increased mandatory training and the deployment of an automated workflow system for NSLs that is designed to facilitate compliance with statutes, guidelines and policies and to improve the accuracy of the FBI's Congressional reporting. Our most significant actions are discussed below:

- Mandated that all information received in response to an NSL be reviewed prior to uploading the information into FBI databases. Because all reviews of the FBI's NSL usage (*i.e.*, those conducted by FBI and OIG) have found frequent examples of overproduction of materials by NSL recipients, this policy change alone should result in substantially fewer potential intelligence oversight board violations connected to the use of NSLs.
- Prohibited the issuance of exigent letters, and issued clear policy, with audit trails, for acquiring communications records in truly exigent circumstances.
- Prohibited the issuance of NSLs solely from control files.
- Mandated legal review of all NSLs either by attorneys in the Office of General Counsel (OGC) or by Chief Division Counsel and clearly delineated the scope of that review to include the predication for the NSL and the predication for the underlying investigation.
- Established an Office of Integrity and Compliance to facilitate the efforts of executive management to identify and mitigate significant areas of risk. The OIC has been functioning for approximately one year and has demonstrated its value in focusing the attention of executive management on aspects of the FBI's operations and business processes that pose compliance risks.
- In conjunction with DOJ, implemented a program for regular reviews of national security investigations in FBI field offices and headquarters units, including but not limited to compliance with NSL statutes, policies and procedures. Those reviews, like the activities of the OIC, have proved valuable in uncovering policies and procedures that pose compliance challenges.

Following NSL 1, all NSL policies and required procedures were combined into a single document that provides clear and comprehensive guidance to FBI employees who issue and approve NSLs during national security investigations. Prior to its issuance, a draft of the new "one-stop" policy document was briefed to Congressional staff and privacy groups and many of their comments were incorporated into the final version of the policy. We also instituted mandatory in-person NSL training and have developed further training that is available on the FBI's Virtual Academy.

We also developed and fully deployed enhanced information technology tools to automate the NSL workflow, including accumulating the data necessary for Congressional reporting. The system (called the NSL Subsystem) is programmed with drop down menus and other user-friendly features to make the NSL process less time intensive for agents and analysts while simultaneously increasing the accuracy of the process and decreasing the sort of human errors noted by the OIG *(e.g.*, failing to cite the appropriate statute in the Electronic Communication ("EC") requesting an NSL; inconsistency between the data requested in the EC and that requested in the NSL). No NSL can now issue unless vital information is included such as: the subject of the NSL, the predication for the NSL, the type of NSL, the recipient, and the specific targets of the NSL. In other words, the automated system captures all the information required for Congressional reporting before generating the NSL. In addition to improving the accuracy of Congressional reporting, the system ensures that each NSL receives the required legal review and each level of required supervisory review. Providing one database for automated generation of NSLs also reduces the time consuming manual process for generating the required documentation and ensures consistency between the documents reviewed and the NSL actually issued. After a pilot project, the NSL Subsystem became operational in all FBI field offices and Headquarters on January 1, 2008.

Finally, as suggested by the OIG in NSL 1, we issued comprehensive guidance to assist our employees in effectuating the requirement that the FBI use, if possible, the "least intrusive alternative" when conducting investigations. We believe this guidance will be valuable in pointing employees to the sorts of considerations they should balance when deciding between investigative alternatives that have differing levels of intrusiveness.

FBI's Response to Specific Recommendations

Overview: the FBI agrees with all of the OIG's recommendations in the Report and will implement each recommendation as discussed below.

Recommendation #1: Create blank mandatory fields in the software supporting the NSL data system for entering the U.S. person/non-U.S. person status of the target of NSLs and for entering the number of NSL requests in order to prevent inaccuracies that may otherwise result from the current default settings.

The FBI agrees with this recommendation: To improve the accuracy of NSL Congressional reporting, the FBI will modify the NSL Subsystem to require the user to select one of the U.S. person status options before an NSL may be approved.

Recommendation #2: Implement measures to verify the accuracy of data entry into the new NSL data system by including periodic reviews of a sample of NSLs in the database to ensure that the training provided on data entry to the support staff of the FBI OGC National Security Law Branch, other Headquarters divisions, and field personnel is successfully applied in practice and has reduced or eliminated data entry errors. These periodic reviews should also draw upon resources available from the FBI Inspection Division and the FBI's new Office of Integrity and Compliance (OIC).

The FBI agrees with this recommendation: The FBI agrees that there should be periodic spot checks to ensure that information is being properly reported and to make system improvements where issues are identified. The FBI will utilize the resources of the Inspection Division to conduct such periodic reviews and the resources of OIC to assist in managing the policy and training changes indicated by the results of such reviews. In addition, it is important to note that the data from which Congressional reports will be prepared will come solely from data contained within the NSL Subsystem. Thus, NSL data will no longer be culled from ECs and transferred manually to a standalone database (a process that generated many data entry errors) but instead will be recorded automatically upon the creation of the NSL. As a result, the data entry role of the support staff of the National Security Law Branch is greatly diminished, and the process under the new system is designed to minimize the likelihood of data entry errors.

Recommendation #3: Implement measures to verify that data requested in NSLs is checked against serialized source documents to verify that the data extracted from the source document and used in the NSL (such as the telephone number or e-mail address) is accurately recorded on the NSL and the approval EC.

The FBI agrees with this recommendation: Data such as a telephone numbers or email addresses that are the basis for NSLs should be verified against authoritative documents. Such an authoritative document will frequently, although not always, be a serialized document. The FBI will continue to train and advise its employees regarding their duty to accurately prepare NSLs and to verify critical data against authoritative documents to avoid clerical errors.

Recommendation #4: Regularly monitor the preparation of NSL-related documents and the handling of NSL-derived information with periodic reviews and inspections. This includes requiring that during quarterly file reviews, squad supervisors should conduct, at a minimum, spot checks of NSL related documents in investigative files to ensure adherence to NSL authorities, Attorney General Guidelines, and internal policies governing use of NSL authorities.

The FBI agrees with this recommendation: The FBI requires an examination of NSL-related documents and return information during quarterly file reviews. Moreover, the National Security Reviews conducted by DOJ-NSD and FBI-Office of General Counsel ("OGC") will help ensure adherence to laws, policies and procedures with respect to all investigative tools in the national security area.

Recommendation #5: Assign NSLB attorneys to participate in pertinent meetings of operational and operational support units in the Counterterrorism and Counterintelligence Divisions.

The FBI agrees with this recommendation: NSLB will continue the well-established practice of requiring attorneys to attend meetings of operational and operational support units.

Recommendation #6: Consider increasing the staffing level of OIC so that it can develop the sufficient skills, knowledge, and independence to lead or directly carry out critical elements of the OIC's work.

The FBI agrees with this recommendation: The mission of the OIC is to develop, implement, and oversee a program that ensures that there are processes and procedures in place that facilitate FBI compliance with both the letter and the spirit of all applicable laws, regulations, rules and policies. The OIC will cultivate an environment committed to these principles, serve as a focal point for the compliance program, and assist FBI management at all levels in maintaining a culture where ethics and compliance are emphasized as paramount considerations in decisions throughout the FBI.

OIC staff engages the leadership of the FBI in integrating the Integrity and Compliance Program into all FBI operations, programs, and activities and promoting a culture of ethical compliance throughout the FBI. The Office is responsible for establishing policy and methodology for compliance standards, risk assessment, workflow, monitoring and auditing, as well as establishing baseline standards for measuring the effectiveness of risk mitigation measures. OIC's responsibilities also include working with the Inspection Division to develop appropriate inspection protocols and procedures, tasking the Inspection Division with conducting targeted audits as needed, and analyzing the results and recommending such actions as may be necessary or appropriate to mitigate identified risks. OIC is also tasked with developing effective and open channels for receiving reports, including anonymous reports, of potential compliance risks; receiving, reviewing and analyzing data from a variety of sources to identify compliance trends, problems, and best practices; delivering training on the Integrity and Compliance Program; and supporting and facilitating the work of the Integrity and Compliance Council and the Integrity and Compliance Executive Management Committees. OIC also coordinates and manages the FBI Standards of Conduct and Ethics Program to include effecting liaison with the Office of Government Ethics and the DOJ Ethics Office, the review of financial disclosure reports, the initiation and maintenance of ethics education and training programs, and the provision of ethics advice and counsel to individual officers and employees.

The OIC is making steady progress in each of these areas of responsibility, and the office workload is increasing as the program matures. The OIC expects two additional personnel to report in the near future—one attorney and one Special Agent—which will bring the office up to its currently-authorized personnel complement. The FBI will continue to evaluate OIC's personnel needs as the program evolves.

Recommendation #7: Reinforce the distinction between the FBI's two NSL authorities pursuant to the Fair Credit Reporting Act (FCRA) throughout all levels of the FBI's National Security Branch at FBI Headquarters, in new agent training, in advanced training provided to agents and supervisors assigned to counterterrorism and counterintelligence programs, and in training provided to Assistant Special Agents in Charge and Special Agents in Charge.

The FBI agrees with this recommendation: The FBI will continue to train employees involved in the issuance of NSLs on the distinction between FRCAv and FCRAu NSLs. In addition, the new NSL subsystem will not allow a 1681 υ NSL to be issued from a counterintelligence investigation further ensuring that agents do not use FCRA NSLs contrary to the authorizing statute.

Recommendation #8: Add procedures to include reviews of FCRA NSLs in counterintelligence investigations to the FBI Inspection Division's periodic reviews and the National Security Division's national security reviews.

The FBI agrees with this recommendation: The Inspection Division is currently undergoing a redesign of its inspection process and will incorporate a review of NSLs, to include FCRA NSLs, in the new inspection protocol for NSB programs.

Recommendation #9: Clarify in its continuing discussions with major credit agencies that the credit agencies should not provide consumer full credit reports in response to FCRAu NSLs and should ensure that they provide only requested information in response to all FCRA NSLs.

The FBI agrees with this recommendation: The FBI continues to have conversations with credit bureaus regarding responses to FCRA NSLs. The credit bureaus have been asked to carefully review NSL requests and to provide only limited credit information in response to a FCRA 1681u NSL request. The appropriate Chief Division Counsels will continue to communicate with the credit bureaus regarding overproduction in response to NSLs. It is important to note that our ability to work collegially with the credit bureaus on an attorney-to-attorney basis has, in recent years, resulted in fewer overproductions by the credit bureaus.

Recommendation #10: Ensure that guidance and training continue to identify the circumstances under which FCRA NSL matters must be reported to the FBI OGC as possible intelligence violations.

The FBI agrees with this recommendation: Current FBI training and policies identify matters that must be reported to OGC as potential Intelligence Oversight Board (IOB) matters. Following receipt of a report identifying a potential IOB matter, OGC reviews the conduct described in the report to determine whether the IOB must be notified of the reported error. The FBI will continue to provide such training and will update guidance relating to IOB matters as appropriate.

Recommendation #11: Issue additional guidance addressing the filing and retention of NSL-derived information that will improve the ability to locate NSL-derived information. The guidance should require all NSL-derived information be appropriately documented, stored, easily identified, and readily available for internal and external audit.

The FBI agrees with this recommendation: FBI will coordinate any guidance on filing and retention of NSL information with the NSL working group as it continues to consider whether NSL-derived data should be tagged or labeled or otherwise subject to new rules to limit retention or dissemination of NSL-derived data. In addition, the FBI now requires all NSLs, NSL approving ECs, and records produced in response to an NSL to be maintained in a "National Security Letter" subfile of the investigative file.

Recommendation #12: Include in its 90-day case file reviews and the National Security Division's national security reviews an analysis of the FBI's compliance with requirements governing the filing and retention of NSL-derived information.

The FBI agrees with this recommendation: The FBI now requires supervisors to, *inter alia,* examine compliance with requirements governing filing and retention of NSL-derived information during regular quarterly file reviews. In addition, an analysis of compliance with FBI requirements governing the filing and retention of NSL-derived information will occur in connection with the National Security Reviews.

Recommendation #13: Periodically reissue guidance and training materials reminding case agents and supervisors assigned to national security investigations that they must carefully examine the circumstances surrounding the issuance of each NSL to determine whether there is adequate justification for imposing non-disclosure and confidentiality requirements on the NSL recipient.

The FBI agrees with this recommendation: The FBI will continue to issue guidance and training materials as appropriate in order to remind employees involved in the issuance of NSLs that the non-disclosure provision of an NSL is not automatic and that a nondisclosure determination must be made for *each* NSL. In addition, the NSL Subsystem has a banner reminding the user that the determination to impose a non-disclosure obligation must be made on a case-by-case basis for each NSL.

Recommendation #14: Periodically reinforce training and guidance provided to case agents and supervisors assigned to national security investigations the FBI OGC directive to timely report to the FBI OGC possible intelligence violations arising from the use of NSL authorities.

The FBI agrees with this recommendation: Current FBI training and policies identify matters that must be reported to OGC as potential IOB matters. Following receipt of a report identifying a potential IOB matter, OGC reviews the conduct described in the report to determine whether the reported error requires notification to the IOB. The FBI will continue to provide training and update guidance relating to IOB matters as appropriate.

Recommendation #15: Require case agents and supervisors assigned to national security investigations to specify in any reports to FBI OGC the precise remedial measures employed to handle any unauthorized information they obtain in response to NSLs and to address whether the inappropriately provided information was used or uploaded into FBI databases.

The FBI agrees with this recommendation: The FBI currently requires remedial measures to be included in the electronic communication that reports to FBI OGC possible intelligence violations. In future training and guidance, the FBI will continue to emphasize the requirement that such remedial measures be included with the reporting EC.

Recommendation #16: Periodically provide case agents and supervisors assigned to national security investigations with examples of common errors in the use of NSLs, such as the examples used in the November 30, 2006, FBI OGC guidance memorandum regarding possible NSL-related intelligence violations.

The FBI agrees with this recommendation: The FBI will continue the practice of incorporating anecdotal information regarding common errors in the use of NSLs in its NSL and intelligence oversight board training. The FBI will update examples of common errors in training as new issues arise. In addition, the FBI is hopeful that the NSL Subsystem will greatly diminish the number of errors in the use and issuance of NSLs, many of which came from inadvertent errors, routing mistakes and typographical errors.

Recommendation #17: Direct the NSL Working Group, with the FBI's and the NSD's participation, to re-examine measures for (a) addressing the privacy interests associated with NSL-derived information, including the benefits and feasibility of labeling or tagging NSL-derived information, and (b) minimizing the retention and dissemination of such information.

The Department of Justice and FBI agree with this recommendation: The Attorney General has directed the working group to continue its work.

Sincerely yours,
[Signature]
Robert S. Mueller, III
Director

U.S. Department of Justice
Office of the Deputy Attorney General
Chief Privacy and Civil Liberties Officer
Washington, D.C. 20530

March 7, 2008

The Honorable Glenn A. Fine
Inspector General
United States Department of Justice
950 Pennsylvania Avenue, NW
Washington, DC 20530

Dear Mr. Fine:

Thank you for the opportunity to comment on behalf of the National Security Letter (NSL) Working Group, on your report entitled "A Review of the FBI's Use of National Security Letters: Corrective Actions and Use in 2006." We welcome the recommendation in your report and are pleased that you consider the NSL Working Group an appropriate vehicle to continue to examine and develop further safeguards for privacy and civil liberties.

The NSL Working Group worked with dedication and commitment over the past year to strengthen safeguards for individuals' privacy and civil liberties in connection with the FBI's use of NSLs. We believe that your recommendation, combined with the work that the group has already done and will do going forward, will help achieve the goal we all share—to make certain that the FBI is carrying out its vital national security mission under the rule of law and in a manner that protects the privacy and civil liberties of Americans.

As you note in your report, the NSL Working Group analyzed additional protective measures including new minimization procedures for the FBI. To do this, the group examined an array of issues concerning the use, storage, and dissemination of NSL-derived information to include consideration of tagging and labeling, potential retention periods for each category of NSL-derived data, and the privacy concerns associated with the type of information collected. Additionally, the group met with FBI operational, policy, and technology personnel to better understand the operational and technical feasibility of different options. The group has also received feedback from outside privacy advocates. As we move ahead and take on your recommendation, we look forward to sharing with your office greater detail about the NSL Working Group's activities and progress.

Again, we appreciate your recommendation and commit that the NSL Working Group will continue to address these important issues and keep your office informed. We look forward to continuing this important effort to ensure that the FBI's policies and procedures regarding the use of NSLs safeguard privacy and civil liberties in a manner that is consistent with the FBI's critical mission to protect the Nation from threats to our national security.

Sincerely,
[Signature]
Kenneth P. Mortensen
Acting Chief Privacy and Civil Liberties Officer

DOCUMENT NO. 8

OIG REPORT ON NATIONAL SECURITY LETTERS

Department of Justice
Statement of Department of Justice

March 13, 2008

"We are pleased with the Office of Inspector General's (OIG) positive assessment of the many actions taken by the Justice Department and FBI to improve oversight of the use of National Security Letters (NSLs) since the first OIG review of NSLs was issued in March 2007.

"This year's OIG report concluded that the Justice Department and FBI have made 'significant progress' in implementing the recommendations outlined in last year's OIG report and have implemented measures that extend beyond those recommendations. Among other actions, the report highlights the creation of an Office of Integrity and Compliance at the FBI; the creation of a dedicated Oversight Section in the Office of Intelligence at the Justice Department's National Security Division; as well as joint efforts by the Justice Department and FBI to launch and complete 15 national security reviews in FBI field offices and headquarters components in 2007.

"These innovations and corrective actions reflect a new level of oversight and an appreciation of the need for strong measures to improve compliance in our national security investigations. Because this year's OIG report examined the use of NSLs in 2006—before deficiencies in the use of NSLs were first identified by the OIG and before the Justice Department and FBI began to take corrective actions—it should come as no surprise that this year's report found problems similar to those identified in the first OIG report, which covered the period 2003 through 2005. The Inspector General correctly emphasizes the need for sustained oversight of the FBI's use of NSLs and concludes that the senior leadership of the Justice Department and the FBI are committed to addressing these issues and continue to devote significant energy, time, and resources to this effort.

"We appreciate the OIG's continued recognition that NSLs are an indispensable investigative tool and have contributed significantly to many counterterrorism and counter-intelligence investigations. The Justice Department is committed to using this critical tool in an appropriate manner that protects the privacy and civil liberties of all Americans. We appreciate the diligent work of the OIG in completing this review."

08-200

C. THE PROTECT AMERICA ACT

THE PROTECT AMERICA ACT

Commentary

The *Protect America Act of 2007* (P.L. 110-55) became law on August 5, 2007. The statute makes a number of additions and modifications to the Foreign Intelligence Surveillance Act of 1978 (FISA, 50 U.S.C. §§ 1801 *et seq*, as amended). The *Protect America Act* (PAA) featured a 180-day sunset provision. Its substantive provisions include amending the FISA's definition of "electronic surveillance" by excluding from the definition surveillance directed at a person reasonably believed to be located outside the United States.

Significantly, the Act provided the Director of National Intelligence (DNI) and the Attorney General (AG) the authority to acquire foreign intelligence information concerning persons outside the United States, if the DNI and AG determine that:

(1) there are reasonable procedures in place for determining that such acquisition concerns persons outside the United States, and such procedures will be subject to review by the Foreign Intelligence Surveillance Court (FISC);

(2) the acquisition does not constitute electronic surveillance;

(3) the acquisition involves obtaining foreign intelligence information from or with the assistance of a communication service provider or other person who has access to communications;

(4) a significant purpose of the acquisition is to obtain foreign intelligence information; and

(5) the minimization procedures (procedures to ensure the smallest level of privacy intrusion while obtaining such information) to be used meet the definition of minimization procedures under FISA.

The statute requires such determinations to be certified and submitted to the FISC. If the criteria are met, the DNI and AG may authorize the acquisition of the foreign intelligence information for periods up to a year. The statute also requires the AG to report to:

(1) the FISC the procedures by which the government determines that such acquisitions do not constitute electronic surveillance; and

(2) the congressional intelligence and judiciary committees semiannually, concerning acquisitions made during the previous six-month period.

Although, by its language, the PAA terminates after 180 days, it makes authorizations for the acquisition of information and directives issued pursuant to such authorizations, effective until their expiration, which is normally one year.

On February 13, 2008, House Republicans blocked a proposed 21-day extension of the PAA, which was scheduled to sunset on February 17, 2008, following a previous extension of fifteen days. As noted above, notwithstanding the sunset provision, since the Act provides that "[a]uthorizations for the acquisition of foreign intelligence information pursuant to the amendments made by this Act, and directives issued pursuant to such authorizations, shall remain in effect until their expiration," the sunset clause has little immediate practical effect. Intelligence officials will still be able to acquire foreign intelligence information for up to a year. As House Speaker Pelosi put it, "Every order entered under the law can remain in effect for 12 months from the date it was issued. Furthermore, the underlying Foreign Intelligence Surveillance Act, . . . remains intact and available to our intelligence agencies."

To understand the political controversy underpinning passage of the Act, one must go back to December 2005, when it was reportedly discovered that the Bush administration had been conducting warrantless domestic wiretapping in cooperation with major telecommunications companies since 2002, and perhaps earlier. Some observers saw that practice not only as a violation of the U.S. Constitution's Fourth Amendment's protections against unreasonable search but also as a criminal violation of the FISA. While the Executive Branch made defensive arguments based on the U.S. Constitution's Article II provisions and the authorization for the use of force it had received from Congress, it readied a legislative proposal that made legal much of what it was alleged to have done. The administration submitted its proposal to Congress on July 28, 2007, and Congress passed the measure before its August recess.

The administration sought to conduct surveillance on individuals (targets) reasonably expected to be living in foreign countries, including individuals conversing (at the time of the surveillance) with U.S. residents, hoping that those conversations would provide foreign intelligence helpful to the war effort. Opponents of the measure argued that such discretion should not be vested in the agency of government responsible for enforcing the law. Opponents observed that obtaining a warrant from the FISC was no longer a time-consuming process and could be accomplished within as little as 24 hours. Still, the administration considered even that length of delay to not be sufficiently responsive.

After providing a copy of the PAA itself, this section presents a Congressional Research Service report on the Act. The report describes the provisions of the PAA, discusses its possible impact on and parallels to existing law, and summarizes the relevant legislative activity. The report correctly notes that in passing the PAA, as well as the FISA itself, Congress was faced with the challenge of striking an appropriate balance between civil liberties and national security. That is easier said than done, because such a balance relies on rather subjective analyses of the nature and severity of the threat posed by global terrorists.

As discussed in preceding paragraphs, assessments of the threat posed by terrorists vary greatly among the American public, their elected legislators, and the Executive Branch. The American public simply does not believe the nation is in a state of war that warrants significant abridgement of civil rights and suspension of constitutional safeguards. The U.S. Congress is reluctant to place too much discretionary power in the hands of the Executive Branch, fearing loss of oversight and potential misuse. The Executive Branch seeks the greatest possible degree of authority and flexibility in waging the Global War Against Terrorists, seeing the conduct of the war not only as principally a presidential responsibility, but moreover a key determinant of a successful presidency. These differing views are likely to continue into the future, unless the upcoming national elections bring about a decisive national reassessment of the nature of the international security environment and the relative threat posed by terrorists.

Thus, an asymmetry in interests between the Legislative and Executive Branches further demonstrates the nebulous nature of the Global War Against Terrorists. The president understandably views himself as principally responsible for protecting the nation from another major terrorist attack and, therefore, suffers from exaggerated conservatism born of a "not on my watch" mentality. Congress, on the other hand, views itself as the closer representative of the American people and realizes fully that many constituents simply do not see the nation as being in a state of war sufficiently dangerous to warrant abridgement or suspension of important constitutional safeguards.

The CRS report notes that to understand the FISA structure, one must understand its definitions. The most important terms are "electronic surveillance" and "foreign intelligence information." In short, the PAA reduces the definitional scope of "electronic surveillance" so that it does not include surveillance directed at a person reasonably believed to be located outside the United States. Although the PAA provides for acquisition of foreign intelligence information, without a court order, by certification of the DNI and the AG, it nonetheless requires review by the FISC of the procedures by which the DNI and the AG determine that such acquisitions do not constitute electronic surveillance, as newly defined.

Additionally, the PAA authorizes the DNI and AG to direct a person with access to the communications involved to furnish aid to the government to facilitate such acquisitions. The PAA also provides a means by which the legality of such a directive may be reviewed via the FISC petition review pool. A decision by a judge of the FISC petition review pool may be appealed to the Foreign Intelligence Surveillance Court of Review, and ultimate review by the U.S. Supreme Court may be sought by petition for writ of certiorari.

Given that the PAA has expired, as will the authorizations that emanated pursuant to its authority, Congress must act to replace it. As it has attempted to do so, it has encountered and engaged in considerable controversy. The discussion of the Restore Act of 2007 that follows will describe the controversy and the state of negotiations between the Congress and the president to resolve it.

DOCUMENT NO. 9

PROTECT AMERICA ACT OF 2007

Public Law No. 110-55

August 5, 2007

110 P.L. 55; 121 Stat. 552; 2007 Enacted S. 1927; 110 Enacted S. 1927

To amend the Foreign Intelligence Surveillance Act of 1978 to provide additional procedures for authorizing certain acquisitions of foreign intelligence information and for other purposes.

Be it enacted by the Senate and House of Representatives of the United States of America in Congress assembled,

SECTION 1. SHORT TITLE.

This Act may be cited as the "Protect America Act of 2007".

SEC. 2. ADDITIONAL PROCEDURE FOR AUTHORIZING CERTAIN ACQUISITIONS OF FOREIGN INTELLIGENCE INFORMATION.

The Foreign Intelligence Surveillance Act of 1978 (50 U.S.C. 1801 et seq.) is amended by inserting after section 105 the following:

"CLARIFICATION OF ELECTRONIC SURVEILLANCE OF PERSONS OUTSIDE THE UNITED STATES

"Sec. 105A. Nothing in the definition of electronic surveillance under section 101(f) shall be construed to encompass surveillance directed at a person reasonably believed to be located outside of the United States.

"ADDITIONAL PROCEDURE FOR AUTHORIZING CERTAIN ACQUISITIONS CONCERNING PERSONS LOCATED OUTSIDE THE UNITED STATES

"Sec. 105B. (a) Notwithstanding any other law, the Director of National Intelligence and the Attorney General, may for periods of up to one year authorize the acquisition of foreign intelligence information concerning persons reasonably believed to be outside the United States if the Director of National Intelligence and the Attorney General determine, based on the information provided to them, that—

"(1) there are reasonable procedures in place for determining that the acquisition of foreign intelligence information under this section concerns persons reasonably believed to be located outside the United States, and such procedures will be subject to review of the Court pursuant to section 105C of this Act;

"(2) the acquisition does not constitute electronic surveillance;

"(3) the acquisition involves obtaining the foreign intelligence information from or with the assistance of a communications service provider, custodian, or other person (including any officer, employee, agent, or other specified person of such service provider, custodian, or other person) who has access to communications, either as they are transmitted or while they are stored, or equipment that is being or may be used to transmit or store such communications;

"(4) a significant purpose of the acquisition is to obtain foreign intelligence information; and

"(5) the minimization procedures to be used with respect to such acquisition activity meet the definition of minimization procedures under section 101(h).

"This determination shall be in the form of a written certification, under oath, supported as appropriate by affidavit of appropriate officials in the national security field occupying positions appointed by the President, by and with the consent of the Senate, or the Head of any Agency of the Intelligence Community, unless immediate action by the Government is required and time does not permit the preparation of a certification. In such a case, the determination of the Director of National Intelligence and the Attorney General shall be reduced to a certification as soon as possible but in no event more than 72 hours after the determination is made.

"(b) A certification under subsection (a) is not required to identify the specific facilities, places, premises, or property at which the acquisition of foreign intelligence information will be directed.

"(c) The Attorney General shall transmit as soon as practicable under seal to the court established under section 103(a) a copy of a certification made under subsection (a). Such certification shall be maintained under security measures established by the Chief Justice of the United States and the Attorney General, in consultation with the Director of National Intelligence, and shall remain sealed unless the certification is necessary to determine the legality of the acquisition under section 105B.

"(d) An acquisition under this section may be conducted only in accordance with the certification of the Director of National Intelligence and the Attorney

General, or their oral instructions if time does not permit the preparation of a certification, and the minimization procedures adopted by the Attorney General. The Director of National Intelligence and the Attorney General shall assess compliance with such procedures and shall report such assessments to the Permanent Select Committee on Intelligence of the House of Representatives and the Select Committee on Intelligence of the Senate under section 108(a).

"(e) With respect to an authorization of an acquisition under section 105B, the Director of National Intelligence and Attorney General may direct a person to—

"(1) immediately provide the Government with all information, facilities, and assistance necessary to accomplish the acquisition in such a manner as will protect the secrecy of the acquisition and produce a minimum of interference with the services that such person is providing to the target; and

"(2) maintain under security procedures approved by the Attorney General and the Director of National Intelligence any records concerning the acquisition or the aid furnished that such person wishes to maintain.

"(f) The Government shall compensate, at the prevailing rate, a person for providing information, facilities, or assistance pursuant to subsection (e).

"(g) In the case of a failure to comply with a directive issued pursuant to subsection (e), the Attorney General may invoke the aid of the court established under section 103(a) to compel compliance with the directive. The court shall issue an order requiring the person to comply with the directive if it finds that the directive was issued in accordance with subsection (e) and is otherwise lawful. Failure to obey an order of the court may be punished by the court as contempt of court. Any process under this section may be served in any judicial district in which the person may be found.

"(h)(1)(A) A person receiving a directive issued pursuant to subsection (e) may challenge the legality of that directive by filing a petition with the pool established under section 103(e)(1).

"(B) The presiding judge designated pursuant to section 103(b) shall assign a petition filed under subparagraph (A) to one of the judges serving in the pool established by section 103(e)(1). Not later than 48 hours after the assignment of such petition, the assigned judge shall conduct an initial review of the directive. If the assigned judge determines that the petition is frivolous, the assigned judge shall immediately deny the petition and affirm the directive or any part of the directive that is the subject of the petition. If the assigned judge determines the petition is not frivolous, the assigned judge shall, within 72 hours, consider the petition in accordance with the procedures established under section 103(e)(2) and provide a written state-ment for the record of the reasons for any determination under this subsection.

"(2) A judge considering a petition to modify or set aside a directive may grant such petition only if the judge finds that such directive does not meet the requirements of this section or is otherwise unlawful. If the judge does not modify or set aside the directive, the judge shall immediately affirm such directive, and order the recipient to comply with such directive.

"(3) Any directive not explicitly modified or set aside under this subsection shall remain in full effect.

"(i) The Government or a person receiving a directive reviewed pursuant to subsection (h) may file a petition with the Court of Review established under section 103(b) for review of the decision issued pursuant to subsection (h) not later than 7 days after the issuance of such decision. Such court of review shall have jurisdiction to consider such petitions and shall provide for the record a written statement of the reasons for its decision. On petition for a writ of certiorari by the Government or any person receiving such directive, the record shall be transmitted under seal to the Supreme Court, which shall have jurisdiction to review such decision.

"(j) Judicial proceedings under this section shall be concluded as expeditiously as possible. The record of proceedings, including petitions filed, orders granted, and statements of reasons for decision, shall be maintained under security measures established by the Chief Justice of the United States, in consultation with the Attorney General and the Director of National Intelligence.

"(k) All petitions under this section shall be filed under seal. In any proceedings under this section, the court shall, upon request of the Government, review ex parte and in camera any Government submission, or portions of a submission, which may include classified information.

"(l) Notwithstanding any other law, no cause of action shall lie in any court against any person for providing any information, facilities, or assistance in accordance with a directive under this section.

"(m) A directive made or an order granted under this section shall be retained for a period of not less than 10 years from the date on which such directive or such order is made."

SEC. 3. SUBMISSION TO COURT REVIEW AND ASSESSMENT OF PROCEDURES.

The Foreign Intelligence Surveillance Act of 1978 (50 U.S.C. 1801 et seq.) is amended by inserting after section 105B the following:

"SUBMISSION TO COURT REVIEW OF PROCEDURES

"Sec. 105C. (a) No later than 120 days after the effective date of this Act, the Attorney General shall submit to the Court established under section 103(a), the procedures by which the Government determines that acquisitions conducted pursuant to section 105B do not constitute electronic surveillance. The procedures submitted pursuant to this section shall be updated and submitted to the Court on an annual basis.

"(b) No later than 180 days after the effective date of this Act, the court established under section 103(a) shall assess the Government's determination under section 105B(a)(1) that those procedures are reasonably designed to ensure that acquisitions conducted pursuant to section 105B do not constitute electronic surveillance. The court's review shall be limited to whether the Government's determination is clearly erroneous.

"(c) If the court concludes that the determination is not clearly erroneous, it shall enter an order approving the continued use of such procedures. If the court concludes that the determination is clearly erroneous, it shall issue an order directing the Government to submit new procedures within 30 days or cease any acquisitions under section 105B that are implicated by the court's order.

"(d) The Government may appeal any order issued under subsection (c) to the court established under section 103(b). If such court determines that the order was properly entered, the court shall immediately provide for the record a written statement of each reason for its decision, and, on petition of the United States for a writ of certiorari, the record shall be transmitted under seal to the Supreme Court of the United States, which shall have jurisdiction to review such decision. Any acquisitions affected by the order issued under subsection (c) of this section may continue during the pendency of any appeal, the period during which a petition for writ of certiorari may be pending, and any review by the Supreme Court of the United States."

SEC. 4. REPORTING TO CONGRESS

On a semi-annual basis the Attorney General shall inform the Select Committee on Intelligence of the Senate, the Permanent Select Committee on Intelligence of the House of Representatives, the Committee on the Judiciary of the Senate, and the Committee on the Judiciary of the House of Representatives, concerning acquisitions under this section during the previous 6-month period. Each report made under this section shall include—

(1) a description of any incidents of non-compliance with a directive issued by the Attorney General and the Director of National Intelligence under section 105B, to include—

(A) incidents of non-compliance by an element of the Intelligence Community with guidelines or procedures established for determining that the acquisition of foreign intelligence authorized by the Attorney General and Director of National Intelligence concerns persons reasonably to be outside the United States; and

(B) incidents of noncompliance by a specified person to whom the Attorney General and Director of National Intelligence issue a directive under this section; and

(2) the number of certifications and directives issued during the reporting period.

SEC. 5. TECHNICAL AMENDMENT AND CONFORMING AMENDMENTS.

(a) In General.—Section 103(e) of the Foreign Intelligence Surveillance Act of 1978 (50 U.S.C. 1803(e)) is amended—

(1) in paragraph (1), by striking "501(f)(1)" and inserting "105B(h) or 501(f)(1)"; and

(2) in paragraph (2), by striking "501(f)(1)" and inserting "105B(h) or 501(f)(1)".

(b) Table of Contents.—The table of contents in the first section of the Foreign Intelligence Surveillance Act of 1978 (50 U.S.C. 1801 et seq.) is amended by inserting after the item relating to section 105 the following:

"105A. Clarification of electronic surveillance of persons outside the United States."105B. Additional procedure for authorizing certain acquisitions concerning persons located outside the United States."105C. Submission to court review of procedures."

SEC. 6. EFFECTIVE DATE; TRANSITION PROCEDURES

(a) Effective Date.—Except as otherwise provided, the amendments made by this Act shall take effect immediately after the date of the enactment of this Act.

(b) Transition Procedures.—Notwithstanding any other provision of this Act, any order in effect on the date of enactment of this Act issued pursuant to the Foreign Intelligence Surveillance Act of 1978 (50 U.S.C. 1801 et seq.) shall remain in effect until the date of expiration of such order, and, at the request of the applicant, the court established under section 103(a) of such Act (50 U.S.C. 1803(a)) shall reauthorize such order as long as the facts and circumstances continue to justify issuance of such order under the provisions of the Foreign Intelligence Surveillance Act of 1978, as in effect on the day before the applicable effective date of this Act. The Government also may file new applications, and the court established under section 103(a) of the Foreign Intelligence Surveillance Act of 1978 (50 U.S.C. 1803(a)) shall enter orders granting such applications pursuant to such Act, as long as the application meets the requirements set forth under the provisions of such Act as in effect on the day before the effective date of this Act. At the request of the applicant, the court established under section 103(a) of the Foreign

Intelligence Surveillance Act of 1978 (50 U.S.C. 1803(a)), shall extinguish any extant authorization to conduct electronic surveillance or physical search entered pursuant to such Act. Any surveillance conducted pursuant to an order entered under this subsection shall be subject to the provisions of the Foreign Intelligence Surveillance Act of 1978 (50 U.S.C. 1801 et seq.), as in effect on the day before the effective date of this Act.

(c) Sunset.—Except as provided in subsection (d), sections 2, 3, 4, and 5 of this Act, and the amendments made by this Act, shall cease to have effect 180 days after the date of the enactment of this Act.

(d) Authorizations in Effect.—Authorizations for the acquisition of foreign intelligence information pursuant to the amendments made by this Act, and directives issued pursuant to such authorizations, shall remain in effect until their expiration. Such acquisitions shall be governed by the applicable provisions of such amendments and shall not be deemed to constitute electronic surveillance as that term is defined in section 101(f) of the Foreign Intelligence Surveillance Act of 1978 (50 U.S.C. 1801(f)).

Approved August 5, 2007.

DOCUMENT NO. 10

PROTECT AMERICA ACT OF 2007: MODIFICATIONS TO THE FOREIGN INTELLIGENCE SURVEILLANCE ACT

CSR Report
RL 34143

August 23, 2007

Elizabeth B. Bazan
Legislative Attorney
American Law Division

Summary

On August 5, 2007, P.L. 110-55, the Protect America Act of 2007, was signed into law by President Bush, after having been passed by the Senate on August 3 and the House of Representatives on August 4. The measure, introduced by Senator McConnell as S. 1927 on August 1, makes a number of additions and modifications to the Foreign Intelligence Surveillance Act of 1978 (FISA), as amended, 50 U.S.C. §§ 1801 *et seq.*, adds additional reporting requirements, and sunsets in 180 days. This report describes the provisions of P.L. 110-55, discusses its possible impact on and parallels to existing law, and summarizes the legislative activity with respect to S. 1927, H.R. 3356, and S. 2011.

The Foreign Intelligence Surveillance Act of 1978 was enacted in response both to the Committee to Study Government Operations with Respect to Intelligence Activities (Church Committee) revelations with regard to past abuses of electronic surveillance for national security purposes and to the somewhat uncertain state of the law on the subject. In creating a statutory framework for the use of electronic surveillance to obtain foreign intelligence information, the Congress sought to strike a balance between national security interests and civil liberties. Critical to an understanding of the FISA structure are its definitions of terms such as "electronic surveillance" and "foreign intelligence information." P.L. 110-55 limits the construction of the term "electronic surveillance" so that it does not cover surveillance directed at a person reasonably believed to be located outside the United States. It also creates a mechanism for acquisition, without a court order under a certification by the Director of National Intelligence (DNI) and the Attorney General, of foreign intelligence information concerning a person reasonably believed to be outside the United States. The Protect America Act provides for review by the Foreign Intelligence Surveillance Court (FISC) of the procedures by which the DNI and the Attorney General determine that such acquisitions do not constitute electronic surveillance. In addition, P.L. 110-55 authorizes the Attorney General and the DNI to direct a person with access to the communications involved to furnish aid to the government to facilitate such acquisitions, and provides a means by which the legality of such a directive may be reviewed by the FISC petition review pool. A decision by a judge of the FISC petition review pool may be appealed to the Foreign Intelligence Surveillance Court of Review, and review by the U.S. Supreme Court may be sought by petition for writ of certiorari.

The report will be updated should subsequent developments require it.

Introduction

In response to concerns raised by the Director of National Intelligence, Admiral Mike McConnell, that the Foreign Intelligence Surveillance Act (FISA), 50 U.S.C. §§ 1801 *et seq.*, required modernization to meet the current intelligence needs of the nation, a number of bills were introduced in the Senate and the House of Representatives. Intense legislative activity with respect to proposed amendments to FISA in both bodies resulted in the enactment of the Protect America Act of 2007, P.L. 110-55 on August 5, 2007. The measure was introduced as S. 1927 by Senator McConnell, for himself and Senator Bond, on August 1, 2007. The bill was considered in the Senate on August 3, in conjunction with S. 2011, entitled The Protect America Act of 2007, introduced by Senator Levin, for himself and Senator Rockefeller. The Senate agreed by unanimous consent to an amendment to S. 1927 offered by Senator McConnell, for himself and Senator Bond, providing that sections 2, 3, 4, and 5 of the bill would sunset 180 days after its enactment.[1] As amended, S. 1927 passed the Senate the same day.[2] S. 2011 did not receive the requisite 60 votes, and was placed on the Senate calendar under general orders.[3]

That evening, the House considered H.R. 3356, the Improving Foreign Intelligence Surveillance to Defend the Nation and the Constitution Act

[1] S. Amdt. No. 2649 to S. 1927.
[2] Record Vote Number 309, 60-28 (August 3, 2007).
[3] Record Vote Number 310, 43-45 (August 3, 2007).

of 2007, introduced by Representative Reyes for himself, Representative Conyers, Representative Schiff, and Representative Flake. After a motion to suspend the rules and pass H.R. 3356 fell short of the required two-thirds vote of the Members[4] on Friday night, the House took up S. 1927 the following day. At 10:19 p.m. Saturday night, August 4, the House passed S. 1927.[5] It was signed by the President on August 5, 2007.

This report discusses the provisions of P.L. 110-55 and their impact on or relationship with the prior provisions of FISA.

Sec. 1. Short Title

Sec. 1 of S. 1927 states that the short title of the law is the Protect America Act of 2007.

Sec. 2. Additional Procedures for Authorizing Certain Acquisitions of Foreign Intelligence Information

Section 2 of the law contains its first substantive provisions. They are summarized in order below.

New Section 105A of FISA, "Clarification of Electronic Surveillance of Persons Outside the United States"

New Section 105A of FISA, as added by Section 2 of P.L. 110-55, states:

> Nothing in the definition of electronic surveillance under section 101(f) shall be construed to encompass surveillance directed at a person reasonably believed to be located outside of the United States.

Section 101(f) of FISA, 50 U.S.C. § 1801(f), sets forth the definition of "electronic surveillance" under the statute. It provides:

> (f) "Electronic surveillance" means—
>
> (1) the acquisition by an electronic, mechanical, or other surveillance device of the contents of any wire or radio communication sent by or intended to be received by a particular, known United States person[6] who is in the United States, if the contents are acquired by

---

[4] The August 3, 2007, vote on the motion to suspend the rules and pass H.R. 3356 was 218–207 (Roll no. 821).

[5] The bill was passed by the Yeas and Nays: 227–183 (Roll no. 836).

[6] As defined in section 101(i) of FISA, 50 U.S.C. § 1801(i),

> "United States person" means a citizen of the United States, an alien lawfully admitted for permanent residence (as defined in section 1101(a)(20) of Title 8), an unincorporated association a substantial number of members of which are citizens of the United States or aliens lawfully admitted for permanent residence, or a corporation which is incorporated in the United States, but does not include a corporation or an association which is a foreign power, as defined in subsection (a)(1), (2), or (3) of this section.

intentionally targeting that United States person, under circumstances in which a person has a reasonable expectation of privacy and a warrant would be required for law enforcement purposes;

(2) the acquisition by an electronic, mechanical, or other surveillance device of the contents of any wire communication to or from a person in the United States, without the consent of any party thereto, if such acquisition occurs in the United States, but does not include the acquisition of those communications of computer trespassers that would be permissible under section 2511(2)(i) of Title 18;

(3) the intentional acquisition by an electronic, mechanical, or other surveillance device of the contents of any radio communication, under circumstances in which a person has a reasonable expectation of privacy and a warrant would be required for law enforcement purposes, and if both the sender and all intended recipients are located within the United States; or

(4) the installation or use of an electronic, mechanical, or other surveillance device in the United States for monitoring to acquire information, other than from a wire or radio communication, under circumstances in which a person has a reasonable expectation of privacy and a warrant would be required for law enforcement purposes.

To what extent would the new section 105A affect the scope of "electronic surveillance" as defined in section 101(f) of FISA? Absent the interpretation required by section 105 A, two of the four definitions of "electronic surveillance" under section 101(f) of FISA, by their terms, appear to be broad enough to encompass electronic surveillance directed at a person abroad where the communications involved transcend U.S. borders.[7] Subsections 101(f)(2) and (f)(4) of FISA, on their face, appear to have the potential of reaching electronic surveillance of such communications targeted at a person outside the United States. In addition, it might be argued

---

"Foreign power," as defined in section 101(a)(1), (2), or (3), 50 U.S.C. § 1801(a)(1), (2), or (3), means:

(1) a foreign government or any component thereof, whether or not recognized by the United States;

(2) a faction of a foreign nation or nations, not substantially composed of United States persons;

(3) an entity that is openly acknowledged by a foreign government or governments to be directed and controlled by such foreign government or governments[.]

7 Because new section 105 A of FISA explicitly addresses electronic surveillance "directed at a person reasonably believed to be located outside the United States," it would not appear to affect subsection 101(f)(1), which deals with electronic surveillance of the contents of wire or radio communications acquired from an *intentionally targeted U.S. person within the United States* under specified circumstances. "Electronic surveillance" as defined in subsection 101(f)(3) of FISA involves the intentional acquisition of the contents of radio communications in specified circumstances *where the sender and all the intended recipients to the communication are in the United States,* so it would not seem to be impacted by new section 105 A.

that the language of subsection 101(f)(4) might encompass the possibility of reaching some foreign to foreign communications in limited circumstances. This would suggest that, under FISA prior to the passage of section 105A of P.L. 110-55, some interceptions directed at a person abroad covered by the language of these subsections might have been regarded by the FISC as requiring court authorization.[8]

In pertinent part, "electronic surveillance," as defined by subsection 101(f)(2), covers acquisition of the contents of wire communications to or from a person in the United States where the acquisition occurs within the United States and no party to the communication has consented to the interception. Unlike subsection 101(f)(1), there is no express requirement that the person in the United States be known, that he or she be United States person, or that he or she be intentionally targeted by the electronic surveillance.

To the extent that an electronic surveillance under subsection 101(f)(2) intercepts communications between persons in the United States, it would not be impacted by section 105Aof FISA, as added by P.L. 110-55, nor would section 105A affect electronic surveillance targeted at a person within the United States. However, to the extent that the language in subsection 101 (f)(2) might encompass interception of communications between a person in the United States and one or more parties outside the United States, where the surveillance is targeted at a person outside the United States, section 105A would seem to restrict the previous reach of the definition of "electronic surveillance" in section 101(f)(2).

Subsection 101(f)(4) defines "electronic surveillance" under FISA to include "the installation or use of an electronic, mechanical, or other surveillance device in the United States for monitoring to acquire information, other than from a wire or radio communication,[9] under circumstances in which

[8] *See*, Greg Miller, *Spy chief reveals details of operations*, L.A. Times, August 23, 2007, available at [http://www.latimes.com/news/nationworld/nation/la-na-intel23aug23,0,6229712.story?coll=la-home-center].

[9] Section 101(l) of FISA, 50 U.S.C. § 1801(l), defines "wire communication" to mean:

> (1) "Wire communication" means any communication while it is being carried by a wire, cable, or other like connection furnished or operated by any person engaged as a common carrier in providing or operating such facilities for the transmission of interstate or foreign communications.

It does not have a separate definition of "radio communication." However, subsection 101(f)(4) of FISA appears to contemplate that communications can be transmitted using technologies other wire or radio. For example, in Title III of the Omnibus Crime Control and Safe Streets Act, as amended, 18 U.S.C. § 2510(12), "electronic communication" includes other technologies. Under § 2510(12), this term is defined to mean:

> any transfer of signs, signals, writing, images, sounds, data, or intelligence of any nature transmitted in whole or in part by a wire, radio, electromagnetic, photoelectronic or photooptical system that affects interstate or foreign commerce, but does not include—
>
> (A) any wire or oral communication;
>
> (B) any communication made through a tone-only paging device;

a person has a reasonable expectation of privacy and a warrant would be required for law enforcement purposes." This subsection does not explicitly address the location of the parties to the communication or the location of the acquisition of the information involved. Thus, by its terms, it could conceivably be interpreted to cover some communications between parties in the United States, between a party in the United States and a party outside the United States, or between parties abroad, if the other requirements of the subsection were satisfied. The restrictions in this section are two-fold: the information must be acquired other than from a wire or radio communication; and the circumstances of the acquisition must be such that a person would have a reasonable expectation of privacy and a warrant would be required for law enforcement purposes. To the extent that "electronic surveillance" under subsection 101 (f)(4) of FISA could have been or has been directed at a person or persons abroad, prior to the enactment of P.L. 110-55, new section 105A may also have the effect of limiting the scope of this subsection of the definition of "electronic surveillance" as it was previously interpreted.

New Section 105B of FISA, "Additional Procedure for Authorizing Certain Acquisitions Concerning Persons Located Outside the United States"

New section 105B(a) of FISA permits the Attorney General and the Director of National Intelligence, for periods of up to one year, to authorize acquisition of foreign intelligence information concerning persons reasonably believed to be outside the United States, if the Attorney General and the DNI determine, based on the information provided to them, that five criteria have been met. Under these criteria, the Attorney General and the DNI must certify that:

> (1) there are reasonable procedures in place for determining that the acquisition of foreign intelligence information under this section concerns persons reasonably believed to be located outside the United States,[10] and such procedures will be subject to review of the Court pursuant to section 105C of this Act;[11]

(c) any communication from a tracking device (as defined in [18 U.S.C. § 3117]);

or

(D) electronic funds transfer information stored by a financial institution in a communications system used for the electronic storage and transfer of funds[.]

[10] The reporting requirements in Sec. 4 of the P.L. 110-55 require, in part, that the Attorney General report to the House Permanent Select Committee on Intelligence, the Senate Select Committee on Intelligence, and the House and Senate Judiciary Committees regarding incidents of non-compliance by an element of the Intelligence Community with guidelines or procedures for determining that the acquisition of foreign intelligence authorized by the DNI and the Attorney General under section 105B "concerns persons reasonably [sic?] to be outside the United States."

[11] Section 105B(a)(1) states that the "procedures for determining that the acquisition of foreign intelligence information under this section concerns persons reasonably believed to be located outside the United States" are to be submitted to the FISC for review pursuant to section 105C of FISA. There

(2) the acquisition does not constitute electronic surveillance;

(3) the acquisition involves obtaining the foreign intelligence information from or with the assistance of a communications service provider, custodian, or other person (including any officer, employee, agent, or other specified person of such service provider, custodian, or other person) who has access to communications, either as they are transmitted or while they are stored, or equipment that is being or may be used to transmit or store such communications;

(4) a significant purpose of the acquisition is to obtain foreign intelligence information; and

(5) the minimization procedures to be used with respect to such acquisition activity meet the definition of minimization procedures under section 101(h).[12]

---

appears to be some ambiguity in the language of section 105B, particularly as compared with section 105C, as to what the procedures cover and what procedures are to be submitted to the FISC. The phrasing of section 105B(a)(1) on its face, seems to require submission to the FISC only of "reasonable procedures for determining that the acquisition of foreign intelligence information under this section concerns persons reasonably believed to be located outside the United States." This is the only mention in section 105B of procedures being submitted to the FISC. Thus, there is no mention in section 105B of creation of, or submission to the FISC of, procedures upon which the government bases its determination that the acquisition does not constitute electronic surveillance.

However, section 105C, by its terms, addresses only the submission by the Attorney General to the FISC of the procedures by which the government determines that acquisitions conducted pursuant to section 105B do not constitute electronic surveillance, making no mention of the procedures referred to in section 105B(a)(1). In light of this apparent inconsistency, it is unclear what review, if any, the FISC is intended to give the procedures for determining that the acquisition of foreign intelligence information under section 105B "concerns persons reasonably believed to be located outside the United States." It is also not made clear in the language of either section by whom the procedures to be reviewed by the FISC under section 105C are to be promulgated.

On the other hand, section 105A provides that the definition of "electronic surveillance" shall not be "construed to encompass surveillance directed at a person reasonably believed to be located outside of the United States." In light of this, it might be argued that the procedures by which the DNI and the Attorney General determine whether an acquisition of foreign intelligence information under section 105B concerns persons reasonably believed to be located outside the United States could be regarded as part of the FISC's analysis as to whether the procedures to determine that the acquisitions under 105B constitute electronic surveillance are clearly erroneous.

[12] Section 101(h) of FISA, 50 U.S.C. § 1801(h), defines "minimization procedures" for purposes of title I of FISA, dealing with electronic surveillance, to mean:

(h) "Minimization procedures", with respect to electronic surveillance, means —

(1) specific procedures, which shall be adopted by the Attorney General, that are reasonably designed in light of the purpose and technique of the particular surveillance, to minimize the acquisition and retention, and prohibit the dissemination, of nonpublicly available information concerning unconsenting United States persons consistent with the need of the United States to obtain, produce, and disseminate foreign intelligence information;

(2) procedures that require that nonpublicly available information, which is not foreign intelligence information, as defined in subsection (e)(1) of this section, shall not be disseminated in a manner that identifies any United States person, without such person's consent, unless such person's identity is necessary to understand foreign intelligence information or assess its importance;

(3) notwithstanding paragraphs (1) and (2), procedures that allow for the retention and dissemination of information that is evidence of a crime which has been, is being, or is about to be committed and that is to be retained or disseminated for law enforcement purposes; and

Except in circumstances where immediate government action is required and there is not sufficient time to prepare a certification, the determination by the Attorney General and the DNI that these criteria have been satisfied must be in the form of a certification, under oath, supported by affidavit of appropriate officials in the national security field appointed by the President, by and with the advice and consent of the Senate, or the Head of any agency of the Intelligence Community. Where imminent government action is required, the determination must be reduced to a certification as soon as possible within 72 hours after the determination is made.[13] The certification need not identify specific facilities, places, premises, or property at which the acquisition will be directed.[14]

A copy of a certification made under section 105B(a) must be transmitted under seal to the FISC as soon as practicable, there to be maintained under security measures established by the Chief Justice of the United States and the Attorney General, in consultation with the DNI. The copy of the certification must remain sealed unless needed to determine the legality of the acquisition involved.[15]

Where a certification has been prepared, an acquisition under section 105B of FISA must be conducted in accordance with that certification and minimization procedures adopted by the Attorney General. If a certification has not yet been prepared because of inadequate time, the acquisition must comply with the oral instructions of the DNI and the Attorney General and the applicable minimization procedures.[16] Section 105B(d) requires the DNI and the Attorney General must report their assessments of compliance with "such procedures"[17] to the House Permanent Select Committee

---

(4) notwithstanding paragraphs (1), (2), and (3), with respect to any electronic surveillance approved pursuant to section 1802(a) of this title, procedures that require that no contents of any communication to which a United States person is a party shall be disclosed, disseminated, or used for any purpose or retained for longer than 72 hours unless a court order under section 1805 of this title is obtained or unless the Attorney General determines that the information indicates a threat of death or serious bodily harm to any person.

It may be noted that, while section 105B of FISA appears to be located in title I of FISA, which deals with electronic surveillance, the DNI and the Attorney General, under section 105B(a)(2) of FISA, are expressly required to certify that the acquisitions under section 105B do *not* constitute electronic surveillance. Similarly, the minimization procedures in section 101 (h) of FISA, 50 U.S.C. § 1801(h), deal explicitly with minimization in the context of electronic surveillance, while, under subsection 105B(a)(5) of FISA, the DNI and the Attorney General must certify that "the minimization procedures to be used with respect to such acquisition[s] meet the definition of minimization procedures under section 101(h)." This seems likely to be intended to mean that the minimization procedures applicable to such acquisitions must set parallel standards to those applicable to electronic surveillance under the minimization procedures in section 101 (h) of FISA, 50 U.S.C. § 1801(h).

[13] Protect America Act of 2007, P.L. 110–55, Sec. 105B(a), 121 Stat. 552 (August 5, 2007) (hereinafter P.L. 110-55).

[14] P.L. 110-55, Sec. 105B(b).

[15] P.L. 110-55, Sec. 105B(c).

[16] P.L. 110-55, Sec. 105B(d).

[17] In the context of the subsection 105B(d), the reference to "such procedures" might be seen to be susceptible of two possible interpretations. Perhaps the more likely and more limited interpretation

on Intelligence and the Senate Select Committee on Intelligence under section 108(a) of FISA, 50 U.S.C. § 1808(a).[18]

In connection with an acquisition authorized under section 105B, the DNI and the Attorney General may issue a directive to a person to immediately provide the government with all information, facilities, and assistance needed to accomplish the acquisition in a manner which will protect the secrecy of the acquisition and minimize interference with the services provided by that person to the target of the acquisition.[19] The government must compensate the person furnishing such aid at the prevailing rate.[20]

---

would be that this may be a reference to the applicable minimization procedures referenced earlier in the subsection. Alternatively, a more expansive view might interpret this as a reference to the applicable minimization procedures plus the relevant certification, including the "reasonable procedures in place for determining that the acquisition of foreign intelligence information under this section concerns persons reasonably believed to be located outside the United States," or oral instructions regarding the acquisition at issue.

[18] Section 108 of FISA, 50 U.S.C. § 1808, provides:

> § 1808. Report of Attorney General to Congressional committees; limitation on authority or responsibility of information gathering activities of Congressional committees; report of Congressional committees to Congress
>
> (a) (1) On a semiannual basis the Attorney General shall fully inform the House Permanent Select Committee on Intelligence and the Senate Select Committee on Intelligence, and the Committee on the Judiciary of the Senate, concerning all electronic surveillance under this subchapter [title I of FISA, 50 U.S.C. §§ 1801 *et seq*.]. Nothing in this subchapter [title I of FISA] shall be deemed to limit the authority and responsibility of the appropriate committees of each House of Congress to obtain such information as they may need to carry out their respective functions and duties.
>
> (2) Each report under the first sentence of paragraph (1) shall include a description of—
>
> (A) the total number of applications made for orders and extensions of orders approving electronic surveillance under this subchapter where the nature and location of each facility or place at which the electronic surveillance will be directed is unknown;
>
> (B) each criminal case in which information acquired under this chapter has been authorized for use at trial during the period covered by such report; and
>
> (C) the total number of emergency employments of electronic surveillance under section 1805(f) of this title and the total number of subsequent orders approving or denying such electronic surveillance.
>
> (b) On or before one year after October 25, 1978, and on the same day each year for four years thereafter, the Permanent Select Committee on Intelligence and the Senate Select Committee on Intelligence shall report respectively to the House of Representatives and the Senate, concerning the implementation of this chapter. Said reports shall include but not be limited to an analysis and recommendations concerning whether this chapter should be (1) amended, (2) repealed, or (3) permitted to continue in effect without amendment.

It may be noted that the reporting requirements under subsection 108(a) of FISA deal explicitly with electronic surveillance under FISA, and impose responsibility only upon the Attorney General. While section 105B has been added to title I of FISA, which deals with electronic surveillance, the DNI and the Attorney General, under subsection 105B(a)(2) are required to certify, with respect to each acquisition under section 105 B, that such acquisition "does not constitute electronic surveillance." The reporting requirement in section 105B(d) may be intended to direct the DNI and the Attorney General to include their assessments with respect to the procedures involved in the semi-annual report of the Attorney General required by section 108(a), or it may be intended to require that the DNI and the Attorney General fully inform the House and Senate Intelligence Committees of their assessments on a semi-annual basis.

[19] P.L. 110-55, Sec. 105B(e)(1).

[20] P.L. 110-55, Sec. 105B(f).

Any records that person wishes to keep relating to the acquisition or the aid provided must be maintained under security procedures approved by the DNI and the Attorney General.[21] P.L. 110-55 bars any cause of action in any court against any person for providing information, facilities or assistance in accordance with a directive under this section.[22] If a person receiving such a directive fails to comply therewith, the FISC, at the Attorney General's request, shall issue an order to compel such compliance if the court finds that the directive was issued in accordance with section 105B(e) and is otherwise lawful.[23]

A person receiving a directive under section 105B(e) may challenge its legality by filing a petition before the petition review pool of the FISC.[24] Under subsection 105B(h)(1)(B) as written, the presiding judge of the Foreign Intelligence Surveillance Court of Review (Court of Review)[25] shall

[21] P.L. 110-55, Sec. 105B(e)(2).

[22] P.L. 110-55, Sec. 105B(l).

[23] P.L. 110-55, Sec. 105B(g). Service of process may be made upon such person in any judicial district in which he or she is found.

[24] Section 103(e)(1)of FISA, 50U.S.C. § 1803(e)(1), established this pool. As amended by Sec. 5 of P.L. 110-55, section 103(e) provides:

> (e) (1) Three judges designated under subsection (a) of this section who reside within 20 miles of the District of Columbia, or, if all of such judges are unavailable, other judges of the court established under subsection (a) of this section as maybe designated by the presiding judge of such court, shall comprise a petition review pool which shall have jurisdiction to review petitions filed pursuant to section *105B(h) or 501(f)(1)* of [FISA].
>
> (2) Not later than 60 days after March 9, 2006, the court established under subsection (a) of this section shall adopt and, consistent with the protection of national security, publish procedures for the review of petitions filed pursuant to section *105B(h) or 501(f)(1)* of [FISA] by the panel established under paragraph (1). Such procedures shall provide that review of a petition shall be conducted in camera and shall also provide for the designation of an acting presiding judge. [Emphasis added.]

Subsection 103(a) requires the Chief Justice of the United States to publicly designate 11 U.S. district court judges from seven of the United States judicial circuits to become the FISC judges. The reference to section 501(f)(1) of FISA, 50 U.S.C. § 1861(f)(1), may be intended to be a reference to section 501(f), 50 U.S.C. § 1861(f). Section 501(f), as added to FISA by P.L. 109-177, § 106(f), was rewritten by P.L. 109-178, § 3. Current section 501(f)(1) of FISA contains two subsections, defining the terms "production order" and "nondisclosure order," respectively, for purposes of section 501.

[25] Section 105B(h)(1)(B) states that the "presiding judge designated pursuant to section 103 (b) shall assign a petition filed under subparagraph (a) to one of the judge serving in the pool established by section 103(e)(1)." This may be intended to refer to the presiding judge of the FISC designated pursuant to section 103(a), rather than the presiding judge of the Foreign Intelligence Surveillance Court of Review designated pursuant to section 103(b). The petition review pool established by section 103(e)(1) is made up of FISC judges. *See* footnote 24, *supra*. Section 501 (f)(2)(A)(ii) provides that, when a petition under that section is filed with the petition review pool of the FISC, "the presiding judge" shall immediately assign it to one of the judges in the pool. The rules, effective May 5, 2006, promulgated by the FISC under section 103(e)(2) of FISA are more explicit. Under title III, sections 8 and 9, of the "Procedures for review of Petitions filed pursuant to Section 501(f) of the Foreign Intelligence Surveillance Act of 1978, As Amended," the "Presiding Judge of the Foreign Intelligence Surveillance Court," where available, assigns petitions received under section 501(f) of FISA to one of the FISC judges in the petition review pool. If the Presiding Judge of the FISC is unavailable, the local FISC judge with the most seniority, other than the Presiding Judge, becomes Acting Presiding Judge, and assigns the petition to an FISC judge in the petition review pool. If no local judge is available, the most senior FISC judge who is reasonably available becomes the Acting Presiding Judge, and makes the assignment of the petition.

assign a petition filed with the petition review pool to one of the FISC judges in the pool. The assigned judge must conduct an initial review of the directive within 48 hours after the assignment. If he or she determines that the petition is frivolous, the petition is immediately denied and the directive or that portion of the directive that is the subject of the petition is affirmed. If the judge does not find the petition frivolous, he or she has 72 hours in which to consider the petition and provide a written statement for the record of the reasons for any determination made. A petition to modify or set aside a directive may only be granted if the judge finds that the directive does not meet the requirements of section 105B or is otherwise unlawful. Otherwise the judge must immediately affirm the directive and order its recipient to comply with it. A directive not explicitly modified or set aside remains in full effect.[26] Within seven days of the assigned judge's decision, the government or a recipient of the directive may petition the Foreign Intelligence Surveillance Court of Review for review of that decision. The Court of Review must provide a written statement on the record of the reasons for its decision. The government or any recipient of the directive may seek review of the decision of the Court of Review by petition for a writ of certiorari to the U.S. Supreme Court.[27] All judicial proceedings under this section are to be concluded as expeditiously as possible.[28]

All petitions under this section are filed under seal. Upon request of the government in any proceeding under this section, the court shall review ex parte and in camera any government submission or portion of a submission which may contain classified information.[29] The record of all proceedings, including petitions filed, orders granted, and statements of reasons for decision, must be maintained under security measures established by the Chief Justice of the United States in consultation with the Attorney General and the DNI.[30] A directive made or an order granted under this section must be retained for at least ten years.[31]

Effect on or parallels to existing law

Section 105B is a new section added to title I of FISA, 50 U.S.C. §§ 1801 *et seq.* It differs from the other provisions of title I of FISA in that it does not deal with electronic surveillance, but rather with acquisitions that do not constitute electronic surveillance. Because section 105B does not specify where such acquisitions may occur or from whom, it appears that such foreign intelligence information concerning persons reasonably believed to

[26] P.L. 110-55, Sec. 105B(h).
[27] P.L. 110-55, Sec. 105B(i).
[28] P.L. 110-55, Sec. 105B(j).
[29] P.L. 110-55, Sec. 105B(k).
[30] P.L. 110-55, Sec. 105B(j).
[31] P.L. 110-55, Sec. 105B(m).

be outside the United States may be acquired, at least in part, from persons, including U.S. persons, who are located within the United States.[32]

Similar to electronic surveillance under section 102of FISA, 50U.S.C. § 1802, which may be authorized for up to one year by the President, through the Attorney General, without a court order if the Attorney General certifies in writing under oath that certain requirements are satisfied,[33] acquisitions under section 105B of FISA, may be authorized by the DNI and the Attorney General without a court order if they certify in writing under oath that certain criteria are met. However, section 105B has no parallel to section 102(a)(1)(B)'s requirement that "there is no substantial likelihood that the surveillance will acquire the contents of any communication to which a United States person is a party."

Similar to section 105B(d)'s reporting requirements, section 102(a)(2) requires electronic surveillance under that section to be carried out in accordance with the Attorney General's certification and applicable minimization requirements, and directs the Attorney General to assess compliance with "such procedures" and report his assessments to the House and Senate intelligence committees under the provisions of section 108(a) of FISA.

---

32 It may be noted that the description of an acquisition under section 105B of FISA appears broad enough to encompass future collection of phone calling records for pattern analysis, but does not appear intended to address any past use of such investigative techniques. *Cf*, Hepting v. AT&T Corp., 439 F. Supp. 2d. 974 (N.D. Cal. 2006); In re: National Security Agency Telecommunications Records Litigation, MDL No. 06-1791-VRW (March 13, 2007) (stipulation and order staying all cases except *Hepting* against AT&T Defendants); Hepting v. United States, Nos. 06-80109, 06-80110 (9th Cir. 2006) (order granting appeal).

33 Section 102(a), 50 U.S.C. § 1802(a) provides:

> (a)(1) Notwithstanding any other law, the President, through the Attorney General, may authorize electronic surveillance without a court order under this subchapter to acquire foreign intelligence information for periods of up to one year if the Attorney General certifies in writing under oath that—
>
> (A) the electronic surveillance is solely directed at—
>
> (i) the acquisition of the contents of communications transmitted by means of communications used exclusively between or among foreign powers, as defined in section 1801(a)(1), (2), or (3) of this title; or
>
> (ii) the acquisition of technical intelligence, other than the spoken communications of individuals, from property or premises under the open and exclusive control of a foreign power, as defined in section 1801(a)(1), (2), or (3) of this title;
>
> (B) there is no substantial likelihood that the surveillance will acquire the contents of any communication to which a United States person is a party; and
>
> (C) the proposed minimization procedures with respect to such surveillance meet the definition of minimization procedures under section 1801(h) of this title; and
>
> if the Attorney General reports such minimization procedures and any changes thereto to the House Permanent Select Committee on Intelligence and the Senate Select Committee on Intelligence at least thirty days prior to their effective date, unless the Attorney General determines immediate action is required and notifies the committees immediately of such minimization procedures and the reason for their becoming effective immediately.

Section 102(a)(4), which permits the Attorney General to direct a specified communication common carrier to provide information, facilities, or technical assistance to the government needed to carry out the electronic surveillance involved and to compensate that communication common carrier at the prevailing rate for its aid, is structurally similar to section 105B(e) and (f). However, subsections 105B(e) and (g)-(i) permit the Attorney General and the DNI to direct "a person," rather than a "specified communication common carrier," to "immediately" furnish such aid; provide authority for the Attorney General to seek the aid of the FISC to compel compliance with such a directive; give the recipient of the directive a right to challenge the legality of the directive before the petition review pool of the same court; and permit both the government and the recipient of the directive to appeal that court's decision. The authority to challenge the legality of such a directive and to appeal the decision appears modeled, to some degree, after the process set forth in section 501(f) of FISA, 50 U.S.C. § 1861(f), dealing with challenges to the legality of production and nondisclosure orders.

Unlike electronic surveillance pursuant to a court order sought under section 104 of FISA, 50 U.S.C. § 1804, and authorized under section 105 of FISA, 50 U.S.C. § 1805, where the government provides the FISC with specific categories of substantive information about the electronic surveillance involved upon which the court can base its determinations; the government submits certain procedures[34] for review to the FISC, but does not provide the court with substantive information about the acquisitions themselves.

Sec. 3. Submission to Court Review and Assessment of Procedures

Section 3 of the act creates a new section 105C of FISA, creating a review process for the procedures under which the government determines that acquisitions of foreign intelligence information from persons reasonably believed to be located outside the United States do not constitute electronic surveillance.

New Section 105C of FISA. "Submission to Court Review of Procedures"

Subsection 105C(a) requires the Attorney General, within 120 days of enactment of the act,[35] to submit to the FISC the procedures by which the government determines that acquisitions conducted pursuant to section 105B

[34] Compare section 105B(a)(1) with section 105C.

[35] Under Sec. 6(a) of the act, except as otherwise provided, the amendments made by the act are to take effect immediately after the date of enactment of the act. Sec. 105C(a) states that it will take effect within 120 days of the effective date of the act. For purposes of Sec. 105C(a), that would be 120 days after enactment.

of the act do not constitute electronic surveillance.[36] The procedures are to be updated and submitted to the FISC annually. Within 180 days after enactment, the FISC must assess whether the government's determination under section 105B(1) of FISA that the procedures are "reasonably designed to ensure that acquisitions conducted pursuant to section 105B do not constitute electronic surveillance"[37] is clearly erroneous.[38]

If the FISC deems the government's determination not clearly erroneous, the court must enter an order approving the continued use of the procedures. On the other hand, if the government's determination is found to be clearly erroneous, new procedures must be submitted with 30 days or any acquisitions under section 105B implicated by the FISC order must cease.[39] Any order issued by the FISC under subsection 105C(c) may be appealed by the government to the Foreign Intelligence Surveillance Court of Review. If the Court of Review finds the FISC order was properly entered, the government may seek U.S. Supreme Court review through a petition for a writ of certiorari.[40] Any acquisitions affected by the FISC order at issue may continue throughout the review process.

Comparison of this provision with court review

The section 105C procedure review process is new and does not appear to have a parallel in the other provisions of FISA.

Other possible effects of new sections 105A, 105B, and 105C

The Terrorist Surveillance Program has been characterized as involving "intercepts of contents of communications where one . . . party to the communication is outside the United States" and the government has

---

[36] Section 105B(1) on its face refers only to "reasonable procedures in place for determining that the acquisition of foreign intelligence information under this section concerns persons reasonably believed to be located outside the United States," and requires "such procedures [to be] subject to review of the [FISC] pursuant to section 105C of this Act." *See* footnote 11, *supra,* for further discussion of the seeming ambiguities in the statutory language of sections 105B and 105C with respect to the procedures to be reviewed by the FISC.

[37] There appears to be some ambiguity regarding the procedures referenced in section 105B(a) and section 105C of FISA. Section 105B permits the DNI and the Attorney General to authorize acquisition of foreign intelligence information concerning persons reasonably believed to be outside the United States if the DNI and the Attorney General determine, based upon information provided to them, "that—(a)(1) there are reasonable procedures in place for determining that the acquisition of foreign intelligence information under this section concerns persons reasonably believed to be located outside the United States, and such procedures will be subject to review of the Court pursuant to section 105C of this Act[.]" However, section 105C requires the Attorney General to submit to the FISC "the procedures by which the Government determines that acquisitions conducted pursuant to section 105B do not constitute electronic surveillance." For further discussion, see 15, *supra.*

[38] Section 105C(b) of FISA, as added by P.L. 110-55, Sec. 3.

[39] Section 105C(c) of FISA, as added by P.L. 110-55, Sec. 3.

[40] Section 105C(d) of FISA, as added by P.L. 110-55, Sec. 3. If the Court of Review affirms the FISC order, the Court of Review must immediately prepare a written statement of each of the reasons for its decision. Should the government file a certiorari petition, that written record would be transmitted under seal to the U.S. Supreme Court.

"a reasonable basis to conclude that one party to the communication is a member of al Qaeda, affiliated with al Qaeda, or a member of an organization affiliated with al Qaeda, or working in support of al Qaeda."[41] In a letter from the Attorney General to Senator Leahy and Senator Specter on January 17, 2007, the Attorney General indicated that, based upon classified orders issued by a judge of the Foreign Intelligence Surveillance Court (FISC), electronic surveillances previously carried out under the Terrorist Surveillance Program would thereafter be under the court's supervision. His letter stated, in part:

> I am writing to inform you that on January 10, 2007, a Judge of the Foreign Intelligence Surveillance Court issued orders authorizing the Government to target for collection international communications into or out of the United States where there is probable cause to believe that one of the communicants is a member or agent of al Qaeda or an associated terrorist organization. As a result of these orders, any electronic surveillance that was occurring as part of the Terrorist Surveillance Program will now be conducted subject to the approval of the Foreign Intelligence Surveillance Court. . . .[42]

A question may arise as to whether new section 105A's interpretation of the definition of "electronic surveillance" under FISA, might impact the FISC's jurisdiction over some or all of the interceptions to which the Attorney General referred. Under section 103(a) of FISA, 50 U.S.C. § 1803(a):

> The Chief Justice of the United States shall publicly designate 11 district court judges from seven of the United States judicial circuits of whom no fewer than 3 shall reside within 20 miles of the District of Columbia who shall constitute a court which shall have jurisdiction to hear applications for and grant orders approving electronic surveillance anywhere within the United States under the procedures set forth in this chapter, except that no judge designated under this subsection shall hear the same application for electronic surveillance under this chapter which has been denied previously by another judge designated under this subsection . . .

Section 102(b) of FISA, 50 U.S.C. § 1802(b), provides that:

> Applications for a court order under [title I of FISA, 50 U.S.C. §§ 1801 *et seq.*] are authorized if the President has, by written authorization, empowered the Attorney General to approve applications to the court having jurisdiction under section 1803 of this title, and a judge to whom an application is made may, notwithstanding any other law, grant an order, in conformity with section 1805 of this title, approving electronic surveillance of a foreign power or an agent of a foreign power for the purpose of obtaining foreign

---

[41] *See* Press Release, White House, Press Briefing by Attorney General Alberto Gonzales and General Michael Hayden, Principal Deputy Director for National Intelligence (December 19, 2005).

[42] 153 *Cong. Rec.* S646-S647 (January 17, 2007) (Letter of Attorney General Alberto Gonzales to the Chairman and Ranking Member of the Senate Judiciary Committee ordered printed, without objection, in the *Record* during Senator Leahy's remarks on the FISA Program).

> intelligence information, except that the court shall not have jurisdiction to grant any order approving electronic surveillance directed solely as described in paragraph (1)(A) of subsection (a) of this section unless such surveillance may involve the acquisition of communications of any United States person.

The answer to the jurisdictional question raised above would seem to depend on whether those interceptions were directed at the communications of a person reasonably believed to be located outside the United States. If so, then, by virtue of section 105 A, such interceptions would not be construed to fall within the definition of "electronic surveillance" under FISA, and therefore a review of the underpinnings of such interceptions would not be within the FISC's jurisdiction in connection with an application to authorize electronic surveillance. If treated instead as acquisitions under new section 105B of FISA, then the FISC would seem to be limited to reviewing, under a clearly erroneous standard, the general procedures under which the Director of National Intelligence (DNI) and the Attorney General would make determinations that acquisitions did not constitute electronic surveillance;[43] and judges of the FISC petition review pool would have jurisdiction to consider petitions challenging the legality of directives to persons to furnish aid to the government to accomplish those acquisitions.[44]

Implicit in the previous discussion is the question what impact, if any, any possible narrowing of the interpretation of the definition of "electronic surveillance" under FISA might have upon the scope of "acquisitions" under new section 105B of FISA. In other words, if an interception of communications directed toward a person reasonably believed to be located outside the United States does not constitute "electronic surveillance" for purposes of FISA, regardless of where the other parties to the communication may be located or whether some or all of those other parties may be U.S. persons, could some or all such interceptions be deemed "acquisitions" under the provisions of section 105B?

For this to be the case, it would appear that the interception would have to be authorized by the DNI and the Attorney General under section 105B of FISA to acquire foreign intelligence information concerning persons reasonably believed to be outside the United States, and would have to satisfy the five criteria set forth in section 105B(a), including the use of minimization procedures.[45] If these requirements are met, then it appears that some

---

43 Section 105C(a) of FISA, as added by P.L. 110-55, Sec. 3.
44 Section 105B(h) of FISA, as added by P.L. 110-55, Sec. 2.
45 Section 105B(a)(5)of FISA, as added by Sec. 2of P.L. 110-55. For further discussion of minimization procedures in section 105B(a)(5), see footnote 12, *supra,* and accompanying text. Under section 105(f) of FISA, 50 U.S.C. § 1805(f), in approving an application for electronic surveillance under FISA, an FISC judge must find, in part, that the proposed minimization procedures applicable to that surveillance meet the definition of minimization procedures under section 101(h) of FISA, 50 U.S.C. § 1801(h).

communications to which U.S. persons located within the United States might be parties could be intercepted for periods of up to one year without a court order under section 105B.

This contrasts markedly with the detailed information to be provided by the government to the FISC in an application for a court order for electronic surveillance under section 104 of FISA, 50 U.S.C. § 1804,[46] and the level of FISC review provided for such applications. To the extent that new section 105 A circumscribes the previous interpretation of "electronic surveillance" as defined under section 101(f) of FISA, 50 U.S.C. § 1801(f), it could be argued that this might significantly diminish the degree of judicial review to which such interceptions might have here to fore been entitled. On the other hand, if the interpretation of the definition of "electronic surveillance" contemplated in new section 105 A of FISA is consistent with prior practice, then this concern with respect to section 105A's impact would appear to be eliminated.

A somewhat closer parallel might be drawn between the statutory structure for acquisitions contemplated in section 105B and that for electronic surveillance under section 102 of FISA, 50 U.S.C. § 1802. The latter section permits the President, through the Attorney General, to authorize electronic surveillance for up to one year without a court order, if the Attorney General certifies in writing under oath that the electronic surveillance is solely directed at the acquisition of the contents of communications transmitted by means of communications used exclusively between or among foreign powers, as defined in section 1801(a)(1), (2), or (3) of this title;[47] or the acquisition of technical intelligence, other than the spoken communications of individuals, from property or premises under the open and exclusive control of such a foreign power. In addition, the Attorney General must certify that there is no substantial likelihood that the surveillance will acquire the contents of any communication to which a United States person is a party; and that the proposed minimization procedures with respect to such surveillance meet the definition of minimization procedures under section 1801(h) of this title; and he must comply with reporting requirements regarding those minimization procedures.

In authorizing an acquisition under section 105B, the DNI and the Attorney General must certify in writing under oath, in part, that "the minimization procedures to be used with respect to such acquisition activity meet the definition of minimization procedures under section 101(h)."

[46] Section 104 of FISA, 50 U.S.C. § 1804, which deals with application for FISC court orders authorizing electronic surveillance, requires eleven categories of detailed information to be submitted by a federal office in writing under oath or affirmation to an FISC judge. Each application must be approved by the Attorney General based upon his finding that the application satisfies the criteria and requirements set forth in title I of FISA. Section 105 of FISA, 50 U.S.C. § 1805, sets out the findings that a FISC judge must make in approving such an application.

[47] *See* footnote 6, *supra*, for the definition of "foreign power" under section 101(a)(1), (2), or (3) of FISA.

Subsection 102(b) of FISA denies the FISC jurisdiction to grant any order approving electronic surveillance directed solely at the acquisition of communications used exclusively between or among such foreign powers or the acquisition of such technical intelligence from property or premises under the exclusive and open control of such foreign powers, *unless such surveillance may involve the acquisition of communications of any United States person*. Section 105B provides the FISC no similar jurisdiction if an acquisition involves the communications of a United States person. Again, if the interpretation of the definition of "electronic surveillance" contemplated in new section 105A of FISA is consistent with prior practice, then this concern regarding section 105A's effect would appear to be eliminated.

To the extent that any intentional interceptions of communications which were previously deemed to be covered by the definition of "electronic surveillance" under FISA are now excluded from that definition, another question which may arise is whether any of those interceptions may now be found to fall within the general prohibition against intentional interception of wire, oral, or electronic communications under Title III of the Omnibus Crime Control and Safe Streets Act of 1968, as amended, 18 U.S.C. § 2511. Under 18 U.S.C. § 2511(2)(f), "electronic surveillance," as defined in section 101 of the Foreign Intelligence Surveillance Act, is an exception to this general prohibition.[48] If such interceptions were deemed to violate 18 U.]S.C. § 2511, then the intentional use or disclosure of the contents of such communications, knowing that the information was obtained through the interception of a wire, oral, or electronic communication in violation of 18 U.S.C. § 2511 would also be prohibited under that section.

Sec. 4. Reporting to Congress

Section 4 of P.L. 110-55 requires the Attorney General to inform the Senate Select Committee on Intelligence, the House Permanent Select Committee on Intelligence, the Senate Judiciary Committee and the House Judiciary Committee semi-annually concerning acquisitions "under this section"[49] during the previous six-month period. Each report is to include descriptions of any incidents of non-compliance with a directive issued by the DNI and the Attorney General under section 105B, including noncompliance by an element of the Intelligence Community with guidelines or

[48] If there are any types of intentional interceptions of communications previously covered by FISA's definition of electronic surveillance, which may now be prohibited under 18 U.S.C. § 2511, this, in turn, might give rise to the question whether, if the President were to carry out such interceptions under an assertion of his constitutional authority under Article II, the application of Title III's prohibition to those interceptions would be found by a court to be unconstitutional, or whether the application of this prohibition to such interceptions would withstand constitutional scrutiny. *Cf.*, In re Sealed Case, 310 F. 3d 717, 742, 746 (U.S. Foreign Intell. Surveillance Ct. Rev. 2002).

[49] This appears to be a reference to section 105B of FISA, as added by P.L.1 10–55, Sec. 2.

procedures for determining that "the acquisition of foreign intelligence authorized by the Attorney General and the [DNI] concerns persons reasonably to be outside the United States,"[50] and incidents of noncompliance by a specified person to whom a directive is issued under section 105B. The report is also required to include the number of certifications and directives issued during the reporting period.

Sec. 5. Technical Amendment and Conforming Amendments

Section 5(a)(1) and (a)(2) make technical amendments to section 103(e)(1) and (2) of FISA, 50 U.S.C. § 1803(e)(1) and (2), to reflect the jurisdiction of the FISC petition review pool over petitions under section 105B(h) of FISA, dealing with challenges to the legality of directives issued under section 105B(e) of FISA to a person by the Attorney General and the DNI, and over petitions under section 501(f)[51] of FISA, 50 U.S.C. § 1861, dealing with challenges to production orders or nondisclosure orders issued by the FISC under section 501(c) of FISA, 50 U.S.C. § 1861(c).

Section 5(b) makes conforming amendments to the table of contents of the first "section"[52] of FISA, 50 U.S.C. § 1801 *et seq.*, to reflect the additions of new sections 105 A, 105B, and 105C of FISA.

Sec. 6. Effective Date; Transition Procedures

Effective Date

Under Section 6(a) of P.L. 110-55, the amendments to FISA made in the act are to take effect immediately after its enactment except as otherwise provided.

Transition Procedures

Section 6(b) of P.L. 110-55 provides that any order issued under FISA in effect on the date of enactment of P.L. 110-55 (August 5, 2007) shall remain in effect until the date of expiration of the order, and, at the request of the applicant for the order, the FISC shall reauthorize the order as long as the

[50] This may be intended to read "the acquisition of foreign intelligence *information* authorized by the Attorney General and Director of National Intelligence concerns persons reasonably *believed to* be outside the United States." (Emphasis added.)

[51] Sec. 5(a)(1) and (2) of the act refer here to section "501(f)(1)," rather than to section "501(f)," of FISA. The reference to section 501(f)(1) of FISA, 50 U.S.C. § 1861(f)(1), may be intended to be a reference to section 501(f), 50 U.S.C. § 1861(f). Section 501(f), as added to FISA by P.L. 109-177, § 106(f), was rewritten by P.L. 109-178, § 3. Current section 501(f)(1) of FISA contains two subsections, defining the terms "production order" and "nondisclosure order," respectively, for purposes of section 501. For further discussion, see footnote 24, *supra*.

[52] This appears to be intended to refer to the title I of FISA, dealing with electronic surveillance.

facts and circumstances continue to justify its issuance under FISA as in effect the day before the applicable effective date of P.L. 110-55. This appears to refer to orders and applications for orders under FISA authorizing electronic surveillance,[53] physical searches,[54] pen registers or trap and trace devices,[55] or production of tangible things and related nondisclosure orders.[56]

Section 6(b) provides further that the government may also file new applications and the FISC shall enter orders granting such applications pursuant to FISA, as long as the application meets the requirements set forth in FISA as in effect on the day before the applicable effective date of P.L. 110-55. This seems to indicate that preexisting authorities under FISA remain available in the wake of P.L. 110-55's enactment. At the applicant's request, the FISC shall extinguish any extant authorizations to conduct electronic surveillance or physical searches pursuant to FISA. Any surveillance conducted pursuant to an order entered under subsection 6(b) of P.L. 110-55 is to be subject to the provisions of FISA as in effect before the effective date of P.L. 110-55.

Under Section 6(c) of P.L. 110-55, sections 2, 3, 4, and 5 of that act sunset 180 days after the date of enactment of the act, except as provided in section 6(d). Under section 6(d), any authorizations for acquisition of foreign intelligence information or directives issued pursuant to those authorizations issued under section 105B shall remain in effect until their expiration. Section 6(d) also provides that such acquisitions shall be governed by the applicable amendments made to FISA by P.L. 110-55, and shall not be deemed to constitute electronic surveillance as that term is defined in section 101(f) of FISA.[57]

---

53 Applications for electronic surveillance are covered by section 104 of FISA, 50 U.S.C. § 1804, while orders authorizing such surveillance are addressed in section 105 of FISA, 50 U.S.C. § 1805. These sections were not amended by P.L.110–55.

54 Applications for physical searches are addressed in sections 302(b) and 303 of FISA, 50 U.S.C. §§ 1822(b) and 1823, while orders authorizing such physical searches are addressed in section 304 of FISA, 50 U.S.C. § 1824. These sections were not amended by P.L.110-55.

55 Applications for installation and use of pen registers and trap and trace devices are addressed in subsections 402(a), (b), and (c) of FISA, 50 U.S.C. § 1842(a), (b), and (c); while orders authorizing installation and use of such pen registers and trap and trace devices are covered by subsection 402(d), 50 U.S.C. § 1842(d). No amendments to these subsections were made in P.L. 110-55.

56 Applications for orders "requiring the production of any tangible things (including books, records, papers, documents, and other items) for an investigation to obtain foreign intelligence information not concerning a United States person or to protect against international terrorism or clandestine intelligence activities, provided that such investigation of a United States person is not conducted solely upon the basis of activities protected by the first amendment to the Constitution" are addressed in subsections 501(a) and (b) of FISA, 50 U.S.C. § 1861(a) and (b). Production orders are covered in subsection 501(c) of FISA, 50 U.S.C. § 1861(c), while related nondisclosure orders are addressed in subsection 501(d) of FISA, 50 U.S.C. § 1861(d). These subsections were not amended by P.L. 110-55.

57 The provisions in section 6(c) and (d) were added by Senate amendment 2649 to S. 1927, proposed by Senator McConnell, for himself and Senator Bond. It was agreed to by unanimous consent on August 3, 2007. As amended, the bill passed the Senate by Yea-Nay vote, 60-28 (Record Vote Number 309), 153 *Cong. Rec.* S10861–S10872 (August 3, 2007).

D. THE RESTORE ACT OF 2007

RESTORE ACT OF 2007, H.R. 3733

Commentary

The Respected Electronic Surveillance That is Overseen, Reviewed and Effective (RESTORE) Act (RA) was a bill introduced on October 9, 2007 by House of Representatives Majority Leader Steny Hoyer (D-Md.) and written by Judiciary Chairman John Conyers (D-Mich.) and Intelligence Chairman Silvestre Reyes (D-Texas). However, House Democratic leaders pulled the bill from the floor on October 17, 2007, because they lacked the votes to overcome Republican opponents and parliamentary maneuvers. Conservative Democrats feared having to respond to Republican charges that the Democratic bill gave too many rights to suspected terrorists. House Republican leaders offered a motion that would have sent the bill back to the House Intelligence and Judiciary Committees with the requirement that they add language specifying that nothing in the measure would apply to surveilling the communications of Osama bin Laden, al-Qaeda, or other foreign terrorist organizations. If approved, such a motion would have restarted the legislative process, effectively killing the bill by delay. It was the first time Democrats withdrew a major bill from consideration before a scheduled vote since they took control of the House.

On November 15, the House passed the RA with a self-executing rule that addressed Republican concerns. The rule provided that a manager's amendment, containing language the Republicans demanded, shall be considered as adopted upon adoption of the rule. The manager's amendment:

1. Clarifies that nothing in the bill shall be construed to prohibit lawful surveillance necessary to:
    a. prevent Osama bin Laden, al-Qaeda, or any other terrorist organization from attacking the U.S., any U.S. person, or any ally of the U.S.;
    b. ensure the safety and security of our Armed Forces or other national security or intelligence personnel;
    c. protect the U.S., any U.S. person, or any U.S. ally from the threat of WMD or any other threats to national security;
2. Clarifies that the bill shall not be construed to prohibit surveillance of, or grant any rights to, undocumented aliens;

3. Provides that the National Security Agency (NSA) and other agencies can only disseminate identifying information of a U.S. person to other government agencies, if a Senior Executive determines that such dissemination is necessary to understand the value of the intelligence and to protect national security;
4. Establishes criteria for the FISC to determine whether the targeting procedures for ensuring that surveillance is reasonably designed to target only people outside the United States sufficiently protects U.S. person communications intercepted by the NSA.

The Senate passed its version of the Act, S. 2248: FISA Amendments Act of 2008, on February 12, 2008. On March 14, 2008, the House voted to agree with an amendment to the Senate amendment or the RA. The bill may now proceed to a conference committee of senators and representatives to work out differences in the versions of the bill each chamber approved, before it is presented to the president for signature.

The RA would replace the Protect America Act (PAA) and tighten oversight on foreign-intelligence surveillance, addressing several contested provisions in the PAA. In short, the RA would permit the conduct of foreign electronic surveillance, through December 2009, for the purpose of defending against terrorism and other national security threats, without the need for individual court orders for overseas targets. It would do so while protecting the constitutional rights of Americans whose communications may be intercepted in the process. The RA would prohibit warrantless physical searches inside the U.S. and restrict the scope of the program to a narrower range of threats, including terrorism and sabotage. The RA would expire on Dec. 31, 2009, giving Congress time to review the new procedures.

One of the most controversial aspects of the RA is whether it should provide retroactive immunity for the telecommunications companies that participated in the Bush administration's warrantless Terrorist Surveillance Program (TSP), a key demand by the White House and many Republicans. The argument for providing immunity basically is two-part. First, immunity proponents argue that the telecommunication companies acted in good faith to assist the government in gathering information that might be helpful to waging the Global War Against Terrorists, and that the companies therefore should not be subject to hundreds, if not eventually thousands, of lawsuits for doing so. Second, the immunity proponents raise, as a pragmatic argument, the bogeyman of the compromise of sensitive government secrets during the course of discovery and trial. These concerns led the Senate to reject, by a large margin, a proposed amendment to its version of the Act which would have removed the language providing immunity from civil liability for electronic communication service providers for certain assistance provided to the Executive Branch in the past.

The argument against providing immunity has two facets as well. First, some lawmakers believe that granting immunity would in effect prevent the administration from being held accountable for conducting illegal surveillance. This view holds that dismissing the many pending lawsuits against the telecommunication companies would cut off the only feasible way of conducting an unbiased assessment of the legality of the TSP. Second, denying victims their days in court would not only run counter to American principles of jurisprudence, it would also encourage similar illegal activity in the future, if the TSP were in fact illegal.

Some lawmakers favor a compromise in which the federal government would indemnify telecommunications companies, or even more radically, substitute the government as the defendant in the suits. But, there is considerable resistance to allowing the taxpayers to assume the legal liability alleged to have been caused by the Bush administration. That counterargument rings somewhat hollow, however. Of course taxpayers are responsible for the liabilities incurred by those elected to public office. Interestingly, no one seems to question the apparent assumption that the highly educated, sophisticated management of the telecommunications companies that cooperated with the Administration in the TSP should be excused for doing so, even though they did not seriously question, in the courts if necessary, whether what they were being asked to do was illegal. The strident resistance to placing the potential litigation liability on the public combined with the desire to provide immunity to the telecommunication companies resulted in the the Senate soundly rejecting a proposed amendment to the Act that would substitute the U.S. Government for telecommunication companies, as the defendant in civil lawsuits.

The RA's sponsors pragmatically recognize that immunity of some sort will likely have to be included for President Bush to sign the bill. However, they will probably not offer to agree on an immunity clause until they are satisfied that the Administration has provided sufficient information about the TSP, to a sufficient number of lawmakers, to enable them to assess the program's legality. It is unclear that the disclosures made by the Administration thus far satisfactorily answer that demand.

The RA provides that the FISC would issue "basket" or "blanket" warrants that apply to a designated group for up to a year (extendable for a year), so long as there are reasonable procedures in place to ensure that only foreigners are targeted and Americans' rights are preserved. The AG and DNI could authorize wiretapping on those foreign targets, without individual probable cause warrants, on the condition that the court would review the targeting procedures and verify that information collected on non-suspect Americans was expunged from the surveillance. The AG and DNI would be required to certify that the targets were not Americans or U.S. entities, and that the goal of such actions was foreign surveillance and foreign intelligence collection. Additionally, the warrant would have to explain how the collection of data would be minimized, as well as how much of the communication could be collected before a regular warrant would be needed to continue the surveillance.

The FISC would have to approve the procedures under which surveillance is conducted, ensuring that appropriate safeguards are in place to protect the privacy of Americans whose communications with foreigners happen to be intercepted. Specifically, the FISC would review and approve the government's minimization procedures to reduce the aggregation and retention of sensitive information about U.S. citizens, the targeting procedures to ensure that surveillance is reasonably designed to target only people outside the United States, and the guidelines to ensure that if a target becomes a person in the United States for whom collection requires a court order, an individualized order will be sought. Each order applies to a group of suspected foreign terrorists, and the Administration can seek as many orders as it wants.

Supporters of the RA readily point out that it does not extend Fourth Amendment protections to overseas targets such as Osama bin Laden and other members of terrorist organizations. It also clears up any "foreign-to-foreign" ambiguity by plainly stating that purely foreign-to-foreign communications do not require a court order, even when the communication transits the U.S. or when the acquisition is in the United States. This clarification is needed because some communications between foreign persons located overseas pass through routing stations in the United States.

As for housekeeping, the RA requires regular audits by the DOJ IG on communications collected under the RA's authority and the number of U.S. persons identified in intelligence reports disseminated pursuant to this collection. The audits would be provided to the FISC and to Congress. Additionally, the RA requires an audit and a report to Congress on the President's Terrorist Surveillance Program and other warrantless surveillance programs. The RA requires recordkeeping on any interception of the communications of U.S. persons and adds funding to increase the capability of the FISC, to ensure the expeditious handling of applications.

As of this writing, the specific fate of the RA is unclear. Executive session briefings and meetings are occurring in Congress, and it is almost certain that this Congress will reach appropriate compromises and complete action on the bill. One could also reasonably conclude that President Bush will sign it before the authorizations made under the PAA expire. There certainly will be more to follow on this important piece of legislation.

DOCUMENT NO. 11

RESTORE ACT OF 2007

Congressional Record,
Vol. 153, No. 177
House

November 15, 2007

SPEAKER: Mr. CONYERS; Mr. SMITH of Texas; Mr. REYES; Mr. FORBES; Mr. SCHIFF.; Mr. FLAKE.; Mr. GOHMERT; Mr. BOSWELL.; Ms. ESHOO.; Mr. NADLER.; Mr. SHADEGG.; Mr. BLUNT; Ms. WASSERMAN SCHULTZ; Mr. HOEKSTRA; Mr. THORNBERRY; Mr. TIAHRT.; Ms. SCHAKOWSKY; Mr. LANGEVIN; Mrs. WILSON of New Mexico; Mr. KIRK.; Mr. SCOTT of Virginia; Ms. PELOSI; Mr. MAHONEY of Florida; Mr. BLUMENAUER; Ms. BEAN; Mr. UDALL of New Mexico; Mr. DINGELL; Mr. STARK; Mr. GORDON of Tennessee; Mr. UDALL of Colorado; Mr. SMITH of Texas (during the reading); Ms. ZOE LOFGREN of California; Ms. HARMAN.; Mr. WESTMORELAND; Mr. FRANK of Massachusetts; Ms. SLAUGHTER; Mr. HIGGINS; Mr. HAYES

TEXT:

The SPEAKER pro tempore. Pursuant to House Resolution 746, proceedings will now resume on the bill (H.R. 3773) to amend the Foreign Intelligence Surveillance Act of 1978 to establish a procedure for authorizing certain acquisitions of foreign intelligence, and for other purposes.

The Clerk read the title of the bill.

The text of the bill is as follows:

H.R 3773

Be it enacted by the Senate and House of Representatives of the United States of America in Congress assembled,

SECTION 1. SHORT TITLE; TABLE OF CONTENTS

(a) Short Title.—This Act may be cited as the "Responsible Electronic Surveillance That is Overseen, Reviewed, and Effective Act of 2007" or "RESTORE Act of 2007".

(b) Table of Contents.—The table of contents for this Act is as follows:

SEC. 2. CLARIFICATION OF ELECTRONIC SURVEILLANCE OF NON-UNITED STATES PERSONS OUTSIDE THE UNITED STATES

Section 105A of the Foreign Intelligence Surveillance Act of 1978 (50 U.S.C. 1801 et seq.) is amended to read as follows:

> **"CLARIFICATION OF ELECTRONIC SURVEILLANCE OF NON-UNITED STATES PERSONS OUTSIDE THE UNITED STATES**
>
> "Sec. 105A. (a) Foreign to Foreign Communications.—Notwithstanding any other provision of this Act, a court order is not required for the acquisition of the contents of any communication between persons that are not United States persons and are not located within the United States for the purpose of collecting foreign intelligence information, without respect to whether

the communication passes through the United States or the surveillance device is located within the United States.

"(b) Communications of Non-United States Persons Outside of the United States.—Notwithstanding any other provision of this Act other than subsection (a), electronic surveillance that is directed at the acquisition of the communications of a person that is reasonably believed to be located outside the United States and not a United States person for the purpose of collecting foreign intelligence information (as defined in paragraph (1) or (2)(A) of section 101(e)) by targeting that person shall be conducted pursuant to—

"(1) an order approved in accordance with section 105 or 105B; or

"(2) an emergency authorization in accordance with section 105 or 105C.".

SEC. 3. PROCEDURE FOR AUTHORIZING ACQUISITIONS OF COMMUNICATIONS OF NON-UNITED STATES PERSONS LOCATED OUTSIDE THE UNITED STATES

Section 105B of the Foreign Intelligence Surveillance Act of 1978 (50 U.S.C. 1801 et seq.) is amended to read as follows:

"PROCEDURE FOR AUTHORIZING ACQUISITIONS OF COMMUNICATIONS OF NON-UNITED STATES PERSONS LOCATED OUTSIDE THE UNITED STATES

"Sec. 105B. (a) In General.—Notwithstanding any other provision of this Act, the Director of National Intelligence and the Attorney General may jointly apply to a judge of the court established under section 103(a) for an ex parte order, or the extension of an order, authorizing for a period of up to one year the acquisition of communications of persons that are reasonably believed to be located outside the United States and not United States persons for the purpose of collecting foreign intelligence information (as defined in paragraph (1) or (2)(A) of section 101(e)) by targeting those persons.

"(b) Application Inclusions.—An application under subsection (a) shall include—

"(1) a certification by the Director of National Intelligence and the Attorney General that—

"(A) the targets of the acquisition of foreign intelligence information under this section are persons reasonably believed to be located outside the United States;

"(B) the targets of the acquisition are reasonably believed to be persons that are not United States persons;

"(C) the acquisition involves obtaining the foreign intelligence information from, or with the assistance of, a communications service provider or custodian, or an officer, employee, or agent of such service provider or custodian, who has authorized access to the communications to be acquired, either as they are transmitted or while they are stored, or equipment that is being or may be used to transmit or store such communications; and

"(D) a significant purpose of the acquisition is to obtain foreign intelligence information (as defined in paragraph (1) or (2)(A) of section 101(e)); and

"(2) a description of—

"(A) the procedures that will be used by the Director of National Intelligence and the Attorney General during the duration of the order to determine that there is a reasonable belief that the targets of the acquisition are persons that are located outside the United States and not United States persons;

"(B) the nature of the information sought, including the identity of any foreign power against whom the acquisition will be directed;

"(C) minimization procedures that meet the definition of minimization procedures under section 101(h) to be used with respect to such acquisition; and

"(c) Specific Place Not Required.—An application under subsection (a) is not required to identify the specific facilities, places, premises, or property at which the acquisition of foreign intelligence information will be directed.

"(d) Review of Application.—Not later than 15 days after a judge receives an application under subsection (a), the judge shall review such application and shall approve the application if the judge finds that—

"(1) the proposed procedures referred to in subsection (b)(2)(A) are reasonably designed to determine whether the targets of the acquisition are located outside the United States and not United States persons;

"(2) the proposed minimization procedures referred to in subsection (b)(2)(C) meet the definition of minimization procedures under section 101(h); and

"(3) the guidelines referred to in subsection (b)(2)(D) are reasonably designed to ensure that an application is filed under section 104, if otherwise required by this Act, when the Federal Government seeks to conduct electronic surveillance of a person reasonably believed to be located in the United States.

"(e) Order.—

"(1) In general.—A judge approving an application under subsection (d) shall issue an order—

"(A) authorizing the acquisition of the contents of the communications as requested, or as modified by the judge;

"(B) requiring the communications service provider or custodian, or officer, employee, or agent of such service provider or custodian, who has authorized access to the information, facilities, or technical assistance necessary to accomplish the acquisition to provide such information, facilities, or technical assistance necessary to accomplish the acquisition and to produce a minimum of interference with the services that provider, custodian, officer, employee, or agent is providing the target of the acquisition;

"(C) requiring such communications service provider, custodian, officer, employee, or agent, upon the request of the applicant, to maintain under security procedures approved by the Attorney General and the Director of National Intelligence any records concerning the acquisition or the aid furnished;

"(D) directing the Federal Government to—

"(i) compensate, at the prevailing rate, a person for providing information, facilities, or assistance pursuant to such order; and

"(ii) provide a copy of the portion of the order directing the person to comply with the order to such person; and

"(E) directing the applicant to follow—

"(i) the procedures referred to in subsection (b)(2)(A) as proposed or as modified by the judge;

"(ii) the minimization procedures referred to in subsection (b)(2)(C) as proposed or as modified by the judge; and

"(iii) the guidelines referred to in subsection (b)(2)(D) as proposed or as modified by the judge.

"(2) Failure to comply.—If a person fails to comply with an order issued under paragraph (1), the Attorney General may invoke the aid of the court established under section 103(a) to compel compliance with the order. Failure to obey an order of the court may be punished by the court as contempt of court. Any process under this section may be served in any judicial district in which the person may be found.

"(3) Liability of order.—Notwithstanding any other law, no cause of action shall lie in any court against any person for providing any information, facilities, or assistance in accordance with an order issued under this subsection.

"(4) Retention of order.—The Director of National Intelligence and the court established under subsection 103(a) shall retain an order issued under this section for a period of not less than 10 years from the date on which such order is issued.

"(5) Assessment of compliance with minimization procedures.—At or before the end of the period of time for which an acquisition is approved by an order or an extension under this section, the judge may assess compliance with the minimization procedures referred to in paragraph (1)(E)(ii) and the guidelines referred to in paragraph (1)(E)(iii) by reviewing the circumstances under which information concerning United States persons was acquired, retained, or disseminated.".

SEC. 4. EMERGENCY AUTHORIZATION OF ACQUISITIONS OF COMMUNICATIONS OF NON-UNITED STATES PERSONS LOCATED OUTSIDE THE UNITED STATES

Section 105C of the Foreign Intelligence Surveillance Act of 1978 (50 U.S.C. 1801 et seq.) is amended to read as follows:

"EMERGENCY AUTHORIZATION OF ACQUISITIONS OF COMMUNICATIONS OF NON-UNITED STATES PERSONS LOCATED OUTSIDE THE UNITED STATES

"Sec. 105C. (a) Application After Emergency Authorization.—As soon as is practicable, but not more than 7 days after the Director of National Intelligence and the Attorney General authorize an acquisition under this section, an application for an order authorizing the acquisition in accordance with section 105B shall be submitted to the judge referred to in subsection (b)(2) of this section for approval of the acquisition in accordance with section 105B.

"(b) Emergency Authorization.—Notwithstanding any other provision of this Act, the Director of National Intelligence and the Attorney General may jointly authorize the emergency acquisition of foreign intelligence information for a period of not more than 45 days if—

"(1) the Director of National Intelligence and the Attorney General jointly determine that—

"(A) an emergency situation exists with respect to an authorization for an acquisition under section 105B before an order approving the acquisition under such section can with due diligence be obtained;

"(B) the targets of the acquisition of foreign intelligence information under this section are persons reasonably believed to be located outside the United States;

"(C) the targets of the acquisition are reasonably believed to be persons that are not United States persons;

"(D) there are reasonable procedures in place for determining that the acquisition of foreign intelligence information under this section will be acquired by targeting only persons that are reasonably believed to be located outside the United States and not United States persons;

"(E) the acquisition involves obtaining the foreign intelligence information from, or with the assistance of, a communications service provider or custodian, or an officer, employee, or agent of such service provider or custodian, who has authorized access to the communications to be acquired, either as they are transmitted or while they are stored, or equipment that is being or may be used to transmit or store such communications;

"(F) a significant purpose of the acquisition is to obtain foreign intelligence information (as defined in paragraph (1) or (2)(A) of section 101(e)); and

"(G) minimization procedures to be used with respect to such acquisition activity meet the definition of minimization procedures under section 101(h); and

"(2) the Director of National Intelligence and the Attorney General, or their designees, inform a judge having jurisdiction to approve an acquisition under section 105B at the time of the authorization under this section that the decision has been made to acquire foreign intelligence information.

"(c) Information, Facilities, and Technical Assistance.—Pursuant to an authorization of an acquisition under this section, the Attorney General may direct a communications service provider, custodian, or an officer, employee, or agent of such service provider or custodian, who has the lawful authority to access the information, facilities, or technical assistance necessary to accomplish such acquisition to—

"(1) furnish the Attorney General forthwith with such information, facilities, or technical assistance in a manner that will protect the secrecy of the acquisition and produce a minimum of interference with the services that provider, custodian, officer, employee, or agent is providing the target of the acquisition; and

"(2) maintain under security procedures approved by the Attorney General and the Director of National Intelligence any records concerning the acquisition or the aid furnished.".

SEC. 5. OVERSIGHT OF ACQUISITIONS OF COMMUNICATIONS OF NON-UNITED STATES PERSONS LOCATED OUTSIDE OF THE UNITED STATES

The Foreign Intelligence Surveillance Act of 1978 (50 U.S.C. 1801 et seq.) is amended by inserting after section 105C the following new section:

"OVERSIGHT OF ACQUISITIONS OF COMMUNICATIONS OF NON-UNITED STATES PERSONS LOCATED OUTSIDE OF THE UNITED STATES

"Sec. 105D. (a) Application; Procedures; Orders.—Not later than 7 days after an application is submitted under section 105B(a) or an order is issued under section 105B(e), the Director of National Intelligence and the Attorney General shall submit to the appropriate committees of Congress—

"(1) in the case of an application, a copy of the application, including the certification made under section 105B(b)(1); and

"(2) in the case of an order, a copy of the order, including the procedures and guidelines referred to in section 105B(e)(1)(E).

"(b) Quarterly Audits.—

"(1) Audit.—Not later than 120 days after the date of the enactment of this section, and every 120 days thereafter until the expiration of all orders issued under section 105B, the Inspector General of the Department of Justice shall complete an audit on the implementation of and compliance with the procedures and guidelines referred to in section 105B(e)(1)(E) and shall submit to the appropriate committees of Congress, the Attorney General, the Director of National Intelligence, and the court established under section 103(a) the results of such audit, including, for each order authorizing the acquisition of foreign intelligence under section 105B—

"(A) the number of targets of an acquisition under such order that were later determined to be located in the United States;

"(B) the number of persons located in the United States whose communications have been acquired under such order;

"(C) the number and nature of reports disseminated containing information on a United States person that was collected under such order; and

"(D) the number of applications submitted for approval of electronic surveillance under section 104 for targets whose communications were acquired under such order.

"(2) Report.—Not later than 30 days after the completion of an audit under paragraph (1), the Attorney General shall submit to the appropriate committees of Congress and the court established under section 103(a) a report containing the results of such audit.

"(c) Compliance Reports.—Not later than 60 days after the date of the enactment of this section, and every 120 days thereafter until the expiration of all orders issued under section 105B, the Director of National Intelligence and the Attorney General shall submit to the appropriate committees of Congress and the court established under section 103(a) a report concerning acquisitions under section 105B during the previous 120-day period. Each report submitted under this section shall include a description of any incidents of non-compliance with an order issued under section 105B(e), including incidents of non-compliance by—

"(1) an element of the intelligence community with minimization procedures referred to in section 105B(e)(1)(E)(i);

"(2) an element of the intelligence community with procedures referred to in section 105B(e)(1)(E)(ii);

"(3) an element of the intelligence community with guidelines referred to in section 105B(e)(1)(E)(iii); and

"(4) a person directed to provide information, facilities, or technical assistance under such order.

"(d) Report on Emergency Authority.—The Director of National Intelligence and the Attorney General shall annually submit to the appropriate committees of Congress a report containing the number of emergency authorizations of acquisitions under section 105C and a description of any incidents of non-compliance with an emergency authorization under such section.

"(e) Appropriate Committees of Congress Defined.—In this section, the term 'appropriate committees of Congress' means—

"(1) the Permanent Select Committee on Intelligence of the House of Representatives;

"(2) the Select Committee on Intelligence of the Senate; and

"(3) the Committees on the Judiciary of the House of Representatives and the Senate.".

SEC. 6. FOREIGN INTELLIGENCE SURVEILLANCE COURT EN BANC

Section 103 of the Foreign Intelligence Surveillance Act of 1978 (50 U.S.C. 1803) is amended by adding at the end the following new subsection:

"(g) In any case where the court established under subsection (a) or a judge of such court is required to review a matter under this Act, the court may, at the discretion of the court, sit en banc to review such matter and issue any orders related to such matter."

SEC. 7. AUDIT OF WARRANTLESS SURVEILLANCE PROGRAMS

(a) Audit.—Not later than 180 days after the date of the enactment of this Act, the Inspector General of the Department of Justice shall complete an audit of all programs of the Federal Government involving the acquisition of communications conducted without a court order on or after September 11, 2001, including the Terrorist Surveillance Program referred to by the President in a radio address on December 17, 2005. Such audit shall include acquiring all documents relevant to such programs, including memoranda concerning the legal authority of a program, authorizations of a program, certifications to telecommunications carriers, and court orders.

(b) Report.—

(1) In general.—Not later than 30 days after the completion of the audit under subsection (a), the Inspector General shall submit to the Permanent Select Committee on Intelligence and the Committee on the Judiciary of the House of Representatives and the Select Committee on Intelligence and the Committee on the Judiciary of the Senate a report containing the results of such audit, including all documents acquired pursuant to conducting such audit.

(2) Form.—The report under paragraph (1) shall be submitted in unclassified form, but may include a classified annex.

(c) Expedited Security Clearance.—The Director of National Intelligence shall ensure that the process for the investigation and adjudication of an application by the Inspector General or the appropriate staff of the Office of the Inspector General of the Department of Justice for a security clearance necessary for the conduct of the audit under subsection (a) is conducted as expeditiously as possible.

SEC. 8. RECORD-KEEPING SYSTEM ON ACQUISITION OF COMMUNICATIONS OF UNITED STATES PERSONS

(a) Record-Keeping System.—The Director of National Intelligence and the Attorney General shall jointly develop and maintain a record-keeping system that will keep track of—

(1) the instances where the identity of a United States person whose communications were acquired was disclosed by an element of the intelligence community (as defined in section 3(4) of the National Security Act of 1947 (50 U.S.C. 401a(4)) that collected the communications to other departments or agencies of the United States; and

(2) the departments and agencies of the Federal Government and persons to whom such identity information was disclosed.

(b) Report.—The Director of National Intelligence and the Attorney General shall annually submit to the Permanent Select Committee on Intelligence and the Committee on the Judiciary of the House of Representatives and the Select Committee on Intelligence and the Committee on the Judiciary of the Senate a report on the record-keeping system created under subsection (a), including the number of instances referred to in paragraph (1).

SEC. 9. AUTHORIZATION FOR INCREASED RESOURCES RELATING TO FOREIGN INTELLIGENCE SURVEILLANCE

There are authorized to be appropriated the Department of Justice, for the activities of the Office of the Inspector General, the Office of Intelligence Policy and Review, and other appropriate elements of the National Security Division, and the National Security Agency such sums as may be necessary to meet the personnel and information technology demands to ensure the timely and efficient processing of—

(1) applications and other submissions to the court established under section 103(a) of the Foreign Intelligence Surveillance Act of 1978 (50 U.S.C. 1803(a));

(2) the audit and reporting requirements under—

(A) section 105D of such Act; and

(B) section 7; and

(3) the record-keeping system and reporting requirements under section 8.

SEC. 10. REITERATION OF FISA AS THE EXCLUSIVE MEANS BY WHICH ELECTRONIC SURVEILLANCE MAY BE CONDUCTED FOR GATHERING FOREIGN INTELLIGENCE INFORMATION

(a) Exclusive Means.—Notwithstanding any other provision of law, the Foreign Intelligence Surveillance Act of 1978 (50 U.S.C. 1801 et seq.) shall be the exclusive means by which electronic surveillance may be conducted for the purpose of gathering foreign intelligence information.

(b) Specific Authorization Required for Exception.—Subsection (a) shall apply until specific statutory authorization for electronic surveillance, other than as an amendment to the Foreign Intelligence Surveillance Act of 1978 (50 U.S.C. 1801 et seq.), is enacted. Such specific statutory authorization shall be the only exception to subsection (a).

SEC. 11. TECHNICAL AND CONFORMING AMENDMENTS

(a) Table of Contents.—The table of contents in the first section of the Foreign Intelligence Surveillance Act of 1978 (50 U.S.C. 1801 et seq.) is amended by striking the items relating to sections 105A, 105B, and 105C and inserting the following new items:

"Sec. 105A. Clarification of electronic surveillance of non-United States persons outside the United States.

"Sec. 105B. Procedure for authorizing acquisitions of communications of non-United States persons located outside the United States.

"Sec. 105C. Emergency authorization of acquisitions of communications of non-United States persons located outside the United States.

"Sec. 105D. Oversight of acquisitions of communications of persons located outside of the United States.".

(b) Section 103(e) of FISA.—Section 103(e) of the Foreign Intelligence Surveillance Act of 1978 (50 U.S.C. 1803(e)) is amended—

(1) in paragraph (1), by striking "105B(h) or"; and

(2) in paragraph (2), by striking "105B(h) or".

(c) Repeal of Certain Provisions of the Protect America Act.—Sections 4 and 6 of the Protect America Act (Public Law 110-55) are hereby repealed.

SEC. 12. SUNSET; TRANSITION PROCEDURES

(a) Sunset of New Provisions.—

(1) In general.—Except as provided in paragraph (2), effective on December 31, 2009—

(A) sections 105A, 105B, 105C, and 105D of the Foreign Intelligence Surveillance Act of 1978 (50 U.S.C. 1801 et seq.) are hereby repealed; and

(B) the table of contents in the first section of such Act is amended by striking the items relating to sections 105A, 105B, 105C, and 105D.

(2) Acquisitions authorized prior to sunset.—Any authorization or order issued under section 105B of the Foreign Intelligence Surveillance Act of 1978, as amended by this Act, in effect on December 31, 2009, shall continue in effect until the date of the expiration of such authorization or order.

(b) Acquisitions Authorized Prior to Enactment.—

(1) Effect.—Notwithstanding the amendments made by this Act, an authorization of the acquisition of foreign intelligence information under section 105B of the Foreign Intelligence Surveillance Act of 1978 (50 U.S.C. 1801 et seq.) made before the date of the enactment of this Act shall remain in effect until the date of the expiration of such authorization or the date that is 180 days after such date of enactment, whichever is earlier.

(2) Report.—Not later than 30 days after the date of the expiration of all authorizations of acquisition of foreign intelligence information under section 105B of the Foreign Intelligence Surveillance Act of 1978 (as added by Public Law 110-55) made before the date of the enactment of this Act in accordance with paragraph (1), the Director of National Intelligence and the Attorney General shall submit to the Permanent Select Committee on Intelligence and the Committee on the Judiciary of the House of Representatives and the Select Committee on Intelligence and the Committee on the Judiciary of the Senate a report on such authorizations, including—

(A) the number of targets of an acquisition under section 105B of such Act (as in effect on the day before the date of the enactment of this Act) that were later determined to be located in the United States;

(B) the number of persons located in the United States whose communications have been acquired under such section;

(C) the number of reports disseminated containing information on a United States person that was collected under such section;

(D) the number of applications submitted for approval of electronic surveillance under section 104 of such Act based upon information collected pursuant to an acquisition authorized under section 105B of such Act (as in effect on the day before the date of the enactment of this Act); and

(E) a description of any incidents of non-compliance with an authorization under such section, including incidents of non-compliance by—

(i) an element of the intelligence community with procedures referred to in subsection (a)(1) of such section;

(ii) an element of the intelligence community with minimization procedures referred to in subsection (a)(5) of such section; and

(iii) a person directed to provide information, facilities, or technical assistance under subsection (e) of such section.

(3) Intelligence community defined.—In this subsection, the term "intelligence community" has the meaning given the term in section 3(4) of the National Security Act of 1947 (50 U.S.C. 401a(4)).

The SPEAKER pro tempore. Pursuant to House Resolution 824, the further amendment printed in House Report 110-449 is adopted.

The text of the bill, as amended, is as follows:

H.R 3773

Be it enacted by the Senate and House of Representatives of the United States of America in Congress assembled,

Strike all after the enacting clause and insert the following:

SECTION 1. SHORT TITLE; TABLE OF CONTENTS

(a) Short Title.—This Act may be cited as the "Responsible Electronic Surveillance That is Overseen, Reviewed, and Effective Act of 2007" or "RESTORE Act of 2007".

(b) Table of Contents.—The table of contents for this Act is as follows:

SEC. 2. CLARIFICATION OF ELECTRONIC SURVEILLANCE OF NON-UNITED STATES PERSONS OUTSIDE THE UNITED STATES

Section 105A of the Foreign Intelligence Surveillance Act of 1978 (50 U.S.C. 1801 et seq.) is amended to read as follows:

"CLARIFICATION OF ELECTRONIC SURVEILLANCE OF NON-UNITED STATES PERSONS OUTSIDE THE UNITED STATES

"SEC. 105A. (a) Foreign to Foreign Communications.—

"(1) In general.—Notwithstanding any other provision of this Act, a court order is not required for the acquisition of the contents of any communication between persons that are not known to be United

States persons and are reasonably believed to be located outside the United States for the purpose of collecting foreign intelligence information, without respect to whether the communication passes through the United States or the surveillance device is located within the United States.

"(2) Treatment of inadvertent interceptions.—If electronic surveillance referred to in paragraph (1) inadvertently collects a communication in which at least one party to the communication is located inside the United States or is a United States person, the contents of such communication shall be handled in accordance with minimization procedures adopted by the Attorney General that require that no contents of any communication to which a United States person is a party shall be disclosed, disseminated, or used for any purpose or retained for longer than 7 days unless a court order under section 105 is obtained or unless the Attorney General determines that the information indicates a threat of death or serious bodily harm to any person.

"(b) Communications of Non-United States Persons Outside of the United States.—Notwithstanding any other provision of this Act other than subsection (a), electronic surveillance that is directed at the acquisition of the communications of a person that is reasonably believed to be located outside the United States and not a United States person for the purpose of collecting foreign intelligence information (as defined in paragraph (1) or (2)(A) of section 101(e)) by targeting that person shall be conducted pursuant to—

"(1) an order approved in accordance with section 105 or 105B; or

"(2) an emergency authorization in accordance with section 105 or 105C.".

SEC. 3. ADDITIONAL AUTHORIZATION OF ACQUISITIONS OF COMMUNICATIONS OF NON-UNITED STATES PERSONS LOCATED OUTSIDE THE UNITED STATES WHO MAY BE COMMUNICATING WITH PERSONS INSIDE THE UNITED STATES

Section 105B of the Foreign Intelligence Surveillance Act of 1978 (50 U.S.C. 1801 et seq.) is amended to read as follows:

"ADDITIONAL AUTHORIZATION OF ACQUISITIONS OF COMMUNICATIONS OF NON-UNITED STATES PERSONS LOCATED OUTSIDE THE UNITED STATES WHO MAY BE COMMUNICATING WITH PERSONS INSIDE THE UNITED STATES

"SEC. 105B. (a) In General.—Notwithstanding any other provision of this Act, the Director of National Intelligence and the Attorney General may jointly apply to a judge of the court established under section 103(a) for an ex parte order, or the extension of an order, authorizing for a period of up to one year the acquisition of communications of persons that are reasonably believed to be located outside the United States and not United States persons for the purpose of collecting foreign intelligence information (as defined in paragraph (1) or (2)(A) of section 101(e)) by targeting those persons.

"(b) Application Inclusions.—An application under subsection (a) shall include—

"(1) a certification by the Director of National Intelligence and the Attorney General that—

"(A) the targets of the acquisition of foreign intelligence information under this section are persons reasonably believed to be located outside the United States who may be communicating with persons inside the United States;

"(B) the targets of the acquisition are reasonably believed to be persons that are not United States persons;

"(C) the acquisition involves obtaining the foreign intelligence information from, or with the assistance of, a communications service provider or custodian, or an officer, employee, or agent of such service provider or custodian, who has authorized access to the communications to be acquired, either as they are transmitted or while they are stored, or equipment that is being or may be used to transmit or store such communications; and

"(D) a significant purpose of the acquisition is to obtain foreign intelligence information (as defined in paragraph (1) or (2)(A) of section 101(e)); and

"(2) a description of—

"(A) the procedures that will be used by the Director of National Intelligence and the Attorney General during the duration of the order to determine that there is a reasonable belief that the persons that are the targets of the acquisition are located outside the United States and not United States persons;

"(B) the nature of the information sought, including the identity of any foreign power against whom the acquisition will be directed;

"(C) minimization procedures that meet the definition of minimization procedures under section 101(h) to be used with respect to such acquisition; and

"(D) (i) the guidelines that will be used to ensure that an application is filed under section 104, if otherwise required by this Act, when a significant purpose of an acquisition is to acquire the communications of a specific United States person reasonably believed to be located in the United States; and

"(ii) the criteria for determining if such a significant purpose exists, which shall require consideration of whether—

"(I) the department or agency of the Federal Government conducting the acquisition has made an inquiry to another department or agency of the Federal Government to gather information on the specific United States person;

"(II) the department or agency of the Federal Government conducting the acquisition has provided information that identifies the specific United States person to another department or agency of the Federal Government;

"(III) the department or agency of the Federal Government conducting the acquisition determines that the specific United States person has been the subject of ongoing interest or repeated investigation by a department or agency of the Federal Government; and

"(IV) the specific United States person is a natural person.

"(c) Specific Place Not Required.—An application under subsection (a) is not required to identify the specific facilities, places, premises, or property at which the acquisition of foreign intelligence information will be directed.

"(d) Review of Application; Appeals.—

"(1) Review of application.—Not later than 15 days after a judge receives an application under subsection (a), the judge shall review such application and shall approve the application if the judge finds that—

"(A) the proposed procedures referred to in subsection (b)(2)(A) are reasonably designed to determine whether the targets of the acquisition are located outside the United States and not United States persons;

"(B) the proposed minimization procedures referred to in subsection (b)(2)(C) meet the definition of minimization procedures under section 101(h); and

"(C)(i) the guidelines referred to in subsection (b)(2)(D) are reasonably designed to ensure that an application is filed under section 104, if otherwise required by this Act, when a significant purpose of an acquisition is to acquire the communications of a specific United States person reasonably believed to be located in the United States; and

"(ii) the criteria for determining if such a significant purpose exists require consideration of whether—

"(I) the department or agency of the Federal Government conducting the acquisition has made an inquiry to another department or agency of the Federal Government to gather information on the specific United States person;

"(II) the department or agency of the Federal Government conducting the acquisition has provided information that identifies the specific United States person to another department or agency of the Federal Government;

"(III) the department or agency of the Federal Government conducting the acquisition determines that the specific United States person has been the subject of ongoing interest or repeated investigation by a department or agency of the Federal Government; and

"(IV) the specific United States person is a natural person.

"(2) Temporary order; appeals.—

"(A) Temporary order.—A judge denying an application under paragraph (1) may, at the application of the United States, issue a temporary order to authorize an acquisition under section 105B in accordance with the application under subsection (a) during the pendency of any appeal of the denial of such application.

"(B) Appeals.—The United States may appeal the denial of an application for an order under paragraph (1) or a temporary order under subparagraph (A) in accordance with section 103.

"(e) Order.—

"(1) In general.—A judge approving an application under subsection (d) shall issue an order—

"(A) authorizing the acquisition of the contents of the communications as requested, or as modified by the judge;

"(B) requiring the communications service provider or custodian, or officer, employee, or agent of such service provider or custodian, who has authorized access to the information, facilities, or technical assistance necessary to accomplish the acquisition to provide such information, facilities, or technical assistance necessary to accomplish the acquisition and to produce a minimum of interference with the services that provider, custodian, officer, employee, or agent is providing the target of the acquisition;

"(C) requiring such communications service provider, custodian, officer, employee, or agent, upon the request of the applicant, to maintain under security procedures approved by the Attorney General and the Director of National Intelligence any records concerning the acquisition or the aid furnished;

"(D) directing the Federal Government to—

"(i) compensate, at the prevailing rate, a person for providing information, facilities, or assistance pursuant to such order;

"(ii) provide a copy of the portion of the order directing the person to comply with the order to such person; and

"(iii) provide a certification stating that the acquisition is authorized under this section and that all requirements of this section have been met; and

"(E) directing the applicant to follow—

"(i) the procedures referred to in subsection (b)(2)(A) as proposed or as modified by the judge;

"(ii) the minimization procedures referred to in subsection (b)(2)(C) as proposed or as modified by the judge; and

"(iii) the guidelines referred to in subsection (b)(2)(D) as proposed or as modified by the judge.

"(2) Failure to comply.—If a person fails to comply with an order issued under paragraph (1), the Attorney General may invoke the aid of the court established under section 103(a) to compel compliance with the order. Failure to obey an order of the court may be punished by the court as contempt of court. Any process under this section may be served in any judicial district in which the person may be found.

"(3) Liability of order.—Notwithstanding any other law, no cause of action shall lie in any court against any person for providing any information, facilities, or assistance in accordance with an order issued under this subsection.

"(4) Retention of order.—The Director of National Intelligence and the court established under subsection 103(a) shall retain an order issued under this section for a period of not less than 10 years from the date on which such order is issued.

"(5) Assessment of compliance with court order.—At or before the end of the period of time for which an acquisition is approved by an order or an extension under this section, the court established under section 103(a) shall, not less frequently than once each quarter, assess compliance with the procedures and guidelines referred to in paragraph (1)(E) and review the circumstances under which information concerning United States persons was acquired, retained, or disseminated.".

SEC. 4. EMERGENCY AUTHORIZATION OF ACQUISITIONS OF COMMUNICATIONS OF NON-UNITED STATES PERSONS LOCATED OUTSIDE THE UNITED STATES WHO MAY BE COMMUNICATING WITH PERSONS INSIDE THE UNITED STATES

Section 105C of the Foreign Intelligence Surveillance Act of 1978 (50 U.S.C. 1801 et seq.) is amended to read as follows:

"EMERGENCY AUTHORIZATION OF ACQUISITIONS OF COMMUNICATIONS OF NON-UNITED STATES PERSONS LOCATED OUTSIDE THE UNITED STATES WHO MAY BE COMMUNICATING WITH PERSONS INSIDE THE UNITED STATES

"SEC. 105C. (a) Application After Emergency Authorization.—As soon as is practicable, but not more than 7 days after the Director of National Intelligence and the Attorney General authorize an acquisition under this section, an application for an order authorizing the acquisition in accordance with section 105B shall be submitted to the judge referred to in subsection (b)(2) of this section for approval of the acquisition in accordance with section 105B.

"(b) Emergency Authorization.—Notwithstanding any other provision of this Act, the Director of National Intelligence and the Attorney General may jointly authorize the emergency acquisition of foreign intelligence information (as defined in paragraph (1) or (2)(A) of section 101(e)) for a period of not more than 45 days if—

"(1) the Director of National Intelligence and the Attorney General jointly determine that—

"(A) an emergency situation exists with respect to an authorization for an acquisition under section 105B before an order approving the acquisition under such section can with due diligence be obtained;

"(B) the targets of the acquisition of foreign intelligence information under this section are persons reasonably believed to be located outside the United States;

"(C) the targets of the acquisition are reasonably believed to be persons that are not United States persons;

"(D) there are procedures in place that will be used by the Director of National Intelligence and the Attorney General during the duration of the authorization to determine if there is a reasonable belief that the persons that are the targets of the acquisition are located outside the United States and not United States persons;

"(E) the acquisition involves obtaining the foreign intelligence information from, or with the assistance of, a communications service provider or custodian, or an officer, employee, or agent of such service provider or custodian, who has authorized access to the communications to be acquired, either as they are transmitted or while they are stored, or equipment that is being or may be used to transmit or store such communications;

"(F) a significant purpose of the acquisition is to obtain foreign intelligence information (as defined in paragraph (1) or (2)(A) of section 101(e));

"(G) minimization procedures to be used with respect to such acquisition activity meet the definition of minimization procedures under section 101(h); and

"(H)(i) there are guidelines that will be used to ensure that an application is filed under secion 104, if otherwise required by this Act, when a significant purpose of an acquisition is to acquire the communications of a specific United States person reasonably believed to be located in the United States; and "(ii) the criteria for determining if such a significant purpose exists require consideration of whether—

"(I) the department or agency of the Federal Government conducting the acquisition has made an inquiry to another department or agency of the Federal Government to gather information on the specific United States person;

"(II) the department or agency of the Federal Government conducting the acquisition has provided information that identifies the specific United States person to another department or agency of the Federal Government;

"(III) the department or agency of the Federal Government conducting the acquisition determines that the United States person has been the subject of ongoing interest or repeated investigation by a department or agency of the Federal Government; and

"(IV) the specific United States person is a natural person.

"(2) the Director of National Intelligence and the Attorney General, or their designees, inform a judge having jurisdiction to approve an acquisition under section 105B at the time of the authorization under this section that the decision has been made to acquire foreign intelligence information.

"(c) Information, Facilities, and Technical Assistance.—

"(1) Directive.—Pursuant to an authorization of an acquisition under this section, the Attorney General may direct a communications service provider, custodian, or an officer, employee, or agent of such service provider or custodian, who has the lawful authority to access the information, facilities, or technical assistance necessary to accomplish such acquisition to—

"(A) furnish the Attorney General forthwith with such information, facilities, or technical assistance in a manner that will protect the secrecy of the acquisition and produce a minimum of interference with the services that provider, custodian, officer, employee, or agent is providing the target of the acquisition; and

"(B) maintain under security procedures approved by the Attorney General and the Director of National Intelligence any records concerning the acquisition or the aid furnished.

"(2) Parameters; certifications.—The Attorney General shall provide to any person directed to provide assistance under paragraph (1) with—

"(A) a document setting forth the parameters of the directive;

"(B) a certification stating that—

"(i) the emergency authorization has been issued pursuant to this section;

"(ii) all requirements of this section have been met;

"(iii) a judge has been informed of the emergency authorization in accordance with subsection (b)(2); and

"(iv) an application will be submitted in accordance with subsection (a); and

"(C) a certification that the recipient of the directive shall be compensated, at the prevailing rate, for providing information, facilities, or assistance pursuant to such directive.".

SEC. 5. OVERSIGHT OF ACQUISITIONS OF COMMUNICATIONS OF NON-UNITED STATES PERSONS LOCATED OUTSIDE OF THE UNITED STATES WHO MAY BE COMMUNICATING WITH PERSONS INSIDE THE UNITED STATES

The Foreign Intelligence Surveillance Act of 1978 (50 U.S.C. 1801 et seq.) is amended by inserting after section 105C the following new section:

"OVERSIGHT OF ACQUISITIONS OF COMMUNICATIONS OF NON-UNITED STATES PERSONS LOCATED OUTSIDE OF THE UNITED STATES WHO MAY BE COMMUNICATING WITH PERSONS INSIDE THE UNITED STATES

"SEC. 105D. (a) Application; Procedures; Orders.—Not later than 7 days after an application is submitted under section 105B(a) or an order is issued under section 105B(e), the Director of National Intelligence and the Attorney General shall submit to the appropriate committees of Congress—

"(1) in the case of an application—

"(A) a copy of the application, including the certification made under section 105B(b)(1); and

"(B) a description of the primary purpose of the acquisition for which the application is submitted; and

"(2) in the case of an order, a copy of the order, including the procedures and guidelines referred to in section 105B(e)(1)(E).

"(b) Regular Audits.—

"(1) Audit.—Not later than 120 days after the date of the enactment of this section, and every 120 days thereafter until the expiration of all orders issued under section 105B, the Inspector General of the Department of Justice shall complete an audit on the implementation of and compliance with the procedures and guidelines referred to in section 105B(e)(1)(E) and shall submit to the appropriate committees of Congress, the Attorney General, the Director of National Intelligence, and the court established under section 103(a) the results of such audit, including, for each order authorizing the acquisition of foreign intelligence under section 105B—

"(A) the number of targets of an acquisition under such order that were later determined to be located in the United States;

"(B) the number of persons located in the United States whose communications have been acquired under such order;

"(C) the number and nature of reports disseminated containing information on a United States person that was collected under such order; and

"(D) the number of applications submitted for approval of electronic surveillance under section 104 for targets whose communications were acquired under such order.

"(2) Report.—Not later than 30 days after the completion of an audit under paragraph (1), the Attorney General shall submit to the appropriate committees of Congress and the court established under section 103(a) a report containing the results of such audit.

"(c) Compliance Reports.—Not later than 60 days after the date of the enactment of this section, and every 120 days thereafter until the expiration of all orders issued under section 105B, the Director of National Intelligence and the Attorney General shall submit to the appropriate committees of Congress and the court established under section 103(a) a report concerning acquisitions under section 105B during the previous 120-day period. Each report submitted under this section shall include a description of any incidents of non-compliance with an order issued under section 105B(e), including incidents of non-compliance by—

"(1) an element of the intelligence community with procedures referred to in section 105B(e)(1)(E)(i);

"(2) an element of the intelligence community with procedures referred to in section 105B(e)(1)(E)(ii);

"(3) an element of the intelligence community with guidelines referred to in section 105B(e)(1)(E)(iii); and

"(4) a person directed to provide information, facilities, or technical assistance under such order.

"(d) Report on Emergency Authority.—The Director of National Intelligence and the Attorney General shall annually submit to the appropriate committees of Congress a report containing the number of emergency authorizations of acquisitions under section 105C and a description of any incidents of non-compliance with an emergency authorization under such section.

"(e) Appropriate Committees of Congress Defined.—In this section, the term 'appropriate committees of Congress' means—

"(1) the Permanent Select Committee on Intelligence of the House of Representatives;

"(2) the Select Committee on Intelligence of the Senate; and

"(3) the Committees on the Judiciary of the House of Representatives and the Senate.".

SEC. 6. DISSEMINATION OF COMMUNICATIONS OF NON-UNITED STATES PERSONS LOCATED OUTSIDE OF THE UNITED STATES WHO MAY BE COMMUNICATING WITH PERSONS INSIDE THE UNITED STATES

The Foreign Intelligence Surveillance Act of 1978 (50 U.S.C. 1801 et seq.) is amended by inserting after section 105D (as added by section 5) the following new section:

> **"DISSEMINATION OF COMMUNICATIONS OF NON-UNITED STATES PERSONS LOCATED OUTSIDE OF THE UNITED STATES WHO MAY BE COMMUNICATING WITH PERSONS INSIDE THE UNITED STATES**
>
> "SEC. 105E. The contents of communications collected under section 105B or section 105C, and intelligence reports based on such contents, shall not be disclosed or disseminated with information that identifies a United States person unless an officer or employee of the Federal Government whose rate of basic pay is not less than the minimum rate payable under section 5382 of title 5, United States Code (relating to rates of pay for the Senior Executive Service) determines that the identity of the United States person is necessary to—
>
> "(1) understand the foreign intelligence collected under section 105B or 105C or assess the importance of such intelligence; and
>
> "(2) protect the national security of the United States, the citizens, employees, or officers of the United States, or the members of the United States Armed Forces.".

SEC. 7. FOREIGN INTELLIGENCE SURVEILLANCE COURT EN BANC

Section 103 of the Foreign Intelligence Surveillance Act of 1978 (50 U.S.C. 1803) is amended by adding at the end the following new subsection:

> "(g) In any case where the court established under subsection (a) or a judge of such court is required to review a matter under this Act, the court may, at the discretion of the court, sit en banc to review such matter and issue any orders related to such matter.".

SEC. 8. FOREIGN INTELLIGENCE SURVEILLANCE COURT MATTERS

(a) Authority for Additional Judges.—Section 103(a) of the Foreign Intelligence Surveillance Act of 1978 (50 U.S.C. 1803(a)) is amended—

(1) by inserting "(1)" after "(a)";

(2) in paragraph (1) (as so designated)—

(A) by striking "11" and inserting "15"; and

(B) by inserting "at least" before "seven of the United States judicial circuits"; and

(3) by designating the second sentence as paragraph (3) and indenting such paragraph, as so designated two ems from the left margin.

(b) Consideration of Emergency Applications.—Such section is further amended by inserting after paragraph (1) (as designated by subsection (a)(1)) the following new paragraph:

"(2) A judge of the court shall make a determination to approve, deny, or modify an application submitted pursuant to section 105(f), section 304(e), or section 403 not later than 24 hours after the receipt of such application by the court.".

SEC. 9. REITERATION OF FISA AS THE EXCLUSIVE MEANS BY WHICH ELECTRONIC SURVEILLANCE MAY BE CONDUCTED FOR GATHERING FOREIGN INTELLIGENCE INFORMATION

(a) Exclusive Means.—Notwithstanding any other provision of law, the Foreign Intelligence Surveillance Act of 1978 (50 U.S.C. 1801 et seq.) shall be the exclusive means by which electronic surveillance may be conducted for the purpose of gathering foreign intelligence information.

(b) Specific Authorization Required for Exception.—Subsection (a) shall apply until specific statutory authorization for electronic surveillance, other than as an amendment to the Foreign Intelligence Surveillance Act of 1978 (50 U.S.C. 1801 et seq.), is enacted. Such specific statutory authorization shall be the only exception to subsection (a).

SEC. 10. ENHANCEMENT OF ELECTRONIC SURVEILLANCE AUTHORITY IN WARTIME AND OTHER COLLECTION

Sections 111, 309, and 404 of the Foreign Intelligence Surveillance Act of 1978 (50 U.S.C. 1811, 1829, and 1844) are amended by striking "Congress" and inserting "Congress or an authorization for the use of military force described in section 2(c)(2) of the War Powers Resolution (50 U.S.C. 1541(c)(2)) if such authorization contains a specific authorization for foreign intelligence collection under this section, or if the Congress is unable to convene because of an attack upon the United States.".

SEC. 11. AUDIT OF WARRANTLESS SURVEILLANCE PROGRAMS

(a) Audit.—Not later than 180 days after the date of the enactment of this Act, the Inspector General of the Department of Justice shall complete an audit of all programs of the Federal Government involving the acquisition of communications conducted without a court order on or after September 11, 2001, including the Terrorist Surveillance Program referred to by the President in a radio address on December 17, 2005. Such audit shall include acquiring all documents relevant to such programs, including memoranda concerning the legal authority of a program, authorizations of a program, certifications to telecommunications carriers, and court orders.

(b) Report.—

(1) In general.—Not later than 30 days after the completion of the audit under subsection (a), the Inspector General shall submit to the Permanent Select Committee on Intelligence and the Committee on the Judiciary of the House of Representatives and the Select Committee on Intelligence and the Committee on the Judiciary of the Senate a report containing the results of such audit, including all documents acquired pursuant to conducting such audit.

(2) Form.—The report under paragraph (1) shall be submitted in unclassified form, but may include a classified annex.

(c) Expedited Security Clearance.—The Director of National Intelligence shall ensure that the process for the investigation and adjudication of an application by the Inspector General or the appropriate staff of the Office of the Inspector General of the Department of Justice for a security clearance necessary for the conduct of the audit under subsection (a) is conducted as expeditiously as possible.

SEC. 12. RECORD-KEEPING SYSTEM ON ACQUISITION OF COMMUNICATIONS OF UNITED STATES PERSONS

(a) Record-Keeping System.—The Director of National Intelligence and the Attorney General shall jointly develop and maintain a record-keeping system that will keep track of—

(1) the instances where the identity of a United States person whose communications were acquired was disclosed by an element of the intelligence community (as defined in section 3(4) of the National Security Act of 1947 (50 U.S.C. 401a(4)) that collected the communications to other departments or agencies of the United States; and

(2) the departments and agencies of the Federal Government and persons to whom such identity information was disclosed.

(b) Report.—The Director of National Intelligence and the Attorney General shall annually submit to the Permanent Select Committee on Intelligence and the Committee on the Judiciary of the House of Representatives and the Select Committee on Intelligence and the Committee on the Judiciary of the Senate a report on the record-keeping system created under subsection (a), including the number of instances referred to in paragraph (1).

SEC. 13. AUTHORIZATION FOR INCREASED RESOURCES RELATING TO FOREIGN INTELLIGENCE SURVEILLANCE

(a) In General.—There are authorized to be appropriated to the Department of Justice, for the activities of the Office of the Inspector General and the appropriate elements of the National Security Division, and to the National Security Agency such sums as may be necessary to meet the personnel and information technology demands to ensure the timely and efficient processing of—

(1) applications and other submissions to the court established under section 103(a) of the Foreign Intelligence Surveillance Act of 1978 (50 U.S.C. 1803(a));

(2) the audit and reporting requirements under—

(A) section 105D of such Act; and

(B) section 10; and

(3) the record-keeping system and reporting requirements under section 8.

(b) Additional Personnel for Preparation and Consideration of Applications for Orders Approving Electronic Surveillance and Physical Search.—

(1) National security division of the department of justice.—

(A) Additional personnel.—The National Security Division of the Department of Justice is hereby authorized such additional personnel as may be necessary to carry out the prompt and timely preparation, modification, and review of applications under Foreign Intelligence Surveillance Act of 1978 for orders under that Act for foreign intelligence purposes.

(B) Assignment.—The Attorney General shall assign personnel authorized by paragraph (1) to and among appropriate offices of the intelligence community (as defined in section 3(4) of the National Security Act of 1947 (50 U.S.C. 401a(4))) in order that such personnel may directly assist personnel of the Intelligence Community in preparing applications described in that paragraph and conduct prompt and effective oversight of the activities of such agencies under Foreign Intelligence Surveillance Court orders.

(2) Director of national intelligence.—

(A) Additional legal and other personnel.—The Director of National Intelligence is hereby authorized such additional legal and other personnel as may be necessary to carry out the prompt and timely preparation of applications under the Foreign Intelligence Surveillance Act of 1978 for orders under that

Act approving electronic surveillance for foreign intelligence purposes.

(B) Assignment.—The Director of National Intelligence shall assign personnel authorized by paragraph (1) to and among the intelligence community (as defined in section 3(4) of the National Security Act of 1947 (50 U.S.C. 401a(4))), including the field offices of the Federal Bureau of Investigation, in order that such personnel may directly assist personnel of the intelligence community in preparing applications described in that paragraph.

(3) Additional legal and other personnel for foreign intelligence surveillance court.—There is hereby authorized for the court established under section 103(a) of the Foreign Intelligence Surveillance Act of 1978 (50 U.S.C. 1803(a)) such additional staff personnel as may be necessary to facilitate the prompt and timely consideration by that court of applications under such Act for orders under such Act approving electronic surveillance for foreign intelligence purposes. Personnel authorized by this paragraph shall perform such duties relating to the consideration of such applications as that court shall direct.

(4) Supplement not supplant.—The personnel authorized by this section are in addition to any other personnel authorized by law.

SEC. 14. DOCUMENT MANAGEMENT SYSTEM FOR APPLICATIONS FOR ORDERS APPROVING ELECTRONIC SURVEILLANCE

(a) System Required.—The Attorney General shall, in consultation with the Director of National Intelligence and the Foreign Intelligence Surveillance Court, develop and implement a secure, classified document management system that permits the prompt preparation, modification, and review by appropriate personnel of the Department of Justice, the Federal Bureau of Investigation, the National Security Agency, and other applicable elements of the United States Government of applications under the Foreign Intelligence Surveillance Act of 1978 (50 U.S.C. 1804) before their submission to the Foreign Intelligence Surveillance Court.

(b) Scope of System.—The document management system required by subsection (a) shall—

(1) permit and facilitate the prompt submittal of applications to the Foreign Intelligence Surveillance Court under the Foreign Intelligence Surveillance Act of 1978; and

(2) permit and facilitate the prompt transmittal of rulings of the Foreign Intelligence Surveillance Court to personnel submitting applications described in paragraph (1), and provide for the secure elec-

tronic storage and retrieval of all such applications and related matters with the court and for their secure transmission to the National Archives and Records Administration.

SEC. 15. TRAINING OF INTELLIGENCE COMMUNITY PERSONNEL IN FOREIGN INTELLIGENCE COLLECTION MATTERS

The Director of National Intelligence shall, in consultation with the Attorney General—

(1) develop regulations to establish procedures for conducting and seeking approval of electronic surveillance, physical search, and the installation and use of pen registers and trap and trace devices on an emergency basis, and for preparing and properly submitting and receiving applications and orders under the Foreign Intelligence Surveillance Act of 1978; and

(2) prescribe related training on the Foreign Intelligence Surveillance Act of 1978 and related legal matters for the personnel of the applicable agencies of the intelligence community (as defined in section 3(4) of the National Security Act of 1947 (50 U.S.C. 401a(4))).

SEC. 16. INFORMATION FOR CONGRESS ON THE TERRORIST SURVEILLANCE PROGRAM AND SIMILAR PROGRAMS

As soon as practicable after the date of the enactment of this Act, but not later than seven days after such date, the President shall fully inform each member of the Permanent Select Committee on Intelligence of the House of Representatives and the Select Committee on Intelligence of the Senate on the following:

(1) The Terrorist Surveillance Program of the National Security Agency.

(2) Any program in existence from September 11, 2001, until the effective date of this Act that involves, whether in part or in whole, the electronic surveillance of United States persons in the United States for foreign intelligence or other purposes, and which is conducted by any department, agency, or other element of the United States Government, or by any entity at the direction of a department, agency, or other element of the United States Government, without fully complying with the procedures set forth in the Foreign Intelligence Surveillance Act of 1978 (50 U.S.C. 1801 et seq.) or chapter 119, 121, or 206 of title 18, United States Code.

SEC. 17. TECHNICAL AND CONFORMING AMENDMENTS

(a) Table of Contents.—The table of contents in the first section of the Foreign Intelligence Surveillance Act of 1978 (50 U.S.C. 1801 et seq.) is amended by striking the items relating to sections 105A, 105B, and 105C and inserting the following new items:

"SEC. 105A. Clarification of electronic surveillance of non-United States persons outside the United States.

"SEC. 105B. Additional authorization of acquisitions of communications of non-United States persons located outside the United States who may be communicating with persons inside the United States.

"SEC. 105C. Emergency authorization of acquisitions of communications of non-United States persons located outside the United States who may be communicating with persons inside the United States.

"SEC. 105D. Oversight of acquisitions of communications of non-United States persons located outside of the United States who may be communicating with persons inside the United States.".

(b) Section 103(e) of FISA.—Section 103(e) of the Foreign Intelligence Surveillance Act of 1978 (50 U.S.C. 1803(e)) is amended—

(1) in paragraph (1), by striking "105B(h) or"; and

(2) in paragraph (2), by striking "105B(h) or".

(c) Repeal of Certain Provisions of the Protect America Act of 2007.—Sections 4 and 6 of the Protect America Act (Public Law 110-55) are hereby repealed.

SEC. 18. SUNSET; TRANSITION PROCEDURES

(a) Sunset of New Provisions.—

(1) In general.—Except as provided in paragraph (2), effective on December 31, 2009—

(A) sections 105A, 105B, 105C, and 105D of the Foreign Intelligence Surveillance Act of 1978 (50 U.S.C. 1801 et seq.) are hereby repealed; and

(B) the table of contents in the first section of such Act is amended by striking the items relating to sections 105A, 105B, 105C, and 105D.

(2) Acquisitions authorized prior to sunset.—Any authorization or order issued under section 105B of the Foreign Intelligence Surveillance Act of 1978, as amended by this Act, in effect on December 31, 2009, shall continue in effect until the date of the expiration of such authorization or order.

(b) Acquisitions Authorized Prior to Enactment.—

(1) Effect.—Notwithstanding the amendments made by this Act, an authorization of the acquisition of foreign intelligence information under section 105B of the Foreign Intelligence Surveillance Act of

1978 (50 U.S.C. 1801 et seq.) made before the date of the enactment of this Act shall remain in effect until the date of the expiration of such authorization or the date that is 180 days after such date of enactment, whichever is earlier.

(2) Report.—Not later than 30 days after the date of the expiration of all authorizations of acquisition of foreign intelligence information under section 105B of the Foreign Intelligence Surveillance Act of 1978 (as added by Public Law 110-55) made before the date of the enactment of this Act in accordance with paragraph (1), the Director of National Intelligence and the Attorney General shall submit to the Permanent Select Committee on Intelligence and the Committee on the Judiciary of the House of Representatives and the Select Committee on Intelligence and the Committee on the Judiciary of the Senate a report on such authorizations, including—

(A) the number of targets of an acquisition under section 105B of such Act (as in effect on the day before the date of the enactment of this Act) that were later determined to be located in the United States;

(B) the number of persons located in the United States whose communications have been acquired under such section;

(C) the number of reports disseminated containing information on a United States person that was collected under such section;

(D) the number of applications submitted for approval of electronic surveillance under section 104 of such Act based upon information collected pursuant to an acquisition authorized under section 105B of such Act (as in effect on the day before the date of the enactment of this Act); and

(E) a description of any incidents of non-compliance with an authorization under such section, including incidents of non-compliance by—

(i) an element of the intelligence community with procedures referred to in subsection (a)(1) of such section;

(ii) an element of the intelligence community with minimization procedures referred to in subsection (a)(5) of such section; and

(iii) a person directed to provide information, facilities, or technical assistance under subsection (e) of such section.

(3) Intelligence community defined.—In this subsection, the term "intelligence community" has the meaning given the term in section 3(4) of the National Security Act of 1947 (50 U.S.C. 401a(4)).

SEC. 19. CERTIFICATION TO COMMUNICATIONS SERVICE PROVIDERS THAT ACQUISITIONS ARE AUTHORIZED UNDER FISA

(a) Authorization Under Section 102.—Section 102(a) of the Foreign Intelligence Surveillance Act of 1978 (50 U.S.C. 1802(a)) is amended by striking "furnishing such aid" and inserting "furnishing such aid and shall provide such carrier with a certification stating that the electronic surveillance is authorized under this section and that all requirements of this section have been met".

(b) Authorization Under Section 105.—Section 105(c)(2) of such Act (50 U.S.C. 1805(c)(2)) is amended—

(1) in subparagraph (C), by striking "; and" and inserting ";";

(2) in subparagraph (D), by striking "aid." and inserting "aid; and"; and

(3) by adding at the end the following new subparagraph:

> "(E) that the applicant provide such carrier, landlord, custodian, or other person with a certification stating that the electronic surveillance is authorized under this section and that all requirements of this section have been met.".

SEC. 20. STATUTE OF LIMITATIONS

(a) In General.—Section 109 of the Foreign Intelligence Surveillance Act of 1978 (50 U.S.C. 1809) is amended by adding at the end the following new subsection:

(e) Statute of Limitations.—No person shall be prosecuted, tried, or punished for any offense under this section unless the indictment is found or the information is instituted not later than 10 years after the commission of the offense.".

(b) Application.—The amendment made by subsection (a) shall apply to any offense committed before the date of the enactment of this Act if the statute of limitations applicable to that offense has not run as of such date.

SEC. 21. NO RIGHTS UNDER THE RESTORE ACT FOR UNDOCUMENTED ALIENS

This Act and the amendments made by this Act shall not be construed to prohibit surveillance of, or grant any rights to, an alien not permitted to be in or remain in the United States.

SEC. 22. SURVEILLANCE TO PROTECT THE UNITED STATES

This Act and the amendments made by this Act shall not be construed to prohibit the intelligence community (as defined in section 3(4) of the

National Security Act of 1947 (50 U.S.C. 401a(4))) from conducting lawful surveillance that is necessary to—

(1) prevent Osama Bin Laden, al Qaeda, or any other terrorist or terrorist organization from attacking the United States, any United States person, or any ally of the United States;

(2) ensure the safety and security of members of the United States Armed Forces or any other officer or employee of the Federal Government involved in protecting the national security of the United States; or

(3) protect the United States, any United States person, or any ally of the United States from threats posed by weapons of mass destruction or other threats to national security.

The SPEAKER pro tempore. Time for debate pursuant to House Resolution 746 is considered expired.

Pursuant to House Resolution 824, debate shall not exceed 1 hour, with 30 minutes equally divided and controlled by the chairman and ranking minority member of the Committee on the Judiciary and 30 minutes equally divided and controlled by the chairman and ranking minority member of the Permanent Select Committee on Intelligence.

The gentleman from Michigan (Mr. Conyers) and the gentleman from Texas (Mr. Smith) each will control 15 minutes and the gentleman from Texas (Mr. Reyes) and the gentleman from Michigan (Mr. Hoekstra) each will control 15 minutes.

The Chair recognizes the gentleman from Michigan (Mr. Conyers).

General Leave

Mr. CONYERS. Mr. Speaker, I ask unanimous consent that all Members may have 5 legislative days in which to revise and extend their remarks and include extraneous material on H.R. 3773.

The SPEAKER pro tempore. Is there objection to the request of the gentleman from Michigan?

There was no objection.

Mr. CONYERS. Mr. Speaker, I yield myself as much time as I may consume.

Members of the House, the RESTORE Act dealing with FISA addresses the needs of the intelligence community for flexibility in dealing with modern communications networks.

It received the most careful scrutiny and consideration by this Committee on the Judiciary, as well as by the Intelligence Committee, chaired by

Chairman Reyes, to ensure that it meets every concern our intelligence agencies have raised, every single one of them, and does so consistent with the rules of law, our Constitution, and our values.

Let's begin this discussion this evening by clearing up a few things that the bill will not do. The RESTORE Act will never require our intelligence agencies to stop listening to the bad guys. Never. Special emergency provisions allow us to listen first and get the warrant after the fact, if it's needed. No one will ever have to stop listening to a terrorist plotting an attack. I hope I don't hear that raised on the floor this evening.

The RESTORE Act will not make our intelligence agencies have to get thousands of warrants for terrorists outside the country. It will not do that. Instead, a basket authorization will permit surveillance of an entire foreign terrorist organization. This is the most effective way to target Osama bin Laden, al Qaeda, and other threats to our country and our citizens.

The RESTORE Act does not give the government free rein to listen to Americans. As has always been the case under FISA, this bill requires that the government get a warrant to target an American; any American. We have also a manager's amendment, which continues to promote the goals of intelligence flexibility with appropriate oversight, while safeguarding our security and our liberty. It makes clear that the protections of the act will not inhibit gathering intelligence against present dangers, such as Osama bin Laden, or threats to our troops in the field.

It does provide guidelines to make it easier to determine when the significant purpose of the surveillance act is to acquire information on a United States person and a FISA warrant is needed. It provides important safeguards on dissemination of information about individual Americans when it's acquired under the RESTORE Act's more flexible structure. Specifically, an SES-level manager will review such dissemination on a particularized basis.

Importantly, the RESTORE Act has no retroactive immunity for telecommunications carriers who may have assisted the government in conducting unlawful surveillance on Americans. I am sorry to report to you that the other body has a measure that does give that retroactive immunity. The RESTORE Act now on the floor has no retroactive immunity for telecommunications carriers who may have assisted the government in unlawful surveillance on Americans.

Until we receive the information, the data, the letters that we have requested to know what they have done, information we have been waiting for more than 10 months for, we can't even begin to responsibly consider such a request. So as of now, it's out. No retroactive immunity.

The legislation that we have before us now is a much-needed start to restoring our system of checks and balances, preserving our liberty, and ensuring that our government has the tools they legitimately need to combat terrorism. We got pressed up against the wall in August. It's not going to happen again. There's a 6-month run on the present measure before us. Before we get pushed up against the holidays, we are saying, Let's do it now.

We have had a tremendous working relationship with the chairman of the Intelligence Committee, Silvestre Reyes, and his staff and my staff. Majority and minority have been working closely together to bring to you a commonsense and balanced piece of legislation that does what we set out to do, and that is to preserve our liberties and make sure we have effective security. We want our intelligence agencies strong, but we want to bring the FISA Court back into the picture, and we do in the measure before us.

Six years ago, the administration unilaterally chose to engage in warrantless surveillance of American citizens without court review. That decision has—to be charitable—created a legal and political quagmire. Officials resigned, the program was riddled with errors, it was shut down for several weeks, officials rushed to the hospital to ask a sick man to reauthorize it over his deputy's objections, and vital prosecutorial resources were diverted. Most importantly, our own citizens questioned wheher their own government was operating within the confines of the law.

Two months ago, when that scheme appeared to be breaking down, the administration forced Congress to accept an equally flawed statute. This new law gutted the power of the FISA court. It granted the administration broad new powers to engage in warrantless searches within the U.S., including physical searches of our homes, computers, offices and medical records. The law contained no meaningful oversight whatsoever.

The legislation before us today seeks to once again strike the appropriate balance between needed government authority and our precious rights and liberties. It tells the government they need no warrant when foreign agents communicate with other foreigners. It reiterates that warrants are needed when Americans are being targeted. The bill also allows the interception of communications of foreign targets who may communicate with U.S. persons. However, it insists that procedures be in place—approved by the FISA court—to insure that no American is being targeted, and that his or her privacy is protected.

The bill also provides for several critical safeguards. We include periodic audits by the Inspector General, we narrow the scope of the authority to protect against threats to our national security, and we protect the privacy of Americans traveling abroad. We also sunset the legislation in December 2009.

The RESTORE Act, which has received careful consideration by the Judiciary Committee and by the Intelligence Committee, addresses the needs of the intelligence community for flexibility and the ability to deal with modern communications networks.

It meets every concern that our intelligence agencies have raised and does so consistent with the rule of law, our Constitution, and our values.

Let me be clear on a few things this bill will NOT do:

The RESTORE Act will never require our intelligence agencies to stop listening to the bad guys. Never. There are emergency provisions and the ability to get a warrant after the fact. No one will ever have to stop listening to a terrorist plotting an attack.

It will not make our intelligence agencies get thousands of warrants for terrorists outside of the country. Instead, they can get a basket authorization to surveil the entire foreign terrorist organization. This is the most effective way to target Osama bin Laden, al Qaeda, and other threats.

The RESTORE Act does not give the government free rein to listen in to Americans. As has always been the case under FISA, this bill requires the government to get a warrant if it wants to target an American.

The Managers' Amendment also reflects the RESTORE Act's goals of intelligence flexibility and oversight, while ensuring both safety and civil liberties. It makes it clear that the protections of the Act will not inhibit gathering intelligence against present dangers, such as Osama bin Laden or threats to our troops in the field. It provides guidelines to flesh out what should be considered when determining whether a significant purpose of collection is to acquire information about a U.S. person, such that a FISA warrant would be required.

The Manager's Amendment also provides important safeguards on dissemination of information about individual Americans when it is acquired under the RESTORE Act's more flexible structure. Dissemination of U.S. person communications acquired under the RESTORE Act's basket authorities can only happen when an SES-level supervisor determines that the identity of that person is needed to understand or assess the importance of the foreign intelligence, and to protect the national security of the United States. This is not a blanket authorization to unmask everyone intercepted, but must be done on a person-by-person basis.

Importantly, the bill has no retroactive immunity for telecommunications carriers. Until we receive the underlying documents relating to their conduct from the administration—and we have been waiting for more than ten months—we cannot even begin to consider this request. Sending a small set of the documents to a subcommittee of the other body does not begin to meet this test.

There is one of the grave concerns about the Protect America Act that bears mention as we consider the RESTORE Act. The Protect America Act was overbroad in the types of entities from which the government could compel information, reaching into business or medical records or libraries. We have narrowed the scope of the acquisitions in the RESTORE Act to ensure that the government can only seek information under the "basket authorizations" from telecommunications service providers and related companies.

I share the concern of our library community that believes their mission and the chance to bring knowledge and freedom of expression abroad will be diminished if the U.S. government can indiscriminately monitor American libraries when they serve foreign users. This is not a hypothetical concern in an age of distance learning. While a library certainly is not the same kind of "communications service provider" as AOL or AT&T, it may allow patrons to access the internet, to send emails, and to conduct research on-line, so it literally "provides" these communications services to patrons. The Judiciary Committee report indicates that these now-standard library services do not make them "telecommunications service providers" for a 105B or 105C acquisition, but let me be clear—nothing in the bill is intended to leave libraries outside of the protections of the Foreign Intelligence Surveillance Act.

The legislation before us today is a much needed start to restoring our system of checks and balances, to preserving our precious liberties, and to insuring that our government has all the tools they legitimately need to combat terrorism. I urge my colleagues on both sides of the aisle to support this common sense and balanced legislation.

Mr. Speaker, I reserve the balance of my time.

Mr. SMITH of Texas. Mr. Speaker, I yield myself such time as I may consume.

Mr. Speaker, there is a time and place for politics and partisanship. But there are in fact important issues that transcend politics. The security of our Nation outweighs politics, especially when our country is at war.

One of the finest moments of bipartisanship in Washington came after one of the darkest days in our history. On the evening of September 11, 2001, Members of Congress stood shoulder to shoulder on the steps of the Capitol as a symbol of strength and unity in response to the terrorist attacks. In that moment, we stood together, not as Republicans or Democrats, but as Americans resolved to protect our Nation. However, as we stand here today, that same spirit of bipartisanship we shared on 9/11 no longer exists.

We began in August to address a very specific and very urgent issue facing our intelligence community. We learned from the Director of National Intelligence, Admiral McConnell, that the Foreign Intelligence Surveillance Act, or FISA, was outdated for today's technology. But the bill we are considering today does not modernize FISA; it weakens it. Why, after 30 years of lawful foreign intelligence collection, does the Democratic majority suddenly object to a law that their party originally enacted in 1978? Why make it harder to gather intelligence on terrorists after 9/11 than before?

Now, after only a few hours' notice, we are considering the RESTORE Act, which actually restores little. Rather, it undermines our national security and increases the risk of a future terrorist attack on our country. It prevents our intelligence community from gathering critical intelligence information. It ignores the need for legal protection for communications companies that assist law enforcement and intelligence officials. We are at war with terrorists who spend every day plotting attacks against us. Our intelligence community needs to detect and disrupt these plots. To deny this ability could have catastrophic consequences.

Admiral McConnell testified in great detail before the Judiciary Committee about the specific needs of the intelligence community and the need to reform FISA. Admiral McConnell's recommendations are ignored, unfortunately, in the RESTORE Act. Instead, it requires the intelligence community to obtain FISA court orders for all communications of persons reasonably believed to be outside the United States. FISA has never applied to persons outside of the United States.

Under the RESTORE Act, FISA court orders will be required for the first time ever for thousands of overseas terrorist targets. Also, section 18 of the manager's amendment is bluntly titled: "No Rights Under the RESTORE Act for Undocumented Aliens." That is what it says. But the practical effect of the RESTORE Act will be to allow unregulated, warrantless wiretapping of illegal immigrants in the United States. Is this really what the Democratic majority intends?

Finally, the RESTORE Act omits any liability protection for telephone companies and other carriers that assisted the government after September 11, 2001. These companies deserve our thanks, not a flurry of harassing lawsuits. Communications technology has changed since 1978. We can no longer gather foreign intelligence without the assistance of private communications companies. Extending commonsense liability protection to communication providers who acted in good faith to protect the United States from another terrorist attack is completely appropriate. If we fail to provide this protection, we risk losing the future cooperation of communication providers in gathering foreign intelligence.

Democrats made a promise to the American people in 2006 that Members of Congress would put aside politics and work together to find bipartisan solutions to issues facing the American people. That promise has apparently been broken.

Mr. Speaker, I reserve the balance of my time.

Mr. REYES. Mr. Speaker, I yield myself such time as I may consume.

Mr. Speaker, I rise once again in support of H.R. 3773, the RESTORE Act. I would also like the Record to reflect that Congressman Baron Hill intended to be listed as a cosponsor of H.R. 3773, and we are certainly grateful for his support.

In early September, at the direction of Speaker Pelosi, the Intelligence Committee and the House Judiciary Committee took up the call to improve the Protect America Act, or PAA. Passed in August, the PAA modified FISA and gave sweeping and unprecedented surveillance powers to the executive branch, while requiring minimal oversight and without providing a meaningful judicial check on the President's use of the new powers.

While we were charged with undoing the excesses of PAA, we also have the mandate to provide our intelligence professionals the legal authorities required to protect the country from our enemies. Six years after the tragic attacks of 9/11, Osama bin Laden remains at large and America continues to face threats from al Qaeda and other terrorist organizations. The war in Iraq continues to act as a recruitment tool for all our enemies.

Mindful of these threats, we drafted the RESTORE Act as a bill that we can all support and be proud of. The RESTORE Act arms our intelligence community with powerful new authorities to conduct electronic surveillance of targets outside the United States while maintaining our fundamental liberties. First, it exempts truly foreign-to-foreign communications from any judicial review, even when the communication passes through the United States or the surveillance device is still actually located in the United States. Second, it authorizes the acquisition of foreign intelligence information for all matters of national defense, including information relating to terrorism, espionage, sabotage, and other threats to the national security of our country.

Third, the act clarifies that nothing in the act or the amendments to the act shall be construed to prohibit lawful surveillance necessary to prevent Osama bin Laden, al Qaeda, or any other terrorist organization from attacking the United States or our allies. But these powerful authorities are subject to the checks and the balances required by our Constitution.

The RESTORE Act puts the FISA Court back in business where the rights of Americans are at stake. The RESTORE Act tightens overbroad language in the PAA that authorized physical searches of Americans' homes and offices without a warrant. The RESTORE Act restores meaningful, robust, and continuous oversight by the judicial and legislative branches to ensure that the powerful intelligence-gathering tools authorized by the RESTORE Act are being used effectively and within the boundaries set by our Constitution.

In sum, the RESTORE Act provides tools to keep the Nation safe and upholds our constitutional liberties. This debate has gone on long enough, I believe, Mr. Speaker. It has been unnecessarily prolonged bipartisan maneuvering from some in this House. I am sure that we will see more of that partisan gamesmanship tonight. But I urge my colleagues to reject partisan politics in favor of sound policy and support this critically important bill.

I urge all my colleagues to vote "yes" for the RESTORE Act.

With that, I reserve the balance of my time.

Mr. SMITH of Texas. Mr. Speaker, I yield 2 minutes to the gentleman from Virginia (Mr. Forbes), the ranking member of the Crime Subcommittee of the Judiciary Committee.

Mr. FORBES. Mr. Speaker, unfortunately some things never change, and unfortunately this bill happens to be one of them. No matter how dangerous law enforcement says this bill is, it hasn't changed. No matter how dangerous the intelligence community says it is, this bill hasn't changed. And unfortunately there is a cycle that won't change either, and that cycle is simply this.

In the nineties, we cut our intelligence capabilities. On 9/11/2001, we had the worst terrorist attack that has ever hit our shores. Since that time our intelligence community and our law enforcement people have worked hard and they have kept us safe. But if we have another hit, and this bill puts us on the same cycle, because what are we doing now? We are cutting our intelligence capabilities once again, like we did in the nineties. If we have another terrorist attack, the cycle will repeat itself, and they will bring back in law enforcement and they will point their fingers and they will say, why didn't you stop it?

Mr. Speaker, we have an opportunity tonight not to repeat that cycle by not passing this bill and making the amendments necessary to keep our intelligence strong.

Mr. CONYERS. Mr. Speaker, I am pleased now to recognize a very effective member of our committee, Mr. Schiff of California, as well as the gentleman Mr. Flake of Arizona, and I would yield them 2 minutes.

Mr. SCHIFF. I thank the chairman for yielding and for his leadership.

Over the last 2 years, I have worked with my Republican colleague Jeff Flake of Arizona to ensure that the government has all the tools necessary to pursue al Qaeda and all the other terrorists who would seek to harm our country while ensuring that the requirement of court approval of surveillance of Americans on American soil is met.

I am pleased that the committee has included many of the items we proposed, including reiterating FISA's exclusivity, providing robust oversight reporting, requiring FISA Court involvement when U.S. persons are involved, and clarifying that the interception of foreign-to-foreign communications does not require a court order.

To address a concern raised by Mr. Flake, our language makes clear that a court order would not be required for electronic surveillance directed at the acquisition of communications between persons that are not known to be U.S. persons and are reasonably believed to be located outside the U.S., without respect to whether the communication passes through the U.S. or the surveillance device is located in the U.S.

We have also placed additional safeguards to ensure this section is not abused and used to acquire communications of U.S. persons.

I am pleased to yield the balance of my time to my colleague.

Mr. FLAKE. I thank the gentleman for yielding. I have enjoyed working with Representative Schiff on this, and I thank the committee for addressing our concerns. Our concerns had to do mostly, my own concern in particular, with making sure that we are not involving a court when you are talking about foreign-to-foreign communications or communications between persons who are not known to be U.S. residents or not known or reasonably believed to be within the U.S. I believe those concerns were addressed here, and I appreciate the work that was done to do that.

As mentioned, our language also requires that if a U.S. citizen is inadvertently tripped up in the communication, that proper procedures are taken to deal with that and that the information is disseminated to the right people and committees. So I appreciate the committee's work on this.

Mr. SMITH of Texas. Mr. Speaker, I yield 2 minutes to the gentleman from Texas (Mr. Gohmert), the deputy ranking member of the Crime Subcommittee of the Judiciary Committee.

Mr. GOHMERT. Mr. Speaker, to be accused of partisan maneuvering is pretty insulting. Some of us are not concerned about partisan maneuvering; we are concerned about the security of the United States. That is why I am here right now, not because of partisan maneuvering.

Do you want to talk partisan maneuvering? How about when I go out to get a copy of the most current bill and we have got a bait and switch. This isn't even the most current bill out there that we can get ahold of to come in and talk about. But I know the provision, and I appreciate my fine chairman talking about we have taken care of emergency situations, and then we had two Members just talk about emergency situations.

If you take these provisions, and hopefully the part I am talking about is the latest, that is the way I understand from what you are talking about, it says specifically in here, yeah, there is an emergency provision, but in order to get it, the Director of National Intelligence, Admiral McConnell, who was the National Security Advisor for President Clinton, he and the Attorney General have to jointly be able to swear that the targets of their acquisition are not reasonably believed to be located outside of the United States and they are not reasonably believed to be United States persons.

You take that with their testimony, the testimony was I cannot ever swear that. The way you do this intelligence is you go after a foreign target, and I can never testify, he said, as to who the person will be that they call. I can never testify that I reasonably believe they will be outside the United States when they call or that they will not be a United States person.

So, if he comes in and does this after he has testified "I cannot say I reasonably believe that they will not call somebody in the U.S., when I don't know who they will call," then we got problems. This does not protect the problem. We need to vote "no."

Mr. REYES. Mr. Speaker, I yield 10 seconds to the gentleman from Iowa (Mr. Boswell).

Mr. BOSWELL. I thank the gentleman and I support the bill.

I submit for the Record an op-ed by our friend and former colleague, the Honorable Lee Hamilton, co-chair of the 9/11 Commission, regarding the issue of retroactive immunity. The op-ed fully expresses my concerns regarding this issue, and I wish for all Members to have the benefit of reviewing it.

[From the Baltimore Sun, Nov. 4, 2007]

Immunity for Wiretap Assistance Is Right Call
(By Lee H. Hamilton)

If the local fire company asked for your help putting out neighbor's blaze, you would not force the firefighters to justify their request. You would just help, right? That's what the phone companies did when the Bush administration asked them in secret for help with wiretaps to target al-Qaida communications into and out of the country.

However, the president's warrantless wiretap program caused a furor when it became public. The administration had circumvented the Foreign Intelligence Surveillance Act, raising many doubts about the legality and even constitutionality of its wiretap program. The controversy prompted class-action lawsuits against phone companies that cooperated with the government.

The Senate Intelligence Committee has reported out a bipartisan bill that would bring this wiretap program back under the FISA statute and court review. It would ensure the legality and robust congressional oversight so lacking in the original program. It also would give the phone companies immunity for their previous actions.

The committee made the right call. To the extent that companies helped the government, they were acting out of a sense of patriotic duty and in the belief that their actions were legal. Dragging them through litigation would set a bad precedent. It would deter companies and private citizens from helping in future emergencies when there is uncertainty or legal risk.

The help and cooperation of all our citizens are vital in combating the threats we face today. Companies in various sectors of the economy are going to have information that could save the lives of thousands of Americans. When they respond in an emergency, at the call of our highest elected officials and on assurances that what they are doing is legal, they must be treated fairly. To do otherwise would put our security at risk.

This is particularly true of communications companies. They are critical to our intelligence and "early warning" against terrorist attacks. The increasing complexity of communications technology has made the voluntary cooperation of these companies vital.

Government actions require public review. Actions by private companies in response to government requests also should place the burden of accountability on the government. We should not expect private companies to second-guess the propriety and legality of government requests. That is the job of our public servants in the executive branch, the legislators who oversee them, and ultimately the courts.

Unless Congress provides immunity, the clear message will be that private citizens should help only when they are certain that all the government's actions are legal. Given today's threats, that is too high a standard. We should hold public officials accountable for their actions—and hold harmless private citizens and companies when they respond to government requests to help protect us.

Mr. REYES. Mr. Speaker, I yield 3 minutes to the gentlewoman from California (Ms. Eshoo), who serves as the chairwoman of our Subcommittee on Intelligence Community Management.

Ms. ESHOO. I thank the distinguished chairman of the House Intelligence Committee.

Mr. Speaker, this legislation very importantly covers espionage, terrorism, sabotage and all threats to our national security. That sentence alone frames what this issue is about and the seriousness of it.

The other part of it that fills out the frame is that it restores the FISA Court. It restores the FISA Court to its prominence, and, by doing so, it restores a legal framework for surveillance that must be conducted to protect our national security.

This legislation provides every meaningful tool of the legislation that was passed last August. But, unlike that bill, it protects the rights of the American people.

The legislation is true to its name. It restores the role for all three branches of our government by reestablishing the checks and the balances that have protected our security, as well as our rights as Americans. This is what the American people not only expect, it is what they have become accustomed to, and they like it.

This legal framework for the NSA surveillance is absolutely essential. When no Americans are involved, no judicial oversight is required. When an American communication may be intercepted, the court must approve the procedures for handling it. Finally, when an American is targeted, the court must be asked for an order.

The American people know all too well that this administration is now considered the most secretive in the history of our country. It has operated with unchecked power and without judicial or congressional oversight. We now know that the President went around the courts to conduct a program of warrantless surveillance of calls to Americans. We now know that the FBI abused the authorities granted under the PATRIOT Act improperly using National Security Letters to American businesses, including medical, financial and library records, instead of seeking a warrant from the court. In hundreds of signing statements, the President has quietly claimed he had the authority to set aside statutes passed by Congress.

Mr. Speaker, I think enough is enough. This bill says that the executive is not the imperial branch of government. It restores the fundamental balance struck by our Framers, to secure our Nation and to protect the rights of all Americans. Preserving that balance makes our Nation stronger, and this is at the core of the legislation before us. I urge my colleagues to support it.

Mr. SMITH of Texas. Mr. Speaker, I yield 3 minutes to the gentleman from California (Mr. Lungren) who is the senior member of both the Judiciary and Homeland Security Committees.

Mr. DANIEL E. LUNGREN of California. Mr. Speaker, I rise in opposition to this bill, and I am sorry that I have to do that. I respect the gentleman from Michigan (Mr. Conyers). We have worked on many things together. I believe he is a prime time player, but I disagree with his statement that this bill is ready for prime time.

To just give one example, if you look at section 6 of this bill, section 6 of the bill differs with the way we handle minimization under current law by saying that if there is evidence of a crime, it cannot be disseminated to a criminal justice entity. Now, maybe there is a reason for that, but that has never been discussed whatsoever.

Secondly, I would say that in the two 1-hour Special Orders I gave, I raised the problem that exists in the underlying bill as we now see it, which is in the very beginning of the bill, and it deals with a section entitled "treatment of inadvertent interceptions."

It deals with a situation where the intelligence community believes in good faith that they are dealing with foreign-to-foreign, but inadvertently they capture communication that deals with foreign-to-domestic. And what we say here is that you cannot use that information for any purpose, any purpose. It cannot be disclosed. It cannot be disseminated. It cannot be used for any purpose or retained for longer than 7 days, unless what? A court order is obtained or unless the Attorney General determines that the information indicates a threat of death or serious bodily harm to any person, that the information indicates that.

I have stood on this floor on several occasions and said what that means is if we have a conversation or a communication involving Osama bin Laden, and everybody recognizes that might be the case, because in the manager's amendment we talk about Osama bin Laden, if in fact that occurs and the communication deals with someone within the United States, and he doesn't in that communication have information indicating a threat of death or serious bodily harm to any person, but indicates where he happens to be, the exact cave where he is at, we cannot operate on that in a timely fashion.

I would challenge any Member on the other side of the aisle to read the language in the underlying merged text, page 3, entitled "Treatment of Inadvertent Interceptions," and tell me that I am wrong. This is, whether it is by mistake or you intended it to happen, giving greater protection to a terrorist around the world than you give to an American citizen charged with a crime.

I have said it before and I will say it again: I don't believe you intended this, but it is in the bill. As a matter of fact, the gentleman from New York, the chairman of the Constitutional Rights Subcommittee, came to me after we had an exchange on the floor on the issue and said, "You are right. We goofed up. We should get rid of it." Yet we are here with it on the floor. For that reason alone, we ought to defeat the bill.

Mr. CONYERS. Mr. Speaker, I am stunned by my friend from California's comments, but I yield now 2 minutes to the gentleman from New York (Mr. Nadler), the chairman of the Constitution Subcommittee in Judiciary.

Mr. NADLER. I thank the gentleman.

Mr. Speaker, this legislation restores the proper role of the Foreign Intelligence Surveillance Court in the maintenance of our national security infrastructure. Let's get the terms of this debate clear before we begin. Anyone who can read will see that this bill does not inhibit the government's ability to spy on terrorists or on suspected terrorists or to act swiftly and effectively on the information we gather.

The American people expect that their government will keep us all safe and free. This bill does that.

The bill does not require individual warrants of foreign terrorists located outside the United States. That has been the law for three decades; that is still the law.

The bill does provide reasonable FISA Court oversight to ensure that when our government starts spying on Americans, it does so lawfully by getting a warrant from the FISA Court. It will put an end to this administration's well-worn "trust me" routine.

I trust our intelligence community to gather solid intelligence on threats to our Nation. But protecting constitutional rights is not their prime job. That is why we have courts.

This bill provides for Congress to receive independent reports on how the act is working and what our government is doing. This administration's penchant for secrecy and aversion to accountability will come to an end, at least in this area.

Let me say a word for demands for retroactive immunity for the telecom companies. As many of our colleagues have pointed out, any such discussion is premature. We do not even know what we are being asked to immunize or whose rights would be compromised if we did so.

More importantly, Congress should not decide legal cases between private parties; that's for the courts. If the claims are not meritorious, the courts will throw them out. But if the claims do have merit, we have no right to wipe them without even reviewing the evidence. How dare we have the presumption to decide the rights of allegedly injured parties in the blind.

Mr. Speaker, this bill meets every single principle set forth by the Congressional Progressive Caucus. As one of the co-chairs of the caucus' FISA Task Force, I am pleased to support this important bill. It is true to our Constitution. It is true to our values. It is true to our safety. It will keep us safe and free.

This bill gives our intelligence agencies the tools they have told us they need to make us safe, and gives the FISA Court the tools it needs to ensure that the extraordinary powers we are giving to the intelligence community are used correctly and consistently with our laws and our Constitution.

It's called the separation of powers, with each branch of the government doing what it is supposed to do and acting as a check on the others. FISA exists to ensure that the balance between the needs of intelligence gathering and the protection of the rights of all Americans are balanced.

Most importantly, it restores the role of FISA as the exclusive legal basis for foreign intelligence surveillance. No more making it up as you go along.

Did the telecoms break the law? Were they acting appropriately? Were the rights of innocent Americans violated? We don't know.

How dare we have the presumption to decide the rights of allegedly injured parties in the blind?

Mr. SMITH of Texas. Mr. Speaker, I yield 2 minutes to the gentleman from Arizona (Mr. Shadegg), a senior member of the Commerce Committee.

Mr. SHADEGG. I thank the gentleman for yielding.

I think this is a very, very important debate. I understand the frustration of the majority in trying to deal with this issue, but I believe they have created a structure that even they themselves don't understand, and a structure that fundamentally turns the Constitution and the role of at least two branches of the government upside down.

We have the executive branch which is charged with defending the Nation against foreign enemies and we have the judicial branch which is charged with applying and interpreting the laws. But it is charged with judging disputes between American citizens, not with making decisions how about to gather foreign intelligence.

Now, how does this bill work? Number one, it says if the executive branch in carrying out its duty to protect the country from foreign enemies knows in advance that both people, both ends of a telephone communication or some other electronic communication, are in fact foreigners, no warrant is needed.

Well, if we could be mind readers and if we could hire mind readers as intelligence officers, that might be useful. But everyone in the intelligence community tells you that have targeted one person, and without the ability to read the mind of that person, you don't know who the other person they are calling is.

So as a matter of fact, you can never know, never ever know, no CIA agent, no judge, nobody can ever know that both people are foreigners. And so if the law says if you don't know that both are foreigners, you must get a warrant from a judge.

Now they have said we are going to be reasonable about it; it is going to be a basket warrant. But that then gives the duty of protecting the Nation to a judge, an unelected judge.

Mr. REYES. Mr. Speaker, it is my pleasure to yield 2 minutes to the gentleman from New Jersey (Mr. Holt), our chairman of the Select Intelligence Oversight Panel.

Mr. HOLT. I thank my friend and colleague from Texas.

Mr. Speaker, I rise in support of this bill. As many of you know, when the committee reported this bill to the floor, I expressed concerns that it lacked provisions ensuring that the courts would decide whether the executive branch could seize and search communications of Americans.

The RESTORE Act now before us includes provisions via the manager's amendment that will ensure that it is the courts, not an executive branch political appointee, who decides whether or not the communications of an American can be seized and searched and that such seizures and searches must be done pursuant to an individualized court order.

This bill gives our citizens the best protection we can provide them, a sound intelligence collection that will foil our enemies and the review of the executive branch's surveillance actions by the court. In other words, each of us can say to each of our constituents: you have the protection of the court.

Now, it is important to note that this bill will provide better intelligence than existing law, the existing law which was passed in haste and fear. This bill, by applying checks and balances, improves intelligence collection and analysis. It has been demonstrated that when officials establish before a court that they have reason to intercept communications, we get better intelligence, better intelligence than we get through indiscriminate collection and fishing expeditions.

Mr. Speaker, this does it right. Mr. Speaker, I would like to close by thanking the staff of the committee, Jeremy Bash and Eric Greenwald; and from the Judiciary Committee, Lou DeBaca and Burt Wides; as well as the chairmen, Mr. Reyes and Mr. Conyers, who took my concerns to heart and made them their own concerns. It has produced a good bill. I urge my colleagues to vote "yes" for the RESTORE Act.

Mr. Speaker, the RESTORE Act will ensure that it is the courts—and not an executive branch political appointee—who decide whether or not the communications of an American citizen can be seized and searched, and that such seizures and searches must be done pursuant to a court order. This bill gives our citizens the best protection we can provide them: good intelligence collection against our adversaries, and review of the executive branch's surveillance actions by a court.

I was pleased to be able to work with my colleagues on the House Permanent Select Committee on Intelligence to add several key provisions to this bill. For example, the bill's most critical new provision ensures that the government must have an individualized, particularized court-approved warrant based on probable cause in order to read or listen to the communications of an American citizen. Inclusion of this provision was vital. We must be able to assure our citizens that their communications cannot be seized and searched by the government in the absence of a court order, and with this provision now in the bill, we can provide that assurance.

Another provision I worked to include requires the Court to review and approve not only the procedures and guidelines required under this Act, but also the application of those guidelines. This provision provides another important point of review by the courts that will help ensure that the Attorney General and the Director of National Intelligence are actually doing what they claim they are doing.

I also asked that a provision be inserted that makes it clear that the Foreign Intelligence Surveillance Act (FISA) is the sole statutory basis for domestic surveillance. This language was needed to remove any ambiguity. We cannot have any President inventing other claims for secret, warrantless surveillance.

The bill also provides additional resources to both the executive and judiciary branches for processing FISA applications and orders. The bill increases the number of Foreign Intelligence Surveillance Court (FISC) judges from 11 to 15, provides additional personnel to both the FISC and government agencies responsible for making and processing FISA applications, creates an electronic filing, sharing, and document management system for handling this highly classified data, and mandates training for all government personnel involved in the FISA process. All of this will help modernize and streamline the FISA application approval process.

Finally, the bill requires the Bush administration to "fully inform" Congress on all surveillance programs conducted since 9/11. It's outrageous that the Bush Administration has continued to stonewall this Congress over documents for the one program it has acknowledged. If we're to do our job of oversight, we need all the facts about past and current surveillance programs, and this provision will help us get those answers.

I hope our colleagues in the Senate will quickly pass the RESTORE Act, and I call upon the President to end his veto threats and work with Congress to bring America's surveillance activities into compliance with the Constitution.

President Bush has no inherent Constitutional authority to spy on our own citizens in the name of national security. If the President is serious about passing a law that allows us to protect our citizens from all enemies—foreign and domestic—he will sign this bill.

Mr. SMITH of Texas. Mr. Speaker, I am happy to yield 2 minutes to the gentleman from Missouri (Mr. Blunt), the distinguished minority whip of the House.

Mr. BLUNT. Mr. Speaker, I thank the gentleman for yielding and for his hard work on the floor this evening, for the leadership of Mr. Hoekstra and others on this important bill. We need to modernize FISA to keep up with changes in communications technology and the continually evolving tactics of our terrorist enemies.

We made some important steps in this direction only 90 days ago. We all understand that more needs to be done. But rather than responding to this need, this legislation actually impedes the intelligence community's ability to conduct effective investigations and to prevent future terrorist attacks.

This act requires FISA court orders for the first time for thousands of overseas terrorist targets. The Director of National Intelligence, Admiral McConnell, has described this requirement as unworkable and impractical.

This act contains a sunset date which fails to provide the certainty under the law that our intelligence community needs to effectively do its job.

It doesn't provide the liability protections for telephone companies and other carriers that assisted the government after 9/11 who now have a flurry of harassing lawsuits facing them.

Mr. Speaker, the majority claims that this legislation will restore a balance between civil liberties and national security. In fact, this bill will restore the intelligence gap that existed prior to our actions the 1st of August.

I urge this legislation be defeated. The current bill is better than this bill. We need to deal with it certainly between now and the end of the 6 months, but let's not take a step backwards. Let's let the law do what this law was intended to do in 1978 and is doing today.

Mr. CONYERS. Mr. Speaker, it is my pleasure now to recognize the gentlewoman from Florida (Ms. Wasserman Schultz), a member of the Judiciary Committee, for 1 1/4 minutes.

Ms. WASSERMAN SCHULTZ. Mr. Speaker, in August I urged my colleagues to vote against an unconstitutional Senate bill. Simply put, that bill trampled on our constituents' constitutional right to privacy.

Today, I am proud to rise in support of the RESTORE Act, a bill that provides the intelligence community the tools it needs, but that restores the constitutional rights of Americans.

Mr. Speaker, we can be both safe and free, and this bill strikes the right balance.

This bill permits surveillance of foreign-to-foreign communication. It allows us to listen in on Osama bin Laden or any other terrorist who threatens our troops or country. This bill will keep us safe.

But this bill also requires a warrant from the FISA Court in order to eavesdrop on the communications of ordinary Americans, and it requires a court review of targeting procedures to ensure Americans' rights are protected. This bill restores our civil liberties.

Mr. Speaker, our colleagues across the aisle would rather play politics with this bill and unleash arguments of mass distortion, so let me be clear: nothing in this bill gives our constitutional rights to terrorists.

Our Republican colleagues create this smoke screen in order to hide the fact that they have taken away those same constitutional freedoms from Americans.

We need not choose between our secure and liberty. With the RESTORE Act, we can have both.

Mr. HOEKSTRA. Mr. Speaker, I yield myself 1 minute.

This morning as we did the rules debate, I asked some questions of my colleagues on the other side of the aisle, and they said we will cover that during general debate tonight.

So the questions I have that I hope will be answered is in the manager's amendment that was presented this morning and was voted on in the self-enacting rule talks about illegal aliens. The questions I have:

Would it allow surveillance against possible illegal aliens for law enforcement purposes?

Would it allow foreign intelligence surveillance to be conducted against transnational smuggling rings?

Would it allow surveillance to determine whether someone is an alien not permitted to be in or remain in the United States?

Would the amendment exempt undocumented aliens from the physical search requirements of FISA? Exactly how far does this amendment go? What is it intended to do?

These were the questions that I asked this morning that I hope will be answered tonight.

Mr. Speaker, I reserve the balance of my time.

Mr. REYES. Mr. Speaker, could I ask how much time remains on each side.

The SPEAKER pro tempore. The gentleman from Texas (Mr. Reyes) has 6 1/2 minutes remaining. The gentleman from Michigan (Mr. Conyers) has 3 3/4 minutes remaining. The time has expired for the gentleman from Texas (Mr. Smith). The gentleman from Michigan (Mr. Hoekstra) has 14 minutes remaining.

Mr. REYES. Mr. Speaker, I reserve the balance of my time so we can balance the time out with the gentleman from Michigan.

Mr. HOEKSTRA. Mr. Speaker, I yield 2 minutes to the gentleman from Texas (Mr. Thornberry), a member of the committee.

Mr. THORNBERRY. Mr. Speaker, it is unfortunate that here we are again debating a FISA bill that is more about politics than it is about the country. This bill is a cobbled-together mess designed to keep most of the Democratic Caucus together rather than a bill designed to meet the national security needs of the country. It is full of contradictory, unworkable provisions.

Most of this body and most of the American people agree that our intelligence professionals, civilian and military, should be able to gather foreign intelligence on terrorists and others without having a pack of lawyers trail along behind you. Unfortunately, that is exactly what they will need if this bill were to ever become law.

It is also sad that those who have volunteered to help defend us against terrorists are being punished. We debate Good Samaritan laws from time to time. The country needs Good Samaritans, as well, to help prevent errorist attacks.

What the country needs, Mr. Speaker, is an updated law that intelligence professionals can really use, that really works in the field, not some cobbled-together mess designed to achieve a political purpose just before a recess. We can do better. I continue to hope that someday this House actually will.

Mr. REYES. I continue to reserve the balance of my time.

Mr. CONYERS. Mr. Speaker, I reserve the balance of my time.

Mr. HOEKSTRA. I yield 2 minutes to the gentleman on the committee, Mr. Tiahrt of Kansas.

Mr. TIAHRT. I thank the gentleman from Michigan for yielding to me. I rise in opposition to this bill.

I am really surprised by the procedure we have gone through to get to this point in this legislation. You know, under the underlying bill we had open hearings, we had closed hearings, we looked at a lot of the details and openly debated them and I thought we were making pretty good progress. But then, in the self-enacting rule, we have a whole bunch of new language that is dumped into this bill that has had no hearings.

In fact, section 18 says in this bill now, no rights under the RESTORE Act for undocumented aliens. It says: This Act shall not be construed to prohibit surveillance of an alien not permitted to be in the United States.

Undocumented aliens, no rights.

Then we get to what, the rights that the terrorists have in the underlying bill. Section 3 has procedures for authorizing acquisitions of communications, and there are 8 pages telling how we are going to protect the terrorists. They have got some rights protected under this bill.

Then we get to section 4, the emergency authorization. We have 8 more pages explaining how terrorists have more rights than undocumented aliens right here in the United States.

So then we listened to the gentleman from California (Mr. Lungren), who is the former Attorney General of the State of California, and he explains that, through the minimization procedures, that we are actually giving terrorists more rights than we do our own U.S. common criminals.

So what is the deal with this? It is really a mess. You have got terrorists at a higher status than undocumented aliens that are here in America and a lot of them just trying to make a living, and then you have got a higher standard for terrorists than you do for our own criminals. Now, why don't we balance things out here? Why don't we balance things out? You have tried to push this thing through without hearings, you have hodgepodged it together, and it truly is a mess. We ought to send this back to committee and do the right thing on this.

We want to protect the rights of American citizens, and we think that humans have a certain set of rights, too. But this bill does not provide it. It has mixed standards. It is a mess, and I think we should vote it down.

Mr. REYES. Mr. Speaker, I reserve the balance of my time until we balance out the time.

Mr. HOEKSTRA. Mr. Speaker, I think we have balanced the time. We chose on our side to go with the 15 minutes of Judiciary time and then 15 minutes of Intelligence time. I believe the people in opposition to this bill now have 10 minutes; the people who are supportive of this bill have 11. That sounds like balance to me.

I reserve the balance of my time.

Mr. REYES. Mr. Speaker, how much time is remaining?

The SPEAKER pro tempore. The gentleman from Texas (Mr. Reyes) has 6 1/2 minutes remaining. The gentleman from Michigan (Mr. Hoekstra) has 10 1/2 minutes remaining. The gentleman from Michigan (Mr. Conyers) has 3 3/4 minutes remaining.

Mr. REYES. Mr. Speaker, I will now yield 1 1/2 minutes to the distinguished gentlewoman from Illinois (Ms. Schakowsky).

Ms. SCHAKOWSKY. Mr. Speaker, I rise in support of the RESTORE Act because I believe that the way we conduct the fight against terrorism says a great deal about who we are as a people.

We all want to keep the country safe from terrorism and to provide the necessary tools to our intelligence community, but I am not willing to sacrifice who we are and what we stand for just because this President says so.

The President's Protect America Act cut the FISA Court out of the process. The RESTORE Act puts the court back in. Now, the court, not the President, will decide whether the constitutional legal requirements are met. The court will assess in advance a program of surveillance that may intercept the communications of Americans. The court will ensure that the system the NSA establishes will protect the rights of any Americans they come across. The RESTORE Act clarifies the Protect America Act cannot be used to conduct secret searches of Americans' homes, businesses, computers, and medical records. It reiterates the exclusivity of FISA, which would put an end to secret, warrantless spying programs. It makes clear that the President has to obey the laws.

The RESTORE Act requires meaningful reporting to the Congress about the warrantless surveillance programs that have occurred since September 11, and it will require meaningful oversight in the future. The RESTORE Act will make America safer and keeps us true to who we are as a Nation. I urge my colleagues to vote "yes."

Mr. HOEKSTRA. Mr. Speaker, I yield 2 minutes to my colleague from California (Mr. Lungren).

Mr. DANIEL E. LUNGREN of California. I thank the gentleman for yielding.

Once again, I would ask my friends on the other side of the aisle: Can anyone explain why, on page 3, you give stronger rights to someone who is a suspected terrorist, even Osama bin Laden, if he has a communication we intercept believing it was going to be foreign-to-foreign, now foreign to someone in the United States, and in that he reveals where he is, why we cannot use that information as we are able to with a legal wiretap in the United States on an American citizen charged with a crime who calls someone who is not a target of a crime? I do not understand it. Page 3. Is there anybody on your side who can explain why you would have that?

The silence has been deafening for a month now on this.

Mr. CONYERS. Would the former Attorney General of California yield?

Mr. DANIEL E. LUNGREN of California. I would be happy to yield if the gentleman would tell me exactly what I just asked.

Mr. CONYERS. That is why I seek to have you yield to me, sir.

Osama bin Laden is never going to have any rights superior to any citizen.

Mr. DANIEL E. LUNGREN of California. Reclaiming my time, because I asked you to specifically talk about the language in the bill. I have read it and read it and read it, and you have refused to respond to it, even though the chairman of the Subcommittee on Constitutional Rights told me that I was correct in my reading of the bill and that you folks were going to change it. You didn't change it. I expect that is because you forgot about it.

I would invite the gentleman from New York to respond to me, because he intellectually honestly told me just 2 1/2 weeks ago that you folks were going to change it. Why haven't you done it?

Mr. Speaker, the silence I think speaks volumes. This is a bill that is not ready for prime time. It inadvertently protects Osama bin Laden with greater rights than an American citizen charged with a crime.

Mr. CONYERS. Mr. Chairman, it is very important that we understand that Mr. Lungren in his dramatic presentation about the cumbersomeness and the protections that we are affording bin Laden almost begs the question here.

We have been on this bill for several times. We have got a carve-out here. Nothing prevents conducting lawful surveillance that is necessary to, one, prevent Osama bin Laden and al Qaeda or any other terrorists, Mr. Lungren, or any ally of those persons from receiving any of these protections. We can operate against them without giving them any rights, and I think you must know that by now.

Mr. DANIEL E. LUNGREN of California. Mr. Speaker, will the gentleman yield?

Mr. CONYERS. I can't give you time. I have got less than anybody here. No. I reserve the balance of my time.

Announcement By the Speaker Pro Tempore

The SPEAKER pro tempore (Mr. Ross). All Members are reminded to address their remarks to the Chair.

Mr. HOEKSTRA. Mr. Speaker, at this time I yield 2 minutes to my colleague from Arizona (Mr. Shadegg).

Mr. SHADEGG. Mr. Speaker, I want to point out that this bill raises a fundamental question: Do we trust judges, unelected judges, to control foreign intelligence? Are we going to move that responsibility from the executive branch to judges? Or is that not their job?

As I explained earlier, this measure requires that a warrant be obtained every single time you are seeking to gather foreign intelligence. That means that we are asking Federal judges, who are unelected, to decide in 100 percent of the cases whether we can or cannot gather intelligence.

Now, I respect judges. I admire judges. But judges have the duty of deciding disputes between Americans. They do not have the responsibility to protect our Nation. But this bill says you can never gather intelligence from a foreigner without first going and getting a warrant.

So a job that under our Constitution has been given to the executive branch, that is, to conduct foreign intelligence and protect the Nation, we are now taking from the executive branch and giving to judges. Because unelected Federal judges, who have no responsibility to protect our Nation, no responsibility to gather foreign intelligence, now get to decide, this has never been true in the history of our Nation, whether or not the Federal Government will gather any intelligence.

I respect judges. I am all for judges. If I am in a dispute over the civil rights of an American, I want a judge to decide. But when it comes to gathering intelligence about terrorists, we are going to take that authority away from the executive branch, which we have never done in the past, and give it to judges and judges only? Judges whom we cannot defeat in office, judges who are appointed, judges who do not stand for election, judges who cannot be voted out of office? We are going to take the authority away from the executive branch to protect our Nation and in 100 percent of cases give it to unelected judges. That is a mistake.

Mr. REYES. Mr. Speaker, I think we just saw some shrill out of options articulation there.

I now yield 1 1/2 minutes to the gentleman from Rhode Island (Mr. Langevin).

(Mr. LANGEVIN asked and was given permission to revise and extend his remarks.)

Mr. LANGEVIN. Mr. Speaker, I rise in support of H.R. 3773. This legislation does exactly what our Constitution requires us to do: protect security while preserving civil liberties.

Maintaining that balance has sometimes been difficult, and the events of 9/11 have made it even more challenging. However, the RESTORE Act is a carefully crafted solution. We all recognize the gravity of the threats facing our country, and this bill gives the Director of National Intelligence all the authority he has asked for to fight terrorism while at the same time it protects civil liberties.

Further, the RESTORE Act provides for rigorous and independent oversight from the courts, the Congress, and the Department of Justice Inspector General. In our committee markup, I successfully offered an amendment to even strengthen this oversight by preserving the FISA Court's role to review compliance with their rules every 90 days for the life of a court order.

Rigorous oversight is why the Bush administration objects to this bill. They want unfettered authority. Unfortunately, we have seen what happens without checks and balances, and I will not allow that to happen again. As Members of Congress, we took an oath to defend the Constitution and the principles on which it was founded.

I urge my colleagues to support H.R. 3773, which provides security while preserving the fundamental values that make this country so great.

Mr. HOEKSTRA. Mr. Speaker, I yield 3 minutes to my colleague from the State of New Mexico (Mrs. Wilson).

Mrs. WILSON of New Mexico. Mr. Speaker, my colleague from Rhode Island talked about the importance of upholding the Constitution, and there is something in the manager's amendment to this bill that was inserted without any hearing in the committee that I don't understand, that makes no sense to me. It is a provision that says, very plainly: This act and the amendments made by this act shall not be construed to prohibit surveillance of, or grant any rights to, an alien not permitted to be in or remain in the United States.

Now, I think there are probably a lot of people on this side of the aisle who don't have a problem with that provision. What I don't understand is why you all are proposing it.

Here is the irony here. This bill will extend rights under our Constitution to foreigners in foreign countries, while denying the protections of the Constitution to some 12 million people who are not legally in the United States, when the case law is clear that they do have rights. Whether we think they should have rights or not, the case law is absolutely clear. So we will deny those rights to people in the United States while extending them to people in foreign countries?

I think we should be clear with the American people why we insisted on fixing the Foreign Intelligence Surveillance Act, and did so successfully in August. We had soldiers who were kidnapped in Iraq by insurgents.

And because of changes in technology and the demands of the court, the American military had to go to lawyers in the United States to get a warrant to try to intercept the communications of the terrorists trying to kill them. That took time, too much time. And the law had to be fixed.

Soldiers should not need an army of lawyers in Washington to listen to the communications of the enemy that's trying to kill them. This needed to be fixed, and we fixed it the first week of August.

We all remember where we were on the morning of 9/11. We remember who we were with, what we were wearing, what we ate for breakfast.

But people don't remember where they were the day that the British Government arrested 16 people who were within 48 hours of walking on to airliners and blowing them up simultaneously over the Atlantic. We don't remember it because it didn't happen. And the reason it didn't happen is because of exceptional intelligence and the cooperation of the British, Pakistani and American Governments.

Mr. REYES. Mr. Speaker, I'm concerned about the self-induced confusion on the other side.

I now yield 1 3/4 minutes to the gentleman from Pennsylvania (Mr. Patrick J. Murphy) who served in Iraq and also serves with me on the Armed Services Committee, as well as our Intelligence Committee.

Mr. PATRICK J. MURPHY of Pennsylvania. Mr. Speaker, I rise today in support of the RESTORE Act and to set the record straight on an issue that is close to my heart.

In May of 2007, three men from the 10th Mountain Division were captured in Iraq. They're names are Specialist Alex Jiminez, Private First Class Joseph Anzak, and Private Byron Fouty. I recite their names because the right wing attack machine never does. But these are the facts, and they're not pretty.

The intelligence community stood ready to help find these three soldiers. But for 5 hours, for 5 hours, the Bush administration could not decide what to do. When they decided to go ahead, no Bush administration official could authorize it, could be found to authorize it. But when they finally found the Attorney General in Texas, it took an additional 2 hours to authorize the surveillance, even though he could have granted the authority in just minutes. Hours of indecision and incompetence while these three soldiers went missing.

* * * * *

While the RESTORE Act can solve many problems posed by the current FISA law, it will not solve the problem in these soldiers' situations.

Mr. DANIEL E. LUNGREN of California. Mr. Speaker, I ask the gentleman's words be taken down with respect to the use of the word "deceit."

The SPEAKER pro tempore. All Members will suspend.

The Clerk will report the words.

Mr. PATRICK J. MURPHY of Pennsylvania. Mr. Speaker, this has been a very powerful and emotional debate today, and the issue is very close to my heart. I did not mean to offend anyone across the other side of the aisle. And I ask the Speaker and the other side for unanimous consent to withdraw the paragraph that may have given offense to some Members that were on the floor.

The SPEAKER pro tempore. Is there objection to the request of the gentleman from Pennsylvania?

There was no objection.

The SPEAKER pro tempore. In this debate, the gentleman from Texas (Mr. Reyes) has 1 3/4 minutes remaining, the gentleman from Michigan (Mr. Conyers) has 2 minutes remaining, and the gentleman from Michigan (Mr. Hoekstra) has 3 1/2 minutes remaining.

Mr. HOEKSTRA. Mr. Speaker, I yield myself 30 seconds.

I just want to make a couple of points. Again, no one has answered the questions that I asked earlier today and that I asked in the debate tonight. The amendment talking about illegal aliens, would it allow for surveillance against possible illegal aliens? Would it allow for foreign intelligence surveillance to be conducted against transnational smuggling gangs? Would the amendment exempt undocumented aliens from the physical search requirements?

And then just to reiterate the point that my colleague made in the previous speech, this is all about lawyering up the process, and that's what extends the time.

At this point, I yield 1 minute to my colleague, Mr. Kirk of Illinois.

Mr. KIRK. I thank the gentleman. And as the leader of the moderates in this, I would say that this issue should unite us all as Americans, not divide us along partisan lines.

I also speak as a Navy intelligence officer that would say that the provision that was newly included in this legislation says that nothing in this act shall prevent an intelligence officer from monitoring someone related to al Qaeda, Osama bin Laden or Ayman al-Zawahiri to prevent an attack against the United States. But so much of our intelligence is beyond the imminent attack on the United States. So much of us in the intelligence world, we have to watch the earliest signs of this.

Let's be clear, this bill before us has nothing to do with the rights of U.S. citizens; those are already protected. As an intelligence officer, we are always drilled on the code of conduct in dealing with U.S. persons. This bill has everything to do with creating new rights for people overseas. And I think we should let our intelligence community monitor whoever Osama bin Laden is talking with to protect the United States, even if an attack is not imminent.

Mr. CONYERS. Mr. Speaker, I yield for the purpose of making a unanimous consent request to the gentleman from Virginia (Mr. Scott).

(Mr. SCOTT of Virginia asked and was given permission to revise and extend his remarks.)

Mr. SCOTT of Virginia. Mr. Speaker, I rise in favor of the legislation.

Mr. Chairman, I appreciate your leadership on efforts to address warrantless surveillance under the Foreign Intelligence Surveillance Act, or "FISA" and for introducing a bill that corrects many of the shortcomings of the bill that passed the House last August.

The RESTORE Act establishes a strong framework, much stronger than the Administration's PROTECT Act, to fight terrorism effectively, while providing reasonable safeguards to protect personal privacy.

One important change in the Restore Act is that it draws the appropriate distinctions based on the physical location and types of targets. There has never been any controversy over the fact that surveillance directed at people all of whom are overseas does not need any warrant at all. This bill rightly makes it clear that no court orders are required for the government to conduct surveillance on foreign targets outside the United States, even if the technical surveillance is conducted on U.S. soil. But if any surveillance is intentionally conducted on a U.S. person, this bill makes it clear that the government needs to apply for an individual warrant to conduct that surveillance. And if information on U.S. persons is incidentally collected, the Manager's Amendment to the bill rightly limits dissemination of that information among government agencies.

Second, the bill removes vague and overbroad language from the bill passed in August that would allow the wiretapping of conversations without a warrant if the communication was "concerning" a foreign target. That, by its own wording, suggests that if two citizens are in the United States talking about somebody overseas, that you could wiretap their communications without a warrant. The bill before us makes it clear that the persons involved in the communications must be overseas, not just that the subject of their conversation must be overseas.

Third, the RESTORE Act goes a step further than the Administration's bill and allows for the expanded wiretapping authority only in cases involving "national security," as opposed to the over-expansive "foreign intelligence." "Foreign intelligence" could include trade, deals or anything involving general foreign affairs activities.

Finally, the RESTORE Act was made even stronger in Committee by requiring the Department of Justice, in its application to the Court, to identify the "primary purpose" of its wiretapping. Under the original FISA, when an agent wanted to obtain the authority to conduct electronic surveillance or secret searches, a certificate was necessary detailing what the purpose of the surveillance was in order to obtain the warrant. The standard was altered by the Patriot Act, which provided that obtaining foreign intelligence only has to be "a significant purpose."

We have to put this change in context because the Department of Justice has not credibly refuted the allegations that some U.S. Attorneys were fired, because they failed to indict Democrats in time to affect an upcoming election. So if the Department of Justice wiretapped someone when foreign intelligence was not the primary purpose, you have to wonder what the primary purpose was. This bill would allow the surveillance to be conducted but the administration would be required to reveal the true purpose of the wiretap to the secret FISA court.

Mr. Speaker, I want to emphasize that we do not have to balance security and privacy. It is therefore important to note that everything that the administration can do in its own bill, it can do under this bill. We just require them to get a warrant before they do it, or if they are in a hurry, get a warrant after they do it, but they can wiretap and get the information. We just provide a modicum of oversight to ensure that our laws are being obeyed. I urge my colleagues to support the bill.

Mr. CONYERS. Mr. Speaker, I am now pleased to yield 1 minute to the Speaker of the House, the gentlewoman from California, Nancy Pelosi.

Ms. PELOSI. Mr. Speaker, as one who has long served on the Intelligence Committee, I understand full well the threats to our national security.

I understand full well the need for us to have legislation that strikes the proper balance between liberty and security. I think this legislation does just that. And I commend Chairman Conyers, chairman of the Judiciary Committee; and the chairman of the Intelligence Committee, Chairman Reyes, for their important work and their leadership in presenting this legislation to the floor for consideration.

The bill is important and accomplishes the goal of striking the balance between security and liberty in the following ways: it defends Americans against terrorism and other threats; it protects Americans' civil liberties; and it restores checks and balances.

The bill protects Americans by providing the Director of National Intelligence with the flexibility he has requested of Congress to conduct electronic surveillance of persons outside the United States. No warrants are required whenever foreign-to-foreign communications are captured regardless of the point of collection or anywhere in the world.

It protects our civil liberties in a number of ways. The DNI has agreed that when Americans are targeted for surveillance, a warrant is required. We have now included certain criteria that the government must take into account in considering whether a warrant is required. This will help prevent inappropriate warrantless surveillance and "reverse targeting" of Americans under the guise of foreign intelligence.

The bill restores checks and balances. This is very, very important because it, again, is part of our oath of office to protect the Constitution of the United States. The bill rejects groundless claims of "inherent executive authority."

There are those who claim that the President has inherent authority from the Constitution to do whatever he wishes. Long ago our Founders rejected that concept in founding our country. We must do that as well and continue to make that clear.

The legislation also makes clear that FISA is the exclusive means for conducting electronic surveillance to gather foreign intelligence. The government must seek approval from a FISA Court. So we are talking about the Congress of the United States passing legislation, as it did in the late seventies, passing this legislation today which is in light of the new technologies and new reality in the world, and recognizing the authority of the third branch of government: the courts.

This legislation includes extensive reporting to Congress with respect to the interception and dissemination of communications among Americans and from Americans. This is very important because we want to minimize the use of that information and keep it for the purpose for which it is collected.

Most significantly, the bill does not provide immunity to telecommunications companies that participated in the President's warrantless surveillance program. We cannot even consider providing immunity unless we know exactly what we are providing immunity from. And even then, and even then, we have to proceed with great caution.

It is important to note that the bill sunsets on December 31, 2009, the date the PATRIOT Act sunsets, so the next administration and the next Congress can review and reassess the program.

This legislation is supported by organizations dedicated to protecting our national security and protecting our civil liberties, including the Center for National Security Studies, the Center for Democracy and Technology, and many other groups that work to protect privacy rights. The bill protects both national security and civil liberties, reaffirms our constitutional system of checks and balances, and deserves the support of this House.

Mr. Speaker, all of us want our President to have the best possible intelligence, our President and our policymakers, so they can do the best possible job to protect the American people. But no President, Democrat or Republican, should have the authority, to have inherent authority, to collect on Americans without doing so under the law. This legislation establishes that principle; and it establishes it in a very focused way in keeping with the need for flexibility for the Director of National Intelligence, in keeping with honoring our oath of office to the Constitution. I urge our colleagues to support this important legislation.

I, for one, am very, very proud of the work of Mr. Conyers and Mr. Reyes and thank them for their leadership.

Mr. HOEKSTRA. Mr. Speaker, I yield myself 1 minute.

A month after I originally came to the floor to oppose this bill, I now rise in opposition to this flawed legislation, which, disappointingly, has been made worse ever since we started the process.

In August Congress finally acted, after months of prodding from Republicans, to close significant intelligence gaps against potential foreign terrorists in foreign countries that jeopardize America's ability to protect and prevent potential terrorist attacks and to effectively collect intelligence on foreign adversaries.

Now we have a simple choice: Do we do what is necessary to provide long-term legal authority for our intelligence community to conduct necessary surveillance, or do we reopen that intelligence gap?

It now seems that the majority is determined to move a bill intended to make political statements rather than to give intelligence professionals the tools that they need to protect our country.

I urge my colleagues to vote against this bill.

Mr. REYES. Mr. Speaker, I yield 1 minute to our distinguished majority leader, Mr. Hoyer of Maryland.

Mr. HOYER. I thank my friend for yielding. I thank him for his leadership as well. I thank Mr. Conyers for his leadership, and I thank Mr. Hoekstra and Mr. Smith for their participation.

This is a serious issue that confronts us. Mr. Speaker, this legislation, the RESTORE Act, is nothing less than the fundamental reiteration of the most basic concepts of our Constitution, our constitutional form of government that we, indeed, are a Nation of laws and that our Founders deliberately designed our three branches of government to serve as a check and balance on each other.

One of my colleagues, my friend, I believe, from Arizona, stood and said it was not the job of judges to conduct intelligence. He was correct. It is not the job of judges to conduct intelligence. But it is the constitutional duty given by our Founding Fathers, who understood that King George too often abused his sovereign power and who said to all that they would have adopt this Constitution that we will protect you from the abuse of power of government, and we will do it by having it reviewed by independent judges, not by the legislature.

We can be told by judges that we are not acting constitutionally, and that is a protection for our people against congressional abuse of power. And the executive department can be told by judges you are abusing your constitutional power. No power, no protection was felt to be more necessary and important by our Founding Fathers than their right to personal privacy and a lack of intrusion by King George just because he wanted to do it. And they said King George had to have probable cause, in this case, the Government of the United States. So that's why they established the courts. And we, in our wisdom, in my view, established the FISA Court to do just that.

Every single one of us here recognizes that our highest duty is to protect the American people. Indeed, we must detect, disrupt, and eliminate terrorists who have no compunction about planning and participating in the mass killing of innocent people. We saw that tragically on 9/11. We also, each one of us, come to this well or stand at our seats and raise our hand and swear an oath to defend the Constitution of the United States, to protect its laws and to honor the values and principles that are contained therein. That is our oath. That is what we do here this night, including the fourth amendment right that Americans are secure in their persons, houses, papers, and effects against unreasonable searches and seizures. That's not an assertion on any individual or any government or even the legislature. It was an assertion by our Founding Fathers that they had seen too often abuses by the executive agencies of government.

Our basic duties as Members of this Congress, protecting the American people and protecting the values that define us as Americans, are not mutually exclusive. We can protect our country and protect our Constitution. That is our duty.

And that is precisely what this historic act, introduced by Chairman Reyes and Chairman Conyers, has done. This legislation gives our intelligence community the tools it needs to listen in on those who seek to harm us while addressing concerns that the bill passed in August could authorize warrantless surveillance of Americans. That is our concern. That is our focus.

Among other things, this legislation modernizes the technologically outdated Foreign Intelligence Surveillance Act of 1978 by restoring a checks and balances rule for the FISA Court and addressing the intelligence gap asserted by the Director of National Intelligence.

We heard Director McConnell. We want to help Director McConnell. Let us be clear. This legislation does not require a warrant for listening in on suspected and known terrorists, period. An assertion to the contrary is not accurate. In fact, it clarifies that no court order is required for surveillance of conversations where both parties are foreign citizens. It does not extend constitutional rights to suspected or known terrorists, assertions to the contrary notwithstanding. Nor does it delay the collection of intelligence information.

Furthermore, it grants the Attorney General and the Director of National Intelligence authority, authority to apply to the FISA Court for a block order, not an individual order, not a discrete order, but a block order saying that you can pursue this gathering of information to protect America, but you cannot do it simply because you want to do it. You've got to do it consistent with the Constitution of the United States and the laws thereof. You cannot conduct freelance surveillance without some authority of law.

The FISA Court can give a block order to conduct surveillance on large groups of foreign targets for up to a year, and that can be renewed, ensuring that only foreigners are targeted and Americans' rights are preserved. That was the whole reason in a bipartisan way we adopted FISA, to make sure that was the case.

Why do you fear a FISA Court reviewing that basic principle that was its intent at its adoption?

Finally, the legislation is silent on the issue of retroactive immunity for telecommunications companies that possibly violated privacy laws in turning over consumer information to the government. We don't make that judgment today. We need to review information to know what was done before we immunize conduct which we do not know. Simply stated, it would be grossly irresponsible for Congress to grant a blanket immunity for companies without even knowing whether their conduct was legal, appropriate, reasonable or not. Don't you think the American public, each one of our constituents, expects that of us?

In closing, Mr. Speaker, let me quote The Washington Post, which stated in October, the measure produced by the House Intelligence and Judiciary

Committees would alleviate the burden of obtaining individualized warrants for foreign targets while still maintaining a critical oversight for the FISA Court. In other words, we are relieving the administration from the burden of discrete approval. But we are providing for the protections that Americans expect under our Constitution.

Mr. Speaker, we must give our Commander in Chief, the President of the United States and the intelligence community the resources, the authority, and flexibility that is necessary to protect our people and defend our Nation. I believe each of us in this Congress support that objective. But we must also honor the values and principles that make us Americans. This legislation allows us to do both.

I urge my colleagues on both sides of the aisle, facilitate the interception of information and terrorist communication dangerous to our people and our country. And at the same time, redeem that oath of protecting and defending our Constitution.

Mr. HOEKSTRA. Mr. Speaker, may I inquire as to the order of closing.

The SPEAKER pro tempore (Mr. Ross). The Chair will recognize for closing speeches in the reverse order of opening, the gentleman from Michigan (Mr. Hoekstra), the gentleman from Texas (Mr. Reyes) and the gentleman from Michigan (Mr. Conyers).

The gentleman from Michigan (Mr. Hoekstra) has 1 minute remaining. The gentleman from Texas (Mr. Reyes) has 45 seconds remaining. The gentleman from Michigan (Mr. Conyers) has 1 minute remaining.

Mr. HOEKSTRA. Mr. Speaker, I thank my colleagues and thank you for this debate.

At this point in time to close our debate I would like to recognize the distinguished minority leader, Mr. Boehner of Ohio.

Mr. BOEHNER. Let me thank my colleague for yielding.

Mr. Speaker, in August the Congress passed the Protect America Act. Before that bill passed, our intelligence officials did not have the tools they needed to protect our troops and to detect and prevent terrorist plots. This was made clear in a story we read about just last month about our, how our FISA laws failed our soldiers who were kidnapped in Iraq, and I think these outdated laws actually hampered their rescue. That is because our FISA laws in place before the Protect America Act entrusted government lawyers, not our intelligence professionals, to protect our troops and our security.

Yet the bill we are considering today only makes this problem worse. It reopens the terrorist loophole and doesn't ensure that we can act quickly on vital intelligence to protect our troops and the American people. I think it would be a boon to trial lawyers who could take actions against third parties who assisted our government at our request after 9/11. It is yet another example of a troubling pattern of behavior on the part the majority, a pattern of behavior that is undermining our national security. Let me just give you a few examples.

The majority want to extend habeas corpus rights to terrorists. The majority has had over 40 votes in the Congress trying to force retreat in Iraq. The majority wants to close down our Guantanamo detention facility and move those terrorists into American communities. The majority, in their intelligence authorization bill and appropriation bill, are diverting key intelligence resources away from terrorist surveillance to study global warming.

In August, all the Members of this House succeeded in modernizing FISA and closing the terrorist loophole. We did so because terrorists were plotting to kill Americans and our allies, and there is no nice way of saying that. So why on Earth would we tie the hands of our intelligence officials again and open up this loophole that allows terrorists to jeopardize the safety of our troops and jeopardize the safety and security of the American people?

Our country is safer today because of our efforts, and Republicans want to work with Democrats to make the Protect America Act permanent. We were very close to a bipartisan agreement on this bill just about 5 weeks ago, very close. As a matter of fact, there was an agreement in principle until the ACLU got ahold of it and blew the entire bipartisan process up. I think the American people want us to do everything we can to make sure that they are safe and secure. The bill that we have before us will once again tie the hands of our intelligence officials and make America less safe. This is not the bill that I want to vote for.

Mr. REYES. Mr. Speaker, this bill, the RESTORE Act, is about balance. It is about putting checks and balances back in the process. It puts the FISA Court back in the process of protecting Americans. It corrects unchecked authority that we gave through the Protect America Act. Some would want us to continue to rubber-stamp what the administration wants. The American people deserve better.

Mr. Speaker, Halloween is over. Why do our colleagues continue to pull ghouls out of the closet? It is now time to talk turkey.

I yield back the balance of my time.

Mr. CONYERS. Mr. Speaker, I am privileged to yield the balance of our time on our side to the distinguished gentlewoman from Texas, Sheila Jackson-Lee, an invaluable member of the Judiciary Committee.

Ms. JACKSON-LEE of Texas. I thank both chairmen, Chairman Conyers for his leadership and Chairman Reyes. In the month of August, I stood here and shredded paper to reflect that the vote we took on that bill was really a destruction of the Constitution. I am very glad to be able to stand here today to hold the Constitution sacredly in my hand and to indicate that this bill does, in fact, offer a restoration of the civil liberties of Americans but yet does not protect one single terrorist.

It is a bill that avoids reverse targeting of Americans. But it is a bill that provides the opportunity that if there was a pending threat against the United States, the Attorney General, the National Security Director, and three others could, in fact, prevent a terrorist act from occurring in the United States. This restores justice and it protects the American people.

Mr. Speaker, I rise today in support of H.R. 3773, introduced by my colleague Mr. Conyers. Had the Bush administration and the Republican-dominated 109th Congress acted more responsibly in the 2 preceding years, we would not be in the position of debating legislation that has such a profound impact on national security and on American values and civil liberties in the crush of exigent circumstances. More often that not, it is true, as the saying goes, that haste makes waste.

Mr. Speaker, the legislation before us is intended to fill a gap in the Nation's intelligence gathering capabilities identified by Director of National Intelligence Mike McConnell, by amending the Foreign Intelligence Surveillance Act, FISA. It gives our intelligence professionals the tools they need to legally monitor suspect foreigners outside the United States, while protecting the fundamental rights of Americans at home.

Nearly two centuries ago, Alexis de Tocqueville observed that the reason democracies invariably prevail in any martial conflict is because democracy is the governmental form that best rewards and encourages those traits that are indispensable to martial success: initiative, innovation, resourcefulness, and courage.

The United States would do well to heed de Tocqueville and recognize that the best way to win the war on terror is to remain true to our democratic traditions. If it retains its democratic character, no nation and no loose confederation of international villains will defeat the United States in the pursuit of its vital interests. A major challenge facing the Congress today is to ensure that in waging its war on terror, the administration does not succeed in winning passage of legislation that will weaken the Nation's commitment to its democratic traditions.

This is why the upcoming debate over congressional approval authorizing the administration to conduct terrorist surveillance on U.S. soil is a matter of utmost importance. I offer some thoughts on the principles that should inform that debate.

In the waning hours before the August recess, the House acceded to the Bush administration's request and approved the woefully misnamed

"Protect America Act," which gives the Federal Government enlarged powers to conduct electronic surveillance of American citizens under the guise of conducting surveillance of foreign terrorists.

Mr. Speaker, FISA has served the Nation well for nearly 30 years, placing electronic surveillance inside the United States for foreign intelligence and counter-intelligence purposes on a sound legal footing. Given the exigent circumstances claimed by the administration, I am prepared to support a number of temporary changes to FISA legislation, provided that they follow certain principles.

First, I am prepared to accept temporarily eliminating the need to obtain a court order for foreign-to-foreign communications that pass through the United States. But I do insist upon individual warrants, based on probable cause, when surveillance is directed at people in the United States. The Attorney General must still be required to submit procedures for international surveillance to the Foreign Intelligence Surveillance Court for approval, but the FISA Court should not be allowed to issue a "basket warrant" without making individual determinations about foreign surveillance. There should be an initial emergency authority so that international surveillance can begin while the warrants are being considered by the Court. And there must also be congressional oversight, requiring the Department of Justice Inspector General to conduct an audit every 60 days of U.S. person communications intercepted under these warrants, to be submitted to the Intelligence and Judiciary Committees.

This legislation allows the interception of electronic communications between foreigners outside of the United States without a warrant and permits the director of national intelligence and the attorney general to seek "blanket" warrants to intercept communications of people reasonably believed to be outside the United States, even if such communication happens to involve "U.S. persons." Wiretap surveillance could be conducted for 7 days before a warrant must be sought, and the secret Foreign Intelligence Surveillance court would have to act on the application for a blanket warrant within 15 days.

This legislation has many other important provisions. It affirms that FISA is the exclusive source of legal authority for conducting electronic surveillance for foreign intelligence. Crucially, it does not grant amnesty to telecommunications companies for any past violations of law. Finally, it gives the FISA Court more oversight authority and terminates the authorization to conduct foreign surveillance on U.S. soil after 2 years.

In all candor, Mr. Speaker, I must restate my firm conviction that when it comes to the track record of this President's warrantless surveillance programs, there is still nothing on the public record about the nature and effectiveness of those programs, or the trustworthiness of this administration, to indicate that they require any legislative response, other than to reaffirm the exclusivity of FISA and insist that it be followed. This could have been accomplished in the 109th Congress by passing H.R. 5371, the "Lawful Intelligence and Surveillance of Terrorists in an Emergency by NSA" Act, LISTEN Act, which I have cosponsored with the then ranking members of the Judiciary and Intelligence Committees, Mr. Conyers and Ms. Harman.

The Bush administration has not complied with its legal obligation under the National Security Act of 1947 to keep the Intelligence Committees "fully and currently informed" of U.S. intelligence activities. Congress cannot continue to rely on incomplete information from the Bush administration or revelations in the media. It must conduct a full and complete inquiry into electronic surveillance in the United States and related domestic activities of the NSA, both those that occur within FISA and those that occur outside FISA.

The inquiry must not be limited to the legal questions. It must include the operational details of each program of intelligence surveillance within the United States, including: (1) who the NSA is targeting; (2) how it identifies its targets; (3) the information the program collects and disseminates; and most important; (4) whether the program advances national security interests without unduly compromising the privacy rights of the American people.

Given the unprecedented amount of information Americans now transmit electronically and the post-9/11 loosening of regulations governing information sharing, the risk of intercepting and disseminating the communications of ordinary Americans is vastly increased, requiring more precise—not looser—standards, closer oversight, new mechanisms for minimization, and limits on retention of inadvertently intercepted communications.

Mr. Speaker, the legislation before us is necessary. It is incumbent on the Congress to act expeditiously to amend existing laws so that they achieve the only legitimate goals of a terrorist surveillance program, which is to ensure that Americans are secure in their persons, papers and effects, but terrorists throughout the world are made insecure. The best way to achieve these twin goals is to follow the rule of law. And the exclusive law to follow with respect to authorizing foreign surveillance gathering on U.S. soil is the Foreign Intelligence Surveillance Act. It is my sincere hope that my colleagues will join together today in enacting important and much needed reforms to FISA.

Finally, Mr. Speaker, I am proud to support the Manager's Amendment to this legislation. This amendment clarifies that nothing in this act can be construed to prohibit lawful surveillance necessary to prevent Osama Bin Laden, al Qaeda, or any other terrorist organization from attacking the U.S., any U.S. person, or any ally of the U.S.; to ensure the safety and security of our Armed Forces or other national security or intelligence personnel; or to protect the U.S., any U.S. person, or any U.S. ally from the threat of WMD or any other threats to national security.

Mr. Speaker, even as we work to protect our Nation, we must remember the fundamental need to protect Americans. At bottom, America is its people connected to each other, and to past and future generations, as in Abraham Lincoln's unforgettable phrase, by "the mystic chords of memory stretching from every heart and hearthstone." America, in other words, is Americans coming together in a community of shared values, ideals and principles. It is those shared values that hold us together. It is our commitment to those values that the terrorists wish to break because that is the only way they can win.

Thus, the way forward to victory in the war on terror is for this country to redouble its commitment to the values that every American will risk his or her life to defend. It is only by preserving our attachment to these cherished values that America will remain forever the home of the free, the land of the brave and the country we love.

H.R. 3773 does just that. It balances the interest in protecting the Nation from terrorists who would do us harm and, at the same time, ensures that the constitutional rights of American citizens and persons in America are not abridged. I strongly urge my colleagues to join me in supporting this legislation.

Mr. LANGEVIN. Mr. Speaker, I rise in support of H.R. 3773.

Today, as we have so many times in our history, we are wrestling with the question of how best to protect security while preserving liberty. That struggle has always been challenging, and the events of 9/11 made it even more so. But today, the RESTORE Act provides a carefully crafted solution to that problem.

We all recognize the gravity of the threats facing our country, and that is why this bill gives the Director of National Intelligence all the authority he has asked for to fight terrorism. The legislation updates FISA to address new developments in technology so that our intelligence activities are not constrained based on what method of communication suspects happen to be using or where the communication may be routed. The bill also clarifies that no warrant is needed for foreign-to-foreign communications. These are requests that the DNI has made and which are included in the bill.

However, unlike the so-called Protect America Act, which passed in August, the RESTORE Act provides for rigorous and independent oversight from the courts, the Congress, and the Department of Justice Inspector General.

Additionally, during the Intelligence Committee's consideration of the bill, I successfully offered an amendment to strengthen the oversight by preserving the FISA Court's role to review compliance with their rules every 90 days for the life of a court order. By having the FISA Court review the procedures and guidelines used by the DNI and Attorney General when determining that prospective targets are located outside the U.S., we provide another safeguard against the collection of communications of people inside the U.S. Finally, the bill requires greater congressional oversight of the program so that we can monitor how it is being implemented and make any changes that may become necessary.

Such rigorous oversight is why the Bush administration objects to this bill. To them, the Protect America Act that passed in August is just fine the way it is. They want unfettered authority, without checks and balances. But we have seen what happens when the administration is given free rein, and I will not let that happen again.

I want to be clear that this is not a perfect bill. While in theory it is a vast improvement over the Protect America Act, in reality, this legislation will only work if everyone involved follows the rules that Congress establishes and remains within the confines of the law. Like any program, and indeed more so than most, this one could be subject to abuse, and we must remain vigilant in our efforts to ensure that does not happen. We have included meaningful safeguards and significant checks and balances in this measure. However, these provisions are only as strong as the individuals and agencies implementing them. Congress must continue to conduct robust oversight and insist on the briefings and information to which we are entitled. If we fail in these efforts and abuses occur, we will have ourselves to blame.

Mr. Speaker, we have faced grave threats before. Our Constitution was drafted at a time when the very survival of our Nation was in doubt. Yet our Founding Fathers made the preservation of basic liberties part of the fabric of our national identity.

As Members of Congress, it is our sworn duty to defend the Constitution and the principles on which our Nation was founded. I urge my colleagues to support H.R. 3773, which protects security while preserving the liberties that make this country great.

Mr. MAHONEY of Florida. Mr. Speaker, I rise today in support of H.R. 3773, the RESTORE Act.

On my first day, I took an oath of office to support and defend the Constitution. Tonight we will vote to protect our Fourth Amendment rights by passing this bill. Never again will we give any person the ability to conduct surveillance on American citizens without court approval.

America must be vigilant in our fight against terrorism. Congress has a duty to give our intelligence agencies the tools they need to hunt down those who threaten our Nation while protecting the constitutional rights of every American.

The RESTORE Act gives the Attorney General and the Director of National Intelligence the flexibility they need to pursue the terrorists, while keeping the checks and balances enshrined in our Constitution.

Mr. Speaker, it is critical that our intelligence community have the resources necessary to protect America. It is also critical that Americans are protected from unreasonable searches and seizures. This bill accomplishes both of these objectives.

I urge my colleagues to vote in support of the RESTORE Act.

Mr. BLUMENAUER. Mr. Speaker, as a chamber, we have come a long way since August when the disgraceful "Protect America Act" was strong-armed into law. The RESTORE Act, a comprehensive and thoughtful overhaul of the Foreign Intelligence Surveillance Act, could not cut a more striking contrast.

Over the past 7 years I have been highly critical of Republican wiretapping legislation. I have voted against every effort to expand the ability of this administration to intrude in the lives and privacy of innocent citizens.

But this is a Democratic Congress and a Democratic bill. The RESTORE Act strikes an unprecedented balance between civil defense and civil liberties. I deeply appreciate the hard-won progress we've made on this issue and I am heartened by our leadership's determination to end a Republican legacy that so blatantly disregards the rights of ordinary Americans.

The bill before us will not solve every potential abuse of FISA, but it does greatly strengthen legal protections for Americans and introduces robust congressional oversight. As this issue continues to play out into the future, it is my hope that our next steps will include even stronger protections for innocent Americans, clearer legal standards for FISA to judge surveillance procedures, and explicit requirements for the destruction of unnecessary data.

Ms. BEAN. Mr. Speaker, I rise today in support of H.R. 3773.

Giving our intelligence community the tools they need to uncover threats to our Nation's security is one of Congress's most important duties. This bill soundly provides that.

This legislation explicitly clarifies that a warrant is not needed when conducting foreign to foreign surveillance. Importantly this bill also includes reasonable safeguards to ensure U.S. citizens at home and abroad are not subject to surveillance without proper oversight.

It lays out a responsible yet workable framework for the Director of National Intelligence and Attorney General to get FISA certification when U.S. persons may inadvertently be involved yet allows our intelligence community to act immediately in emergency situations prior to FISA court certification.

I commend the committee for its hard work on an issue important to our national security.

While Congress should continue to pursue all relevant information from the administration's surveillance program since September 11, 2001, telecommunications providers should not be held liable for providing requested information that they were told could prevent future attacks on our Nation.

An October editorial in the Washington Post noted that these companies were "acting as patriotic corporate citizens in a difficult and uncharted environment."

Therefore I support retroactive immunity for participating companies and I'm hopeful it will be included in the final bill.

With that, I urge my colleagues to support H.R. 3773.

Mr. UDALL of New Mexico. Mr. Speaker, I rise today to voice my support for H.R. 3773—the Responsible Electronic Surveillance That is Overseen, Reviewed, and Effective (RESTORE) Act of 2007.

In August, Congress unfortunately passed the Protect America Act, a piece of legislation that allowed the surveillance activities of this Administration to go unchecked. Though I opposed that bill, the House was left little choice but to pass that flawed bill. While it is true that modernization of our foreign intelligence laws was necessary to meet the security and intelligence needs of this nation, the Protect America Act went beyond what was essential and instead allowed the continued infringement of American's civil liberties.

Thankfully, today we have before us a piece of legislation that gives the intelligence community the authority it needs to protect Americans while also protecting civil liberties that are the bedrock of our nation. This bill modernizes our foreign surveillance system and authorizes necessary funding for training, personnel and technology resources at DOJ, NSA and the FISA Court to expedite the FISA process. Additionally, it ensures that nothing inhibits lawful surveillance for the purpose of protecting the nation and the troops from threats posed by terrorists.

Also of great importance, unlike previous bills considered by the House, this bill includes vital checks and balances on the Administration. It prohibits warrantless surveillance of Americans and requires a court order before targeting Americans' phone calls or emails. It also requires a finding of probable cause before conducting surveillance on Americans abroad, which was not required under previous legislation. To ensure greater accountability, the legislation mandates audits on the Administration's warrantless surveillance program and the communications collected under the program.

Most importantly, this legislation ensures that it is the courts and not the Administration that decides whether or not an American's communications are targeted. The bill requires the FISA Court to review targeting procedures to ensure that they are reasonably designed to protect Americans and target people outside the United States. It also requires the Court to review the Administration's compliance to ensure that when the government conducts electronic surveillance on Americans, it obtains traditional, individualized warrants from the FISA Court.

Mr. Speaker, for far too long this Administration has been able to extend its power and authority, often to the detriment and subversion of our nation's basic principles. Today, we are passing a bill that will finally curb the Administration's actions and restore a measure of accountability that has been sorely lacking for too long. For these reasons, I support the vitally necessary RESTORE Act.

Mr. DINGELL. Mr. Speaker, I voted against the original Patriot Act, I voted against the reauthorization of the Patriot Act in 2005, I voted against the President's Protect America Act that was signed into law last August, and I was prepared to vote against the RESTORE Act if it did not adequately protect our constitutionally guaranteed civil rights. I had strong reservations about this legislation when it was first reported out of Committee, particularly with respect to the degree it appeared to give the Administration the ability to monitor the conversations of U.S. citizens without an individualized warrant. However, after reviewing the changes made to this legislation in the managers' amendment, I am satisfied that the RESTORE Act now contains adequate Fourth Amendment protections.

I applaud Congressman Holt for working with Chairmen Conyers and Reyes to address this issue. While this legislation is not perfect, I believe that it represents a substantial improvement over existing law. I realize it is likely we will find ourselves revisiting this issue again in the coming months when the Senate is finished with its own legislation on this matter. As this debate continues, I will continue to insist that any legislation I support contains adequate protections for civil rights.

Mr. STARK. Mr. Speaker, I rise today in support of the RESTORE Act. Unlike past national security measures, this bill will prevent the administration from violating our basic civil liberties in the name of its phony war on terror.

I appreciate the hard work of my colleagues, Chairmen Conyers, Reyes and Holt. Thanks to their efforts, this bill is a marked improvement from the legislation President Bush requested and from the Orwellian "Protect America Act" the House passed in August.

Unlike the President's proposal and the legislation I voted against, the RESTORE Act will prevent domestic spying. As its name implies, this bill restores the judiciary's vital role in checking the administration's desire to conduct surveillance on whomever they want, whenever they want.

It prohibits the government from spying on Americans without the explicit approval of the FISA court. It also empowers the FISA court to determine if domestic communications picked up during blanket sweeps directed at international correspondence can be seized or searched.

Importantly, this bill does not grant immunity to telecommunications companies. The RESTORE Act will allow individuals who have had their rights violated to sue the telecommunications companies that made spying possible by sharing telephone conversations and email correspondence with the government.

The President has made it clear that he believes the three branches of government are "me, myself, and I." Thankfully, this legislation dissolves him of that notion and firmly re-establishing the important and necessary role that the judiciary plays in protecting our civil liberties.

I urge my colleagues to stand up in opposition to this President and vote yes to protect our civil liberties.

Mr. GORDON of Tennessee. Mr. Speaker, I would submit the following editorial from the Los Angeles Times for the Record.

[From the Los Angeles Times, Nov. 15, 2007]

When the CIA Comes Calling (By R. James Woolsey)

When I was director of Central Intelligence during President Clinton's first term, I had occasion to go hat in hand to the private sector several times. In one case, it was a detail that, if made public, could have caused a valuable source to be captured or killed; in another, there was a technical feature of a system in production that, slightly modified, was of great help to the nation. In these several cases, executives of American companies heard me out and willingly met my requests, to the substantial benefit of our national security.

They had no legal requirement to do so, and they knew it. They were helping solely out of a sense of patriotism and an understanding that some steps that the nation needs to take in a dangerous world cannot be taken in public, simply because informing the public informs an opponent or an enemy.

Shortly after 9/11, something similar happened. Senior U.S. officials asked telecommunications companies to assist the government in intercepts involving terrorist groups such as those that had just attacked us and killed thousands of people. In these cases, President Bush authorized the intercepts and the senior officials gave written assurances to the companies that their cooperation was legal.

In my judgment, the president acted properly; he had the authority under the Constitution to ask for such intercepts. In addition, his request was reasonable because surveillance of enemy-to-American communications is a time-honored means of intelligence gathering in the U.S. George Washington did it; those under his command intercepted and read correspondence between Benedict Arnold and his spy handler, foiling the plot to turn the fort at West Point over to the British.

But even if one believes the request was illegal and unreasonable—and there are distinguished constitutional lawyers and patriotic citizens on both sides of this debate—the issue currently before the Senate Judiciary Committee is much narrower. It is whether the telecommunications companies that complied with the president's request and trusted the government's assurances of legality should be granted immunity from about 40 lawsuits demanding billions of dollars.

Sen. John D. "Jay" Rockefeller (D-W.Va.), chairman of the Intelligence Committee, has stated that companies "should not be dragged through the courts for their help with national security." And now Sen. Dianne Feinstein (D-Calif.), a member of the Judiciary Committee, has endorsed his statement, saying that the companies should not be "held hostage to costly litigation in what is essentially a complaint about [Bush] administration activities."

Feinstein is a member of the one-vote Democratic majority on the Judiciary Committee, and it is possible that her position will determine the outcome. I hope it does. Her stance is farsighted. Having once, when I was practicing law, taken depositions for months about a single one-hour meeting, I know something about how burdensome litigation can be. If, in the end, the surveillance request made by the government is deemed improper, the government should be held accountable, not those who complied with its request.

We live in a world of terrorism, the possible proliferation of nuclear weapons and a host of other risks to our security. Intelligence, and the cooperation of the private sector in obtaining and protecting it, will be among our most important tools to avoid catastrophes such as 9/11 or worse.

If some future senior government official needs to make a call on a CEO of the sort I did, and that others did after 9/11, we and our children will be better off if the official can answer the question "Can you guarantee that my company won't be sued if we help the country?" with "If it happens, we'll get protective legislation approved as in 2007." We would be in much more danger if, because companies that helped after 9/11 became ensnared in years of litigation and financial losses, that official has to answer the question with a shrug.

Mr. UDALL of Colorado. Mr. Speaker, I have reservations about this bill, but I will vote for it today.

It is similar to one that I supported earlier this year but that failed to receive the two-thids vote necessary for passage under the procedure that applied to its consideration.

In my opinion, the RESTORE Act is far preferable to the legislation—the so-called "Protect America Act"—that I voted against but which the House, to my regret, approved and is now law.

Fortunately, that law will expire early next year, so we have the opportunity—and, I would say, the responsibility—to replace it with a better, more balanced measure.

By a more balanced measure, I mean one that fulfills two equally important requirements—first, that of enabling our intelligence community to do its job to protect us against terrorism and other threats, and second, respecting and safeguarding the rights and liberties of all Americans.

And while this bill is not perfect, I think it does meet those tests and deserves to be passed today.

It is based on the legislation I supported earlier this year but in several important ways it is even better than that bill.

For example, it is more carefully focused, applying not to all foreign intelligence but specifically to intelligence collection related to terrorism, espionage, sabotage and threats to national security. It also provides that the minimization rules—the steps agencies will take to limit their actions so as to avoid inadvertent or unnecessary surveillance—as well as the guidelines for intelligence collection regarding all targets must be approved by the FISA court, not merely by an administrative monitor.

It includes critical language that says that actions in compliance with the Foreign Intelligence Surveillance Act, and with that law's procedural safeguards, will be the exclusive means to conduct surveillance for intelligence purposes. And the bill restates current law stipulating that surveillance targeting Americans requires an individualized FISA court order.

It takes a great step toward greater accountability by requiring an audit of past surveillance activities by the National Security Agency and by mandating record-keeping on any interception of communications by American citizens and legal residents.

The bill eliminates ambiguous language in the "Protect America Act" that appeared to authorize warrantless searches inside the United States, including physical searches of homes, offices, and medical records. And it makes clear that the Administration cannot conduct surveillance against Americans without probable cause—even if they are outside the United States.

Furthermore, this bill, like the one hastily passed earlier this year, is not permanent but will expire at the end of 2009, at which time Congress will be able to reconsider it with the benefit of greater knowledge of how it has worked in practice and whether further refinements should be made.

Also important is what the bill doesn't do. It does not provide constitutional protections to foreign terrorists. The bill does not require the government to obtain a FISA order in order to intercept "foreign to foreign" communications of suspected terrorists, even if these communications pass through the United States. Nor does this bill permit the National Security Agency to collect the communications of Americans through a "basket" court order. Instead, the bill requires the Administration to certify that the targets are not Americans, and if it wants to conduct surveillance on Americans, the Administration must get a formal FISA order.

And, as now amended, it includes additional language to make clear that there are other things it will not do. Specifically, it will not prevent the lawful surveillance necessary to: prevent Osama Bin Laden, al Qaeda, or any other terrorist organization from attacking our country, our people, any of our allies. It will not prevent surveillance needed to ensure the safety and security of our Armed Forces or other national security or intelligence personnel. It will not prevent surveillance needed to protect the United States, the American people, or any of our allies from the threat of weapons of mass destruction or any other threats to national security. And it will not prohibit surveillance of, or grant any rights to, undocumented aliens.

The bill does grant authority to the Director of National Intelligence and the Attorney General to apply to the FISA court for a single court order, or a "basket" order, authorizing surveillance of a suspected terrorist organization abroad for up to one year, as long as there are procedures in place to ensure that only foreigners are targeted and the rights of Americans are preserved.

In general, I am wary of the concept of broad scope "basket warrants," which are not normal under our laws. But I am prepared to support this part of the bill on the understanding that it is limited in scope and not applicable within the United States and with the expectation that the question will be revisited if the audits indicate a need for reconsideration of this part of the legislation. In this context, I am glad to note that this legislation is not permanent and will expire at the end of 2009.

President Bush has criticized the bill, in part because it does not include a provision granting retroactive immunity for telecommunications companies that assisted in the Administration's secret surveillance program without a warrant. I think it might be appropriate to consider such a provision, but not until the Bush Administration responds to bipartisan requests for information about the past activities of these companies under the program. I am not ready to grant immunity for the companies' past activities while we don't know what activities would be covered.

Mr. Speaker, this bill is not perfect, but I am not prepared to insist on perfection at this point. I believe we must do all we can to correct the shortcomings of the "Protect America Act," even if it takes Congress a number of attempts to get it right. The RESTORE Act will give the Administration the authority it says it needs to conduct surveillance on terrorist targets—while restoring many of the protections that the "Protect America Act" has taken away. For that reason, I will vote for this bill today.

The SPEAKER pro tempore. All time for debate has expired.

Pursuant to House Resolution 746, the previous question is ordered on the bill, as amended.

The question is on the engrossment and third reading of the bill.

The bill was ordered to be engrossed and read a third time, and was read the third time.

Motion to Recommit Offered by Mr. Smith of Texas

Mr. SMITH of Texas. Mr. Speaker, I have a motion to recommit at the desk.

The SPEAKER pro tempore. Is the gentleman opposed to the bill?

Mr. SMITH of Texas. I am in its current form.

The SPEAKER pro tempore. The Clerk will report the motion to recommit.

The Clerk read as follows:

> Mr. Smith of Texas moves to recommit the bill, H.R. 3773, to the Committee on the Judiciary with instructions to report the same back to the House promptly with the following amendments:
>
> In section 18 in the heading, strike "ALIENS" and insert "ALIENS, STATE SPONSORS OF TERRORISM, OR AGENTS OF STATE SPONSORS OF TERRORISM".
>
> In section 18, strike "This Act and" and insert "(a) In General.—This Act and".
>
> In section 18, strike "United States" and insert "United States, a State sponsor of terrorism, or an agent of a State sponsor of terrorism".

At the end of section 18 add the following new subsection:

> (b) State Sponsor of Terrorism Defined.—In this section, the term "State sponsor of terrorism" means a country the government of which the Secretary of State has determined, for purposes of section 6(j) of the Export Administration Act of 1979 (as continued in effect pursuant to the International Emergency Economic Powers Act) (50 U.S.C. App. 2405), section 40 of the Arms Export Control Act (22 U.S.C. 2780), section 620A of the Foreign Assistance Act of 1961 (22 U.S.C. 2371), or any other provision

of law, to be a government that has repeatedly provided support for acts of international terrorism.

In paragraph (1) of the undesignated section relating to Surveillance to Protect the United States added to the bill pursuant to the adoption of House Resolution 824, insert "members of the al-Quds Iranian Revolutionary Guard," after "al Qaeda,".

In the undesignated section relating to Surveillance to Protect the United States added to the bill pursuant to the adoption of House Resolution 824, strike "This Act and" and insert "(a) This Act and".

At the end of the undesignated section relating to Surveillance to Protect the United States added to the bill pursuant to the adoption of House Resolution 824 add the following new subsection:

(b) Notwithstanding any other provision of this Act, or the amendments made by this Act, the intelligence community (as defined in section 3(4) of the National Security Act of 1947 (50 U.S.C. 401a(4))) shall be permitted to conduct surveillance of any person concerning an imminent attack on the United States, any United States person, including a member of the United States Armed Forces, or an ally of the United States by Osama Bin Laden, al Qaeda, members of the al-Quds Iranian Revolutionary Guard, or any other terrorist or foreign terrorist organization designated under section 219 of the Immigration and Nationality Act.

Mr. SMITH of Texas (during the reading). Mr. Speaker, I ask unanimous consent that the motion be considered as read.

The SPEAKER pro tempore. Is there objection to the request of the gentleman from Texas?

Mr. CONYERS. Mr. Speaker, I reserve a point of order, and I object to waiving the reading of the motion to recommit.

The SPEAKER pro tempore. The point of order is reserved.

The Clerk will read.

The Clerk concluded the reading of the motion.

The SPEAKER pro tempore. Pursuant to the rule, the gentleman from Texas is recognized for 5 minutes in support of his motion.

Mr. SMITH of Texas. Mr. Speaker, the motion to recommit says "promptly," because the bill needs to go back to committee immediately. Members were given almost no notice of what was going to be in this bill. There are many questions remaining about the text because it has not gone through the regular committee process.

This motion addresses a major problem created by the manager's amendment. Under existing law, court orders are required to conduct certain surveillance of illegal immigrants within the United States. Section 18 of the manager's amendment strips away any rights that illegal immigrants have under FISA, stating clearly that there will be "no rights under the RESTORE Act for undocumented aliens."

If that is really what the Democratic leadership wants to do, then we should ensure that the legislation does not treat terrorists more favorably than illegal immigrants. To fix this problem, the motion adds "state sponsors of terrorism and their agents" to section 18 to ensure that they are treated equally. There is no reason that the law should provide greater protection to terrorists than to illegal immigrants.

Also, the motion preserves the ability of our intelligence community to conduct surveillance of Osama bin Laden, al Qaeda, the Iranian Revolutionary Guard, and other terrorist organizations to protect America from an imminent terrorist attack. When faced with a life-or-death situation, a ticking bomb, an imminent threat of attack, do we really want to subject intelligence agents to unnecessary legal hurdles in order to protect our country?

The RESTORE Act hinders our intelligence community's ability to collect foreign intelligence needed to prevent al Qaeda and other terrorists from attacking our country. It requires the government to obtain court orders to conduct surveillance of overseas terrorists. The implication of this requirement, Mr. Speaker, could be catastrophic.

Mr. Speaker, I yield the balance of my time to the gentleman from Michigan (Mr. Hoekstra), who is the ranking member of the Intelligence Committee.

Mr. HOEKSTRA. Mr. Speaker, the new manager's amendment that self-executed with a rule this morning included broad new language that would treat illegal immigrants differently than other threats to the homeland. This was a poorly conceived and ill-advised provision that has created a lot of confusion.

Through the day, when we discussed the rule this morning, as we had the debate tonight, I had a series of questions: Would this amendment allow surveillance against possible illegal aliens for law enforcement purposes? Would it allow surveillance to determine whether someone is an alien not permitted to be in or remain in the United States?

During the rule, I was told I would get the answers during general debate. During general debate there was nothing but silence.

If we take a look at the bill, for a month we have been dealing with a bill that provided protections and legal protections to terrorists. Overseas terrorists having access to the courts, having warrants, and those types of things were moved. Then today, at the last minute, or yesterday at the last minute, we get an amendment, a manager's amendment, that provides or, it appears, rips away any type of protection for another threat.

Is the majority saying that the threat to the homeland is greater for aliens, illegal aliens living in the United States, than state sponsors of terrorism? It appears that it does because they have 40 or 50 pages of protections and a paragraph of exceptions that says: "No rights under the RESTORE Act for undocumented aliens." Many on our side may think that that is a good idea.

What this manager's amendment says very simply is if there are no rights under the RESTORE Act for undocumented aliens, maybe we should put that same provision in here for state sponsors of terrorism and agents of sponsors of terrorism. It's very clear. We think that if a threat to the homeland, as identified by the other side, are illegal aliens, perhaps it's also time that we recognize that state sponsors of terrorism pose the same type of threat to the United States.

Is the majority saying that illegal aliens are a greater threat to the United States than Cuba, than Iran, North Korea, Sudan and Syria? It appears from the bill that we have before us tonight that is exactly what they are saying, because they have 50 pages of protections and one page of exceptions.

Let's make sure that we treat illegal aliens the same way we treat North Korea and Cuba.

The SPEAKER pro tempore. Does the gentleman from Michigan continue to maintain his reservation?

Mr. CONYERS. Mr. Speaker, I do not insist upon my point of order.

The SPEAKER pro tempore. The reservation is withdrawn.

Mr. CONYERS. Mr. Speaker, I rise to respond to the motion to recommit.

The SPEAKER pro tempore. Is the gentleman opposed to the motion to recommit?

Mr. CONYERS. Mr. Speaker, I am.

The SPEAKER pro tempore. The gentleman from Michigan is recognized for 5 minutes.

Mr. CONYERS. Mr. Speaker, ladies and gentlemen of the House, here we are again at another one of these so-called motions to recommit. Approach them with great care. I strongly oppose this motion.

The minority has just made it clear that they are not seeking to change the bill; they are seeking to kill the bill. The tactic is getting pretty old in the House of Representatives. If they wanted to vote on their proposal today, they would have used the word, doesn't everybody know it now, "forthwith," as I have suggested. But they have refused under well-established House rules and precedents.

Other words do not have that effect, even if they sound like they should. The minority used the word "promptly." It's no accident that they chose that word. The authors of this motion know full well the effect of choosing this word, and so do we. That is why they chose it. They wanted to send the bill back to the graveyard, which is what will happen if this motion is adopted.

I would now yield to the gentlewoman from California (Ms. Zoe Lofgren).

Ms. ZOE LOFGREN of California. Mr. Speaker, I would note that the motion to recommit itself leads to a nonsense sentence, adding "United States, a State sponsor of terrorism," to section 18. It's inexplicable nonsense. It also guts the bill.

On August 2, I rushed to the floor to say that we were passing a bill that was a terrible offense to the Constitution. It gutted the fourth amendment. This bill does not. Mr. Speaker, I urge its passage.

Mr. CONYERS. Mr. Speaker, I am proud to yield to the distinguished chairman of the Intelligence Committee, the gentleman from Texas (Mr. Reyes).

Mr. REYES. I thank the gentleman for yielding.

Mr. Speaker, this is a sham solution in search of a problem. This language is unnecessary, and it would kill this bill. The bill already states that this act and the amendments made by this act shall not be construed to prohibit the intelligence community from conducting lawful surveillance that is necessary, one, to prevent Osama bin Laden, al Qaeda, or any other terrorist or terrorist organization from attacking the United States. It also provides the means to protect the United States, any United States person or any ally of the United States from threats posed by weapons of mass destruction or other threats of national security.

Mr. Speaker, the answer to the ranking member's question about undocumented aliens, all they have to do is check section 235 and 287 of the Immigration and Naturalization Act. This does not confer any additional rights not provided by the Constitution.

Mr. CONYERS. I thank the chairman.

I am really moved by the sudden concern for immigration rights that the other side has begun to display, to my surprise.

I yield now to the gentlewoman from California (Ms. Harman).

Ms. HARMAN. I thank the gentleman for yielding. I think this has been an interesting debate. I have sat through every minute of it. During the debate on the rule, I spoke for this bill and for the rule; and now I speak strongly against this motion to recommit. As you have already heard, it is redundant. We have inserted language in this bill that takes care of the problem. In the manager's amendment, language was added at the request of the Blue Dogs, and I am proud to be a co-chair of the Blue Dog Coalition, and that language specifically refers to terrorist organizations, and the Revolutionary Guards are one such organization.

So I would like to say for two reasons there's no need to support this motion to recommit: one, it kills the bill by using the word "promptly"; number two, it is redundant with excellent language that we added to the bill in the manager's amendment. As I have said before, this is not a zero sum game. We don't get more security and less liberty or more liberty and less security. We either get more of both or less of both.

These amendments carefully restore, it's called the RESTORE Act, the balance of the Foreign Intelligence Surveillance Act, which Congress wisely passed 20 years ago. Vote for this bill and against the motion to recommit. We will restore that balance.

[The vote was taken by electronic device, and there were—yeas 194, nays 222, not voting 16.]

SUBJECT: INTELLIGENCE SERVICES (82%); SURVEILLANCE TECHNOLOGY (82%); ESPIONAGE (63%);

LOAD-DATE: November 16, 2007

SUBJECT INDEX

Doc/Pg

Counterterrorism

Doc/Pg

FBI

Foreign Intelligence Surveillance Act (FISA)

Intelligence

Doc/Pg

Iraq

Legislation – Federal

Military – Role of

National Security – Threats to

Terrorism – Policy

www.ingramcontent.com/pod-product-compliance
Ingram Content Group UK Ltd.
Pitfield, Milton Keynes, MK11 3LW, UK
UKHW051224160926
475595UK00022B/165